An Illustrated
Dictionary of Silverware

HAROLD NEWMAN

An Illustrated

Dictionary of Silverware

2,373 entries, relating to British and
North American wares, decorative techniques
and styles, and leading designers and makers,
principally from *c.*1500 to the present

709 illustrations

Thames & Hudson

To the memory of Wendy,
for thirty-four years
my very beloved wife
and my invaluable aid

© 1987 Thames & Hudson Ltd, London

First published in hardcover in the United States of America in 1987 by Thames & Hudson Inc., 500 Fifth Avenue, New York, New York 10110

First paperback edition 2000

Library of Congress Catalog Card Number 86-51576
ISBN 0-500-28196-3

Printed and bound in Germany by Interdruck

Preface

SILVER, by its inherent qualities, lends itself to being used to make almost any type of article of reasonably small size. Indeed, the range of articles that have been made of silver defies any attempt at making a complete inventory. Silver's appeal lies in the fact that the metal is malleable, and hence can be conveniently worked into many shapes and decorated in many styles by a variety of techniques. Silver is tempting to the purchaser because it has the advantage – unlike readily breakable ceramic ware and glassware – of being durable and hard-wearing, thus ensuring long survival. The ageless attraction, however, is that articles made of silver retain an instant recoverable value simply as metal, so that, as and when methods of use or styles of decoration change, the owner can have the ware altered in shape and style to conform to the current vogue; more important, however, the pieces can be held as a monetary reserve, and thus a portion of the investment can be realized at any time by having the ware melted down for its cash value, any loss being limited usually to the value of the 'fashion' of the pieces. Thus, silver meets the manifold needs and whims of the wealthy and the modestly well-to-do, resulting in its having been used to make an infinite variety of articles. Over the years, silversmiths have been able to satisfy almost every demand, as science progressed and social customs changed, while always maintaining their link with the past by using basically the same manufacturing and decorating processes and adapting the forms of prior generations.

The range of silverware to be covered includes the many types of article for domestic use (serving, drinking, and eating utensils) and the highly important fields of ware made for religious use (Christian and Jewish plate), as well as for commemorative and presentation purposes. In order to keep this dictionary to a convenient size, it has therefore been necessary to concentrate on such articles, and hence to consider as being beyond its range silver jewelry (dealt with in the author's *An Illustrated Dictionary of Jewelry*) and many other small portable articles which, although made entirely or partially of silver, are classified as objects of vertu (e.g., snuff-boxes, scent-bottles), as well as articles for personal use (e.g., writing and sewing accessories, vision aids, small toilet articles, and smoking accessories), scientific, surgical, and astronomical instruments, and some forms of riding equipment. Even after allowing for such exclusions, the range of topics remaining for consideration – extending far beyond the forms of ceramic ware and glassware – has made a world-wide coverage of silverware impossible in a volume of this extent, and hence this book is restricted to the products, silversmiths, and styles of Great Britain (including Ireland up to 1921) and North America, including the United States (which is too often the area implied by the loosely used term 'American silver') and Canada, and also modern Mexico. The American areas are compatible with Britain, for much of the silverware of the Colonial era and of the United States, Canada, and modern Mexico was derived from British prototypes, albeit subject to indigenous modifications. The time span extends principally from *c.* 1500 (before which date few pieces are extant or recorded) to the present day, but also embraces some historic earlier pieces (e.g., the Ardagh Chalice).

There are included here many purposely created presentation and commemorative pieces, ranging from the frequently occurring examples of large two-handled cups to elaborate centrepieces and candelabra decorated with sculptured figures. Also listed are such prosaic categories of household articles as dishes, spoons, and cutlery which, although well known to everybody as to basic forms, here serve as the basis for listing cross-references (in SMALL CAPITALS) to the different named varieties of such articles, to objects of related use or style, and to specific named examples. Definitions have been limited to essentials while noting as cross-references qualifying terms, related subjects or specific examples, as well as names of designers, makers, etc., wherever appropriate. Although basic processes of production and decoration are defined and briefly explained, this book is not intended as a manual for silversmiths, and hence manufacturing techniques, such as the steps involved in raising, sinking, hammering, joining, affixing mounts, polishing, etc., are merely outlined and not explained in detail.

A unique feature of wares made of precious metals is the use of hallmarks, which now usually supplement their original control function by furnishing collectors with authentic data about the makers and dates of marked pieces, such as are not generally available with respect to ceramic ware, which is only infrequently marked, and less so for glassware, which is rarely marked. The principal British hallmarks are briefly described (with specimen illustrations), but for detailed descriptions and extensive listings with illustrations, the reader is referred to the many books and pamphlets on the subject.

In describing various forms of silverware, no distinction is noted here between pieces made of Sterling silver, of Sheffield plate, or of plated ware, for most of the articles discussed have been made in all three media. The plated examples usually came later, but in some instances the plated forms were new ones created by the platers. Although the forms themselves are usually similar, the processes used in making and finishing the articles were quite different.

Gold articles, naturally far fewer than those made of silver, have been made in many of the same forms and styles, as well as by the same processes and with the same styles of decoration. In fact, makers of silverware are often referred to as goldsmiths. However, such gold objects (other than jewelry) are generally beyond the financial reach of individual collectors and are for acquisition only by museums well acquainted with them; hence, with the exception of a very few pieces of special British significance, they are not included in this book.

Many specific pieces of silverware have acquired a particular name, sometimes that of the designer, the modeller, the maker, or a former or present owner. Such pieces are listed here by the acquired name. In view of the format of this book, with its entries arranged alphabetically, it has been necessary for all other pieces that are individually discussed, on account of significant form or history, and which have not heretofore been known by an accepted name, to be identified for the purpose of such listing. In such cases the author has, therefore, assigned a name, usually that of the designer, modeller or maker, or of the person who donated an article to a museum or college, or (in a few cases) that of a past or present owner. Whether such names will hereafter become generally accepted, only time will tell.

This dictionary seeks primarily to define terms and to describe silver objects, hence it does not generally offer descriptions of the historical development of various types of object or of their shapes or styles of decoration, such as can be found in many treatises on silverware that discuss the origin of forms and changes in decorative style through successive periods. As this book is intended for use by English-speaking readers everywhere and not only those in the United Kingdom who are usually better acquainted with the reigns of the successive British Sovereigns, most periods of production and styles are identified here by approximate dates rather than by referring simply (as is the British custom) to, for example, the 'reign of George III'. Besides, styles did not change coincidentally with reigns, many preceding by some years the accession of the Sovereign by whose name they are now known and certainly continuing after the death of the eponymous Sovereign. Nevertheless, some styles of silverware are now universally classified by the rather vague terms that adapt the names of the contemporary (or nearly contemporary) Sovereign, such as 'Caroline', 'Georgian', 'Elizabethan', or 'Victorian' silverware. These broad terms are defined here with their approximate year dates, as also are some terms that are based on names of persons other than Royalty, such as 'Adam style' or 'Chippendale rim'.

Many important pieces of British silverware bear an engraved achievement or coat of arms, either of the original owner or of a subsequent owner, and the presence of such armorials – especially those of a Sovereign or a high-ranking member of the nobility – can add considerable monetary value to a particular piece, as provenance is usually established thereby (but not necessarily either ownership, e.g., as to Ambassadorial silverware, or date of production) and an element of rarity added. Hence, although the heraldic details of armorials are usually stated in auction and museum catalogues, they are irrelevant for the purposes of a dictionary that is concerned mainly with describing style, form, and decoration, and so details of armorials are omitted.

The dimensions stated in the captions to the illustrations are in many instances merely close approximations sufficient to afford a general idea of size. The weight of individual pieces, often stated for articles of silverware and essential in an auctioneer's catalogue or a museum catalogue, is here generally not significant and therefore given in only a few cases of particular interest.

Although this dictionary is devoted mainly to antique silverware of the 17th to 19th centuries, i.e., that which is of greatest interest to collectors, it also discusses some types of article that have come into use only in modern times, especially items of tableware such as the corncob holder and the splayd; even though today such objects are not collectors' items, the inclusion of definitions seems justified, remembering that in their day a set of Apostle spoons, a mazer or a caddy spoon were made not for collectors, but for everyday use. Likewise, although leading designers, modellers, and makers (including firms as well as individuals) of silverware are the subject of entries with particular reference to past centuries, only a few 20th-century silversmiths of acknowledged reputation are included. Contemporary silversmiths, often working for manufacturing firms rather than as independent craftsmen, are so numerous – and opinions and tastes differ so widely in appraising their work – that is has been deemed prudent not to include entries for any individual born after 1950. The choice of those to be included has, subject to considerations of space, been largely based on the opinions of authoritative writers, dealers, and others active in the field of silverware. The inclusion or omission of any firm or craftsman is thus not to be regarded as reflecting a personal judgment or preference.

The function of a dictionary is normally to state briefly the meaning of words as generally understood in contemporary usage, with sometimes a caution that a term has become obsolete. It is not customary for a lexicographer to criticize such usage or to seek to change the accepted meaning of an oft-used word. Here, however, I have in a few cases suggested instances where greater precision could be achieved. All too often, books, magazine articles, and auction catalogues will be found to use ambiguous terminology. This is especially deplorable when distinctive terms are not only available, but whose use, appropriately applied, would convey a clearer image and would enable collectors and museums to avoid the risk of being misled. A number of cases of indiscriminate usage exist with respect to silverware.

Some examples are noted here by way of illustration. (1) In the case of the terms 'lid' and 'cover', clarity and precision would be served by confining the former to a covering that is affixed by a hinge (as on a mug or a tankard, so that 'hinged lid' would become tautological) and the latter to any removable covering (as on a tureen or standing cup). (2) A footed flat waiter or salver intended to be used for serving should always be distinguished from a footed shallow-bowl drinking vessel – a 'tazza' (the word *tazza* being the Italian for 'cup') – although 'tazza' has often been applied to footed flat articles. (3) A 'sconce' is a wall candelabrum, and the term is obsolete when applied to a 'candlestick socket'. (4) A receptacle, whether small or large and ornate, for iced water to cool one or more bottles of wine is a 'wine cooler', and the term 'cistern', often applied to large examples, should be confined to receptacles intended to contain water for washing. (5) The terms 'charger', 'sideboard dish', and 'shield' have been used interchangeably, but the first should be confined to a large serving dish, the second to a large ornamental dish with relief decoration (making it unsuitable for serving purposes) and meant to be stood vertically on a sideboard as an ornament, and the third to a more massive piece decorated with a pictorial medallion in high relief and having small holes by which it can be suspended as a wall decoration. (6) The term 'chafing dish' is often used in Britain to designate not only a receptacle resting on a lamp-stand and used for cooking a light snack (as the term is invariably used in the United States), but also for a stand in which are placed hot coals and which is stood under a pot or grille, the latter type of piece being preferably termed a 'brazier', an object basically intended to provide heat rather than being a receptacle for use in cooking.

Probably the most frequent instance of confused terminology involves the words 'posset-pot' and 'porringer', which have too often been used interchangeably and also to designate a type of small two-handled cup (sometimes with a cover) having two vertical side handles. The former term (and its related term 'caudle-cup', differing only in respect of the ingredients of the beverage drunk from it) is applied in ceramic ware and glassware to a cup-like drinking receptacle that has a thin curving spout extending upward from the bottom so that the liquid can be drunk without the curds on the surface; and that seems a more logical usage than does applying the term to a small silver cup with two vertical side handles which is not suitable for drinking such beverages. The term 'porringer', often applied in Britain to such small two-handled cups, would be preferably reserved (as it invariably is in the United States) for a low flat-bottomed bowl having two side handles extending flush with the rim (similar to the French *écuelle*). With the two terms thus reserved for those special forms, a small cup-like receptacle with vertical side handles (basically similar in form to the many large cups with two vertical side handles) can be called simply a 'small two-handled cup'. However, the existing practices are probably so embedded in British usage that it may prove difficult now to bring about a change; even so, some writers have drawn attention to the confusion, and perhaps it is still not too late for greater clarity to be achieved.

The black-and-white illustrations fall into two main categories: (1) some show objects that are typical of a class with regard to form (e.g., argyll or monteith), decoration (e.g., chinoiserie or embossing), designer (e.g., A. W. N. Pugin, Léonard Morel-Ladeuil), modeller (e.g., Edmund Cotterill) or maker (e.g., Robert Garrard II); (2) others show unique objects or pieces that have an accepted name (e.g., the America's Cup trophy or the Theocritus Cups), or one of the many other named pieces, whether in public collections or not easily accessible for viewing, that are less well known, as well as many individual commemorative and presentation pieces. The choice of colour plates has been influenced by the fact that most silverware can be illustrated equally well in monochrome; hence the plates (see list on p. 12) show mainly pieces that are partially gilded or have enamelled or other decoration which can be better appreciated in colour.

A wide-ranging book of this type must inevitably draw on the writings and expert knowledge of prior and contemporary writers; these include the authors of earlier glossaries, of treatises on silverware of various types, periods or regions, or of relevant magazine articles (of which there is a plethora on the subject of silverware, notably those published in *Apollo, The Connoisseur, Burlington Magazine, Country Life,* and *Antiques*), written by such eminent authorities as the late Charles C. Oman, Norman M. Penzer, G. Bernard Hughes, and Edward Wenham, and by Arthur G. Grimwade and Judith Banister. Although no general bibliography is included, the literature on silverware being far too vast, many individual entries conclude with an appropriate citation of a source book or magazine article which deals with the particular topic in greater detail or which includes relevant illustrations. I gratefully acknowledge my indebtedness to all such prior writers.

I wish also to express my appreciation to the many British and American museums and collections which have made available photographs of pieces in their possession for use as illustrations; in each case the source is noted in the caption. Special thanks are due to the following for having supplied a significant number of photographs:

Hartford, Connecticut	Wadsworth Atheneum
London	British Museum
	The Goldsmiths' Company
	The Jewish Museum
	Science Museum
	Victoria and Albert Museum
New Haven, Connecticut	Yale University Art Gallery
New York City	Metropolitan Museum of Art
Oxford	Ashmolean Museum
Williamsburg, Virginia	Colonial Williamsburg Foundation

I am also grateful to Her Majesty the Queen for graciously permitting photographs of several pieces in the Royal Collection to be reproduced, and to the Controller of Her Majesty's Stationery Office (HMSO) for permission to reproduce photographs of pieces of the Crown regalia in the Tower of London. Thanks are also extended to a number of silverware firms that have generously supplied photographs of pieces owned or handled by them, especially Garrard & Co. Ltd, Brand Inglis Ltd, Asprey & Co. Ltd, Partridge (Fine Arts) Ltd, the Gorham Co., and Tiffany & Co. Appreciation is also expressed to the London and New York offices of Christie's and Sotheby's for photographs supplied by them.

Charles Truman, formerly of the Victoria and Albert Museum and now head of the Silver Department at Christie's, London, read the manuscript and made helpful suggestions, but the responsibility for the content of all entries is solely that of the author.

Finally, I wish to express my recognition of and heartfelt gratitude for all the invaluable assistance, sincere interest, and constant encouragement by my recently deceased wife, Wendy, throughout the years of researching and writing the manuscript, and without which the task could not have been completed.

New Orleans 1987   H.N.

Dictionary of Silverware

Alphabetization of entries is by the word-by-word method: thus, 'arm sconce' precedes 'armband'. Cross-references to related topics are indicated by SMALL CAPITALS within an entry. Initial capitals are used in entry headings to denote a unique or distinctively named piece: thus, 'Berkeley Teapot' refers to a particular teapot with known historical associations, whereas 'Birmingham silverware' refers to all types of ware made in that city. Birth/death dates are given in parentheses; dates between commas indicate reigns or periods of office. For the sake of brevity and as an aid to identification, two or more silversmiths having the same name are distinguished by the use of roman numerals, e.g., Paul Revere I and Paul Revere II (father and son), the number in each case being for convenience only and not part of the individual's name.

Illustrations in black and white will as a rule be found on the same page as the relevant entry or on the facing page, though a few appear on adjacent pages owing to considerations of space. The following abbreviations are used in the captions: D. = diameter; H. = height; L. = length; W. = width.

A

ablution basin. A type of BASIN for holding water intended: (1) in ecclesiastical usage, for rinsing the hands or some object of CHURCH PLATE, such as a CHALICE; or (2) in secular usage, for rinsing the fingers at the dinner table (sometimes called a ROSE-WATER BASIN). Two ecclesiastical ablution basins were donated in 1515–16 to Corpus Christi College, Oxford, by its founder, Bishop Richard Fox. *See* ALMS DISH.

Academic Style. A style of decoration, developed in the United States, based on the copying of earlier English and French styles. The style was in the tradition of the École des Beaux-Arts, Paris, the designs being precise and academic. It was introduced as to FLATWARE in the 1880s, initiated at the GORHAM COMPANY by F. ANTOINE HELLER, and occurs in HOLLOW WARE from the late 1880s; its use continued into the 1920s.

acanthus. A southern European plant, the spiky leaf of which has been used, generally in a vertical position, as a stylized decorative motif since antiquity, especially in architecture on capitals of the Corinthian order. As to silverware, the motif occurs on some HOLLOW WARE, used repetitively to form a band encircling the CALYX of the piece. It was popular as a feature of the RENAISSANCE STYLE and later of the NEO-CLASSICAL STYLE and the ADAM STYLE, and again of the REGENCY STYLE. The leaf, which varies in form in the successive periods, is found as either applied or embossed decoration.

achievement. In heraldry, the armorial bearings of an individual or family, comprising the ESCUTCHEON with, above it, the helmet supporting the CREST, together with the supporters to left and right and the motto below. An achievement is an emblem restricted to one family (unlike a crest, which may be used by several unrelated families). It is found, either engraved or enamelled, on some important articles of silverware, and often serves to establish PROVENANCE and date, as well as being decorative and adding value to the piece.

Achilles Shield. A silver-gilt convex SHIELD having a large central medallion, in high relief, depicting the shield of encrusted iron made by the god Hephaestus for Achilles at Troy, as described by Homer in Book 18 of the *Iliad*; the medallion, which depicts in high relief a figure of the Sun (Apollo) standing in a quadriga (a chariot drawn by four horses), is within a wide border decorated with a continuous frieze depicting seven scenes of war and peace (based on Book 18) and surrounded by a narrow band of stellar formations and an outer border embossed with waves representing the 'Stream of Ocean'. The shield was designed and modelled by JOHN FLAXMAN II from 1809 to 1818, on commission from the Prince Regent, 1811-20 (later George IV). Four such shields were cast in silver at the Soho works of RUNDELL, BRIDGE & RUNDELL, 1821-3, with CHASING done by WILLIAM PITTS II. The original cast, dated 1821, first appeared at the coronation banquet of George IV in July 1821, and is in the Royal Collection. The other casts were sold to: Frederick, Duke of York (1763-1827), brother of George IV; Hugh Percy, 3rd Duke of Northumberland; and the 1st Earl of Lonsdale (1757-1844). The cast owned by the Duke of York was sold by his executors at Christie's, London, in 1827 (the buyer being the Rundell firm, acting for the Duke's youngest brother, the 1st Duke of Cambridge), was sold again at Christie's, London, in 1904 (the buyer being the Dowager Grand Duchess of Mecklenburg-Strelitz, sister of the 2nd Duke of Cambridge), and was sold again at Sotheby's, Los Angeles, California, in May 1973; it is now in the Henry E. Huntington Art Gallery, San Marino, California. The Lonsdale cast was sold by the Earl's descendants at Christie's, London, in 1947, and is now in the Fairhaven Collection at Anglesey Abbey, near Cambridge; it was shown in the exhibition 'Treasure Houses of Britain' at the National Gallery of Art, Washington, D.C., 1985-6. The Northumberland cast (with leather suspen-

acanthus. Jug with applied decoration of acanthus leaves and bunches of grapes, London, 1836. H. 30 cm. Wellcome Collection, Science Museum, London.

Achilles Shield. Designed and modelled by John Flaxman II and made by Philip Rundell, 1821. W. 92 cm. Royal Collection; reproduced by gracious permission of Her Majesty the Queen.

acorn cup. Gold standing cup. London, c. 1610. H. 18·8 cm. British Museum, London.

sion rings on the reverse) was sold by the 10th Duke at Sotheby's, London, on 3 May 1984, when it was acquired for £484,000 (about $678,000) by E. & C. T. Koopman & Son Ltd, London silverware dealers, who have since re-sold it to a private collection in the United Kingdom.

A bronze cast of the shield, together with a plaster cast, was sold in 1911 by Mrs J. E. Bridge, of Manor House, Piddletrenthide, widow of the son of John Gawler Bridge, a partner in Rundells. Bronze casts were given by Rundells in 1842 to the Universities of Oxford and Cambridge. Another bronze cast was given to the Royal Academy, and a fourth to the painter Sir Thomas Lawrence, this last example being sold at Christie's, London, on 6 July 1930. An ELECTROFORM copy was shown by HUNT & ROSKELL at the Great Exhibition, London, 1851.

See Brian Ivon-Jones, 'The Achilles Shield' in *Apollo*, April 1975, p. 447; Shirley Bury and Michael Snodin, 'The Achilles Shield' in Sotheby's *Art at Auction* (1983-4), p. 274.

acorn cup. A type of STANDING CUP, of which the bowl and cover together are in the form of an acorn, the bulging bowl (the cupule) having its surface covered with raised dots in a diaper pattern and the cover (the visible part of the nut) being smooth; the bowl rests on a gnarled tree-trunk stem rising from a high circular foot, and the cover has a globular finial. The only known English silver example is the WESTBURY CUP. A later example, made of 22-carat gold, unmarked but attributed to c. 1610, and said to be the earliest known piece of English secular gold plate, bears a later engraved inscription, 'This cup left to ye Church of Stapleford by ye Rt Honble Bennet Earl of Harborough who departed this life Octr. 16 1732', and the donor's arms and crest, and also the Sacred Monogram 'IHS' in a glory; it was owned by the parish church of Stapleford, Leicestershire, and was bought in 1956 by the British Museum, London.

acorn spoon. A type of SPOON having a straight stem terminating in a finial in the form of an acorn. On some examples the acorn is accompanied by foliage. The acorn was moulded with the stem and not soldered to it. Such spoons are recorded from the early 14th century to the 17th century.

Adam, Robert (1728-92). A Scottish architect, designer, and antiquary who, with his brother, James (1730-94), working in London, developed the style known as ADAM STYLE. Robert was inspired by the archaeological excavations at Herculaneum and Pompeii (which he visited in 1754-7) and by Etruscan art, and, drawing on the design books that depicted the forms and decoration of Greek and Roman vases, created his own version of the NEO-CLASSI-CAL STYLE, mainly in architecture, but also-in seeking to provide an integrated interior décor by designing furniture and furnishings-extended its use to articles of silverware. He and his brother, although they did not design on commission for silversmiths, produced many designs for silverware suggestive of Greco-Roman style. Some of his designs are preserved at Sir John Soane's Museum, London, but not all of these were executed. *See* RICHMOND RACE CUP.

Adam silverware. Articles of silverware made in England, *c.* 1765–95, in ADAM STYLE, including especially dinner-table and sideboard pieces, designed to complement the decoration of a room, e.g., TUREENS, SALVERS, CAKE-BASKETS, JUGS, cube-shaped TEA-CADDIES, EPERGNES, CANDELABRA, CANDLESTICKS, and TEA SERVICES. Many such pieces were the work of London silversmiths, particularly objects made of STERLING SILVER for aristocratic buyers, but much was also made at Birmingham and Sheffield of SHEFFIELD PLATE to cater to the newly developing mass market, in which silverware in the Adam style became popular. *See* E. Alfred Jones, 'Adam Silver' in *Apollo*, February 1939, p. 55; Robert Rowe, *Adam Silver, 1765-95* (1965).

Adam style. A consistent and easily recognizable style of decoration that is especially associated with ROBERT ADAM and that somewhat corresponds with that of the early years, 1765–95, of the NEO-CLASSICAL STYLE (which had followed the ROCOCO STYLE). Although Adam was principally an architect and a designer of furniture, his designs for silverware greatly influenced the work of contempory silversmiths. The HOLLOW WARE, such as the JUGS and HORSE-RACING TROPHIES that he designed, was largely inspired by the forms of Greek and Etruscan ceramic vases, and his decorative motifs featured the flowing designs and motifs of classical style, such as ROSETTES, PATERAE, ACANTHUS leaves, SWAGS, KEY-FRET BORDERS, VITRUVIAN SCROLLS, HUSK BORDERS, GUILLOCHE borders, and rams' heads, and the use of TASSIE SILVER MEDALLIONS. The style, although based on Adam designs, was often modified by contemporary silversmiths.

Admiralty Barge Badge. Parcel-gilt badge with embossed marine motifs and with enamelling, William Lukin, London, 1736-7. W. 15 cm. Victoria and Albert Museum, London.

Admiralty Barge Badge. A type of BADGE worn with full-dress livery by Thames Watermen of the Admiralty Barge. It is decorated with EMBOSSING depicting dolphins and maritime motifs, enclosing an oval decorated with a foul-anchor emblem (an anchor and coiled rope). *See* WATERMAN'S BADGE.

Aeneas Shield. A SHIELD designed by WILLIAM PITTS II in the style of JOHN FLAXMAN II and THOMAS STOTHARD. Pitts showed a plaster model at the Royal Academy in 1828, intending to execute it in gold, but it remained unfinished when in 1840 he committed suicide; HUNT & ROSKELL acquired the model from his widow and made a silver version in 1848, and an ELECTROFORM version in copper which was shown in London at the Great Exhibition of 1851 and again at the London International Exhibition of 1862.

Aesop's Fables Service. A four-piece parcel-gilt combined TEA SERVICE and COFFEE SERVICE made in 1850 by Joseph Angell III (see ANGELL), depicting eight of Aesop's Fables. The body of each piece is of shallow spool shape, made of FROSTED SILVER and encased in a framework of free-standing trees, with the scenes engraved on the frosted silver and with a scroll under each scene bearing the apposite moral. The handles and spouts are of ungilded silver, but the trees and other ornamentation are of silver gilt. The ornamentation is removable to facilitate use when so desired. The service, made to be shown at the Great Exhibition of 1851, was said by Angell to be an example of ware purchasable 'at moderate cost'. It was acquired in 1890 by Benjamin Bridgeman and sold by one of his descendants at Sotheby's Belgravia on 29 March 1973; it is now owned by the Goldsmiths' Company, London.

agate objects. Articles of which the essential part is made of agate, combined with silver MOUNTS, such as certain STANDING CUPS, as well as the handles of some dessert knives, forks, and spoons, and the lids of some SNUFF-BOXES. Comparable ware was made of jasper, including some plates made by Eley & Fearn, 1817, and some of alabaster (*see* DYNELEY CASKET). *See* RUTLAND EWER; MOUNTED OBJECTS.

agate objects. Standing cup with agate bowl and silver-gilt mounts, London, 1567-8. H. 20 cm. Victoria and Albert Museum, London.

Agincourt Sideboard Dish. A silver-gilt SIDEBOARD DISH in the centre of which is depicted in high relief a scene from the Battle of Agincourt (1415) in which Henry V of England routed the French. It was made by RUNDELL, BRIDGE & RUNDELL to the order of Thomas Hamlet, a retail silversmith, to be a birthday gift in 1826 to Adolphus Frederick, 1st Duke of Cambridge (1774–1850), seventh son of George III, from his wife, Princess Augusta, third daughter of the Landgrave Frederick of Hesse-Cassel, whom he had married in 1818. It was sold at Christies's on 7 October 1904, and its subsequent whereabouts is unknown. It is sometimes called the 'Agincourt Shield', and is a companion piece to the CRÉCY SIDEBOARD DISH.

Agnus Dei case. A small receptacle (sometimes of silver or silver gilt) in which was enclosed a roundel of wax bearing a stamped impression of the Agnus Dei (the Lamb of God, as the emblem of Christ), made from the wax of a paschal candle blessed at Rome by a new Pope in the first year of his pontificate, the ceremony being repeated every seventh year thereafter. Such cases, some of which have a cover of glass or transparent horn on the front and back, were distributed to the faithful in the 14th/15th centuries.

Albany pattern. A pattern used on the handle of FLATWARE; the stem, which widens gradually toward the terminal, is decorated along half of its length with FLUTING, broadening into a fluted terminal capped by a tiny ball.

Aldridge, James (fl. 1778-1816). A London silversmith who was apprenticed in 1778 and freed in 1785; he entered his first mark in 1798 with address at 20 The Strand. His work includes articles decorated with engraving in imitation of the enamelled decoration on Chinese porcelain of the reign of Ch'ien Lung, 1736-95, the different enamel colours being conveyed by the use of the appropriate HATCHING. He also decorated porcelain objects with silver MOUNTS. Examples of his work were acquired by William Beckford (1759-1844) for his collection at Fonthill Abbey, Wiltshire, and, after he moved to Bath in 1822, at his house in Lansdown Crescent and later in the tower he had built on Lansdown.

Aldridge, James. Bowl in the style of Ch'ien Lung porcelain, London, 1812. Victoria and Albert Museum, London.

Alhambra Table Fountain. A CENTREPIECE in the form of a Moorish pavilion having a domed roof decorated with CHAMPLEVÉ enamelling and resting on a leafy base; the piece is in the style of the Alhambra, Granada, and is intended to represent a shrine covering a water-hole. On the base and encircling the edifice are figures in-the-round of three Arab horses that had been presented to Queen Victoria, and of their Arabian attendant, and nearby a Negro boy with a dog. Lower on the base are two flamingos, a buzzard, and plants indigenous to Arabia. A fountain in the pavilion spurts scented rose-water, hence the piece is sometimes called 'The Fountain Temple'. It was designed (stated by J. B. Waring) by Edward Lorenzo Percy under the direction of Prince Albert, and the horses were modelled by EDMUND COTTERILL; it was made by ROBERT GARRARD II for R. & S. Garrard & Co., 1852-3. It was shown at the Dublin Industrial Exhibition in 1853, at the London International Exhibition of 1862, and at the Victoria and Albert Museum Centenary Exhibition of 1962; it is now in the Royal Collection. *See* J. B. Waring, *Masterpieces of Industrial Art* (1863), vol. II, pl. 121.

Alhambra Table Fountain. Design by E. Lorenzo Percy; horses modelled by Edmund Cotterill; made by Robert Garrard II for R. & S. Garrard, London, 1852-3. H. 1·09 m. Royal Collection; reproduced by gracious permission of Her Majesty the Queen.

alloy. A mixture of two or more compatible metals (or sometimes a metal and a non-metal, e.g., steel, an alloy of iron and carbon), made by being fused into each other to form a homogeneous mass, the resultant new metal usually being harder, more durable and more fusible than the components but generally less malleable and of a different colour. Non-compatible metals (e.g. nickel and silver) will not dissolve into each other, and hence cannot be alloyed. Some alloys are formed by nature (e.g., electrum), but most are man-made to increase strength or workability, or to alter colour, e.g., a base metal mixed with a precious metal. Alloys made of various metals and in various proportions to meet different industrial needs are produced by refiners for sale, e.g., gold and silver solder supplied to makers of silverware. An alloy differs from a COMPOSITE METAL or PLATED METAL, in which the components are not integrated. *See* SILVER ALLOY; GERMAN SILVER; PAKTONG; BRITANNIA METAL; FINENESS.

alms dish. A large ecclesiastical dish or plate (sometimes called an 'alms basin' or 'alms plate') upon which money, collected in church from the congregation in a smaller COLLECTION PLATE, COLLECTION BOX, or a bag, was assembled and presented at the altar in Anglican churches. Examples vary in size, ranging from about 30 to 60 cm in diameter, and are of indeterminate style of decoration, usually in the prevailing style of the times, but often having the bowl and rim embossed, and the bowl frequently depicting the Last Supper or the Chi-Rho monogram. Some so-called alms dishes were probably originally intended for secular use as an ABLUTION BASIN (ROSE-WATER BASIN); it is often difficult to make a distinction, except in cases where decoration featuring a scriptural motif is present or, in the case of a piece made as an ablution basin, where there is a central depressed circle to position an accompanying EWER. An alms dish is often placed on the altar be-

tween a pair of CANDLESTICKS. *See* ARLINGTON TAZZA; BERMONDSEY DISH; QUEEN ANNE ALMS DISHES; ALTAR DISH; CHURCH PLATE.

altar candlestick. A type of tall CANDLESTICK for use on a church altar, usually having a BALUSTER stem resting on a tripod or circular base. Some have a single SOCKET on the stem, but most examples are in the form of a PRICKET CANDLESTICK. After the Reformation, it was usual Anglican practice to have a pair of candlesticks on an altar; in recusant chapels the candlesticks were usually in sets of four or six. *See* CHURCH FURNISHINGS.

altar cross. A type of large CROSS that stands on an altar, as part of the CHURCH FURNISHINGS. Such crosses are decorated usually on only one side, in the form of a crucifix, but later Protestant examples are simple undecorated crosses. Occasional examples are in the form of a RELIQUARY CROSS.

altar cruet. A type of CRUET used at a church altar as an article of CHURCH PLATE, being generally a pair, one for wine (often marked with a letter 'V' for *vinum*) and one for water (often marked with a letter 'A' for *aqua*). Some have such letters cut out as the finial or engraved on the body or on the top of the cover or stopper. Many were made of silver, but some were of crystal with silver mounts, thus enabling the contents to be readily distinguished. Other pairs were distinguishable by having one receptacle made of silver gilt, by being provided with a gilt stopper, or by being decorated with vine scrolls. Some early altar cruets are in the form of a small MILK-JUG, with loop handle and pouring BEAK; but later examples are often vase-shaped with a high loop handle and a pouring lip, and are usually accompanied by a TRAY. Also called a 'burette'.

altar dish. A type of plate used at the Eucharist. At least five examples are in the Royal Collection. Three, *c.* 1660, are at St George's Chapel, Windsor, the largest one depicting Christ washing the feet of the Disciples, and the other two, presented by the Duchess of York in 1661, having in the well scenes depicting, respectively, Christ blessing the children, and the Last Supper. Another, 1683–4, with a scene of the Last Supper, is at St James's Church, Piccadilly, London. *See* CHARLES II ALTAR DISHES; GARTHORNE ALTAR DISH; STUART ALTAR DISH; ALMS DISH.

Alverstone Cups. A pair of silver-gilt STANDING CUPS having a spool-shaped body and a domed cover with a finial in the form of an *amorino*. They are decorated with FLAT CHASING on panels between stripes of vertical curved fluting. They were made by PAUL STORR, 1832, and were presented to the Goldsmiths' Company, London, by Lord Alverstone, Prime Warden in 1893 and 1897.

America's Cup. Britannia silver, Robert Garrard II, London, 1848. H. 68·5 cm. Courtesy, Garrard & Co. Ltd, London.

ambassadorial silverware. Articles of silverware that were provided, from the 16th century, by the English Sovereign to ambassadors and to certain other important emissaries or officials to enable them to maintain a high standard of living and entertainment. The pieces, usually a SERVICE, and often a COMPOSITE SERVICE, were technically loaned for the recipient's use while posted abroad or holding an office, but by custom after *c.* 1688 many pieces were retained as a perquisite of office. All such pieces bore, for identification when demanded for return, the engraved Royal arms. The practice of furnishing such plate was terminated in 1815 for ambassadors and in 1839 for the Speaker of the House of Commons. Some retained pieces were melted down by the recipient or his heirs, the metal being used to make a new piece, on which was engraved the original Royal arms. Thus, much silverware bearing the Royal arms was never intended for the Sovereign's personal use. *See* WELLINGTON AMBASSADORIAL SERVICE; ARMORIAL PLATE.

America's Cup. A TROPHY, made of BRITANNIA SILVER, in the form of a EWER (originally known as the 'Hundred Guinea Cup' when presented in 1851 by the Royal Yacht Squadron for a yacht race in August 1851 around the Isle of Wight), designed and made in 1848 by ROBERT GARRARD II for GARRARD & CO. In 1857 it was renamed the 'America's Cup' and was deeded to the New York Yacht Club, to be held 'as a perpetual challenge cup for friendly competition between foreign countries' represented by yachts of prescribed measurements, races to be held periodically in the waters of the nation holding the trophy between a yacht representing that nation and a foreign challenger, the result being decided in the best of seven races.

The cup was won first in 1851 by the American schooner *America*, and subsequently retained by the American defender in twenty-four consecutive competitions until 1983, when it was won by the Australian challenger, *Australia II*. The cup, 68·5 cm high, which had been kept (secured to a table by a bolt) by the New York Yacht Club in New York City, was thereupon turned over – together with the bolt – to the Royal Perth Yacht Club in Perth, Western Australia. In 1987 the trophy was won by the challenger, *Stars and Stripes*, from San Diego, Cal., who retained it until the 1995 race, which was won by the Royal New Zealand Yacht Squadron. The cup bears the names of early winners, those since 1950 being recorded on a plinth, 17·8 cm high, added in 1958.

An almost exact copy of the cup, dated 1856, also made by Garrard & Co., bears an inscription recording its having been a gift to John Etensor Heathrate and his wife. Another cup, purporting to be a copy but differing in several aspects, was made by Spink & Co., London, 1899; bearing the engraved arms of the City of London; this version is at the Mansion House, London.

American silverware. A broad term usually confined to North American silverware, and even more often restricted to that of the United States, with sometimes Canada included. *See* CANADIAN SILVERWARE; MEXICAN SILVERWARE; UNITED STATES SILVERWARE.

amphora ewer. A type of EWER in the shape of a Greek amphora (ovoid, with two vertical loop handles attached at the shoulder and just below the neck). Such pieces were popular in the Elizabethan period, 1558–1603, and Jacobean period, 1603–25. *See* GREEK-VASE SILVERWARE.

ampulla. A type of receptacle, of various shapes and sizes, used in churches and at coronations to hold the chrism (the consecrated oil). The ampulla in the British Royal regalia, used during the coronation service, is of gold, being in the form of a standing eagle with spread wings and having the pouring aperture in its beak and its head the screwed-on cover; it was remade for Charles II by using metal from the original ampulla, perhaps the gold eagle ampulla used at the coronation of Henry IV in 1399. *See* CORONATION SPOON; CHRISMATORY; CHURCH PLATE.

ampulla. Silver ampulla used at the coronation of Charles I at Holyrood, Edinburgh, 1633. National Museum of Antiquities of Scotland, Edinburgh.

Anathema Cup. A silver-gilt STANDING CUP having a bowl of inverted bell shape, an ogee-shaped vertical section, a TRUMPET FOOT, and a circular base with vertical sides. The only decoration is a narrow band, depicting floral rosettes and alternating ribbon scrolls, encircling the base between two bands of moulding, and six PELLETS in a row under the bowl. It is said to have had a cover, now missing. A PRINT in the bottom of the bowl was formerly enamelled. The cup bears a Latin inscription, in Gothic letters, 'Qui alienaverit anathema sit' (Who shall take me away, let him be cursed). It bears the London hallmark and the date letter D for 1481–2, and is (apart from some spoons) the earliest-known fully marked English piece of secular plate. It was donated in 1497 to Pembroke College, Cambridge, by Dr Thomas Langton (d. 1500), then Bishop of Winchester and a former fellow of the college. An ELECTROFORM copy is in the Victoria and Albert Museum, London.

Anchor Hallmark. The ASSAY OFFICE HALLMARK used at the Birmingham Assay Office from 1773 (and confirmed by the Hallmarking Act of 1973), being an anchor that is vertical for STERLING SILVER, horizontal for gold and platinum.

andiron. A term (not derived from the word 'iron') applied during the Middle Ages to the article later called a FIRE-DOG.

Angell. A family of three generations of London silversmiths, descended from Joseph Angell I, a weaver, of Cow Cross, London (and possibly also of Battle Bridge, Middlesex). He had three sons — Joseph Angell II, John, and Abraham – all of whom became silversmiths.

Joseph Angell II (d. *c.* 1851-3), was apprenticed in 1796 to Henry Nutting, and freed in 1804; he entered his first mark in 1811 from his address at 55 Compton St, Clerkenwell, his second in 1824, and a third in 1831 (the last jointly with his nephew, John Charles Angell). He made the BATTLE OF ISSUS SHIELD in 1828. He had two sons: Joseph Angell III (1816-91), who became a partner from 1840 (when the firm moved its workshop to Panton St, Haymarket) and later opened a shop at 10 The Strand; and Charles Angell, apprenticed to his uncle, John Angell, in 1825. In 1849 Joseph Angell III took full control of the business, entered his first mark, and showed silverware, including his AESOP'S FABLES SERVICE and the VINTAGE CLARET JUG, at the Great Exhibition of 1851. He had about 35 employees, including as an apprentice his nephew, Richard Angell Green (b. 1836). Joseph Angell III promoted the use of enamelling to decorate silverware, the results receiving mixed critical opinion. His success in business led to his showing, at the New York International Exhibition of 1853, pieces of enamelled silverware and also his CENTREPIECE decorated with a figure group depicting Sir Roger de Coverley having his fortune told by a gipsy. He retired in 1862. Richard Angell Green became a jeweller, showing ware at the London International Exhibition of 1862 and executing in part the silver MOUNTS on one of the BURGES CLARET-JUGS.

John Angell (d. 1850) was apprenticed to William Elliot in 1799; he apparently did not register a mark, but was working with his uncle, Joseph Angell II, in Compton St in 1825. He had two sons: John Charles Angell, who was apprenticed to his father in 1825 and entered a joint mark with his uncle, Joseph Angell II, in 1831; and George Angell, who became his father's partner in 1840 and who made the silver mounts on one of the Burges Claret-Jugs and the lid of another.

Abraham Angell was apprenticed in 1808 to his eldest brother, Joseph Angell II.

animal silverware. Any article of silverware made in the form of or including a realistic representation in-the-round of an animal. Examples have been made depicting many different kinds of wild and domestic animals. They include ornamental pieces representing, e.g., a horse, dog or lion, and articles having a figure of an animal as a decorative element, such as a THUMBPIECE or a finial (e.g., a horse on the cover of a PUNCH-BOWL, a lion on the lid of a TANKARD, or a cow on the cover of a BUTTER-DISH). Sometimes several animal figures are an integral decorative feature on a CENTREPIECE, e.g., the goats on the ASHBURNHAM CENTREPIECE, the horses on the ALHAMBRA TABLE FOUNTAIN, and the dogs on the 'QUEEN VICTORIA'S DOGS' CENTREPIECE. Some pieces in the form of an animal serve a utilitarian purpose, e.g., a COW CREAMER, BEAR JUG, STIRRUP CUP, and the MONKEY SALT. *See* BIRD SILVERWARE.

Anne, Queen. For subjects associated with Queen Anne, *see* QUEEN ANNE ALMS DISHES; QUEEN ANNE STYLE.

annealing. The process of restoring silver (or other metal) to its original state after it has been hammered, rolled, drawn or otherwise worked (resulting in a distortion of the grains and consequent brittleness) by heating it to approximately 700° C. (becoming 'cherry red') and then cooling it so as to recrystallize the grains and make the metal again DUCTILE and MALLEABLE. The metal must be uniformly annealed, requiring varying periods of time for metals of different annealing temperatures and thicknesses; overheating must be avoided, as it would change the surface. After heating, the cooling process varies; some metals are cured by lapse of time, others by immersion (QUENCHING) in water or in pickle. (The process is related to, but must be distinguished from, annealing glass, which requires uniform slow heating and cooling to remove internal stresses.) Annealing is done in a heat-controlled oxygen-free furnace (to prevent oxidation) or by hand torch; if the latter, immersion in an acid bath is essential, to remove the oxidation caused by the heating, and then rinsing to remove the acid. A recent method, not often used, is called 'salt-bath furnace annealing'.

Anchor Hallmark. Birmingham Assay Office hallmarks used (*left*) in cycle 1950-74 (except 1973) and (*right*) from 1 January 1975.

Anathema Cup. Electroform copy of original silver-gilt cup, London, 1481-2, at Pembroke College, Cambridge. Victoria and Albert Museum, London.

animal silverware. Ornament in the form of a rearing stallion, John Mortimer and John Samuel Hunt, London, 1842, H. 41 cm. Courtesy, Partridge (Fine Arts) Ltd, London.

annular base. A term used to describe the bottom of a piece of silverware, including some TWO-HANDLED CUPS, having affixed to it a thin silver FOOT-RING.

anthemion. A Greek decorative motif consisting of stylized foliated and floral forms, derived from the honeysuckle blossom and palmette branches extending in a radiating cluster. It is found, singly or in bands, on silverware of the 18th and early 19th centuries, both on large receptacles and on CUT-LERY.

Apollo and Daphne Candlesticks. Two pairs of FIGURAL CANDLESTICKS, the stem of each being in the form of a standing figure in-the-round; each pair has one figure representing Apollo, the other Daphne, standing on a ROCOCO STYLE triangular base ornately decorated with scrolls, rockwork, and foliage. The upraised arms of the figures support the candle SOCKETS. The form is based on drawings by George Michael Moser, R.A. (1706–83). The pieces, unmarked, attributed to London *c.* 1740–5, were acquired in 1977 by the Victoria and Albert Museum, London.

Apostle spoon. A type of SPOON, about 18 cm long, that has, as the finial (on a straight undecorated stem), a cast full-length figure in-the-round depicting one of the Twelve Apostles, with his attribute (emblem: a symbol of his trade or an instrument of his martyrdom), together with, to form a complete SET, a thirteenth spoon (the 'Master Spoon') having such a figure representing, usually, Christ. Usually the figures have a nimbus (on early examples, at the back of the head, upright and rayed; on later examples, horizontal or inclined forward, and pierced). Such spoons originated on the Continent (especially in Germany and the Netherlands, but also made in France and Spain), the styles varying in each country. In England they were made mainly in the Tudor period, 1490–1650; the earliest known example, *c.* 1450–78, is in the 'Beaufort Set' at Christ's College, Cambridge (see below), and a reference to such a spoon occurs in a York will dated 1494. The spoons made in London have the finial soldered to the stem by a V-joint; provincial examples have a lap joint. The figure, although sometimes cast in one piece with the spoon, was usually cast separately, and sometimes the attribute (often held in the right hand) was cast separately from the figure. Apostle spoons were popular in the 16th and 17th centuries, when a set or a single spoon was often given as a christening present by the sponsor, especially a spoon with the Apostle having the same name as the child or being the patron saint of the sponsor.

Apostle spoon. Detail of finial depicting St Andrew with saltire cross. Approx. twice actual size. British Museum, London.

Many silversmiths made such spoons (usually the figure being cast by a specialist, not the spoonmaker), sometimes making them singly or in incomplete sets varying according to the demand for particular figures. Complete sets of thirteen different spoons having the same maker and date (but sometimes slightly varying in length) are very rare, as also are assembled sets of spoons by different makers and of different years. Complete or assembled sets are in the following collections: (1) Henry E. Huntington Gallery, San Marino, California (*see* MUNRO APOSTLE SPOONS); (2) British Museum, London (*see* ASTOR APOSTLE SPOONS); (3) Goldsmiths' Company, London (*see* LAMBERT APOSTLE SPOONS); (4) Metropolitan Museum of Art, New York (*see* SWETTENHAM-MORGAN APOSTLE SPOONS); (5) Henry Ford Museum (Edison Institute), Dearborn, Michigan (*see* SULHAMSTEAD APOSTLE SPOONS); and (6) Sterling and Francine Clark Art Institute, Williamstown, Massachusetts (an assembled set, five made by Robert Jygges, London, 1628?; all purchased in 1965). Important partial sets are the 'Beaufort Set' of six, unmarked, *c.* 1450–78, at Christ's College, Cambridge (from originally thirteen, as inventoried in 1655, but inventoried as only six in 1688; there is no existing evidence to support the legend that they were bequeathed to the college in 1509 by Lady Margaret Beaufort, its founder); the 'Benson Set' of six; the 'Bute Set' of seven, 1499/1513?; the 'Bernal Set' of eleven, 1519 (silver-gilt and having the figures and attributes cast in one piece; bought by the Rev. Thomas Staniforth on 27 April 1853 and listed in a catalogue of 1898); and the 'Symons Set' of twelve, sold in June 1923.

Apostle spoons have been reproduced in great numbers over many years, including some made of pewter or latten, as well as inexpensive reproductions which often show the figures without a nimbus or an attribute. A silver set, with twisted-vine stems, was made by the GORHAM COMPANY in 1876/1901; in 1974 it was reproduced in a limited edition of 2,750.

Many fake spoons exist, including some with a figure transposed to an unrelated stem, some transposing a different figure to an authentic stem, some substituting a different attribute, and some regilded or having parts repaired by electroplating. Some spoons having a figure of one of the Evangelists may not be English silver examples.

See John S. Sharman, 'English Apostle Spoons and their Symbols' in *The*

Apostle Statuettes. The Twelve Apostles and Christ, formerly thought to be English, early 16th century. H. *c.* 5 cm. Victoria and Albert Museum, London.

Connoisseur, November 1918, p. 138; G. E. P. How and J. P. How, *English and Scottish Silver Spoons* (1953), II, 3-40.

Apostle Statuettes. A group of silver-gilt STATUETTES in the form of standing figures in-the-round depicting Christ and the Twelve Apostles, each with a nimbus and his attribute and each standing on a square PLINTH upon which is inscribed an abbreviated form of his name. The figures, about 5 cm high, are unmarked; they were formerly thought to have been made in England in the 16th century, but in view of the spellings (possibly Flemish or German) of the saints' names, the Victoria and Albert Museum, London, which owns the group, no longer considers them to be of English make.

applied decoration. A decorative element that is affixed by SOLDERING to a silver article after the piece has been given its basic form. Some such work is done using MOUNTS made by MOULDING or CASTING, e.g., FINIALS, BASES of HOLLOW WARE, THUMBPIECES, ornamental legs and feet, as well as some parts essential to the use of the piece, such as a SPOUT or HANDLE. Such applied work is also done with CUT CARD pieces, either solely as decoration or to strengthen the piece, as a surround at the junction of a spout or a handle; WIREWORK is also applied either decoratively or to finish a receptacle with a MOUTH WIRE.

apprentice. In the silverware trade, a person who had signed an indenture binding him to a seven-year period of service with a silversmith who was a freeman, in return for training and care provided by the latter, as well as imposing various subsidiary conditions. An apprentice was sometimes transferred to a new master. He could be freed by one of several methods; by service (satisfactory compliance with the terms of the indenture over the full seven-year period), by patrimony (being the son of a freeman), or by redemption (payment of an agreed sum). Some persons were granted freedom by special grace and favour in exceptional circumstances. Before a freed apprentice could register his mark, he was required to submit an acceptable MASTERPIECE. Freedom was granted by a certificate delivered in a FREEDOM BOX. A newly freed apprentice did not always start his own workshop, some choosing to become 'journeymen' (from French *journée,* day), working for a master at a daily or other periodic wage. Apprentices and journeymen often did preliminary work on a piece that was to be finished by the master.

arabesque. A style of decoration of intricately interlaced motifs which in Islamic art was often of geometric or angular character, and in Renaissance art was composed of flowing curved lines and fanciful intertwining of swags of foliage, fruit, scrolls and part-foliate figures, being derived from GROTESQUES (*grotteschi*) based on frescoes in Nero's Golden House in Rome and often found on Italian maiolica. The style was imported into Europe in the late

15th century and was much used in the 16th century as decoration in all the applied arts. It was a popular form of Moorish decoration, its Spanish version excluding close representations of animal or human figures, those which do occur there being the work of Christian artists. In 19th-century England such designs were often termed MORESQUES. Arabesque decoration is found on some silverware, especially that in RENAISSANCE STYLE.

arcaded. *See* GALLERY.

Archambo, Peter. Two London silversmiths, father and son, of Huguenot ancestry. Peter Archambo I (fl. 1721-50), whose family is said to have emigrated from the Île d'Oléron, near La Rochelle, France, became a freeman of the Butchers' Company, London, in 1720. He registered his first and second marks in 1721 and 1722, with address at Green St, then moved to Hemings Row, and registered his third mark in 1739 from Coventry St, Piccadilly. He did much work for the 2nd Duke of Warrington, examples of which were sold at Christie's, London, in 1921.

His son, Peter Archambo II (1724-68), was apprenticed in 1738 to PAUL DE LAMERIE, turned over to his father, and freed in 1747; he registered his mark in 1750, in partnership with his cousin Peter Meure, when Peter Archambo I retired, and the firm continued until 1755, making mainly dinner plate.

See Edward Wenham, 'Peter Archambo, father and son' in *Antique Collector*, July-August 1945, p. 124.

architectural silverware. Articles of silverware made as a small replica of a building or other edifice. A silver INKSTAND in the form of a replica of the United States Capitol in Washington, D.C., was made in 1898 by the GORHAM COMPANY. *See* EDDYSTONE LIGHTHOUSE SALT; ETON COLLEGE CHAPEL REPLICA; EXETER SALT; HARRODS REPLICA; TEMPLE BAR INKSTAND; VICTORIA AND ALBERT MUSEUM CENTREPIECE; WALKER ART GALLERY REPLICA.

Ardagh Chalice. Silver with filigree bands, inset glass, enamelling, gold granules, etc.; Ireland, 9th century. H. 17·8 cm. National Museum of Ireland, Dublin.

Ardagh Chalice. A large CHALICE, reputedly the finest work of metal in Ireland, of the 9th century and a part of the ARDAGH HOARD. It is a 'Ministerial Chalice' taken to the communicants. Its rounded bowl, of beaten silver, rests on a large conical base with a broad flange, joined together by a cylindrical stem through which there is a copper bolt concealed on the underside by a boss of polished rock crystal surrounded by three encircling bands, each with a different type of decoration. The bowl has two broad vertical loop handles decorated with red and blue enamelling, a gilt-bronze (or brass) rim, and a decorated band of gold filigree panels and glass settings. The ornamentation includes filigree wires, glass, amber, malachite, crystal, enamel, and gold granules. Encircling the bowl is a Latin inscription in plain silver as a reserve on a STIPPLED ground, with the names of eleven ot the original Apostles and St Paul. The piece is in the National Museum of Ireland, Dublin. In the late 19th century the chalice was copied in various sizes and with modified decoration, e.g., as a sugar-bowl by Edmond Johnson. *See* DERRYNAFLAN CHALICE.

Ardagh Hoard. A HOARD consisting of the ARDAGH CHALICE, four silver-gilt brooches, and a bronze chalice. It was found in 1867 during potato digging in Reerasta Rath, near Ardagh, Co. Limerick, Ireland, and is now in the National Museum of Ireland, Dublin.

Argand lamp (2). Sheffield plate, *c.* 1790. H. 32 cm. Smithsonian Institution, Washington, D.C.

Argand lamp. A type of oil LAMP, developed in France and named after the inventor, Aimé Argand (1755-1803) of Geneva, which has an open tubular wick that, when enclosed in a glass chimney (preferably slightly ATTENUATED), admits a current of air on both its inner and outer edges, thus providing a hotter, brighter and almost smokeless flame. The burner which supports the wick is connected with an oil reservoir that must be elevated higher than the burner so that the heavy colza oil then used for oil lamps would feed by gravity, rather than by capillary action as in the case of later oil-lamp wicks. The lamps have a valve beneath the reservoir to control or cut off the flow of the oil, and a small detachable sump beneath the burner to catch any excess oil. Argand had the lamp patented in England on 12 March 1784 and arranged with MATTHEW BOULTON to produce them, first in London and later in Manchester. After the patent was revoked on 24 February 1786, Boulton continued to make the lamps in Birmingham. The lamps were made in two forms: (1) a table lamp (sometimes as a double lamp with one reservoir supplying two burners); and (2) as a wall bracket (SCONCE). They are usually made of brass, but examples made of SHEFFIELD PLATE, ordered by George Washington, are at Mount Vernon, Virginia, and brass examples are at Jefferson's home at Monticello, Virginia. Such lamps were sometimes decorated with Wedgwood plaques or with crystal drops.

argent. The French word for silver, derived from the Latin, *argentum*. In English heraldic usage, the term denotes 'silver' or 'white'; *see* TINCTURE.

Argentan. The name applied in Germany, and later (from *c.* 1835) at Birmingham and Sheffield, to NICKEL SILVER.

argentiferous. Producing or containing silver, as an ore, e.g., galena (a lead ore).

argyll (sometimes, incorrectly, 'argyle'). A gravy-warmer made in various shapes, styles, and sizes, but generally similar to a covered COFFEE-POT with one handle and a SPOUT. The gravy is kept warm by means of hot water contained in (1) a compartment created by a double exterior wall, (2) a compartment created by a false bottom, or (3) a central vertical attenuated tube, or by means of a central vertical cylindrical tube (FIRE-BOX) in which is placed a previously heated iron rod (BILLET). In types (1) and (2) the hot water is inserted through an opening in the upper FERRULE of the handle, through an external tube that extends up to the rim, or through an opening midway down one side which extends into the false bottom. Argylls range in height from 11 cm up to (in rare cases) 28 cm. The argyll is said to have been invented by the 3rd Duke of Argyll (1682–1761). This peculiarly English utensil was made of silver (the earliest known example being from 1755) and SHEFFIELD PLATE (the earliest known being from 1768), and continued to be made until *c.* 1790; reproductions have been made in silver *c.* 1910 and by ELECTROPLATING, and ceramic examples also exist in English creamware and delftware. (The name 'argyll' is the preferred spelling in the *Oxford English Dictionary*, and the name of the Dukes of Argyll has, according to Debrett, always been so spelled since the creation of the title in 1701.) *See* Harold Newman, 'Argylls – Silver and Ceramic' in *Apollo*, February 1969, p. 98. *See* GRAVY-BOAT.

Arlington Tazza. A parcel-gilt TAZZA, 1532–3, having a wide stem, a STEPPED base, and a shallow bowl. The bottom of its bowl is decorated overall with a DIAPER pattern of circular depressions, and encircling the interior of the rim is the inscription, in Lombardic characters, 'BENEDICTVS DEVS DONIS SVIS ET SANCTIS IN OMNIBVS'. The stepped base is encircled with two bands of foliage. The tazza, originally for secular use, served as an ALMS DISH after it was given in the 19th century to the parish church of St James, Arlington, north Devon. It was purchased in 1953 by the Goldsmiths' Company, London. *See* ROCHESTER CATHEDRAL TAZZE.

arm badge. A type of BADGE, often made of silver, that was worn on the sleeve by crews of some ceremonial barges and by inmates of some almshouses. They are usually oval, bearing an identifying inscription, symbol or ARMORIAL.

arm sconce. A type of WALL SCONCE having the projecting branch, extending horizontally from the back-plate, in the form of a human arm with the hand holding the candle SOCKET. An example is in the Victoria and Albert Museum, London.

armband (American Indian). A type of broad penannular band, examples of which were made as INDIAN-TRADE SILVERWARE by some leading early American silversmiths, e.g., Joseph Richardson, Jr (*see* RICHARDSON), *c.* 1790–1820. Such pieces are variously decorated, with STAMPING, ENGRAVING or CHASING, and often have two holes pierced at each end to permit the use of thongs.

argyll. Three forms (*left to right*): (1) With double wall, Augustus Le Sage, London 1771. H. 11·3 cm. Private Collection. (2) With false bottom, *c.* 1790. H. 20·5 cm. Victoria and Albert Museum, London. (3) With central tube for billet, John Emes, London, 1806. H. 15·2 cm. Courtesy, Garrard & Co. Ltd, London.

Arlington Tazza Parcel-gilt tazza, 1532–3. W. 23 cm. Goldsmiths' Company, London.

armband (American Indian). Joseph Richardson II, Philadelphia, Pa, *c.* 1792–6. H. 6·3 cm. Yale University Art Gallery (Mabel Brady Garvan Collection), New Haven, Conn.

Artichoke Bowl. C. & A. G. Fox, London, 1849–50. Victoria and Albert Museum, London.

Ashbee, C. R. Steeple cup, with enamelling and gemstones, 1900. H. 45 cm. Victoria and Albert Museum, London.

armorial. The heraldic device of some families, and some corporate bodies and livery companies, which includes a COAT OF ARMS or a CREST, often within an ESCUTCHEON or CARTOUCHE. Such armorials are found engraved or etched on many pieces of important silverware, as evidence of contemporary ownership and also as decoration, and usually add considerable monetary value, especially when well executed or when establishing PROVENANCE (but not necessarily the date of production of the article, which may be some years before the engraving or etching was done).

armorial plate. Articles of silverware that are decorated, often within an ESCUTCHEON or CARTOUCHE, with a heraldic COAT OF ARMS or CREST, executed by ENGRAVING, ETCHING or striking with a die. As an escutcheon or cartouche is sometimes left with a blank central space to be inscribed later, identification of the arms or the crest does not always establish the date of the piece. Similarly, for an article of SHEFFIELD PLATE, the coat of arms or crest was sometimes executed on a separate silver INSCRIPTION PLATE that was inserted or was affixed by the process of SWEATING; this could have been added to the piece later than the year in which it was made. Much silverware that is engraved with the Royal arms was AMBASSADORIAL SILVERWARE, never having been a part of the Royal plate, and the arms depicted are therefore those of the Sovereign in whose reign it was issued rather than those of the recipient.

Armstead, Henry Hugh (1828–1905). A leading London sculptor and a designer of silverware in the 1850s–60s. He worked for HUNT & ROSKELL, HANCOCKS, and HARRY EMANUEL. He made designs for many sculptural groups for HORSE-RACING TROPHIES, TESTIMONIALS, SHIELDS, and medals, usually in RENAISSANCE STYLE, executed as OXIDIZED SILVERWARE and with varied surface effects. His work was shown in the London International Exhibition of 1862 and the Paris Exposition of 1867. By the early 1870s he worked mainly as a sculptor, seldom designing silverware. *See* OUTRAM SHIELD.

arrow. A missile to be shot from a bow, being a straight wooden shaft with a sharp metal point and, at the other end (butt), feathers (fletchlings or vanes). Silver replicas were made as archery prizes, dating from the 17th century but becoming popular in the 18th century. The SCORTON ARROW is the earliest extant English sporting trophy, awarded from 1673. In Scotland several Companies of Archers had a silver arrow as a permanent trophy retained by the Company, sometimes with attached medals of the winners. Examples are the Musselburgh, Peebles, Selkirk, Stirling, and Edinburgh arrows of the 17th and 18th centuries. They are of varying lengths, ranging from *c.* 28 to 70 cm. A silver arrow was awarded at Harrow School, Middlesex, from 1684 to 1771.

Art Deco style. A decorative style that originated in France in the 1920s and 1930s in protest against the ART NOUVEAU STYLE and later art movements, and that was popularized in the United States. Scorned by many in its early period, it re-acquired some popularity in the 1960s and 1970s. The style emphasized abstract designs and geometric patterns. Examples are found in many branches of the decorative arts, including silverware. The name is derived from 'L'Exposition Internationale des Arts Décoratifs et Industriels Modernes', held in Paris in 1925. Among the leading exponents in English silverware were HAROLD STABLER, BERNARD CUZNER, and REGINALD YORKE GLEADOWE. *See* Bevis Hillier, *Art Deco* (1968).

Art Nouveau style. The style of decoration current in the 1890s and early 1900s, the name being derived from a gallery for interior decoration opened by Samuel Bing in Paris in 1896, called the 'Maison de l'Art Nouveau'. It was introduced in England *c.* 1890, mainly as a product of the movement started by William Morris and the Pre-Raphaelites, which spread to the Continent and America. In Germany the same style was called *Jugendstil*, after a magazine entitled *Die Jugend* (Youth), and in Italy it was known as *Stile Floreale* or *Stile Liberty* (after the London store that featured it). Applicable to all the decorative arts, the style was adapted to silverware in England and on the Continent, but to a much lesser extent than in the other decorative arts. The style resulted from a revolt against the rigid styles of the previously mass-produced wares and a philosophy that sought to revive the craft movement and aestheticism in art. It featured free-flowing, curving lines with asymmetrical natural motifs, such as intertwining floral patterns, butterflies and dragonflies, and ethereal, human, female faces, greatly influenced by Japanese art. Eventually its own extravagances led to its demise, *c.* 1910–14, but it enjoyed a brief revival in the 1950s. Leading exponents in English silverware were C. R. ASHBEE and GILBERT MARKS. *See* CYMRIC SILVERWARE; ATLAS STANDING CUP.

Artichoke Bowl. A bowl in the form of an artichoke, made by C. and A. G. Fox, London, 1849-50. The hemispherical bowl has a jagged rim to simulate the tips of artichoke leaves; it rests on a low foot and a wide base in the form of spreading leaves of the artichoke plant. Similar bowls have been made in recent years.

Asby Maske Cup. A silver-gilt HORSE-RACING CUP, in the form of a covered SMALL TWO-HANDLED CUP, made by William Ramsey, *c.* 1669; it is the second-oldest known such trophy surviving. It was awarded in 1669 at Asby Maske, a small race course near Appleby in Westmorland. Formerly in the collection of Col. F. Curtis, it was sold at Sotheby's, London, on 13 May 1954, and last recorded in the collection of H. T. DeVere Clifton, Lytham, Lancashire.

Ashbee, C(harles) R(obert) (1863-1942). An English designer of silver-ware and jewelry, who was an important figure in the promotion of the ART NOUVEAU STYLE in England. Having been an architect and goldsmith, he became in the 1880s a leader of the Arts and Crafts Movement. In 1888 he founded the Guild and School of Handicraft in London, but in 1895 the school closed; in 1898 he registered the mark of the Guild of Handicraft, which in 1902 moved to Chipping Campden, Gloucestershire, and closed in 1908. In 1912 he published *Silverware and Jewellery*. His designs, which were executed by the Guild, were mainly for TEA-SERVICES and other ware of un-pretentious form and decoration, with much use of WIREWORK. In 1900 he made a modern version of a STEEPLE CUP. His influence was important in developing Art Nouveau ware, especially at Liberty & Co., and at the Wiener Werkstätte. His marks were 'CRA' from 1896, and after 1898 'GOH Ltd'; they were punched beside the HALLMARKS on silverware signed by him. He was originally a strong promoter of the self-taught artist-craftsman, but after *c.* 1902 he advocated the machine as the practical means to carry out his ideals. *See* Shirley Bury, 'An Arts and Crafts Experiment: Ware by C. R. Ashbee' in *Victoria and Albert Museum Bulletin* 7 (1969); Alan Crawford, *C. R. Ashbee: Architect, Designer and Romantic Socialist* (1985).

Ashburnham Centrepiece. Stand with covered bowl supported by two figures of goats, Nicholas Sprimont, London, 1747-8. H. 46·5 cm. Victoria and Albert Museum, London.

Ashburnham Centrepiece. A CENTREPIECE made by NICHOLAS SPRIMONT, 1747-8, in ROCOCO STYLE, having a stand with four feet in the form of crowned lion's heads, a bowl resting on the backs of two figures in-the-round of standing goats, and a cover with a finial of two pears (*see* BOLTON CENTREPIECE). The bowl (without a liner) has overall openwork decoration in a DIAPER pattern, so that the piece is not, as formerly stated, a SOUP-TUREEN, but more likely a fruit-basket or merely a centrepiece. It bears two CARTOUCHES enclosing the coats of arms of, respectively, John, 2nd Earl of Ashburnham (1724-1812), and his wife, who were married in 1756, so that it would seem–as confirmed by indications on the shields–that the piece was acquired from a prior owner and that the shields were re-engraved to change the armorials. It was sold at Christie's, London (in the Ashburnham sale of 24 March 1914), and was acquired in 1971 by the Victoria and Albert Museum, London. *See* CRESPIN TUREEN.

ashet. A Scottish term (derived from French *assiette*) for a meat PLATTER.

Ashmole Cup. A STANDING CUP having a bowl of bucket shape resting on a plain baluster stem with a wide slightly domed base and having a cover with a conical finial surmounted by the figure of a standing *putto*. The bowl, foot, and cover are decorated with EMBOSSING depicting masks of grotesque monsters, in the style of CHRISTIAN VAN VIANEN. The cup was given in 1666 to the Corporation of Lichfield, Staffordshire, by Elias Ashmole (1617-92), Windsor Herald, 1666, and founder of the Ashmolean Museum, Oxford; it bears the engraved seal of the Corporation and an inscription recording the gift. The cup belongs to the City Council of Lichfield, and is now kept on display at the Lichfield Treasury at the church of St Mary, Lichfield.

askos jug. A type of JUG in the form of an askos (a type of Greek pottery vase used for pouring oil into lamps); such jugs have an overhead arched handle extending from the back of the spout to the opposite end of the body. The name is derived from the fact that some examples were said to have been made in the shape of a wine-skin or leather bottle (*askos*). A silver example with a LID, granulated surface, and gilt interior, was made by Storr & Mortimer (*see* PAUL STORR), London, 1836, based on a bronze prototype milk-jug. *See* GREEK-VASE SILVERWARE.

asparagus butter-bowl. A type of small, shallow, cup-like BOWL, about 7·5 cm in diameter, having one flat lateral handle. It was intended for individual use. The form is similar to a *godet* for a VEILLEUSE and to a BLEEDING BOWL.

Ashmole Cup. Standing cup with embossed decoration, maker's mark 'WM', London, 1666. H. 45·8 cm. City Council, Lichfield.

askos. Granulated surface and gilt interior, Storr&Mortimer, London, 1836. H. 22·2 cm. Courtesy, Sotheby's, London.

asparagus butter-dish. A type of oval DISH in the centre of which there is a BUTTER-DISH; used for serving asparagus.

asparagus-dish. A receptacle for bringing asparagus to a dinner table, being an oblong dish upon which rests a separate utensil in the form of a frame made of a series of joined parallel straight rods bent upward vertically at each end to hold the stalks.

asparagus holder. A utensil for a diner to hold a stalk of asparagus. It is made of a single strip of metal, bent in the form of U-shaped tongs, with a small square plate at each end to grip the stalk. Early examples were made with two arms joined (like a pair of scissors), with claws or discs at each end.

asparagus server. A utensil for serving individual portions of several stalks of asparagus. Some examples are in the form of U-shaped tongs, similar to but larger than an ASPARAGUS HOLDER, having a small metal plate at each end to grip the stalks and sometimes a sliding band around the two arms. Others are made with the two arms joined (like a pair of scissors), sometimes with claws or discs at each end and sometimes with indentations along the inside of the arms to grip the stalks and with one arm having a turned end.

aspergillum. An article of ecclesiastical use in the form of a small brush or a perforated globe (containing a saturated sponge) attached to an elongated handle; it is used for sprinkling holy water. *See* CHURCH PLATE.

aspersorium. *See* STOUP.

Assay Office. An office established for ASSAYING the precious metal content of articles of silver, gold, and platinum, and attesting – by applying its ASSAY OFFICE HALLMARK to individual pieces tested – its findings that the relevant fixed standard has have been complied with by the maker. In Great Britain the four offices still active are the LONDON ASSAY OFFICE, the BIRMINGHAM ASSAY OFFICE, the SHEFFIELD ASSAY OFFICE, and the EDINBURGH ASSAY OFFICE, each with its own distinctive hallmark. The other provincial offices in England – at Chester, Exeter, Newcastle-upon-Tyne, Norwich, and York – have been terminated, as has the GLASGOW ASSAY OFFICE in Scotland. In Ireland the DUBLIN ASSAY OFFICE has been the country's sole office since 1637.

Originally, articles had to be submitted to the designated office for a prescribed area, but since 1854 each maker may submit any article to the office of his choice.

Assay Office Hallmark. The HALLMARK required to be punched on articles that have been tested and approved by an ASSAY OFFICE; the mark attests the place where the ASSAYING was carried out. Each Assay Office has its own distinctive authorized hallmark, although variations of style and details have occurred from time to time.

assaying. The process of testing the purity of metal in an article, e.g., ascertaining the proportion of silver (or gold or platinum) in relation to other metals that are constituents of an ALLOY, but without making a complete analysis. Assaying has been legally required in Great Britain since *c.* 1300 for articles of gold or silver, and also (as provided in the Hallmarking Act of 1973) since 1 January 1975 for platinum; the Act of 1790 exempted certain SMALLWARE (except CADDY-SPOONS), but the Act of 1973 lists specified exceptions (including any article made before 1975). All articles of silver made before 1975 (with a few exceptions, such as some small pieces) had previously been required to be hallmarked before being offered for sale, but since 1 January 1975 any article weighing more than 7·78 grams must be marked only before it can legally be described by the seller as 'silver'.

The process formerly involved rubbing with a TOUCHSTONE, but today

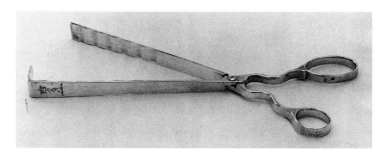

asparagus server. Scissors style, London, *c.* 1790. L. 25·5 cm. Colonial Williamsburg, Va.

technical procedures are used to test the scrapings (DIET) of each component part of an article submitted; gold and silver are tested by CUPELLATION, silver by the 'volumetric method', and in both cases the precious metal content must be established to the nearest 0·1 %. When an article contains metal of two different qualities, the assaying applies only to that of lower quality, and the mark ignores the metal of higher quality. Assaying was done in ancient Egypt and Rome, and has been carried out in continental Europe for centuries; there is no governmental assaying of silverware in the United States. *See* ASSAY OFFICE; HALLMARK(S); SPECTROSCOPIC EMISSION.

Assistants' Cups. The group of WINE-CUPS, of no fixed or uniform shape or style of decoration, which since 1957 have been commissioned by each newly elected member of the Court of Assistants of the GOLDSMITHS' COMPANY. They are designed and made by various craftsmen, and usually bear the name or a decoration symbolic of the Assistant. Each cup remains the property of the Assistant, but usually is left for display at Goldsmiths' Hall, London; some have been bequeathed or donated by heirs to the Company.

Aston Tankard. A TANKARD of which the bowl is the shell of an ostrich egg, held by four vertical hinged straps connecting the neck rim and the stem. It has a stepped spreading foot, a vertical scroll handle, and a hinged lid (made of ostrich egg) surmounted by a finial in the form of an animal head. The tankard, made in England in 1609, bears the Aston crest. It was included in the Franks Bequest to the British Museum, London. *See* OSTRICH-EGG CUP.

Astor Apostle Spoons. A complete set of thirteen APOSTLE SPOONS, having ungilded finials and all bearing the same unrecorded maker's mark resembling a sheaf of corn (wheat) and the same London date letter for 1536–7. The set is unique in that the finial on the Master Spoon depicts, instead of Christ, a figure of the Virgin Mary, probably originally holding a figure of the Child, now missing (*see* VIRGIN SPOON, an example of which dated London, 1577–8, is in the Victoria and Albert Museum, London). The set is unusual in that the figures are depicted without a nimbus. The bowls are engraved with the Sacred Monogram 'IHS' (perhaps explaining the name 'Abbey Spoons' which has sometimes been unjustifiably applied to the set, probably on the uncorroborated theory that they might have been made as a gift for some abbey). The figures (with St Paul substituted for St Philip) were cast from individual models and the attributes were cast separately and affixed. The monogram shows traces of gilding. The set was acquired by the British Museum, London, in 1981, at the sale at Christie's, London, of the collection formed by William Waldorf Astor, lst Viscount Astor (1848–1919), of Hever Castle, Kent, who had purchased the set at Christie's, London, on 16 July 1903 from a member of the Ludlow-Bruges (or Bryce) family. The set (having engraved on the back of each bowl the Bruges anchor crest) had descended from Thomas Bruges (1751–1835), of Seend, near Melksham, Wiltshire, to whom it had been given by his wife, Katherine Long (1717–1810); she was the heiress of Henry Long (d. 1611), of Whaddon, Wiltshire, an inventory of whose estate included two sets of such spoons, one of which may have been the set given by Katherine Long to Bruges.

Athenic. A trade name for articles of silverware produced by the GORHAM COMPANY, *c.* 1901, which were composed of a combination of STERLING SILVER with copper, glass, and ivory. In contrast to the exclusively handmade MARTELÉ ware, the bodies were made on a spinning lathe, but with some handwork on the decoration. The ware included pieces made in a variety of styles, ranging from ART NOUVEAU STYLE to the ACADEMIC STYLE.

Atlas Cup. (1) A STANDING CUP having as its stem a figure of a nude Atlas kneeling and holding on his head the bowl, which is decorated with vertical fluting and has a domed cover; the cover bears a spool-shaped ornament surmounted by a draped female figure emblematic of Fortune, holding over her head a fold of drapery. Made in 1692, the piece bears the mark 'AR'. It was formerly in the collection of Louis Huth, and was sold by him at Christie's, London, in May 1905 to T. H. Noble, and again at Christie's, by Lord Astor of Hever, on 31 March 1976, the buyer being E. & C. T. Koopman & Son Ltd, London. (2) A standing cup in ART NOUVEAU STYLE, having a a semi-ovoid bowl held on the upraised arms of a kneeling figure of Atlas and having a cushion-shaped cover with a finial in the form of three supports for an artichoke-like globe. It was made in 1902 by Holland, Aldwinkle and Slater, London, and is now in the Art Institute of Chicago.

attenuated. Having a tapering shape, such as the SPOUT on some COFFEE-POTS that narrows toward the lip.

Aston Tankard. Ostrich-egg bowl and lid, with silver mounts, London, 1609. H. 30·5 cm. British Museum, London.

Atlas Cup (2). Cup in Art Nouveau style, Holland, Aldwinkle & Slater, London, 1902. H. 41 cm. Art Institute of Chicago (photo courtesy, Brand Inglis Ltd, London).

auricular style. A style of shaping silverware in the form of the auricle (the ear lobe) or of a conch shell, with decoration - executed in relief by EMBOSS-ING - consisting of foliage and scrolls, often combined with dolphins and sinuous nudes. The style, possibly based on Italian Late MANNERIST STYLE, was a development of early-17th-century BAROQUE STYLE, and was popularized by Wendel Dietterlin, of Strasbourg, from 1598 and by Lucas Kilian, of Augsburg, from 1619, and in the Low Countries by Hans Vredeman de Vries from *c.* 1600. Its use in silverware is said to have been developed *c.* 1613 by Paulus van Vianen and later by his brother Adam and especially his son CHRISTIAN VAN VIANEN. Some of the designs by Adam were used by Christian and were published, together with some of his own, by Christian, *c.* 1652, in *Modelles Artificiels,* a copy of which is at the Victoria and Albert Museum, London. The style was brought, *c.* 1630, by Christian van Vianen from the Netherlands to England, where it was extensively copied, as well as being copied in the Netherlands by the Dutch silversmiths Thomas Bogaert and Jan Lutma the Elder. It influenced English silverware in the period 1660–70 and was revived in the period of the ROCOCO STYLE, in the era of ART NOUVEAU STYLE in the late 19th century, and again in the 1950s. Also called 'lobate style' and 'cartilaginous style', and in Germany *Knorpelwerk* and in the Netherlands *Ohrmuschel* and *Kwabornament.*

B

baby's set. A PAIR of small eating implements for use by a baby, comprising a SPOON and a pusher (an implement having a flat vertical rectangle attached to a straight handle).

bacchanal. A type of FIGURAL FLATWARE of the Regency period, having the handle in the form of a cast standing figure in-the-round of a girl supporting on her head a wicker basket; such a figure has been mistakenly thought to depict a bacchante, but is a CANEPHOROS, derived from Greek architecture. Examples were made by EDWARD FARRELL from 1816 as FRUIT SERVERS, and others were made as silver-gilt dessert spoons, knives, and forks. They are to be distinguished from Bacchanalian spoons, having a flat handle decorated with relief figures of two or three bacchanalian figures, silver-gilt examples of which, designed by THOMAS STOTHARD, 1812, for RUNDELL, BRIDGE & RUNDELL, are now in the Royal Collection.

Bacchus and Ariadne Sideboard Dish. A silver-gilt circular SIDEBOARD DISH having in the well a decoration of a group of figures in high relief depicting the 'Triumph of Bacchus and Ariadne', with Bacchus and Ariadne, each holding a thyrsus, standing in a chariot drawn by four centaurs holding a thyrsus and musical instruments and with two *amorini* flying alongside them. The group is encircled by a band of laurel leaves and a second decorative band, and the wide rim is decorated with trellis-work and vines with interspersed bacchanalian masks, trophies, and musical instruments. The original version was designed by THOMAS STOTHARD, and four examples were made by PAUL STORR for RUNDELL, BRIDGE & RUNDELL. One example, 1814–15, was purchased by the Prince Regent (later George IV) in 1815 and bears the Royal arms; it is in the Royal Collection. Other examples include: (1) a pair, 1813, acquired by Hugh Percy, 3rd Duke of Northumberland, at the 1822 sale of Wanstead House, Essex, and sold by the present Duke at Sotheby's, London, on 3 May 1984; (2) one, 1817, without the second band encircling the well, made for Charles Noel-Hill, 2nd Earl of Ailesbury, and bought by William Butlin at Christie's, London, in 1944, and sold by him at Christie's on 17 July 1968; (3) two examples made in 1815 for the Duke of Cumberland. A comparable piece, with a similar rim but having the central decoration depicting a winged male figure and four horses in profile, was made by PHILIP RUNDELL, 1820, for Rundell, Bridge & Rundell, to the order of Sir Isaac Lyon Goldsmid, and bears the Goldsmid arms.

bachelor coffee-pot. A small type of COFFEE-POT about 15 cm high, with a capacity sufficient to serve only one person.

bachelor teapot. A small type of TEAPOT, about 11 cm high, with a capacity sufficient to serve only one person.

Bacchus and Ariadne Sideboard Dish.
Silver gilt, designed by Thomas
Stothard and made by Paul Storr,
1814-15. W. 78 cm. Royal Collection;
reproduced by gracious permission of
Her Majesty the Queen.

back-stamping. Placing on a piece of silverware a MAKER'S MARK other than
that of the actual maker, by impressing it over the original mark or along
with it. Such marking has been done by some retailers who wish a piece to
show the firm's own name. Also called 'double marking' or 'store marking'.
It differs from the practice of adding a SPONSOR'S MARK to a piece made by
an unregistered silversmith.

Bacon Cups. Three silver-gilt SEAL CUPS in the form of STANDING CUPS, London, 1573-4, each having a low hemispherical bowl resting on a vase-shaped
stem and having a spreading foot; each cup has a flat-domed cover with a
finial in the form of a small three-handled cup, atop which there is an ungilded figure of a standing boar. The cups are examples of SEAL WARE, having
been made for Sir Nicholas Bacon (1509-79) as Lord Keeper of the Great
Seal of England to Elizabeth I in 1558, from the Great Seal of Mary I (Tudor), 1553-8, and Philip II of Spain, which became obsolete and was defaced
and melted down, and was superseded by the new seal of Elizabeth I. From
the metal the three cups were made, each bearing three coats of arms, those
of Sir Francis Bacon as a bachelor and as a married man and that of Anthony,
his eldest son. One cup was made for each Bacon house, and they are referred to by name as inscribed on them, to wit: (1) the Redgrave Cup (for
his house at Redgrave), which remained in the possession of Anthony
Bacon's descendants until it was lent to the British Museum by the Rt Hon.
Edmond Wodehouse, M.P., later being bequeathed to the museum in 1915
by his widow; (2) the Stewkey (alternative name for Stiffkey, in Norfolk)
Cup, which passed to Sir Nathaniel Bacon, second son of Sir Nicholas, and
then to the family of Viscount Charles Townshend, who sold it at Christie's,
London, in 1904 to Joseph A. Holms, from whom it passed to Sir Ernest Cas-
sel who bequeathed it to his daughter Edwina (Lady Louis Mountbatten), by
whom it was loaned to the Burlington Fine Arts Club Exhibition in 1926,
and later to the Victoria and Albert Museum, London; and (3) the Gorhambury Cup (for Gorhambury House, St Albans), which passed to Anthony
Bacon, and then to his younger brother, the writer Francis Bacon
(1561-1629), 1st Baron Verulam, Viscount St Albans, and was last reported to
be in a private collection in Canada. Encircling the rim of each cup is the inscription 'A THYRDE BOWLE MADE OF THE GREATE SEAL OF ENGLANDE, 1574'.
The cups were all made by an unidentified silversmith whose mark was a
bird. They are similar in shape to a Ming porcelain cup of the Chia Ch'ien
period, 1522-66.

Bacon Cups. The Redgrave Cup,
London, 1573-4. H. 29·2 cm. British
Museum, London.

bail handle. Cream-pail, Samuel Herbert, London, 1752-3. H. (of pail) 6·7 cm. Colonial Williamsburg, Va.

badge. An insigne·of membership or office, sometimes made of silver. Early examples, worn from the 17th century, were sewn on the upper part of the sleeve of a garment; later ones, of silver or other metal, and made to be either pinned on or suspended, were issued by some City of London Livery Companies and other bodies. For various types, *see* ARM BADGE; ADMIRALTY BARGE BADGE; BARGE-MASTER'S BADGE; CRIPPLEGATE BADGE; DOGGETT'S BADGE; GREYHOUND BADGE; MASONIC BADGE; PORTER'S BADGE; WATERMAN'S BADGE; WHITTINGTON COLLEGE BADGE; BELT PLATE; SHOULDER-BELT PLATE.

bail handle. An arched overhead HANDLE, either fixed or swivelling, found on certain open articles, such as a PAIL or CAKE-BASKET, and on certain covered objects, such as a KETTLE. The handle is sometimes made entirely of the same metal as the article to which it is attached, but often it has – between the upright side arms – a horizontal handgrip made of wood (sometimes ebony), ivory or ceramic ware, or is occasionally wicker-covered. The shape of the handle is usually a continuous curve, but on some cake-baskets in ROCOCO STYLE the handle is ornate and asymmetrical, becoming almost vertical at one end. The incorrect spelling 'bale handle' has sometimes been used.

Baily, Edward Hodges (1788-1867). A sculptor and designer, originally from Bristol, who went to London in 1807 and became a pupil of JOHN FLAXMAN II until 1814. In 1815 he was employed by RUNDELL, BRIDGE & RUNDELL, working as a designer under WILLIAM THEED II until 1817; he became chief designer in 1826 upon the death of Flaxman. In 1833 he became chief designer for Storr & Mortimer (*see* PAUL STORR), and from 1839 for HUNT & ROSKELL, where he worked until 1857, making original designs and adapting designs made by others. He is said by Charles C. Oman to have made all the designs in an album at the Victoria and Albert Museum formerly attributed to Flaxman, this claim being based on the fact that his name appears on the leather binding; the album includes 48 undated designs on 27 pages, all said to have been made between 1815 and 1833. Some of his designs were original, but many were alterations to make more practical the designs of others, and some were to change a design by another in order to adapt it to a different type of ware. *See* Charles C. Oman, 'A Problem of Artistic Responsibility: The Firm of Rundell, Bridge & Rundell' in *Apollo*, March 1966, p. 174. *See* GOODWOOD 'CUP', 1833; KEMBLE CUP.

Bainbridge Snuffer. A SNUFFER operating like a pair of scissors, having at the ends of the arms two similar boxes to cut off and retain the snuff and having two loop handles. The piece is decorated with PARCEL GILDING, and on the boxes are the seals, in gold and red enamelling, of Henry VII and of Cardinal Bainbridge, who was Archbishop of York and Ambassador from Henry VIII to the Pope in 1509. The piece is English, *c.* 1510; it is now in the British Museum, London.

balance scale. A type of instrument for weighing. Small balance scales made of silver were sometimes used by apothecaries. An English example, *c.* 1702-14, has the beam, chains, and pans, as well as eight weights, made of silver, all in a fitted morocco case; it is in the Wellcome Collection at the Science Museum, London. *See* POSTAL SCALE.

Balfour/Bothwell Centrepiece. A sculptural CENTREPIECE with figures in-the-round of equestrian combatants suggested by an episode in Sir Walter Scott's *Old Mortality* (1816), where Balfour of Burleigh slew Sergeant Bothwell. The piece was designed and modelled by EDMUND COTTERILL and made by ROBERT GARRARD II for R., J. & S. Garrard (*see* GARRARD & CO. LTD), 1831-2, and was acquired by the Duke of Buckingham and Chandos. After the Duke's financial losses, the piece was sold in 1838 to Richard Gunter, the well-known London confectioner, who used it as a rental centrepiece. In 1893 it was awarded as a HORSE-RACING TROPHY (the Manchester Cup), as attested by a plaque affixed to a plinth. On 24 June 1974 it was bought at Christie's, London, by Garrard & Co. Ltd. A companion piece depicts a scene suggested by an episode in Scott's *Waverley* (1814), with an equestrian group of Robert Bruce in combat with Lord Bohun at the Battle of Bannockburn, 1314.

Balfour Freedom Box. A FREEDOM-BOX given by the Goldsmiths' Company to Arthur J. Balfour (1848-1930), British statesman (created 1st Earl of Balfour in 1922), upon his being granted the freedom of the Company. It was made in 1888 by Isaac Bathecary, London, and is decorated with the arms of the Company and of Balfour.

ball foot. A type of FOOT in the form of a sphere.

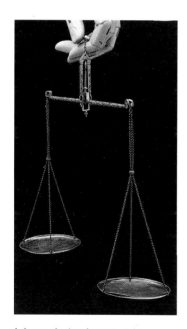

balance scale. Apothecary's scale, English, *c.* 1702-14. H. 25·5 cm. Wellcome Collection, Science Museum, London.

Balfour Freedom Box. Isaac Bathecary, London, 1888. W. 40 cm. Goldsmiths' Company, London.

baluster. A bulging shape on articles of circular section, similar to that of the upright supports of a balustrade, the upper and lower parts being cylindrical or slightly flaring; the wider part of the bulge is usually toward the bottom, and when it is toward the top, the shape is termed 'inverted baluster'. It differs from pear-shaped (pyriform) in being less bulbous and more elongated. It occurs in silverware as the shape of some VASES, JUGS, and TEAPOTS, and of the stem of some CANDLESTICKS and of some STANDING CUPS. It was introduced into England by the Huguenots, *c.* 1690–1710.

baluster-top spoon. A type of SPOON having a straight stem terminating in a finial of BALUSTER form, the baluster varying in length on different spoons. An early example dates from 1553.

Bancks Cup. A GOURD-SHAPED STANDING CUP, 1594–5, of the usual form, with its stem in the form of a gnarled and twisted tree trunk and the CALYX at the bottom of the bowl ungilded and standing free of the bowl. The original finial has been replaced by a figure of a 'Bluecoat boy' (hatless, unlike the original figure), representing a pupil wearing the uniform of Christ's Hospital, London (founded in 1552 as a charity school; in 1902 the school was moved to Horsham, Sussex), to which the cup was presented in 1602 by John Bancks.

Bank of England Inkstand. A parcel-gilt INKSTAND designed by LESLIE G. DURBIN and bearing the maker's mark of Durbin and Leonard Moss, made in 1950 as a presentation piece to the Bank of England from its Court of Directors to commemorate its 250th anniversary in 1944. The rectangular tray, resting on four feet in the form of lions sejant, has upcurved ends; at the front is a depression for pens, behind which are two inkwells with gilded dolphin finials and between them, standing upright, is a gilded replica of the

Bank of England Inkstand. Leslie Durbin, London, 1950. L. 43·3 cm. Bank of England, London.

Bank of England Wine Cooler. George Garthorne, London, 1694–5. W. 77·5 cm. Bank of England, London.

bannock-rack. Three rows, Patrick Robertson, Edinburgh, 1773–4. Royal Scottish Museum, Edinburgh.

baptismal pot. Paul Morand, Montreal, *c.* 1835. H. 7·6 cm. Musée du Québec, Quebec.

Bank's Britannia medallion. Engraved on the piece in script are the names of the Bank's Governor, Deputy Governor, and the twenty-four members of its Court of Directors in 1944.

Bank of England Wine Cooler. A WINE COOLER of oval shape with bulging sides and an everted rope rim, resting on four CLAW-AND-BALL FEET (lion's paws). At each end there is a DROP-RING HANDLE, each ring being suspended from the mouth of a lion's-head mask. The interior of the rim is decorated with a band of ACANTHUS leaves. The cooler was made by GEORGE GARTHORNE, 1694–5, and was acquired by the Bank of England in 1932.

Bannatyne (Bute) Mazer. A MAZER having a silver rim band and a silver base ring that are connected by four vertical strips, and having a silver PRINT, *c.* 1314–18, on the interior bottom (embossed, depicting a lion) that is surrounded by six coats of arms of Scottish families in six-lobed medallions of CHAMPLEVÉ enamelling. It has been said to be the only mazer recorded from before the 16th century. It is accompanied by a 16th-century cover made of carved whalebone.

bannock-rack. The Scottish version of a TOAST-RACK, with partitions for holding bannocks (flat roundish unleavened cakes of oatmeal or barley-meal). It sometimes has three rows of partitions, each row holding nine bannocks.

banqueting plate. A collection of many pieces of silverware for use and to serve as table decoration at a formal banquet, including centre and side CANDELABRA, PLATTERS, BASKETS, WINE-BOTTLE HOLDERS, EPERGNES, and PLATES. A silver-gilt COMPOSITE SERVICE, most of which was made by PAUL STORR and supplied to the 1st Earl of Harewood in 1812–15, was sold at Christie's, London, on 3 June 1965.

baptismal basin. A receptacle, circular or oval, used for the sacrament of baptism by aspersion (sprinkling water on the head). Some examples were in the form of a shallow bowl with a wide, slightly concave rim, but occasionally they were made as a deep bowl to fit into a FONT; later examples were intended to be used instead of a font. Such basins were usually unpretentious and undecorated, and occasionally a ROSE-WATER BASIN or an ALMS DISH was used for the purpose. *See* CHRISTENING BOWL; ROYAL FONT; CHURCH PLATE.

baptismal pot. A term used in Canada for an object derived from the English TEAPOT but which is used to pour holy water on the head of a child being baptised by affusion. Such pieces are usually in the form of a cylindrical pot with a long ATTENUATED spout extending upward from near the bottom of the pot, and having on the cover a finial in the form of a cross. Sometimes called a 'baptismal ewer.' *See* QUEBEC SILVERWARE.

barber's bowl. The same as a SHAVING BOWL.

barge-master's badge. A type of BADGE worn by a barge-master of a Livery Company of the City of London; such badges were worn for river processions and on ceremonial occasions. The oval badge of the Goldsmiths' Company was of silver gilt, having a REED-AND-TIE BORDER and, in the centre, the arms of the Company embossed in high relief; an example was made by John Payne, London, 1761. (The Company's barge was not used after 1865.) *See* WATERMAN'S BADGE.

Barlow's, Bishop, Cup. A silver-gilt STANDING CUP, 1608–9, of which the bowl and cover together are of ovoid form, and are decorated on a matted surface with engraved SCALLOP shells and FLEURS DE LIS. The stem is decorated with BRACKETS having scrolled dragon forms, and the cover has a finial with scrolled dragon brackets surmounted by a standing figure holding a spear (possibly a replacement for a former steeple). The cup was donated to Trinity Hall, Cambridge, by William Barlow (d. 1613), Bishop of Rochester and from 1608 Bishop of Lincoln.

Barnard, Edward, & Sons Ltd. The London firm of silversmiths that is the present-day successor to the firm started in 1689 by ANTHONY NELME and continued by FRANCIS NELME, Thomas Whipham, Charles Wright, THOMAS CHAWNER, HENRY CHAWNER, JOHN EMES, and REBECCA(H) EMES. Edward Barnard I (fl. 1781–1846) became associated with the firm in 1781, when he was apprenticed to Charles Wright. He transferred in 1784 to Thomas Chawner, was freed in 1789, and became foreman for Henry Chawner from 1786 to 1796, and from 1796 to 1798 for the successor firm of Henry Chawner and John Emes, and then became manager for John Emes from 1798 to 1808. Upon the death of Emes, he became a partner of the widow Rebecca(h) Emes (together with Henry Chawner II) and entered a joint mark with her ('RE/EB'). After entering three other marks, his fifth was entered in 1829, when Rebecca(h) Emes retired; this last was a joint mark ('EEJWB') with his sons – Edward Barnard II (d. 1867), John I (d. 1877), and William (d. 1851) – whom he took as partners in the firm then known as Edward Barnard & Sons, and later as E. J. & W. Barnard. The firm continued, after the death of Edward Barnard I in 1846, as W. & J. Barnard, with family descendants (including Edward Barnard III, Walter, John II, Michael, Stanley, and Eric) and others, using a succession of marks and becoming in 1910 Edward Barnard & Sons Ltd, and from 1933 using the present mark 'EBSs'. Eric, the last one of the family connection, retired in 1973, and the firm is now owned by the Padgett & Braham Group (which also owns other silversmith firms, including WAKELY & WHEELER LTD). The firm's addresses have been successively: 9 Ave Maria Lane (from 1689); Amen Corner (from 1773); Angel St, St Martin's Le Grand (from 1838); 22/24 Fetter Lane (from 1898); and 54 Hatton Garden (from 1910), where it has since remained. In the 1830s and 1840s the firm executed orders for RUNDELL, BRIDGE & RUNDELL (including the LILY FONT) and for ELKINGTON & CO.

baroque style. A style in art and decoration that emerged shortly before 1600 and remained current in Europe until the development of the ROCOCO STYLE began *c.* 1730. It was started in Italy, and spread to southern Germany, Austria, the Low Countries, and Spain and Portugal, with only a somewhat classic version being popular in France under Louis XIV. The style was a development of the RENAISSANCE STYLE and is characterized by lively curved and exuberant forms, by vigorous movement, and by ornament, based on classical sources, that is symmetrical (as distinguished from the asymmetry of the following rococo style). In English silverware, the style was influenced by the French émigrés producing HUGUENOT SILVERWARE and by a few native silversmiths, such as GEORGE GARTHORNE and ANTHONY NELME.

barrel beaker. One of a pair of BEAKERS that are made to be joined together at their rims so as to form a barrel-shaped piece and that are usually decorated with several bands of REEDING to simulate barrel hoops, and sometimes decorated with vertical stripes to simulate barrel staves. English silver examples are known from the second half of the 16th century, but such beakers were more frequent in the late 18th century.

barrel-tap. A type of TAP to be driven into a barrel and used for drawing off its contents (wine or ale). It has a down-turned spout and is provided with a SPIGOT to control the flow. The handle of the spigot is sometimes removable (to prevent unauthorized use). On some examples there is, at the projecting end of the tap, above the curve of the spout, a metal projection ('anvil') to be struck when driving the tap into the barrel. One such piece, with the London marks for 1830, bears the maker's mark 'WW'.

barrel teapot. A type of TEAPOT having the body shaped with bowed sides, taking the form of a miniature barrel. Such teapots were made principally in Scotland.

barge-master's badge. Goldsmiths' Company badge, John Payne, London, 1761, W. 24 cm. Goldsmiths' Company, London.

baseband. A band soldered around the bottom of the body of certain receptacles, including some TANKARDS. Such a band applied midway up the receptacle is called a 'midband'.

basin. Any concave receptacle, usually circular, of a size sufficient to hold water for rinsing the hands. It has sloping sides and its width is greater than its depth. Some examples were used as an ABLUTION BASIN accompanied by a FLAGON, but more often such pieces were passed around, with a EWER, to diners after a meal in the 16th/17th centuries. *See* BOWL; BAPTISMAL BASIN; ROSE-WATER BASIN.

basket. A receptacle for bread, cake, fruit or sweetmeats, circular or oval, and made usually in OPENWORK with sides decorated with PIERCED WORK and some examples having a BAIL HANDLE. Some early examples from the 17th century are circular with an everted rim and flat bottom and have either no handle or two opposed handles. Later oval ones have an everted rim and rest on a spreading base, a foot-ring, or four ornamented feet, the end handles being replaced with a bail handle, at first fixed and later swinging. Only very rare examples have a cover. Many such baskets of all types were made of SHEFFIELD PLATE at Birmingham and Sheffield, some by hand but many mass-produced by assembling machine-made parts. Some with openwork sides are of WIREWORK or pierced sheet with elaborate decoration of SAW-CUTTING, PUNCHING and CHASING and have rims with ornate MOUNTS. Large examples used indiscriminately for bread, cake or fruit are preferably called 'table baskets'. Small sizes were made for sweetmeats, and also some with a glass LINER to hold cream or sugar. The decorative style varied, many baskets being in ROCOCO STYLE or NEO-CLASSICAL STYLE. *See* G. Bernard Hughes, 'Pierced Silver Table Baskets' in *Country Life*, 10 November 1950, p. 1603. *See* BREAD-BASKET; CAKE-BASKET; FRUIT-BASKET; SWEETMEAT-BASKET; CREAM-BASKET; SUGAR-BASKET; WICKERWORK SILVERWARE.

basting spoon. A type of SPOON having a long handle (from 46 to 60 cm) and a large deep bowl, usually similar in shape to that of the normal TABLE-SPOON. It is similar to but longer than a GRAVY SPOON. *See* STUFFING SPOON.

bat-wing fluting. A variant form of GADROONING, in which the shape is curved to resemble the outline of a bat's wing.

bat-wing rim. A type of RIM on some receptacles (e.g., a SALT-CELLAR, SUGAR-BASKET) that is oval, slightly higher at the ends, and has four curved indentations on each side so that it bears a resemblance to the wing of a bat. usually the foot of a receptacle with such a rim has a conforming base.

Bateman. A family of London silversmiths, the prominent members of which were Hester Bateman, her sons John, Peter, and Jonathan, her daughter-in-law Ann, and her grandson William. John Bateman (*c.* 1704-1760) was a chain-maker, never apprenticed as a goldsmith or a member of any Livery Company; in 1732 he married Hester (1709?-1794), the youngest daughter of John Needham and his third wife Ann Booth, and trained her as a silversmith. They worked together, moving in 1747 from St Giles, Cripplegate, to a house at 106 Bunhill Row, and they and their descendants lived and worked in several houses there for many years. When John died, Hester, having become a skilled and creative silversmith, carried on the business with her three apprentice sons, John (d. 1778), Peter (1740-1825), and Jonathan (1747-91); in 1761 she registered her first mark 'HB' in script. For the period from 1761 to 1774 few extant pieces bear her mark, as her workshop made ware for other silversmiths (including the predecessor firm of RUNDELL, BRIDGE & RUNDELL) and retailers who by BACK-STAMPING defaced her mark with their own. She was greatly assisted by John Linney, as apprentice; by Richard Clarke (b. 1728), a Master Silversmith in her workshop, who married her daughter Letticia; and by Sir James Esdaile, a friend and banker, who was her patron and sponsor.

Before Hester retired in 1790, the business prospered and became the dominant silversmiths of England in the period 1770-1810, producing, it has been estimated, some 11,000 pieces bearing her mark. Most of the ware in the early years consisted of spoons and other FLATWARE, later of TEA EQUIPAGE and SMALLWARE, including many JUGS and SALTS. Her reputation was based on the gracefulness of the forms she created and her decorative style; she favoured sparsely decorated ware, featuring edges of tiny BEADING, urn-shaped finials topped with a small ball, and occasional use of BRIGHT CUTTING and elaborate SAW CUTTING.

After Hester retired, the business was carried on by her surviving sons, Peter and Jonathan, who on 7 December 1790 registered their joint mark 'PB/IB', the rarest Bateman mark as this partnership lasted only until Jona-

Bath rim. Detail of applied rim on salver, London, 1735-6. Wadsworth Atheneum (Elizabeth B. Miles Collection), Hartford, Conn.

beadle's staff. Silver-gilt staff-head, Samuel Courtauld I, London, 1755. W. 26 cm. Clothworkers' Company, London.

than died on 19 April 1791. Thereafter the partnership consisted of Peter and his very competent and active sister-in-law Ann (*née* Dowling; 1748–1813), widow of Jonathan (whom she had married in 1769), and a fine craftsman of Huguenot descent; in 1791 they registered their joint mark 'PB/AB' and continued the successful career of the firm, but changed the style of the ware, substituting a thread decoration for Hester's well-known beading.

In 1800 Ann's youngest son, William Bateman I (1774–1850), a superior craftsman, became a partner (the mark then included three sets of initials, 'PB/AB/WB'), and when Ann retired in 1805, he and Peter became partners, registering their joint mark 'PB/WB'. In 1815 Peter retired and William became sole owner, the first time that there was only one Bateman in the firm. He soon departed from its previous restrained style to make lavishly decorated ware (e.g., the CRÉCY SIDEBOARD DISH) of the sort which became typical of VICTORIAN SILVERWARE. When he retired, his son, William Bateman II (d. *c.* 1874–7), assumed control, taking as a partner for a few years Daniel Ball; thereafter he worked alone in the Victorian style, registering his mark 'WB' in 1827 and making pieces foreign to the Bateman tradition.

Although there are very many extant pieces of silverware in a great variety of forms that bear the Bateman marks, they are much sought after by collectors, especially in the United States, notwithstanding that in England Bateman pieces are often deprecated as to design and workmanship. There are known FAKES, some bearing a false Hester Bateman mark.

See David S. Shure, *Hester Bateman* (1959); G. Bernard Hughes, 'An 18th-Century Woman Silversmith' in *Country Life,* 6 September 1960, p. 508; 'A Unique Discovery' in *The Connoisseur,* December 1965, p. 225 (Hester Bateman coffee service, 1790, in a private Scottish collection).

Bath rim A curving ribbed RIM found on some TRAYS, WAITERS, and SALVERS; it is in the form of a series of two long shallow curves meeting at a point (a 'brace', as used in typography) separated by a straight line, making basically a circular border. *See* CHIPPENDALE RIM; SCROLL-AND-SHELL RIM.

baton. A type of STAFF, shorter and less ornate than a MACE, that is carried as a symbol of authority of public officials or military commanders. Some have been made of silver, although most are of gold or of wood covered with leather or velvet. *See* SCEPTRE; STICK.

bay-leaf garland. A pattern in the form of a continuous series of stylized bay leaves, used as a border decoration.

bayonet cover. A type of cover which is secured to an article by a BAYONET JOINT, as on some CASTERS, etc. It is sometimes called a 'slip-lock cover'.

bayonet joint. A type of coupling on certain composite articles, by which the removable part (such as the cover on some CASTERS) has two small projecting lugs that fit into vertical slots on the receptacle, and is made secure by rotating it to engage with the slots, extending horizontally on the receptacle. A variant type of fitting is found on the removable handle or knop on the cover of some VEGETABLE-DISHES.

bead pattern. A pattern on FLATWARE having the entire border of the stem in the form of a continuous row of small circular beads. When the beads are tiny, it is sometimes called a 'fine bead pattern'. *See* BEADING.

bead-and-reel pattern. A decorative pattern in the form of a series of alternating circles (beads) and narrow vertically elliptical forms (reels), singly or in pairs. *See* KNURLING.

beading. A decorative motif in the form of a continuous row of small relief hemispheres resembling beads. It has been used along the edge of pieces such as a TRAY, SALVER, etc., and also along the vertical handle of some drinking vessels and along the entire length of both edges of the handles of some FLATWARE and CUTLERY. Sometimes called a 'beaded edge'.

beadle's staff. A type of STAFF carried by a beadle (an official who walks before a dignitary in a ceremonial procession, summons members to meetings, etc., especially at an English University; at Oxford, spelled *bedel*, at Cambridge, *bedell*). Such staves usually consist of a long wooden pole sheathed with silver or silver gilt, the decoration divided lengthwise into sections by knops, and have a large ornamental emblematic staff-head and a smaller foot-knop. The staff-head usually bears an inscription, symbol or motto identifying the college, company or corporation to which the beadle is attached. Examples, dating from the 16th century, average about 1·20 m in length. *See* PORTER'S STAFF; TIPSTAFF; VERGE.

beak. Beer-jug by Francis Soilsbury, London. Courtesy, Asprey & Co. Ltd, London.

beaker. Beaker with stamped decoration, Cornelius van der Burch, New York, 1685. H. 20·5 cm. Yale University Art Gallery (Mabel Brady Garvan Collection), New Haven, Conn.

bear jug. Performing bear, with jewelled eyes and collar, Hands & Son, 1855. H. 17·5 cm. Courtesy, Garrard & Co. Ltd, London.

beak. A type of LIP on a JUG (pitcher) or other pouring vessel; it extends to a point, being usually in the form of the lower mandible of a sparrow. *See* BEAK SPOUT.

beak spout. A type of SPOUT with a pouring LIP in the shape of a BEAK; it occurs on some JUGS, BIGGINS, and COFFEE-POTS.

beaker. A type of drinking vessel of cylindrical shape tapering slightly down and inward to a flat base and having a slightly to boldly flared rim (probably derived from early examples made from a section of a horn). A few are supported by a stemmed foot or three BUN FEET. Only rare examples have a handle, sometimes in scroll loop form, or a cover. Decoration includes EMBOSSING, ENGRAVING, and HATCHING, but seldom applied MOUNTS. The height is usually about 15 cm, but some examples are up to 23 cm high. A number of examples made in England and the United States follow the form and the STRAPWORK decoration of 17th-century Dutch prototypes. Some large examples were used in Protestant churches to pass the wine among the congregation at the Eucharist. *See* G. Bernard Hughes, 'Old English Silver Beakers' in *Country Life*, 8 August 1956, p. 293. *See* BARREL BEAKER; HORN BEAKER; HANDLED BEAKER; BEAUFORT BEAKER; MAGDALEN CUP; NEST.

beaker set. A type of TRAVELLER'S DINING SET composed of a BEAKER into which are fitted several dining implements, such as knife, fork, and spoon (the implements sometimes having folding or detachable handles). The set is sometimes fitted into a wooden case covered with leather or shagreen.

bear jug. A type of JUG in the form (derived from pottery jugs made in England in the 18th century) of a bear in-the-round standing upright on a decorated base. The head, which is detachable, serves as the cover, and its collar is connected by a chain to the base on which the bear stands. An example by Hands & Co. has ruby eyes, and turquoises and rubies on the collar.

Beaufort Beaker. A silver-gilt covered BEAKER, 1507-8, the bowl and cover of which are engraved with a DIAPER PATTERN of STRAPWORK enclosing Tudor roses, fleurs de lis, and portcullises that were the device of Lady Margaret Beaufort (1443-1509), Countess of Richmond and Derby (wife of Edmund Tudor and mother of Henry VII), who founded Christ's College, Cambridge, in 1505 and bequeathed the beaker to it (hence called there 'The Foundress' Tun'). At the intersections of the diaper pattern are engraved flowers, perhaps daisies derived from the badge of Humphrey, Duke of Gloucester (1391-1447), but sometimes said to be marguerites, a heraldic rebus for the donor's name. The bowl rests on a lobed base, and the cover has a hexagonal ornament of which the sides are pinnacled portcullises, surmounted by a finial in the form of four daisies topped by a Tudor rose. Around the vertical sides of the base are a number of small holes that have been said to be possibly intended for the insertion of gemstones that are now missing.

Beaufort Cup. A silver-gilt STANDING CUP, 1438–40, having a hemispherical bowl resting on a TRUMPET FOOT and having a conical cover tapering upward to the finial (added at a later date) which is surmounted by an ornament with six crocketed (*see* CROCKET) pinnacles and bears on the top an engraved Tudor rose. The bowl, cover, and base are decorated with spiral bands of embossed oak, vine, and rose branches on granulated surfaces, alternating with spiral plain bands. The rim of the bowl and the top of the base are decorated with CRESTING. Inside the bowl are, in translucent enamel, the arms of Humphrey, Duke of Gloucester (1391–1447; uncle of Henry VI), for whom the cup was made, and his second wife, Eleanor Cobham. The cup was bequeathed to Christ's College, Cambridge, by Lady Margaret Beaufort (1443–1509), Countess of Richmond and Derby (wife of Edmund Tudor and mother of Henry VII), who founded the College in 1505 (hence the piece is called there 'The Foundress' Cup').

Beaufort Cup. Silver-gilt standing cup, 1438-40. H. 32·4 cm. Christ's College, Cambridge.

bed. A silver bed, no longer in existence, was made for Nell Gwynn (1650-87) in 1674 by JOHN COOQUS, as evidenced by an existing bill for £906 owned by the Duke of St Albans. *See* FURNITURE.

Bedingfield Chalice. A parcel-gilt CHALICE, having a hexafoil base, a stem with a large embossed KNOP, and a plain hemispherical bowl, accompanied by a circular parcel-gilt PATEN with a central sexfoil painted decoration depicting the head of Christ surrounded by a 26-pointed star. It bears a London hallmark of 1518-19, and a later mark 'EH' that is said to be possibly for Elizabeth Howard, daughter of William Howard of Naworth, who married Sir Henry Bedingfield (d. *c.* 1607). It is in the Victoria and Albert Museum, London.

Bedingfield Chalice. Parcel-gilt chalice and accompanying paten, London, 1518–19. Victoria and Albert Museum, London.

beehive coffee-pot. A type of COFFEE-POT, ovoid in shape, the bowl being in the form of an inverted beehive resting on a stemmed base and the cover being in the form of a vertical beehive, all decorated with a series of parallel horizontal ridges. An example made of SHEFFIELD PLATE, *c.* 1805, by Roberts, Cadman & Co., Sheffield, is in the Folger's Coffee Collection.

beehive honey-pot. A type of HONEY-POT of semi-ovoid shape, in the form of a skep (a beehive made of layers of horizontal coils of tied straw). The upper third of the pot is the close-fitting cover, having usually a finial depicting one or more bees. The pot often rests on a circular saucer-like tray having a REED-AND-TIE BORDER and wide enough to allow a small serving spoon to rest on it; such trays have a depressed centre to position the pot. Sometimes the interior is gilded. On later examples, the reed-and-tie bands of the skep were replaced by bands with engraved decoration. The skep form has also been used as the bowl of a tea-urn, *c.* 1800, and as a BEEHIVE COFFEE-POT.

beer-jug. A type of large JUG, for serving beer or ale, usually of baluster shape, but some examples are of bulging cylindrical shape and some have a globular lower half and a cylindrical upper half. Such jugs generally have a vertical loop or scroll handle, opposite which there is a pouring BEAK. Some rest on a spreading foot. Occasionally such jugs are decorated with an engraved barrel and ears of barley or are inscribed 'Small' or 'Strong' or with the letter 'A' or 'B' (for ale or beer).

Beeston Salt. A STEEPLE DOUBLE-SALT with two-tiered SALT-CELLARS and narrow decorative bands encircling top and bottom of the cylindrical base. It bears the maker's amrk 'RB' and the London date mark for 1614–15. It was formerly owned by the Company of Painter Stainers, and is now in the Victoria and Albert Museum, London.

bell. A hollow metallic object that vibrates and emits a musical note when struck. The main types made in silver are: (1) A bell in the form of an inverted cup (krater) with a flaring mouth, a vertical handle, and a clapper (tongue). Such bells have a sound-bow (the thick lower rim against which the clapper strikes), waist (the large cup-like section), shoulder (the upper incurved rim of the waist), and crown (the top, to which the handle is affixed). Usually the sound-bow is decorated only with bands of ribbing, but the waist and crown sometimes are decorated with EMBOSSING or ENGRAVING. *See* HAND BELL; TABLE BELL; FIGURAL BELL; CORONATION CANOPY BELL; SACRING BELL; HALLAMSHIRE BELL. (2) A hollow metallic perforated sphere containing a loose ball that causes it to emit a ringing sound when shaken, such as is attached to a baby's RATTLE. *See* RACING BELL; TORAH BELLS. (3) An electrical device with a push-button that causes a musical note to be sounded when the button is pressed. Other types made in silver include the mechanical bell.

bell salt. A type of SALT consisting of three sections that are made to fit together vertically: two open-bottomed bell-shaped sections, each having a shallow depression at the top for salt, the larger lower section resting on

beehive coffee-pot. Sheffield plate, Roberts, Cadman & Co., *c.* 1805. H. 26·8 cm. Folger's Coffee Collection, Procter & Gamble Co., Cincinnati, Ohio.

beehive honey-pot. Cover and tray (with glass liner), Paul Storr, London, 1799 and 1805. H. 11·5 cm. Courtesy, Partridge (Fine Arts) Ltd, London.

Beeston Salt. Steeple double-salt, London, 1614–15. H. 41·5 cm. Victoria and Albert Museum, London.

bell salt. Two bell-shaped sections surmounted by a small caster, London, 1599. Courtesy, Christie's, London.

three ball feet or CLAW-AND-BALL FEET and the smaller central section having an attached slip-on band around the base to enable it to fit over the bottom section; and, at the top, a small dome-shaped container (also with a slip-on band around the base) having a removable ball finial that is pierced so as to allow this part to serve as a CASTER (for spice). Such salts, about 23 cm high, are not as elaborately decorated as STANDING SALTS, having usually a MATT-CHASED ground with decoration of floral and foliage motifs and STRAPWORK; some examples are of silver gilt. Bell salts, the known examples of which are exclusively of English make, are mostly from the late 16th and early 17th centuries, but some are recorded from *c.* 1550; they were not of sufficient size or importance to be used as a GREAT SALT.

bellows. A type of instrument, having a leather body and two projecting handles, used to blow air at burning coals or wood in a fireplace. The alternating expansion and contraction of the body causes air to be drawn in through an orifice and then expelled through a tube at the end of the bellows. A number of examples with silver mounts are known, dating from *c.* 1670–90. There are three at Ham House, Richmond, and one in the Farrar Collection at the Ashmolean Museum, Oxford; another is in the Untermyer Collection at the Metropolitan Museum of Art, New York. *See* HEARTH FURNITURE.

belt plate. A type of ornamental plaque worn on a shoulder belt or a waist belt, especially by United States military personnel prior to 1821. Although such plaques were often made of a base metal, some examples were made of silver or were silver-plated, being produced by leading silversmiths. The decoration usually consisted of a figure of an American eagle or a military motif. Some comparable plates were worn as military cap plates. *See* SHOULDER-BELT PLATE.

Benney, (Adrian) Gerald (Sallis) (1930–). A leading English silversmith, born in Hull and trained in London, who established his first workshop in London in 1955. In 1964 he developed a new technique for texturing the surface of silverware, now generally used. Since 1968 he has developed his own process of applying enamel to large areas of flat or curved silver (*see* ENAMELLING). He has designed and made important CENTREPIECES and TROPHIES for many institutions, and is noted for having made, in modern style, almost all types of articles of JEWISH RITUAL SILVERWARE. He holds Royal Warrants from the Queen, the Duke of Edinburgh, the Queen Mother, and the Prince of Wales. He has exhibited in many cities world-wide and was given a retrospective one-man exhibition at Goldsmiths' Hall, London, in 1973. From 1974 to 1983 he was Professor of Silversmithing and Jewellery at the Royal College of Art, London. He has a studio and workshop at his home, Beenham House, near Reading, and a workshop in London at Bear Lane, Southwark. *See* Graham Hughes, 'Gerald Benney' in *The Connoisseur*, December 1963, p. 234; Kenneth Snowman, 'Gerald Benney–Silversmith' in *The Connoisseur*, May 1973, p. 18. *See* CONTEMPORARY SILVERWARE.

Berden Cup. A silver-gilt GOURD-SHAPED 'STEEPLE CUP', 1602, in the typical form of several other such cups. It was recorded in 1686 as having been a gift of Elizabeth Aldersey, Lady Coventry (d. 1653), to the parish church of St Nicholas, at Berden, Essex. The cup bears the coat of arms of the Newcomen family. Elizabeth married in 1610 Thomas, Lord Coventry, having previously lived at Berden and been married since 1600 to William Pritchard (d. 1609); it has been suggested that possibly the latter had some connection with Edward Newcomb (both being members of the Grocers' Company), who was related to the Newcomen family, and that Pritchard received the cup from Newcomb (hence the coat of arms) and bequeathed it to his wife, who left it to the parish of her youth in memory of her former husband. The cup bears the maker's mark 'IE' and the initials 'PB', possibly for the Parish of Berden, inscribed when the cup was repaired in 1708. The cup is on loan from the church at Berden to the Victoria and Albert Museum, London.

Beresford Hope Collection. Various articles of silver, silver gilt, and SHEFFIELD PLATE first recorded as owned by William Carr Beresford (b. 1768), the illegitimate son of the 1st Marquess of Waterford, who married his cousin, the widow of Thomas Hope; the couple had no children, and her children prefixed the name of Beresford to their patronymic, Hope. Through their descendants the collection passed to Harold Beresford Hope (d. 1917), a British diplomat posted to Warsaw, Poland, and was used at the British Legation (later Embassy) there. He married a Pole and upon his death he bequeathed the collection of 176 pieces to Poland if the country became independent within five years after his death, otherwise to the British Mission in Warsaw. After the British Probate Court had awarded the silver to the

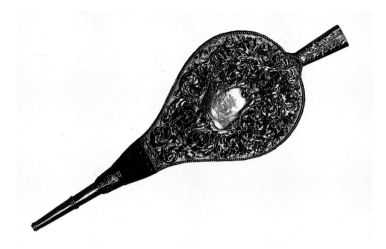

bellows. Silver-mounts, with chased and embossed decoration on one side only, London, *c.* 1660–85. Ham House, Richmond (Victoria and Albert Museum, London).

Mission, it was shipped from the London depository to Warsaw in 1921 and kept in the Mission vault when the Embassy was evacuated in 1939. When the Embassy was reopened in 1945, it was found that the vault had been broken into and the silver stolen. Later, a number of the pieces were found and identified in Warsaw, London, New York, and elsewhere. Some were exhibited in 1960 at the Victoria and Albert Museum, and in 1962 the 26 recovered pieces were sent to the National Museum in Warsaw (pending transfer to the British Mission), and delivered to the new British Embassy when it was opened in 1964. The recovered pieces include the silver-gilt Buenos Aires Cup (designed by JOHN FLAXMAN II and made by BENJAMIN SMITH I and his brother James in 1809, being one of the LLOYD'S PATRIOTIC FUND VASES), a WINE COOLER made by B. and J. Smith, 1814, a SOUP-TUREEN made by them, 1811, and a VENISON-DISH, 1814, a pair of FIGURAL CANDELABRA, 1814, and a SOUP-TUREEN, 1812, made by B. Smith, all bearing the engraved Beresford coat of arms or crest. The whereabouts of many of the pieces (including a CENTREPIECE made by PAUL STORR and many plates) is still unknown. *See* note 'Where is the Beresford Plate?' in *The Connoisseur*, April 1957, p. 179; Mary Henderson, 'The Beresford Hope Silver' in *Apollo*, January 1974, p. 34.

Berkeley Teapot. The earliest-known English silver TEAPOT, being in the form of a truncated cone with smooth sides and having a LID of smaller conical shape. It has a D-shaped leather-covered handle set at right-angles to the straight SPOUT. Although it resembles an early type of COFFEE-POT, it bears an inscription 'This silver teapot; it was given to the East India Company by George Lord Berkeley in 1670'; it also bears the engraved arms of the donor and the donee, the maker's mark 'TL' and the London ASSAY OFFICE HALLMARK and date mark for 1670–1. It is in the Victoria and Albert Museum, London. *See* EAST INDIA COMPANY COFFEE-POT.

Bermondsey Dish. A circular parcel-gilt ALMS DISH having a central medallion engraved with a scene depicting a lady placing a helmet on the head of a kneeling knight, with a background of a fortified gatehouse. Encircling the medallion is a narrow band (once gilded) of embossed vine leaves and grapes, surrounded by a wide border of sixteen spirally-curving tear-drop motifs, alternately raised and depressed. Enamelling formerly on the medallion has almost entirely disappeared. The piece is unmarked except for an engraved leopard's head on the back, now considered to be an OWNERSHIP MARK (possibly of Edward III) rather than a hallmark. The dish was formerly regarded as being of Spanish origin, but has been attributed by Charles C. Oman to English make, *c.* 1325. The dish is owned by the parish church of St Mary Magdalen, Bermondsey, London, and has been said to have possibly been given to the Abbot of Bermondsey by Edward III, *c.* 1350, or to have been received by the parish church following the dissolution of the monasteries in the 16th century. The medallion has been said to be possibly of Italian origin, brought to England by a monk and inserted into the dish. The piece, which has sometimes been incorrectly referred to as the 'Bermondsey Mazer' and as the 'Battersea Dish', is on loan at the Victoria and Albert Museum, London. An ELECTROFORM reproduction made in 1880 is on loan from the museum to the church. *See* Charles C. Oman, 'The Bermondsey Dish' in *Burlington Magazine*, January 1952, p. 23, fig. 11.

Berden Cup. Silver gilt, London, 1602–3. H. 35·7 cm. Parish church of St Nicholas, Berden, Essex (on loan to the Victoria and Albert Museum, London).

Berkeley Teapot. London, 1670–1. H. 34·5 cm. Victoria and Albert Museum, London.

Bermondsey Dish. Parcel-gilt alms dish, English, *c.* 1325. D. 26 cm. Victoria and Albert Museum, London.·

Bermuda silverware. Articles of silverware made in Bermuda by a number of local silversmiths in the 18th and 19th centuries. Earlier, some silverware owned by residents had been brought from England and France or salvaged from wrecks. The earliest silversmiths immigrated from England and France; they trained local apprentices who by the 18th century had established a flourishing trade. Over 25 local silversmiths have been recorded; among the best known was George Hutchins (1777–1856). Much of the ware was made from melted-down pieces or salvaged silver, most of the new work being domestic ware, especially spoons. *See* Katherine M. McClinton, 'A round-up of eighteenth-century Bermuda silversmiths' in *The Connoisseur*, January 1961, p.56; Erica Manning, 'Art of the Bermuda Silversmiths' in *Country Life*, 27 February 1964, p. 452.

Berry Cup. A silver-gilt GOURD-SHAPED STANDING CUP of typical shape, with decoration of ACANTHUS leaves on the lower part of the bowl and on the base. It bears the arms of Sir Benjamin Berry and his wife, the arms of the City of Portsmouth, Hampshire, and the London date mark of 1610. Berry was a professional soldier and later a Deputy-Governor of Portsmouth; in his will he bequeathed £10 with which his executors were instructed to buy a cup and donate it to the city. A cup of identical form (but with a different maker's mark) was acquired before 1889 by Sir Charles James Jackson, the writer on English silver, and he has suggested that his cup (marked London, 1570) was copied in 1610 on the orders of the Berry executors and donated to Portsmouth; the Jackson cup is now in the National Museum of Wales, Cardiff.

berry spoon. (1) A type of SPOON having a straight stem terminating in a finial in the form of a globular berry. (2) A trade name for a type of spoon that is usually an ordinary TEASPOON or DESSERT SPOON altered at a later date by the addition, on the bowl, of embossed decoration depicting fruit, and sometimes having the interior gilded.

bezel. As applied to silverware, that part of an article or its cover intended to secure the cover firmly in place, such as: (1) the lower part of a SLIP-ON COVER that extends downward and outside the collar at the top of the body of some JARS and CASTERS; (2) the projecting ring on the bottom of some covers, the projection fitting inside the rim of the neck of the piece; or (3) the rim inside the neck of an article to secure the cover.

bifurcated. Divided into two branches, as the lower terminal on some HANDLES or the THUMBPIECE on some TANKARDS. *See* FORKED HANDLE; WARWICK VASE.

biggin. An early type of COFFEE DRIPPER, sometimes said to have been named after George Biggin, a London silversmith whose mark and date letter for 1799 appear on one example; however, examples by other silversmiths, bearing earlier date letters, are recorded, and the term 'biggin' was used centuries earlier for a child's conical cap and for a fabric used to clarify wine. The coffee-biggin, made of silver or SHEFFIELD PLATE, was of cylindrical shape or sometimes barrel-shaped (with simulated staves and encircling hoops), and was produced in several sizes. Inside the biggin, just below the rim, was a ledge with a wire ring for suspending the conical fabric (usually muslin) 'biggin' into which the ground coffee was placed, hot water then being poured over it. The SPOUT was usually placed opposite the vertical loop wooden handle, and sometimes was fitted with a small SPOUT FLAP to reduce heat loss. The covering was either a low-domed COVER or a hinged LID, having a finial which occurs in various forms. The handle, varying in shape, was usually of hardwood, occasionally ebony or ivory. The interior of the pot was heavily tinned. The base of the pot was usually flat, so that the contents could be warmed by placing the pot on a stand containing a spirit lamp, but some were footed so that the pot could be heated by being placed on a fireplace hob. With the advent of the COFFEE PERCOLATOR, the coffee-biggin lost its popularity *c.* 1820.

billet. (1) The THUMBPIECE on the LID of a TANKARD or other vessel. (2) A decorative motif, usually found on an architectural MOULDING but also on some silverware, in the form of a continuous series of short raised cylinders or squares with regular spaces between them, sometimes in two parallel bands having the raised portions opposite the spaces on the adjacent band. (3) A short metal rod, that, after being made red-hot, is placed in a FIRE-BOX to heat the surrounding liquid in some TEA-URNS or some ARGYLLS or to keep warm the contents of an ENTRÉE-DISH.

bird silverware. Any article of silver made as an ornament or a receptacle in the form of or including a realistic representation of a bird, such as an owl, falcon, grouse, partridge, fighting cock, swan, peahen or pelican. Sometimes a bird is realistically depicted as an ornamental part of an object, such as the eagles on the SEYMOUR SALT. Some bird figures are utilitarian articles, e. g., CASTERS made in the form of an owl or cups made in the form of a bird, such as the COCKEREL CUPS, PELICAN CUP, GLYNNE CUP, OSTRICH CUP, PEAHEN CUP. *See* OWL SILVERWARE; ANIMAL SILVERWARE.

Birks, Henry, & Sons Ltd. Well known as the leading Canadian retailer of silverware, the company has a long tradition as silversmiths. In 1879 a retail store was established in Montreal by Henry Birks (1840-1928), whose father, John Birks, had migrated there in 1832. The latter was descended from a long line of English cutlers and silversmiths since 1564. The firm's silver manufacturing business began in 1887 and was augmented by the acquisition in 1898 of the silversmith business of Hendery & Leslie of Montreal (successors to the firm founded by ROBERT CRUICKSHANK). The company expanded throughout Canada, and is directed today by the fifth generation of the founder's family. The Henry Birks Collection of Silverware includes important Canadian ecclesiastical and secular articles and INDIAN TRADE SILVERWARE made from the early 18th century to the present time.

Birmingham Assay Office. The ASSAY OFFICE opened in 1773 in Birmingham, England; it has used, and still does use, as its ASSAY OFFICE HALLMARK on silverware a vertical anchor, accompanied by a STANDARD HALLMARK, a MAKER'S MARK, and a DATE HALLMARK commencing in 1773. In 1973 a special COMMEMORATIVE MARK was adopted to celebrate the 200th anniversary of the office; it was the usual anchor mark, with a Roman numeral 'C' on each side.

Birmingham silverware. Articles of silverware, as distinguished from PLATED METAL, made in Birmingham, England. Silverware had been made there for several centuries before the BIRMINGHAM ASSAY OFFICE was established by the Act of 1773, the articles having been sent from 1765 to Chester for ASSAYING. The 1773 Act greatly stimulated the production of silverware in Birmingham, and a wide range of types of ware was produced by the MATTHEW BOULTON factory. Boulton, being ambitious to surpass the quality of the London silversmiths, in the 1770s sought designs from, among others, ROBERT ADAM, James Wyatt and Robert Mylne, but he also used designs made by his own craftsmen and adapted designs of Continental ware and contemporary English ware. In 1773 there were more than 2,000 firms producing silverware in Birmingham, as the locally made articles could be sold more cheaply than London ware. Local ware continued to be mainly SMALLWARE, especially such articles as BOTTLE TICKETS, BUTTONS, BUCKLES, CADDY SPOONS, VINAIGRETTES, and CASTLE-TOP WARE. Birmingham became known as the capital of the world for the making of TOYS. New production methods were patented and mass-production thrived, but as a result quality diminished. *See* Shirley Bury, 'Assay Silver at Birmingham' in *Country Life*, 13 June 1968, p.1610, and 20 June 1968, p.1699; Margaret Holland, 'Silverware made at Birmingham' in *Antiques*, April 1976, p.760; Kenneth Crisp Jones (ed.), *The Silversmiths of Birmingham and their Marks, 1750-1980* (1981).

biscuit-box. A covered receptacle for biscuits (in the United States, cookies), usually a circular container with a tight-fitting SLIP-ON COVER, but occurring in various shapes and styles. Some are in the form of a silver frame and cover with a glass LINER. *See* FOLDING BISCUIT-BOX.

black-coffee set. A type of small COFFEE-SERVICE, for serving after-dinner coffee, consisting of small coffee-cups (*see* CANN), a coffee-pot, cream-jug, and sugar-bowl, and sometimes a small serving tray. Such sets, sometimes so called in the United States, were popular there from *c.* 1880 to *c.* 1910, and were made in many styles. *See* DEMI-TASSE.

blackjack. A type of TANKARD made of treated leather, intended for drinking beer or ale. Some examples from the 17th and 18th centuries have silver MOUNTS and, rarely, a silver lining. Such tankards have a distinctive bulge midway on the body. They were a speciality of Chester, having been made there by members of the Richardson family and by George Walker. *See* MOUNTED OBJECTS.

bleeding bowl. A small, shallow, flat-bottomed BOWL with straight or slightly convex sides, and having one flat, horizontal, triangular, pierced handle extending from (or near) the rim. Such cups, from 10 to 13 cm in diameter, have been said to have been employed by barber-surgeons in the 17th and 18th centuries for bleeding a patient. Although some writers have

Berry Cup. Silver gilt, London, 1610. H. 39 cm. City of Portsmouth.

biggin. Coffee-biggin with stand, spirit lamp, and tray, Robert Salmon. London, 1796. H. 29·2 cm. Folger's Coffee Collection, Procter & Gamble Co., Cincinnati, Ohio.

blackjack. Leather tankard with silver mounts, English, *c.* 1690. Courtesy, Brand Inglis Ltd. London.

bleeding bowl. Bowl with pierced handle, Exeter, 1704. Wellcome Collection, Science Museum, London.

Bodkin Cup. Silver gilt, London, 1525–6. H. 12 cm. City of Portsmouth.

doubted such usage, some old engravings depict such bowls with surgical instruments, thus confirming their use; but bowls can be identified as having served this purpose only when horizontal, graduated measuring lines are present on the interior. Bowls so used have a capacity of not more than 3 fl. oz. (85 ml), the maximum amount of blood formerly taken in blood letting. The form resembles that of the larger PORRINGER, the smaller TEA MEASURE, and the even smaller ASPARAGUS BUTTER-BOWL and WINE TASTER. It has been sometimes called in Britain a 'cupping bowl', but incorrectly, as in cupping the blood was drawn by a vacuum, usually into a glass receptacle. It has been suggested that some early pieces in such form may have been made to serve as the cover of a SKILLET, but this has been repudiated. Some were donated to churches and used as an ALMS DISH. *See* Charles Noon, 'Bleeding Bowl or Skillet Cover?' in *The Connoisseur*, January 1942, p. 142.

blind caster. *See* MUSTARD CASTER.

blind hinge. A type of HINGE where the pin-joints and the tube through which they pass are made within the hinge itself so as to be concealed (as on some TOOTHPICK-CASES and high-quality SNUFF-BOXES and on the flat lid of some teapots). Sometimes called a 'hidden hinge', 'sunken hinge' or 'flush hinge'.

blow hole. A small hole (or slit) found in some HOLLOW WARE (such as at the base of the handle on some TANKARDS), the purpose of which was to permit the escape of air that was heated while the two parts were being soldered together. Without the hole, the enclosed air would expand during heating and contract during cooling, resulting in a distortion of the shape of the piece. The hole served to facilitate detection of any fraudulent filling of the hollow handle to increase the weight of the piece. The hole on the handle of some tankards (sometimes called a 'whistle tankard') has sometimes been explained erroneously as being a whistle to call for another drink; this is disproved by such holes occurring on some church FLAGONS. Sometimes called a 'whistle slot'.

Bobrinsky Centrepiece. A large CENTREPIECE, made by PAUL DE LAMERIE, 1734, in the form of a central bowl resting on a stand supported by four shell-decorated feet and having extending from each end of the stand curved arms to support, on each side, a pair of CANDLESTICKS and a set of three CASTERS and two CRUETS. The piece, which is 81 cm long, is now in the Russian State Museum, Moscow.

Bodkin Cup. A silver-gilt 'FONT-SHAPED' cup having a typical shallow vertical-sided bowl resting on a wide TRUMPET FOOT decorated on its spreading base with spiral GADROONING. The bowl has gadrooning on its bottom, and encircling it is the Latin inscription 'SI DEVS NOBISCVM QVIS CONTRA NOS' (If God be with us, who shall be against us). Encircling the edge of the foot is a narrow vertical band decorated with a repeating pattern of small vase-like motifs alternating with floral sprays. Inside the bowl are the initials 'FB' of the original owner, Francis Bodkin (d. 1591), who was Mayor of Portsmouth, Hampshire, in 1553, 1560 and 1579, and whose widow, Grace, donated the cup to the City of Portsmouth. The cup bears the London date mark for 1525. A silver-gilt replica of the cup, identical except for the unidentified maker's mark and the London date mark for 1622, was formerly in the collection of the Earl of Breadalbane, and was purchased *c.* 1968–9 by the City of Portsmouth.

Bodmin Cup. A tall silver-gilt STEEPLE CUP, 1617, its bowl and cover together being of ovoid shape. The bowl rests on a vase-shaped stem (with three brackets), supported by a high foot on a circular base. The cover is surmounted by a four-sided pierced obelisk-type steeple topped by a standing figure of Minerva holding a spear and shield (the steeple is a later replacement, presumably – in view of the three brackets on the stem – for a three-sided one). The cup is owned by the church of St Petroc, Bodmin, Cornwall.

body. The main portion of a vessel or object, as distinguished from the BASE, SPOUT, HANDLE, COVER, LID or FOOT.

Boleyn Cup. A silver-gilt STANDING CUP, marked London, 1535, having an inverted conical bowl and a circular foot, between which there is a merese (collar) decorated with applied ACANTHUS leaves. The lower part of the bowl, the low-domed cover, and the foot are decorated with applied radiating REEDING and the upper part of the bowl has an encircling engraved band of scrolling foliage. The cover rises to a finial upon which, standing on a circular support with descending roots, there is a figure of a falcon holding a sceptre and standing alongside a rose tree. The falcon was the personal badge of Anne Boleyn as queen. The cup is said to have been given, *c.* 1653, to the parish church of Cirencester, Gloucestershire, by Dr Richard Masters, physician to Elizabeth I, and it is presumed that she presented to him the cup that she had inherited from her mother, Anne Boleyn. It has been suggested that the cup may have been imported and given a London hallmark. A design almost identical to that of the bowl of the cup occurs in a design book, *c.* 1545, by Hans Brosamar, and the form of the cup is similar to that of Venetian glass goblets of the 16th century. *See* RICHMOND, JOHN, CUP.

Bolsover, Thomas. *See* BO(U)LSOVER.

Bolton Centrepiece. A fantasy CENTREPIECE made in ROCOCO STYLE, *c.* 1760, by JOHN PARKER and EDWARD WAKELIN. The oval base, resting on four scroll feet, has at each end a sculptured head of a goat, and in the centre, supporting the bowl, two figures-in-the-round of standing hinds. Near each end of the base are trees with their branches extending outward beyond the rim of the base. The bowl (a fruit-basket with an everted rim) has a cover with a finial in the form of fruit and leaves. The piece is 1·03 m long. It bears the arms of Powlet, having been made for Charles Powlet, 5th Duke of Bolton; it was sold by Lord Bolton at Christie's, London, in 1965, and is now in the Museum of Fine Arts, Boston, Massachusetts. *See* ASHBURNHAM CENTREPIECE.

bombé. A curved, bulging, convex shape occurring usually in articles of rectangular, square or oval section, such as some TEAPOTS, TEA-CADDIES, TUREENS, CASKETS, and JARDINIÈRES, often those in ROCOCO STYLE.

Bonnie Prince Charlie's Canteen. The travelling CANTEEN captured from Prince Charles Edward Stuart ('Bonnie Prince Charlie'; 1720–88), the Young Pretender, after the Battle of Culloden, 16 April 1746. It consists of thirteen pieces: the flask-shaped, heavily embossed outer case, which has a hinged lid, encloses two plain nesting BEAKERS, into which is fitted a wooden block with holes for holding vertically several dining implements (two knives, two forks, two tablespoons, a cruet set, a combined nutmeg grater/corkscrew, a combined teaspoon/marrow spoon), and – stored in the lid – a small two-handled cup (possibly a wine taster). The canteen was made by Ebenezer Oliphant, Edinburgh, 1740–1. It was given by the Duke of Cumberland to George Kepple, son of the 2nd Earl of Albemarle, and it remained in the Albemarle family until 1963, when it was sold at Christie's, London; it was subsequently resold several times and, after an export licence was refused, was acquired by the National Museum of Antiquities of Scotland, Edinburgh. *See* George Dalgleish, 'Prince Charlie's Canteen' in *Antique Collector*, October 1985, p. 66.

book cover. A hinged covering for a book, either made of silver (or gold or other metal) and decorated with EMBOSSING, CHASING, ENAMELLING, and sometimes set with gemstones, or made of leather and decorated with silver mounts. Some examples for church use were books of the Gospels and Epistles, and later the Old and New Testaments and the Book of Common Prayer. Other small books so bound were various devotional texts, the cover having an attached suspensory ring to provide for carrying on a CHATELAINE or from a girdle (*see* GIRDLE BOOK). *See* BOOK MOUNTS; MISSAL COVER.

book hinge. A type of HINGE where the pin-joints (made of a base metal and left unsilvered) and the tube through which they pass project (as on a door hinge) outside the edge of the article, and have a rounded back resembling the spine of a book. Sometimes the terminals of the pin-joints are hidden by small ornamental silver caps.

book mounts. Decorative MOUNTS affixed to the cover of a book (often a Bible or the Gospels), generally in the form of eight corner mounts, a central inscribed mount, and two hinged clasps over the open end.

boot hook. A type of device for pulling on a boot that has a loop provided at the top; it is in the form of a long hook at right-angles to a straight cross-bar handle, and sometimes occurs as one of a pair. A silver-gilt pair was made by EDWARD FARRELL, London, 1814, and a silver pair by PAUL STORR, London, 1825, was sold at Sotheby's, London, on 22 November 1984. Sometimes erroneously called a 'boot jack' (a device made of wood and used to take off a boot by gripping the heel).

Booth Cup. A silver-gilt STANDING CUP, its design being in MANNERIST STYLE, having a spool-shaped bowl resting on a stem with a central bracketed vase-shaped knop. The bottom of the bowl has two bulging bands, the lower

Bodmin Cup. Silver gilt, English, 1617. H. 64·8 cm. Church of St Petroc, Bodmin, Cornwall (photo courtesy, Historic Churches Preservation Trust, London).

Boleyn Cup. Silver gilt, English, 1535. H. 31·5 cm. Parish church, Cirencester, Glos. (photo courtesy, Historic Churches Preservation Trust, London).

embossed with GADROONING and the upper with lion's-head masks, alternating with cartouches enclosing sea-monsters. The cylindrical part of the bowl is decorated with circular cartouches enclosing embossed figures of Jupiter, Diana, and Venus, and such cartouches on the base depict Mercury, Mars, and Diana. The cover, of CUSHION SHAPE, has a bracketed vase-shaped finial topped by a standing figure of Hercules wearing the skin of the Nemean lion. The piece, bearing the London mark for 1616–17, is said to have been made probably by a Dutch craftsman in London. It was purchased *c.* 1636 by St John's College, Cambridge, with funds from a cash legacy left to the College by Robert Booth, a Fellow in 1572–3.

Borg-Warner Trophy. A TROPHY awarded since 1936 for the annual Indianapolis Speedway 500-mile auto race. Its tall ovoid bowl has two wing-shaped handles and is engraved with a chequered pattern to symbolize the racing finish flag. After each race a sculptured portrait head of the winner is affixed to a vacant square and in the one immediately below it his name, the date, and the winning speed are recorded. The finial on the cover is in the form of a nude male figure waving the chequered finish flag. The mammoth trophy, 1·29 m high, was designed in ART DECO STYLE by Robert J. Hill, and was made in 1935 by the GORHAM COMPANY. The trophy (registered trademark of the Borg-Warner Corporation) is on permanent display at the Indianapolis Speedway Hall of Fame Museum. Each winner receives a tiny silver replica.

Boscobel Oak box. A type of BOX, usually oval and with a hinged LID, that depicts on the lid the Royal Oak in Boscobel Wood in which Charles II is seen hiding when fleeing the country after his defeat by Cromwell at Worcester in 1651; some examples also show, below the tree, Cromwell's horsemen searching for the king. Such boxes were popular *c.* 1690–1730.

boss. (1) A protuberant, domed, circular ornament, such as is found on some pieces decorated by EMBOSSING. (2) The raised central ornament (sometimes referred to tautologically as a 'convex boss') in the well of some PLATES or BOWLS or in the bowl of some MAZERS (upon which there is usually affixed a PRINT). (3) As a verb, to beat up from the back, as in embossing.

bo'sun's call. A type of WHISTLE used by a bo'sun (boatswain) or his mate to give various signals and commands, often to establish the rhythm for rowers. An English silver example is recorded from 1671. A so-called 'Mariner's Whistle' was referred to in 1574.

bottle. A vessel for holding liquids, usually having a long neck and a narrow mouth. Bottles are often cylindrical, but they may be globular, ovoid, pear-shaped or of square section, with a great many variations. They have either flat or rounded sides. Examples of small size, for perfume, are often a unit of a TOILET SERVICE, especially glass SILVER-CASED BOTTLES. *See* PILGRIM FLASK; WINE-BOTTLE; CASTING BOTTLE; SCENT-BOTTLE.

bottle coaster. A type of COASTER in the form of a circular flat-bottomed receptacle used as a rest for a wine-bottle on a table. Originally it was merely a wooden stand (known as a 'slide'), used to protect the table from being scratched by the encircling rim of a bottle with a high kick. It was superseded in the 1780s by a circular stand of silver or SHEFFIELD PLATE, the size varying to suit different bottles. It has a low vertical gallery (known as a 'bar'), about 5 to 10 cm high, with its rim slightly everted and decorated with BEADING or REEDING, and the gallery decorated with pierced work, applied swags, or BRIGHT CUTTING. The metal bottom of early examples was soon superseded by a wooden disc (mahogany or boxwood), with its upper surface having an inlaid central metal BOSS engraved with a cipher. The underside was covered with baize. Also called a 'bottle stand', a 'bottle slide' or a 'bottle tray'. *See* DECANTER WAGON; DECANTER STAND; WINE-BOTTLE STAND; WINE-BOTTLE COASTER; HOCK-BOTTLE COASTER; TUMBLER STAND; WELLINGTON BOTTLE COASTER.

bottle cork. A type of cork (for recorking an opened bottle) topped by an ornamental silver mount. The mount is sometimes in the form of a vine-branch pulling ring, a standing figure, or a label with the name of the contents. The mount usually has a long stem which extends through the cork to a fastening cap at the bottom.

bottle handle. A type of handle that can be attached to a wine-bottle for carrying it. One example, of scrolled shape, has arms that can be fitted around the neck of the bottle and secured by a screw. A different form has a coaster-type base from which a handle extends upward, and has hinged arms that encircle the neck.

Booth Cup. Silver-gilt cup and cover, London, 1616. H. 63·5 cm. St John's College, Cambridge.

bottle holder. A cylindrical receptacle in which to place a bottle; it is both decorative and useful, serving to protect the surface on which it stands from any moisture on the bottle. Such pieces, which usually fit closely around the lower part of the bottle and extend part-way up its sides, have either a flat bottom or small feet. Small examples are intended for use with a bottle that is part of a TOILET SERVICE, and large ones with a wine-bottle (*see* WINE-BOTTLE STAND).

bottle lock. A device for preventing theft of the contents of a wine-bottle or a decanter. Such articles were made of silver in a variety of forms from the latter half of the 19th century. Some decanters were made with a silver mount that incorporated a lock. *See* TANTALUS FRAME.

bottle ring. A type of BOTTLE TICKET in the form of a ring with sloping sides, designed to fit snugly on the shoulder of a bottle. Such rings, variously inscribed with the names of wines, were a speciality of Chester. *See* CHESTER SILVERWARE.

bottle stand. The precursor of the BOTTLE COASTER, being in the form of a compressed oval bowl resting on a low spreading foot, and shaped to hold a flask-type round-bottomed bottle. An early example was made in 1723 by Augustin(e) Courtauld II (*see* COURTAULD). The term was sometimes applied to a CRUET STAND or to a galleried bottle coaster.

bottle ticket. A small plaque to be suspended by a chain around the neck of a bottle (usually a wine-bottle) and lettered with the name of the contents; such plaques were made mainly in four shapes – oblong, oval, crescent, and escutcheon – and were slightly curved so as to fit closely on the bottle. The chain was attached through two holes pierced near the top or through an eyelet on an extension of the upper edge. The names (about 1,500 – including misspellings – are recorded, many now unknown, the most popular wine names having been madeira, port, sherry, and claret) were engraved in thick lines, filled in with close HATCHING or sometimes black NIELLO, or were cut out through the ticket. Examples in silver are known from the 1730s and in SHEFFIELD PLATE from the 1760s. The plaques were decorated in various styles and had beaded or other ornamental edges, and after *c.* 1780 some included the owner's crest or cipher, usually on a CRESTING to the ticket. A rare Scottish series has the suspended label cut out in the form of a pointing dog; other unusual examples are in the form of a bugle, foul anchor, vine leaf or SCALLOP shell. A variant style was a BOTTLE RING. Some tickets bear only a single letter, cut out or forming the shape of the ticket; such letters were the initial of the owner and not of the wine. The utilitarian wine-bottle tickets were supplemented by elaborately decorated DECANTER LABELS. Both types differ from a 'bin label' which, usually made of ceramic ware, was used to identify the contents of a wine-barrel in the cellar. As such plaques often bear the name of a distilled spirit, the term 'bottle ticket' is preferable to the modern phrase 'wine label'. *See* Norman M. Penzer, *The Book of the Wine Label* (1947). *See* SLOT WINE LABEL; CONDIMENT LABEL; TOILET-WATER LABEL; CRUET LABEL; MEDICAL LABELS.

Bouget Hallmark. A mark used by the Dublin Assay Office as a FOREIGN ORIGIN MARK on silverware imported into Ireland or sent there for ASSAYING. The mark is a heraldic M-shaped symbol, adopted in 1906 (replacing the 1904–6 shamrock mark), representing a stylized depiction of a medieval water carrier ('water bouget') in the form of two leather pouches suspended one at each end of a carrying cross-bar or yoke. The mark is accompanied by the FINENESS MARK (being an oval enclosing the numerals 925 for STERLING SILVER and 9584 for BRITANNIA SILVER, both permitted to be imported) and the current DATE MARK.

bougie-box. A cylindrical type of BOX to hold a wax-taper coil, to protect it when not in use. It is about 8 cm in diameter and has a SLIP-ON COVER and usually a single loop handle. The cover was originally flat, but later ones were cone-shaped and dome-shaped. A tube or socket at the top of the cover permits the coiled taper to emerge. Such pieces were variously decorated, e.g., with BRIGHT CUTTING or PIERCED WORK; some with pierced decoration were provided with a glass LINER to act as protection for the taper within. Some examples had a glass chimney to protect the flame, and some had a chain-attached CANDLE EXTINGUISHER. The name is derived from the French *bougie*, candle, derived in turn from B(o)ugia, the Algerian town which exported the wax. Also called a 'taper-box'. *See* WAX-JACK; WAX-BALL TAPER-HOLDER.

bouillon-cup. The same as a SOUP-CUP.

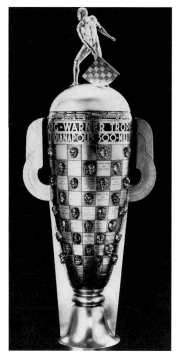

Borg-Warner Trophy. Designed by Robert J. Hill and made by the Gorham Company, 1935. H. 1·29 m. Courtesy, Borg-Warner Corporation, Chicago, Ill.

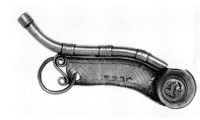

bo'sun's call. Whistle, London, *c.* 1740. L. 11·2 cm. Courtesy, Sotheby's, London.

Bouget Hallmark

bourdalou. Silver with gilt interior, Robert Garrard II, London, 1845–6. L. 24 cm. Trinity Hall, Cambridge.

Bowes, Sir Martin, Cup. Silver gilt with rock-crystal bowl, London, 1554–5. H. 49 cm. Goldsmiths' Company, London.

bouillon spoon. A type of small SPOON with a circular bowl, used for soup or bouillon served in a SOUP-BOWL or a SOUP-CUP (bouillon-cup). *See* SOUP SPOON.

Bo(u)lsover, Thomas (1704–88). A cutler of Sheffield, England, noted for having made the discovery in 1743 of the process of PLATING by which silver and copper, when united by FUSION, would retain, after rolling, their original proportions and would expand in unity, thus laying the foundation for all SHEFFIELD PLATE. Having experimented with sheets of SILVER LEAF fused to rolled copper plates (*see* CLOSE PLATING), he manufactured, with Joseph Wilson as his partner, silver-plated buttons. He then fused a plate of silver to copper, rolled the resulting bimetallic sheet, and (calling it 'Copper Rolled Plate') used it to make boxes. Although he did not patent his process, he was sole user of it until 1758, when Joseph Hancock (1711–91), a former apprentice, established himself as a competitor. From 1762 the process was used ever increasingly by MATTHEW BOULTON and other silversmiths.

Boulton, Matthew (1728–1809). A renowned manufacturer and industrial innovator of Birmingham, England, known best for his production of many and various types of articles of silver and of SHEFFIELD PLATE. From 1745 he worked for his father (d. 1759), who was a maker of buttons and buckles at Snow Hill, Birmingham, and became his partner in 1749. He inherited the firm in 1759, and by 1762 it began making Sheffield Plate ware and soon became its largest producer. Boulton moved in 1762 to Soho, near Birmingham, and soon took as a partner John Fothergill (d. 1782), the firm becoming Boulton & Fothergill until 1781. The firm at first made only SMALLWARE, much of cut steel, but by 1765 began making articles of STERLING SILVER, including SUGAR-BASKETS, CAKE-BASKETS, TEA SERVICES, etc., said not to be up to the quality of the London silversmiths. The firm grew and by 1770 employed over 700 artisans; it engaged some outside designers, but mainly used its own employees. Boulton was actively involved in promoting the establishment of the BIRMINGHAM ASSAY OFFICE, opened in 1773, to deal with the large production there. Initially the firm used hand processes but these were supplemented by machine work for ROLLING, STAMPING, and PIERCED WORK, and for mass-producing parts for sale to others for finishing and assembling. In partnership, *c.* 1775–87, with James Watt, he financed the development of the steam engine and introduced its use into his business. The firm departed from the current ROCOCO STYLE to use the more practical and popular NEO-CLASSICAL STYLE. The name of the firm was from 1781 Matthew Boulton Plate Co., then from 1794 Boulton, Watt & Sons, and after Boulton's death and until 1834 M. R. Boulton, and thereafter until it closed in 1844 the Soho Plate Co. *See* exhibition catalogue, *Matthew Boulton and the Toymakers*, Goldsmiths' Hall, London, November 1982. *See* GODMAN TEA-URN.

bourdalou. A small urinary receptacle for female use, of compressed elliptical shape and generally made of porcelain or earthenware, *c.* 1710–1850, by the leading Continental and English potteries, but also made occasionally of silver. Sometimes confused with a SAUCE-BOAT, it is basically different in form in that the front end has an incurved rim rather than an EVERTED pouring lip. There is usually a simple foot-ring (or none at all) rather than a stemmed foot. The single handle, at the end of the long axis, is usually a simple loop. Silver examples are known from France and England, and some have been attributed to Russian (including a miniature example by Carl Fabergé) and Eastern European origin. A silver example, made by ROBERT GARRARD II, 1845–6, was donated by Lawrence Strangman to Trinity Hall, Cambridge, in 1977 to mark the occasion of its admitting women as undergraduates for the first time. Such pieces were also made of plated metal; an example of SHEFFIELD PLATE, *c.* 1790, is in the City Museum, Sheffield. An apocryphal explanation of the origin of the name attributes it to Père Bourdaloue (1632–1704), a Jesuit preacher at the Court of Louis XIV, whose long discourses detained the ladies of the Court so as to necessitate this practical receptacle; however, the earliest known examples are of Dutch delftware made *c.* 1710, after Bourdaloue's death. The terms used in England are 'coach-pot', 'oval chamber-pot', and (incorrectly) 'slipper'. *See* Harold Newman, 'Bourdalous' in *The Connoisseur*, December 1970, p. 258, and May 1971, p. 22. *See* CHAMBER POT.

Bowes, Elizabeth, Cup. A silver-gilt STANDING CUP having a shallow hemispherical bowl resting on a knopped stem supported by a circular STEPPED base; its low-domed cover has a bell-shaped finial surmounted by several alternating knops and mereses (flat collars). The bowl and cover are decorated with engraving in the form of symmetrical scrolling flowers and foliage. The piece bears a maker's mark 'IS', for John Spielman (or Spilman), and London marks for 1589. It is traditionally said to have been given by Elizabeth I to her god-daughter, Elizabeth Bowes, on the occasion of her marriage in 1592 to Timothy Hutton (hence it is sometimes called the 'Hutton Cup'); however, an inscription on the cup states that the gift was made in 1570. It is now in the Royal Collection.

Bowes, Sir Martin, Cup. A large silver-gilt STANDING CUP that was presented by Sir Martin Bowes (1497–1556), Lord Mayor of London, 1545-6, and Prime Warden, 1558, of the Goldsmiths' Company, to the Company in 1561. The cup is marked London, 1554-5. The original bowl of the cup was a rock-crystal cylinder, enclosed within four vertical CARYATID straps; the bowl was damaged in 1829 and sent to RUNDELL, BRIDGE & RUNDELL for repairs, but the firm replaced it with a bowl made of lead glass. The stem has set within it a rock-crystal polyhedron, around which are two male and two female figures in-the-round standing on a crystal disc. The domed cover is surmounted by a crystal hemisphere supporting a vase-shaped finial, on top of which is a standing female figure holding a shield decorated with the donor's arms in enamels (the figure was affixed before the presentation of the cup in 1561). According to an unsubstantiated tradition, it is the coronation cup of Elizabeth I, following the custom from very early times that the Lord Mayor, as Cup-bearer, would attend the coronation banquet, and receive as his fee a standing cup from which the Sovereign had drunk; but Bowes was not Lord Mayor in 1558 (when Elizabeth was crowned) and records do not show his attendance at the coronation. *See* ELIZABETH II CORONATION CUP.

bowl. A receptacle that is deeper than a SAUCER and whose width is generally greater than its height. It usually, but not invariably, has a spreading base or a FOOT-RING. Small bowls for table purposes often have two side handles, and some have a COVER. They vary in size, depending on the purpose, and occur in many forms and styles. Some examples are accompanied by a STAND decorated EN SUITE. *See* STUDLEY BOWL; PUNCH-BOWL; SUGAR-BOWL; ÉCUELLE; PORRINGER; MAZER; MONTEITH; TUREEN; VOIDER; SLOP-BOWL; SHAVING BOWL; WASH BOWL; CHRISTENING BOWL; SPITTOON; FRUIT-BOWL; ROSE-BOWL; NEW YORK BOWL.

box. A closed receptacle, usually circular, oval or polygonal, having a cover or hinged lid, and, as to silver examples, of small size and readily portable. They have been made in a great many shapes, sizes, and styles, and for a vast number of purposes. Some small boxes are part of a TOILET SERVICE (such as a COMB-BOX, SOAP-BOX, JEWEL-BOX, patch-box, rouge-box, salve-box, and TOILET CASKET). Some larger boxes are units of a DINNER SERVICE (such as a BISCUIT-BOX, SPICE-BOX, and SUGAR-BOX). Many types of box have been made or used for some special purpose, e.g., a BOUGIE-BOX, CASKET, CIGAR-BOX, CIGARETTE-BOX, FREEDOM BOX, KNIFE-BOX, SEAL-BOX, SNUFF-BOX, TOBACCO-BOX, TOOTHPICK-CASE, VESTA-BOX. Some are made in fanciful form as an ornament. Other types, e.g., the BOSCOBEL OAK BOX, have been made to commemorate a particular event. Some types of box have the bottom slightly recessed to protect the decoration on the bottom or the surface of the table upon which they rest. Boxes are sometimes made in similar shapes, but graduated in size so as to nest into each other.

box cruet stand. A type of CRUET STAND that has a platform with, along the rim, a GALLERY topped with a flat plate with cut-out recesses to hold the cruets. The plate is attached to the platform by a central post.

box hinge. A type of HINGE found on some STONEWARE JUGS having the top of the handle level with the stoneware rim of the jug, but having the hinge joined at the top of the applied silver mouth rim, so that the lid must be raised by a box set atop the handle. Such box hinges are also found on other ceramic jugs having an applied silver mouth rim.

box salt. A type of dinner-table accessory in the form of a DOUBLE-LIDDED BOX with two compartments for salt; it is similar to certain 18th-century SPICE-BOXES, but without the NUTMEG GRATER(/ under the hinge. A pair of silver-gilt examples, made by NICHOLAS CLAUSEN and marked 1721, are in the Royal Collection; they bear the engraved arms of William and Mary, 1789-94, and the monogram 'WM', and the discrepancy between the date mark and the reign of William and Mary has suggested to Arthur Grimwade that these are later replacements for an original pair.

bracket. A scroll-shaped vertical piece primarily used as a support, but in silverware often used ornamentally. On some STANDING CUPS and STEEPLE CUPS, three such brackets are found on the stem as ornament, as well as on

Boulton, Matthew. Krater-shaped wine cooler with gadrooning and vitruvian-scroll decoration, Sheffield plate, Birmingham, 19th century. H. 25 cm. City Museums and Art Gallery, Birmingham.

box. Ornamental box with cover (its form based on the shape of a tropical fruit seed). H. 16·5 cm. Courtesy. Tiffany & Co., New York.

box salt. One of a pair, silver gilt, with engraved arms and cipher of William and Mary; replacement made by Nicholas Clausen, London, 1721-2, H. 4 cm. Royal Collection; reproduced by gracious permission of Her Majesty the Queen.

brandy-saucepan. David Willaume II, London, 1740. H. 4·5 cm. Ashmolean Museum, Oxford.

brazier. Charcoal burner, Jonathan Madder, London, 1708–9. W. 14·8 cm. Wadsworth Atheneum (Elizabeth B. Miles Collection), Hartford, Conn.

the cover just below the finial. On some STANDING SALTS and STEEPLE SALTS, such brackets are found on the rim of the salt-bowl as supports for the cover, raising it above the bowl, and on the cover as supports for the finial. *See* CHESTER CUP; HERCULES SALT; VYVYAN SALT; WARDEN HILL'S SALT; CROCKET.

brandy-bowl. A type of drinking vessel derived from the Dutch *brandewijn-kom*, ranging in size from small bowls up to 25 cm in diameter. Such pieces are generally in the shape of a shallow uncovered bowl resting on a FOOT-RING and having two opposed vertical loop handles. Examples are known made in New York in the first quarter of the 18th century; such bowls were used on festive occasions, being filled with brandy and raisins and passed among the guests. They differ from a WINE TASTER in being wider and having a flat bottom without EMBOSSING.

brandy-saucepan. A small SAUCEPAN used for warming brandy or mulling wine. The deep bowl is cylindrical or bulging toward the bottom, and has an everted rim, a beak-shaped pouring lip, and, at right-angles, a long uplifted handle. The handle, pinned in a silver FERRULE (attached to the bowl with a reinforcing encircling plate) is made of ivory or a hard wood. The bowl has a flat bottom and sometimes three or four short legs. It often has a cover with a finial of silver or wood; the cover sometimes has a projection extending over the lip. Some examples have decoration of ENGRAVING. Sometimes called a 'pipkin'. *See* BRANDY WARMER.

brandy warmer. (1) A BRANDY-SAUCEPAN or 'pipkin'. (2) A modern utensil for warming brandy over a spirit lamp. It consists of a large glass brandy snifter which is placed at a 45° angle in a silver wire frame that supports the spirit lamp under the bowl of the snifter. *See* TODDY WARMER.

brazier. A type of utensil that provides heat from burning charcoal; it is sometimes used for warming or cooking certain foods in a pan placed upon it over the charcoal. The piece is in the form of a bowl-shaped circular basin having: (a) a metal grille, either removable or screwed to the bottom of the interior, upon which to place the burning charcoal; (b) a pierced base and rim to provide air circulation to keep the coals burning; (c) three outward-curved, vertical brackets on the rim, upon which to rest a dish or bowl to be kept warm; (d) three short scroll legs to elevate it above the table, (e) usually a long straight wooden handle projecting horizontally from an attached FER-RULE; and (f) a plate, with an upcurved rim, placed below the grille to catch and hold the ashes. An unusual example has, instead of the brackets, three hinged flaps on the rim, to be turned in or out in order to support receptacles of different sizes. The brazier is derived from ancient utensils to hold burning charcoal, of which the larger examples were for warming a room, and some smaller ones were used as foot-warmers. Braziers have frequently been, and sometimes still are, called CHAFING DISHES, but that term is preferably applied to the type of utensil of which the cooking receptacle is an integral part rather than a separate piece to be placed on brackets above heated coals. *See* H. E. K., 'Braziers as Collectibles' in *Antiques*, September 1933, p. 106. *See* PIPE LIGHTER; PERFUME-BURNER.

bread-basket. A type of BASKET that is usually either circular or oval, with an everted rim and a BAIL HANDLE, and generally decorated with PIERCED WORK, sometimes in the form of plaited osier strips. Some have four decorated feet, but usually they rest on a flat bottom. Such baskets are indistinguishable from a CAKE-BASKET, except when a wheat motif is included in the decoration. An osier-type example, London, 1791–2, was donated to King's College, Cambridge, in 1792 by Thomas Orde (from 1797, Lord Bolton).

bread-fork. A type of FORK having three prongs or tines in trident fashion, used for serving bread from a BREAD-BASKET or a BREAD-TRAY.

bread-tray. A shallow receptacle, not flat like the usual serving TRAY, for serving bread at a dinner table. Some are rectangular with upcurved sides and a wide horizontal rim; some, intended for a long loaf, are long and narrow, of extended elliptical shape. The rim is usually ornately decorated with relief mounts or EMBOSSING.

Breadalbane Candelabrum. An ornate parcel-gilt CANDELABRUM, the upper part having four curving branches extending upward which, together with the central stem, are surmounted by globes encircled by gold bands set with translucent gemstones that are illuminated by interior lighting. The removable upper part rests on a support that can also serve as a vase. The bowl is decorated with two plaques depicting, in low relief, figures of Venus, and on the shoulder are two reclining figures of Mars and Venus; on the base are figures symbolic of the birth of Genius. The piece is made of silver and iron, decorated with DAMASCENED gold. It was designed and made by ANTOINE VECHTE for HUNT & ROSKELL at the request of the Marquess of Breadalbane, to provide a setting for some of the celebrated engraved gemstones of the Poniatowski Collection, some of which are set on the stem, the bowl, and the base. It was shown at the London International Exhibition, 1862. *See* J. B. Waring, *Masterpieces of Industrial Art* (1863), vol. III, pl. 202.

breakfast dish. A type of DISH for serving hot food on a breakfast side-board; it is usually in the form of an oval PLATTER resting on four tall legs and having a high-domed COVER that rotates vertically so as to be under the platter when opened. Sometimes there is a bowl (smaller than the cover) be-low the platter, acting as a reservoir for hot water to keep the food warm. Some dishes or platters are used in a similar way, when placed on a STAND or a DISH CROSS above a spirit lamp. It is similar to, but smaller than, a VENISON DISH. Sometimes called a 'bacon dish'.

breakfast service. A type of SERVICE for use at breakfast, the components varying according to the needs, taste, and means of the owner. Among the articles (all made EN SUITE) which such a service might include are a TEAPOT, COFFEE-POT, EGG-CUPS (or EGG-CUP STAND), TOAST-RACK, MUFFIN-DISH, JAM-POT, CUPS and SAUCERS, BOWLS and PLATES, CASTERS for salt and pepper, and FLATWARE and CUTLERY. *See* BREAKFAST DISH; CABARET SERVICE.

bridal cup. (1) A CUP or MAZER which, in the 16th century, was carried be-fore the bride at a wedding, and in which special small cakes were soaked in wine for the bride and groom; there was no special form for a receptacle so used, but some English churches kept a cup especially for the purpose. *See* WAGER CUP.

Bridge, John (1755–1834). An English silversmith from Dorset who was ap-prenticed in 1769 to William Rogers, of Bath, and came to London in 1777 to work for the firm of WILLIAM PICKETT and PHILIP RUNDELL (founded in 1772) at Ludgate Hill. He became a partner of Philip Rundell in 1785. By 1803 Edmund Waller Rundell, nephew of Philip Rundell, had joined the firm, and in 1805 its name was changed to RUNDELL, BRIDGE & RUNDELL. In 1804 Bridge's nephew, John Gawler Bridge (d. 1849), had joined the firm and he, having been freed by redemption in 1816, became a partner in 1817. Bridge entered his first mark in 1823, with address at 76 Dean St, Soho, after Philip Rundell had retired, and a second mark soon after, also in 1823. When Edmund Rundell retired in 1830, Bridge formed a new firm with his above-mentioned nephew and Thomas Bigge, known as Rundell, Bridge & Co., which continued until Bridge's death. In 1842 its stock was sold at Christie's, London, the goodwill being said to have been purchased in 1839 by Francis Lambert (d. 1841) and transferred to Coventry St. The work of Bridge was greatly influenced by NICHOLAS SPRIMONT and PAUL DE LAMERIE. *See* ROYAL WINE COOLER; BRIDGE CUP.

Bridge Cup. A silver-gilt TWO-HANDLED CUP having a cylindrical bowl rest-ing on a short stem supported by a spreading foot, and having two foliated DOUBLE-SCROLL HANDLES. The cup is cast in relief with straps of flowers and of vine foliage, the latter enclosing grotesque masks. It bears the engraved arms of John Gawler Bridge (d. 1849), and was given by him to the Gold-smiths' Company at about the time that he was its Prime Warden in 1839. It was made by PAUL DE LAMERIE, 1739, *See* BRIDGE, JOHN.

bridge spout. A type of SPOUT that is attached to the body of a JUG, EWER, CRUET, TEAPOT or COFFEE-POT by a horizontal bar or decorative ornament. *See* GUILLE CRUET.

bright cutting. A process of ENGRAVING by which the metal is cut in small gouges at an angle and removed by a tool (burin) having a sharp bevelled cutting edge and two cutting points (the front one to cut, the other to bur-nish), so that the engraving is cut in narrow channels and of varying depths with variously slanting sides, thus giving a faceted, bright, and sparkling ap-pearance. It was popular for ADAM SILVERWARE and was done best in the period 1770–90. Although engraving was not ordinarily suitable for SHEF-FIELD PLATE (due to its revealing the copper layer beneath the silver), bright cutting was executed in the 1770s in Birmingham and in the 1780s in Shef-field, and continued into the 1820s, but it required a heavily plated metal with a layer of silver deeper than usual.

bright vine pattern. A pattern on FLATWARE having a stem that is double curved and decoration in relief of bunches of grapes with foliage, spaced

Bridge Cup. Silver gilt, Paul de Lamerie, London, 1739. H. 34·3 cm. Goldsmiths' Company, London.

bright cutting. Detail of tray with bright
cutting on marli, Hannan & Crouch,
London, 1792. Courtesy, Asprey & Co.,
London.

along the stem, at the terminal, and at the junction of the stem with the
bowl.

Brighton Cup, 1805. A silver-gilt HORSE-RACING CUP in the form of a
covered urn. It was made in 1805 to the order of the Prince of Wales (later
Prince Regent and George IV) as a prize to be awarded at the Brighton
Races that year, being executed by JOHN EMES for RUNDELL, BRIDGE & RUN-
DELL. On one side of the cup a panel bears a depiction in relief of the Royal
Pavilion, Brighton, in its early form, below which is inscribed 'The Brighton
Cup/1805/Won by Orville', and on the other side is depicted a figure of Vic-
tory presenting a crown to the winner of a classical horse-race, below which
is an inscription 'The Gift of His Royal Highness the Prince of Wales to
Chris Wilson' (the winner, owned by the Prince, having been bought from
Christopher Wilson, whose descendants owned the cup until it was acquired
by Brighton Corporation). Encircling the rim of the cup is a FRET pattern
and encircling the bottom above the stem is a band of ACANTHUS leaves. Below each horizontal side handle is a relief mask. The cover has a finial surmounted by a coronet with the Prince of Wales's feathers.

Brighton Cup, 1805. Silver gilt, made by
John Emes for Rundell, Bridge &
Rundell, 1805. H. 45 cm. Royal
Pavilion, Brighton.

Bristol silverware. Articles of silverware made at Bristol, England, from the
early 15th century until the mid-18th century. A statute of 1423 'nominated'
Bristol as an 'Assay Town', and a charter for silversmiths was recorded in
1462; it provided for a mark of a bull's head, but no article with such a mark
is known. More than 100 silversmiths were recorded there prior to 1700. An
ASSAY OFFICE was established by the Act of 1701, and an Assay Master was
appointed; the Office was active between 1720 and 1740, but in 1773 there
was no evidence of an Assay Office there. Later silversmiths, including the
firm of John and Josiah Williams, sent their ware to Exeter to be assayed and
marked. Few surviving pieces bearing a Bristol mark are recorded; a few
bear a mark with a ship issuing from a castle. *See* Mrs. G. E. P. How, 'The
Goldsmiths of Bristol' in *The Connoisseur*, August 1974, p. 252

Britannia Cup. A vase-shaped PRESENTATION CUP having two handles in the
form of dolphins extending from the shoulder upward to the rim of the
mouth and having on the base cast coral and shell motifs. On the bowl is an
engraved depiction of a three-masted bark, and on the neck are profiles of
Neptune and Mercury. The cup bears a label 'Manufactured by Low, Ball &
Co., Boston, USA' (the predecessor of the present-day firm Shreve,
Crump & Low), but in addition it has a maker's mark of OBADIAH RICH, of
Boston. The cup was commissioned by Boston merchants for presentation
to Sir Samuel Cunard (1787–1865), founder of the Cunard Line, to commemo-
rate the arrival at Boston in July 1840 of the *Britannia*, the first transatlantic
mail steamship, which was owned by his company. The cup's whereabouts
remained unknown until it was found in 1967 and presented to the Cunard
Line; it is now kept on the liner *Queen Elizabeth 2. See* Martha Gandy Fales,
'The Britannia Cup' in *Antiques*, July 1982, p. 166.

Britannia Hallmark. The STANDARD HALLMARK required in England on
BRITANNIA SILVER from 30 May 1697 (when the standard for silver had to be
raised to deter the melting down of silver coins made of STERLING SILVER)
until 1 June 1720, in order to attest compliance with the higher standard;
during the same period the LION'S HEAD ERASED HALLMARK was also required. The Britannia Hallmark has since been permitted optionally in England for silversmiths who have elected to work with silver of the higher
standard. The Britannia Hallmark depicts the seated 'figure of a woman commonly called Britannia', holding a shield and a trident. It was never used in
Scotland or Ireland. A variant hallmark, depicting Britannia standing, was
used from 1 December 1784 to 24 July 1785 on silver articles exported from
England; *see* DRAWBACK MARK.

Britannia Hallmark

Britannia metal. An ALLOY, unrelated to BRITANNIA SILVER and containing no silver, being a silver-white leadless alloy of tin (about 90%), regulus of antimony (about 8%), copper (about 2%), and a trace of bismuth. It somewhat resembles, and is occasionally confused with, polished pewter, as both mellow to the same tones, but it contains no poisonous lead and can be more readily fabricated, being harder and tougher. When polished, Britannia metal takes on a highly lustrous silver-white appearance; it emits a ringing tone when struck (unlike pewter). It was developed in 1790 by James Vickers, of Sheffield, as an improvement of his VICKERS METAL, and until 1817 ware made of it was impressed on the bottom 'Vickers' in small Roman capitals. Britannia metal was used, usually after the development of ELECTROPLATING, for making inexpensive tableware, being cheaper than SHEFFIELD PLATE. It differs from pewter in the method of fabrication in that it can be worked by SPINNING, ROLLING or STAMPING, then polished and partly burnished (*see* BURNISHING), producing ware that is thin and light, while pewter is worked by CASTING and turning and may also be strengthened by HAMMERING. It was used in the United States first by the firm of Isaac Babbitt and William Crossman, founded in 1824 (the predecessor of REED & BARTON). A related metal, called 'Britannia Metal Plating', was developed in the 1820s by Kelly, Smith & Co., Sheffield; this was produced by pouring molten Britannia metal over a heated sheet of pure silver, which was picked up by the alloy and then rolled (however, the rolled metal proved impracticable and was seldom used). A process for hardening Britannia metal was developed in 1884 by James Shaw. The metal was also used for lids of ceramic drinking vessels and for export, especially variants made by other silversmiths in Sheffield and Birmingham, and some fakes were produced. It was called, *c.* 1850, 'Britannia Metal'; when electroplated, the ware was sometimes referred to by the abbreviation 'EPBM' (electroplated Britannia metal). *See* G. Bernard Hughes, 'The Story of Britannia Metal', in *Country Life*, 20 August 1953, p. 562.

Britannia silver. An ALLOY of silver having a greater FINENESS (958·4) than STERLING SILVER (925) and a troy weight of 11 oz. 10 dwt of silver to 10 dwt of copper. The higher standard was made the only legal standard for wrought silver in England (but not in Scotland or Ireland) from 30 May 1697, following a period when there was a widespread practice of clipping and melting down newly minted coins to obtain the scarce sterling silver. After severe penalties had proven inadequate to stop the CLIPPERS and others from debasing the coinage, the higher standard was enacted, all articles to be marked with the usual HALLMARKS except that instead of the LEOPARD'S HEAD HALLMARK and the LION PASSANT HALLMARK, the LION'S HEAD ERASED HALLMARK and also the BRITANNIA HALLMARK were substituted. The Hallmarking Act of 1973 restored the Leopard's Head Hallmark as the London Assay Office Hallmark, instead of the Lion's Head Erased Hallmark, conforming to the marks formerly used on sterling silver. The metal of the higher standard was called at first 'New Sterling Silver'. When the higher standard was no longer required after 31 May 1720 (when the sterling standard was restored, but subject to duty), Britannia silver continued to be used by some silversmiths (e.g., PAUL DE LAMERIE, who used it for twelve years, preferring it to harder sterling silver), and has since been an alternative optional standard, attested by the Britannia Hallmark. *See* G. Bernard Hughes, 'Britannia Standard Silver' in *Country Life*, 6 December 1956, p. 1351.

British Commemorative marks. Three COMMEMORATIVE MARKS used by the British Assay Offices: (1) Silver Jubilee mark, for the Silver Jubilee of George V and Queen Mary (their profiles facing left), 1934-5; (2) Coronation mark, Elizabeth II (her profile facing right), 1953-4; and (3) Silver Jubilee mark, Elizabeth II (her profile facing left, without an ESCUTCHEON), 1977. As such marks were punched only at the maker's request, they are not strictly HALLMARKS.

British Commemorative marks. George V Silver Jubilee, 1934-5 (*left*); Elizabeth II Coronation, 1953-4 (*centre*); and Elizabeth II Silver Jubilee, 1977.

British plate. A COMPOSITE METAL, developed *c.* 1835, of a thin sheet of silver fused over a core of a NICKEL SILVER (instead of over copper, as for SHEFFIELD PLATE). It was harder and more durable than Sheffield plate, had a colour and lustre similar to silver, did not reveal a pink tinge when worn, resisted acids, could be fused with hard SOLDER, and required less silver for the coating; consequently it largely supplanted Sheffield plate, but in turn was superseded in 1840 by ware made by ELECTROPLATING. Articles of British plate were made by stamping sheets with a drop hammer and soldering them to form the desired piece, then adding mounts of silver either stamped or, later, made by ELECTROFORMING. It was used to make all the types of articles that were made of Sheffield plate. British plate had no legal HALLMARKS, but was often given marks resembling silver hallmarks, usually not by the makers but by merchants, thus violating the 1772 and 1819 laws forbidding

Bryant Vase. Designed by James H. Whitehouse and made by Tiffany & Co., New York, 1875. Metropolitan Museum of Art (Gift of William Cullen Bryant), New York.

the use of marks on plated ware except those registered at the SHEFFIELD ASSAY OFFICE; the law was not strictly enforced, and a number of deceptive marks have been noted. The ware was sometimes advertised as 'plated by fire' to promote its sale over electroplated ware. *See* G. Bernard Hughes, 'Successor to Sheffield Plate' in *Country Life*, 28 January 1960, p. 160. *See* GERMAN SILVER; ARGENTAN; ROBERTS PLATE; MERRY PLATE.

British silverware. Articles made of silver or SHEFFIELD PLATE or by ELECTROPLATING, produced in the United Kingdom. *See* ENGLISH SILVERWARE; IRISH SILVERWARE; SCOTTISH SILVERWARE; WELSH SILVERWARE; CHANNEL ISLANDS SILVERWARE.

Bryant Vase. A VASE of ovoid shape, having a spool-shaped neck and two vertical incurving side handles extending upward from the shoulder, and resting on a square plinth. It was made by TIFFANY & CO. in 1875, from a prize-winning design by James H. Whitehouse, on order of a committee of prominent United States citizens formed to honour the 80th birthday of William Cullen Bryant (1794–1878), the American poet and journalist. The decoration, covering the entire body of the piece, depicts various flowers and motifs associated with Bryant; a central medallion has a portrait of Bryant, flanked by medallions with scenes of his life. The vase, presented on 20 June 1876, was shown at the Centennial Exposition at Philadelphia, 1876, and was donated by Bryant in 1877 to the Metropolitan Museum of Art, New York.

bubby-pot. A type of feeding pot in the form of a SPOUT POT, but having at the end of the thin upcurved spout a teat-like protuberance with one or more small holes. It was invented in 1777 by Dr Hugh Smith for feeding infants. Most examples were of pewter, but some were made of silver.

Buccleuch Wine Cooler. A WINE COOLER decorated with medallions enclosing classical busts and having handles in the form of a griffin and a unicorn, respectively. It was made by FRANCIS NELME, 1731, and is owned by the Duke of Buccleuch and Queensberry.

bucket. The same as a PAIL.

bucket-shaped. Made in the form of a bucket or PAIL, cylindrical or tapering slightly inward toward the bottom, as some CREAM-PAILS, ICE-PAILS, and SUGAR-BOWLS.

buckle. A type of fastener for a belt, girdle, etc.; first developed in England in the late 17th century, buckles were used there to replace shoe-laces. Later buckles, of various shapes and sizes, were used for other purposes, and were sometimes attached as an ornament to a ribbon (throatlet) worn around a woman's neck; a buckle is also used, as a fastener or as an ornament, on some shoes or on a wristband.

A buckle is usually in the form of a rectangular or curved frame, with a horizontal tongue attached to one side or to a vertical bar across the centre of the frame; the tongue is long enough to allow its tip to rest on the opposite side of the frame. Sometimes there are two or more tongues, or a single tongue may be forked so as to have two points. The buckle is attached to the belt, shoe, etc., by means of a loop of material folded and sewn or riveted around the vertical bar. Buckles have been used since Roman times, made of silver (or gold) or other metal (sometimes covered with fabric); some have been decorated with marcasite, cut steel, jet, paste or other material, and expensive ones have been set with gemstones.

Buddha spoon. A type of English provincial SPOON having a straight stem and a finial in the form of a half-length figure in-the-round of Oriental appearance, sometimes said to depict Buddha or a Far Eastern deity, but with no established basis for such belief. Such spoons, possibly derived from examples with half-length female figures, are known from *c.* 1620 to *c.* 1670, made in the West Country of England, principally at Barnstaple and Plymouth.

buffing. The final process in POLISHING an article of silver, done by use of a buff-stick charged with a mild abrasive, such as rouge. New articles of silver are so buffed, but if old silver is buffed, the PATINA will be destroyed and the value of the piece diminished.

bugle. A musical wind instrument similar to, but shorter than, a valveless TRUMPET. An example, 37·5 cm long and entirely of silver, was made by William Tant, 1811. *See* MUSICAL WARE.

bullet teapot. A type of TEAPOT of which the bowl is of oblate spherical shape (so-called 'bullet-shaped'), and which has a loop handle or a DOUBLE-SCROLL HANDLE opposite the spout. The handle, if of wood, is pinned into silver FERRULES or, if of silver, usually has insulating rings. The spout occurs in various forms, curved or straight and ATTENUATED, or is sometimes a FACETED SPOUT. The cover (generally a DROP-IN COVER) is small and almost flat, usually flush with the top of the teapot, and has a small decorative finial. The pot usually rests on a FOOT-RING, but sometimes has three small legs. The form was featured in Scotland in the period 1720–60. Such teapots are usually sparsely decorated. Examples are usually small, but some similarly shaped pieces are large, in the form of a TEA-KETTLE WITH STAND. *See* HERBAL POT.

bullet teapot. Pot with attenuated spout, by James Ker, Edinburgh, 1743–4. H. 13 cm. Ashmolean Museum, Oxford.

bullion. As to silver: (1) The pure metal in bars or ingots, without regard to value being imparted to it by form. (2) A rounded ornament or boss of silver, as on certain finger-rings, book-covers, bridles, etc. (3) Silver wire twisted into threads, as used in church vestments and in epaulets; sometimes called 'bullion lace'. (4) Braid or fringe of silver (more often of gold) thread, as used on officers' epaulets.

bun finial. A type of FINIAL in the form of a flattened (oblate) sphere.

bun foot. A type of FOOT in the form of a flattened (oblate) sphere.

bun pepper. A type of PEPPER-CASTER having a cover which, instead of being of the usual high-domed shape, is in the form of a very low, flat, bun-shaped dome (the neck of the caster being consequently longer), and which has, instead of a finial, overall pierced holes. It has been said to be more effective in scattering pepper than is the type of caster having a high-domed cover.

Bunyan Shield. A SHIELD designed and made by LÉONARD MOREL-LADEUIL in 1878 in emulation of his MILTON SHIELD. It depicts scenes from Bunyan's *Pilgrim's Progress*, hence has sometimes been called the 'Pilgrim Shield'. It was shown at the Paris Exposition of 1878, but was less successful than his previous shield.

Bunyan Shield. Designed and made by Léonard Morel-Ladeuil, London, 1878. Victoria and Albert Museum, London.

burette. The same as an ALTAR CRUET.

Burges Claret-Jugs. Three almost identical pear-shaped bottles made of tinted glass, each mounted in parcel-gilt silver as a CLARET-JUG; they were designed in 1865 in Gothic Revival style by the English architect William Burges (1827–81) on the basis of a watercolour drawing made by him in 1858. Each bottle is encased in wide horizontal and vertical bands of silver, rests on a spreading foot, has an ivory handle in the form of a winged monster (inspired by an Assyrian ivory pommel of a dagger-hilt, 8th-7th century BC, which Burges presented in 1864 to the British Museum) with a head of mother-of-pearl, and has a spout in the form of the head of an antelope holding in its mouth a stopper attached by a chain to its neck. The neck of each jug is made of four plaques of green malachite, and the hinged lid has a woven gallery (palisade) rim and a THUMBPIECE, but with a different form of finial in each case. The bands are variously decorated with amethysts, lapis lazuli, opals, crystal, pearls, Persian seals, intaglio gemstones, and Roman and Greek coins. The three jugs, made in London, are:

(1) That made for James Nicholson, of *sang-de-boeuf* glass with silver mounts bearing the 1865-6 mark of Richard Angell Green (*see* ANGELL) and having as its finial a crystal seated lion; it is in the Victoria and Albert Museum, London.

(2) That made of green glass with silver mounts bearing (apart from the lid) the 1864-5 mark of George Angell, cousin of Richard Angell Green, and the lid bearing the mark of Josiah Mendelson, and having as its finial a Chinese jade carving of two horses and a monkey under a silver loop; it is in the Cecil Higgins Art Gallery, Bedford.

(3) That made of dark-green glass with silver mounts bearing (apart from the lid) the 1864-5 mark of Josiah Mendelson, and the lid bearing the mark of George Angell, and having as its finial a crystal seated lion under a silver loop; it is in the Fitzwilliam Museum, Cambridge.

Jugs (2) and (3) were made for the private use of Burges, paid for by him out of the proceeds of his specified writings, as recorded around each neck in a Latin inscription with the name of Burges. They were exhibited (as items from the Charles Handley-Read Collection) in 1972 at the Royal Academy of Arts, London.

A related piece is a DECANTER, without a handle or spout, having a globular body and a narrow neck, made of a Chinese *sang-de-boeuf* glass bottle

Burges Claret-Jug (1). Jug designed by William Burges and made for James Nicholson: glass bottle with silver mounts by Richard Angell Green. London, 1865-6. H. 28·8 cm. Victoria and Albert Museum, London.

Burghley, Lord, Tankard. Colourless glass with silver-gilt mounts, *c.* 1575. H. 21·3 cm. British Museum, London.

Burghley Nef. Parcel gilt with nautilus shell, Paris, 1527. H. 35·2 cm. Victoria and Albert Museum, London.

mounted in a network of narrow silver-gilt bands decorated with enamelling, jade, and other gemstones and having a hinged lid surmounted by a finial in the form of a carved coral figure. The piece was designed by Burges *c.* 1867 for his own collection and was made (by an unidentified silversmith) in 1870. It was financed from the proceeds of the sale of his book *Architectural Designs*, as recorded in an inscription reserved on a blue-and-green enamelled foot-band. After the death of Burges, the piece passed to his patron, the 3rd Marquess of Bute, and was donated in 1972 to the Victoria and Albert Museum.

Burghley, Lord, Tankard. A TANKARD in the form of a tall cylinder of colourless English glass on a silver-gilt base and with a silver-gilt handle with a thumbpiece and a hinged lid; the MOUNTS are English. The glass has been attributed to Jacopo Verzelini, *c.* 1572-5, and was possibly a test piece made for Lord Burghley (William Cecil; 1520-98), the piece bearing his enamelled coat of arms encircled by the Garter (hence dating from 1572 or after) on the lid and having the thumbpiece in the form of an escutcheon. Its form resembles contemporary silver and crystal tankards.

Burghley House porcelain objects. Four Chinese Ming porcelain objects of the Wan-Li period (1573-1619), having English silver MOUNTS, 1583-90, made by a London silversmith. The pieces are: (1) a circular basin, with a rim band and a base connected by vertical straps; (2) a EWER, with a handle in the form of a mermaid with an intertwined double tail; and (3) two bowls with such mermaid handles. The MAKER'S MARK on the mounts is a trefoil within a shaped shield, the mark of a specialist in mounting porcelain who featured such mermaid handles and CARYATID handles. The pieces were once owned by Lord Burghley (William Cecil; 1520-98), Lord Treasurer from 1572 to 1578 to Elizabeth I, and were sold in the Burghley House sale at Christie's in 1888 to William Agnew; later they were in the J.P.Morgan Collection and are now in the Metropolitan Museum of Art, New York. *See* PORCELAIN OBJECTS; MOUNTED OBJECTS.

Burghley Nef. A NEF of parcel gilt, having a NAUTILUS SHELL as its hull, with silver bands simulating timbers and resting on the back of a mermaid supported by a hexagonal base on six CLAW-AND-BALL FEET. The forecastle and poop (which encloses a detachable salt) and the full sails and rigging are of parcel gilt. Figures of four sailors are on outboards and the rigging, and tiny cast figures (probably fragments from a 14th-century piece) on the deck are said to depict Tristan and Iseult playing chess when returning to Cornwall from Ireland. The pennons on the three masts are 1959 replacements. The piece bears a Paris mark and, though previously dated to 1482 and attributed possibly to Pierre le Flamand (fl. 1462-89), it has recently been dated to 1527.

Although not English, the piece is included here as representative of such nefs used in England, having been at Burghley House, Stamford, until it was sold by the 6th Marquess of Exeter (d. 1981) at Christie's, London, on 17 July 1959, and acquired by the Victoria and Albert Museum, London. *See* R. W. Lightbown, *French Silver* (1978), p. 28.

Burghley Wine Cooler. A very large WINE COOLER made in QUEEN ANNE STYLE, having a bulbous bowl with everted rim and being decorated with an encircling band of floral swags. It has four scroll feet from which rise heads of dragons. The two handles are in the form of figures of lions, each standing on a projecting scroll and resting its forefeet on the rim of the bowl. It has a maker's mark (no other mark) of PHILIP ROLLOS I, *c.* 1710. It is engraved with the arms of Brownlow Cecil, 8th Earl of Exeter. The piece was owned by the 6th Marquess of Exeter (d. 1981), and is at Burghley House, Stamford, the family seat of the Cecils.

burnishing. The process of making the surface of a metal object smooth and shiny by friction, using a hard smooth tool called a 'burnisher' (a pointed hand tool having a rounded end of steel, ivory, or agate, extending from a ferrule to a straight wooden haft). The technique involves first a thorough cleaning of the article and rubbing it with soft soap, then rubbing it with sand and water to remove any grease, then vigorously rubbing back and forth with a steel burnisher, next with one of agate, then with one of bloodstone, and finally hand-polishing with wet jeweller's rouge. The process results in concealing join marks and in imparting a brilliant finish, though not the 'mirror finish' of polishing that sometimes removes the PATINA. As to electroplated ware, burnishing forces the crystals of silver into the pores of the base metal, thus adding durability.

Burrell Inkstand. *See* WALPOLE INKSTAND.

Burghley Wine Cooler. Maker's mark of Philip Rollos I, *c.* 1710. L. 1·60 m. Burghley House, Stamford.

Burt, Benjamin (1729–1805). A silversmith of Boston, Massachusetts, son of JOHN BURT. He made a number of pieces now in United States museums. He was so eminent that he led the Boston goldsmiths in the memorial procession in 1800 for President Washington. *See* MASSACHUSETTS SILVERWARE.

Burt, John (*c.* 1692–1745). A silversmith of Boston, Massachusetts, who had been apprenticed to JOHN CONEY. He made a variety of silver pieces, including some for Harvard University, among them a pair of CANDLESTICKS (seldom made in Colonial silverware). His three sons were also silversmiths: Samuel (1724–54), William (1726–51), and BENJAMIN BURT.

Burton's, Captain, Cup. A CUP of vase shape, having a stemmed foot, two vertical loop side handles, and a pointed COVER with a pine-cone finial. On the front is an engraved depiction of a two-masted schooner. The cup, made in 1792 by WILLIAM PITTS and JOSEPH PREEDY, London, was donated by the Prince of Wales (later George IV) to Captain Burton for 'having preserved the life of Countess Noel [the Duchesse de Noailles]' in 1792, as inscribed on a plaque on the reverse.

bushell. An obsolete term for a circular silver plate set into the cover of some receptacles to provide a place for a coat of arms to be engraved, but which was sometimes left blank. *See* INSCRIPTION PLATE.

Butleigh Salt. A massive and elaborate COVERED STANDING SALT, *c.* 1606, standing on a square base resting on four corner feet in the form of winged dragons and having at each corner a Corinthian column; in the centre there is a massive column with IMBRICATED decoration, at the top of which there is a recessed hemispherical salt-bowl with a large domed cover having a finial (from which a figure is now missing). The name is based on its association with Butleigh Court in Somerset. It was acquired in 1949 by the Barber Institute of Fine Arts, University of Birmingham.

Butleigh Salt. Silver gilt, London, *c.* 1606. H. 31·3 cm. Barber Institute of Fine Arts, University of Birmingham.

butter-boat. A type of small receptacle in the shape of a SAUCE-BOAT, for serving melted butter.

butter-dish. (1) A type of small DISH, for use at a dinner table by an individual diner, upon which to place a pat of butter. Such pieces are usually circular or square, with decoration (varying in style) including a raised rim having an embossed pattern, and differ from a bread-and-butter plate (upon which each diner can place bread as well as a pat of butter). (2) A type of BOWL, usually circular or oval and with pierced decoration and a cover, for

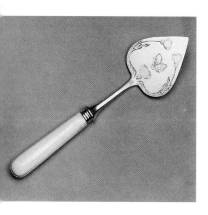

butter trowel. Parcel gilt, George Adams, London, 1864. Courtesy, Brand Inglis Ltd, London.

holding and serving butter at the dinner table; it usually has a glass LINER with a silver cover (often with a finial in the form of a cow), and often an accompanying matching silver tray. Some examples are globular, resting on tall legs, and having a hemispherical cover that rotates vertically under the tray when opened. *See* GIBBS BUTTER-DISH.

butter-shell. A type of small DISH, in the form of a SCALLOP shell, for serving butter; such dishes are usually of thin GAUGE and rest on two or three whelk feet. The GRIP opposite the scalloped rim varies in size: some are straight, but later ones are shaped and some elaborately decorated.

butter spreader. A type of KNIFE, for use by a diner, for spreading butter; it is small and has a wide blade with a curved unsharpened edge. Examples with a silver blade were made in the late 18th century with a handle of green-dyed ivory or of mother-of-pearl. Sometimes called a 'butter-knife'.

butter trowel. A type of small, flat, triangular implement, shaped like a TROWEL, with a straight handle (sometimes made of ivory), used for slicing and serving butter. Some are appropriately decorated with engraved buttercups and butterflies. Sometimes called a 'butter spade' or a 'cheese spade'.

button. A small object used usually to fasten together two sides of a garment by being attached to one side and passed through a slit, button-hole or loop on the other side, but sometimes being only ornamental and attached to a single piece of material by a prong or by sewing, without any corresponding button-hole. Buttons were used in ancient Greece and Rome, but were first employed generally in southern Europe in the 13th century and had become useful and fashionable by the 14th century. By the 16th/17th centuries they had come to be used almost exclusively by men and were made in highly decorative styles, including some made of gold set with gemstones or pearls, of enamelware, or of cameos. Less luxurious varieties have been made of a great variety of materials, including silver and SHEFFIELD PLATE, which were decorated in various styles, including decoration by EMBOSSING, CHASING, and ENAMELLING. Buttons occur in many shapes (although usually circular), styles, and sizes. Some are attached by thread through two or more eyelets or by a shank attached to the back, or by a fixed or twisting bar (as some studs or collar-buttons). In England a vast trade was built up at Birmingham, the principal manufacturers in the 18th century being John Taylor and MATTHEW BOULTON. *See* Victor Houart, *Buttons* (1977). *See* COURSING BUTTON.

C

cabaret service. The term 'cabaret', originally referring to a tea-table, came to apply to a set of vessels comprising a small BREAKFAST SERVICE or TEA SERVICE, together with a TRAY. A small service for a Continental breakfast was sometimes called a 'déjeuner service', or, if for one person, a SOLITAIRE SERVICE, and, if for two persons, a TÊTE-À-TÊTE SERVICE.

cabriole. A type of leg (derived from Chippendale furniture and found on some QUEEN ANNE STYLE silverware) which curves outward from the body of the piece and descends to a tapering inward curve, terminating in an ornamental foot.

cachepot (French). An ornamented pot (the name derived from *cacher*, to hide), to contain and conceal a utilitarian flower-pot. *See* JARDINIÈRE.

Cadboll Cup. A STANDING CUP having a wide shallow bowl resting on an ovoid stem supported by a spreading foot. The decoration of the bowl consists of vertical tapering stripes, alternately plain and decorated, the latter alternately decorated with STRAPWORK and floral motifs, a style of decoration peculiar to the Western Highlands of Scotland. The cup bears no maker's mark or date mark, but was made in Scotland in the 16th century. It was owned originally by the Macleods of Cadboll, of Invergordon Castle, Ross-shire, and it has engraved on the inside the arms of Maclean, the cup probably having descended from a 16th-century Maclean-Macleod marriage. It was acquired in 1970 by the National Museum of Antiquities of Scotland, Edinburgh, after having been on loan for many years at the Victoria and Albert Museum, London.

caddinet. A dining-table accessory for use only by Royalty in England and also, in France, by high nobility. The type originated in France in the 18th century, where it is called a *cadenas*; such pieces were very rare in England. Each consists of a raised flat oblong tray about 30·5 cm wide, upon which to rest a napkin, having along the rear end an oblong box divided into two (in England) or three (in France) compartments with hinged lids, a long one for a knife, fork, and spoon, and the small one(s) for salt (and pepper). The earliest known English example was recorded in 1672 as having been used by Charles II at his coronation banquet on 23 April 1661. Others were used by later Sovereigns and also by the respective Queens Consort at the coronations of James II and George II. The only two known surviving English examples (although records mention five) are both silver-gilt, each resting on six small feet in the form of lions couchant, and bearing the coat of arms of William and Mary: (1) one dated 1683, of a pair ordered by Sir Gilbert Talbot (with coat of arms added later); and (2) one of a pair made by ANTHONY NELME, dated 1689, the arms being without the Scottish unicorn. Each is accompanied by a small pear-shaped secular vinegar-jug with a finial in the form of a V. The three missing caddinets are unaccounted for. The two extant examples were probably sold by the Crown in 1808 to defray the expenses of the Princess of Wales and came into the possession of the 1st Earl of Lonsdale (1757–1844), of Lowther Castle, Penrith, They were sold at Christie's, London, in 1975 from the estate of the 6th Earl of Lonsdale (d. 1953), and acquired by the Queen and the Government, and have been on display in the Jewel House at the Tower of London since 1975. *See* Charles C. Oman, 'Caddinets' in *Burlington Magazine*, December 1958, p. 431, figs 28, 33.

caddy. *See* TEA-CADDY. The term 'caddy' (originally *catti*) is derived from the Malay word *kati* which was a unit of weight used for tea, 75 *katis* equalling 100 lbs. The *kati* was the weight–about one and one-third lbs (600 g.)–of the standard 18th-century package of tea.

caddy-box. A type of wooden container to hold loose tea or two or more TEA-CADDIES, the earliest form of container for dry tea. Some examples were decorated with silver mounts. Early examples are rectangular and flat-topped, with shagreen covering; they were made of a variety of woods, ornately carved or having veneers of rare wood, ivory or mother-of-pearl. Later ones are more elaborately shaped and carved. Some include a SUGAR-BOWL or SUGAR-BOX and a MILK-JUG, and some were provided with a lock to prevent pilferage of the tea. *See* TEA-CHEST.

caddy spoon. A type of SPOON for use in taking and measuring dry tea from a TEA-CADDY, usually small enough to fit inside the caddy. English examples (called *c.* 1770 'caddy ladle' and *c.* 1800-15 'caddy scoop' or 'caddy shell') were developed in the mid-18th century, when the Chinese tea-bottle was superseded by the tea-caddy having an orifice large enough to accommodate a small spoon to dispense and measure the tea, and when the cover (the 'thimble top') was no longer used as a measurer. The earliest type was the short MEDICINE-SPOON CADDY SPOON, *c.* 1755-60. In the period of the ADAM STYLE, *c.* 1770, the style developed into the SCALLOP-SHELL CADDY SPOON. Later a vast variety of forms was adopted, including spoons having the bowl in the shape of a leaf, flower, bird's wing, heart, salmon, shovel, etc. Most have a short handle (a shaped flat handle or a vertical ring), but many have no handle, while a few have a massive figural handle. Some examples are gilded and some have PARCEL GILDING. On some examples the bowl is decorated with REPOUSSÉ work, BRIGHT CUTTING or CHASING, or with FILIGREE patterns (to permit shaking out the tea dust). Unusual caddy spoons have a bowl made of an actual shell with MOUNTS of silver and some are set with a translucent slice of a gemstone; occasionally the handle is made of jade or ivory. In some cases the spoon is fitted into a notch in the cover of a caddy. A few have an elongated bowl set at right-angles to the stem. Those with a pierced bowl served as a SIFTER SPOON or as a TEA-STRAINER. The usual length ranges from 6·3 to 7·5 cm, but exceptionally spoons may be 12·5 cm long. Caddy spoons were always required to be hallmarked, being excluded from the exemption of the English Act of 1790 relating to small articles. For some of the many varieties of spoon, *see* CHINESE MANDARIN CADDY SPOON; EAGLE-WING CADDY SPOON; HAND CADDY SPOON; HAREBELL CADDY SPOON; FIGURE-TERMINAL CADDY SPOON; JOCKEY-CAP CADDY SPOON; LEAF CADDY SPOON; PISCATORIAL CADDY SPOON; ROCAILLE CADDY SPOON; ROMAN-LEAF CADDY SPOON; SERPENT-AND-SHELL CADDY SPOON; *See* G. Bernard Hughes, 'Sil-

café-au-lait pots. Pair, Sheffield plate, c. 1810. H. 19 cm. Folger's Coffee Collection, Procter & Gamble Co., Cincinnati, Ohio

cagework cup. Small two-handled cup, pierced silver sleeve over gilt bowl, Thomas Jenkins, London, c. 1670. H. 19·8 cm. Goldsmiths' Company, London.

cake-basket. Basket with swinging bail handle, Peter Archambo II and Peter Meure, London, 1749-50. W. 39·5 cm. Museum of Fine Arts, Montreal.

ver Caddy Ladles' in *Country Life*, 13 July 1951, p. 109; Eric Delieb, 'The Caddy-Spoon' in *Apollo*, April 1960, p. 113; *Catalogue of Loan Exhibition of tea-caddy spoons*, Goldsmiths' Hall, London, June 1965; Judith Banister, 'The Cult of the Caddy Spoon' in *Antique Dealer & Collectors Guide*, September 1965, p. 38; —, 'Sixty Glorious Years of Silver Caddy Spoons' in *Antique Dealer & Collectors Guide*, April 1961, p. 244.

Cafe, John (fl. 1740-57). An English silversmith best known for his many CANDLESTICKS and SNUFFER TRAYS. He was apprenticed to James Gould in 1730 and freed in 1741. His first mark was entered in 1740 at Foster Lane, London; he moved to Carey Lane in 1741 and to Gutter Lane in 1743. He was succeeded by his brother, William (died c. 1802), who was apprenticed to him in 1742 and freed in 1757, and who continued their prolific production of candlesticks, but became bankrupt in 1772. He apparently continued in business at High St, Marylebone, taking Thomas Neale as an apprentice in 1777 and his own son Thomas in 1784.

café-au-lait pots. A pair of COFFEE-POTS of similar shape and decoration, having projecting uplifted wooden handles, but with one handle on the left side of the SPOUT, the other on the right side, to enable one person to hold both pots and pour coffee and milk simultaneously into a cup. An example, made of SHEFFIELD PLATE, c. 1810, was made presumably for the French market (in France the drinking of *café au lait* antedated its popularity in England, where it became common only during the Victorian period).

cagework. A type of decoration on SHEATHED WARE that may have been inspired by the decoration on Roman glass cage cups of *vasa diatretum* type which have a network of glass carved on and surrounding an inner glass cup. *See* CAGEWORK CUP.

cagework cup. A type of SMALL TWO-HANDLED CUP decorated with CAGE-WORK, being of cylindrical shape and having two foliated SCROLL HANDLES or DOUBLE-SCROLL HANDLES and having a CUSHION-SHAPE cover. Such cups have a plain silver-gilt bowl set within a pierced silver sleeve embossed and chased with foliage and with relief figures (often birds of various types, and sometimes different on the two sides). Such cups rest on four feet, sometimes in the form of birds, and the finial is sometimes in the form of a different bird. Several examples are known: (1) One having depicted on one side a peacock and on the other side a turkey, and having the finial in the form of a sitting phoenix. The piece, c. 1670, bears no hallmark; the maker's mark, 'TI', formerly said to be that of Thomas Issod, is now attributed to THOMAS JENKINS. It was aquired in 1923 by the Goldsmiths' Company, London. (2) One, London, c. 1670, also bearing the mark 'TI' and having a pierced silver sleeve, but differing in having a flower finial and handles in the form of female TERMS, as well as in the style of its openwork decoration; it is in the British Museum, London, where it has now likewise been attributed to Thomas Jenkins. (3) One, with foliated double-scroll handles and with openwork decoration including figures of a peahen, has CLAW-AND-BALL FEET and a tiered knop finial; it bears a maker's mark 'CG' in monogram and a London mark for 1669-70, and was purchased by the South Kensington Museum (now the Victoria and Albert Museum, London) in 1854 (thus being one of the earliest acquisitions of silverware for the museum's collection). (4) A pair of cups, each having the silver sleeve decorated with eagles with wings spread and having an eagle finial, made by Nicholas Wollaston, London, c. 1670; one is on loan to the City Museums and Art Gallery, Birm-

Calverley Toilet Service. Complete service, London, 1683–4. Victoria and Albert Museum, London.

ingham, and the other was sold at Sotheby's, London, on 3 May 1984. (5) An example, also with figures of eagles on the sleeve, and having claw-and-ball feet, debased CARYATID HANDLES, and a flower finial, is marked 'IA', London 1677–8; formerly in the Elizabeth Miles Collection, it is now in the Museum of Art, Cleveland, Ohio. *See* SHEATHED WARE.

cake-basket. A type of BASKET, usually circular, oval or boat-shaped, with everted rim and a high arched BAIL HANDLE, sometimes fixed but more often swivelling. The sides are usually of PIERCED WORK, often resembling wicker-work (*see* WICKERWORK SILVERWARE). The basket usually rests on a support-ing rim, often also pierced, but sometimes on ornamental feet or, rarely, on a spreading foot. The rim is often wavy or decorated with GADROONING. Some baskets are made with WIREWORK. Cake-baskets resemble BREAD-BASKETS, but the latter are identifiable by having a wheat motif as decoration.

cake-slice(r). A flat implement, shaped somewhat like a TROWEL, with a single projecting handle (haft), used for slicing and serving cake. The blade is broad, curved on one unsharpened edge and with the other edge straight and slightly sharpened.

calumet. A ceremonial tobacco PIPE of the North American Indians, used when ratifying a treaty or on ceremonial occasions; it has a long curving stem and a small bowl. A silver example, with an inscribed bowl, was pre-sented in 1814 to the Delaware Indians by General William Henry Harrison (later 9th President of the United States); it is now at the Smithsonian Insti-tution, Washington, D.C. Also called a 'peace pipe'.

Calverley Toilet Service. A TOILET SERVICE consisting of a TOILET MIRROR, several BOXES, CASKETS, SALVERS, JARS, etc., all dated London, 1683–4; the decoration features EMBOSSING and CASTING of high quality, characteristic of CAROLINE SILVERWARE, in the form of ACANTHUS leaves, flowers, and fruit. It belonged formerly to the Calverley family of Yorkshire, and was bequeathed in 1879 by Sir Walter Calverley Trevelyan, Bt, of Wellington, Northumber-land, to the Victoria and Albert Museum, London.

calyx. By analogy to the outer leaves (sepals) of a flower, the applied decora-tion sometimes encircling the lower part of the bowl of a TWO-HANDLED CUP, often in the form of a band of vertical GADROONING, ACANTHUS leaves, or SPOON-HANDLE STRAPS. On some silver-gilt STEEPLE CUPS, the calyx is un-gilded in contrast to the body.

Cambon Cup. A three-handled CUP made by TIFFANY & CO. for presentation by William McKinley (24th President of the United States) to Jules Cambon, French Ambassador to the United States, in appreciation of his friendly ser-vices in the negotiation of the Protocol of Peace between the United States and Spain, 12 August 1898, ending the Spanish-American War. The cup has three hollow handles pierced with holly-leaf motifs, and below each handle there is a CARTOUCHE bearing, respectively, the emblem of the three countries involved in the negotiations. The stem of the cup is in the form of three standing eagles holding floral garlands in their mouths. The cup is now exhibited in the Treaty Room of the White House, Washington, D.C.

Cambridge Colleges Plate. Articles of silverware owned by individual col-leges of the University of Cambridge. *See* E. Alfred Jones, *The Old Plate of the Cambridge Colleges* (1910), which discusses articles from the earliest example,

Cambon Cup. Three-handled cup, Tiffany & Co., New York, 1899. H. 29·8 cm. The White House Collection, Washington, D.C.

camp cup. Richard Humphreys, Philadelphia, Pa, *c.* 1780. H. 4·3 cm. Yale University Art Gallery (Mabel Brady Garvan Collection), New Haven, Conn.

Campion Cup. 'Font-shaped' cup, London, 1500-1. H. 9·5 cm. Victoria and Albert Museum, London.

a DRINKING HORN from the first half of the 14th century, until 1836, with 120 photographs of pieces from sixteen colleges; Charles C. Oman, 'Cambridge College Plate' in *The Connoisseur*, April 1959, p. 166; R. A. Crighton, *Cambridge Plate* (1975); John A. Goodall, 'Cambridge Plate' in *The Connoisseur*, August 1977, p. 291.

camp cup. A type of CUP of cylindrical shape tapering slightly downward to a flat base and having a slightly FLARED rim, similar to a BEAKER but only about 4·5 cm high. Such cups, for use on military campaigns, were made for George Washington, Nathaniel Greene, and others. They can be stacked in sets as a NEST of cups. They have been reproduced because of their historical significance.

camp kettle. A type of cooking utensil used on military campaigns. A silver example used by the Duke of York (1763-1827), son of George III, when in command of the Grenadier Guards, 1805-27, is now owned by that regiment; it is of plain cylindrical bucket shape, with a BAIL HANDLE and a flat cover with a ring finial, and bears the Duke's engraved coat of arms and the maker's mark, 'EF', 1790.

campaign étui. A type of BEAKER or TUMBLER CUP that has fitted into it several small implements for use by a soldier on campaign, such as folding CUTLERY, CASTERS, CORKSCREW, SPICE-BOX, etc., all enclosed in a sharkskin carrying case. *See* ÉTUI; TRAVELLER'S DINING SET; CANTEEN.

campana cup. A type of STANDING CUP having the bowl of inverted bell-shape, like that of a Greek krater of the bell type. *See* WARWICK VASE.

Campion Cup. A 'FONT-SHAPED' CUP (the earliest-known surviving example of such cups) in English GOTHIC STYLE, having a shallow, vertical-sided, thick, plain bowl supported by an undecorated short wide TRUMPET FOOT. The bowl has an encircling engraved band bearing the inscription, in Lombardic characters, 'SOLI DEO HONOR ET GLORIA' (Honour and glory be to God alone). The cup has an unidentified maker's mark and a London hallmark for 1500-1. It was owned by the Campion family of Danny, near Hurstpierpoint, Sussex, and later was in the Willett and Swaythling Collections; it was acquired in 1924 by the Victoria and Albert Museum, London. Resembling this cup are the St Mary, Sandwich, Cup, *c.* 1510, and the Wymesfold Cup 1512-13. *See* Norman M. Penzer, 'Tudor "Font-shaped" Cups' in *Apollo*, December 1957, p. 174, fig. 1.

can. *See* CANN.

Canadian hallmarks. Although HALLMARKS on silverware were not legally required in Canada before 1906, some silversmiths did mark their ware in various ways. The French makers in Quebec Province, especially in the early period, adopted a style similar to that of France, using a FLEUR DE LIS or a crown, with the maker's initials or surname and sometimes 'Quebec' or 'Montreal'. The English makers used various marks resembling the English ASSAY OFFICE HALLMARKS and STANDARD HALLMARKS, with initials or symbols for the place name. Date marks were not used.

Canadian silverware. Articles of silverware made in Canada during successive periods of its history. In the first period, during the 'New France' era, *c.* 1730-59, the principal Canadian silverware centres were in Quebec Province, at Montreal and Quebec City, where the French and native French-trained silversmiths (who, unlike the French Huguenots who emigrated to England and the American colonies, were Catholics) produced mainly ecclessiastical ware. There was little Canadian raw silver and the main source of the metal was old silverware and coins melted down. The second period followed the British conquest in 1759, when English silversmiths came in the 1760s to Quebec Province, producing principally domestic articles in English styles, but also much INDIAN-TRADE SILVERWARE. The third period began after the American Revolution in 1776, when many Loyalists moved to the Maritime Provinces (Nova Scotia and New Brunswick), and they and the Quebec silversmiths built thriving businesses in domestic silverware. In the mid-19th century mass production, by means of STAMPING and SPINNING, began, as well as the making of SHEFFIELD PLATE and SILVER-PLATED WARE. Individual silversmiths were superseded by craftsmen employed by dealers, especially the Montreal firm of Hendery & Leslie. Later the making of hand-wrought silverware was revived. The leading firm today is HENRY BIRKS & SONS LTD. *See* John Emerson Langdon, *Canadian Silversmiths and their Marks, 1667-1867* (1960); —, *Canadian Silversmiths 1700-1900* (1966). *See* CANADIAN HALLMARKS; QUEBEC SILVERWARE.

candelabrum. A type of ornamental candle-holder for table use, having several (usually two to six) fixed or detachable scroll branches supporting candle SOCKETS (sometimes the branches having been added at a later date). The branches extend from a central shaft in twisting manner and sometimes there is also a socket at the top of the shaft. The shafts and the bases are of varying styles, similar to the styles of contemporary CANDLESTICKS. Some have figures on the base around the shaft. They were often made as a PAIR. The plural form 'candelabra' is now sometimes used to refer to a single piece. The term 'table lustre', sometimes applied to such pieces, should, strictly, be reserved for a table candelabrum having faceted glass or rock-crystal lustre drops. *See* G. Bernard Hughes, 'Elaboration by Candlelight' in *Country Life*, 7 October 1965, p. 899. *See* FIGURAL CANDELABRUM; TELESCOPIC CANDELABRUM; MENORAH; HANUK(K)A(H) LAMP; CHANDELIER.

candle extinguisher. A type of small hollow cone to be placed over a lighted candle to extinguish the flame without causing the snuff to smoke. It frequently accompanied a CHAMBER CANDLESTICK, being attached by a hook to the stem of the candlestick, to which was sometimes also attached a SNUFFER. A variant form, for use with a HURRICANE CANDLESTICK, has attached to the top of the cone a wire, with a ball or ring finial, to be lowered in the chimney to extinguish the flame. Some modern examples have the cone attached to the end of a long handle. Sometimes called a 'dunce'. *See* SNUFFER STAND.

candle snuffer. *See* SNUFFER; CANDLE EXTINGUISHER.

candlestick. A type of utensil for supporting a single candle, usually having a flat base (although some rest on four feet) and having at the top of the vertical stem (shaft) a SOCKET or NOZZLE, and also usually a DRIP-PAN. They were made in a great variety of shapes, sizes, and styles, with bases being circular, square or polygonal. The decoration is very varied, with some having cast ornaments or decoration of ENGRAVING or CHASING. The earliest examples were made from sheet metal, with a hollow stem and a single vertical soldered seam; later ones were made by CASTING, and still later by STAMPING (in sections soldered together and LOADED to provide stability). Often they were made as a PAIR or as a SET of four or more. *See* G. Bernard Hughes, 'Silver Candlesticks from the Factory' in *Country Life*, 12 April 1973, p. 1063.

See ALTAR CANDLESTICK; CARYATID CANDLESTICK; CHAMBER CANDLESTICK; COLUMN CANDLESTICK; DESK CANDLESTICK; DWARF CANDLESTICK; FIGURAL CANDLESTICK; FLAT CANDLESTICK; HAND-GUARD CANDLESTICK; HAREBELL CANDLESTICK; HAVDALAH CANDLESTICK; HURRICANE CANDLESTICK; PALM-TREE CANDLESTICK; PIANO CANDLESTICK; PRICKET CANDLESTICK; SUNKEN-BASE CANDLESTICK; TABLE CANDLESTICK; TELESCOPIC CANDLESTICK; TAPERSTICK; SAVE-ALL; SCONCE; CANDELABRUM; HARTHILL CANDLESTICKS; ROMSEY CANDLESTICKS.

canephoros. A draped standing female figure supporting on her head a wicker basket containing sacred utensils and offerings; it was originally used in ancient Greek architecture and is found in silverware as a figure in-the-round forming the handle on some flatware in a DESSERT SERVICE. *See* CARYATID.

canister. A type of small container for dry tea; *see* TEA-CANISTER. By the end of the 18th century the style had undergone several changes, and the term then used was TEA-CADDY.

cann. A type of CUP, cylindrical (sometimes slightly tapering) and having a flat base with a low FOOT-RING and one vertical loop handle. Examples range in height from 10 to 12·5 cm. Such silver cups, intended for drinking coffee, are rare. They are similar to the porcelain coffee-cups made in Europe and known as a 'coffee-can', and especially those smaller ones made in England at Derby and known as a 'can'. It has been said that the term is an old name ('canne') for any MUG, and is applied (spelled 'cann') in the United States (and sometimes in England) to a small mug popular as a gift to children and to some mugs of pear-shaped form with a SCROLL HANDLE or a DOUBLE-SCROLL HANDLE, sometimes having an ACANTHUS-motif THUMBPIECE and a FLARED rim. Only rarely do such canns have a cover. *See* DEMI-TASSE.

cannelated. Shaped with sides in the form of FLUTING in vertical parallel grooves.

cannon handle. A type of handle for a KNIFE in the form of a cannon barrel, slightly tapering toward the muzzle (joined to the blade) and having at the terminal a small spherical knob.

candelabrum. Two-armed, one of a pair, John Schofield, London, 1784–5. H. 39·5 cm. Courtesy, Garrard & Co. Ltd, London.

candelabrum. Four-armed, Benjamin Smith and Digby Scott (for Rundell, Bridge & Rundell), London, 1805–6. H. 90 cm. Colonial Williamsburg, Va.

cann. With scroll handle, John Edwards, Boston, Mass., *c.* 1828–35. H. 12 cm. Yale University Art Gallery (Mabel Brady Garvan Collection), New Haven, Conn.

canoe shape. The shape of an article having an oval horizontal section and its two ends higher than the centre, such as some CRUET STANDS, SALTS, SAUCE-TUREENS, and INKSTANDS.

canopy stave. A long pole, being one of a set employed to support a canopy, e.g., in a coronation procession, as has been done in England since 1199, the canopy being held over the head of the Sovereign (and Consort) by the Barons of the Cinque Ports. One such set (eight staves, each 2·40 m long), used at the coronation of George IV in 1820, was made in that year, the staves being fitted with silver finials made by WILLIAM PITTS II and JOSEPH PREEDY. *See* CORONATION CANOPY BELL.

canteen. Originally, from the 17th century, a case for use by travellers and military officers to carry basic articles of silverware for eating and drinking, such as a KNIFE, FORK, and SPOON (usually with screw-on handles and fitted into a CAMPAIGN ÉTUI), a BEAKER, SALT, SPICE-BOX, CORKSCREW, and NUTMEG GRATER, with sometimes NAPKIN HOOKS and TOOTHPICKS. Such cases were made of wood, shagreen (untanned animal skin, polished and coloured, usually green) or fish skin. Later, the term was extended to refer to a wooden fitted case for domestic use for storing silver FLATWARE and CUTLERY (and sometimes 'canteen extras', such as GRAPE SHEARS), usually having a hinged LID or two or three drawers (some luxury examples being built as a table supported by four legs). The capacity is usually for an 8- or 12-person PLACE SETTING, with several serving pieces. *See* BONNIE PRINCE CHARLIE'S CANTEEN.

Canterbury Processional Cross. A silver-gilt PROCESSIONAL CROSS having a hexagonal staff surmounted by two tiers of six niches (in each of which is a standing figure of a saint) and topped by a cross pattée set with gemstones: it is carried before the Archbishop of Canterbury on formal occasions. The cross was made by Messrs Hardman of Birmingham, under the direction of Messrs Bodley and Garner, and was presented in 1883 to Archbishop Benson by the local clergy. To the original cross have been added three sapphires and three opals which were presented to Archbishop Fisher during his visit to Australia in 1950.

cape teapot. A type of TEAPOT, popular from *c.*1790, that is usually oval and has at the front of the mouth a rim or gallery which curves upward and outward towards the SPOUT so as to form a sort of shield. Examples in silver are similar to the ceramic type made by Wedgwood and other English potteries in the early 19th century, and called a 'parapet teapot'.

capstan salt. A type of SALT-CELLAR shaped somewhat like a ship's capstan, circular or of polygonal section, with the side waisted between the bands encircling the wide base and the narrower rim. Such salts were made mainly in the 17th and early 18th centuries.

card-case. A type of small, thin BOX used (especially in the Victorian era) to carry personal visiting cards. Such cases in silver, of rectangular shape, with a LID hinged on one of the narrow sides, were often decorated with stamped, chased or engraved scenes (particularly of a castle, abbey or cathedral) or with ENGINE-TURNING. *See* CASTLE-TOP WARE.

card holder. a small dinner-table accessory serving as a MENU HOLDER or PLACE-CARD HOLDER. Such pieces are sometimes part of a DINNER SERVICE; made in SETS, they occur in various styles of decoration, some having as a finial a figure of a different animal or bird on each holder.

Caroline Mathilda Toilet Service. A silver-gilt TOILET SERVICE of 30 pieces, of which 23 were made by THOMAS HEMING, London, 1760, for Caroline Mathilda (1752-75), posthumous daughter of Frederick, Prince of Wales, and sister of George III, as a wedding gift from an unidentified donor upon her marriage by proxy to Christian VII of Denmark. She brought it with her in a leather-covered box when she went to Denmark to meet her husband. The set includes a TABLE MIRROR, EWER and BASIN, SNUFFER TRAY (bearing the mark of EMICK ROMER), and a pair of SMALL TWO-HANDLED CUPS. Most of the pieces are decorated with naturalistic floral sprays in ROCOCO STYLE. The service was inherited by Caroline Mathilda's daughter, Louisa Augusta (1771-1843), who left it to her second son, in whose family it remained until after World War I; it was bought by the Meyer Fuld family, from which it was acquired in 1954 by the present owner, the Danske Kunstindustriemuseum, Copenhagen. *See* Charles C. Oman, 'A Queen's Silver Toilet Set' in *Country Life*, 25 November 1954, p. 1850; Arthur G. Grimwade, 'Royal Toilet Services in Scandinavia' in *The Connoisseur*, April 1956, p. 175. For an almost

cape teapot. London, *c.* 1800. Victoria and Albert Museum, London.

identical toilet service, also by Thomas Heming, *see* WILLIAMS-WYNN TOILET SERVICE.

'Caroline of Brunswick Silverware'. A group of pieces by different makers and dating from the reigns of Charles II, 1660-85, James II, 1685-8, and William III, 1689-1702, which RUNDELL, BRIDGE & RUNDELL received from the Jewel House in the Tower of London when the Prince of Wales (eldest son of George III and later Prince Regent, 1811-20) commissioned the firm in 1808 to supply silver plate to his wife, Caroline of Brunswick (1768-1821), then separated from him since 1796; although it was intended that the old pieces be melted down and the metal used to make new pieces, the firm instead allowed the bullion price for the Royal plate, which it sold to collectors. Eight SCONCES (out of a set of twelve), London, *c.*1765, from the group are now at Colonial Williamsburg, Virginia.

Caroline silverware. Articles of silverware made in England between 1625 and 1688 in the periods of Charles I, 1625-49, Cromwell (the Protectorate), 1649-60, Charles II (the Restoration), 1660-85, and James II, 1685-8. In the early years the forms and decoration were simple, with little gilding, due to the decline of the economy and the fear of financial loss of the value of the workmanship in case melting down became necessary; the work was characterized by grounds of MATTING and by decoration of FLAT CHASING and CHINOISERIES. In the later more prosperous years of the Restoration period, the styles became elaborate, with the revival of the use of EMBOSSING and CASTING and the production of articles of luxury. *See* Charles C. Oman, *Caroline Silver 1625-1688* (1970). *See* CALVERLEY TOILET SERVICE; RESTORATION SILVERWARE.

Carr, Alwyn (Charles Ellison) (1872-1940). A silversmith born in Sheffield, who was a long-time friend and from 1898 partner of OMAR RAMSDEN, working mainly as a designer. He designed the Chancellor's MACE for the University of London in 1902. His partnership with Ramsden was dissolved in 1919; its work bore their joint mark.

Carrington, John Bodman (d. 1926). A leading London silversmith who was in 1903-4 Prime Warden of the Goldsmiths' Company. His firm executed some pieces adapted from designs of Wedgwood ceramic ware, e.g., one of the OVOID CUPS and pairs of WINE-AND-WATER EWERS, and made a variety of articles, several of which are owned by the Goldsmiths' Company. He was the author, with George Ravensworth Hughes, of *The Plate of the Worshipful Company of Goldsmiths* (1926).

Carter, John (fl. 1769-77). A London silversmith who is said to have specialized almost exclusively in CANDLESTICKS and SALVERS. His first mark was entered in 1776, but he is recorded as supplying candlesticks from 1769 to JOHN PARKER I and EDWARD WAKELIN. His address was Westmoreland Buildings, Aldersgate St, in 1770, and Bartholomew Close in 1776. Richard Carter, said to have been probably a younger brother or a cousin of John Carter, entered his first mark with Robert Makepeace (with whom he had worked since 1772) in 1777, when he took over the workshop of John Carter upon his retirement, and a second mark in 1778 with Daniel Smith and Robert Sharp, at Westmoreland Buildings.

cartouche. Strictly, a decoration in the form of a scroll of paper with curling edges, on which there is a picture, a design, an ornamental monogram, an inscription, a CREST, a COAT OF ARMS or an ACHIEVEMENT. The term is often used loosely to refer to any frame decorated with scrollwork. It is found executed in ENGRAVING or CHASING on many articles of silverware. Sometimes the cartouche on a piece is executed before the piece is sold, to be completed with the buyer's coat of arms; hence it is occasionally found with a blank centre. The design is usually symmetrical, except those in ROCOCO STYLE. Sometimes the crest of an achievement is omitted and replaced by a decorative shell, leaves or scroll.

carving fork. A type of large FORK used to hold securely meat that is being carved with a CARVING KNIFE; it has two long TINES, usually curved slightly outward and tapering to a point. *See* CARVING SET; CARVING SKEWER.

carving knife. A type of large KNIFE that is used to carve, the meat being held securely by a CARVING FORK or CARVING SKEWER; the blade is very sharp, slightly curved, and pointed. *See* CARVING SET.

carving set. A CARVING KNIFE and CARVING FORK, made and decorated EN SUITE, often with a conforming knife sharpener.

carving skewer. Close plate, W. Scot, Birmingham, 1807. L. 24·8 cm. City Museum, Sheffield.

caryatid handle. Detail of covered two-handled cup, John Coney, Boston, Mass., *c.* 1679–85. H. (of handle) 10 cm. Yale University Art Gallery (Mabel Brady Garvan Collection, Gift of Francis P. Garvan), New Haven, Conn.

caster stand. Stand by William Spackman, 1723, with three lighthouse casters by John Porter, London, 1699. Wadsworth Atheneum (Elizabeth B. Miles Collection), Hartford, Conn.

carving skewer. A type of culinary utensil used for holding securely a large joint of meat or a haunch of venison while it is being carved. It has two long TINES attached to a straight handle which has at its end a ring-shaped handle. Sometimes there is on the TANG, just below the handle, a circular disc to serve as a guard for the carver. *See* SKEWER.

caryatid. A female figure, draped or partially draped, that in architecture serves as a column to support an entablature; in silverware, such a figure–standing or sometimes reclining–is used to form the handle of some HELMET JUGS or of some SMALL TWO-HANDLED CUPS or forming the stem of some CANDLESTICKS. *See* CARYATID HANDLE; CARYATID CANDLESTICK; CANEPHOROS.

caryatid candlestick. A type of TABLE CANDLESTICK having its stem in the form of a CARYATID or part-caryatid. A related form has the stem in the form of a telamon (a male figure in the style of a caryatid).

caryatid handle. A type of handle, made by CASTING, in the form of a reclining female figure, sometimes loosely called a CARYATID. Such handles were often used on a SMALL TWO-HANDLED CUP, but the shape became so debased that it was often very thin and rudimentary, being in effect a DOUBLE-SCROLL HANDLE with, at the top, a female head or only a small ball, and sometimes even a mermaid with a double intertwined tail.

casket. An ornamental BOX, usually with hinges for a lid, rather than having a cover. Some rest on a flat base, others have four short legs or ball feet. Such caskets are usually intended to hold jewelry, as part of a TOILET SERVICE. *See* DYNELEY CASKET; CASKET INKSTAND; FREEDOM BOX.

casket inkstand. A type of INKSTAND in the form of a circular covered CASKET having the interior divided into compartments to hold, in a glass liner, two INKPOTS and a pair of quill holders, the space around them being filled with lead shot.

cassolette. A type of covered vase (usually ceramic) to contain liquid perfume for scenting a room, and hence having holes on the shoulder or the cover, or pierced decoration, or being mounted in silver (or ormolu) with openwork decoration. Such pieces, the mounts for which were made by MATTHEW BOULTON, were called by him an 'essence vase' or an 'essence pot'. *See* POT-POURRI BOWL; POT-POURRI VASE; PERFUME BURNER.

cast chasing. A type of CHASING that is executed to sharpen or to add details to the decoration on a decorative piece that was made by CASTING, such as a CANDLESTICK or a cast figure or mask applied to an object where the result of the casting process requires some refinement.

cast filigree. A type of decoration made of FILIGREE work produced by CASTING. It is used by applying it to the surface of a piece of metalware. A fine example is a silver-gilt STANDING CUP having a semi-ovoid bowl decorated with horizontal encircling decorative bands of cast filigree in the form of vine scrolls, alternating with bands of engraved hunting scenes; it was made by an unidentified silversmith, mark 'TYL', London, 1611–12, and is of unknown provenance except that it was stated to belong to a Lincolnshire family in 1859 when it was sold to the South Kensington Museum (now the Victoria and Albert Museum), London.

caster (formerly, castor). A type of small receptacle, having a pierced cover, that is used for sprinkling sugar, salt, ground pepper or spices or dry mustard powder. Such pieces are made in many styles and sizes, and of various vertical easily held shapes, such as cylindrical, baluster-shaped, pear-shaped, vase-shaped, etc., and, though usually of circular section, are sometimes polygonal. The cover is generally dome-shaped, with piercing in intricate and varied patterns (scrolls, hearts, quatrefoils) and with a small finial surrounded by a CUT CARD ornament. The cover, secured to the receptacle by various methods, may be a SCREW COVER, BAYONET COVER or CAP COVER (seldom an impracticable SLIP-ON COVER). A caster usually rests on a flat base, but some examples have a STEPPED or a footed base. They were often made in sets of two (one for mustard and one for pepper), with sometimes a third (for sugar); some were for two varieties of pepper, each caster having a slightly different LINER (often now missing), one with larger holes for coarse Jamaica pepper, and one with smaller holes for black pepper, but each having a similarly pierced cover. *See* LIGHTHOUSE CASTER; VASE-SHAPED CASTER; SALT CASTER; PEPPER CASTER; PEPPERETTE; KITCHEN PEPPER-POT; DREDGER; MUSTARD CASTER; MUFFINEER; CASTING BOTTLE.

caster stand. A type of receptacle for holding several types of CASTER, often in the form of a circular tray with a stemmed foot.

casting. The process of making and shaping a silver object by pouring molten metal into a hollow mould which has been made from a model of the desired article. In ancient times a hand-carved stone mould was used, but later a clay mould was formed around a solid object. These early methods (known as 'open casting') produced a solid object. Later, hollow moulds were made by suspending a close-fitting object within the mould so that the molten metal flowed between it and the walls of the mould (known as 'hollow casting'); but *see* SPINNING. Later methods were CIRE PERDUE, CUTTLEFISH CASTING, SAND CASTING, and, in modern times, for mass-production, centrifugal (investment) casting for objects of complex patterns. Open casting was used to produce some complete objects such as CANDLESTICKS and such small parts of objects as HANDLES, FINIALS, FEET, SPOUTS, THUMBPIECES, and applied MOUNTS. Most objects made by casting were produced by specialists who furnished them to other silversmiths. The process is sometimes called 'founding'.

casting bottle. A type of BOTTLE, made in various shapes, used for sprinkling scented essence over the hands of diners at the end of a meal in lieu of their rinsing their hands by using a ROSE-WATER EWER and BASIN. Sometimes called a 'sprinkler'. (1) One type is in the form of certain WINE-BOTTLES that were adaptations of the PILGRIM FLASK, having a flattened, rounded body, a long neck, and a pierced cover, but smaller (being about 12·5 cm high) and with, instead of two long chains, only one short chain attached to the shoulder of the bottle. Examples were made in TUDOR SILVERWARE, *c.* 1540–55. Related is a circular bottle of crystal with silver mounts, *c.* 1540. (2) Another type is exemplified by a silver-gilt bottle, *c.* 1550–65, that has a globular body and a tall tapering neck with, at the top, a pierced ball; it has overall IMBRICATED decoration. It was purchased in 1958 by the British Museum, London.

Castle Hallmark. (1) The ASSAY OFFICE HALLMARK used at the EDINBURGH ASSAY OFFICE both before 1974 and since for articles of silver and gold, being the three-turret castle of the City of Edinburgh. (2) An Assay Office Hallmark used at Newcastle-upon-Tyne, from 1672 to 1883, being in the form of three turrets (two small above a larger one).

castle-top ware. Articles, principally SNUFF-BOXES, CARD-CASES, and VINAIGRETTES, of which the flat rectangular hinged lid is decorated with an inserted PLAQUE depicting a scene of a British castle, e.g., Windsor or Kenilworth, or manor house, e.g., Abbotsford. The decoration, in low relief, is produced by DIE STAMPING. Such ware was made in Birmingham in the 1830s, a specialist there being Nathaniel Mills. *See* TOPOGRAPHICAL WARE.

Cathach, Shrine of the. An Irish reliquary SHRINE, made in the form of a book, to preserve the 6th-century vellum manuscript known as the Cathach Psalter which is traditionally associated with St Columba (521–97). It is a wooden box encased in metal plates and decorated with motifs executed in silver with NIELLO inlay, as well as panels sheathed in gold foil and also set with crystal cabochons. It was made between 1062 and 1098 to house the relic brought to Kells in 1090. Additions were made to it *c.* 1400. The shrine (its name being a nickname meaning 'battler') was owned by the O'Donnells and was traditionally carried around the O'Donnell army before battle to ensure victory. It was kept by the O'Donnells at Kells, and in the 19th century was deposited in the museum of the Royal Irish Academy, and in 1891 passed to the National Museum of Ireland, Dublin.

caudle-cup. The same as the unspouted SMALL TWO-HANDLED CUP (often called in England a POSSET-POT or a PORRINGER) used for drinking caudle (a warm thin gruel made from wine or ale, with eggs, bread or crushed oatmeal, and sugar and spices, usually intended for invalids, but formerly also served on ceremonial occasions). The term has sometimes, and preferably, been applied to a SPOUT CUP used for caudle. Drinking 'The Queen's Caudle' was a ceremony held at StJames's Palace, London, until 1793 on the occasion of the birth of each of the fifteen children of Queen Charlotte, the Ladies of the Court being invited to participate on successive days.

ca(u)ldron salt. A type of SALT-CELLAR having a bowl of low bulbous shape, similar to that of a ca(u)ldron, and resting on three or four short legs or on a low FOOT-RING. Such salts usually have a gilded interior or are provided with a glass LINER. An example was made by PAUL DE LAMERIE, 1737.

ca(u)lking. *See* RAISING.

casting bottle (1). Flattened body, London, 1546-7 (stopper, chain, and crest of later date). H. 12 cm. Victoria and Albert Museum, London.

casting bottle (2). Globular body with imbricated decoration, *c.* 1550-65. H. 18 cm. British Museum, London.

castle-top ware. Vinaigrette with hinged lid, the plaque bearing a die-stamped depiction of Abbotsford, Roxburghshire (home of Sir Walter Scott); Taylor & Perry, Birmingham, 1835(?). Courtesy. Sotheby's, London.

censer. Insense-burner by Laurent Amyot, Quebec, *c.* 1820. H. 24·2. Musée du Québec, Quebec.

ceramic-style silverware. Teapot with crabstock handle and spout and applied decoration of vine leaves and grapes, John Wirgman, London, 1748–9. H. 11·5 cm. Victoria and Albert Museum, London.

caviar server. A hemispherical or vase-shaped receptacle, resting on a spreading foot or base, within which is a smaller covered bowl (usually of glass) to hold and serve caviar, with space between the two receptacles for crushed ice; sometimes the cover has a finial in the form of a sturgeon. Most examples are modern, but one is known dating from *c.* 1820. Some modern pieces have, in the cover that bridges the two bowls, notches for suspending a number of vodka glasses. A recent example is in the form of a sturgeon in-the-round, with space in the head and tail for crushed ice and, in the central portion, a glass LINER with a DROP-IN COVER.

cayenne-scoop. A type of SPOON used for cayenne (red pepper), having a long handle and a small circular bowl, sometimes attached to a CRUET. Sometimes called a 'kyan scoop'.

celadon objects. Articles of which the essential part is made of celadon ware (porcelain, or sometimes pottery, having a celadon glaze) and which have English silver or silver-gilt MOUNTS in the form of the mouth-rim, stem, foot, and cover (comparable to many porcelain articles with mounts of gilded bronze or ormolu). Examples include some Ming dynasty pieces, such as the WARHAM BOWL. *See* PORCELAIN OBJECTS; POTTERY OBJECTS; MOUNTED OBJECTS.

censer. A type of receptacle in which incense is burned, especially as used in churches. Early ecclesiastical censers are usually spherical or baluster shaped, having a tall pierced cover and several chains by which to be suspended or swung by the bearer to increase the combustion and provide a continuous stream of smoke. After *c.* 1200 censers were made in architectural form, sometimes as a Gothic chapel with ogival windows and a pointed roof. Sometimes called a 'thurible'. *See* RAMSEY ABBEY CENSER; INCENSE BOAT; CHURCH PLATE.

centrepiece. A type of large ornamental object, often of silver gilt, that is used to decorate the centre of a formal dining table, but without the branching arms to support dishes, etc., that characterize an EPERGNE (although an epergne was sometimes used as a centrepiece). It often includes candle SOCKETS, as well as a small bowl or dish for fruit or sweetmeats, sometimes as separate pieces made EN SUITE and intended to be grouped together. Some elaborate examples by NICHOLAS SPRIMONT and others in the mid-18th century included in the decoration representations in-the-round of animals and fruit set in a landscape with trees, or sometimes mythological persons and animals. Some Victorian examples include flower VASES or branching arms for candlesticks. *See* ALHAMBRA TABLE FOUNTAIN; ASHBURNHAM CENTREPIECE; BOBRINSKY CENTREPIECE; BOLTON CENTREPIECE; CENTURY VASE; COLONNADE CENTREPIECE; EGLINTON TESTIMONIAL; JUBILEE CENTREPIECE; JUSTICE CENTRE-PIECE; NEPTUNE CENTREPIECE; NEWDIGATE CENTREPIECE; 'QUEEN VICTORIA'S DOGS' CENTREPIECE; TALISMAN CENTREPIECE; WELLINGTON CENTREPIECES.

Century Vase, The. An immense symbolic CENTREPIECE intended to summarize the story of the United States. It was designed by THOMAS J. PAIR-POINT and made by the GORHAM COMPANY for the 1876 Philadelphia Centennial Exposition; it was exhibited at the Paris Exposition of 1889 and the World's Columbian Exposition of 1893 in Chicago. On the base are sculptured groups and at the top a figure symbolizing America. The base is 1·57 m wide. *See* Alexander Farnum, *The Story of the Century Vase* (1876).

ceramic-style silverware. Articles of silverware that are in the form and decorative style of earlier ware made of pottery or porcelain, as distinguished from the more usual pieces of ceramic ware in SILVER SHAPE. An example is the silver TEAPOT made by John Wirgman, 1748–9, in the form of a Staffordshire earthenware teapot, *c.* 1740, with a crabstock handle and spout and having a finial in the form of a cat. Other examples include: BEAR JUGS; silver teapots having the body decorated overall with vertical cabbage leaves and having a conforming cover; and the silver TEA WARMER type of VEILLEUSE that copied the earlier Wedgwood creamware form. Two OVOID CUPS are adapted from Wedgwood designs, as are the WINE-AND-WATER EWERS. *See* BACON CUPS; GOAT-AND-BEE JUGS.

chafing dish (from French, *chauffer*, to warm). (1) A type of utensil, for a dinner table or a sideboard, for preparing or keeping warm certain foods. It is in the form of a covered circular skillet that rests on a stand supported by three or four legs so as to afford space for a heating device (usually a spirit lamp or a short fat candle). Some examples have a water-pan in which the skillet rests. The legs often have CLAW-AND-BALL FEET with wooden balls to protect the surface of the table from the heat. Such chafing dishes have been said to be derived from DISH RINGS and DISH CROSSES. Modern examples are made in various shapes and styles. A variant form is called a TODDY WARMER. Chafing dishes were often made in the American colonies and states along the eastern seaboard. *See* Helen Comstock, 'Chafing Dishes by New York Silversmiths' in *The Connoisseur*, July 1942, p. 66. (2) The term applied in former times, and still frequently, to a BRAZIER, but preferably to be avoided for utensils that provide heat from hot coals placed on a grille and used to warm the contents of a receptacle placed upon the brazier.

chalice. A type of ecclesiastical drinking vessel used at the Eucharist (the Catholic Mass), originally akin to the secular GOBLET or WINE-CUP and made of various materials, but after the 12th century required to be made only of precious metals. It varied in form, but had two characteristics: (1) the stem, for secure holding, has one central KNOP, to be held above and below by the index and middle fingers; and (2) the foot must be so shaped that the chalice cannot be easily overturned, hence from the 14th century was generally hexagonal and from *c.* 1500 was hexafoil (often with incurved sides) in lieu of the previous (but sometimes later) circular base which created the risk of its rolling away when laid on its side on the PATEN at the ablutions at the conclusion of the Mass. After the Reformation in England in 1534, the form of the Protestant cup (thereafter called a COMMUNION CUP) was simplified to differentiate it from the more ornate Catholic chalice. Although medieval chalices were often still used in recusant churches, new forms were developed for such use, including some that could be unscrewed into three parts for ready concealment. Later, many early chalices were converted into Communion cups, especially after the accession of Elizabeth I in 1558. After the Reformation, with the introduction of the extension of the cup to the laity, the cups were made larger and of secular design. In the 20th century new designs tend to follow contemporary secular styles. The term 'chalice' is still used by Catholics, especially in Ireland. The chalice is always accompanied by a paten. *See* BEDINGFIELD CHALICE; KEITH CHALICE; NOBLE CHALICE; PUGIN CHALICE; FUNERARY CHALICE; CHURCH PLATE.

chalice spoon. A type of ecclesiastical SPOON that accompanied a CHALICE and was used to add water to the wine in the chalice.

chamber candlestick. A type of CANDLESTICK that is intended to be carried to light the way indoors; it consists of a small flat tray or shallow saucer-like base about 15 cm wide with a central support for the candle. The form and styles are varied. The base is usually circular, but a few are rectangular or octagonal. In the centre of the base there is usually a mounted low stem with a SOCKET, or merely an affixed socket; the socket sometimes has an inserted removable NOZZLE. Some early examples have a flat or curved handle extending from the rim, but on later ones there is a ring-shaped handle (extending upward from the rim in a loop to rejoin the rim) with usually a THUMBPIECE. The handle sometimes supports, in a pierced slot, a CANDLE EXTINGUISHER or a SNUFFER, or both. In a few cases the stem has two curved arms, each having a socket and a candle extinguisher. The base is usually undecorated, but some have a rim that is upcurved or is decorated with REEDING, BEADING or GADROONING; it sometimes rests on low feet. The base serves as a DRIP-PAN, there usually being none either on the stem or on the socket. The socket sometimes has a pierced slot, occasionally with a sliding knob, to facilitate ejecting the candle stub. Such candlesticks were often made in pairs, but more often in sets of four, six, ten or more. To minimize the fire hazard, some examples are provided with a cylindrical glass chimney. Originally called a 'low-footed candlestick' or a 'flat candlestick', they were later variously termed a 'chamberstick', a 'bedroom candlestick' or a 'hand candlestick', and are sometimes still referred to (using an obsolete term) as a SCONCE. *See* G. Bernard Hughes, 'Silver Chamber Candlesticks' in *Country Life*, 5 January 1956, p. 12. *See* GIMBAL CHAMBER CANDLESTICK; TRAY CANDLESTICK; OIL LAMP.

chamber pot. A bedchamber receptacle for urine, usually in cylindrical form with shaped convex sides, a flat bottom, and a single loop or scroll handle. Some have a cover. Although usually made of porcelain or glazed earthenware, some were made of silver, especially in the 17th and early 18th centuries. The earliest recorded English silver example was made by Marmaduke Best, 1670–1, and was presented to the City of York for the use of the Lord Mayor. From the time of Samuel Pepys, *c.* 1700, until the mid-Victorian period, a silver chamber pot was often placed in a cupboard in the dining room for the men to use after dinner when the ladies had withdrawn. Examples were often present in AMBASSADORIAL PLATE. At least five, possibly as many as eleven, are recorded as probably having been in the collection of Sir John Foley-Grey sold at Christie's, London, on 20 April 1921; one, 1744, by DAVID WILLAUME II, was sold at Sotheby's, London, on 14 June 1984. *See* Nor-

chalice. Parcel gilt, Laurent Amyot, Quebec, *c.* 1800–39. H. 31·4 cm. Musée du Québec, Quebec.

chamber pot. One of a pair, David Williaume II, London, 1743–4. D. 19·2 cm. Colonial Williamsburg, Va.

Chantilly pattern. Salad spoon and fork. L. 22 cm. Courtesy, Gorham Collection, Providence, R.I.

man M. Penzer, 'The Silver Chamber Pot' in *The Antique Collector*, October 1958, p.174, and December 1958, p.225. *See* YORK CHAMBER POT; BOURDALOU.

chamfered corner. A corner on a square, rectangular or other polygonal object formed by trimming away the angle made by two adjacent faces. Also called a 'canted corner'.

champagne-flute. A type of drinking vessel for champagne, in the form of a narrow tall goblet on a stemmed foot. The shape is deemed by champagne connoisseurs to be preferable to the type of glass with a shallow saucer-shaped bowl long associated with champagne, as the flute's deep bowl and narrow mouth prevent the bubbles from escaping too quickly.

champagne spigot. A type of article for dispensing champagne from its bottle over a period of time, but without removing the cork. It consists of a pointed tube encircled by a worm (as of a corkscrew) and having, on the end that projects above the cork, a SPOUT with a SPIGOT. Some silver examples have an ornamented spout. Patented types were made in France, *c.*1820–40, and an English design was registered at the Patent Office on 6 October 1874 by William Ryder.

champlevé (French). Literally, raised field. The technique of decoration by enamelling in which the design was made by cutting lines or cells into the metal base and filling these with powdered enamel of various colours, the piece being then fired to fuse the enamels and develop the colours. In early examples, only lines of the design were incised and filled, but later more of the metal was cut away, leaving only walls of thin metal to form the design and separate the colours, thus simulating early CLOISONNÉ work (except that the partitions were part of the base rather than being affixed to it). After firing, the entire surface was smoothed and levelled with pumice and then polished. Decorating in *champlevé* enamelling was done mainly on bronze and copper, but occasionally on silverware. *See* KING JOHN'S CUP; NIELLO.

chandelier. A type of lighting fixture, made to be suspended from a ceiling, equipped with a varying number (usually six to sixteen) of curving arms terminating with SOCKETS for candles (later oil lamps, then electric-light bulbs). Although silver examples are rare, several made by English silversmiths and one made in Ireland are known to survive, mainly in large manor houses; these include one by GEORGE GARTHORNE at Hampton Court, the SNEYD CHANDELIER now at Colonial Williamsburg, Virginia, and the KNESWORTH CHANDELIER. A pair made by PAUL DE LAMERIE, 1734–5, now in the Kremlin, Moscow, have sixteen arms each, and are decorated with a Russian Imperial crown. In order to facilitate their being lowered for cleaning, some examples have a handle at the bottom, with a balancing counterweight. Some chandeliers were made in the 1930s by ELECTROFORMING.

Channel Islands silverware. Articles of silverware made on the islands of Jersey, Guernsey, and Sark. Some of the early examples were made by immigrant Huguenot silversmiths. The leading local silversmith, designer, and engraver was Guillaume Henry (fl. 1740–55), of Guernsey. The ware included many types of domestic objects, especially CHRISTENING CUPS and BEAKERS. There were no local ASSAY OFFICES or HALLMARKS, but the silversmiths used distinctive MAKER'S MARKS, usually with three letters from their names. The retailers frequently overstruck, by BACK-STAMPING, the marks of London silversmiths. *See* Richard H. Mayne, *Old Channel Islands Silver* (2nd ed., 1985); Judith Banister, 'Silver of the Channel Islands' in *Country Life*, 22 April 1971, p.960.

Chantilly pattern. A design for the handles of FLATWARE, patented in 1895 by WILLIAM CHRISTMAS CODMAN for the GORHAM COMPANY, and named after the town near Paris. The design consists of overlapping scrolls surrounding a plain surface for a monogram, topped by a FLEUR DE LIS. It is still the most popular flatware pattern.

charger. A large PLATTER or PLATE, usually circular or oval and having a shallow WELL, used for serving meat on a sideboard or a dining-room table. Many are decorated with GADROONING, and sometimes have a lobed or shaped rim. Some highly ornamented pieces with relief decoration, preferably called a SIDEBOARD DISH, were made only for display, or sometimes to be hung on the wall as a plaque, in which case they often have two holes in the FOOT-RING for a suspensory cord and are preferably called a SHIELD.

Charing Cup. A silver-gilt STEEPLE CUP having an ovoid bowl and cover resting on a vase-shaped stem supported by a high foot; the stepped-domed

Charing Cup. Silver gilt with overall scallop-shell decoration, London, 1599–1600. H. 49 cm. Photo courtesy, Historic Churches Preservation Trust, London.

cover is surmounted by a plain triangular obelisk-like steeple with a baluster finial. The bowl, cover, and foot are decorated overall with a DIAPER pattern of REPOUSSÉ and chased SCALLOP shells of graduated sizes. Around the rim of the bowl is an engraved inscription recording the gift from Mrs Elizabeth Ludwell to the parish church of Charing, Kent, in 1765. It bears a London hallmark for 1599–1600. A cup with similar decoration but lacking the cover belongs to St Mary Abbot's church, Kensington, London. A similarly shaped silver-gilt standing cup, London, 1598, also has a diaper decoration of scallop shells, but with interspersed diamonds (lozenges); it was sold at Sotheby's, London, on 26 February 1981.

Charlecote Cup. A silver-gilt 'FONT-SHAPED' CUP having a typical shallow vertical-sided bowl resting on a wide TRUMPET FOOT; it is decorated on the upper part of the stem with a chased IMBRICATED pattern and on the lower part with applied tongue-shaped lobes. The bowl is encircled by a band decorated with engraved ovals, five containing depictions of various animals alternating with five containing foliage patterns. The inside of the bowl is decorated with a honeycomb pattern and is gilded (later restored by ELECTRO-GILDING). The maker's mark has not been identified; the cup bears a London hallmark of 1534–5. The history of the cup is not known before it was found in 1945 at Charlecote Park (built in 1558 by Sir Thomas Lucy, whose family had lived at Charlecote since 1189), near Stratford-upon-Avon; the cup is now owned by Sir Edmund Fairfax-Lucy, Bt, and is on display at Charlecote Park. The initials 'RE' are pounced on the bottom of the bowl, but they have not been identified and no record has been found of a person with those initials connected with the Lucy family. Resembling this cup, in form and imbricated decoration, is the J. A. Holms Cup, 1521–2 (privately owned in 1957), of which miniature copies have been made in modern times. *See* Charles C. Oman, 'The Charlecote Cup' in *Apollo*, November 1945, p. 259; Norman M. Penzer, 'Tudor "Font-Shaped" Cups' in *Apollo*, December 1957, p. 179 and fig. viii.

Charles II Altar Dishes. (1) A pair of circular silver-gilt ALTAR DISHES, each having a well with chased decoration to represent waves in which are twelve different types of swimming fish, and having in the centre a medallion bearing a large rose surmounted by a crown. The wide border has embossed decoration in the form of four oval panels, separated by large embossed cuttlefish; the panels of one dish have scenes with figures symbolizing Love, Death, Industry, and Strength, and on the other are figures of Faith, Hope, Justice, and Fortitude. The pair are unmarked, attributed to *c.* 1685–7, and according to an inventory of William IV they were part of the Communion Plate of the Royal Coronation Service. They are now in the Jewel House at the Tower of London. (2) A circular silver-gilt dish having in the well an engraved coat of arms of Charles II, and having a wide concave border decorated with foliage, surrounded by a rim decorated with embossed floral motifs. It was made *c.* 1660 by an unidentified silversmith using the mark 'RF'. It is accompanied by the ROYAL FONT; the measurements of the piece indicate that it was the base on which the font rested, but it is considered to be, and is used as, an altar dish.

Charles II Salt. A silver-gilt GREAT SALT (one of a set of four) in modified hourglass form, having a large lower part and, separated by a bulging knop, a smaller upper part (with a recessed receptacle for salt). From its rim there are three out-curved scrolls. From the rim of the salt-cellar three scroll brackets extend upward to support a domed canopy cover which has a finial in the form of a figure in-the-round of an equestrian warrior. The body and cover are decorated with embossed foliage. All four bear a maker's mark 'FL' and are dated 1660; their heights differ, varying from 14·8 to 26·6 cm. They are now in the collection of Royal Plate in the Jewel House at the Tower of London.

Charles II Statuette. A STATUETTE depicting Charles II, made by WILLIAM PITTS I, 1790. It was last reported to be in the Royal Collection.

chasing. The technique of decorating by handwork the front surface of an article of silver (or other metal) by indenting it and so raising the design (without cutting into the metal and removing any of it, as in ENGRAVING), using a great number of differently shaped tracing tools ('tracers') and a chasing hammer. When used to make a design on a flat surface, rather than to develop relief work, it is called FLAT CHASING. When used to enhance from the front the design made by EMBOSSING from the back and to sharpen the relief work, it is called REPOUSSÉ CHASING; when used to enhance from the front a design made by CASTING, by sharpening or adding details not satisfactorily formed by the casting process, it is called CAST CHASING. The

Charles II Altar Dishes. One of a pair; silver gilt, *c.* 1685–7. D. 57 cm. Tower of London (Crown copyright, HMSO).

Charles II Salt. Silver gilt, London, 1660. H. *c.* 25 cm. Tower of London (Crown copyright, HMSO).

Chatsworth Cup. Silver gilt, attributed to Thomas Heming, *c.* 1700. H. 39·3 cm. Devonshire Collection, Chatsworth (reproduced by permission of the Chatsworth Settlement Trustees).

technique involves laying the article on a bed of pitch (mixed with resin and plaster of Paris so as to be resilient but firm enough to support the article), and working the metal with the tracers and hammer. Chasing is coarser than ENGRAVING and can be distinguished by its leaving a blurred impression on the underside of the metal. The process has been used since antiquity. During the 18th century the French are said to have excelled at such work, but English artisans also produced good results; in England its popularity fluctuated in the various periods of decorative styles. *See* DE-CHASING.

chatelaine. An ornamental clasp worn in daytime at a woman's waist, attached to a belt or girdle with a hook-plate from which are suspended several (usually five, but up to nine) short chains terminating with rings or swivel catches to which are attached various small objects for daily household use. Early examples had attached a SEAL and a watch; later more articles were added, e.g., keys, watch-keys, ÉTUI, POMANDER, SCISSORS, thimble-case, bodkin-case, household notebook in a metal case, small purse, penknife, pin-cushion and tape measure, as well as sometimes a GIRDLE BOOK, cameo charm, and pendants. Some chatelaines made for men were longer and were worn suspended at each thigh to conceal the openings on breeches; early examples held a watch, seals, and charms, but after *c.* 1800 they were simpler and no longer held a watch. Some chatelaines had two suspensory chains joined at the belt by a short chain. Chatelaines were made of silver, gold, pinchbeck, cut steel, and later polished steel, and were ornamented with enamelling, beads, beaded tassels, and sometimes medallions of Wedgwood's jasper; they very rarely had a gemstone. They came into use in England in the 17th century and were very popular in the 18th and 19th centuries, but *c.* 1830 declined in use as fashionable jewelry and were worn only for utilitarian purposes. *See* G. Bernard Hughes, 'Georgian and Victorian Chatelaines' in *Country Life*, 4 October 1956, p. 727.

Chatsworth Cup. A silver-gilt TWO-HANDLED CUP, generally similar to the TATTON CUP, having a bowl of baluster shape with FLYING SCROLL HANDLES in the form of TERMS, one holding a tabor (but without any engraved ARMORIALS) and the other holding pipes in the right hand and a bunch of grapes in the uplifted left hand. The cover has a finial in the form of an infant Bacchus holding a bunch of grapes in his uplifted left hand. The cup is unmarked but, on account of its form and decoration, has been attributed to THOMAS HEMING, *c.* 1760; the cover bears the mark of EMICK ROMER, with the London mark of 1761–2. The piece is part of the Devonshire Collection at Chatsworth, Derbyshire, and was acquired probably by the 4th Duke of Devonshire (1720–64), who held the title at the date the cup was made. *See* HEMING TWO-HANDLED CUPS.

Chawner, Henry (1764–1851). A London silversmith, son of THOMAS CHAWNER. He was freed by patrimony in 1785 and registered his first mark in 1786, having succeeded that year to his father's business at Amen Corner, Paternoster Row, where he worked until 1796. In that year he was joined by JOHN EMES, and they entered a joint mark and worked at Paternoster Row; in 1798 Chawner retired to Hampshire, but retained an interest in the firm for the rest of his life.

Chawner, Thomas (1734–1805/11?). A London silversmith who was born in Derbyshire, apprenticed in 1754, and freed by patrimony in 1762. From 1759 until 1773 he worked in London at 60 Paternoster Row in partnership with WILLIAM CHAWNER I, probably his brother, entering joint marks from 1763 to 1768, and at Red Lion St, Clerkenwell, from 1767. They were known as spoon-makers. He registered his first mark alone in 1773 from Paternoster Row, his second in 1775, and a third in 1783 from 9 Ave Maria Lane. In 1783 he succeeded to the business managed by Charles Wright and formerly owned by FRANCIS NELME, and in 1786 the firm passed to his son HENRY CHAWNER.

Chawner, William (I) (fl. 1759–84). A London silversmith, the partner and probably brother of THOMAS CHAWNER, with no record of apprenticeship or freedom. From 1759 to 1773 he worked with Thomas Chawner at 60 Paternoster Row, registering joint marks from 1763 until 1768. In 1774 he entered a joint mark with GEORGE HEMING, with address at King's Arms, New Bond St, where – from 1773 to 1781 – they made the dinner service and dessert service commissioned by Catherine the Great. In 1782 they succeeded to the business of THOMAS HEMING, but after 1784 George Heming continued the business alone.

Chawner, William (II) (d. 1834). A London silversmith, apprenticed in 1797 and freed in 1804, who was a spoon-maker. He registered seven marks between 1808 and 1833. His family was unrelated to that of WILLIAM CHAWNER I.

Chawner & Co. A London firm of silversmiths, located at Hosier Lane, Smithfield, which specialized in making forks, spoons, and other SMALLWARE, some of which it sold to HUNT & ROSKELL. In 1830 its director was George Williams Adams.

cheese knife. A type of KNIFE having a curved blade, used for cutting cheese, and usually having the end of the blade curving away from the cutting edge and bifurcated, with two points to pick up a piece of cut cheese.

cheese scoop. A type of serving implement having a straight handle connected to a wide curved blade occurring in a variety of shapes, used to scoop an individual portion from a large cheese, such as Stilton. The handle may be of silver, ivory, bone or wood. Some examples have an attached sliding pusher to eject the cheese from the scoop. *See* MARROW SCOOP; CORER.

cheese stand. A type of receptacle for serving cheese, made in two forms: (1) flat and circular like a cheese-board, for a cheese resting flat, an example of which was made by PIERRE HARACHE, 1689, perhaps not originally for cheese; and (2) in the form of a cradle, to hold upright a circular cheese resting on its side; two examples were made by EDWARD WAKELIN and JOHN PARKER, 1760 and 1764, of rectangular shape with incurved ends and overall pierced work, and one by ROBERT HENNELL II, 1812, of shallow hemispherical shape with flowing curved lines.

cheese stand (2). Cradle type, Edward Wakelin, London, 1760. W. 36 cm. Victoria and Albert Museum, London.

cheese toaster. A type of utensil for toasting cheese on bread before an open fire. It is in the form of a rectangular hot-water dish with a horizontal divider midway inside, and having resting upon the divider six to twelve small removable pans; it has a hinged domed lid and at the rear, set in a FERRULE, is a long projecting straight handle (made of wood or ivory). Extending from the finial on the lid to a hook on the ferrule is a short chain. A piece of toast is placed in each pan and covered with cheese; then the toaster, with its lid partially raised and kept open by the chain, is held before the fire and the heat, reflected by the brightly burnished interior of the raised lid, melts and browns the cheese. Sometimes the pans have a short flat lip or a low handle to facilitate removal from the dish. The hot-water compartment below the interior plate is filled through: (1) the orifice in the ferrule after removing the handle; or (2) an orifice in the handle created when a flat plug screwed into the handle is removed; or (3) a lip with a hinged lid on one side of the compartment. The hot water suffices to keep the toast warm while the cheese is browning. The pans became scratched by the knives used in removing the toasted squares and so were frequently tinned or replaced. The toasters, from 23 to 30 cm wide, were introduced *c.* 1760–80, and during the 1810–20 Regency period they were very elaborately decorated on the sides and lids, and they sometimes have four small feet. Some dishes were oval, and in such cases the corner pans were rounded at the corner. Rare examples were made with a replica of a mouse-trap on the lid, and some with the figures of a mouse on each leg, e.g., one by BENJAMIN SMITH II, 1826. Few such pieces were made after *c.* 1830. Sometimes called a 'toasted-cheese dish'. *See* G. Bernard Hughes, 'The Georgian Way with Toasted Cheese' in *Country Life*, 30 May 1968, p. 1467.

cheese toaster. Sheffield plate, Boulton, Watt & Sons, Birmingham, *c.* 1800. L. 24 cm. City Museum, Sheffield.

chessmen. The 32 pieces used in the game of chess. For many centuries and in many countries sets have been made of various materials and in widely differing styles. Only a few antique silver sets are known to have been made in England, but modern English sets include some modelled in the form of the 1835 Staunton design, others in fantasy form, but all having the opposing sides differentiated by being, respectively, of silver and silver gilt.

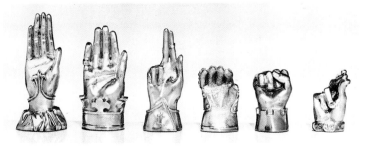

chessmen. Pieces from a set designed by Ringo Starr and Robin Cruikshank (queen, king, bishop, knight, rook, pawn), Asprey & Co., London, 1972. Courtesy, Asprey & Co. Ltd.

chinoiserie. Silver-gilt salver, Thomas Jenkins, London, 1682. D. 32·4 cm. Metropolitan Museum of Art (Gift of Irwin Untermyer), New York.

Although A. E. J. Mackett-Beeson states, in *Chessmen* (1968), that no English silver examples were made before the 19th century, a set, probably of English make (but unmarked and of uncertain date), has the kings and queens depicting Charles I, 1625-45, and Queen Henrietta Maria; the set, together with its silver-mounted fitted case, is in a private collection and is on loan to the Victoria and Albert Museum, London. In another set the pieces are in the form of various busts on scrolled pedestals and bear the maker's mark 'EF'; this set is said by Mackett-Beeson to be by E. Fennel, 1815. Another early set, made of BRITANNIA SILVER and bearing a maker's mark 'EF', has pieces in the form of figures wearing Roman and Oriental garb, some being mounted on camels, elephants, and horses; it was illustrated in the sale catalogues of 15 June 1961 and 15 October 1970 of Sotheby's, London, and there attributed probably to EDWARD FARRELL, 1816.

Among the modern English versions are: (1) sets designed by Ringo Starr and Robin Cruikshank and made by Asprey & Co., London, 1972, the pieces being in the form of a hand, each with an appropriate attribute or gesture; (2) sets commemorating the United States Independence Bicentennial, made by John Townley, London, 1976, the pieces representing soldiers in uniforms of the American Revolutionary War, with the opposing kings depicting, respectively, George III and George Washington, and the pawns tea-chests and American Indians. (3) sets with Staunton-type pieces, some of standard size and some of small size as travelling sets; and (4) a set designed by Cy Enfield, 1972, with the pieces cut from tubes of silver and silver gilt in shapes that can be fitted together for storing on a perspex rod.

Chester, Richard, Cup. A silver-gilt STEEPLE CUP having a U-shaped bowl resting on a footed stem, a cover of CUSHION SHAPE with a triangular pierced steeple finial, and having scroll brackets on the stem and on the finial; it is decorated overall with leaves and fruit in EMBOSSING and CHASING. It bears the maker's mark 'FT' for Fred Terry (fl. 1612-41) and the London mark for 1625-6. The piece, weighing 23 oz 9 dwt, was acquired by Trinity House, London, with funds bequeathed to that body - to acquire a cup weighing 20 oz - by Captain Richard Chester (d. 1632) in commemoration of his term as Master (1616-19); earlier, he had been in command of a naval vessel against the Spanish Armada in 1588. The inscription pricked on the lip of the cup states merely 'Richard Chester guift'. In view of the known dates of the cup and of Chester's death, as well as the difference between the specified and actual weights, it is apparent that an existing cup was purchased with the legacy instead of a new cup being specially made. It is not known how or when the cup left Trinity House (some of its records having been destroyed in World War I). It was shown on loan from Viscount Clifden in June 1862 in a Special Exhibition at the South Kensington Museum (now the Victoria and Albert Museum), London (Catalogue, p. 481, item 5,784). It was sold by Viscount Clifden at Christie's, London, on 4 May 1893, and at the Joseph Dixon sale at Christie's on 14 March 1911. In 1924 the Victoria and Albert Museum requested the Drapers' Company, London, to buy the cup for the museum (allegedly to prevent its being exported), and the Company did so, acquiring it from Heigham & Co., London, and re-selling it to the museum.

Chippendale rim. Detail of salver by Charles Kandler, London, 1739. Folger's Coffee Collection, Procter & Gamble Co., Cincinnati, Ohio.

Chester silverware. Articles of silverware made at Chester, England, which had its Guild of Goldsmiths from the early 15th century. The local ASSAY OFFICE HALLMARK before 1701 was a shield bearing the arms of the city (a vertical sword amid three wheat sheaves), together with a shield bearing the word 'Sterling'; from 1701 to 1779 it was a dimidiated shield having on one side the three lions of England and on the other side a wheat sheaf; and from 1779 to 1962 it was a shield with a variant of the earliest mark. The LEOPARD'S HEAD HALLMARK as a STANDARD HALLMARK was discontinued in 1839. The Assay Office closed on 24 August 1962. The earliest-known extant Chester pieces are four COMMUNION CUPS from 1570, made by William Mutton (d. 1583). The local ware consisted mainly of domestic articles, specialities being BLACKJACKS and BOTTLE RINGS. Among the leading silversmiths were Ralph Walley (1661-1703), Peter Edwardes II (fl. 1680-90), Peter Pemberton I (fl. 1676-1703), Richard Richardson I (1674-1729), and George Lowe (1768-1841), and members of their families. *See* Maurice Ridgway, *Some Chester Goldsmiths and their Marks* (1973); —, *Chester Silver 1727-1837* (1985); Christopher Lever, '400 Years of Chester Goldsmiths' in *Country Life*, 4 July 1974, p. 40; C. N. Moore, 'Chester silver of the Georgian period' in *Antique Dealer & Collectors Guide*, September 1985, p. 70; —, 'Silver from the city of Chester' in *Antiques*, June 1986, p. 1292.

chocolate-cup. Cup with reversible cover, Ralph Leake, London, *c.* 1685. H. 12·5 cm. Courtesy, Sotheby's, London.

chevroned. A style of decoration in the form of a band of connected chevrons, sometimes found vertically on the steeple of a STEEPLE CUP. *See* DEVIZES CUP.

child's cup. A type of small CUP for use by a child. Examples in silver are usually cylindrical, with an EVERTED rim and one SCROLL HANDLE. The height ranges from about 5 to 7·5 cm.

Chinese mandarin caddy spoon. A type of CADDY SPOON having in the bowl a low-relief bust depicting a Chinese mandarin wearing a conical hat and holding a tea-plant, the bowl being bordered by a scrolled CARTOUCHE; the handle is in the form of a massive floral bouquet. Examples were made by CASTING by EDWARD FARRELL, dated 1816 and 1830.

chinoiserie. European decoration inspired by Oriental sources, particularly Chinese. Chinoiseries are pseudo-Chinese figures, pagodas, monsters, landscapes, etc., with imaginative fantasy elements derived from an idealized 'Cathay'. Chinoiseries were introduced at the end of the 17th century in the designs of such *ornementistes* as Jean Bérain *père* (1640-1711) and others, and were widely used in France and England in decoration of all kinds. The use of such decoration on English silverware occurred principally in the 1680s, when the motifs were executed by ENGRAVING and FLAT CHASING, and in the 1700s, when it was done in chasing in relief, and later, *c.* 1750, with chasing and REPOUSSÉ and PIERCED WORK; there was a revival of the style in the period 1810-20. Some such decorations may have been added later on ware of an early date, perhaps by a single specialist in the style. *See* P. H. Honour, *Chinoiserie: The Vision of Cathay* (1961); Carl C. Dauterman, 'Dream-pictures of Cathay – Chinoiserie on Restoration Silver' in *Bulletin of The Metropolitan Museum of Art*, Summer 1964, p. 11.

Chippendale rim. A decorative ribbed RIM found on some TRAYS, WAITERS, and SALVERS in the basic form (subject to variations in detail) of a series of long concave-curved sections alternating with short concave-curved sections, connected by short angular sections, making together a basically circular rim. It is sometimes decorated at intervals around the rim with relief shells, fans, ACANTHUS leaves or other motifs. The name is a trade term, derived from the resemblance to the raised and carved 'piecrust' rim of some tripod tip-top tables with a circular top made by Thomas Chippendale (1718-79), the noted English furniture designer and cabinet-maker; but it has been pointed out that some silver pieces with such a rim were hallmarked before 1730, whereas Chippendale did not publish his designs until 1754. *See* BATH RIM; SCROLL-AND-SHELL RIM.

chocolate-cup. A type of large CUP for drinking hot chocolate, usually having a cover and accompanied by a saucer. Cups for hot beverages are not practicable in silver due to the heat-conducting quality of the metal. The only known English example of such a silver cup was made by Ralph Leake, London, *c.* 1685, and was sold at Sotheby's. London, on 23 May 1985; it is decorated with CHINOISERIE, has one vertical scroll handle, and has a cover on the top of which are three upcurved brackets which enable the cover, when removed and inverted, to serve as a saucer, with the brackets as legs. The cup is similar in form to a gold cup also made by Leake, *c.* 1685. The term 'chocolate-cup' has sometimes been applied to a TREMBLEUSE (which is equally suitable for other beverages), perhaps because a well-known advertising picture (taken from a 1745 painting, based on a ceramic figure) shows a girl drinking hot cocoa from a trembleuse.

chocolate-pot. A type of covered vessel for preparing and serving hot chocolate. It is usually pear-shaped, baluster-shaped or of tapering cylindrical or octagonal shape, closely resembling the contemporary COFFEE-POT, except that (1) it often rests on a heavy FOOT-RING or sometimes on three small feet, so as to raise it from the surface of the table upon which it stands and to add stability while the contents is being stirred, and (2) it invariably has provision for inserting a notched muddler (called a MOLINET or a 'mill') used to whisk the contents without its losing heat, by having a hole (a) at the top of the cover or domed hinged lid, covered by a small sliding, hinged or removable finial, or (b) in the side of the cover or of the hinged lid. The pot usually has a SWAN-NECK SPOUT, rising to the level of the rim, which sometimes has a SPOUT FLAP. The pot often has a projecting straight handle at right-angles to the spout, although this feature is not, as often supposed, proof that the vessel is a chocolate-pot rather than a coffee-pot. Some chocolate-pots have a SCROLL HANDLE, at right-angles to the spout, made of wood (sometimes leather-covered) set in two silver FERRULES. The aperture for the muddler can be closed, when the muddler is removed, by various types of sliding, hinged or slip-on covers or by a detachable cover which is sometimes connected to the upper ferrule by a short chain. The hinged lid on some examples has a scroll THUMBPIECE or a CORKSCREW THUMBPIECE. Some examples rest on a stand furnished with a spirit lamp. A rare example, made

chocolate-pot. Pot with hinged lid and removable finial, Edward Winslow, Boston, Mass., *c.* 1700-10. H. 24·3 cm. Yale University Art Gallery (Mabel Brady Garvan Collection), New Haven, Conn.

chocolate-pot. Pot with hinged lid and hinged finial and with cut-card decoration, Robert Cooper, London, 1705. H. 24 cm. Museum of Fine Arts, Montreal.

by Thomas Parr I, 1706, has an applied socket on the side of the pot in which to stand the muddler when not in use. *See* Edward Wenham, 'Silver Chocolate Pots' in *Antique Collector*, September/October 1946, p. 167; G. Bernard Hughes, 'Silver Pots for Chocolate' in *Country Life*, 20 October 1960, p. 856.

chrismatory. Three joined receptacles, each with identifying initial letter on lid. H. 3·2 cm. Burrell Collection, Glasgow.

chrismatory. A type of sacred vessel in which is kept the chrism (the consecrated oil, mixed with balm, which is blessed in the Western Christian Church by the bishop on Holy Thursday). Some examples are in the form of a cylindrical receptacle with a SCREW COVER surmounted by a cross, especially in Catholic Canada. More often it is a container for three small flasks for sacramental oils. Such containers are of two types: (1) an oblong box with a sloping lid and having a plate fitted with three holes for the flasks, or (2) a trefoil container for the three flasks. Examples were made of silver or silver gilt, some elaborately decorated, especially in Canada. A variant type is fitted with crystal flasks having silver mounts. A Scottish silver example in the Burrell Collection, Glasgow, has three joined receptacles, each marked on its hinged lid with an identifying letter – C, S, and I (for *Olium Catechumenorum, Olium Sacrationis*, and *Olium Infirmorum*) – for the appropriate oils to be used for, respectively, confirmation, baptism, and anointing the sick. Also called an 'oil stock'. *See* AMPULLA; CHURCH PLATE.

christening bowl. A type of bowl used for baptism by aspersion or affusion; no special form is recognized, but often a bowl presented to and used in a church for that purpose was originally either a PUNCH-BOWL or a MONTEITH. Only a bowl bearing an inscription designating its baptismal use or an example known to have been made for the purpose can be definitely so classified. Sometimes, especially when the bowl is elevated on a tall stem, it is called a 'christening font' or a 'baptismal font'. *See* BAPTISMAL BASIN; FONT; LILY FONT; ROYAL FONT.

christening goblet. A GOBLET, appropriately inscribed, presented by a godparent to an infant as a christening gift, differing in form from the more usual small CHRISTENING MUG destined for use by the infant. A silver-gilt example with a cover was purchased in 1963 by the Victoria and Albert Museum, London; it was made by John Mortimer and John Samuel Hunt (*see* HUNT & ROSKELL), and bears London marks for 1842-3. It has a waisted bowl resting on a stem in the form of intertwined vines bearing clusters of grapes and having midway on the stem a knop set with four carbuncles. The wide circular base is decorated with an applied serpent encircling the roots of the vine. The bowl is decorated with seated figures of *putti* and the flanged cover has a finial with figures of a lion and a lamb. The goblet was given by Queen Victoria to her godchild, the Hon. Victoria Alexandrina Emily Jocelyn, on the occasion of her christening on 19 October 1842, as recorded in an engraved inscription encircling the rim of the base. It has been said that other goblets of such design were presented on several occasions by Queen Victoria and the Prince Consort when they acted as godparents. Such gifts, being goblets, may have been chosen by the donors not merely for presentation, but also to be used to drink a toast to the infant.

christening mug. A type of MUG often given to a child as a christening present, being of no fixed shape and style but frequently made with an octagonal bowl and foot and a single loop or angular handle.

christening set. Various articles intended as gifts to an infant on the occasion of christening. A complete set would include a plate, feeding bowl, mug or cup, knife, fork, spoon, and pusher. Partial sets of two or more pieces are more often given. Some sets have been made of silver gilt and provided with a fitted case. A set, given by Queen Victoria to Albert Victor Arthur Wellesley (great-nephew of the 1st Duke of Wellington), was made by George Adams, London, 1864; it is now in the Institute of Art, Minneapolis, Minnesota. Some examples, *c.* 1880-5, are decorated with characters after drawings by Kate Greenaway (1846-1901), the well-known children's-book illustrator.

christening set. Silver gilt, George Adams, London, 1864. Minneapolis Institute of Art, Minn. (photo courtesy, Brand Inglis Ltd).

chrysanthemum pattern. A pattern of FLATWARE and CUTLERY, designed in 1880 by Charles T. Grosjean for TIFFANY & CO., named from the design of a stylized chrysanthemum on the terminal of the stem. The stem is decorated along its entire length with EMBOSSING depicting swirling leafage.

church furnishings. Articles used on altars in Christian churches, often made of silver and enriched with gemstones, pearls, and enamelling, including ALTAR CANDLESTICKS, ALTAR CROSSES, ALTAR RELIQUARIES, PRICKET CANDLESTICKS, SANCTUARY LAMPS, and large BOOK-COVERS, as well as items of

CHURCH PLATE. Many such articles, despite the iconoclasm of past periods, have survived due to their value as ecclesiastical patrimony and their sacred nature. *See* MITRE.

church plate. Various articles for Christian ecclesiastical use, including the AMPULLA, ALMS DISH, ALTAR CRUET, ASPERGILLUM, BAPTISMAL BASIN, BEAKER, CANDELABRUM, CANDLESTICK, CENSER, CHALICE, CHRISMATORY, CHRISTENING BOWL, CHURCH SALT, CIBORIUM, COMMUNION-BREAD KNIFE; COMMUNION CUP, CROSIER, EWER, FAN, FLAGON, FONT, HAND WARMER, INCENSE BOAT, MONSTRANCE, PATEN, PAX, PROCESSIONAL CROSS, PYX, SACRING BELL, SCALLOP, STRAINER SPOON, TRIPTYCH. In England the confiscation and destruction of church plate under Henry VIII and the melting down of much that was not confiscated resulted in the survival of little pre-Reformation plate. Much Canadian church plate is extant. Although such items are generally not disposed of by the owning churches, some have in recent years been sold unofficially or after formal proceedings and consent, usually to provide funds either for the acquisition of other church plate or for the maintenance of the fabric of the church. A sale of 157 examples was held by Christie's, London, in January 1955. *See* J. F. Hayward, 'Early Church Plate' in *Country Life*, 6 January 1955, p. 20; Charles C. Oman, *English Church Plate 697-1830* (1957); James Gilchrist, *Anglican Church Plate* (1967). *See* RECUSANT PLATE; JEWISH RITUAL SILVERWARE.

church salt. A type of SALT CASTER used in some churches in the baptism service. No special form is recognized (a secular salt caster having sometimes been used), but a known example – at Corpus Christi church, Oxford – was possibly made expressly for church use; it is of hourglass form, the body and cover having openwork decoration of religious motifs.

ciborium. A receptacle, usually shaped like a GOBLET and having a tightly fitting COVER, in which are kept the consecrated wafers for the Eucharist. The cover is usually surmounted by a cross, sometimes resting upon an orb or a monde, and occasionally closed by a latch. It is for use only in a church, as distinguished from a PYX which is smaller and may be taken out by the priest when visiting the sick. Sometimes called a Custodial or, in French-speaking Canada, a *Porte-Dieu*. *See* CHURCH PLATE.

cigar-box. A type of BOX used as a container for cigars, either (1) a portable flat container for carrying a few cigars, or (2) a large rectangular hinged container for table or desk use. A box originally made for some other purpose but having appropriate dimensions may have been adapted for such use, but a cigar-box made in 1938 expressly for such use is at the Mansion House, London.

cigar lighter. A type of lighter for cigars, usually a non-portable utensil resting on a table and sometimes made in fantasy form. *See* ROYAL ACADEMY CIGAR LIGHTER.

cigarette-box. A type of small rectangular BOX for use on a table or desk as a container for cigarettes. A box made as part of a TOILET SERVICE or for some other purpose may sometimes have been adapted to such use.

cipher (sometimes **cypher**). A monogram, formed by the intertwining of letters, such as the initials of a person's names. It is found engraved on silverware as a decorative motif or as evidence of ownership.

cire perdue (French). Literally, lost wax. A process of CASTING metal, originally used in casting bronze ware, but later for much gold jewelry. Its use was primarily for articles of intricate design in-the-round that could not readily be made by shaping the metal by chiselling, HAMMERING or ordinary methods of casting. The technique for a solid object involved carving a model in wax, then encasing ('investing') it in a clay, plaster or steatite mould, and applying heat to cause the wax to melt and run out of a hole (sprue) in the mould, after which the mould was filled under pressure with molten gold or silver. In the modern technique the mould, before having the molten metal poured into it, is placed in a vacuum to force the metal into the entire space. For making a hollow object, it was necessary to insert a core inside the mould, leaving a thin surrounding space for the wax, with the core held in position by small pegs (called 'chaplets'). The method was used in ancient times by the Egyptians in the 15th/14th centuries BC. It is sometimes called the 'lost-wax process', and a modern mass-production method is called 'centrifugal casting' or 'investment casting'. As the mould must be broken to retrieve the object, only one reproduction can be made from each wax model and from each mould.

chrysanthemum pattern. Fork and spoons with decorated handles. Courtesy, Tiffany & Co., New York.

ciborium. Covered receptacle, by Ignace-François Delzenne, Quebec, *c.* 1769. H. 28 cm. Musée du Québec, Quebec.

Cirencester Flagons. One of a pair, parcel gilt, English, 1576. H. 36·2 cm. Cirencester parish church (photo courtesy, Historic Churches Preservation Trust, London).

Cirencester Flagons. A pair of parcel-gilt FLAGONS, 1576, each having a plain undecorated body with a bulbous lower half and a high cylindrical neck, resting on a spreading foot and having a flat cover with a winged-figure thumbpiece. The two covers bear engraved views of a church and houses, and the inscription 'Villa Cirencistrie 1577'. They are the earliest recorded examples of this type of flagon and are owned by the parish church at Cirencester, Gloucestershire.

cistern. A large receptacle for holding water or other liquid not in a bottle or other container. No example in silver is known. The term 'wine-cistern' has often been used to refer to the type of WINE COOLER that is large and oval, but as such receptacles were intended to hold bottled wine, they are now preferably termed a 'wine cooler', although they were probably used sometimes as a cistern for washing drinking glasses.

cladding. The technique of covering an inferior metal with a coating of a noble metal. In the Middle Ages, the process involved hammering on a thin sheet of silver (or gold), this method being superseded by a process of laminating a thin sheet of silver (or gold) to a base metal and rolling the laminate to produce a PLATED METAL. Laminating was in turn superseded by the processes of FRENCH PLATING and CLOSE PLATING, and in 1842 by the technique of ELECTROPLATING.

claret-jug. A type of JUG used for serving decanted claret (Bordeaux red wine) and often other beverages. Some early examples were of ovoid shape and made entirely of silver, but most are made of cut (sometimes frosted) glass, the body being generally globular (but sometimes cylindrical or ovoid), with a tall narrow neck of silver that broadens to fit over the top of the glass body. It has a lid that is hinged to the collar of the neck and a loop handle that extends from the top of the collar down to the bottom of the neck or to the bulge of the bowl. The lid usually has a THUMBPIECE, often ornamented with a figure. The silver mounts are usually decorated with grapes. Some such jugs are made in fantasy form representing, e.g., a monkey or a sea-lion, the body being made of glass and the detachable head, made of silver, being the cover. Sometimes called a 'decanter jug'. *See* G. Bernard Hughes, 'The Charm of the Claret Jug' in *Country Life*, 4 February 1970, p. 242. *See* BURGES CLARET-JUGS; DRESSER CLARET-JUG; VINTAGE CLARET-JUG; WALRUS AND CARPENTER CLARET-JUGS.

Clausen, Nicholas (fl. 1709-31). A London silversmith of Swedish or German(?) origin who emigrated to England, and was naturalized in 1709, the year in which he was freed by the Haberdashers' Company. His first mark was entered in 1709, from Orange St, near Leicester Fields, where he worked until 1723. His second mark was registered in 1720. His work is of Huguenot style, his greatest piece being the THRONE and footstool, made in 1731 for Peter the Great, that are now in the Hermitage, Leningrad. *See* BOX SALT.

claw-and-ball foot. A type of FOOT in the form of the claw of an animal or bird clasping a ball. Such feet are usually found on furniture, but also occur on silverware, especially on a SALVER, TEAPOT STAND or CHAFING DISH, also infrequently on HOLLOW WARE such as a CREAM-JUG. A foot incorporating a wooden ball is intended to serve as a heat insulator for a piece with a warming device; if made entirely of metal, such a piece could damage the surface of the table.

Clay, Henry, Urn. A TWO-HANDLED CUP with a cover, having a bell-shaped bowl, two foliated vertical loop handles, and on the cover a finial in the form of a gilded spread eagle. The cup was made in 1840 by William Adams (b. 1801), of New York, as a tribute by six silversmiths to Henry Clay (1777-1852), the United States statesman. The urn, which bears a cartouche with a testimonial inscription, was carried on the funeral car at Clay's funeral on 29 June 1852 in Washington, D.C. The cup was given by Robert Clay to Ashland, Clay's home in Kentucky.

claymore. A type of large two-edged, sometimes two-handed, sword formerly used by Scottish Highlanders. The term is sometimes inaccurately applied to the basket-hilted broadsword, often one-edged, used by them in the 16th century. An example of the latter type, with the basket-guard hilt made of silver by CHARLES (FREDERICK) KANDLER, London, 1740-1, accompanied by a leather scabbard with silver mounts, is owned by the National Museum of Antiquities of Scotland, Edinburgh; it is said to have been given by Prince Charles Edward Stuart, the 'Young Pretender', to Reginald George Macdonald, and was bequeathed by a descendant to the museum.

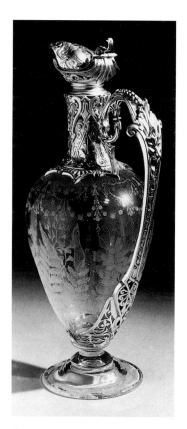

claret-jug. Glass with silver mounts, Sheffield, 1866. Courtesy, Asprey & Co. Ltd, London.

Clements, Eric (1925–). A designer of silverware who studied at the Birmingham College of Arts & Crafts, 1942–3 and 1947–9, and at the Royal College of Art, London, 1949–52, and travelled and studied extensively abroad in the years 1948–74. He teaches industrial design at Birmingham. His designs for silverware include pieces of ceremonial ware, such as maces, swords, and centrepieces, and articles of domestic ware, generally in contemporary style.

Clements, Eric. Teapot, sugar-bowl, and milk-jug, designed for Wakely & Wheeler, London, 1974. Courtesy, Eric Clements.

Cleopatra Cup. A silver-gilt STANDING CUP, 1579, the cover of which is surmounted by a standing figure said to depict Cleopatra. The cup is engraved with birds, arabesques, and garlands of fruit, and is partly embossed with fruit and STRAPWORK. It is owned by the Goldsmiths' Company, London.

Clinton Vase. A VASE basically in the form of the WARWICK VASE, but having on the front and reverse of the bowl engraved views of the Erie Canal in New York State, completed in 1825. It was designed and made by Thomas Fletcher and Sidney Gardiner, of Philadelphia, in 1824–5, for presentation by the merchants of Pearl St, New York City, to De Witt Clinton (1769–1828), Governor of New York, who sponsored the building of the canal. The finial is a figure for an eagle, and the vase rests on a square plinth engraved with a frieze of classical figures and a testimonial inscription. The vase is owned by the New York Chamber of Commerce.

clipper. A person who, in the reign of William III, 1689–94, fraudulently clipped small triangular chips from the edge of silver coins and sold them to silversmiths, being enabled to do so by reason of the crude quality of the hammered coins from the reign of Charles II, 1660–85. Despite severe penalties imposed by the Government and its refusal to accept clipped coins in payment of taxes, the practice continued and counterfeiting of coins increased, being finally ended by the legalization of BRITANNIA SILVER with its higher FINENESS and the adoption of the BRITANNIA HALLMARK from 1697 to 1720.

clock-case. (1) A type of ornamental piece made to accommodate a table clock. Few examples made entirely of silver are known, but there are several instances of wooden cases with silver MOUNTS. *See* TOMPION CLOCK. (2) A type of case in which to suspend a large watch (sometimes called a 'Goliath watch'), giving the appearance of a table clock.

clock salt. A type of GREAT SALT that combines a clock with a STANDING SALT. Such pieces were produced in the 16th century, and seven, probably of Continental make, are recorded as having been in the inventory of Elizabeth I. A design for one was prepared by Hans Holbein the Younger (1497–1543), to be executed as a New Year's gift in 1545 from Sir Anthony Denny to Henry VIII. The design for another (formerly in the collection of Duke Albrecht V of Bavaria, but no longer extant) is shown in a drawing in a contemporary inventory, believed to have been illustrated by Hans Meihlich, 16th century, The only known extant example is the TUDOR CLOCK SALT.

cloisonné (French). A type of decoration using enamel on a metal base in which the design is outlined by metal fillets *(cloisons)* secured to the metal, the enclosed spaces being filled in with coloured enamels which are then fired. The process has not generally been used to decorate silverware, but in the 1870s, when Japanese decoration had become popular, ELKINGTON & CO. produced some silverware imitative of true *cloisonné*, by substituting for the affixed *cloisons* an electroformed ground with cavities for the enamels; but the work was abandoned *c.*1880 due to the superiority of imported Japanese *cloisonné* work.

close plating. The process of PLATING with SILVER LEAF an article of steel (used especially on knives and scissors), patented in 1779 by Richard Ellis, a goldsmith of London, as a technique less expensive than FRENCH PLATING. It involved using silver leaf to overlay small domestic objects of steel or iron which required strength and had a cutting edge or a sharp point, where the acid of the base metal might impair the flavour of food. The technique involved first cleaning, smoothing, and polishing the article, heating it red-hot over a charcoal BRAZIER, plunging it into a solution of sal ammoniac (as a flux), and then into molten tin; after the removal of all the tin except a thin coating, the article was closely coated with silver leaf and rubbed with a hot soldering iron which fused the silver to the tin. After BURNISHING with agate or bloodstone to conceal the join, it was rubbed with rottenstone. Some small fittings were close plated over brass. An almost perfect resemblance to SHEFFIELD PLATE was achieved, but the effect lacked permanence, as extreme heat, dampness, and long use tended to cause blistering and flaking of the

Cleopatra Cup. Silver gilt, London, 1579. H. 30·5 cm. Goldsmiths' Company, London.

cluster-column candlestick. One of a pair by Jeremiah Dummer, Boston, Mass., *c.* 1680-90. H. 27·5 cm. Yale University Art Gallery (Mabel Brady Garvan Collection). New Haven, Conn.

Cockayne Cups. Two of a set of five, 1605. H. 42 cm. Skinners' Company, London.

silver. In 1810 an improved but costlier process was developed by Edward Thomason, of Birmingham, using rolled SILVER FOIL instead of silver leaf, binding it on the base metal, and then at red heat the silver became attached and the tin was expelled. Many artisans used close plating in various ways and over a long period. In 1806 they were allowed to stamp an identifying mark on close-plated metal, registering it at the SHEFFIELD ASSAY OFFICE; but the mark had to be of four components on one punch and so was not often used on SMALLWARE. *See* G. Bernard Hughes, 'The Art of Close Plating' in *Country Life*, 19 December 1968, p. 1663. *See* ELECTROPLATING.

cluster-column candlestick. A type of TABLE CANDLESTICK having its stem (shaft) either (1) composed of two or four similar columns placed adjacently or close together and held (or apparently held) together by a binding, or (2) of square section with two flutes on each side and with encircling binding, giving the appearance of a cluster of columns. The base is wide and square, and there are usually square flanges at the top and near the bottom of the stem. The form, adapted from a furniture design by Thomas Chippendale (1718-79), was popular in England in the 18th century, and was used also in the United States.

coach pot. The term used in England for a BOURDALOU, based on its use.

coaster. A type of dinner-table accessory, usually circular, that was used originally to protect the surface of a dinner table from being scarred by the woven osier covering on early wine-bottles, and later was used to protect the table from being scratched by the irregular or rounded bottom of some wine-bottles or from being damaged by the heat or moisture of a drinking vessel resting on it. Those used to support a bottle or decanter have an encircling vertical or everted GALLERY (*see* WINE-BOTTLE COASTER; WINE-BOTTLE STAND; DECANTER STAND), but those for use with drinking glasses (such as a modern highball glass) are smaller and have a low rim. The early name for such pieces was a 'stand' or a 'slider'; the term 'coaster', first recognized in 1887, was derived from the custom that, after finishing dinner, the cloth was removed from the table, the ladies withdrew, and the bottle of port was 'coasted' around the table by the men. *See* G. Bernard Hughes, 'Old English Wine Coasters' in *Country Life*, 10 May 1956, p. 1003. *See* DECANTER WAGON; BOTTLE STAND.

coat of arms (from French *cotte d'armes*, a garment of lightweight material worn over armour in the 15th/16th centuries). A heraldic emblem that shows the bearings or devices of a family or the branches of a family. It is usually shown on an ESCUTCHEON between the supporters (the standing figures or animals on each side). It was often shown on silverware, especially pieces of importance, and its appearance today enhances the value of the piece, as usually establishing PROVENANCE (unless added later), as well as being ornamental. Usually it was engraved, but sometimes affixed by striking with a die, an economical method for use on a number of similar pieces. Sometimes referred to as an 'armorial'. *See* CREST; ACHIEVEMENT; ARMORIAL WARE.

cobbler tube. A type of drinking tube used in the United States and Canada for drinking sherry cobbler (sherry, orange or lemon juice, and sugar, with ice), usually drunk through such a tube or a straw. The tube was usually (1) straight and ATTENUATED, or (2) scroll-shaped with one end closed except for piercing and with a hook halfway down one side for suspending it on the rim of a glass.

Coburg pattern. A pattern of FLATWARE where the stem is double-curved and is decorated along its length with a series of shell-like forms supplemented by foliage designs at the terminal and at the junction of the stem with the bowl.

Cockayne Cups. Five silver-gilt CUPS made in the form of figures in-the-round of cockerels having long spurs and each standing on a small circular base in the form of a turtle. The heads are removable covers. The maker's mark is a 'G', and the cups are dated 1605. They were made for William Cockayne, whose coat of arms, which includes five cockerels, appears on each piece; he bequeathed them to the Skinners' Company, London.

cockfighting spur. A sharp pointed spur (gaff) for a fighting cock, examples of which have been made of silver and many of SHEFFIELD PLATE. They were used in Ireland and in certain of the North American colonies, such as Virginia. The top of the silver spur is encased in a leather holder to secure it to the cock's leg. Some examples were made in sets of six.

cockle shell. A shell similar in shape to a SCALLOP shell and used as the model for various articles, such as a SALT-CELLAR, but such pieces are more often made in the form of the scallop shell.

cocktail shaker. A modern type of receptacle for mixing and pouring cocktails. It is cylindrical with sides sloping slightly outward, and has a domed cover with a central opening for pouring, upon which fits a small cylindrical SLIP-ON COVER.

coconut cup. A type of STANDING CUP having as its bowl part of a coconut shell (with its fibrous husk removed and the shell polished and often carved), which is set with silver MOUNTS consisting of a TRUMPET FOOT or domed base, a stem (some ornamented with brackets), an encircling everted rim band (to protect the shell's brittle edge), and vertical bowed straps (usually three) connecting the rim and the stem so as to position the shell and leave the greater part of its surface exposed. Some examples have a handle and some a hinged lid, and some rest on silver feet. As the straps could not be soldered to the rim and the stem either before enclosing the shell or after it was enclosed, they were joined by rivets or short rods passing through tubular sections somewhat like a door hinge. Some examples have the shell carved to depict a biblical, battle or tropical scene, or animals, birds or fish, and sometimes a coat of arms; these scenes were often carved by early European explorers bringing back the coconuts from the tropics. English examples of such cups are known from the late 15th century to the mid-18th century; a New College, Oxford, inventory of 1508 lists seven. Some TWO-HANDLED CUPS and OX-EYE CUPS have a coconut-shell bowl. *See* MOUNTED OBJECTS.

coconut cup. Cup with silver mounts, *c.* 1580. H. 21·5 cm. Victoria and Albert Museum, London.

Codman, William Christmas (b. 1839). A designer of silverware who studied art at Norwich, England, and designed ecclesiastical silverware for ELKINGTON & CO., and others. In 1887 Edward Holbrook, later President of the GORHAM COMPANY, 1894–1919, met him in Europe, and engaged him to come to Gorham in 1891 as Chief Designer. He originally designed conventional Victorian ware in Gothic Revival style, some pieces being made for the World's Columbian Exposition at Chicago in 1893. In the 1890s he became an exponent of the ART NOUVEAU STYLE, developing by 1898 his own versions of the European forms. In 1897 he joined with Holbrook in the development and introduction of MARTELÉ ware, which was exhibited at the Paris Exposition of 1900 and which he continued to develop until he retired in 1914. In 1895 he was granted a patent for the CHANTILLY PATTERN for flatware, and he designed for Gorham over 50 other flatware patterns. His work was awarded prizes at the St Louis Exposition of 1904. *See* DEWEY CUP.

Codrington Punch Bowl. The largest-known covered PUNCH-BOWL, its diameter being 44·5 cm, having a hemispherical shape with a STEPPED cover and a finial in the form of a ball, and having two DROP-RING HANDLES. The decoration overall consists of vertical bands of REEDING of varying lengths. The bowl bears the London mark of BENJAMIN PYNE, 1701, and is made of BRITANNIA SILVER. The bowl was made for Christopher Codrington (1668–1710), of Dodington, Gloucestershire, Commander-in-Chief of the Leeward Islands and founder of Codrington College there.

coffee-and-tea machine. A large apparatus for use on a breakfast sideboard to make both coffee and tea. It consists of three urns (each with a TAP and supported by a plinth) that stand on a platform (usually cruciform) which rests on four or six ball feet. The urns are spherical, the central one being larger and considerably higher than the other two. Each urn is fitted with a FIRE-BOX or a small spirit lamp to heat the contents. The central urn (holding about 3·4 litres, or 6 pints) is for hot water and the side urns (about 1·7 litres, or 3 pints each) for tea and coffee. The hot-water urn swivels so that its tap can be used to fill the other two urns, and each small urn has a tap for filling cups. Each urn is removable and portable. At the front of the platform there is sometimes a small projection to support a hemispherical waste (drip) bowl. A variant form has the small urns (sometimes all three) on a rotating platform instead of having a swivelling top urn. The height of the piece is about 60 cm. The globular urns were made in two sections, with the join concealed by a wide horizontal band, usually decorated with various motifs, and some urns were completely decorated with adjacent horizontal bands of REEDING. Such pieces were made *c.* 1790–1820. *See* G. Bernard Hughes, 'Dual-purpose Elegance at Breakfast' in *Country Life*, 4 April 1968, p. 816.

Codrington Punch Bowl. Covered bowl, Benjamin Pyne, London, 1701. W. 44·5 cm. William Rockhill Nelson Gallery of Art (Gift of Mr and Mrs Joseph S. Atha), Kansas City, Mo.

coffee-cup. A type of CUP, of various sizes and in many styles, having one or two handles, or none, for drinking coffee, either black or with milk. The dia-

coffee-and-tea machine. Urns for coffee, tea, and (centre) hot water, Sheffield plate, *c.* 1800–10. H. 61 cm. Folger's Coffee Collection, Procter & Gamble Co., Cincinnati, Ohio.

coffee-jug. Covered jug with beak and thumbpiece, John Gibbons, London, 1706. H. 28 cm. Folger's Coffee Collection, Procter & Gamble Co., Cincinnati, Ohio.

coffee percolator. Sheffield plate, T. & J. Creswick, London, *c.* 1805. H. 35·7 cm. Folger's Coffee Collection, Procter & Gamble Co., Cincinnati, Ohio.

meter is usually smaller than the height, which is the opposite of the proportions of a TEACUP. The usual size for post-prandial coffee is much smaller, and is called a 'can' (*see* CANN) or – especially in the United States – a *'demitasse'*. No full-size coffee-cup of English silver has been recorded. *See* TREMBLEUSE.

coffee dripper. A device for infusing coffee by causing hot water to drip slowly through ground coffee a single time, unlike the repeated filtering characteristic of a COFFEE PERCOLATOR. Various forms are used, but the basic version is a cylindrical receptacle into which is suspended a perforated-bottom container for the coffee, above which is suspended another perforated container for hot water. Some are of fantasy form. *See* BIGGIN; 'ENGINE' COFFEE DRIPPER.

coffee-jug. A vessel in the form of a JUG for serving coffee, having a pouring LIP or BEAK instead of a spout and having a hinged LID with a THUMBPIECE. Some such pieces rest on a stand provided with a heating device.

coffee percolator. A device for infusing coffee by causing heated water to filter repeatedly through ground coffee. Various forms are used, but one type has a cylindrical receptacle (in the form of a cylindrical COFFEE-POT) that is fitted with an interior perforated-bottom container in which is suspended a perforated-bottom receptacle for the ground coffee; a flat circular strainer with a narrow vertical tube is in the perforated receptacle, and the water, when heated, is forced upward through the tube as steam, and then, on condensing in the upper part of the container, descends through the ground coffee, running back into the lower part of the receptacle for the cycle to be repeated. The interior fittings are removable so that the receptacle can be used as an ordinary coffee-pot to serve the coffee when made. An example made of SHEFFIELD PLATE, *c.* 1805, rests on a separate stand with a spirit burner. *See* COFFEE DRIPPER; BIGGIN.

coffee-pot. A type of covered vessel for serving coffee, first made in England soon after the earliest importation of coffee in the mid-17th century (*see* EAST INDIA COMPANY COFFEE-POT). Such pieces have been made in many forms, styles, and sizes. The early examples are straight-sided in the form of a truncated cone or with almost vertical sides having various geometrical sections (e.g. square, octagonal); later pieces are incurved toward the bottom, then pyriform (sometimes on a stemmed foot). In early examples the SPOUT is straight (sometimes ATTENUATED), but later ones have a curved spout or a SWAN-NECK SPOUT; it is set into the body midway, on the bulge of the pyriform pieces. The spout is sometimes decorated at its base or along its entire length with GADROONING, scroll work, CUT CARD pieces or applied mounts. At the tip of some spouts there is a small hinged SPOUT FLAP to conserve heat. The HANDLE is usually opposite the spout, but sometimes is at right-angles to it; it is generally curved or scroll-shaped (plain, double or foliated), but it often occurs in other styles, such as D-shaped. The handle is usually made of wood, set into two metal FERRULES; sometimes it is of silver, attached directly to the body and then preferably separated by ivory insulat-

ing discs or wrapped in a protective covering of raffia or leather. Occasionally there are applied mouldings on the pot, encircling the junction of the handle and the spout, to act as decoration and reinforcement. The cover, usually having an ornamented THUMBPIECE, is generally a high or low dome (but on early examples it is conical) with a decorative finial. The flat base is often encircled, for decoration and strengthening, with several narrow bands. Rococo examples have applied decoration, and neo-classical ones are urn-shaped. Sometimes a coffee-pot rests on a stand in which is set a heating device such as a spirit lamp; *see* COFFEE-POT WITH STAND. The Folger's Coffee Collection, owned by the Procter and Gamble Company, Cincinnati, Ohio, includes many important and varied examples and related articles; *see* its *Catalogue*. *See* SQUARE COFFEE-POT; TURKISH COFFEE-POTT; BEEHIVE COFFEE-POT.

coffee-pot with spigot. A rare type of COFFEE-POT having (instead of a SPOUT) a TAP and a SPIGOT. An early example, London, 1704, in the QUEEN ANNE STYLE, has a tap with a sea-horse spigot, and is decorated with CUT CARD work. *See* COFFEE-URN.

coffee-pot with stand. A type of COFFEE-POT which rests on a stand that supports a heating device, usually a small spirit burner. The coffee-pot has a flat bottom and the stand is usually a tripod composed of three legs (sometimes on decorative feet) joined at their bottom by arms that connect at a central ring in which the burner rests; the top of the stand is encircled by a grooved ring to support the coffee-pot. A coffee-pot of octagonal section resting on a square stand is known. Sometimes a coffee-pot has a stand, such as a flat conforming plate, without a heating device.

coffee-pot/teapot combined. A combined utensil for making and serving coffee and tea, in the form of a TEAPOT upon which rests a coffee dripper; when used as a teapot, the upper unit can be removed and its cover fits the teapot.

coffee service. A type of SERVICE for serving coffee, including a COFFEE-POT, SUGAR-BOWL, CREAM-JUG or MILK-JUG, and often a large TRAY, but not articles of CUTLERY or FLATWARE. The earliest known examples of a MATCHED SERVICE made by the same silversmith and with the same hallmarks (but not necessarily the same date mark) date from the early years of the reign of George I, 1714–27, but such examples are rare, and even a matched service from that period with different pieces made by more than one well-known silversmith is seldom found. *See* BLACK-COFFEE SET; TEA SERVICE.

coffee spoon. A very small SPOON, about 10 cm long, used for stirring coffee in a small coffee-cup (CANN or DEMI-TASSE); it is often decorated by being made of silver gilt or decorated by having the handle enamelled.

coffee-urn. A type of vessel for serving coffee, in the form of a COFFEE-POT but having, instead of a SPOUT, a TAP and SPIGOT. Some large examples have two or three taps and spigots. In order to permit drinking receptacles to be placed under the spigot, the urn has supporting legs or rests on a STAND, sometimes a stand enclosing a warming device. *See* COFFEE-POT WITH SPIGOT; TEA-URN; HOT-WATER URN; COFFEE-AND-TEA MACHINE.

coffin-end spoon. A type of SPOON, made in the United States from the end of the 19th century, having a squared end to the terminal of the handle.

coin holder. A type of container for coins, being cylindrical in form, to hold a stack of circular coins of identical size. Examples were made for British gold sovereigns, usually with an interior spring which propelled the stack to the top of the container for easy removal of the uppermost coin. A modern version is designed to hold British £1 coins (first issued in 1984). *See* COUNTER HOLDER.

coin mount. A coin affixed to an object as a decorative MOUNT, as on the lid or on the TERMINAL of the handle of some TANKARDS.

coin silver. Silver of the standard of FINENESS used for coins. In the United Kingdom it is STERLING SILVER, having a fineness of ·925; in the United States, where the standard of fineness is now ·900, the term 'coin silver' is sometimes used rather than 'sterling silver'. *See* UNITED STATES SILVER MARKS.

coin-silver spoon. A type of SPOON made in the United States *c.* 1800–60, but especially in the 1830s and 1840s, produced from metal derived from melted-down silver coins of various countries, mainly U.S. dollars. Such

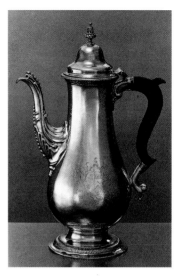

coffee-pot. Pear-shaped, with rococo spout, Joseph and Nathaniel Richardson, Philadelphia, Pa, *c.* 1780–90. H. 30·5 cm. Yale University Art Gallery (Mabel Brady Garvan Collection), New Haven, Conn.

coffee-pot with spigot. Cut-card decoration and sea-horse spigot, William Charnelhouse, London, 1704. H. 24·8 cm. Folger's Coffee Collection, Procter & Gamble Co., Cincinnati, Ohio

coffee-pot with stand. Octagonal pot, Robert Timbrell and Benjamin Bentley, London, 1714, with lamp-stand by Isaac Liger, London, 1709. H. (overall) 38 cm. Folger's Coffee Collection, Procter & Gamble Co., Cincinnati, Ohio.

coffee-urn. Urn with three taps (with ivory spigots), John Swift, London, 1700. H. 48·3 cm. Folger's Coffee Collection, Procter & Gamble Co., Cincinnati, Ohio.

spoons were of varying degrees of FINENESS, depending on the coins used, but all were light in weight and flimsy due to use of minimum metal in order to reduce cost. Such spoons were hand wrought until *c.* 1850, thereafter made by a drop press using steel dies. Most of the examples were in simple styles.

coin weights. A set of small weights, made of silver, in various sizes, to be used to test the weight of a variety of gold coins. They were issued in England by the Royal Mint from 1205, and in 1587 a Royal Proclamation ordered the production of a small case with a set of such weights, together with a small balance. One such case with a set and a balance is in the British Museum, London.

Coker, Ebenezer (fl. 1738–83). A London silversmith apprenticed in 1728 to Joseph Smith and freed in 1740. He registered his first mark in 1738 and several thereafter. He made mainly candlesticks and salvers.

collar. (1) The removable rim on some MONTEITHS. (2) A DOG COLLAR.

collection box. An offertory BOX, circulated among the congregation in a church, having a detachable cover with a slot for inserting money. An English example, *c.* 1677, is in the St Peter Chapel, Tabley Hall, Cheshire. A variant piece was made in the form of a TANKARD with a funnel-shaped opening on the lid. *See* ALMS-DISH; COLLECTION PLATE.

collection plate. An offertory plate, circulated among the congregation in a church; it is generally similar in form to a DINNER PLATE (such secular plates having often been converted for church use). Its form developed into a plate with a projecting handle (sometimes called a 'collecting shoe'), and later, to conceal the amount of each individual donation, a covered box or a bag was used. *See* ALMS-DISH; COLLECTION BOX.

college cup. *See* OX-EYE CUP.

college plate. *See* CAMBRIDGE COLLEGES PLATE; OXFORD COLLEGES PLATE.

collet foot. A type of FOOT that is wide and spreading, found on a bowl or other receptacle; sometimes called a 'spreading foot'.

Collis, G. R. & Co. A silversmith firm of Birmingham, England, the predecessor firm having been founded by Sir Edward Thomason, of Birmingham, who had been apprenticed to MATTHEW BOULTON and was later a rival of RUNDELL, BRIDGE & RUNDELL. When Thomason retired in 1835, the business was taken over by George Richmond Collis, who acquired some of the PAUL STORR models sold by the Rundell firm. The firm showed various pieces at the Birmingham Exhibition of 1849, including copies of the WELLINGTON COASTER.

Colman Monteith. A MONTEITH bearing on the inside of the bowl the engraved arms of John Colman (1670–1751), a wealthy Boston merchant, and having on the bottom the initials 'TB' for Dr Thomas Bullfinch (1694–1757), his son-in-law. The piece has a wide deep hemispherical bowl decorated with encircling FLUTING and resting on a foot decorated with encircling GADROONING; the rim is lavishly decorated with scrolled indentations for hanging glasses, alternating with cartouches surmounted by heads of cherubs. The two DROP-RING HANDLES are suspended from lion's-head masks. It was made by JOHN CONEY, *c.* 1700–10. Two almost identical monteiths (differing from the Colman piece mainly in the gadrooning and the fluting), made by Robert Timbrill, London 1699, and given in 1699 by William Sydenham to the Mercers' Company, London, bear on the inside of the bowls the arms of the Mercers' Company and of the Sydenham family; small reproductions of these were presented by the Mercers' Company to its members in 1894. A reproduction of the Sydenham monteith was made by GARRARD & CO. and presented to the Prince of Wales (later Edward VIII) upon his being admitted to the freedom of the Mercers' Company in 1919.

Colonial Revival style. A style of decoration that has been popular in the United States from the 1870s to recent times, involving the use of a minimum of applied ornament, decoration mainly of ENGRAVING or FLAT CHASING, and reliance upon classic forms rather than decoration.

colonnade centrepiece. A type of CENTREPIECE made in the form of a circular colonnade having the columns resting on a circular base and surmounted by a dome-shaped roof, with usually a figure or other ornamental motif

Colman Monteith. Fluted bowl with scrolled indentations around rim, John Coney, Boston, Mass., c. 1700-10. H. 22 cm. Yale University Art Gallery (Mabel Brady Garvan Collection), New Haven, Conn.

standing in the centre of the base. *See* JUSTICE CENTREPIECE; WILLIAMSBURG CENTREPIECE.

colour-pike finial. The FINIAL secured to the top of a colour pike bearing the colours of a military unit. Two examples, of silver gilt, were presented by William IV to the Grenadier Guards and the Household Cavalry, respectively. The former, presented on 20 June 1830, is in the form of a crown surmounted by the figure of a crowned lion passant guardant; it was made by John George Nutting and is used only on State occasions when the Sovereign is present.

columbine cup. A type of tall STANDING CUP, so called from its resemblance to the columbine flower. It was prescribed, in Nuremberg in the 16th century and later, as a MASTERPIECE to be completed by apprentices, the earliest reference being to one from 1531. The earliest extant example has been attributed, but without established basis, to Wenzel Jamnitzer (1508-85), a German goldsmith. There are two German examples in the Victoria and Albert Museum, London, and one in the British Museum. The complete cups usually remained the property of the guild and hence were not marked. An English example of a cup in substantially such form is in the Royal Collection; made by JOHN BRIDGE, for RUNDELL, BRIDGE & RUNDELL, 1825-6, it is of two-coloured gilded silver. Its bowl and base are lobed and decorated with alternating panels of engraved flowers and foliage, and its cover has a finial in the form of a figure of St George and the Dragon (the finial made from the same mould as that used for the finial of the NATIONAL CUP, but slightly altered). *See* RICHMOND, JOHN, CUP.

Columbus Statue. A life-size statue of Christopher Columbus, modelled by Frédéric Auguste Bartholdi (1834-1904) in Paris and cast in solid silver by the GORHAM COMPANY for exhibition at the World's Columbian Exposition of 1893, held in Chicago. It contained 30,000 troy ounces of silver, and was reputed to be the largest silver sculpture in the world. Although the original statue was subsequently melted down, bronze casts were made.

Columbus Statue. Solid silver, life-size, from model by F. A. Bartholdi, cast by the Gorham Company, 1893 (subsequently melted down). Courtesy, Gorham Collection, Providence, R.I.

column candlestick. A type of TABLE CANDLESTICK having its stem (shaft) in the form of a classical Greek or Roman column, with the stem usually fluted and the capital of either the Corinthian or the Ionic order; the NOZZLE is recessed into the capital and its flat rim serves as the DRIP-PAN. Such candlesticks rest on a circular, square or hexagonal base (often a STEPPED base), and the stem is correspondingly shaped. They are sometimes LOADED to provide stability. *See* CLUSTER-COLUMN CANDLESTICK; MONUMENT CANDLESTICK.

comb-box. A type of BOX, of rectangular shape, for holding combs as part of a TOILET SERVICE. Some examples rest on ornamented feet and have a hinged LID, and are decorated, especially on the lid, with FLAT CHASING or EMBOSSING, sometimes with CHINOISERIE patterns.

Commemorative mark. A mark authorized to be punched on articles of silverware by an Assay Office to commemorate an important anniversary or public event (its individual use being limited to articles assayed during the period specified), but added only at the maker's request. *See* BRITISH COMMEMORATIVE MARKS; IRISH HALLMARKS; BIRMINGHAM ASSAY OFFICE.

Communion-bread knife. A type of KNIFE, known examples being similar in form to the usual domestic bread knife with a broad blade, used in a church to cut household bread (formerly used as an element of the Eucharist). An example made by James Shruder, 1753, is at the parish church of Melbury Sampford, Dorset; it is accompanied by an oblong silver-gilt box. Another example, 1755, accompanied by a silver-gilt sheath, is at Stinsford, Dorset. *See* CHURCH PLATE.

Communion cup. A type of ecclesiastical drinking vessel, sometimes in the form of a GOBLET or WINE-CUP but more often a BEAKER, used for the wine at the Eucharist in Protestant churches from the time of Edward VI, 1547-53. The term was adopted, after the Reformation in the 16th century, to be used instead of CHALICE by the Protestants who did not accept the Catholic doctrine of transubstantiation and hence decided to simplify the form of the cup to differentiate it from the Roman Catholic chalice. In the early 17th century, with the return of ritualism, more elaborate cups, of Gothic design, were introduced, especially in High Church practice; and after the 1840s cups of medieval style were again used. In the 20th century new designs tend to follow contemporary secular styles.

Communion set. A SET of articles used for the Eucharist, including a CHALICE (or COMMUNION CUP), PATEN, and FLAGON. Some small sets, about 10 cm high, were made as portable pocket sets, to be used away from the church.

companion piece. An object that is one of a PAIR, SET or GROUP, in relation to the other(s).

compass-case. A small thin container for a pocket compass. Some silver examples from the late 17th century are engraved with names of towns in Europe and other data possibly useful to a traveller.

composite metal. The same as PLATED METAL.

composite service. A SERVICE which was not made originally by a factory or maker as a complete matching set, but which includes one or more pieces of similar but not identical form and decoration, perhaps made at different times and even by a different factory or maker, or even sometimes by the same maker, possibly supplied as a REPLACER. It differs from a MATCHED SERVICE, where the assembled pieces are made EN SUITE, of identical form and decoration. Pieces of AMBASSADORIAL SILVERWARE usually formed a composite service. *See* GRAND SERVICE; WELLINGTON AMBASSADORIAL SERVICE.

compotier. A small shallow DISH for serving compote (whole fruit cooked in syrup). Usually called in the United States a 'compote'.

condiment frame. *See* WARWICK CRUET STAND.

condiment label. A type of BOTTLE TICKET made to be attached to bottles of varieties of condiments, such as soy, ketchup, chili, garlic, and anchovy.

condiment set. A set of small receptacles for serving various condiments, usually including a SALT-CELLAR, a PEPPER CASTER, and a MUSTARD-POT (or a pair of each), small SPOONS, and, rarely, a tiny paprika-jar, generally all resting on a small TRAY. Sometimes such sets were assembled as a COMPOSITE SERVICE, such as one example with a salt by PAUL STORR, 1814, and the pepper caster and mustard-pot by S.H.Garrard, for GARRARD & CO. LTD, 1922. *See* Michael Snodin, 'Silver Vases and their Purpose' in *The Connoisseur*, January 1977, p.37. *See* DURBIN CONDIMENT SETS.

Coney, John (1655/6-1722). A highly reputed silversmith of Boston, Massachusetts, whose father had emigrated from Boston, Lincolnshire, England. After his apprenticeship ended, *c.*1675, he became one of the most prolific New England silversmiths, having a number of apprentices (including PAUL REVERE II). Silver coins were entrusted to him to be melted down and the metal fashioned into silver objects. In 1702 he engraved the plates for the printing of the paper money to be used in Massachusetts. The range of his work included almost all types of domestic silverware, especially TANKARDS and other drinking vessels, most being made in styles derived from English

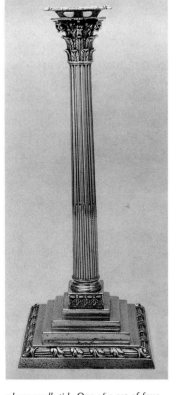

column candlestick. One of a set of four, Corinthiam column, with square stepped base, John Robinson, London, 1704-5. H. 31·5 cm. Colonial Williamsburg, Va.

condiment set. Salt-cellar with spoon (left) by Paul Storr, London, 1814, and pepper caster and mustard-pot by Sebastian Henry Garrard, London, 1922. Goldsmiths' Company, London.

ware. Many of his pieces survive in U.S. museum collections. *See* Hermann Frederick Clarke, *John Coney, Silversmith* (1932). *See* STOUGHTON CUP; MASSACHUSETTS SILVERWARE.

Connecticut silverware. Articles of silverware made in Connecticut, the earliest, from *c.*1700–40, being made by silversmiths coming from Massachusetts and Rhode Island, who were influenced by English styles, and from New York, who were influenced by Dutch and Huguenot styles. From *c.*1740 to *c.*1776 indigenous patterns and styles were developed by locally born craftsmen. Later, when machine-produced ware was introduced, individual craftsmanship was superseded by quantity-production methods. The article most frequently produced was the spoon, and HOLLOW WARE was seldom made in the early years other than some teapots, tankards, and porringers, and later beakers as presentation pieces. Among the total of more than 900 silversmiths recorded as having worked in Connecticut (some only part-time), well-known early craftsmen included Pygan Adams (1712–76), Cornelius Kierstede (1675–1757), John Potwine (1698–1792), and Ebenezer Chittenden (1726–1812). *See* George Munson Curtis, *Early Silver of Connecticut and its Makers* (1913); Peter Bohan and Philip Hammerslough, *Early Connecticut Silver, 1700–1840* (1970).

contemporary silverware. Articles of silverware made since World War II, from *c.*1945 to the present. The making of hand-wrought plate by individual craftsmen, sponsored by the Arts and Crafts Movement of the late 19th century, diminished as the cost of the metal and of labour increased and the use of stainless steel for tableware became more socially acceptable. Design became simplified, influenced by Scandinavian prototypes, and much of the production of silverware was done by firms whose mark was punched on the ware rather than that of the individual craftsmen. Although some talented individual designer-makers have been recognized, the range of contemporary silversmiths and of the forms produced is so wide as to make their inclusion impracticable within the scope of this book, except for a few recognized silversmiths and designers, such as in England GERALD BENNEY, STUART DEVLIN, LESLIE DURBIN, and ALEX STYLES, and in the United States ERIK MAGNUSSEN. *See* Judith Banister, 'Silver for Today and Tomorrow' in *Country Life*, 30 January 1969, p.220; —, 'Silver for the New Universities' in *Country Life*, 29 January 1970, p.236; W. Scott Braznell, 'The Advent of Modern American Silver' in *Antiques*, January 1984, p.236.

contemporary silverware. Parcel-gilt altar cross, Gerald Benney, London, 1982. H. 82 cm. Charterhouse School, Godalming, Surrey.

Convention Hallmarks. A series of new HALLMARKS established under the 'Convention for the Control and Marking of Articles of Precious Metals', arranged through the European Free Trade Association (hence sometimes called 'EFTA Hallmarks'), now ratified by eight European countries, including the United Kingdom and the Republic of Ireland. The Convention provides for the use of standard assaying methods so that articles tested by any Assay Office of a member country and marked with the Convention Hallmarks can be accepted for import and sale in any other member country without the need for any additional testing or marking. A complete set of Convention marks includes: (1) a SPONSOR'S MARK; (2) the Convention Common Control Mark, which depicts a set of balance scales; (3) a FINENESS mark (arabic numerals showing the standard, which for silver to be imported into the U.K. is 925); and (4) the ASSAY OFFICE HALLMARK indicating the place where the piece was assayed (being, in the U.K., that of any of the country's four Assay Offices, or elsewhere that of any recognized Assay Office of member countries). There need be no DATE HALLMARK. Any article made in the U.K. for export may be stamped either, if for export to a member country, with the aforesaid Convention Hallmarks, or, if to a non-member country, with the usual British hallmarks. For articles made abroad for import into the U.K., *see* IMPORTED GOODS HALLMARKS.

Conyngham Inkstand. An elaborate silver-gilt columnar INKSTAND resting on a triangular plinth upon each corner of which is a seated sculptured figure, depicting, respectively, Homer, Milton, and Virgil; in the centre rises a tall palm-tree column surmounted by a sculptured figure of a winged Victory. Between each pair of figures there is an inkwell covered by a Royal crown. It bears the London date mark of 1821-2 and the maker's mark of PHILIP RUNDELL. It was a gift from George IV to the Marquess of Conyngham (whose wife was a member of the Royal Pavilion set at Brighton, Sussex), and has been acquired by the Brighton Museum and Art Gallery.

Cooqus, John (d. 1697). A silversmith who was a native of the Low Countries and settled *c.* 1664 in London, near Pall Mall, but was refused registration by the Goldsmiths' Company due to opposition from London silversmiths. He gained the favour of Charles II, 1660-85, and consequently made silverware for the King's mistress, Nell Gwynn (1650-87), including a MIRROR and a STANDISH. He also made silverware for the Royal Chapel in Whitehall Palace and in 1687 for the Royal Chapel in Dublin, as well as for James II. He was the maker of the famous silver BED for Nell Gwynn in 1674. *See* E. Alfred Jones, 'The Maker of Nell Gwynn's Silver Bedstead' in *Apollo,* July 1942, p. II.

coral objects. Articles of which an essential part is made of coral but which also have silver MOUNTS, such as a TEETHING STICK or a RATTLE. *See* WHISTLE WITH CORAL AND BELLS.

Corbridge Lanx. A 4th-century Roman silver lanx (from Latin, a shallow dish or platter) found in 1735 on the bank of the River Tyne, at Corbridge, Northumberland, England. Although outside the scope of British silverware, it is included here because of its significance as an important example of Roman silverware found in England. The piece is rectangular, completely decorated in the slightly recessed central area with a scene depicting, in the shrine of Apollo on the Greek island of Delos, the figures of five mythological deities; the rim is decorated, as a frame, with alternating grapes and vine leaves. The subject of the decoration has led to the suggestion that the piece was made in the reign, 361-363, of the Roman Emperor Julian the Apostate, who visited Delos in 363, and that the lanx may be a commemorative piece. It belongs to the Duke of Northumberland, and has been on loan at the British Museum, London.

corded. A style of decoration in the form of a twisted rope, found on the edge of some BASKETS or as the form of some swinging BAIL HANDLES.

cordial-pot. A type of small covered pot, with a spout and a handle, similar in appearance to a small TEAPOT, but said to have been used to serve a warmed cordial. It has no strainer where the spout joins the bowl and no insulating rings on the handle, but has a small air-hole in the top of the finial on the cover. Such pieces are said to have been placed, in the late 17th and early 18th centuries, on a tea table when a cordial was customarily drunk with tea. A gilded example, without a hallmark, but with the mark of DAVID WILLAUME I, *c.* 1690-1700, is in the Wilding Bequest at the British Museum, London.

corer. A utensil for removing the core of an apple, in the form of a long thin cylindrical handle extending to a hemispherical tube (early examples are of narrow diameter) having the end sharpened and pointed for cutting. Some examples are in two parts, having the separate corer thin so as to fit into the hollow handle; and some have a small spice CASTER at the end of the handle. Some are entirely of silver, others have an ivory or bone handle. An example made of Sheffield plate has a detachable hollow handle, and the corer has at its other end a blade; the end not in use can be enclosed in the hollow handle. *See* MARROW SCOOP.

Cork silverware. Articles of silverware made from the 15th century in Cork, Ireland, where a guild of GOLDSMITHS was established in 1656 and existed

Conyngham Inkstand. Silver gilt, Philip Rundell, London, 1821-2. H. 72 cm. Brighton Museum and Art Gallery, Sussex.

Corbridge Lanx. Romano-British, 4th century. W. 48·4 cm. The Duke of Northumberland (photo British Museum, London).

until 1842. From *c.*1714 to *c.*1813 Cork sought to have its own ASSAY OFFICE, but was denied it due to opposition from Dublin. Silversmiths in Cork used until *c.*1714, as a mark to indicate quality, a two-sail galley ship between two castles, but later used the word 'Sterling' or 'dollar' (derived from the Spanish dollars that were melted down into ingots), and sent the ware from 1709 to Dublin for assaying and hallmarking. The ware was of high standard of design and technique, and consisted of many types of domestic ware, and especially the FREEDOM BOX. Leading makers of the 18th century were Carden Terry, John Williams, and William Teulon.

corkscrew. An implement with a spiral steel rod ('worm') for drawing a cork from a bottle. The basic form has a ring handle or a T-shaped crossbar, and is often provided with a protective cylindrical sleeve that fits over the rod; the sleeve can sometimes be inserted crosswise through a hole in the rod to form the T-shaped crossbar. Examples have been made in many forms, some with fantasy handles. Some are hinged so as to fold the worm into the ring handle; and some are made for multiple use, having attached an EAR-PICK, a TOOTHPICK, a button-hook, or combinations of these, and some have in the crossbar a WHISTLE on one end and a tobacco-tamper on the other. They are pocket-size except in the case of some large ones intended for cellar or tavern use. An unusual form has an attached sleeve that fits around the neck of the bottle to centre the worm over the cork. Early examples were called *c.* 1657, a 'bottle screw' and from *c.* 1720 a 'corkscrew'. Some have silver handles decorated with ENGRAVING and CHASING. In recent years they have been made for use by various mechanical methods. *See* Charles R. Beard, 'Corkscrews' in *The Connoisseur,* July 1929, p. 28; Bernard M. Watney and Homer D. Babbidge, *Corkscrews for Collectors* (1981). *See* CHAMPAGNE SPIGOT.

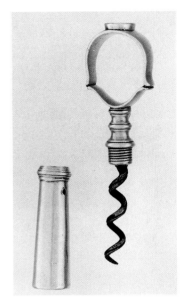

corkscrew. Ring-handle type with protective sleeve, John Harvey, London, *c.* 1750. L. 8·6 cm. Colonial Williamsburg, Va.

corkscrew thumbpiece. Detail of tankard showing lid and part of handle, Jacob van der Spiegel, New York, *c.* 1690–1700. Yale University Art Gallery (Mabel Brady Garvan Collection), New Haven, Conn.

Coronation Canopy Bell. Silver gilt, made for the coronation of George IV by Phipps & Phipps, London, 1820. Courtesy, Asprey & Co. Ltd, London.

corkscrew thumbpiece. A type of THUMBPIECE of elliptical shape, made of a spirally twisted wire, wide at the centre and tapering to the two extremities. Sometimes called a 'scrolled thumbpiece'. A similarly shaped corkscrew terminal is sometimes found on the handle of a spoon.

corncob holder. One of a PAIR of small implements for individual use when eating corn (maize) on the cob, each consisting of a short straight handle with an attached pointed steel prong to be inserted into an end of the cob; the handle is variously shaped and decorated, sometimes as a replica of an ear of corn.

Coronation Canopy Bell. A silver BELL that is attached to each of the CANOPY STAVES used to support the canopy that is held over the head of a British Sovereign in a coronation procession. The number of bearers (each of whom retains a bell as a perquisite of office) has varied from six to probably sixteen. Each bell is about 12·5 cm high. Known examples survive from the coronations of George I (1714), George II (1727), George III (1761), and George IV (1820). The first three are of simple campana (inverted krater) shape, but that of 1820 (silver-gilt, made by Phipps & Phipps, London) has cast decoration and has, instead of a ring handle, an ornate handle topped by a crown above the Royal floral symbols and motto.

Coronation Cup. (1) A silver-gilt GOBLET, decorated with gemstones and enamelling. The bowl is cylindrical, supported by a twisting stem that has a

Coronation Cup (1). Silver-gilt goblet, John Bridge, London, 1826-7. H. 28 cm. Royal Collection; reproduced by gracious permission of Her Majesty the Queen.

Coronation Cup (2). Silver-gilt cup presented to the Earl Marshal on the occasion of the coronation of George V, 1911. Arundel Castle, Sussex. Courtesy, the Duke of Norfolk.

gem-set knop and is decorated with an engraved DIAPER PATTERN; it rests on a domed base having eight encircling ARCADED feet. The lower part of the bowl is embellished with eight shields enamelled with the arms of George IV and of England, Scotland, and Ireland, each shield held by a figure of a kneeling angel. The upper part of the bowl is decorated with chased quatrefoils set with gemstones within wavy lines, below which are diamond rosettes alternating with cabochon sapphires set within arches. The bottom of the bowl is modelled as a fan vault, supported by pierced brackets. The cup, made by JOHN BRIDGE, 1826-7, is in the Royal Collection.

The piece, although called a 'Coronation Cup' in an inventory of 1872 and again in an inventory of George V, has had no connection with any coronation. It was made apparently for a chapel, and was called by E. Alfred Jones, in 1911, a 'George IV Sacramental Cup'. Hence, the usual name is a misnomer. The designer has not been identified. Charles Oman has noted (*The Connoisseur*, April 1954, p. 190) the similarity of its Gothic Revival style to that of A. W. N. PUGIN, but avoided attributing the piece to him (Pugin having been only fourteen years old when the cup was made); nevertheless, in a later article by Shirley Bury, Alexandra Wedgwood, and Michael Snodin (*Burlington Magazine*, June 1979, p. 353), the piece is ascribed to Pugin on stylistic grounds – based on five unexecuted designs signed by Pugin and countersigned by John Gawler Bridge – with the suggestion that a more appropriate name for it would be the 'Pugin Cup'.

(2) One of a series of TWO-HANDLED CUPS that have, by tradition, been given by successive British Sovereigns – since George III in 1760 – at the date of the coronation to the Duke of Norfolk, as hereditary Earl Marshal, in recogniton of his services in arranging the coronation ceremonial. The cups (the latest having been given by Elizabeth II in 1953) vary in style and decoration on each occasion; those of earlier years are of gold, and later ones of silver gilt.

See BOWES, SIR MARTIN, CUP; ELIZABETH II CORONATION CUP.

Coronation Service. A COMPOSITE SERVICE, the articles of which were ordered by, and bear the 1801 arms of, George III. The pieces, made mainly by THOMAS HEMING, *c.* 1760, include WAITERS, TUREENS, BASKETS, and SALTS. The service is in the Royal Collection.

Coronation Spoon. (1) A silver-gilt anointing spoon that is part of the British coronation regalia. It is 26.1 cm long, and is believed to date from the 12th century, possibly having been used at the coronation of King John, 1199 (although possibly rebuilt when regilded for the coronation of Charles II in 1661). The bowl has chased decoration and a central ridge, possibly to permit two fingers of the anointing priest to be dipped into the consecrated oil. The ATTENUATED handle is set with four freshwater pearls, and is decorated with chasing up to its WRITHEN top. It holds the oil poured from the Royal AMPULLA and used to anoint the new Sovereign's head, breast, and palms. (2) One of a set of four silver-gilt spoons made by EDWARD BARNARD & SONS LTD, London, 1902, at the time of the coronation of Edward VII; each spoon has its terminal and bowl differently decorated, with emblems of, respectively, England, Scotland, Wales, and Ireland.

Coronation 'Wine Fountain'. A silver-gilt ornament included in the Coronation Plate preserved in the Jewel House of the Tower of London and there designated the 'Coronation Wine Fountain', but more correctly called in an early document a 'perfume fountain', as the piece has a receptacle for burning perfume and has pipes at the sides as outlets for perfumed water. It was presented by the City of Plymouth to Charles II upon his restoration in 1660. The form is a wide circular basin, embossed with figures of Neptune, Amphitrite, and sea-monsters, which is supported by a domed base having four feet in the form of mermaids. The basin supports a square column that has on each side a niche in which is set, alternately, figures in-the-round of Neptune and a sea-nymph. Above the column there is a finial (removable when the perfume is being burned) in the form of a standing female figure grasping two snakes, said possibly to depict Medusa. Although it has been claimed to be the earliest English 'Wine Fountain' (albeit it is without a spigot), it bears no mark, and has been said to be more likely by a Hamburg goldsmith, Peter Oehr I, an example of whose work, *c.* 1650, it is said to resemble. *See* Charles C. Oman, 'The Civic Gifts to Charles II' in *Apollo*, November 1968, p. 336. *See* WINE FOUNTAIN.

Corpus Christi College (Oxford) Hourglass Salt. A parcel-gilt HOURGLASS SALT of hexagonal section, having three tiers of six triangular silver panels on the bowl, base, and cover, respectively, each decorated with openwork ARABESQUE tracery, over a ground of silver gilt, with depictions of hunting scenes with hares, hounds, and stags, each alternate panel having on it a pelican. At the junction of the hourglass panels there is a large pierced knop with a scene, on a green ground, depicting the 'Coronation of the Virgin'. The cover has an elaborate finial upon which are small figures of three pelicans with pearls suspended from their beaks and supporting a silver-mounted crystal. The rim of the salt and of the cover are decorated with motifs of pelicans, between which are the initials 'R d' for Ricardus Dunelmensis, being Richard Fox (1447/8-1528) as Bishop of Durham, 1494-1501 (not 'RE' for Ricardus Exoniensis, as was formerly alleged, signifying his earlier appointment as Bishop of Exeter, 1487-92), and the founder, 1515-16, of Corpus Christi College, Oxford (hence the salt being sometimes called there the 'Founder's Salt'), where the date now attributed to the salt is *c.* 1494-1501.

Corpus Christi College (Oxford) Pomegranate Cup. A silver-gilt covered 'FONT-SHAPED' CUP of which the bowl, base, and low-domed cover are each decorated with EMBOSSING with a double row of circular lobed ornaments. The wide vertical stem is decorated with thick stalks and rests on a spreading foot. The decoration on the contemporary cover includes a chased Tudor rose, a fleur de lis, and two pomegranates, and atop it there is a finial in hemispherical form decorated with relief foliage and, at the flat top, an engraved Tudor rose. The rim of the bowl and of the finial have edges of ROPE MOULDING. The piece bears London hallmarks of 1515-16 and an unidentified maker's mark. The cup was presented to Corpus Christi College, Oxford, by Bishop Richard Fox (1447/8-1528), the college's founder in 1515-16, and the tradition (supported by the Tudor roses and the pomegranates) is that it had been received by him as a gift from Catherine of Aragon (one of whose emblems was a pomegranate) for his services in advocating her marriage to Henry VIII; hence it is usually referred to as the 'Pomegranate Cup' rather than as the College's 'Founder's Cup'. See Norman M. Penzer, 'Tudor "Font-shaped" Cups' in *Apollo*, December 1957, p. 177, fig. VI.

corrugated teapot. A type of TEAPOT that has vertical sides which are wholly or partially corrugated by adjacent alternating ridges and grooves, sometimes with flat areas between the corrugation.

Cotterill, Edmund (fl. 1795-1860). An English sculptor, with address at 67 John St, Fitzroy Square, London, whose works were exhibited at the Royal Academy from 1822 to 1858. He became a designer and modeller of silverware, and was engaged by GARRARD & CO. LTD, as head of its design department from 1831 until his death in 1860. He designed also for RUNDELL, BRIDGE & RUNDELL. He was especially skilled in designing and modelling figures of horses, as depicted on a number of HORSE-RACING TROPHIES (including the QUEEN'S CUP) and CENTREPIECES (e.g., the MARLBOROUGH CENTREPIECE and the ALHAMBRA TABLE FOUNTAIN). He also designed pieces depicting scenes from English history (e.g., the CRÉCY SIDEBOARD DISH), from mythology (e.g., the HERCULES VASE), and from the novels of Sir Walter Scott (e. g., the BALFOUR/BOTHWELL CENTREPIECE and the TALISMAN CENTREPIECE). Some of such pieces were awarded as prizes for horse races at Ascot and Goodwood. *See* EGLINTON TESTIMONIAL; QUEEN'S TANKARD; 'QUEEN VICTORIA'S DOGS' CENTREPIECE.

counter holder. A type of container for gaming counters, being cylindrical in form, to hold a stack of similar circular counters. Some examples have openwork sides to reveal the stacked counters within. *See* COIN HOLDER.

coursing button. A type of BUTTON worn by members of coursing clubs in the last quarter of the 18th century and the early 19th century, bearing the engraved depiction of a greyhound and the name of the wearer's greyhound. (Coursing is the pursuit of running game by dogs that follow by sight instead of by scent.)

Courtauld. A family, of Huguenot ancestry, highly reputed for its three generations of silversmiths. Augustin(e) Courtauld (1665-1706), a Protestant, fled in 1687 from his native St Pierre, on the Île d'Oléron, near La Rochelle, France; he was a merchant but after settling in London in 1687/9 he became a cooper. His eldest son, Augustin(e) Courtauld II (1685/6-1751), was born in France, travelled to London in 1687 with his father and was granted Letters of Denization (Naturalization) in 1696; he was apprenticed in 1701 to SIMON PANTIN until 1708 when he was made by service a Freeman of the Goldsmiths' Company. He established himself as a plateworker in 1708/9 in Church St, St Martin's Lane, where he remained until moving to Chandos St in 1729. In 1708 he registered his first mark 'CO' for use on BRITANNIA SILVER, which he continued to use after 1720. In 1729 he registered his second mark 'AC' for use on STERLING SILVER, and made much domestic

Coronation Spoon. Silver-gilt anointing spoon, *c.* 12th century, with the ampulla re-made in the reign of Charles II. Tower of London (Crown copyright, HMSO).

Coronation 'Wine Fountain'. Silver gilt, London, *c.* 1660. W. 76·2 cm. Tower of London (Crown copyright, HMSO).

counter holder. English, *c.* 1660. H. 7 cm. Courtesy, Brand Inglis Ltd, London.

covered jug (pitcher). One of a pair, with acanthus decoration and thumbpiece on lid, Charles Kandler, London, 1733. H. 27·3 cm. Courtesy, Garrard & Co. Ltd, London.

covered porringer. Peter van Dyck, New York, *c.* 1705–25. W. (of bowl) 13·7 cm. Yale University Art Gallery (Mabel Brady Garvan Collection), New Haven, Conn.

plate. In 1739 he registered his third mark 'AC' in script capitals. He was the most prolific silversmith of the family; he is best known for his pieces in QUEEN ANNE STYLE and restrained form, especially his TRAYS, SALVERS, and PRESENTATION CUPS. Examples of MINIATURE SILVERWARE formerly attributed to him have recently been ascribed to David Clayton.

Peter Courtauld (1690-1729), second son of Augustin(e) Courtauld I by his second marriage, was born in England, was apprenticed from 1705 to 1712, also to Simon Pantin, and was freed in 1712. He registered his first mark for Britannia Silver in 1721, while still employed by Pantin, and his second mark for Sterling silver a month later. His address was Litchfield St. No silverware identified with him is known.

Samuel Courtauld I (1720-65), second son of Augustin(e) Courtauld II, was apprenticed to his father from 1734 to 1741 and then worked for him as a journeyman until 1746. He registered his first mark 'SC' when he started under his own name, but still working from his father's premises in Chandos St. When his father died in 1751 he registered his second mark and moved to 21 Cornhill in the City, staying there until his death. He departed from the style of his father, adopting the ROCOCO STYLE and making many pieces of great importance. He bequeathed the business to his widow, Louisa Perina Ogier (*c.*1730-1807), who registered her own mark 'LC' in 1765; she continued the business but not working herself as a goldsmith, being assisted mainly to George Cowles (d. 1811), a former apprentice. He was made a Freeman in 1765, and in 1768 was made a partner, registering the joint mark 'LC/GC'. They continued work in rococo style but also adopted the NEO-CLASSICAL STYLE, with which they excelled. The partnership ended in 1777 when Cowles was succeeded by Louisa's eldest son, Samuel Courtauld II (1752-1821), at 21 Cornhill and they registered the joint mark 'LC/SC' in 1777; they sold the business in 1780 to another goldsmith, John Henderson, and Samuel emigrated to America where he became a merchant. (Cowles entered his second mark in 1777 as a plateworker in Lombard St.)

A collection of Courtauld silverware has been assembled by the Courtauld family and Courtaulds plc, and is occasionally lent to museums for display. *See* E. Alfred Jones, *Some Silver Wrought by the Courtauld Family* (1940); Edward Wenham, 'The Courtauld Family' in *Antique Collector*, January-February 1945, p. 12; Christopher Lever, 'The Courtauld Family of Goldsmiths' in *Apollo*, August 1974, p. 138; John F. Hayward, *The Courtauld Silver* (1975); Judith Banister, 'Three Generations in Silver' in *Country Life*, 3 June 1982, p. 1628.

Courtenay Waiters. A set of four WAITERS of hexagonal shape, made by BENJAMIN PYNE, 1698-9, having a central medallion engraved with the arms of Sir William Courtenay (ancestor of the Earls of Devon, of Powderham Castle, Devon), and a surround completely decorated with EMBOSSING; the engraving is in the style of SIMON GRIBELIN and the embossing in the style of Jean Lepautre. Two are in the Victoria and Albert Museum, London, and two in the United States.

covered monteith. Bowl, London, 1806, and cover, London, 1831. W. 30·5 cm. City Council, Lichfield.

cover. An unattached removable covering or top (as distinguished from a LID which is usually hinged) for closing the mouth of a BOWL, TUREEN, VASE or other open vessel. It occurs in various shapes – flat, conical, domed – and is usually surmounted by a decorative HANDLE termed a KNOP or FINIAL; *see* CUSHION SHAPE; DISH COVER; DOME COVER; THIMBLE COVER. Various methods are used to secure a cover on a receptacle; *see* BAYONET COVER; DROP-IN COVER; SCREW COVER; SLIP-ON COVER.

covered jug. A type of JUG (pitcher) that has a hinged LID with a THUMB-PIECE, and usually a BEAK SPOUT and a scroll handle. Some unusual examples made in Massachusetts are barrel-shaped with encircling applied reeded bands, and have a TAU HANDLE.

covered monteith. An unusual type of MONTEITH which is accompanied by a low-domed COVER having a finial. An example owned by the City Council of Lichfield, Staffordshire, has its bowl and cover decorated with embossed and chased fruit, flowers, and a mask, its cover surmounted by a seated figure of a boy pouring from a jug into a cup, and its handles in the form of demi-figures of satyrs emerging from cornucopias; the bowl bears the maker's mark 'SH', London, 1806, and the cover the maker's mark 'EF', London, 1831.

covered porringer. A type of PORRINGER, of the shallow one-handled form, having a COVER, usually flat or low-domed, with a finial in the form of a ring or shaped object.

covered posset-pot. A SMALL TWO-HANDLED CUP (of the type sometimes called in England a POSSET-POT or a PORRINGER) that has a COVER. The cover sometimes has a short cylindrical hollow handle with a horizontal flat flange at the top. Such pieces were not uncommon in England, and some were made in Massachusetts and New York, *c.* 1670–1700.

covered sauce-boat. A SAUCE-BOAT, usually of the type with one pouring lip and a single handle, that is provided with a COVER. Such pieces are found only infrequently, the usual type of covered receptacle for sauce being a SAUCE-TUREEN.

covered standing salt. A type of STANDING SALT that is often massive, tall and elaborately decorated, differing from the usual cylindrical PEDESTAL SALT by having an elevated cover above the salt receptacle which is often concealed within an imposing architectural framework. Sometimes the cover is supported by scrolled BRACKETS resting on the rim of the base. Such salts were used as a GREAT SALT. *See* BUTLEIGH SALT; HERCULES SALT; LEAKE SALT; STEEPLE SALT; VYVYAN SALT.

covered tazza. A rare type of TAZZA that has a COVER; usually the saucer-shaped bowl is shallow and has sloping sides, the cover being an inverted form of the bowl but having a tall finial, sometimes surmounted by a figure. An example, 1584, owned by the Goldsmiths' Company, London, is engraved and embossed with fruit, insects, fish, and shells, has a knopped stem resting on a TRUMPET FOOT, and has a finial surmounted by a figure of a standing warrior holding a lance and a shield; on the BOSS of the bowl is an embossed bust of a Roman warrior with a helmet. *See* SALISBURY TAZZA.

cow creamer. A type of CREAM-JUG in the form of a cow with a covered opening on its back for filling, its open mouth serving as the SPOUT and its recurved tail as the handle. On some examples a hinged lid on the cow's back is decorated with flowers in relief, and sometimes a relief fly or bee serves as its handle; a few have a textured representation of hair on the cow. On some there is a collar encircling the neck. Some are gilded to conceal FIRE MARKS. Such pieces were a speciality of John Schuppe (fl. 1753–73), of London, but an earlier example by DAVID WILLAUME II is known. A variant type is in the form of a goat, made by J. and J. Aldous, 1834. *See* Charles C. Oman, 'English Silver Cow Milk Jugs' in *Apollo*, August 1944, p.42; G. Bernard Hughes, 'Silver Cow Milk-Jugs' in *Country Life*, 7 January 1954, p. 26.

Cowper Cup. A thistle-shape CUP that incorporates, in the lower half of the bowl and in the base, symbolic rings of oak wood and has, below the rim, a band of applied silver oak leaves; it bears an engraved tribute to the English poet William Cowper (1731–1800) and his poem 'Yardley Oak'.

cowrie (or cowry) shell. The shell of a small gastropod mollusc, found mainly in the Indian Ocean and the Red Sea, that was used in ancient times as an amulet or as a form of money, but later was made into a serviceable ob-

covered tazza. Silver gilt, London, 1584. H. 34·5 cm. Goldsmiths' Company, London.

Cowper Cup. Thistle shape, with oak rings around bowl and base. Courtesy, Asprey & Co. Ltd, London.

crab server. Silver with gilt interior, accompanied by serving spoon, Asprey & Co. Ltd, London, 1983. W. 16·5 cm. Courtesy, Asprey & Co. Ltd, London.

ject by the addition of silver MOUNTS. The shell is found in many varieties, but is usually yellowish with dark spots. Objects so made include a SAUCE-BOAT (the base, rim, lip, and handle being of silver), NUTMEG GRATER, PAP-BOAT, SPOON, and SNUFF-BOX.

crab server. A dinner-table or sideboard receptacle for serving dressed crab, made in the form of a blue crab, with hinged lid and accompanied by a serving spoon. A silver-gilt SALT in the form of a crab was made by NICHOLAS SPRIMONT in 1742–3.

cradleboard cover. An article made for and used by the Indians of north-eastern North America, including Canada. It is used to secure a well-wrapped papoose to its cradleboard. The piece is composed of wide bands pinned together, two upright forming the sides and three horizontal, all decorated with pierced hearts, diamonds, and other motifs and surface engraving, and having small heart-shaped ornaments dangling from the lower edge of the horizontal bands. An example, made by Pierre Huguet called Latour, Montreal, *c.* 1771–1829, was found in 1916 near Ottawa, and another has since been found. A related article is a 'cradle shade' made of wool and silk ribbons with silver brooches.

cream-basket. A type of small BASKET for serving cream, similar in form to other types, but usually boat-shaped and having a glass LINER. Examples were made EN SUITE with a SUGAR-BASKET.

cream-boat. A type of boat-shaped receptacle used for serving cream, usually having an undulating rim, a handle at one end, and an everted pouring lip at the other end; it is similar in general form to a SAUCE-BOAT but smaller. Early examples stand on three legs, one being under the pouring lip, and have a SCROLL HANDLE or a FLYING SCROLL HANDLE; later ones have a loop handle and rest on a spreading base. Such pieces were made from the 1730s into the 1760s. *See* G. Bernard Hughes, 'Georgian Silver Cream-Boats and Pails' in *Country Life,* 25 October, p. 960; Joan Sayers Brown, 'Selected Silver Cream Boats' in *Antiques,* February 1979, p. 357.

cream-jug. A type of small JUG (pitcher) for pouring cream, similar to a MILK-JUG but smaller and sometimes having a wider pouring lip for the thick cream. It is often pear-shaped, but is sometimes baluster-shaped, melon-shaped, vase-shaped, or in the form of a HELMET JUG. It has an everted pouring lip (sometimes a BEAK), opposite which is a single handle, usually in the form of a SCROLL HANDLE or DOUBLE SCROLL HANDLE. Many have a wavy rim. It rests on a spreading base or on three small feet. The decoration is ENGRAVING, CHASING, GADROONING or, in the ROCOCO STYLE, much EMBOSSING; some chased examples have depictions of farmyard scenes or of milkmaids, but such work is sometimes not contemporary. Sometimes called a 'cream-pot'. *See* G. Norman-Wilcox, *English Silver Cream-jugs of the 18th Century* (1952); G. Bernard Hughes, 'Georgian Milk and Cream Jugs' in *Apollo,* June 1956,

cradleboard cover. Pierced decoration and dangling ornaments, Pierre Huguet called Latour, Montreal, *c.* 1771–1829. W. 36·8 cm. National Museums of Canada, Ottawa.

p. 199; Jonathan Stone, 'English and Irish Cream Jugs' in *Antiques,* January 1965, p. 94. *See* CREAMER; CREAM-BOAT; CREAM-PAIL; COW CREAMER.

cream ladle. A small type of LADLE that has a curved handle and usually a lipped bowl, for use with a CREAM-PAIL or CREAM-BASKET.

cream-pail. A small pail for serving cream. Early examples, *c.* 1730–60, are BUCKET-SHAPED with a swinging BAIL HANDLE; most, from the period 1760–80, are cylindrical. Some are decorated with encircling bands of REEDING, and some with pierced work have a glass LINER. *See* CREAMER; PIGGIN.

cream scoop. A type of implement for skimming cream off milk. Examples are in the form of a flat semicircular band, attached vertically to a long straight wood handle. Examples were made in Scotland, *c.* 1790–1800.

creamer. A receptacle for holding and serving cream. *See* CREAM-JUG; CREAM-BOAT; CREAM-PAIL; CREAM-BASKET; COW CREAMER. Such articles date from the early 18th century, when tea-drinkers first added milk or cream to their tea. *See* Francis Townshend, 'Silver for Cream in Ireland' in *Country Life,* 23 September 1965, p. 757.

cream-jug. Jug with decoration of flat chasing and engraving, Charles Leslie, Dublin, *c.* 1735. H. 11·5 cm. Courtesy, Asprey & Co. Ltd, London.

Crécy Sideboard Dish. A silver-gilt oval SIDEBOARD DISH in the centre of which there is depicted in high relief a scene from the Battle of Crécy (where in 1346 Edward III defeated Philip VI of France); in the battle the English under Edward, the Black Prince (son of Edward III), armed with longbows, met and defeated horsemen under the blind King of Bohemia, John of Luxembourg. The wide border is decorated with a wreath of oak leaves and acorns, together with interspersed masks and a rim of GADROONING. The dish was designed by EDMUND COTTERILL and made in 1834–5 by William Bateman I (*see* BATEMAN) for Rundell, Bridge & Co. (*see* RUNDELL, BRIDGE & RUNDELL) for the 1st Duke of Cambridge (1774–1850), seventh son of George III. The dish was made as a companion piece for the AGINCOURT SIDEBOARD DISH. It was sold on 7 June 1904 at Christie's, London, by the executors of the 2nd Duke of Cambridge, to D. Davis. It bears an inscription stating that it was presented in 1905 by the citizens of Glasgow to Robert Gourlay, a lawyer in that city, one of whose descendants sold it at Sotheby's Belgravia, London, on 10 July 1975, when it was acquired by an undisclosed private collector. It is sometimes called the 'Crécy Shield'.

cream scoop. Semicircular band, by Charles Jamieson, Edinburgh, *c.* 1800. Courtesy, Christie's, London.

creeper. A type of small FIRE-DOG (andiron), a pair of which are placed between a pair of large firedogs and serve as the main support for the logs, the large fire-dogs, often made of or cased with silver, being primarily for display. The creepers also sometimes have silver mounts.

Crespin, Paul (1694–1770). A London silversmith of Huguenot family, apprenticed to John Pons in 1713 and freed in 1720. He entered his first and

Crécy Sideboard Dish. Silver gilt, William Bateman I, London, 1834–5. W. 81·5 cm. Courtesy, Sotheby's, London.

Crespin Tureen. Tureen with stand, Paul Crespin, London, 1740, L. 55 cm. Toledo Museum of Art (Gift of Florence Scott Libbey), Toledo, Ohio.

second marks in 1720/1, and three later marks in 1739, 1740, and 1757, all from the address of the 'Golden Ball', St Anne's, Compton St, Soho, where he was a neighbour of NICHOLAS SPRIMONT. In 1724 he made a 'vessel for bathing', weighing 6,030 oz., for John V of Portugal, but nothing more is now known of it; he also made two other large basins, 1722, both having Portuguese provenance (indicating that he had other commissions from the Portuguese Royal Family). He made many pieces for members of the English nobility, including the 2nd Duke of Portland (some of them now at Welbeck Abbey), the 4th Duke of Devonshire, the 3rd Duke of Marlborough, and the 4th Earl of Dysart. His best-known work is a CRUET STAND, 1721, now at Colonial Williamsburg, Virginia. With other Huguenot silversmiths, he made in 1720 a large service for Catherine I of Russia; this, together with two silver-gilt TWO-HANDLED CUPS, is now in the Hermitage, Leningrad. Several pieces of original design were made *c.* 1740–1, including a CENTREPIECE now in the Royal Collection and the CRESPIN TUREEN. Examples of his work made *c.* 1743 feature coral and sea-shells. His surviving work is of the highest standard of design and execution. In 1747 he became bankrupt, but settled his debts and continued as a silversmith until he retired to Southampton in 1760. *See* Edward Wenham, 'Paul Crespin' in *Antique Collector,* November-December 1945, p. 202; Tessa Murdoch, 'Harpies and Hunting Scenes: Paul Crespin, Huguenot Goldsmith' in *Country Life,* 29 August 1985, p. 556.

Crespin Tureen. A massive SOUP-TUREEN, with a stand and LINER, made by PAUL CRESPIN, 1740, with the bowl resting on two figures in-the-round of recumbent goats or hinds, and with a cover decorated with various fruits and a finial in the form of two apples with cherries and leaves. The piece bears a striking resemblance to the ASHBURNHAM CENTREPIECE with its goat supports and its fruit finial, bearing the mark of Crespin but attributed to NICHOLAS SPRIMONT. The liner is engraved with a ducal coronet and the Seymour crest. The piece was possibly made for Charles Seymour, 6th Duke of Somerset (1662–1748). It was sold at Christie's, London, on 15 June 1888 to Baron Ferdinand de Rothschild for Waddesdon Manor, Aylesbury, and was inherited by his sister Alice, who left it to her great-nephew, James de Rothschild. Baroness James de Rothschild sold it at Christie's, London, on 13 May 1964. Since 1964 it has been at the Toledo Museum of Art, Toledo, Ohio. *See* Arthur G. Grimwade, 'Crespin or Sprimont? An unsolved problem of Rococo silver' in *Apollo,* August 1969, p. 126, fig. 1. *See* BOLTON CENTREPIECE.

Cressener Cup. A covered silver-gilt 'FONT-SHAPED' CUP in English GOTHIC STYLE, having a shallow circular bowl with a plain straight-sided rim and supported by a wide TRUMPET FOOT whose edge has a rolled moulding. The low-domed cover has a flattened ball finial that encloses a rock-crystal disc covering a PRINT depicting, in CHAMPLEVÉ enamelling, the owner's coat of arms. The cup bears the date letter for 1503–4. It was made for John Cressener

Cressener Cup. Silver gilt, 1503–4. H. 16·5 cm. Goldsmiths' Company, London.

(d. 1536) of Hinckford Hundred, Essex, and was owned by members of the Cressener family until 1722, then by descendants in the Tufnell family until 1908, when it was acquired by the Goldsmiths' Company. *See* Norman M. Penzer, 'Tudor "Font-shaped" Cups' in *Apollo,* December 1957, p. 175, fig. III.

crest. A heraldic device formerly displayed on a helmet, not on a shield, and sometimes inscribed inexpensively on silverware to indicate ownership in lieu of a costly, engraved COAT OF ARMS. A crest may be common to more than one family, unlike a coat of arms or an ACHIEVEMENT, and hence its presence on a piece of silverware does not establish PROVENANCE. *See* ARMORIAL WARE.

cresting. A decorative motif which, in silverware, is in the form of an ornamental border, often foliated, protruding upward along the horizontal top rim of a SALT, MIRROR, CUP or other article, or along the crook of a CROSIER. When the ornament points downward, it is called 'inverted cresting'. *See* WARDEN HILL'S SALT; LIMERICK CROSIER; CROCKET.

Cripplegate Badge. Silver, *c.* 1693. H. 21·6 cm. Cripplegate Foundation, London.

Cripplegate Badge. A BADGE, *c.* 1693, worn on special occasions by the Beadles of Cripplegate Parish (now Ward) in the City of London. The badge depicts, within a foliated CARTOUCHE, the so-called Cripplegate which was one of the four original gates of the Roman city of Londinium and stood in present-day Fore Street north of London Wall and close to the church of St Giles; the gate was the entrance for a covered footway leading from the city to the Barbican outpost defences. The Anglo-Saxon word for a 'covered footway' was 'crepel', and presumably that word and the proximity of the church of St Giles, the patron saint of cripples, led to the adoption of the name Cripplegate. The badge depicts apocryphal figures of cripples passing through the gate; at its top is a plaque inscribed 'The Gift of ye Stewards for ye Year 1693' below which are four names. The badge bears a maker's mark of a crowned monogram 'DA'. It is now owned by the Cripplegate Foundation, London, established in 1891.

Cripplegate Tazza. A parcel-gilt TAZZA having a knopped stem decorated with STRAPWORK and a domed foot. The bowl has a BOSS with embossed decoration depicting the head of a Roman warrior in profile within a circular frame, accompanied by engraved scrolls. The mark is a Tudor rose, 1586. The tazza is owned by the Cripplegate Foundation, London. (The piece has similarities to a silver-gilt tazza marked with a grasping hand between the letters 'HC' – perhaps for Hugh Crook, 1579 – sold at Christie's, London, in 1966.)

Cripplegate Tazza. Parcel gilt, 1586. H. 12·5 cm. Cripplegate Foundation, London.

crocket. A type of ornament, often resembling curved and bent foliage, projecting upward along the sloping side of a pinnacle, finial, etc. It should be distinguished from the BRACKET that serves as an ornament or support on some STANDING CUPS and STANDING SALTS. *See* WARDEN HILL'S SALT; CRESTING.

Cromwell Mazer. A shallow MAZER having an everted and deep silver rim band and a silver PRINT with an engraving depicting a seated figure of the Virgin and Child. Made in the 15th century, it was formerly owned by the Lambert family who had received it as a gift from Oliver Cromwell's son Richard Cromwell (1626–1712), Lord Protector, 1658–9. Since 1914 it has been owned by the Victoria and Albert Museum, London.

Crosby Cup. A silver-gilt TWO-HANDLED CUP having a spreading foot on a square base, an ovoid bowl, and two vertical loop handles, each in the form of a satyr holding a bunch of grapes in his left hand and with uplifted right hand holding the end of the chain of husks that decorate the bowl. The piece was commissioned in 1772 by the Court of Common Pleas of the City of London, to be presented to Sir Brass Crosby (1725–93) who in 1770-1 had been Lord Mayor of London, and, with the support of Aldermen John Wilkes (1727–97) and Richard Oliver, had resisted the attempt of the House of Commons to restrain printers from printing criticism of George III and to arrest them. The bowl of the cup has two applied scenic plaques, one depicting the triumphant carriage procession of the Lord Mayor returning to the Mansion House and the other an allegorical scene with a crowned figure symbolizing London, flanked by figures of Fame, Justice, Liberty, and Britannia, and having on the shoulder medallions with relief portraits of the Lord Mayor and the two Aldermen. There is, engraved on the plinth supporting the finial upon which a *putto* is kneeling, an inscription 'United in the Cause of Liberty'. Encircling the neck is a commemorative inscription. The piece was probably made by John Romer and the plaques (possibly also the portraits) were probably modelled by George Daniel Gaab (d. 1784); it is

Cromwell Mazer. Central print depicting the Virgin and Child, second half of the 15th century. D. 20·5 cm. Victoria and Albert Museum, London.

inscribed on the base 'Portal and Gearing Fecit Ludgate Hill', but they were the retailers, not the makers. The cup was presented by Lord Wakefield, Lord Mayor of London in 1935, to the Mansion House to commemorate the City's struggle for freeedom of the press. Two other cups, made by Charles Wright, were presented to Wilkes and Oliver; vase-shaped in NEO-CLASSICAL STYLE, having on the cover a figure of Liberty wearing a Liberty Cap, the Wilkes cup, 1772, is lost, but the Oliver cup has been at the Mansion House since 1867. *See* Judith Banister, 'In the Cause of Liberty' in *Country Life*, 12 November 1981, p.1671. *See* SONS OF LIBERTY BOWL (which had been presented at an earlier date to American supporters of John Wilkes); 'I LOVE LIBERTY' SPOON.

crosier (or **crozier**). The pastoral STAFF of a bishop, abbot or abbess, resembling a shepherd's crook and borne as a symbol of office. A few dating from the 12th century, and several from the 14th and 15th centuries, have survived, the highly decorated silver-gilt and enamelled examples including: (1) the WILLIAM OF WYKEHAM CROSIER, (2) the LIMERICK CROSIER, and (3) that made *c.* 1489-91 for Richard Fox (1447/8-1528), Bishop of Exeter, 1487-92, and of Durham, 1494-1501, the founder in 1515-16 of Corpus Christi College, Oxford. These are decorated along the staff and under the crook with figures of saints standing in Gothic niches and along the crook with CRESTING. The term 'crosier' has sometimes been erroneously applied to an archbishop's processional cross-staff bearing a crucifix.

cross. An ornamental or devotional article usually in the form of an upright joined at the top by a horizontal arm as a T (a tau cross) or with a transverse arm (a Latin cross), or made in a number of other forms and styles, such as a Maltese Cross, cross pattée, etc. Silver examples were made in different forms and sizes and for a variety of purposes. When the cross bears a painted or relief figure of Christ, it is termed a 'crucifix'. *See* ALTAR CROSS; PECTORAL CROSS; PROCESSIONAL CROSS; ROSARY CROSS.

'Crown Goldsmith'. The goldsmith (silversmith) – being an individual or, after *c.*1760, a firm – appointed by the British Sovereign to be responsible for maintaining the Crown Regalia and Royal silverware, and for preparing the pieces used in the course of the coronation service. The earliest such appointment was made by Henry VII before 1509; from *c.*1660 the appointee was called the 'Principal Goldsmith' (several others being appointed as 'Subordinate Goldsmiths'), and from *c.*1782 the title became 'Goldsmith in Ordinary to His Majesty'. Individuals so appointed before 1660 were not necessarily practising goldsmiths, but persons who often farmed out the work. The designation 'Goldsmith to the Crown' (sometimes called 'Crown Goldsmith') was first used by RUNDELL, BRIDGE & RUNDELL, and from 1830 to the present by its successors, the firm that is today GARRARD & CO. LTD.

At present, any firm (or individual) having completed a three-year period during which it has supplied goods or services directly to the Queen, the Duke of Edinburgh, the Queen Mother or the Prince of Wales, may qualify for an appropriate Royal Warrant (bearing the relevant coat of arms and the description 'By Appointment to . . .'), which the holder is entitled to display. A holder of a Royal Warrant is not necessarily the sole purveyor of silverware to the Royal household.

Crown Mark. (1) A mark, not an official HALLMARK, often used in Great Britain between 1765 and 1825 by various makers of SHEFFIELD PLATE, along with a MAKER'S MARK, to indicate ware of high quality and to distinguish it from imitations imported from France and Austria. (2) The ASSAY OFFICE HALLMARK used at Sheffield on STERLING SILVER from 1773 until 1975, when it was superseded by the Rose Hallmark. As the Crown mark used on some Sheffield Plate from 1765 to 1825 was deemed to resemble too closely the Assay Office Hallmark of Sheffield, its use on Sheffield Plate was prohibited thereafter.

Crown silverware. The articles of silverware (sometimes referred to as the 'Royal Plate' or as being in the 'Royal Collection') owned by the British Crown, some of which are kept with the regalia in the Jewel House at the Tower of London, and some at various royal residences, principally at Buckingham Palace and Windsor Castle. Such pieces must be distinguished from: (1) articles owned privately by the Sovereign, e.g., in the case of Elizabeth II, gifts made to her and to the Duke of Edinburgh at the time of their marriage and thereafter while she was H.R.H.Princess Elizabeth, before succeeding to the throne in 1952 (which pieces were kept at Clarence House, London, until they moved to Buckingham Palace), as well as silverware acquired by them privately since the accession; and (2) articles owned privately by other members of the Royal Family (*see* ROYAL WEDDING SILVER-

WARE). *See* E. Alfred Jones, *The Gold and Silver at Windsor Castle* (1911); Arthur G. Grimwade, *The Queen's Silver* (1953).

cruet (or **cruet bottle**). A receptacle for serving oil, vinegar, soy, and other liquid condiments; it is usually in the form of a small thin bottle or vial of circular section with a tapering and elongated neck, an everted pouring lip, a stopper, and sometimes a narrow vertical loop handle rising above the rim. Cruets are usually made of glass, but often have silver mounts, such as a silver cap on the stopper, a silver handle, and a silver band around the neck forming the lip. They are generally made in SETS (of 2 to 5) and are often accompanied by a CRUET STAND (sometimes the stand is referred to as a 'cruet'). The type with a pierced cover is preferably called a CASTER. Originally, a cruet was a receptacle for oil, wine or holy water used at a church altar in the Eucharist; *see* ALTAR CRUET. *See* G. Bernard Hughes, 'Old English Cruets' in *Country Life,* 20 January 1955, p. 178. *See* GUILLE CRUET; SOY-BOTTLE.

cruet label. A type of BOTTLE TICKET, made in small size for use on a CRUET, to distinguish different condiments in a CRUET STAND or sauces in a SOY STAND.

cruet stand. Stand with cruets and casters, Paul Crespin, London, 1721-2. Colonial Williamsburg, Va.

cruet stand. A receptacle, often part of a DINNER SERVICE, for holding several CRUETS (2 to 8), with some examples also holding two or more CASTERS for spices and pepper, and more elaborate ones also holding one or more receptacles for mustard and other condiments. Such stands were made in a great variety of styles, many having a platform (of various shapes – oval, rectangular, boat-shaped) and a number of guard rings to secure the cruets and other pieces and sometimes to hold the stoppers after removal; the rings were supported by short legs with decorative feet, so that glass cruets were completely exposed. Some examples have a handle at each end of the stand, but usually the stand has a central vertical post topped with a ring or other type of handle. Some such stands hold, instead of glass cruets, a silver MUSTARD-POT and small GINGER-JAR, and some, intended for only two cruets, are termed an OIL-AND-VINEGAR STAND. Also sometimes called a 'cruet frame'. *See* SOY STAND; CRUET STAND/SOY STAND; WARWICK CRUET STAND; BOX CRUET STAND.

cruet stand/soy stand. A dinner-table or sideboard accessory combining a CRUET STAND and a SOY STAND. It was made in a number of forms, often as a rotating platform with supports for soy-bottles (5 to 8) and cruets (3 or 4); some are stands with a high gallery and central vertical handle. They were made in PAIRS and also in SETS (of 6, 8 or 12). Some were also combined with an EPERGNE rising on a central pillar, topped with a bowl and having extended arms to support small dishes. Sometimes called a 'cruet and soy frame'.

crumb scoop. Electroplated scoop with ivory handle, Elkington & Co., Birmingham, *c.* 1880. Courtesy, Brand Inglis Ltd, London.

Crystal Cup. Faceted rock crystal bowl with silver-gilt mounts and straps, London, 1545-6. H. 24·7 cm. Goldsmiths' Company, London.

Cruickshank, Robert (d. 1809). A London silversmith, born in Aberdeen, who emigrated to Boston, *c.* 1768, and fled to Montreal, *c.* 1773. There he founded the silversmith business that was succeeded in 1895 by Hendery & Leslie (which firm was acquired in 1898 by HENRY BIRKS & SONS). He introduced into Canada English forms and styles which by *c.* 1800 were superseding the old French styles.

crumb scoop. A dinner-table accessory used to remove crumbs from the table during a meal before serving the dessert (sweet). It has a wide flat horizontal blade with, on the rear side, a low curved rim to retain the crumbs, and a long horizontal handle, often of a material other than silver, e.g., of ivory. *See* CRUMBER.

crumber. A dinner-table accessory used in modern times to remove crumbs from the table during a meal before serving the dessert (sweet). It is of two types: (1) A small tray having one flat undecorated edge, into which the crumbs are swept by means of an accompanying brush or a CRUMB SCOOP. (2) A small roller fitted with an interior rotating brush which sweeps in the crumbs.

Crump, Francis (fl. 1741–73). A London silversmith, apprenticed in 1726 to GABRIEL SLEATH and freed in 1741, in which year he entered his first mark from Newcastle St. He moved to Fenchurch St, and entered a mark in 1753 in partnership with Sleath. Later marks were entered alone from his address at Gutter Lane, 1753–73.

crystal articles. Articles of which an essential part is made of rock crystal, combined with silver MOUNTS. Examples include some SALT-CELLARS, GREAT SALTS, MACES (*see* NORWICH MACE), CUPS (*see* CRYSTAL CUP, THE; BOWES, SIR MARTIN, CUP; METHUEN CUP; TONG CUP: YATELY CUP), CANDLESTICKS, CASTING BOTTLES, SPOONS, and also, but rarely, the bowl of a EWER or base of a TANKARD. Among the Great Salts with a crystal component are the GIBBON SALT, HUNTSMAN SALT, MONKEY SALT, SEYMOUR SALT, STONYHURST SALT, WALKER SALT and WOBURN SALT. *See* PILLAR SALT.
   Crystal was often used in the Early Middle Ages for its beauty, its symbolic significance as expressive of Christ's purity, and even its supposed magical properties of detecting poison and curing various ailments. It was frequently used as a hollow tube to display relics or figures, as well as for knops on CHALICES and arms of crucifixes. The crystal used on silver-mounted articles was often from a reliquary that had been destroyed during the Reformation.

Crystal Cup, The. A silver-gilt STANDING CUP having a tall, slender vertical bowl of rock crystal cut with twelve vertical facets and contained within three thin vertical silver straps hinged to the everted lip at the top and to the shallow bowl at the bottom which is decorated with concave and convex fluting. The stem rests on a crystal collar and disc enclosed within three brackets that connect the stem to the foot. The cup bears an indistinct maker's mark and the rare crowned LION PASSANT GUARDANT HALLMARK for the year 1545–6. It was acquired in 1914 by the Goldsmiths' Company, London.

Cubic Style. A decorative style created for the GORHAM COMPANY in 1927 by ERIK MAGNUSSEN, who designed and executed the work. The forms of the pieces are broken down into flat irregular triangles, some being burnished and others being gilded or oxidized brown, thus producing a contrasting overall effect.

cucumber slice(r). A type of implement for cutting a cucumber into thin slices, some examples being made of silver or being SILVER-PLATED WARE. One example is in the form of a horizontal tube resting on a weighted foot, having at the ejecting end a sharp circular blade that rotates on a spindle turned by a hand crank and having an internal sliding rod, with a projecting

Cubic Style. Serving spoon and fork, designed and made by Erik Magnussen for the Gorham Company, 1927. Gorham Collection, Providence, R.I.

handle, that propels the cucumber as it is being sliced. (Cucumbers could be grown straight to fit into the tube by being cultivated in a straight glass cucumber-trainer made expressly for the purpose.)

cuff. A cylindrical armband (made as one of a pair) sometimes called a 'gauntlet', but without finger coverings, made as a split cylinder to be worn around the wrist and joined by a clasp. Although rare in silver, an example is known, made by Hester Bateman (*see* BATEMAN) in 1783, to be worn by a Lady-in-Waiting to the Queen; each cuff is decorated on the front with a profile bust (of George III and Queen Charlotte, respectively) and on the reverse with an embossed figure of a lion, and with saw-cut borders. *See* cover of *The Antique Collector,* November 1936; David Shure, *Hester Bateman* (1959), pl. XLIV.

Cumberland Tankard. A large silver TANKARD, 32·5 cm high, engraved with an encircling panel depicting scenes associated with the Battle of Culloden, 1746, and the victory of George II's son, William Augustus, Duke of Cumberland (d. 1765), over the Jacobites under Charles Edward Stuart. The bowl is cylindrical, tapering slightly, with a low-domed lid and a DOUBLE-SCROLL HANDLE, and is supported by three feet in the form of lions couchant, each fitted with a swivelling castor; the feet are attached by brackets, each including the coronet of Cumberland. A similar lion forms the thumbpiece. Set into the domed lid is a mortuary medallion, made *c.* 1766 by John van Nost, which depicts on the obverse a profile bust of Cumberland and on the reverse a monumental obelisk; it probably replaced a contemporary medal. The body and the lid of the tankard bear the mark of GABRIEL SLEATH, London, 1746–7. It was perhaps made either on the order of Cumberland for presentation by him to one of his generals or as a gift to him from his father in recognition of the victory. The tankard was sold on 27 June 1843 at Christie's, London, from the estate of the Duke of Sussex (1773–1843), sixth son of George III and Cumberland's great-nephew, and again (its history in the interim being unknown) at Christie's on 13 March 1968 by the Countess of Breadalbane; an export licence was refused, and the tankard was subsequently acquired, with the aid of grants, by the National Army Museum, London. *See* William Reid, 'The Cumberland Tankard' in *The Connoisseur,* November 1971, p. 154.

Cumberland Tankard. Engraved with scenes depicting the Battle of Culloden, Gabriel Sleath, London, 1746-7. H. 32·5 cm. National Army Museum, London.

Cuny, Louis (fl. 1703–33). A Huguenot immigrant silversmith who was naturalized in England in 1697 and registered his first mark in 1703, his address being Panton St, London, until 1727. Among the pieces that he made were TWO-HANDLED CUPS, TEAPOTS WITH STAND, SALT-CELLARS, CHAMBER CANDLESTICKS, etc., usually of unpretentious style.

cup. (1) A small vessel employed by an individual primarily for drinking. It occurs in various shapes, styles, and sizes, usually bowl-shaped or cylindrical and generally having one side handle (but sometimes two or none) and a low FOOT-RING. Small drinking cups are generally accompanied by a SAUCER of similiar style and decoration. *See* CAMP CUP; CANN; CAUDLE-CUP; CHILD'S CUP; CHOCOLATE-CUP; COFFEE-CUP; COMMUNION CUP; CUSTARD-CUP; DRAM-CUP; MAGDALEN CUP; OX-EYE CUP; POSSET-POT; SPOUT CUP; TAZZA; TEACUP; TOT-CUP; TREMBLEUSE; WAGER CUP; WINE-CUP. (2) A large tall drinking vessel, having a bowl resting on a stem and supported by a spreading foot. Such cups are intended usually for use on formal or ceremonial occasions, as in the case of a LOVING CUP, STANDING CUP, TWO-HANDLED CUP or STEEPLE CUP. *See* PRESENTATION CUP.

cup. Cylindrical shape, John Dixwell, Boston, Mass., 1710-20. H. 6·5 cm. Yale University Art Gallery, New Haven, Conn.

cupellation. A process of separating silver from ARGENTIFEROUS lead ore (galena); used since the third millennium BC, it is still employed by many ASSAY OFFICES for testing silver. The assaying technique involves taking scrapings (the DIET) from the article to be tested and after careful weighing, wrapping them in a lead sheet; the mass is then melted in a porous bowl (a 'cupel') made of bone-ash (now magnesia) at a high temperature (1100 °C.) both the lead and any copper in the ALLOY under test become oxidized, and the lead oxide (known as 'litharge') and any copper oxide are absorbed in the cupel, leaving 98 % pure silver. Further refinement can then be done electrically. By subtracting the weight of the silver remnant from the original weight of the sample, the amount of base metal that was in the alloy is determined. *See* SCORIFICATION.

cupping bowl. A small utensil of globular form with one open side, used formerly for bleeding a patient by producing a partial vacuum; such pieces were made of glass and without any handle, hence the term is a misnomer when, as sometimes happens, it is applied to a silver BLEEDING BOWL or to a PORRINGER.

cut card. Covered bowl with flying scroll handles and applied cut-card foliage, Pierre Harache II, London, *c.* 1695. Courtesy, Asprey & Co. Ltd, London.

cushion shape. The shape of a COVER or LID that is slightly raised, with a flat top and rounded sides, resembling a cushion. Some examples are two-tiered, with one cushion on top of a larger one.

custard cup. A type of small CUP for serving custard (or jellies) having usually a single loop handle and sometimes a cover; such cups are generally made in sets which rest on a serving tray or stand, and sometimes each cup is accompanied by a small serving spoon. Such sets, usually made of ceramic ware, have occasionally been made of silver. One pair of such silver sets consists of two circular footed stands, upon each of which rests seven uncovered cups (six encircling the seventh which is elevated on a central post), with each cup accompanied by a small silver spoon; the stands and cups, made by PHILIP RUNDELL, 1820, and the spoons, made by JOHN BRIDGE, 1823–4, are in the Royal Collection, having been purchased by George IV in July 1824.

cut card. A very thin plate of silver cut from a rolled sheet to produce a border and/or a surface silhouette design and affixed by SOLDERING to a silver object as an integral part of its decoration in relief. Originally, *c.* 1650, the cutting required great skill by the artisan, especially in producing intricate patterns of scrolling and foliage and in applying the plate with care to avoid any seepage of solder from behind the design, thus ensuring that the card appears to be an integral part of the piece. Later, *c.* 1690, the technique was developed by the Huguenot silversmiths. The applied cut-card work was sometimes itself decorated by ENGRAVING or CASTING, e.g., to depict veins of leaves, by affixing cast motifs or BEADING, or by being applied in several layers. The process was altered, *c.* 1860, by cutting with a piercing saw. The cut design was required to be affixed to a piece before ASSAYING and having the HALLMARK applied. The cut plates served not only as decoration (especially as a CALYX-pattern around the bottom of a stemmed bowl), but also to strengthen the joint of a handle or a foot of thin-gauge metal and to mask the join. On a few articles the cut-card ornament was detachable. Although some cut-card work is found in CAROLINE SILVERWARE, it was used more elaborately in the reign of William III, 1695–1702, especially on HUGUENOT SILVERWARE.

cutlery. Articles of FLATWARE (strictly, those that have a cutting edge) used for cutting, carving or serving food, especially various types of KNIFE. However, the term is generally used in modern times to embrace all types of flatware, including FORKS and SPOONS. *See* exhibition catalogue *Masterpieces of Cutlery,* Victoria and Albert Museum, London (1979).

cutlery-urn. A sideboard accessory for holding various articles of CUTLERY, being a receptacle, in the form of an urn, made of wood (mahogany), often with silver MOUNTS, and having interior slots for holding upright the individual pieces; it has a central stem that rises, with the cover attached, to permit access to the cutlery when releases are pressed. Such pieces, related to a KNIFE-BOX, were made *c.* 1790–1800 (then called a 'vausis') and have been reproduced in the 20th century.

cuttlefish casting. A process of CASTING silver objects by using a mould of cuttlefish bone. The bone is cut in half lengthwise and the faces rubbed flat; next a model of the desired article is placed between the two sections which are then pressed firmly together so that an impression (mould) of the model is made in the soft bone. A small groove is cut in the mould to permit molten silver to be poured in. The two sections are then joined to complete the mould, and molten metal is poured in to make the casting.

Cuzner, Bernard (Lionel) (1877–1956). A designer and silversmith of Birmingham, apprenticed to his father. He was for forty years a leading silversmith instructor at Birmingham schools until he retired in 1942. His own work was of the highest standard, and he influenced many of the younger silversmiths. He was a staunch adherent of the Arts and Crafts Movement. His principal craftsman was the designer Stanley G. Morris. Cuzner's most important piece is the OLYMPIC TORCH, commissioned following several torch trophies he had made for the Walker Technical College. He designed and made, without maker's mark, some pieces of LIBERTY SILVERWARE. He was the author of *A Silversmith's Manual* (1935; 2nd ed. 1979).

cylindrical caster. *See* LIGHTHOUSE CASTER.

Cymric silverware. Articles of silverware introduced *c.* 1899 by Liberty and Co., London (founded by Arthur Lazenby Liberty in 1875) and made for it originally by an unidentified London workshop but after *c.* 1900 by its associated company, Liberty & Co. (Cymric) Ltd, which it founded with W. H. Haseler, Birmingham. The ware features decoration in ART NOUVEAU STYLE of Celtic (Cymric or Welsh) designs and is characterized by the marks of hammering being left on the metal without burnishing or polishing and by decoration with enamelling and the use of gemstones. It adapted the style of hand craftsmanship introduced by C. R. ASHBEE, the pieces, however, not being hand-wrought but mass-produced by die-stamping and then hammered to give the appearance of hand craftsmanship. The pieces were stamped with the mark of Liberty & Co. without identifying maker's marks, but some have been attributed to the designs of the artist Archibald Knox. Other ware of the same style and designs was made also by William Hutton & Sons Ltd, of Sheffield and London, and was stamped with that company's mark. *See* LIBERTY SILVERWARE.

D

damascened. Inlaid with narrow strips of silver or gold set in an incised metal surface to produce an ornamental design (as distinguished from the similarly termed watered pattern of wavy character found on Damascus steel blades). Examples include the MILTON SHIELD and the VECHTE SHIELD.

Date Hallmark. The HALLMARK stamped by an ASSAY OFFICE on an article of silver to indicate the year (usually, but not necessarily, the year of its make) in which the article was marked after ASSAYING. The use of a Date Mark was introduced at Montpellier, France, in 1355, and copied in Paris in 1461. In England the use of the Date Hallmark was commenced in 1478 as a means of identifying the Assay Master responsible for any year. The mark thereafter has been a letter of the alphabet enclosed within a shield, each Assay Office having, until 1975, a different series of letters and types of shields used in cycles. The date letter was changed every year (not a calendar year before 1975, but a mid-year date ending differently at each Assay Office, hence most pre-1975 dates must be stated by naming two consecutive years). The cycle of letters used in London ran from A to T, omitting J, and included either U or V. Until 1975 each cycle of 20 letters used a different style of lettering, and also a changed style of shield when necessary. The British Hallmarking Act of 1973 required that the Date Hallmark should be uniform for all four Assay Offices in Great Britain, that the cycles should extend through 26 letters, and that the annual change should coincide with the calendar year. Booklets are available showing all date letters, and hence – except in cases where a letter bas become worn – the date of assaying of an article can normally be readily ascertained. The Date Mark was sometimes called a 'Warden's Mark' (referring to the Warden of the Goldsmiths' Company).

Davenport, Burrage (fl. 1773–83). An English silversmith at 6 Foster Lane, London. He is best known for his pierced and decorated BREAD-BASKETS and CAKE-BASKETS, also DISH CROSSES.

Davis Cup. A TROPHY awarded annually by the International Lawn Tennis Association to the winning country (but not retained by it) in an international lawn tennis tournament; the matches, played in the various countries, being between men's singles and doubles teams. (Preliminary matches to select a challenger to play the winner of the preceding year were abolished in 1971.) The cup is bowl-shaped, rotating on its base, and gilt-lined; it was designed and made in 1900 by Shreve, Crump, and Low of Boston, and was donated by Dwight F. Davis (1879–1945), American diplomat. Engraved on the cup are the details of the first 14 matches (1900–19). When there was no more space, Mr Davis in 1921 donated a tray, of similar style, designed and made by Black, Starr, and Frost of New York; this bears engraved details about the matches of 1920–32. When more space was needed, Mr Davis designed and donated in 1935 the plinth which has 15 plaques for 30 matches, 1933–62. After 1968, another plinth, with 16 plaques for 32 matches, was provided which will permit inscriptions until 1994.

Deane Cup. A parcel-gilt 'FONT-SHAPED' CUP having a circular spreading base and a shallow, vertical-sided bowl. The bowl is slightly waisted and

Davis Cup. Trophy with tray and plinth, 1900/1921/1935. Width of cup 32 cm. United States Lawn Tennis Association.

Deane Cup. Parcel-gilt, London, 1551-2, maker's mark 'RD'. W. 15 cm. Hampshire County Museum Service, Winchester.

decanter. Parcel-gilt, filigree decoration on neck and stopper, Stuart Devlin, London, 1977. H. 51 cm. Courtesy, Stuart Devlin.

bears the inscription, engraved in Lombardic capitals, 'GYVE GOD THAKES EOR ALL THYNGS [*sic*]'. The interior of the bowl has engraved decoration depicting a helmeted head and shoulders in profile. The thick short stem is decorated with seeded roses on stalks, and the foot with applied SPOON-HANDLE STRAPS. The cup bears the mark 'RD', perhaps for Robert Danbe, and the London date mark for 1551–2. Under the bowl there is the inscription 'Ex dono Dorotheae Wither de Hall, Viduae 1698'. The cup was never owned by George Wither (d. 1586), as has been written, but research in 1958 has indicated that it was brought into the Wither family by Agnes, wife of the second George Wither, son of Gilbert Wither, and was bequeathed to Joan, her niece-by-marriage, and then to Joan's husband, George Wither, of Winchester, who left it to his daughter Mary; she bequeathed it to her cousin Charles (d. 1697), whose widow, Dorothy Wither, of Oakley Hall, donated the cup in 1698 to All Saints church, Deane, near Basingstoke, in Hampshire, where it (although a secular cup) was used as a PATEN. It was sold in 1971 by the church to raise funds to repair the church roof, and was acquired by the Winchester Museum in 1973. A comparable 'font-shaped' cup, 1557, bearing the same maker's mark, is in the Kremlin, Moscow; it was presented by Anthony Jenkinson to Ivan IV (the Terrible), possibly as a gift in 1561 from Elizabeth I. *See* Norman M. Penzer, 'Tudor "Font-shaped" Cups' in *Apollo,* February 1958, pp. 48–9, fig. v; and also *Apollo,* March 1958, p. 86.

de-bruising. Removing dents from an article of silverware without reducing the metal content or altering the decoration, hence a process that does not detract from value.

decanter. A type of decorative bottle used originally for serving wine at table after it had been decanted from the bottle to leave the dregs, but today used for serving various alcoholic beverages. Although usually made of glass, some modern examples have been made of silver.

decanter frame. A receptacle designed to support two, three or four glass DECANTERS. Such pieces were made in a variety of styles, but generally have a platform of silver mounted on a wooden base and a central vertical handle from which extend silver guard rings to encircle the decanters, and sometimes are also provided with small attached rings to hold the stoppers when removed. The frames may be circular, oval, rectangular or cruciform. *See* DECANTER STAND; LIQUEUR FRAME.

decanter label. A small plaque intended to be suspended by a chain around the neck of a wine DECANTER, appropriately lettered with the name of the wine; it substituted for the utilitarian BOTTLE TICKET by being larger and more elaborately decorated, especially with patterns of vine leaves and tendrils, as well as foliage and scrollwork.

decanter stopper. Figural stoppers (from 'The Vintagers' set designed by J. C. Horsley; copies, 1855–6, of originals by Benjamin Smith II, 1848). H. 11·5 cm. Victoria and Albert Museum, London.

decanter wagon. Old Sheffield plate, Walker, Knowles & Co., Sheffield, *c.* 1840. L. 45 cm. City Museum, Sheffield.

decanter mounts. Ornamental mounts, made to decorate a glass DECANTER, encircling the upper portion of the bottle as a collar and conforming in style to a close-fitting DECANTER STAND at the bottom. Both sections were made in the same style, with PIERCED WORK to reveal the glass decanter.

decanter stand. A type of COASTER to support a glass DECANTER or a wide wine-bottle. Originally it was similar to a BOTTLE STAND, but from *c.* 1780 was made with a wider base, about 15 cm in diameter, and a deeper GALLERY, from about 4 to 9 cm high. The gallery may be decorated with PIERCED WORK, CHASING, EMBOSSING or BRIGHT CUTTING. Later examples have either an EVERTED rim or a TURNED-OUT RIM, decorated with GADROONING or relief vine wreaths or leaves. Such pieces originally had a bottom with a silver surface, often with an engraved cipher, but this proved unsuitable to protect the surface of the table and was replaced by a turned wood disc of mahogany or boxwood, occasionally having on the top an inlaid BOSS decorated with a cipher; the underside of the coaster is covered with baize. *See* DOUBLE DECANTER STAND; DECANTER WAGON; TANTALUS FRAME.

decanter stopper. A type of ornate stopper for a glass DECANTER. Some were made of silver in the form of a figure in-the-round, such as a set of three, depicting figures of nude *putti* and called 'The Vintagers', designed in 1847 by the painter John Colcott Horsley (1817–1903), and made by BENJAMIN SMITH II, 1848, for the SUMMERLY ART MANUFACTURES, of which copies were made by STEPHEN SMITH and William Nicholson in 1855–6.

decanter wagon. A type of stand, designed to hold two glass DECANTERS, that is mounted on four wheels with a swivel pulling handle. Some examples have two recesses to hold the decanters, and some are in the form of two DECANTER STANDS joined by a coupling. Such pieces were used to pass decanters (usually of port wine) around a dinner table. The origin is said to have been a suggestion by George IV, 1820–30, to avoid the need for a guest sitting beside the King to rise and pass the port to a guest on his other side. One example, made by BENJAMIN SMITH II, 1828, bearing the arms of the 1st Earl of Hastings, consists of two decanter stands joined together and having a handle at each end. An example in the MACKAY SERVICE was in the form of a sleigh having runners that concealed small wheels. Modern examples occur in many forms and styles. Sometimes called a 'decanter carriage', a 'coaster wagon' (as it 'coasts' around the table), a 'wine wagon' or a 'wine coaster'. *See* WELLINGTON DECANTER WAGONS; JOLLY-BOAT DECANTER WAGON; DOUBLE DECANTER STAND.

decanting siphon. A long thin U-shaped tube of which the slightly shorter end was placed in a filled bottle of wine so that the wine could be decanted throught the longer tube, and having affixed to the side of the longer tube a device to start the flow, such as a tap and pump or a tap and mouthpiece. An example of the former type was made by Thomas Harache, London, *c.* 1750–60, and of the latter type by JOHN EMES, London, *c.* 1805. Some examples have a reinforcing plate or band attached to the bend of the tube. *See* TODDY LIFTER.

Deccan Candelabra/Tureens. Parcel-gilt candelabra and tureens that are part of the WELLINGTON DECCAN SERVICE.

de-chasing. A fraudulent process of removing from a silver object embossed work that was considered to detract from the value of the piece. The process

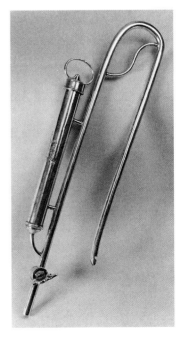

decanting siphon. Maker's mark 'TH', *c.* 1768, L. 35·5 cm. Courtesy, Richard Kihl Ltd, London.

involved hammering flat the embossing and then repolishing the surface to conceal the work. The process is revealed by the loss of PATINA and by the remaining tiny nicks on the surface, as well as by any remains of original embossing near the untouched handles.

decoration. Ornamentation and embellishment of silver articles by several processes: (1) APPLIED DECORATION, by SOLDERING on to the piece some decorative motif, such as a CUT CARD or WIREWORK ornament; (2) surface decoration, by CHASING, EMBOSSING, HATCHING, MATTING or PUNCHING, which involve no removal of metal, as well as by GILDING, PARCEL GILDING, ENAMELING, and NIELLO; and (3) ENGRAVING, ETCHING, ENGINE-TURNING or PIERCING which involve removal of some metal. There are some examples of GEM-DECORATED SILVERWARE.

demi-tasse. A small COFFEE-CUP, so called principally in the United States. It is generally used for serving post-prandial coffee. Some examples are cylindrical, in the form of a CANN, but many are of inverted-bell shape or fancifully shaped. *See* COFFEE SPOON.

depletion silvering. The process used on some articles made of an ALLOY of silver and copper to produce a silver surface. The process involves applying an acid that brings the copper to the surface as a black scale which is then removed either by repeated cold HAMMERING and then heating or by applying a pickle solution that dissolves the copper oxide. By repeating the process, the surface of the article is left with a thin film of brilliant-white pure silver. The process differs from ELECTROPLATING in that no additional metal is added; no silver of the alloy is lost, as the silver content remains on the surface. The process was used by the Colombian Indians before 1000 BC. It is related to the process used to produce FROSTED SILVER.

Derrynaflan Chalice. Silver, with silver-gilt handles, gold filigree decoration, and inset amber beads, Ireland, 9th century. H. 19 cm. National Museum of Ireland, Dublin.

Derrynaflan Chalice. A large CHALICE, attributed on stylistic grounds to the 9th century, that is part of the DERRYNAFLAN HOARD; it closely resembles the earlier ARDAGH CHALICE. Its rounded bowl, of beaten silver, rests on a gilt-bronze hollow stem that is supported by a silver conical foot with a broad flange. The body, stem, and foot are joined by a pin and washer. Two vertical loop handles are riveted to the sides of the bowl. The decoration of the piece consists of two large bands of FILIGREE panels, just below the everted rim and encircling the flange of the foot, and two smaller filigree bands just below and above the stem. The bands of filigree panels are decorated with interlaced animal and bird forms and with tendrils, and other decoration consists of gilt-copper ornaments separated by amber studs, some *en cabochon,* some faceted. Similar amber studs and filigree work decorate the handles.

Derrynaflan Hoard. A HOARD consisting of the DERRYNAFLAN CHALICE, a bronze Communion basin and strainer, and a silver PATEN. It was found on 17 February 1980 at Derrynaflan Monastery, near Cashel, Co. Tipperary, Ireland, buried below an upturned bronze basin. The pieces, which are now regarded as treasure-trove, are in the National Museum of Ireland, Dublin.

Design Registration Mark. A mark (not a HALLMARK) required by the British Patent Office from 1842 to be placed, for protection against plagiarism, on certain articles using a registered design in Great Britain, to indicate the year, month, and date when the design was registered (not the name of the designer or the date of production). Such marks are recorded in the Patent Office Design Register, and must be renewed each three years. The mark used was, from 1842 to 1883, in the form of a lozenge, having in the centre 'Rd'. From 1842 to 1867 it had at the top point a circle enclosing a Roman numeral to indicate the class of the article (metalware was Class I) and below it a code letter for the year of registration, at the right point a numeral for the day (date), at the bottom point the parcel number, and at the left point a code letter for the month; from 1868 to 1883 the class and the date were at the top, the year at the right, the month at the bottom, and the parcel number at the left. After 1883 only serial numbers were used in a continuous sequence usually preceded by the abbreviation 'Regd.' or 'Regd. No.' Sometimes termed the 'Registry mark'.

designer. A person, of whatever occupation, who has made designs for silverware. Such individuals include (1): professional designers, e.g., JOHN FLAXMAN II, WILLIAM THEED II, EDWARD HODGES BAILY, THOMAS STOTHARD, Charles Cotton (1756–1819), Sir Francis Chantrey (1781–1814), Charles Heathcote Tatham (1772–1842), WILLIAM CHRISTMAS CODMAN, EDWARD CHANDLER MOORE, and THOMAS J. PAIRPOINT; (2) designer-craftsmen, who executed their own designs, e.g., LÉONARD MOREL-LADEUIL, ALEX STYLES, and

ROBERT WELCH; (3) engravers, e.g., BENEDETTO PISTRUCCI and G. B. PIRANESI; (4) architects, e.g., C. R. ASHBEE, A. W. N. PUGIN, ROBERT ADAM, WILLIAM KENT, and Philip Webb (1831–1915); (5) sculptors, e.g., EDMUND COTTERILL and AUGUSTE ADOLPHE WILLMS; and (6) occasionally Prince Albert.

desk candlestick. A type of CANDLESTICK of which the height of the light is adjustable by having a central pole upon which an arm holding two candle SOCKETS can be slid upward or downward; attached to the pole is a curved shield to protect the reader's eyes and to reflect the light on to the desk. Sometimes called a 'library candlestick' or a 'reading candlestick'.

desk set. The same as LIBRARY SET.

dessert dish. A type of DISH or BOWL for serving a dessert (sweet), usually elaborately decorated as an ornamental piece for the DESSERT-TABLE SERVICE. It has no established form; some examples are flat-bottomed, with ornamental feet, and some rest on a spreading foot; some others are made with fluted sides and a scalloped rim. *See* TOLLEMACHE DESSERT DISH; 'STRAWBERRY DISH'.

dessert dish. Decorated in Portuguese style, maker's mark 'WS', London, 1627. W. 21·5 cm. Courtesy, Brand Inglis Ltd, London.

dessert fork. A type of FORK used for eating a dessert (sweet). The handle is usually short and the tines, three or four, are flat. The fork is frequently accompanied by a DESSERT SPOON.

dessert knife. A type of KNIFE used for eating a dessert (sweet). The handle is usually short, and the blade sometimes curved and pointed.

dessert plate. A type of PLATE for eating a dessert (sweet), similar to but larger than a DESSERT DISH.

dessert service. The SERVICE that is used at a dinner table for the dessert course served as the last course, after the cheese. Such services (often made of silver-gilt pieces) include DESSERT PLATES, DESSERT DISHES, DESSERT FORKS, DESSERT KNIVES, DESSERT SPOONS, and sometimes a SERVING SPOON and FINGER BOWLS. *See* DESSERT-TABLE SERVICE.

dessert spoon. A type of SPOON used for eating a dessert (sweet). It is intermediate in size between a TABLESPOON and a TEASPOON. The bowl of such a spoon is often gilded as a protection against discoloration by certain foods and also as a decorative feature. Some rare examples are ornately cast and chased, but most conform with contemporary styles of FLATWARE. *See* DESSERT SERVICE; DESSERT STAND.

dessert stand. A dinner-table or sideboard receptacle, usually a type of decorated DISH or shallow BOWL that rests on a wide spreading foot. The decoration varies in style, including EMBOSSING, CHASING, FLUTING or PIERCED WORK. Ornate examples have an elaborate stand, sometimes with a triangular base upon which figures (e.g., dolphins) or animal legs support the receptacle. Such stands were intended for serving the nuts and dried and fresh fruits that in England traditionally followed the sweet and cheese, but they could also be used for cakes, pastries, etc. They were often made in pairs or in sets of four, to be placed alongside a CENTREPIECE. *See* FOOTED SALVER; EPERGNE; GARNITURE DE TABLE.

dessert-table service. The SERVICE that was used in former days of formality and elegance to set a separate table in the dining room for fresh and dried fruits, nuts, and sweetmeats, but not the cooked preparations that were served at the dinner table. The dessert-table service included articles from the DESSERT SERVICE, and also elaborate and decorative FRUIT-BASKETS, EPERGNES, and sometimes CANDELABRA, all laid out on the dessert table for the guests to admire before starting the meal. The separate formal dessert table originated in France, where it was used to display elaborate preparations and a multitude of creations of the chef, formally arranged with pyramids of fruits.

Dethick Salt. A silver-gilt SCROLL SALT in circular 'pulley' form with a waisted body and three upright scroll-terminal BRACKETS on the rim. It bears the maker's mark 'FC' and the London date mark for 1638. It also bears the engraved arms of the Mercers' Company and of Sir John Dethick (Master of the Company in 1649 and in 1656, and also Lord Mayor of London in 1656, the year in which he was knighted), who donated the piece to the Company with funds remitted to him in 1638 out of a fine he had paid to the Company at the time he was admitted to it. Until the beginning of the Civil War (1642) under Charles I, the salt stood on the table in the Company hall, but was then placed in the vaults (where it is still kept).

Devizes Cup. A silver-gilt STEEPLE CUP having a bowl and cover that, combined, are of ovoid shape. The cup has a TRUMPET FOOT and a knopped stem with two collars, and the bowl is decorated with an overall DIAMOND PUNCHED pattern. The cover is decorated conversely with REPOUSSÉ work in an overall pattern of small raised diamond motifs. Surmounting the cover is a finial in the form of a three-sided pyramidal steeple decorated with a CHEVRONED pattern. The lower part of the bowl has a CALYX decoration of applied SPOON-HANDLE STRAPS. The cup, dated 1606–7, bears the maker's mark 'AB' (perhaps for Anthony Bull) and the municipal arms of Devizes, Wiltshire, the date 1620 (when apparently it was given to the town), and the names of the Mayor and twelve Chief Burgesses (Councillors) at the time. The cup is carried before the Mayor, when making formal visits to church, by a cup-bearer. It is sometimes called the 'Hanap Cup'. *See* HANAP.

Devizes Maces. Two silver-gilt MACES belonging to the town of Devizes, in Wiltshire, dated respectively 1660 and 1661. The stems are decorated with the rose and thistle. The bowl of the head has, in four panels, the Royal Badges, all crowned, and the cap bears the Royal arms in relief. Each mace bears an inscription as to the time of the making. The maces are now carried before the Mayor on ceremonial occasions by two mace-bearers.

Devlin, Stuart (1931–). A leading London silversmith, born in Australia, who studied and taught as a silversmith, 1950–62, in Melbourne, London, and New York. He settled in London in 1965, with his first workshop in Clerkenwell, moving in 1972 to his present showroom at 90 St John St, and establishing in 1979 a workshop-showroom (now closed) at 25 Conduit St. He has executed commissions for the Goldsmiths' Company, members of the Royal Family, and many private clients and industrial and public bodies world-wide. He designed the new decimal coinage for Australia in 1965 and has executed numismatic designs for many other countries. His work, which displays a wide variety of styles and textures, including FILIGREE decoration, embraces CENTREPIECES, ceremonial ware, ecclesiastical ware (including pieces for the altar of Canterbury Cathedral), and a series of animal-shaped paperweights cast by the CIRE PERDUE process. Much of his work is characterized by richness and elegance, especially some pieces set with gemstones. In 1982 he received a Royal Warrant as Goldsmith and Jeweller to Her Majesty the Queen. In November 1983 he was given a one-man retrospective exhibition at Goldsmiths' Hall, London. He has engaged also in designing jewelry since 1971 and furniture since 1975. *See* David Coombs, 'Stuart Devlin and the Idea of Richness' in *The Connoisseur*, May 1974, p. 18. *See* MENZIES MEMORIAL TROPHY.

Dewey Cup. A tremendous PRESENTATION CUP made for Admiral George Dewey (1837–1917) in 1899 after the United States naval victory over the Spanish fleet in Manila Bay, Philippines. It was made by the GORHAM COMPANY under the direction of WILLIAM CHRISTMAS CODMAN in four months when, in anticipation of Dewey's return home, the *New York Journal* proposed a fund to be raised by persons sending a dime each; the metal for the cup was derived from the 70,000 silver dimes so donated. The cup is ovoid, with three handles surmounted by eagles with upraised wings and perched on red, white, and blue shields. On the bowl are three panels, depicting the battle of Manila Bay, the Admiral's home, and his reception at Grant's Tomb, New York. The three-cornered base is decorated with dolphins and has a testimonial inscription. The cover, with decoration depicting the prows of three gunboats, is surmounted by a winged Victory figure holding an oval porcelain miniature bearing a portrait of Dewey. The cup rests on a circular plinth, bearing a laurel wreath and a band of oak leaves. Silver dimes are affixed to the cup and cover. The piece rests on a square oak platform with a drawer that holds a book listing the names of all the donors. It is now owned by the Chicago Historical Society, having been donated to it in 1934 by Dewey's son.

diamond-point spoon. A type of SPOON having a straight stem terminating in a finial made in the form of a faceted and pointed pyramid. Examples made in England are known from the 14th/15th centuries.

diamond punched. A style of decoration in the form of an overall pattern consisting of closely placed small indentations of diamond shape, as sometimes found on the surface of the bowl of a STANDING CUP, and occasionally made from within, forming a REPOUSSÉ pattern. *See* DEVIZES CUP.

diaper pattern. An ornamental pattern in the form of contiguous repetitions of one or more units of design, usually a chequered pattern of square-, diamond- or lozenge-shaped units enclosing some decorative motif or mo-

diaper pattern. Tea-caddy with engraved decoration, John Thompson, London, 1790. H. 12·7 cm. Courtesy, Brand Inglis Ltd, London.

tifs. The outline of each unit generally forms part of the outline of adjoining units so as to make an overall pattern for a ground or a border. Examples of such symmetrical patterns are occasionally found on silverware. *See* BEAU-FORT BEAKER.

die-rolled border. An applied border made of a decorative strip of silver produced by passing the metal through small patterned steel rollers.

die stamping. The process of STAMPING silver (or other metal) by the use of a die that forms the design on a sheet of the metal forcibly pressed between it and another surface. The die is made by skilled artisans called 'die sinkers', and can be made with detailed patterns requiring great expertise; it can be used repeatedly for mass-production. The process is sometimes used for stamping and cutting out complete objects (such as SPOONS and FORKS) or some MOUNTS. *See* MACHINE STAMPING.

diet. The metal scraped from articles submitted for ASSAYING and retained at the ASSAY OFFICE, kept in a securely locked 'diet-box' and periodically as-sayed as a check on the work of the assayer. (A silversmith who submits a piece that is approved receives a quantity of silver equal in weight to that which has been removed.) Sometimes called 'assay scrape'.

dinner fork. A type of dining FORK for individual use; the largest of the eat-ing forks, it has four equal and similar tines. It is used with a DINNER KNIFE.

dinner knife. A type of dining KNIFE for individual use; the largest of the eating knives, it has a straight blade and is moderately sharp. It is used with a DINNER FORK. *See* STEAK KNIFE.

dinner plate. A type of PLATE for serving the main course at dinner; also called a 'meat plate'. Until recently such plates were always circular, but modern examples are sometimes oval or octagonal. The central space is usually left undecorated (as use would impair any decoration) except for an occasional coat of arms; but the rim is often decorated with GADROONING, a REED-AND-TIE BORDER or REEDING. Such plates are usually found in a set of six or more; the diameter is about 25 cm. Some 17th-century examples have at the centre a pin-point, as evidence of the silversmith's use of a compass to ensure an accurate circular shape.

dinner service. A type of SERVICE intended for use at a dinner table by a number of diners, silver examples being intended especially for banquets. Originally it consisted only of PLATES and DISHES of different sizes, but later other articles decorated EN SUITE (and sometimes several of a kind) were added, such as TUREENS, SAUCE-BOATS, PLATTERS, BOWLS, CASTERS, BASKETS, and MAZARINES. Early examples were usually decorated only with an en-graved coat of arms on individual pieces, but later GADROONING and other types of decoration were added. *See* SIDEBOARD SERVICE; LEINSTER SERVICE; THANET SERVICE.

Directoire style. A French decorative style that was a transition between the NEO-CLASSICAL STYLE of the Louis XVI period and the EMPIRE STYLE, be-ing in vogue *c.* 1793–1804, approximating to the period of the Directory, 1795–99, that was overthrown by Napoleon. The style is characterized by simplicity and absence of excess ornamentation; it occurs mainly in the fields of the decorative arts, occasional examples being found in silverware.

disc-end spoon. A type of SPOON having a straight flat stem terminating in a finial in the form of a flat disc. On some examples the disc is decorated with a chased or engraved design or with initials, and sometimes the stem with ACANTHUS foliage. Such spoons were popular in northern England and in Scotland, examples being known from the mid-16th century until the mid-17th century.

dish. A shallow utensil upon which food is served or from which it is eaten. It is usually circular or oval (but some are hexagonal or shaped) and has a MARLI (ledge) and a WELL. The term is usually reserved for utensils about 30 cm in diameter (those smaller and circular being called a PLATE or SAUCER) and not over 3 cm deep (those deeper being called a BASIN or BOWL). Dishes have been made in many forms and styles, and for many purposes (e.g., ENTRÉE DISH, MEAT-DISH, SECOND-COURSE DISH, VEGETABLE-DISH, SALAD-DISH, VENISON-DISH, and SUPPER SET). The well of a dish is usually undecorated (use would damage the design), but some examples are highly ornamented with EMBOSSING and were used only as ornaments. *See* SAUCER-DISH; SIDE-BOARD DISH.

dish cover. Pierced decoration with rustic scene, Charles Townsend, Dublin, 1773. W. 30 cm. National Museum of Ireland, Dublin.

dish cover. A high-domed covering of silver (more often SHEFFIELD PLATE) to be used with a PLATTER or MEAT-DISH to keep the course warm while being brought to the dining room or while standing on a sideboard. The size varies, from large ones for a VENISON-DISH to smaller ones ranging from 24 to 60 cm. Some are circular or oval, sometimes undecorated (except for an ARMORIAL), but some are elaborately decorated with FLUTING, EMBOSSING, CHASING and GADROONING. They have a ring handle or a large knop for lifting. They were often made in pairs or sets of four or six. One Irish example, with pierced-work decoration depicting characteristically a barnyard scene, was perhaps intended for a POT-POURRI BOWL, having openwork to emit the scent.

dish cross. A type of dinner-table or sideboard accessory used to support and warm a serving receptacle, while protecting the table surface from the heat. It has at the centre two rings of equal size, one rotating above the other, each ring having extending from it horizontally in opposite directions two arms of square section, so that the four arms radiate as an X, their position being adjustable by rotating the upper ring. Each arm is supported at its end by a fixed scrolled leg and a flat-bottomed foot, and on each arm there is a sliding bracket to support a receptacle, so that the piece, when the brackets and arms are suitably adjusted, can support a dish or platter in a wide range of sizes and shapes. In the centre, suspended in the rings, there is a spirit lamp, raised high so as not to rest on the table; as its heat would normally be concentrated at the centre of the receptacle on the cross, there is sometimes placed above the lamp a heat disperser in the form of a circular concave disc with perforations or radiating PALES. The arms are of square section so that the brackets can slide smoothly along the arm and be held rigidly in place.

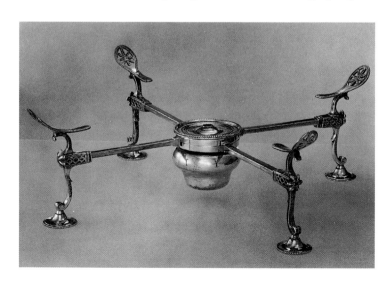

dish cross. Burrage Davenport, London, 1783–4. W. 26·5 cm. Wadsworth Atheneum (Elizabeth B. Miles Collection), Hartford, Conn.

The brackets are variously shaped and ornamented, rising about 2·5 cm above the arms so as to hold the receptacle well above the flame of the heater. At the back of each bracket there is a small THUMBPIECE that is used to adjust the position. A variant type of cross, used only to support a circular receptacle, has fixed arms extending at right-angles to each other. The dish cross was invented in Ireland *c.* 1730; it is sometimes called a 'spider' or 'table cross'. For alternative pieces used to support and warm a food receptacle, *see* DISH RING and DISH STAND. *See* G. Bernard Hughes, 'Keeping Georgian Food Hot', in *Country Life,* 26 December 1968, p. 1702.

dish ring. A dinner-table or sideboard accessory in the form of a hollow cylindrical or spool-shaped ring, formerly used to protect the surface from heat by supporting on top (not within it) a hot-food receptacle (probably of wood, pottery or glass, as no example is known with an accompanying silver receptacle). Some are of the same width at top and bottom, but most have a diameter of 18 to 21 cm at one rim, and 21 to 23 cm at the other, so that they could be reversed to support receptacles of different sizes; the height is usually from 8 to 13 cm. They were made principally in four types: (1) a vertical openwork band between the rims; (2) a sloping concave band entirely decorated with openwork and EMBOSSING; (3) a vertical band decorated with openwork in the form of PALES; and (4) a simple form made entirely of wire, with two horizontal circles joined by four connecting vertical arms. Such pieces were a speciality of Dublin (called there a 'dish ring'), the first from there being dated *c.* 1740, although they were made earlier in England (one is recorded from 1704) and there called a 'dish ring'. They continued to be made in the late-19th and 20th centuries in Ireland, England, and also in the United States. They have erroneously been called an 'Irish potato ring' (*see* POTATO RING). Some examples have a blue glass liner, but that is a later addition, solely decorative and not meant to serve as a receptacle. For other types of article used to support a heated receptacle, *see* DISH CROSS and DISH STAND. *See* M.S.D. Westropp, 'Irish Dish Rings' in *The Connoisseur,* July 1936, p. 213; G. Bernard Hughes, 'Irish Dish Rings' in *Country Life,* 21 April 1950, p. 1116; —, 'Irish Dish Rings' in *Apollo,* August 1953, p. 52.

dish ring. Pierced decoration and applied ornament, John Lloyd, Dublin, *c.* 1770. National Museum of Ireland, Dublin.

dish stand. A dinner-table or sideboard accessory for supporting and warming a food receptacle. It is in the form of a WIREWORK open frame composed of a pair of parallel horizontal wire rings, one above the other, connected by wire supports and having a centre wire frame for a spirit lamp. The rings are of different sizes (or one may be circular and the other oval), and the piece is reversible so that the different rings can support receptacles of different sizes or shapes. The reversible spirit lamp is sometimes between two heat dispersers that have a surface pierced with radiating PALES and circular holes to diffuse the heat over the width of the receptacle. For alternative pieces used to support and warm a food receptacle, *see* DISH RING, DISH CROSS and DISH WARMER.

dish warmer. A dinner-table or sideboard accessory composed of (1) a stand to which is affixed a heating device, such as a spirit lamp, (2) a dish or platter on which to place the food to be kept warm; and (3) a high-domed cover. *See* ROYAL DISH WARMER; VENISON-DISH; BREAKFAST DISH.

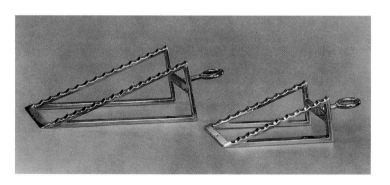

dish wedge. Two examples by Robert Hennell, London, 1792-3. L. 10 cm. and 6 cm, respectively. Wadsworth Atheneum. (Elizabeth B. Miles Collection), Hartford, Conn.

dish wedge. A dinner-table accessory with a sloping surface, to be placed under one end of a DISH or PLATTER (especially a WELL PLATTER), thus raising it so that the gravy would flow down to the other end. Some examples have a flat sloping rectangular surface with openwork and retarding protuberances, while others have only sloping bars with retarding ridges, to enable the dish to be securely positioned on it and allow the angle of the slope to be adjusted. Large sizes are intended for a platter, small ones are to tilt a plate so that gravy or sauce can be spooned or sopped with bread. Some have at the rear a ring-shaped handle. Sometimes called a 'platter tilter'.

dispensary, pocket. A small case with compartments (sometimes removable) for holding an assortment of medicines. *See* MEDICAL SILVERWARE.

Dixon, James, & Sons Ltd. A leading English firm of silversmiths at Sheffield, still making some ware of BRITANNIA METAL. It was founded in 1806 by James Dixon (1776–1852), who in 1811 took as a partner Thomas Smith (the name becoming Dixon & Smith until 1822) and made a great variety of wares of Britannia metal. In 1822 the factory was moved to Cornish Place (named for the extensive use of Cornish tin in its Britannia metal and pewter ware), still the location of its now greatly enlarged plant. When Smith left in 1822, Dixon's eldest son, William Frederick Dixon, became a partner (the name being changed to Dixon & Son, and later James Dixon & Son) and trade greatly increased, including exports to the United States. In 1829 the firm began making ware (especially hunting accessories) of SHEFFIELD PLATE, and registered in Sheffield as a silversmith. In 1835 a second son, James Willis Dixon, Sr (1814–76), became a partner (the name becoming James Dixon & Sons). When James Dixon retired in 1842, a third son, Henry Isaac Dixon, and a son-in-law, William Fawcett, became partners, and James Willis Dixon, Sr, took over the management. In 1849 ELECTROPLATING was begun, using Britannia metal as a base, and in 1851 the word 'Sheffield' was added to the firm's mark on such ware. A limited amount of Sheffield plate was made, less after 1850. In 1859 James Willis Dixon, Jr (1838–1917) became a partner, and in 1876 became head of the firm. In 1917 his son, Lennox Burton Dixon (d. 1941), who had become a partner in 1889, became head of the firm. In 1921 the firm became a limited company. In 1941 W. Milo Dixon (1901–76), grandson of James Willis Dixon, Jr, became head of the firm, the last member of the Dixon family to do so, and upon his death control passed to a group of Sheffield and London silversmiths who still operate the company as James Dixon & Sons Ltd, producing STERLING SILVER ware, SILVER-PLATED WARE, and pewter ware. Dixon ware was never dated, the numerals on individual pieces being the pattern numbers; some pieces bear a trumpet trade-mark.

dog bowl. A small bowl used for feeding a dog; silver examples for pampered canines have been made in recent years by ASPREY & CO., London.

dog collar. A collar to fasten to a dog's neck. Silver examples are usually a narrow cylindrical band, with an affixed ring to attach to a chain, and sometimes with provision for adjusting the size. Some are inscribed with the name of the dog and/or its owner. Some examples have been converted into COASTERS. A type of dog collar, called a 'coursing collar', has been awarded as a prize for coursing; such collars are wide bands with padlocks. *See* COURSING BUTTON.

dog-nose spoon. A type of SPOON having a flat stem widening toward the terminal which then narrows to a rounded point, said to resemble a dog's head viewed from above. The terminal is similar to that of a TRIFID SPOON with the two notches eliminated. The pattern was used from *c.* 1690 to *c.* 1710.

Doggett's Badge. A silver BADGE that was first donated in 1716 by Thomas Doggett (d. 1721), actor and joint owner of the Drury Lane Theatre, London, as a prize to be awarded to the winner of a race rowed by six Thames watermen between London Bridge and Cadogan Pier, Chelsea, in honour of the accession to the throne in 1714 of George I (the first Hanoverian king). The race is still held annually in August, the badges (together with an orange livery) being now given by the Fishmongers' Company from the Doggett bequest. The badges are embossed with a depiction of the White Horse of Hanover and the word 'Liberty'. Several examples, in slightly varying forms, are at the National Maritime Museum, Greenwich, England, and at the Watermens' Company, London. *See* WATERMAN'S BADGE.

dome cover. A type of circular SLIP-ON COVER that is domed in shape and fits on the upright smooth collar of a receptacle, as on some types of SALT.

Donald, John (1928–). A London silversmith, and also a designer-maker of jewelry and an industrial designer, who established his first workshop in 1962 at Queen's Mews, Bayswater, and in 1967 opened a new workshop in Cheapside. He has a staff of craftsmen who execute his designs, and has had his own retail shop in London since 1968 and another in Geneva since 1978.

dispensary, pocket. Gilt-lined, with six (possibly later) removable compartments, Birmingham, 1835. W. 8·5 cm. Wellcome Collection, Science Museum, London.

dog collars. Adjustable collars, maker's mark 'WC', Edinburgh, 1838. D. (of collar) 12·8 cm. Courtesy, Sotheby's, London.

Doncaster Cup, 1828. Trophy, Rebecca(h) Emes and Edward Barnard, London, 1828-9. H. 35 cm. City Art Galleries (Lotherton Hall), Leeds.

He won, in 1959, a competition for the BADGE of the Warden of the Goldsmiths' Company, London. In 1963 he made a modern version of an OX-EYE CUP for Balliol College, Oxford. *See* Graham Hughes, 'John Donald' in *The Connoisseur,* October 1963, p. 99.

Doncaster Cup, 1828. A silver-gilt HORSE-RACING CUP awarded at the Doncaster Racecourse, South Yorkshire, in 1828. It has an ovoid bowl resting on a trumpet foot and having two bifurcated handles, each formed by two serpents with their heads resting on the lip of the bowl. The cup, decorated with grape vines and *amorini,* is unusual in having no cover. The form is based on an engraving by G.B. PIRANESI, inspired by a marble vase excavated by Gavin Hamilton in 1769 and sold by him in 1774 to George, Marquess of Buckingham (hence it is sometimes called the 'Buckingham Vase') for the Stowe Collection. The silver version, made by REBECCA(H) EMES and Edward Barnard, is now in the City Art Galleries, Leeds (Lotherton Hall).

Dopping Posset Pot. A SMALL TWO-HANDLED CUP with ogee-shaped sides, two vertical debased CARYATID HANDLES, and a low-domed cover with a finial of upright leaves. It is decorated with embossed foliage, and depicted on one side is a lion and on the other the arms of Anthony Dopping, Bishop of Meath, 1643–97. It bears the marks of John Phillips, Dublin, the dates on the cup and the cover being 1685 and 1687 respectively.

dot repoussé. Decoration of REPOUSSÉ work made in the form of dots hammered into a sheet of metal with a punch, usually massed together to form a pattern or to depict an animal or other motif. *See* MATTING.

double beaker. A pair of BEAKERS which, when placed together rim to rim, fit together so as to appear as one piece. An English example, with mark 'RF', 1572, is in the Hermitage, Leningrad; it also has added Russian engraving dating from 1640.

double cup. A pair of CUPS of identical form which fit together, rim to rim, sometimes having, when joined, the appearance of a barrel, its staves bound with hoops of wire bands. A pair was made by Peter and William Bateman (*see* BATEMAN), 1806.

double decanter stand. A pair of DECANTER STANDS resting in recesses on an oblong tray. Some types are joined by a wire coupling formed into two rings as holders for the decanter stoppers, and occasionally having a wire ring at each end for use in moving it along the table. The earliest type, *c.*1790, consisted of a hardwood slider support for two decanters, its top surface being covered with silver or SHEFFIELD PLATE and its underside with baize to facilitate sliding on a polished surface. The double decanter stand was superseded in the 1830s by the DECANTER WAGON, which differs in having wheels.

double-lapped edging. An improved method of EDGING objects made of SHEFFIELD PLATE, the use of which succeeded the SINGLE-LAPPED EDGING process, employed to conceal the copper line at the edge. The later process, patented in 1768 by George Whateley, involved first making a length of PLATED WIRE and passing it between rollers to make a thin ribbon having plated silver on both sides and both edges, then SOLDERING it to the edge of the article of Sheffield plate so that it protruded somewhat and lapped over the edge so as to be flat on the underside, the resulting join being difficult to detect. Sometimes called a 'double-lapped copper mount'. *See* SILVER-LAPPED EDGING.

double-lidded box. A type of BOX or CASKET of rectangular form, with chamfered or shaped corners, and divided crosswise into two compartments, each having a hinged lid. Some examples, made in the 18th century, were intended for use as a SPICE-BOX, and have, under the hinge, a NUTMEG GRATER. Others were intended as a BOX SALT. A modern example, probably intended merely as a casket, was made by H.J. Brown, 1947, and is in the collection of Her Majesty the Queen; it bears the crest of Princess Elizabeth as Duchess of Edinburgh and the arms of the City of Norwich.

double-lipped sauce-boat. An early type of SAUCE-BOAT having a pouring LIP at each end and, instead of a single handle at one end, one on each side, usually a low SCROLL HANDLE rising from the raised central section of the rim that curves upward and inward. Such pieces usually rest on a spreading foot and often have a wavy rim. As the presence of two side handles makes such pieces inconvenient for pouring, it seems preferable to designate them GRAVY-BOATS, to be used with a GRAVY-LADLE.

Dopping Posset Pot. John Phillips, Dublin, 1685/7. H. 24·8 cm. Ulster Museum, Belfast.

double decanter stand. One of a pair, E., J. & W. Barnard, London, 1829. W. 50·5 cm. Courtesy, Sotheby's, London.

double-lipped sauce-boat. One of a pair, Thomas Heming, London, 1765. W. 23 cm. Courtesy, Garrard & Co. Ltd, London.

double salt (1). Twin wells separated by intertwined-dolphin handle, Stephen Smith, London, 1872. Courtesy, Brand Inglis Ltd, London.

double plated. The type of PLATED METAL that is covered with a layer of silver on both sides, so that it can be used for making articles of HOLLOW WARE when both sides are intended to show. *See* SINGLE PLATED.

double salt. (1) A type of SALT-CELLAR or TRENCHER SALT that has two wells for salt. *See* TRIPLE SALT. (2) A type of STANDING SALT that has two receptacles for the salt, in tiers one above the other, which could be removed and used separately.

double-scroll handle. A type of HANDLE in the form of two connected scrolls curving in opposite directions from the point where they meet. It occurs on many JUGS, MUGS, CANNS, and TWO-HANDLED CUPS, and on Scottish BULLET TEAPOTS. Sometimes called a 'broken-scroll handle' or an 'S-C scroll handle'. *See* SCROLL HANDLE.

double tea-caddy. A TEA-CADDY divided into two sections, each for a different variety of tea, such as green and black.

double wine cooler. A type of circular WINE COOLER having a central vertical partition and made to hold two wine bottles.

douceur. A gift which, by custom from 1679 to 1778, was made annually to the incoming Lord Mayor of London by the Sephardic Congregation of Spanish and Portuguese Jews (founded in 1657), which in 1701 founded the Bevis Marks Synagogue, the oldest synagogue in London. The term 'douceur' means a conciliatory gift, and in this context serves as a reminder of the community's claim for protection. The gift originally was a silver DISH or SALVER, then from *c.*1740 a silver TWO-HANDLED CUP; it was accompanied by a quantity of sweetmeats and later a purse of 50 guineas. A similar practice was also followed by the Dutch Protestants and the French Huguenots in London. *See* LORD MAYOR'S CUP; LORD MAYOR'S SALVER.

douter. A type of article with two arms joined like SCISSORS or U-style TONGS, having at the end of each arm a flat disc. Such articles were used in the 18th century to extinguish the flame of a candle or of a lamp, by compression rather than by cutting the wick as done by a SNUFFER or a WICK TRIMMER. The name has been said to be derived from the expression 'Dout the candle'.

drainer. A flat pierced false bottom resting on a PLATTER for draining the liquid from food, as the juices from roast meat. The type used to drain cooked fish is called a MAZARINE.

'Drake Cup'. (1) A parcel-gilt STANDING CUP so called because it was traditionally said to have been presented by Sir Francis Drake in 1582 as a New Year's gift to Elizabeth I, but now considered to have been made probably *c.*1595 and hence not the piece so donated (see 2 below). This so-called Drake Cup is composed of a bowl and cover which together form a terrestrial globe divided at the equator and engraved on Mercator's projection, with the land gilt and the seas in matt silver. The bowl rests on a stem resembling an ovoid vase chased with marine deities and a circular high base on a spreading foot. The cover is surmounted by a vase-shaped finial upon which rests an armillary sphere supported by brackets terminating with griffins. This piece was purchased by Dr George Lockett in 1919 from Captain Gerald Thomas-Peter; it was sold at the Lockett sale at Christie's, London, in 1942 and bought by the National Art-Collections Fund and presented by it to the City of Plymouth to commemorate the role of the city in World War II. It is now in the City Museum and Art Gallery, Plymouth. The cup was made, probably (on the basis of the cartography of the globe) *c.*1595, by Abraham Gessner, a silversmith of Zurich who became Master of the Zurich guild in 1571. Although the piece would normally fall outside the scope of this book as not being of British make, it is included due to its having often been confused with the piece discussed in (2) below.

(2) A SALT of unknown whereabouts today but described in a book by Lady Eliot-Drake (d. 1937), published in 1911, as being in the form of a globe resting upon two naked men, being Jupiter and Pallas, and having at the top the figure of a woman holding a trumpet, and having the foot enamelled with flowers. This is presumably the piece presented by Drake to Elizabeth I.

'Drake Cup' (1). Silver-gilt standing cup, Abraham Gessner, Zurich, 1595(?). H. 51·5 cm. City Museum and Art Gallery, Plymouth.

dram cup. A type of CUP of no fixed shape or capacity, but of small size. Such cups were popular in England, Ireland, and the American colonies from the 17th century (and variously named) for drinking a draught (dram) of distilled spirit.

drawback mark. A mark that was struck in England from 1 December 1784 to 24 July 1785 on articles of silver (or gold) which were to be exported and on which the duty paid (6*d* per oz.) had been refunded. It showed a standing figure of Britannia (differing from the BRITANNIA HALLMARK) punched as an INCUSE MARK making an intaglio impression. Unlike other hallmarks that are struck before finishing and polishing, this mark was punched on a finished article and risked causing damage, so it was withdrawn and the duty drawback was thereafter claimed on the shipping bills. *See* DUTY MARK.

dredger. A type of CASTER which, when made of silver, was used presumably for sprinkling ground spices. It is cylindrical and undecorated, except for some horizontal moulding, and has a simple scroll or ring handle. *See* KITCHEN PEPPER-POT.

Dresser, Dr Christopher (1834–1904). A designer of silverware in Birmingham, England; he was born in Glasgow, and trained at the Government School of Design, London, in the late 1840s and early 1850s. He became interested in plant structure, the subject of two books that he published in 1862 and 1873, and received an Honorary Doctorate in Botany from the University of Jena. In 1877 and 1882 he travelled in Japan and became influenced by Japanese art and design; later he became interested in techniques for mass production of silverware and in functional considerations. From 1878 he produced designs for SILVER-PLATED WARE which he sold to HUKIN & HEATH (becoming the firm's Art Director in 1879), to JAMES DIXON & SONS, and to ELKINGTON & CO. His designs were primarily functional, seeking economy of material and minimum use of decoration, using it mainly where it would strengthen a piece; many pieces of his design were intended for middle-class buyers. Some designs provided for use of encrusted non-silver materials, but such pieces could not be hallmarked in England. Many of his pieces bear the DESIGN REGISTRATION MARK of the firms he worked for, but some bear his stamped facsimile signature. *See* Shirley Bury, 'The Silver Designs of Dr Christopher Dresser' in *Apollo,* December 1962, p. 766. *See* DRESSER CLARET-JUG.

Dresser Claret-Jug. A glass CLARET-JUG mounted in silver, with an ivory handle. It was designed by CHRISTOPHER DRESSER, and made by HUKIN & HEATH, 1881. It is accompanied by six BEAKERS, all owned by the Victoria and Albert Museum, London.

drinking horn. A medieval arc-shaped drinking vessel, made of HORN, tapering to a point, and sometimes having silver mounts, such as a lip band around the open end (the mouthpiece), encircling decorative rings, and a decorative finial at the pointed end, and sometimes a cover with a decorative finial. Many are provided with two legs toward the large end and sometimes also a short leg at the other end so that the horn can be rested in a level position when not empty. Such horns, used in Anglo-Saxon times for drinking wassail (and sometimes called a 'wassail horn'; *see* WASSAIL-BOWL), became in the Middle Ages a feudal symbol of land tenure by cornage. *See* Peter Stone, 'Some Famous Drinking Horns in Britain' in *Apollo,* April 1961, p. 102, and May 1961, p. 143. *See* PUSEY HORN; QUEEN'S COLLEGE (OXFORD) DRINKING HORN; POWDER-HORN.

drip-pan. The small fixed or removable tray surrounding the NOZZLE of a CANDLESTICK, for the purpose of collecting dripping wax or tallow. Some examples are attached to a nozzle that fits into the SOCKET on the shaft. A few candlesticks, *c.* 1690–1710, have – between the stem and the base – a slight encircling horizontal projection which served as a drip-pan. Sometimes called a 'wax-pan' or a 'grease-pan'.

drop-in cover. A type of cylindrical COVER that fits closely inside the circular mouth of, e.g., a BULLET TEAPOT. It is held in place by friction, not by being secured as is a SCREW COVER or a BAYONET COVER. *See* SLIP-ON COVER.

drop-ring handle. A type of HANDLE, usually found as one of a pair on opposite sides of various types of receptacle; it is loosely suspended, in the form of a ring hanging from a BRACKET, or often from the mouth of a lion's head mask. Such handles are usually found on a receptacle that, with its contents, is heavy, e.g., a SOUP-TUREEN, MONTEITH, WINE COOLER, WINE FOUNTAIN or PUNCH-BOWL.

drop spoon. A type of SPOON having on the back, at the juncture of the stem and the bowl, a rounded extension of the stem as a reinforcement. Later examples having an overlapping protuberance were called a 'double-lap spoon' or 'double-drop spoon'.

Druid Group. Silver figures on bronze base overlaid with silver, Hancock & Co., London. H. 60·5 cm. Courtesy, Garrard & Co. Ltd, London.

drum-shaped teapot. Joseph and Nathaniel Richardson, Philadelphia, Pa, *c.* 1780–90. H. 17 cm. Yale University, Art Gallery (Mabel Brady Garvan Collection), New Haven, Conn.

Ducie Ostrich-Egg Cup. Silver-gilt mounts (the egg a modern replacement), London, 1584. H. 36·8 cm. Toledo Museum of Art, Toledo, Ohio (photo courtesy, Christie's, London).

Druid Group. An ornamental piece of FIGURAL SILVERWARE on a bronze base overlaid with silver, depicting ancient Britons, inspired by a Druid, awaiting the landing of the Romans at Pevensey Bay, Sussex. It was made by Hancock & Co. (*see* HANCOCKS), London, 1865.

drum. A type of percussion instrument occurring in various forms, some of which have been reproduced in silver, e.g., a KETTLE-DRUM and a side drum (snare drum) are found as REGIMENTAL SILVERWARE.

drum-shaped mustard-pot. A type of MUSTARD-POT that is of cylindrical (drum) shape, having a flat bottom, a hinged flat or domed LID with a THUMBPIECE, and an S-shaped or scroll handle. The lid usually has an indentation to retain the stem of a MUSTARD SPOON. The pot is about 7·5 cm high and 5 cm in diameter. Such pieces were often undecorated, but frequently had pierced work on the sides (often in the form of PALES, sometimes embellished with connecting circular motifs or overlaid swags of foliage); with such pierced examples there was a removable glass LINER, and the bottom was sometimes also pierced to facilitate pushing out the liner. Sometimes called a 'mustard-can'.

drum-shaped teapot. A type of TEAPOT that is of tapering cylindrical (drum) shape, slightly wider at the bottom than at the top; it has a flat bottom, a sunken-hinged flat LID (without a THUMBPIECE) and a C-shaped handle of wood riveted in silver FERRULES. Such pots were made *c.*1770–90. They are sometimes decorated with ENGRAVING and CHASING and sometimes a chain connects the finial on the cover to the upper ferrule provided for the handle.

dry-mustard jar. The same as a MUSTARD CASTER.

Dublin Assay Office. The ASSAY OFFICE established in Dublin in 1637, and the only Assay Office in Ireland. *See* IRISH HALLMARKS; HIBERNIA HALLMARK.

Dublin silverware. Articles of silverware made in Dublin, Ireland, some from very early periods but mainly from 1637 when the Company of Goldsmiths of Dublin was chartered, the local Assay Office was established, and the STERLING SILVER standard was adopted. More than 1,100 names of Dublin silversmiths have been recorded in the period 1714–1830. Almost all types of domestic silverware, and much ecclesiastical silverware, were made; for the different styles produced in successive periods, *see* IRISH SILVERWARE. *See* IRISH HALLMARKS.

Ducie Ostrich-Egg Cup. An OSTRICH-EGG CUP (the present ostrich egg being a modern replacement for an earlier silver-gilt replacement egg), with silver-gilt mounts for the slightly domed circular foot, the plain vase-shaped stem, the high vertical neck-band, and the baluster finial, and having four vertical, hinged, decorated straps securing the bowl and four others securing the section of egg forming the cover. The stem is decorated with four dolphin brackets whose upraised tails support the silver CALYX in which the bowl rests; the four straps are decorated with caryatid-like figures. The cup was made in 1854 for William Rose (d.1588), of Bockmer, Buckinghamshire; it was sold by the 6th Earl of Ducie at Christie's, London, on 7 October 1959 and was resold there on 13 May 1964. It is owned by the Toledo Museum of Art, Toledo, Ohio, as a gift from Edward Drummond Libbey.

Ducie Standing Cup. A silver-gilt STANDING CUP having a thistle-shaped bowl resting on a baluster-shaped stem and a domed base. The low-domed finial is surmounted by a standing male figure holding a spear. It is similar in form and decoration to the LEE CUP except for the stem, the finial, and different arms and inscriptions; both cups feature the work of the same engraver. It was made for Robert Ducie and bears the London mark for 1607. It is in the Hermitage, Leningrad.

duck's-head spout. A type of S-shaped SPOUT for a TEAPOT or COFFEE-POT, having its pouring lip shaped somewhat like a duck's head, with a split opening for the beak and a small ornament on the top.

ductile. Susceptible of being drawn into a desired shape, as in making silver WIRE. *See* MALLEABLE.

Dummer, Jeremiah (1645–1718). A leading silversmith who worked in Boston, Massachusetts, having been apprenticed in 1659 to the firm of HULL AND SANDERSON. He is known for having engraved the plates used in printing the first paper money issued in Connecticut and for making a wide var-

iety of pieces of silverware, many examples of which are extant, especially
PORRINGERS and SPOONS. He is said to have introduced in the Colonies the
use of CUT CARD decoration. *See* Hermann Frederick Clarke and Henry
Wilder Foote, *Jeremiah Dummer* (1970); Frederick Clarke, 'Jeremiah Dummer' in *Antiques,* October 1935, p. 142. *See* MASSACHUSETTS SILVERWARE.

Durbin, Leslie G. (1913–). An outstanding English designer-silversmith.
He was apprenticed as an engraver in 1929 to OMAR RAMSDEN and stayed
with him as a journeyman until 1938, when he won a scholarship to study
silversmithing. After World War II, he opened his own workshop in 1945 at
62 Rochester Place, Camden Town, London, with his partner, Leonard Moss
(d. 1982), until the latter retired in 1970. He obtained many prestigious commissions, and designed and made a wide range of articles, including maces
(*see* SMITHSONIAN MACE), swords, boxes, BADGES, medals, CANDELABRA, and
animal figures, but principally commemorative pieces for public bodies (*see*
BANK OF ENGLAND INKSTAND) and prominent individuals, as well as important ecclesiastical articles (e.g., the PROCESSIONAL CROSS for Coventry Cathedral and the ALTAR CROSS and CANDLESTICKS for Guildford Cathedral) and
domestic ware (*see* DURBIN CONDIMENT SETS). His designs varied so that each
should be appropriate for the particular donor or recipient, and his work recognized both traditional and modern styles. He made the gold- and silverwork on the quillons and fittings of the STALINGRAD SWORD, and modelled
the Queen's head for the 1977 Silver Jubilee BRITISH COMMEMORATIVE MARK.
Much of his work bears the mark of WAKELY & WHEELER LTD, London. He was
awarded the C.B.E. in 1976, and was given a one-man retrospective exhibition (170 pieces) at Goldsmiths' Hall, London, in July 1982, catalogued in
Leslie Durbin, Fifty Years of Silversmithing (1982). He is now semi-retired at his
home in Richmond, Surrey. *See* Judith Banister, 'Inspired by Minerva' in
Country Life, 15 July 1982, p. 172.

Durbin Condiment Sets. (1) A CONDIMENT SET consisting of a pair of SALT-
CELLARS and a pair of PEPPER CASTERS made in 1947 by LESLIE G. DURBIN, having the receptacles supported by stems in the form of figures of a pelican in-

duck's-head spout. Coffee-pot with
faceted octagonal spout, Augustine
Courtauld II, London, 1716. H.
22·3 cm. Folger's Coffee Collection,
Procter & Gamble Co., Cincinnati, Ohio.

Durbin, Leslie. Teapot, designed by
Robert Y. Goodden, with chased
decoration and cast foot, London, 1951
(from a service for the Royal Pavilion
at the Festival of Britain). H. 17·8 cm.
Photo courtesy, Robert Y. Goodden.

Durbin Condiment Sets (2). Designed by
and made at the workshop of Leslie
Durbin, London, 1963. H. 10 cm.
Photo courtesy, Leslie Durbin.

her-piety, motifs from the arms of Corpus Christi College, Oxford, to which the set was donated by the late Sir Alan Barlow, upon his being made a Fellow. (2) A comparable set made in 1963 by Durbin, but with the stems in the form of the heads of antlered stags having a Latin cross on the heads, as in the vision of St Hubert, taken from the family crest of Miss Beryl le Poer Power, who donated the set to Girton College, Cambridge, for use at High Table.

Dürer Cup. A silver-gilt STANDING CUP, based on a design, *c.* 1500, by Albrecht Dürer (1471–1528), the famous German artist and engraver from Nuremberg, and made by JOHN BRIDGE, 1826-7, for RUNDELL, BRIDGE & RUNDELL. The lobed bowl is decorated with chased flowers; the stem is in the form of a gnarled tree-trunk rising from a base of curved leaves upon which are figures of two frogs and a lizard, each having inset gemstones for eyes. The foot and bowl are also set with gemstones. The piece is in the Royal Collection.

duty-dodger. Any unscrupulous silversmith who sought to evade the 1720-57 duty (tax) at 6*d* per oz. on silverware, payable at the ASSAY OFFICE where the ASSAYING was performed and the HALLMARKS stamped on individual pieces. Several methods were used: (1) inserting into a new article an existing set of hallmarks removed from an old piece, possibly acquired for melting down, and sometimes punching his own maker's mark over thar of the original maker; (2) inserting into a piece made to special order several of his own punches so that an unwary buyer might think them to be official marks of the Assay Office; or (3) inserting into a large heavy piece, e.g., a TWO-HANDLED CUP, a small disc bearing marks from an article on which a low tax had been paid for the deliberate purpose of its being so used (e.g., the WARRINGTON WINE FOUNTAIN). The term is applied also to the piece so marked, and also to a piece altered and considered a FAKE and illegal, even though legal when first made and hallmarked in its original form. *See* Judith Banister, 'Forgers, Furbishers and Duty-Dodgers' in *Apollo*, October 1961, p. 104.

Duty Mark. A 19th-century mark showing the head of Queen Victoria in profile.

duty mark. A mark (not a HALLMARK) punched on certain articles of silver (or gold) submitted to the ASSAY OFFICES during parts of the 18th and 19th centuries to attest that the then required excise duty had been paid. Excise duty was levied in England from 1 June 1720 to 1757 (but no Duty Mark) and from 1 December 1784 to 30 April 1890. The mark used in England from 1 December 1784 was the head in profile of the reigning Sovereign in an ESCUTCHEON, and was punched on articles of silver in the first period and of gold or silver (except some small articles) in the second period until the duty was abolished in 1890. Such duty was imposed on Irish silver from 1730; until 1807 the mark used there was the seated figure of Hibernia, and thereafter that mark was continued along with the Duty Mark of the Sovereign's head. The Duty Mark of the Sovereign's head was introduced in Scotland in 1819. The marks show successively: from December 1784 to 29 May 1786, the head of George III (facing left) punched in intaglio (*see* INCUSE MARK) in an octagonal escutcheon; then from 1786 (facing right) in relief in an oval escutcheon; thereafter the heads of George IV and of William IV (both facing right) and of Victoria (facing left), all punched in relief in oval escutcheons. In 1797 the duty mark was punched twice, as evidence of the doubling of the duty in that year. The Duty Mark is sometimes called the 'Sovereign's Head Mark'. *See* DRAWBACK MARK.

dwarf candlestick. A type of CANDLESTICK of small size, about 10 to 15 cm high; it has a base supporting the SOCKET, either with a very short intervening stem or with no stem. Such pieces were made in the period 1660 to 1770 in various forms and styles of decoration. Sometimes called a 'desk candlestick'.

Dyneley Casket. Alabaster with silver-gilt mounts, London, *c.* 1620. Victoria and Albert Museum, London.

Dyneley Casket. A circular CASKET, having an alabaster body and low-domed hinged lid, decorated with stamped silver-gilt mounts, *c.* 1620. The mounts on the body consist of bands encircling the base and the rim, connected by four vertical hinged strips, and four CLAW-AND-BALL FEET, and those on the lid consist of a spiked finial and a hinged hasp. It was formerly owned by the Dyneley family, of Brenhope Manor, Yorkshire, and since 1865 has been in the Victoria and Albert Museum, London.

E

eagle-wing caddy spoon. A type of CADDY SPOON having on its circular bowl relief decoration of simulated feathers extending to a handle in the form of an eagle's neck and terminating in an eagle's head with a hooked beak and a burnished eye. Examples are fairly rare; they were made by DIE-STAMPING silver of light gauge. They were made from *c*. 1790 to c 1850, but also in flimsy versions in the later Victorian period.

ear-pick. An instrument with a small scoop for removing wax from the ear. Some silver examples were made with a TOOTHPICK on the end opposite the scoop, and some have an ear-pick and a toothpick joined by a swivel. English examples are recorded in the inventories of James II of Scotland (1488), of Henry VIII (1530) and of Elizabeth I (1573-7). Some were enclosed in a WHISTLE (such as one said to have been owned by Anne Boleyn) or in an ÉTUI.

ear-trumpet. A hearing aid, usually in the form of a straight musical trumpet, sometimes in two or more parts to be telescoped when not in use. In some rare cases an amplifying device is set into an article such as the handle of a walking stick. Two silver telescopic examples (London, 1814, and Dublin, 1829, respectively) are in the Wellcome Collection at the Science Museum, London, which also owns a Sheffield plate example, 1845; another plated example was made by W.B. Pirie, *c*. 1820. *See* MEDICAL SILVERWARE.

East India Company Coffee-pot. The earliest-known English silver COFFEE-POT, being in the same form as the BERKELEY TEAPOT, exept that the wooden handle is scroll-shaped and is opposite the spout. It bears an engraved inscription, 'The Gift of Richard Sterne Esq to Ye Honorable East India Comp.'; it also bears the engraved COAT OF ARMS of the donor, the maker's mark 'GG', and the London hallmark for 1681-2. It is in the Victoria and Albert Museum, London.

écuelle (French). A shallow, flat-bottomed BOWL with vertical sides, having two flat horizontal lateral handles that are level with the rim, and usually a domed cover, and sometimes having a conforming STAND. Such pieces were used mainly for serving an individual portion of soup; they were used by holding the two handles and drinking from the bowl before the SOUP SPOON came into general use. They are similar in shape to the type of PORRINGER that is a shallow bowl with one flat handle. Such bowls were introduced into England from France by immigrant Huguenot silversmiths, and also were made in QUEBEC SILVERWARE.

Eddystone Lighthouse Salt. A GREAT SALT, *c*. 1698,. of the architectural type, made in the form of the original Eddystone Lighthouse (designed by Henry Winstanley, completed in 1698, ans swept away by a storm on 26/27 November 1703), off Plymouth. The circular edifice, with an external ladder and stairway, has an open gallery surmounted by a cupola, a pieced and windowed lantern, and a finial in the form of a weather-vane. The cupola and the lantern form a sugar caster, and there is a depression for salt in the gallery; the lower part divides into three compartments. Thus, the piece has six compartments, making it impracticable for use; although it has been suggested that it might have been used as a SPICE-BOX, it seems more probable that it was made primarily as a decorative article. The four lower parts each

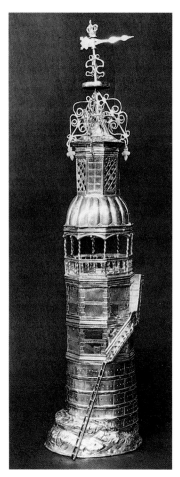

Eddystone Lighthouse Salt. Britannia silver, maker's mark 'Rowe', Plymouth, c. 1698. H. 48·3 cm. City Museum and Art Gallery, Plymouth.

Edinburgh Assay Office. Assay Office Hallmark depicting castle.

egg boiler. Old Sheffield plate, John Edwards, London, c. 1800. H. 12·5 cm. City Museum, Sheffield.

bear a maker's mark 'Rowe', probably Peter Rowe (fl. 1685–1711), of Plymouth, and three parts bear marks 'Plinᵒ' (Plymouth, before 1701) and also 'Britan' (indicating use of BRITANNIA SILVER). The piece was owned by the Morgan family of Tredegar Park, Monmouthshire, and Sir Charles Morgan is reputed to have given it to a cousin, Mrs Caye, in whose family it descended until acquired in 1948 by the City Museum and Art Gallery, Plymouth.

A replica is owned, appropriately, by Trinity House, London (the corporation with responsibilities for lighthouses around the coasts of England, Wales and the Channel Islands), and was shown at the 'Rule Britannia' Maritime Exhibition held for the benefit of the Royal National Lifeboat Institution at Sotheby's, London, 1–29 January 1986, the catalogue attributing it to R. & S. Garrard & Co. (*see* GARRARD & CO. LTD), 1880. There is no record of the piece before it was found at Trinity House, c. 1948 (some of its records were destroyed in World War I). The replica is generally similar to the Plymouth piece, but differs as to the brackets on the lantern, the form of the weather-vane finial, and the angle of the ladder, and the structure rests on a granite base; it bears, on each of its six parts, the mark of ROBERT GARRARD II and the London marks for 1880. Although the Garrard firm states that it has no record of such a piece in 1880, it must be inferred that it was asked to make a replica and (it being normal practice at that time for the firm to make replicas of various pieces of silverware) that it made this example, but altered some details.

The Plymouth Museum catalogue notes two references to such a piece: (1) a journal of 1703 which mentions a silver model of the Plymouth lighthouse seen by the writer when visiting Winstanley's house, Littlebury; and (2) a record of the Lord Chamberlain, dated 24 June 1727, at the Public Record Office, which mentions a silver model of the Eddystone lighthouse brought from Leicester House for the Queen's Apartment at St James's Palace. However, there is nothing to identify either piece with the Plymouth example.

See ARCHITECTURAL SILVERWARE.

edging. The process used by makers of SHEFFIELD PLATE to conceal the copper line at the edge of DOUBLE PLATED ware that became visible when a piece of such ware was sheared. There were three methods: (1) SINGLE-LAPPED EDGING; (2) DOUBLE-LAPPED EDGING; and (3) SILVER-LAPPED EDGING. *See* MOUNTS.

Edinburgh Assay Office. The ASSAY OFFICE established in 1552, and now the only Assay Office in Scotland. Its oldest HALLMARK is its distinctive ASSAY OFFICE HALLMARK, in the form of the 'castle of Edinburgh' with three turrets, accompanied by a varying 'Deacon's Mark' (Assay Master's Mark) and also, since 1847, a MAKER'S MARK. The use of the DATE HALLMARK commenced in 1681 and continued in alphabetical cycles (omitting J) until 1975, when new cycles based on the calendar year were introduced. The STANDARD HALLMARK, introduced in 1759 to replace the Deacon's Mark, was a thistle (*see* THISTLE HALLMARK), and this continued to be used until 1975 when (under the provisions of the Hallmarking Act of 1973) the LION RAMPANT HALLMARK was substituted, whereas the existing practices relating to the use of the Castle Assay Office Hallmark and Maker's Marks remained unchanged. A DUTY MARK, with the Sovereign's head, was used from 1784 until 1890. *See* Malcolm Baker, 'Late 18th Century Edinburgh Silver Trade' in *The Connoisseur*, August 1973, p. 289.

Edward VIII Cup. A TWO-HANDLED CUP of original shape, having a high bowl that is cylindrical and sloping slightly inward toward the domed base, and two thin unconventional handles; the cover is surmounted by a finial in the form of a crown. The cup was designed by HAROLD STABLER, 1936, and made by WAKELY & WHEELER LTD, on commission from Captain Llewellyn Amos, Director of the National Jewellers Association; the order was placed shortly before the abdication of Edward VIII, 1936, and engraved on the bowl are two leopards and the inscription 'To commemorate the Accession Year of His Majesty King Edward VIII'. The engraving was by G. T. Friend. The cup is owned by the Goldsmiths' Company, London.

egg-and-dart border. A border pattern consisting of a series of alternating ovoid motifs and darts (arrowheads) pointed at both ends, or of alternating semi-ovals with darts all pointing in the same direction.

egg-and-tongue border. A border pattern consisting of a series of alternating ovoid and tongue-shaped motifs.

egg boiler. A vessel for boiling or coddling one or more (up to eight) eggs. It is usually in the form of a cylindrical or vase-shaped receptacle having a flat or dome-shaped LID (sometimes divided into two sections and opened by two hinges). The receptacle contains a frame of wire formed into four to six rings, each to hold an egg while being cooked, and has a central vertical HANDLE with a loop at the top to lift it from the water. Such receptacles are sometimes accompanied by a stand for a spirit lamp and sometimes a sand-glass egg-timer set in a wire frame on the lid. A variant form is an EGG-CUP with a semi-ovoid cover, both parts pierced, to be set into boiling water and, after cooking, to be used to serve the egg. Also called an 'egg coddler'.

egg-cup. A small semi-ovoid cup on a stemmed base, used for serving a boiled egg in the shell. The cups are usually plain but some have openwork decoration of pierced patterns or vertical PALES, and all have a rim around the top or an everted rim in order to support the cup when placed in the ring of an EGG-CUP FRAME. The interior of the cup is often gilded to preclude discoloration caused by egg-yolk on silver. Sometimes the cup has a base that is an inverted second cup of a slightly different size; such a piece is called a 'double egg-cup'. *See* EGG-RING; MEDICINE-CUP.

egg-cup frame. Silver-gilt stand with six egg-cups, central salt-cellar, and rope handle, Richard Cook, London, 1803; silver-gilt egg-spoons, A. Fogelberg and S. Gilbert, London, 1783. H. 35 cm. Courtesy, Partridge (Fine Arts) Ltd, London.

egg-cup frame. A stand, sometimes made of WIREWORK, for holding several EGG-CUPS, usually four to six, with sometimes a supporting TRAY (square, oval, triangular or of CANOE SHAPE) and occasionally a SALT-CELLAR. Such stands were made in numerous forms and styles. They sometimes support circular guard-rings in which the egg-cups are suspended, and sometimes loops are formed between the rings to support EGG SPOONS in a vertical position, bowl upward. Unusual examples have three cups and two spoons, apparently for husband-and-wife use, or two cups and one spoon, or even one cup and spoon but with extendable guard-rings for two more cups and spoons. Some trays have a central column or framework with a ring handle at the top and also a support for several egg spoons and occasionally 'a central support for a salt-cellar. Some such stands are combined with a TOAST-RACK. Sometimes called an 'egg cruet'. *See* G. Bernard Hughes, 'Stands for Georgian Egg-cups' in *Country Life*, 21 November 1968, p. 1334.

egg-ring. A small waisted cylindrical receptacle for serving a boiled egg, the upper part being shaped to hold the egg. *See* EGG-CUP.

egg spoon. A type of small SPOON that is sometimes found accompanying an EGG-CUP STAND. The bowl is sometimes slightly elongated and is often gilded in order to give protection against the discoloration that egg-yolk produces on silver.

Eglinton Testimonial. An ornamental CENTREPIECE in architectural form, having an indented 20-sided polygonal base decorated with Gothic arches in each of which is a heraldic shield; from the base rises an edifice around which are figures of mounted knights in armour, and above them on a balcony are female figures bestowing flowers and wreaths, all surmounted by a high battlemented finial. It was designed and modelled by EDMUND COTTERILL, with architectural details by Sibron, and was executed by R. & S. Garrard (*see* GARRARD & CO. LTD), 1843. It was presented to Lord Eglinton by subscribers as a testimonial for the lavish tournament he had presented at Eglinton Castle, near Kilmarnock, Scotland.

Egyptian Service. A SERVICE ordered by George III in 1803, commissioned from RUNDELL, BRIDGE & RUNDELL, and made for them by PAUL STORR and by BENJAMIN SMITH I and DIGBY SCOTT. It was completed in 1811 and purchased by the Prince Regent (later George IV) for use on state occasions. The pieces are decorated with sphinxes and other Egyptian motifs; the tureen has handles in the form of the many-breasted Artemis of Ephesus. The service is in the Royal Collection.

Election Cup. A silver-gilt STANDING CUP having a bowl of inverted bell shape resting on a stemmed base and having a domed cover with a finial surmounted by a globe encircled by a crown. The bowl is removable, being attached to the stem by a BAYONET JOINT. The bowl, base, and cover are embossed with repeating shell-like motifs in a DIAPER pattern, and are set at intervals, along the rim of the bowl and the base, with paste jewels of different colours, some now missing. The unmarked piece was attributed formerly to c. 1520, but later (*Burlington Magazine*, July 1977) to c. 1500. It was presented in 1555 to Winchester College, Winchester, Hampshire, by John White, Bishop of Lincoln and, from 1541 to 1554, Warden of the College. The name of the cup is derived from the donor's wish that it 'Supplement the Election'.

electroform. A facsimile made by the process of ELECTROFORMING.

Elgin Jug. Silver gilt, Paul Storr, London, 1799. H. 33·7 cm. Courtesy, Sotheby's, London.

Elizabeth I Salt (1). Silver-gilt standing salt, London, 1572. H. 29·2 cm. Tower of London (Crown copyright, HMSO).

electroforming. The technique of making an exact facsimile of a model by depositing a thin layer of metal (e.g., silver or copper), by means of an electric current, on a replica of the model. (The process was formerly called 'electrotyping', which is the term used in the printing trade for block-making.) The model is sometimes made of wax, but often it is an actual article of which reproductions are sought, ranging from a natural flower or a prosaic baby's shoe to a large and ornate piece of silverware. The process involves first making a negative mould, of plaster of Paris, from the model, then casting a metal positive (a replica of the model and called a 'mandrel') of a lightweight metal, gutta-percha, silicon, rubber, plastic, etc., and finally depositing, by an electric current, on the mandrel a thin layer of metal, usually silver. When mass production is desired, a second negative mould is made from the cast, and the mandrel is made from it. The deposit varies in thickness (and consequent durability) according to the length of time that the current is switched on. The final article (sometimes called an 'electrotype' or an 'electroform') is then perfected by BURNISHING. The fact that the silver is deposited particle by particle (rather than being poured in molten form) is usually perceptible unless the piece has been well polished. Electroforms may not be legally hallmarked as they are not made entirely of silver, but some bear the mark of the maker, e.g., ELKINGTON & CO.

The technique was first demonstrated in 1838 by Prof. H. H. Jacobi, of St Petersburg, and at about the same time by Thomas Spencer, a framemaker of Liverpool and also by C. J. Jordan, a London craftsman, and was published in England in 1839; it was developed by Elkington & Co. in the 1840s in making copies of Celtic jewelry, and was then expanded to make copies of ancient jewelry and important silverware. Unlike ELECTROPLATING, in which the surface layer is deposited on a heavy metal base, the use of a light-weight mandrel permits the production of relatively large articles of reasonably light weight. The second (metal) mould can be re-used so that the process is commercially practicable for mass-production. The process has been used in England in recent years for silverware articles by ALEX STYLES and by LOUIS OSMAN, and in the United States by Stanley Lechtzin.

For security reasons during exhibitions open to the public, the Goldsmiths' Company sometimes displays on the buffet, where its ceremonial plate is normally placed, only electroforms. Some silver electroforms are in the Royal Collection and in many leading museums, e.g., the Victoria and Albert Museum electroform of the JERNINGHAM-KANDLER WINE COOLER.

Some Elkington electroforms, made in 1850–70, of important antique silverware were acquired by Metro-Goldwyn-Mayer in the 1920s and used in film productions; the collection was dispersed in 1971.

See Shirley Bury, *Victorian Electroplate* (1971); G. Bernard Hughes, 'An Elegant Use for Electricity' in *Country Life*, 12 November 1973, p. 1722.

electro-gilding. The process of GILDING by means of an electric current. Experiments, started in 1805 by the Italian scientist Luigi Vincenzo Pignatelli, to gild silver by use of Volta's battery (although commercially unsuccessful) led to the making of the GALVANIC GOBLET by PAUL STORR in 1814. In 1840 the publication of the results of work by Arthur Smee started the commercial development of electro-gilding which was pioneered by ELKINGTON & CO. By the 1860s–70s the process superseded that of mercury gilding, which was more costly and had proven dangerous to the health of the workers. Although most of the gilding is reddish-gold, lighter hues similar to those of fire-gilding can be produced. *See* VERMEIL.

electroplating. The technique of changing the surface of a metal (usually a base metal) object by depositing a thin layer of a different metal by means of an electric current. Articles so plated with silver are called SILVER-PLATED WARE. The object and the plating metal are immersed in a plating bath after being connected to electric terminals and, when a low-voltage current is passed through, particles of the plating metal are deposited as a thin film on the object. The object is then hammered to secure the adhesion of the silver. The thickness of the plating varies according to the amount of current and the duration of the process, and is measured in 'microns' (1 micron = one thousandth of a millimetre). When the layer of the plating metal is less than 2 microns thick, it is known as 'washed' or 'flashed'. Sometimes silver is so plated with rhodium to prevent tarnishing. The process for plating with gold or silver, discovered by John Wright of Birmingham in 1840, was patented in England by G. R. and H. Elkington (*see* ELKINGTON & CO.). It has been used extensively in modern times to plate TABLEWARE and large articles of silverware. The process differs from making an object of PLATED METAL by reason of the fact that in electroplating the object is completely made before being silvered, while in the latter the piece is formed after the metal has been plated. Pieces made by the two processes can be distinguished by the fact that electroplated ware will not show the seams and joins which are concealed by the film of electrically deposited silver, and also the colour is whitish rather than the faintly bluish tone of plated ware. In England the centres for the industry are in Birmingham and Sheffield. There are no HALLMARKS for such ware, but a number of symbols (or initials, such as 'EP', 'EPNS' or 'EPGS', or the words 'hard soldered') have been used to stamp articles so made. *See* Shirley Bury, *Victorian Electroplate* (1971). *See* SHEFFIELD PLATE; SILVER DEPOSIT.

electro-texturing. A modern technique which produces on a metal article a textured surface. Grant MacDonald, of London, is a leading English exponent of the process, which is used principally on silverware

electrotype. A facsimile made by ELECTROFORMING.

electrotyping. *See* ELECTROFORMING

Elgin Jug. A silver-gilt JUG in NEO-CLASSICAL STYLE, having a bowl of inverted pear shape resting on three vertical supports terminating in claw feet, and having on the shoulder an encircling band of horned-satyr masks; it has a vertical scroll ivory handle and a hinged domed lid with a finial in the form of a Royal Crown. It was made by PAUL STORR, 1799. It bears the engraved arms of George III and of Thomas Bruce, 7th Earl of Elgin (1766–1841), who in 1803-12 purchased the Elgin Marbles, removed from the Parthenon in Athens during the Turkish occupation of Greece and brought by him to England. The jug was originally a gift to him from the Crown in recognition of his services as a diplomat at Vienna, Brussels, and Berlin prior to his Ambassadorship to Turkey, 1799-1803; it was sold by the 10th Earl of Elgin in 1926 and since then has been sold a number of times, the last recorded sale being at Sotheby's, London, on 18 March 1982.

Elizabeth I Salt. Two different silver-gilt STANDING SALTS, both referred to as Queen Elizabeth Salts and both having been made during her reign, 1558-1603, but having no known connection with her except possibly the virtues depicted in the decoration.

(1) A standing salt, having a drum-shaped body resting on three paw feet and having at the top of the body a shallow recessed receptacle for salt; from its rim four scroll brackets extend upward to support a domed canopy cover which has an urn-shaped finial surmounted by a figure in-the-round of a standing warrior holding a sword and a shield. The body is decorated with three circular panels with EMBOSSING depicting the figures of the three Theological Virtues (Faith, Hope, and Charity) after engravings by Peter Flötner (*c.* 1485–1546) of Nuremberg; between each pair of panels is a thin figure of a CARYATID. On the cover are three medallions depicting Dido, Cleopatra, and Lucretia. The piece is dated 1572 and is said to have been made probably by Thomas Bird. It is now in the collection of Royal Regalia at the Tower of London.

(2) A standing cup, having a square body and base resting on four feet in the form of sphinxes, and having a square cover with an urn-shaped finial surmounted by a standing female figure holding a shield upon which is engraved the arms of the Vintners' Company, London. The four panels on the sides are decorated with CHASING depicting landscapes in which are the figures of the Four Cardinal Virtues (Justice, Fortitude, Temperance, and Prudence) also after engravings by Peter Flötner. It has on the bottom the engraved inscription 'Y^e gift of Mr John Powel Master of the Worpf[11] Company of Vintners Ann^0 Dom 1702'. It bears the mark of a bird, said to be possibly that of Thomas Pampton or of Affabel Partridge. It is marked London, 1569, and is owned by the Vintners' Company. A salt of similar shape, but smaller, marked London, 1573-4, and having a finial in the form of a figure of a boy holding a shield and staff, was formerly owned by a Mr Chancellor.

Elizabeth I Statuette. A silver-gilt STATUETTE depicting Elizabeth I on horseback entering Kenilworth Castle, Warwickshire, in 1575. Two different such pieces are known: (1) that with the horse and figure modelled by Baron Charles Marochetti (1805-67) and the accompanying dogs by H. McCarthy, the whole being executed by a predecessor firm to HANCOCKS; and (2) that designed by Pierre-Emile Jeannest (1813-57), a Parisian artist working in London, and made by ELKINGTON & CO. as a prize for the Warwick Races in 1850-1 (it was shown at the Great Exhibition of 1851).

Elizabeth II Coronation Cup. A silver-gilt STANDING CUP designed by ROBERT Y. GOODDEN and made in 1953 by WAKELY & WHEELER LTD, with engraving by T.C. Wise. The bowl and cover together form a sphere, with the hemispherical bowl resting on a fluted stem rising from a stepped foot; both bowl and cover are decorated with tapering GADROONING. The cover has a

Elizabeth I Salt (2). Silver-gilt standing salt, London, 1569. H. 31 cm. Vintners' Company, London.

gadrooned steeple finial supported by six brackets and topped by an orb covered with many small wavy spikes representing the sun's rays. The foot rests on a circle of short brackets joined to the round base, on the centre of which are the Royal Arms and the inscription 'The Coronation Cup of Her Majesty Queen Elizabeth II 1953'. The cup was made from the winning design in a competition to commemorate the coronation. In the tradition of the SIR MARTIN BOWES CUP, the Queen used the cup to drink a toast to the City of London at the banquet at the Mansion House in 1954, held to commemorate her return with Prince Philip from a royal tour to Australia and other Commonwealth countries. The usual hallmarks are supplemented by the COMMEMORATIVE MARK for the coronation. The cup was commissioned by the Goldsmiths' Company, London, which owns it.

Elizabeth, Princess, Statuette. A silver-gilt equestrian STATUETTE depicting Princess Elizabeth (before her accession to the throne as Elizabeth II in 1952) riding her horse Tommy; it was cast by an unknown maker from the 1947 model by Doris Lindner which was reproduced in porcelain by the Worcester Porcelain Co. It bears the hallmark of the LONDON ASSAY OFFICE, and the 1953 Coronation Commemorative mark (sss BRITISH COMMEMORATIVE MARKS); it also bears, in lieu of a maker's mark, the initials 'LAO' (for London Assay Office), indicating that it was submitted by an unregistered maker (possibly the modeller herself or a commercial silver-casting firm with no registered mark). It is signed on the base by Doris Lindner. It was donated to the Corporation of the City of London by Sir Leslie Boyce, Lord Mayor in 1951-2, and is kept at the Mansion House, London. *See* ELIZABETH I STATUETTE; VICTORIA STATUETTE.

Elizabethan silverware. Articles of silverware made in England during the reign of Elizabeth I, 1558-1603, and the decades following. The style included the adaptation of Renaissance motifs, featuring STRAPWORK, GROTESQUES, and mythological subjects.

Elkington & Co. Ltd. A leading firm of silversmiths at Birmingham, England, in the 19th century and the first half of the 20th century. It was founded in the 1830s by Josiah and George Richards, to whom their nephew, George Richards Elkington (1801-65) had been apprenticed in 1815. The latter soon became a partner and, when his uncles died, the sole proprietor. He took as his partner his cousin, Henry Elkington (c. 1810-52). In the 1840s they formed a partnership with Josiah Mason (d. 1859), the firm becoming Elkington, Mason & Co. until Mason's retirement in 1856, when the name became Elkington & Co. After Henry died in 1852, George continued to direct the firm until his death in 1865, when it passed to his son Frederick, and later became Elkington & Co. Ltd. The Company was purchased in the 1950s by the Delta Metal Group, which continued the silverware production until 1963 when such production was joined with GARRARD & CO. LTD and MAPPIN & WEBB LTD, to form British Silverware Ltd. Later the silverware operation of Elkington was transferred from Goscote, near Walsall, to Sheffield, and Elkington has ceased to be a silverware producer.

In 1836-8 the firm patented several processes, including ELECTROGILDING. In 1838 it acquired from O. W. Barrett the process of coating metal with zinc. In 1840 it acquired from John Wright, of Birmingham, his patent for ELECTROPLATING. Further patents were taken out by the firm, and it also acquired patents from outsiders for improving its processes. The firm granted licences to many firms, including EDWARD BARNARD & SONS LTD and, in Paris, Christofle & Cie, but it marked pieces made by it 'E and Co.'. During the 1850s it engaged as designers several French sculptors, including LÉONARD MOREL-LADEUIL as special designer and AUGUSTE ADOLPHE WILLMS as head of the art department. In this period it developed new processes for STAMPING silverware, and acquired a steam-operated machine for the production of large objects. The firm made SILVER-PLATED WARE in the 1880s, some from designs by CHRISTOPHER DRESSER. It sent technicians to Russia to reproduce by ELECTROFORMING some important English silverware in the Kremlin; many of the copies were exhibited in London at the Great Exhibition of 1851 and the International Exhibition of 1862, and some are now at the Victoria and Albert Museum, London.

Emanuel, Harry (fl. 1860-70). A retail silversmith and jeweller of Bond St, London, and 70 Brook St, London, noted for the unusual types of silver articles that he exhibited. Pieces associated with him do not bear his mark as maker, and they were probably commissioned by him from outside silversmiths, e.g., the 'Faerie Queen Group' made by Benjamin Preston. Some of his ware was made from models by the sculptor HENRY HUGH ARMSTEAD. He exhibited pieces at the London International Exhibition of 1862, e.g., the 'Perseus and Andromeda Vase', designed and made by Aimé Cherneau, and

Elizabeth II Coronation Cup. Silver-gilt, designed by Robert Y. Goodden for Wakely & Wheeler Ltd, London, 1953. H. 45·8 cm. Goldsmiths' Company, London.

embossing. Relief decoration on salver, London, 1661. Wadsworth Atheneum (Elizabeth B. Miles Collection), Hartford, Conn.

at the Paris Exposition of 1867, e.g., the SWAN AUTOMATON. Other silver-smiths with similar surnames but not known to be related include: (1) E. & E.Emanuel of Portsmouth, who also showed silverware at the International Exhibition of 1862, and (2) H.M.Emanuel & Son of Portsea.

embossing. The technique of producing relief decoration by raising the surface of thin metal from the reverse so as to form the design on the front. The technique is the same as that used in REPOUSSÉ work, but the term is some-times strictly applied only to work done by mechanical means, such as the use of metal or stone dies (called 'embossing dies'), as distinguished from *repoussé* work which is done by hand using punches ('embossers') and hammers. The process is usually applied to flat metal, but it is sometimes used to decorate HOLLOW WARE by means of a SNARLING IRON that impresses the design from the interior, the result then being refined by REPOUSSÉ CHASING on the outside. *See* POUNCE.

Emes, John (d. 1808). An English silversmith, apprenticed in 1778 and freed in 1786. His first mark was entered in 1796 in partnership with HENRY CHAWNER, at Amen Corner, Paternoster Row, London. Later marks were registered alone. He appointed Edward Barnard to manage the business (*see* BARNARD, EDWARD, & SONS LTD). His wife, REBECCA(H) EMES, worked with him and, after his death in 1808, continued the business with Edward Barnard as partner. Emes made mainly TEA SERVICES and COFFEE SERVICES, and some TANKARDS. *See* TEA WARMER.

Emes, Rebecca(h) (fl. 1808-29). An English silversmith who worked with her husband JOHN EMES and upon his death in 1808 carried on the business with her brother-in-law, William Emes, registering in 1808 their joint mark 'RE/WE'. Soon after in 1808 she took as her partner Edward Barnard I, the workshop foreman, registering their joint mark 'RE/EB', with later marks in 1818, 1821, and 1825. The firm became large and prosperous, supplying plate to RUNDELL, BRIDGE & RUNDELL, and continued until 1829, when Edward Barnard, in partnership with his three sons, continued it (*see* BARNARD, EDWARD, & SONS LTD). *See* WEYMOUTH REGATTA CUP.

Empire style. A French decorative style which was introduced after the French Revolution and which spread throughout Europe. It is named after the First Empire, 1804-14, but it continued until *c.*1830 when a Gothic Revival style commenced. It followed the DIRECTOIRE STYLE, adding motifs, such as sphinxes, inspired by Napoleon's campaigns in Egypt and by archaeological discoveries. It corresponds to the REGENCY STYLE in England. An example of a transatlantic adaptation is an INKSTAND having supports in the form of sphinxes, each wearing a feathered head-dress typical of North American Indians.

enamel. A pigment of a vitreous nature composed of powdered potash and silica, bound with oil, coloured with metallic oxides, and applied on various materials, including silver, as a surface decoration by low-temperature firing (*c.*750 °C.); enamels are usually mixed with a flux to facilitate melting at this temperature. *See* ENAMELLING.

enamelling. The technique of decorating silver (and other materials) by the application of ENAMEL on the surface. The process, known since ancient times, has been used on ecclesiastical silverware in Britain from the Tudor period in the 16th century on, and more extensively from the mid-19th century on secular ware by A.W.N. PUGIN. PIERRE-ÉMILE JEANNEST, Joseph Angell III (*see* ANGELL), and others. Such decoration was used mainly on small articles, such as SNUFF-BOXES, and on some household silverware such as small CUPS and the HANDLES of some COFFEE SPOONS. The process used is that generally known as 'painted enamelling' or 'en plein enamelling', being painted on the flat surface, rather than deposited in grooves or depressions, as in CHAMPLEVÉ or CLOISONNÉ work, although the latter processes were sometimes used on the PLINTH of some sculptural ware. Examples of such painted enamelling on Tudor ware are found on the PARKER EWER and the HENSLOWE EWER, the inscriptions on some MAZERS and on some covered STANDING CUPS, e.g., the LEIGH CUP of 1499-1500, and on some CANDLE-STICKS. The process was developed in the 19th century on ware produced by ELKINGTON & CO. A new process of enamelling on large flat surfaces was developed in 1964 by GERALD BENNEY.

'engine' coffee dripper. A fantasy type of COFFEE DRIPPER in the form of a railway steam locomotive. At the front end a decorative tall, slim funnel rests on a container for ground coffee. The coffee is spooned from here onto a perforated plate inside the large cylindrical receptacle at the rear end. In

Empire style. Inkstand, Harvey Lewis, Philadelphia, Pa, *c.* 1815-25. H. 9·2 cm. Yale University Art Gallery (Mabel Brady Garvan Collection), New Haven, Conn.

enamelling. Teapot with black enamelled lid, Gerald Benney, London, 1983. H. 12·5 cm. Courtesy, Gerald Benney.

'engine' coffee dripper. Old Sheffield plate, *c.* 1828. H. 48·3 cm. Folger's Coffee Collection, Procter & Gamble Co., Cincinnati, Ohio.

the middle is the horizontal 'boiler' which, when filled with water, is heated by a spirit lamp beneath it; steam then rises and passes through a curved tube that enters the top of the cylinder, so that as it condenses it drips down through the coffee into a lower receptacle which has a TAP and SPIGOT. The wheels of the 'engine' revolve so that it can be moved along rails. An example was made of SHEFFIELD PLATE, c. 1828.

engine-turning. The technique of ENGRAVING and decorating silverware with an overall pattern of continuous, encircling, and contiguous narrow grooves, usually of a wavy character. The process involves the use of an engine-turning lathe which usually has an eccentric motion that enables it to cut a variety of patterns, the more elaborate of which were done using a guide called a 'rosette', hence the term 'rose-engine-turned' which is applied to a pattern executed in this manner. The decoration is found on silver BOXES of various types, especially those made in the second half of the 18th century. *See* GUILLOCHE.

English hallmarks. The HALLMARKS required to be punched on silverware in England since the reign of Edward I, 1272–1307, and that have been extended to include the ASSAY OFFICE HALLMARK, the STANDARD HALLMARK, and the DATE HALLMARK. These have taken various forms at different times. Other marks have sometimes been punched, such as the MAKER'S MARK, the DUTY MARK and the DRAWBACK MARK, as have the IMPORTED GOODS HALLMARKS and COMMEMORATIVE MARKS (not strictly hallmarks). A DESIGN REGISTRATION MARK (not a hallmark) has been used to indicate the date of registration of a design (not the date of manufacture of the piece). No hallmark has ever been required on SHEFFIELD PLATE, which is not subject to compulsory ASSAYING, but marks (*see* CROWN MARK) have been permitted, and sometimes required to be registered. *See* FOREIGN ORIGIN MARK.

Booklets listing British hallmarks can be obtained from most British silver retailers and jewellers, such as the latest editions of *Hallmarks*, published by the Assay Offices of Great Britain, and of *Bradbury's Book of Hallmarks*. For more complete data about British marks, *see* Sir Charles J. Jackson, *English Goldsmiths and their Marks* (1921, 1964); Arthur G. Grimwade, *London Goldsmiths, 1697–1837* (1976); Judith Banister, '500 Years of Hallmarking' in *Country Life*, 9 November 1978, p. 196; exhibition catalogue (Goldsmiths' Hall), *Touching Gold and Silver: 500 Years of Hallmarks* (1978).

English plate. Ware having silver plated on copper, as in the case of SHEFFIELD PLATE, as distinguished from ware plated on a core of white ALLOY such as NICKEL SILVER.

English silverware. Articles made of silver or SHEFFIELD PLATE or by the process of ELECTROPLATING produced in England during successive periods and in changing styles, and generally referred to by the name of the contemporary Sovereign. *See* TUDOR SILVERWARE; ELIZABETHAN SILVERWARE; CAROLINE SILVERWARE; QUEEN ANNE SILVERWARE; WILLIAM AND MARY SILVERWARE; GEORGIAN SILVERWARE; VICTORIAN SILVERWARE. Such nomenclature is imprecise, for styles did not automatically change with the accession of a new Sovereign, and the designations are often used to include ware made in the years shortly before and after the span of a named reign. Few examples of early ware are extant, due to the melting-down of silver articles for revenue, especially in the era of Cromwell, or for conversion to articles of new style. The greater part of surviving English silverware dates from the period after Charles II, c. 1660. Some English silverware is referred to by the name of the style, e.g., ADAM SILVERWARE; HUGUENOT SILVERWARE. *See* BRITISH SILVERWARE.

engraving. The technique of decorating the surface of silver (or other metal) from the front by incising lines, characters, patterns, portraits, etc., in the surface, with consequential removal of some metal. Engraving has been done since the third millennium BC with crude tools of flint, bronze, copper, and later iron; in Germany in the 15th century it was done by dry-point needle. In modern times engraving is executed (1) by hand, by means of a sharply pointed steel tool (called a burin or graver, or, when two-edged, a scorper), while the metal object is held on an engraver's block, or (2) by machine, as on some trophies. A speciality of engravers is reproducing CIPHERS and COATS OF ARMS. Engraving of monograms and commemorative inscriptions has been done by craftsmen skilled in calligraphy. Engraving, being a special skill, is not done by a silversmith but by a technician-artist selected by him. Some engravers who decorated articles made by leading silversmiths are known by name, such as BENJAMIN RHODES, SIMON GRIBELIN, and WILLIAM HOGARTH, although engravers on silverware by custom did not sign their work (as they did on work intended for printing); however, an exception was JOSEPH SYMPSON, who signed some SALVERS which he engraved. *See* Charles C. Oman, 'English Engravers on Plate' in *Apollo*, May 1957, p. 173; June 1957, p. 218; July 1957, p. 286; and November 1957, p. 109; also Katherine C. Buhler, 'Some American Engraved Silverware' in *Antiques*, November 1945, p. 268; and December 1945, p. 348; Charles C. Oman, *English Engraved Silver, 1150–1900* (1978); Judith Banister, 'Six Centuries of Engraved Silver' in *Country Life*, 14 December 1978, p. 2108.

entrée dish. A type of DISH used for serving at dinner the entrée (in early English usage, the first cooked course, before the roast). It is shallow, usually rectangular, but sometimes oval or octagonal, generally with a flat bottom or standing on four low feet, and having a low-domed flat-top COVER. Such dishes were made in several sizes. The cover has a detachable finial (screw or bayonet type) as a vertical ring HANDLE; when removed, the cover can be inverted and used as a slightly smaller serving dish. Early examples were placed on a DISH CROSS; later ones had provision for keeping the food warm by means of: (1) a lower receptacle into which was placed a heated iron BILLET on a frame and a perforated plate above the frame to support the dish, (2) a HOT-WATER PLATE, or (3) a spirit lamp. Such dishes were decorated with ornamental GADROONING or floral MOUNTS on the rim of the bowl and on the cover. Some examples had at each end a sturdy handle by which to carry the loaded dish. Such pieces were often sold in sets of four. Sometimes called a 'double dish', 'steak stew dish', 'curry-dish' or 'hash-dish', and in Victorian times a 'corner dish' or 'side-table dish'. Such entrée dishes are often used today to serve vegetables accompanying the main course. *See* VEGETABLE-DISH.

entrée fork. A type of table FORK of medium length, having four equal and similar tines; it is somewhat smaller than a DINNER FORK.

entrée knife. A type of table KNIFE of medium length; it is similar to but smaller than a DINNER KNIFE.

epaulet (or **epaulette**). A shoulder ornament worn on a military uniform, usually terminating in a fringe. Some worn in England have been made of either silver or PLATED METAL.

epergne. A type of CENTREPIECE for a dinner table or a sideboard, introduced *c*. 1715 from France into England; it is in the form of an elaborate stand characterized by having several branching arms (usually from four to six, but up to twelve) with, either suspended from or supported by the arms, several small removable receptacles (such as CRUETS, SALT-CELLARS, PICKLE-DISHES or SWEETMEAT-DISHES), sometimes made of silver but more often of

entrée dish. One of a set, Paul Storr, London, 1816–17. W. 36·8 cm. Collection of Roselinde and Arthur Gilbert, Beverly Hills, Cal. (photo courtesy, Los Ángeles County Museum of Art).

epergne. Thomas Pitts I, London, 1776. H. 36·8 cm. Courtesy, Garrard & Co. Ltd, London.

glass. On the usual central support there is a larger receptacle, often a BOWL or a BASKET. The piece rests on a spreading foot or on four legs. It is sometimes combined with a CANDELABRUM, having curved arms supporting candle SOCKETS. Some are combined with a CRUET STAND, having at the bottom, just above the stemmed foot, a rotating TRAY with rings to hold various types of cruets and CASTERS. The epergne was made in very many forms and in several styles of decoration; some are in ROCOCO STYLE, decorated with shells and flowers, some are decorated with pagoda-like canopies having suspended bells. The height varies from about 30 to 45 cm. The pedestal or branches of some examples rotate to facilitate use. Some were made as a pair. Although the epergne is sometimes called a *surtout de table*, that phrase is primarily the French term for an article of ceramic ware consisting of a flat, raised centrepiece upon which are placed various cruets, TUREENS, DISHES, and other small receptacles, and sometimes ornamental pieces. In some early 18th-century Royal inventories an epergne is referred to as an 'Aparn'. The name is derived from the French *épargner* (to save), i.e., to save space on the table and the trouble of passing several receptacles. Some centrepieces that are not functional and have no provision for receptacles, but are merely decorative, are occasionally incorrectly termed an 'epergne'. *See* G. Bernard Hughes, 'English Silver Epergnes' in *Country Life*, 19 May 1955, p. 1317. *See* PAGODA EPERGNE; SURTOUT; CRUET STAND/SOY STAND; THOMAS PITTS.

epergne-candelabrum. A type of CENTREPIECE that combines the features of an EPERGNE (having extended arms to support dishes) and a CANDELABRUM (having branches for candles). An elaborate silver-gilt example, at the Mansion House, London, stands on a separate plinth; the epergne, with eight branching arms, was made by PAUL DE LAMERIE, 1738, and the plinth by PAUL STORR, for RUNDELL, BRIDGE & RUNDELL, 1811. *See* KENT EPERGNE.

Epping Forest Centrepiece. A tall CENTREPIECE having three branching arms for candle NOZZLES and, at the top of the centre stem, a pierced ornament holding a glass bowl. The triangular base rises to a circular platform upon which are the figures of three stags. The piece, bearing the initials J. T. B. and a donative inscription, was a public testimonial in June 1880 to John Thomas Bedford for his services in the preservation of Epping Forest, 5,600 acres of park in Essex. It was made by W. & T. Barnard (*see* BARNARD), 1879, and is now at the Mansion House, London.

(e)scallop shell. *See* SCALLOP.

escutcheon. The ornamental form, usually shield-shaped, on which armorial bearings are displayed. *See* COAT OF ARMS; ACHIEVEMENT; CARTOUCHE; ARMORIAL.

essence-box. A small BOX to hold perfumed pastilles, having a pierced LID to permit the scent to be released. It was a forerunner of the VINAIGRETTE, except that is had no pierced metal grille under the lid. It was superseded by the vinaigrette when more aromatic and pungent scented vinegar was introduced for use instead of less volatile pastilles.

Essex Cup. A silver-gilt STANDING CUP, 1592–3, having a hemispherical bowl resting on a stem of vase shape between discs and having a spreading foot; the low-domed cover is topped by a bell-shaped ornament surmounted by a vase-shaped finial. The bowl is encircled by an engraved band of laurel leaves, above and below which are rectangular panels, in chequerboard effect, alternately plain or decorated with faintly engraved close vertical lines (except one panel that bears a coat of arms). The cup was donated in 1598 to Cambridge University by Robert Devereux, 2nd Earl of Essex (1567–1601), when he was Vice-Chancellor of the University. It is now the symbol of the University's Vice-Chancellor's office. The cup was exhibited in 1959 at Goldsmiths' Hall, London, and in 1975 in the Exhibition of Cambridge Plate at the Fitzwilliam Museum, Cambridge, and at the Victoria and Albert Museum, London.

etching. The technique of decorating a metal surface by use of acids. The usual process is to cover the design on the surface with an acid-resisting substance and then to immerse the piece in acid, which eats away (corrodes) the uncovered portions; but for decoration of fine lines, the entire piece is covered with the acid-resisting substance and the design is scratched through it with a sharp tool and then the piece is immersed in the acid. The covering is often a type of wax or varnish, and the usual acids for metalwork are nitric acid for silver and copper. The process has sometimes been used in modern times in lieu of ENGRAVING or CHASING, but seldom in England

epergne-candelabrum (2). Parcel gilt, designed by Thomas Pairpoint, Gorham Co., 1871. Gorham Collection, Providence, R.I.

ethrog box. Bombé shape with citron finial, maker's mark 'AM', London, 1867. W. 17·8 cm. Jewish Museum, London (photo courtesy, Warburg Institute, University of London).

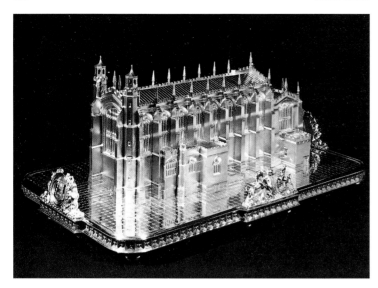

Eton College Chapel Replica. John Tapley, 1834, for Rundell, Bridge & Rundell. L. 82·7 cm. Eton College.

except on VICTORIAN SILVERWARE. It is similar to the process of etching glassware and ceramic ware, except that there hydrofluoric acid is used. Sometimes tautologically called 'acid etching'.

ethrog-box. A type of BOX used in certain Jewish communities in which to keep the *ethrog*, a symbolic citron. anciently used with palm branches in the celebration of the harvest Feast of Tabernacles *(Sukkoth)* and still used as a symbol. It has no prescribed form. Some were made in the form of a citron lying on its side and divided midway to form a bowl and cover, and occasionally resting on a small tray; and sometimes the box has a finial in the form of a citron. A London example, 1867, is of BOMBÉ shape and is embossed and chased with depictions of biblical scenes. *See* JEWISH RITUAL SILVERWARE.

Eton College Chapel Replica. A parcel-gilt silver miniature replica, resting on a large rectangular PLATEAU, of Eton College Chapel, Eton (near Windsor), made in 1834 by John Tapley for RUNDELL, BRIDGE & RUNDELL, to a commission from William IV, for presentation to the Provost and Fellows of Eton College, with the expressed desire that it be used each year at the Eton anniversary dinner. On one side of the plateau are the engraved arms of the College, and on the other side are the Royal arms of William IV. On each end of the plateau there is a plate bearing an inscription recording the gift. *See* ARCHITECTURAL SILVERWARE.

étui (French). A small ornamented case fitted with miniature implements for a woman's daily use, such as scissors, bodkins, needles, tweezers, thimble, a tiny knife, pencil, ivory writing tablet, etc. The cases were variously shaped, delicately decorated with enamels, and richly mounted with gilt hinges and collars. A case, known as a 'gentleman's étui' and used to contain a set of small knife, fork, and spoon, and sometimes an EAR-PICK, was used by travellers. *See* G. Bernard Hughes, 'Elegance of the Etui' in *Country Life*, 19 July 1973, p. 182. *See* CAMPAIGN ÉTUI.

everted. Turned outward, as in the shape of the LIP of a JUG or SAUCE-BOAT, with a sharp angle between the lip and the side of the piece; the curve is more pronounced than on a FLARED lip. *See* TURNED-OUT RIM.

ewer. A type of large JUG (pitcher) that has a tall, deep bowl on a stemmed base and has a single vertical scroll handle, figural handle or HARP-SHAPED HANDLE extending upward to slightly above the rim of the mouth. The bowl is sometimes of ovoid shape with a narrow tall neck, but is usually cylindrical, baluster-shaped or helmet-shaped. Examples have a pouring lip or a beak, and only occasionally a hinged LID. Often a ROSE-WATER EWER and a ROSE-WATER BASIN decorated EN SUITE were used together until the mid-18th century for rinsing the hands at a dinner table before or after a meal. Smaller examples sometimes formed part of a TOILET SERVICE. *See* AMPHORA EWER; HELMET JUG; MERMAID EWER; HENSLOWE EWER; HORNICK EWER; HOWARD EWER; PARKER EWER; WYNDHAM EWER; WINE-AND-WATER EWERS.

ewer (1). Harp-shaped handle, and gadrooning, Anthony Nelme, London, 1794–5. H. 24·8 cm. Bank of England London.

Exeter Salt. Silver-gilt great salt. H. 46 cm. Tower of London (Crown copyright, HMSO).

Exeter Salt. A silver-gilt GREAT SALT, of architectural type, made in the form of a square, four-turret castle with a circular tower and keep, surmounted by a Royal crown; the rocky base is decorated with embossed lizards, frogs, etc., and with gemstones. It was presented to Charles II, on the occasion of his coronation, by the City of Exeter. The piece bears a maker's mark 'IH', but no hallmarks. It was said by E. Alfred Jones to be of English make, but today it is attributed to Johann Haas (fl. 1622–49), a silversmith of Hamburg, Germany, *c.* 1630: it is nevertheless included here because of its historical associations and because it is kept in the Tower of London and there known sometimes as the 'State Salt'. It is now believed not to have been specially commissioned, but rather bought from stock in Hamburg by an English diplomat as a presentation piece and later sold to Exeter. *See* ARCHITECTURAL SILVERWARE.

Exeter silverware. Articles of English silverware bearing the ASSAY OFFICE HALLMARK of the City of Exeter, which mark from the mid-16th century was an 'X' (in a circular shield, later in a rectangular shield) surmounted by a crown, but after 1701 was a three-tower castle (the arms of the city). Much fine plate bearing the Exeter mark was made by silversmiths from Exeter and from Plymouth and Barnstaple, also in Devon, until 1882 when the local Assay Office was closed. Especially notable are examples of CHURCH PLATE and drinking vessels made in the 16th century. Among the leading silversmiths of Exeter were John Jons (fl. *c.* 1575), John Eydes (fl. *c.* 1580), and John Elston (fl. 1701–17); and of Plymouth, Robert Rowe (fl. 1697–1706) and Henry Muston (fl. 1690–94). *See* Christopher Lever, 'West Country Goldsmiths' in *Country Life*, 16 January 1975. p. 146.

Exeter Wine Cooler and Fountain. A WINE COOLER with related WINE FOUNTAIN, both made by THOMAS FARREN, 1728. The cooler is oval, resting on an oval base with a spreading foot, a bowl decorated with applied male masks and floral swags, and two handles in the form of the fore-half of lions emerging from the ends of the bowl and with their backs joined to the rim. The wine fountain has a thistle-shaped body resting on a spreading foot; the lower part is decorated with STRAPWORK, the middle part with baroque cartouches enclosing masks; and the bulging upper part, decorated with floral swags, has two lion's-mask DROP-RING HANDLES. The tap has a spigot surmounted by a figure of a dolphin. The domed cover has a pineapple finial. Both pieces are at Burghley House, Stamford, ancestral home of the Cecil family and seat of successive Marquesses of Exeter (the 6th and last Marquess having died in 1981).

extinguisher. *See* CANDLE EXTINGUISHER.

eye bath. A small cup-like utensil having a rim made to conform to the shape of the eye, and usually resting on a stemmed foot. Silver examples were sometimes a unit of a TOILET SERVICE, and sometimes kept separate in a hinged case.

Eyre Salvers. Two SEAL SALVERS made from two seals rendered obsolete by the death of George I in 1727, both seals having been held by Sir Robert Eyre

Exeter Wine Cooler and Fountain. Thomas Farren, London, 1728. H. (of cooler) 80 cm; (of fountain) 70 cm. Burghley House, Stamford.

(1666–1736), one in his capacity as Chief Baron of the Exchequer (the salver having been made by Edward Vincent, London, 1728) and the other as Chancellor of the Principality of Wales (the salver, marked 'IL', having been made probably by John Liger, London, 1735), and both salvers having been engraved by Samuel Gribelin, son of SIMON GRIBELIN. The salvers were sold in one lot from the collection of Donald S. Morrison at Sotheby's, New York, on 6 June 1980 for $180,000 (£76,596) *See* John Hayward, 'The seal salvers of Lord Chief Justice Robert Eyre' in *Art at Auction 1979-80* (Sotheby-Parke-Bernet, 1980), p. 477.

F

faceted spout. A type of SPOUT made in the form of a series of narrow adjacent parallel plane surfaces, as on some BULLET TEAPOTS. The same style is found on the FERRULES on some teapots with such a spout.

fairing. An article offered for sale at one of the many fairs held in Britain from the earliest days, including some made expressly for such sale and bearing the name of the fair. Silversmiths customarily opened temporary shops at the fairs, especially the annual Bartholomew Fair held in August at West Smithfield, London. The pieces ranged from some quality examples to those of poor workmanship and low standard of FINENESS.

fake. As applied to silverware, an article that in genuinely old but that has been altered or added to, in respect of its HALLMARKS, body or decoration, for the purpose of deceptively enhancing its value, e.g.: (1) altering or substitution of the hallmark (practised by DUTY DODGERS to evade the tax, and by other fakers) but revealed by the different SOLDER; (2) distortion of the hallmark; (3) altering an article by changing or adding a handle, spout, or other part without obtaining a new hallmark; (4) adding decoration without obtaining a new hallmark; (5) converting an article into an article of different purpose; or (6) removing a section which bore a monogram and substituting a blank section. *See* Graham Hughes, 'Silver Stumers' in *Artiques*, April 1961, p. 378; Arthur G. Grimwade, 'A Study of English Silver Fakes' in *Apollo*, September 1982, p. 181. *See* FORGERY; REPRODUCTION; PATCH LINE.

false filigree. A style of decoration on metal, including silverware, that is an imitation of FILIGREE. False filigree is made mainly: (1) by soldering ornamental wire to a punch and then hammering it into a sheet of metal from the back; (2) by CASTING a piece from a model that was already decorated with true filigree; or (3) by DIE STAMPING. Examples of false filigree are found on the bowls of some CADDY SPOONS. Sometimes called 'simulated filigree'.

Falstaff Cup. A silver-gilt GOURD-SHAPED STANDING CUP, 1590, of typical shape. The bowl has an overall decoration of engraved tear-drop motifs. The cup bears an inscription stating that it was a gift from Francis Withens, a former Master of the Vintners' Company, to the vestry of the church of St Michael, Crooked Lane, London (now demolished). The cup is now owned by the church of St Magnus the Martyr, Lower Thames St, London. The cup is so called because vestry meetings were held in the Boar's Head tavern, where the cup was kept until 1830; some Falstaff scenes from Shakespeare's *Henry IV, Part II*, are set in that tavern, and it has been suggested that the cup may be one mentioned by Mistress Quickly as a 'parcel-gilt goblet' (Act II, sc. 1).

fan. A type of device to create circulation of air, examples of which were used in English churches to keep flies from the elements of the Eucharist. Although seldom made of silver, a silver example is listed in an inventory of 1222 of Salisbury Cathedral. *See* CHURCH PLATE.

fan tray. A type of triangular TRAY in fantasy form, shaped like an extended folding fan. A parcel-gilt example, made by Frederick Elkington, of ELKINGTON & CO., in 1877, is decorated in the contemporary fashion with Japanese motifs of birds in branches.

Falstaff Cup. Silver-gilt, London, 1590. H. 30 cm. Church of St Magnus the Martyr, London (photo courtesy, Goldsmiths' Company, London).

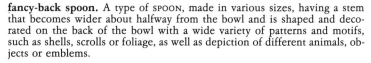

fan tray. Parcel gilt. Frederick Elkington, Birmingham, 1877. Goldsmiths' Company, London.

fancy-back spoon. A type of SPOON, made in various sizes, having a stem that becomes wider about halfway from the bowl and is shaped and decorated on the back of the bowl with a wide variety of patterns and motifs, such as shells, scrolls or foliage, as well as depiction of different animals, objects or emblems.

Farrell, Edward (Cornelius) (1779/81?–1850). An English silversmith, born in Middlesex, who entered his first and second marks in 1813, the latter from King's Head Court, Holborn Hill, London, and his third in 1819 from 24 Brydges St, Covent Garden. Little is known of him except that he was the principal supplier – from *c.* 1815 to the mid-1830s – to the retailer KENSINGTON LEWIS, who sold most of his work (*see* YORK, DUKE OF, SOUP-TUREENS). Much of it was influenced by antique models; he made some unusual pieces of REGENCY SILVERWARE, including massive TEA SERVICES decorated with Dutch peasant scenes (after paintings in the style of Teniers) and heavy ornamental pieces, such as the HERCULES CANDELABRUM. In his later years he undertook refurbishing and chasing of old silverware. It has been suggested that he was probably the silversmith for Thomas Hamlet, whose name as retailer is found stamped on some silverware.

Farren, Thomas (fl. 1707–43). An English silversmith (whose name was sometimes spelled Farrer), apprenticed in 1695 and freed in 1707. He entered his first mark in 1707, from St Swithin's Lane, London, and later marks in 1720 and 1739. He was a Subordinate Goldsmith to the King, 1723–42. It is possible that his wife was Ann Farren; her mark was entered in 1743 by Thomas Whipham (as attorney), an apprentice of Farren. *See* EXETER WINE COOLER AND FOUNTAIN.

fashion. The combined factors relating to an article of silverware which, in addition to its WEIGHT, contribute to establishing its PRICE; these factors include the style of the piece (and the consequent labour it required) and the quality of the workmanship or of its decoration (but disregarding the reputation of the maker or the age of the piece). Invoices for articles of silverware sometimes specify separately the price of the silver content based on weight and the price for 'fashion'.

Feake Cup. A tall silver-gilt STANDING CUP having a cylindrical bowl, a knopped stem, and a low chased foot; the cover rises in a sharp curve to a cone which is surmounted by a figure of a demi-lion rampant. The cup is embossed with floral motifs with reserved panels on each side, bearing, respectively, the arms of William Feake (a London goldsmith who in 1621 was Prime Warden of the Goldsmiths' Company) and his wife, Mary Weatherall (d. 1619). The maker's mark on the cup is 'AM', formerly ascribed to Andrew Moore, but more recently to Arthur Mainwaring, 1663, and the date mark on the cover is 1665. The cup, owned by the Goldsmiths' Company, was made to replace a cup donated by Feake in the early 17th century which, with four other cups, had been melted down during the Civil War; of the five only the Feake Cup is now extant. For a very similar piece by the same maker, *see* HANBURY CUP.

Feake Cup. Silver gilt, Arthur Mainwaring, London, 1663 (cover, 1665). H. 50·2 cm. Goldsmiths' Company, London.

feather-edge pattern. A pattern on the handle of some FLATWARE, having the entire border of the stem in the form of continuous oblique RIBBING, sometimes with alternate short ribs of different width.

feathered flagon. A type of FLAGON having a globular body, a tall cylindrical neck, a TRUMPET FOOT, a flat hinged lid, and a SCROLL HANDLE. It is decorated overall with a pattern of embossed, vertically-arranged, adjacent ostrich feathers. Several examples are known: (1) a pair, with maker's mark 'TB' but not hallmarked, made 1661, in St George's Chapel, Windsor Castle, and recorded in the chapel archives as having been bought in 1662; (2) a silver-gilt pair, in the Royal Collection, made by CHARLES SHELLEY, London, 1664–5, having on the front a reserved plaque with the engraved arms of Charles II as Duke of Lancaster and on the lid the device of the Duchy of Lancaster; (3) one, known as the 'Smythier Flagon', made by Robert Smythier, London, 1664–5, for the private chapel of James, Duke of York, whose arms it bears, it being in the Royal Collection; (4) a pair, with maker's mark of Charles Shelley, London, 1664–5, having on the cover the monogram 'DL' (possibly for Lionel Sackville, Duke of Dorset), at Colonial Williamsburg, Va. Other similarly shaped flagons were made for Royal Chapels, some of which were destroyed during the 17th-century Civil Wars.

Federal style. A style of decoration that was developed in the United States, between c. 1790 and c. 1820, being the transitional phase from the ROCOCO STYLE to the Classical Revival style. Although the style, based on the ADAM STYLE, was used mainly for architecture and furniture, it also influenced the work of some American silversmiths, such as MYER MYERS. It is characterized by the use of straight lines, MOULDINGS featuring BEADING and REEDING, bands of ornament produced by BRIGHT CUTTING, and urn-shaped finials, and it also reflects the influence of shapes of ceramic objects that were imported into the country.

feeding cup. A type of CUP for feeding children and invalids. Early examples were cylindrical or bucket-shaped but later, after c. 1790, they were sometimes hemispherical with a FOOT-RING or flaring base. Characteristically, the front half of the cup has an integrated covering, flat on early examples but convex on later ones; but some examples have a detachable complete cover. Such cups have a SPOUT (usually straight on early examples, curved on later ones) and generally two lateral handles level with the RIM, but sometimes a curved handle opposite the spout. See SPOUT CUP; MEDICAL SILVERWARE.

feeding spoon. A type of small SPOON for feeding an infant. Such spoons occur in either of two forms. (1) The bowl is oval in shape, wider at the feeding end; it is joined to the handle with its longer axis at right-angles to the handle, and with the handle nearer to the back end of the bowl. (2) The elongated bowl is partially covered, with an orifice at the feeding end and, at the other end, a loop or curled handle; some examples of this type were originally made as a TABLESPOON and fitted later with the partial cover.

feeding tube. A type of curved tube (usually S-shaped) to be used by an invalid to suck food from a cup. The lower end is broadened and is covered by a pierced sliding plate that serves to strain the food, and the upper end is tapered and serves as the mouthpiece, sometimes terminating with a nipple. There is at the side of the piece a hook for suspending it at the side of the cup. Early examples in silverware are known from c. 1750, and marked pieces from 1813. The length ranges from 9 to 15 cm. Sometimes called a 'sick syphon'. See MEDICAL SILVERWARE.

Fejø Bowl. A cup-shaped bowl with sides tapering inward toward the rim and having neither cover nor handles; it is decorated in NIELLO depicting

feathered flagon. Silver gilt, one of a pair, Charles Shelley, London, 1664–5. Royal Collection; reproduced by gracious permission of Her Majesty the Queen.

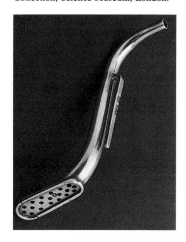

feeding tube. Phipps & Robinson, London, 1813. L. 9·2 cm. Wellcome Collection, Science Museum, London.

fender. Miniature fender at Ham House, Richmond. Courtesy, Victoria and Albert Museum, London.

Festival of Britain Rose Bowl. Covered shallow bowl, Jack E. Stapley, London, 1953. D. 35·5 cm. Goldsmiths' Company, London.

figural candlestick. One of a pair, Anthony Nelme, London, 1693. Bank of England, London.

birds and beasts within interlacing (on which evidence Charles Oman ascribed the piece to southern England, late 8th century). It is now in the National Museum, Copenhagen.

fender. An article of HEARTH FURNITURE, in the form of a low metal frame to be placed before an open fireplace. A miniature example in silver is at Ham House, Richmond, Surrey.

ferrule. A tube-like metal projection: (1) affixed to the body of an article as one of a pair (one being placed above the other), and into each of which is fitted one of the ends of a handle (of ebony or other wood, bone or ivory, but not of silver), as on a COFFEE-POT, TEAPOT or BRANDY WARMER; or (2) affixed to the handle of a piece of cutlery, and into which is fitted the blade of a knife or the TANG of a fork. The end of the handle in each case in secured in the ferrule(s) by means of silver pins.

Festival of Britain Rose-bowl. A ROSE-BOWL in the form of a very shallow circular dish with an everted rim, almost concealed by the slightly concave overlapping cover, from the centre of which rises a spiralling stem-like column surmounted by a finial in the form of two intertwined unicorns holding shields engraved with the arms of the Goldsmiths' Company, London. The holes pierced in the cover are interspersed with applied flower stems and foliage. Around the rim of the cover is an inscription recording that the bowl was made for the Goldsmiths' Company to commemorate the Festival of Britain, held in 1951. The piece was made in 1953 by JACK E. STAPLEY, the winner of the Company's competition for such a commemorative piece.

festoon. The same as a SWAG.

fiddle pattern. A pattern used for the handle of some FLATWARE, the shape somewhat resembling a fiddle (violin); the stem is like an elongated fingerboard and the body has smooth parallel sides extending toward a rounded terminal. There are several variants: (1) fiddle thread, where a single or double line of incised THREADING runs unbroken around the edges; (2) fiddle shell, where a relief shell occurs at the terminal of the handle; and (3) fiddle thread and shell, which combines the preceding two forms. The shape was introduced into England from *c.* 1800.

fig-shaped. The shape, resembling the section of a fig cut lengthwise, of the bowl of some SPOONS; somewhat ovoid, the bowl tapers slightly toward the stem.

figural bell. (1) A type of TABLE BELL, made in the form of a human figure, having the movable head of the figure attached to the clapper so that the bell is rung by shaking the head. Many such bells have been made in brass as curios, but some rare silver examples are also known. (2) A type of table bell of which the vertical handle is made in the form of a human figure.

figural candelabrum. A type of CANDELABRUM decorated with one or more sculptured figures, such as: (1) having its stem in the form of a figure or figures that support the candle SOCKETS; (2) having no stem but with the candle sockets supported by part of a figure or figures (*see* HERCULES CANDELABRUM); or (3) having a figure or figures as decoration on the base and surrounding the stem, without any supportive function. *See* WELLINGTON CANDELABRUM; GOLDSMITHS' COMPANY CANDELABRA.

figural candlestick. A type of TABLE CANDLESTICK having its stem in the form of, or supporting, a sculptured figure or figures. On some examples the figure is a CARYATID (*see* CARYATID CANDLESTICK), a telamon, or a draped classical figure, but various other figures have been so used, e.g., a kneeling blackamoor, a standing *putto*, a harlequin, a sailor, a knight in armour. The figure usually supports the candle SOCKET either on its head or by an upraised arm. In an example by ANTHONY NELME, 1693, the socket rises from a cornucopia held by the upraised arms. Examples are usually decorated in ROCOCO STYLE, with an asymmetrical base and swirling decoration. *See* J. F. Hayward, 'Candlesticks with Figure Stems' in *The Connoisseur*, January 1963, p. 16.

figural flatware. Articles of FLATWARE (KNIVES, FORKS, SPOONS, FISH SLICES, FRUIT SERVERS) having the handle in the form of a human figure. *See* BACCHANAL.

figural salt-cellar. A type of SALT-CELLAR featuring in its design: (1) a human or animal (e.g., a lion rampant) figure that supports the salt receptàcle either on its head or in extended arms or forelegs; (2) a figure standing between two salt receptacles on a flat stand and serving as an upright handle for the piece. *See* HUNTSMAN SALT.

figural silverware. Articles of silverware that include a figure or figures, human or animal, in-the-round. The figures are: (1) functional, such as (a) a supporting stem of a FIGURAL CANDLESTICK, FIGURAL BELL, FIGURAL SALT-CELLAR, (b) the support of some CUPS, e.g., a WAGER CUP, or (c) a handle of FIGURAL FLATWARE; or (2) solely ornamental, often depicting an episode of mythology, history or literature, as found on the PLINTH of many CENTRE-PIECES and TESTIMONIALS of the Victorian period (*see* VICTORIAN SILVERWARE) or as the finial on many TROPHIES. The figures are generally made by CASTING from a sculptured model, and many have been produced by leading designers and silversmiths. Sometimes called 'sculptural silverware'. *See* STATUETTE; FIGURE-TERMINAL CADDY SPOON; ANIMAL SILVERWARE; BIRD SILVERWARE.

figure-terminal caddy spoon. A type of CADDY SPOON, of which the bowl may occur in various forms, often shell-shaped, and having its handle in the form of a figure in-the-round. Known examples have the handle depicting a fisherman or a lady-in-crinoline holding a parasol.

filigree. A type of decoration on metalware made usually by the use of fine WIRE, plain, twisted or plaited, which is formed into a delicate and intricate design of foliate or geometric form. Filigree work is usually Continental, but is sometimes applied as decoration in England; however, in a few instances the filigree work has been made in England. It is applied by either of two techniques: (1) unsupported by any backing, and affixed as an openwork border, mainly on jewelry; or (2) by SOLDERING work of CAST FILIGREE to a flat metal plate where, in silverware, it is found mainly on book-covers, small boxes, purses, and buttons. English examples are principally from the late 17th century, but in the early 19th century there was in Birmingham a revival of such work for SMALLWARE. *See* LOCKET; FILIGREE CANDLESTICK; FALSE FILIGREE.

filigree candlestick. A type of CANDLESTICK having its entire decoration made of FILIGREE work. A rare pair, unmarked, *c.*1675, is in the Metropolitan Museum of Art, New York.

fillet. A narrow band separating two MOULDINGS; usually an architectural feature, but also found in silverware.

findings. Various small component parts of articles of silverware (e.g., feet, spouts, handles, finials, etc.), that are made separately (usually mass-produced by manufacturers in Birmingham and Sheffield) and supplied to other silversmiths who assemble them when making up complete pieces.

fineness. The proportion of pure SILVER in an article made of silver ALLOY, usually expressed in parts per thousand, e.g., 925 in the case of STERLING SILVER.

finger bowl. A type of small bowl used by a diner at table to rinse the fingers; it is often accompanied by a supporting dish decorated EN SUITE. A set of 24, made by JOHN DIGBY and BENJAMIN SMITH I, London 1805–6 (and called in the William IV inventory 'verriers'), is in the Royal Collection.

finial. The terminal ornament on the top of an article, but particularly on the COVER of a receptacle (where it also serves as the HANDLE) or on the stem of a SPOON. It is sometimes termed a 'knop'. Finials are made in a great variety of forms, such as a flower, fruit, acorn, flame, animal, human figure, shell, baluster, loop, mushroom, button, pine-cone, pineapple, etc. Certain finials are characteristic of particular periods, such as flowers and fruits of the ROCOCO STYLE, pine-cones and acorns of the NEO-CLASSICAL STYLE, and sphinxes of the EMPIRE STYLE. *See* JANUS FINIAL; COLOUR-PIKE FINIAL.

fire-box. A thin vertical metal cylinder, affixed within some TEA-URNS and ARGYLLS, and into which can be inserted a red-hot iron rod (BILLET) to keep the surrounding liquid warm. The device was invented by John Wadham, London.

fire-dog. One of a pair of metal objects used in a fireplace to support burning logs. It consists of a horizontal iron bar resting on two front legs and one leg at the back, and having a vertical shaft at the front end. The front end and the shaft are sometimes of silver, but often consist of an iron core sheathed with silver; the shaft, up to about 50 cm in height, is sometimes surmounted by a figure or a vase-shaped or ball-shaped ornament, with in-

figural salt-cellars. Two of a set of twelve, Robert Garrard II, 1855–6. H. *c.* 18 cm. Courtesy, Garrard & Co. Ltd, London.

filigree. Purse, silver gilt, English, *c.* 1660. Courtesy, Brand Inglis Ltd, London.

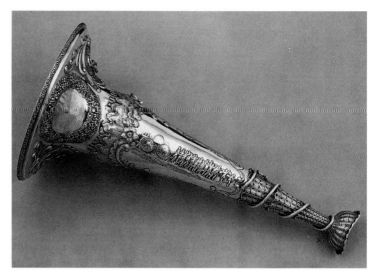

fireman's trumpet. American, *c.* 1852. L. 55 cm. Yale University Art Gallery (Mabel Brady Garvan Collection), New Haven, Conn.

fire-dog. One of a pair, Andrew Moore, London, 1696–7 (with canephoros and plinth by Rundell, Bridge & Rundell, 1821). H. 43·5 cm. Royal Collection; reproduced by gracious permission of Her Majesty the Queen.

termittent knops. Silver examples exist in the Royal Collection and in several manor houses. Also called an 'andiron'. A small type to be placed between the fire-dogs and to carry the main weight of the burning logs, or to be used in a small fireplace, is termed a CREEPER. *See* J. Hartley Beckels, 'Fire-dogs' in *The Connoisseur*, September 1907, p. 151, and December 1907, p. 227; Norman M. Penzer, 'The Royal Fire Dogs' in *The Connoisseur*, June 1954, p. 9. *See* HEARTH FURNITURE.

fire-irons. Utensils for use at a fireplace, including TONGS, a poker, hook, shovel, and hearth brush. Examples with silver handles are known from *c.* 1674. There exist some FAKES and REPRODUCTIONS made *c.* 1900. *See* HEARTH FURNITURE.

fire marks. Discoloration on the surface of silver left by the formation of cuprous oxide due to overheating in ANNEALING or to the heat of soldering or of repair work, e.g., in straightening or strengthening the rim of a bowl of a spoon. The presence of such marks on any piece tends to diminish its market value. They can be removed (if the oxide has not penetrated too deeply) by vigorous polishing, by use of a pickle solution, or by 'stripping' (removing some surface metal), or they can be concealed by ELECTROPLATING; in recent years the use of special furnaces or the addition of a small amount of aluminium to the ALLOY has made possible the prevention of fire marks. Also known as 'fire-stain'.

fire-pan. A receptacle for holding coals in a fireplace. An example, *c.* 1675, made of iron has silver mounts on three sides and is supported by front feet of silver; it is engraved with a ducal coronet and intertwined initials 'JL/ED'. *See* HEARTH FURNITURE.

fire screen. A screen placed before a fireplace as a guard. An iron screen with silver mounts, *c.* 1675, is among the HEARTH FURNITURE at Ham House, Richmond, Surrey.

fireman's trumpet. A trumpet-shaped instrument used by firemen as a loud-hailer or megaphone at the scene of a fire. Examples have been made of silver, especially as presentation pieces. *See* TRUMPET.

fish drainer. *See* MAZARINE.

fish feeders. A conforming FISH FORK and FISH KNIFE, to be used as a PAIR, each made of silver in one piece, unlike other such contemporary utensils made with steel blades and tines that were thought to rust when used with fish. The knife has a blade with a curved edge similar to later fish knives. Some sets have figural handles (*see* FIGURAL FLATWARE).

fish fork. A type of FORK for use with a conforming FISH KNIFE when eating fish; it usually has three or four flat unsharpened tines, the outer one being wider and sometimes having a curved point. A larger type was used as a fish server, with a conforming FISH SLICE. *See* FISH FEEDERS.

fish kettle. A type of cooking utensil in the form of a circular pan with high sloping sides and having a removable pierced strainer to which is attached a vertical conical handle for use in lifting it out. Below the strainer is a plate having a vertical handle that passes through the conical handle, by which the plate can be raised to remove the fish from the kettle. The cooking liquid rises through the strainer and returns to the pan below. A silver example was made in 1881 by JOHN EMES.

fish knife. A type of KNIFE for use with a conforming FISH FORK when eating fish; the blade is flat and decoratively shaped, and has no sharp edge; one edge is smooth and gently curved, the other being incurved and undulating. *See* FISH SLICE; FISH FEEDERS.

fish slice. A type of flat implement, shaped basically like a TROWEL, for use in serving, and sometimes dividing, fish at a dinner table. The earliest examples, from *c*. 1735 (the earliest-known extant example was made by PAUL DE LAMERIE, 1740, and is now in the Ashmolean Museum, Oxford), were shaped like a mortar trowel (i.e., triangular and pointed, though often with rounded corners) with overall pierced decoration; their main purpose was to drain and serve fried whitebait direct from the frying pan, hence they have sometimes been called a 'whitebait server'. After *c*. 1745, the outline was usually symmetrically elliptical or fish-shaped, intended for use in separating and serving portions of a larger fish, but later the shape was changed so as to be asymmetrical (like a fish fin) with one blunt and undulating edge rising to a point nearly midway, while the other edge was convex and sharp; some examples also have overall pierced or cut-out patterns, sometimes rows of PALES, sometimes depicting a fish, all surrounded by a narrow plain border. Rare examples have on the upper edge a row of several projecting teeth. The handle (haft) of all types is straight, sometimes made of silver and shaped like a contemporary knife handle, but often made of ivory, bone, boxwood or ebony. A few examples were made with a rectangular outline, sometimes with chamfered corners. Some, with decoration on one side only, are for left-handed use, as one of a pair. An unusual form has two blades, one (smaller) above the other, joined together and provided with a lever that, when pressed, brings the blades together to hold a fish when lifting it from a serving dish. The fish slice is sometimes called a 'fish trowel' or a 'fish server'; and some, accompanied by a conforming fork with four flat tines, are together called 'fish servers'. *See* G. Bernard Hughes, 'Designs for Silver Fish-Slices' in *Country Life*, 19 July 1956, p. 141; H. W. Smart, 'A Slice of Culinary History' in *Country Life*, 26 December 1974, p. 1994.

fish-soup tureen. A type of SOUP-TUREEN intended for serving fish soup or bisque, hence decorated with applied figures of marine forms, such as Triton and mermaids, dolphins, shellfish, sea shells, and modelling suggestive of waves. *See* TURTLE TUREEN.

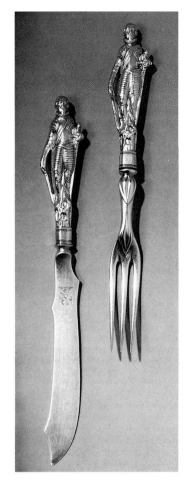

fish feeders. Silver gilt, with figural handles, William Cooper, London, 1842. Courtesy, Asprey & Co., London.

fish slice (1). Paul de Lamerie, London, 1741-2. L. 31·8 cm. Ashmolean Museum, Oxford.

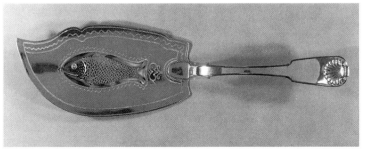

fish slice (2). Nelson Walker, Montreal (made in England *c*. 1845-55). L. 30 cm. Museum of Fine Arts, Montreal.

Fisher Cup. Presentation cup, Thomas Fletcher and Sidney Gardiner, Philadelphia, Pa, 1830. H. 53·3 cm. Yale University Art Gallery (Mabel Brady Garvan Collection), New Haven, Conn.

Fisher Cup. A TWO-HANDLED CUP having a semi-ovoid bowl resting on a spreading foot and supported by a square PLINTH with four lion's feet. The bowl has two vertical bifurcated handles in the form of two twisted vine stems, and is decorated with a band of ACANTHUS leaves encircling the bottom, together with, at the top, a band of grapes and vine leaves. The high-domed cover is surmounted by a figure in-the-round depicting a river god standing on a shell. On two opposite sides of the plinth are oval plaques depicting a reclining river god; on the other two sides are engraved plaques, one depicting a horse towing a canal barge under a bridge, and the other bearing an inscription recording the gift of the piece in 1830 to James C. Fisher by the proprietors of the Chesapeake and Delaware Canal. It was made by FLETCHER AND GARDINER, Philadelphia, 1830. It is in the Garvan Collection, Yale University Art Gallery, New Haven, Connecticut.

flagon. A pouring vessel, so called from *c.*1640, that is tall and has a single handle and a hinged LID, either dome-shaped or cushion-shaped, with a finial and a THUMBPIECE. The body of some examples from the mid-17th century is cylindrical ('drum'- or 'barrel'-shaped), sloping slightly upward, but some earlier examples have a bulbous lower half and a high cylindrical or waisted neck. A flagon usually has no LIP or SPOUT, but some examples have a thin tall BRIDGE SPOUT (connected by a bar to the neck). Most examples are undecorated, but some have elaborate EMBOSSING, ENGRAVING or CHASING. They were used for serving wine at table, by replenishing CUPS and TANKARDS. As many made for secular use were later given to a church, the term has sometimes been applied to a church vessel that is used to replenish the wine in a CHALICE or COMMUNION CUP at the Eucharist. The cylindrical form was probably derived from the Scandinavian stoneware vessels, the French *canette,* and the Siegburg *Schnelle* (the *Jacobus Kannetje*). Called in the 17th century a 'stoup' and later a 'LIVERY POT'. *See* CIRENCESTER FLAGONS; FEATHERED FLAGON; WESTWELL FLAGONS.

flared. Spread slightly outward, as in the case of the rim of some BEAKERS, CUPS and CANNS. *See* EVERTED.

flask. A type of narrow-necked receptacle for holding a liquid. Silver examples, usually made for carrying spirits on the person, are of flattened rectangular shape, with a short neck and a small mouth, and generally have a SCREW COVER; sometimes the cover is telescopic, extending to form a drinking cup. In some cases the lower half is encased in a removable silver drinking cup, and examples have been made in fantasy forms, e.g., as a book. The height ranges from about 15 to 25 cm. Those of modern make, of various sizes, are called a 'pocket flask' or a 'hip flask'. *See* PILGRIM FLASK; SCENT-FLASK.

flat candlestick. A type of CANDLESTICK having its SOCKET rising from a flat tray that has an upcurved rim and a long straight handle, instead of a loop handle as on a CHAMBER CANDLESTICK. An early example, 1688, is at Exeter College, Oxford.

flat chasing. A type of CHASING done to decorate a flat surface rather than to develop relief decoration. The technique differs from PUNCHING (which makes a design by a series of strokes) by making a continuous line produced by repeated hammering as in the technique of chasing. It was used not only to form conventional patterns, but also to decorate a matted ground, as well as in conjunction with EMBOSSING and ENGRAVING. It was particularly used for decorating with CHINOISERIE motifs, especially in the 1660s–80s. On thin metal the pattern may be visible on the reverse side. As chased decoration may have been added some time after a piece was assayed, the DATE HALLMARK is not necessarily an indication of the year in which the chasing was done. *See* MATT-CHASED.

flat-bowl cup. The same as a 'FONT-SHAPED' CUP.

flat hammering. The process of shaping a flat silver article (e.g., a TRAY, SALVER, PLATTER, WAITER), which involves first SOLDERING to a previously shaped flat plate of silver the border, either cast or of wire, then HAMMERING the edge of the heated piece; such work causes the piece to buckle under the heat and it must then be hammered flat by extruding the metal toward the edge, a process which is more difficult when the piece has a shaped rather than a circular or oval form.

flatware. Articles of TABLEWARE that are basically flat (such as SPOONS, FORKS, SIFTERS, and SLICES) and that have no cutting edge, but in modern usage embracing CUTLERY and hence also including KNIVES, but distin-

flagon. John Potwine, Boston, Mass., *c.* 1720–30. H. 34·5 cm. Yale University Art Gallery (Mabel Brady Garvan Collection), New Haven, Conn.

guished from HOLLOW WARE (such as BOWLS, pouring vessels, and drinking vessels). Such pieces are now usually made in sets having, on the handles, similar or related decorative patterns. *See* Ian Pickford, *Silver Flatware 1660-1980* (British; 1983); Richard F. Osterberg and Betty Smith, *Silver Flatware Dictionary* (American; 1981). *See* CHRYSANTHEMUM PATTERN.

Flaxman, John (I) (fl. 1770-5). A sculptor and modeller who moved to London in 1755, with a studio in New Street, Covent Garden, and from 1755 at 420 The Strand. He made plaster casts for Wedgwood & Bentley, as evidenced by a bill in 1775 for the celebrated EWERS that were produced in black basaltes and in other ware in several editions – *see* WINE-AND-WATER EWERS – and that were copied in silver in 1900. He was the father of JOHN FLAXMAN II.

Flaxman, John (II) (1755-1826). The son of JOHN FLAXMAN I, he became a noted sculptor and also a designer of silverware as well as of ceramic ware in the NEO-CLASSICAL STYLE. He began by making, from 1775 to 1787, designs and wax models for cameos, classical friezes, and portrait medallions for Josiah Wedgwood; a TEA SERVICE designed by him for Wedgwood, 1784, was produced but its whereabouts today is unknown. From 1787 to 1794 he worked in Rome, achieving a reputation for his designs of classical subjects. After returning to England in 1794, he designed imposing pieces of silverware, some of which were executed by PAUL STORR for RUNDELL, BRIDGE & RUNDELL, for whom Flaxman was head designer from 1817 until 1826 (including the GALVANIC GOBLET; THEOCRITUS CUPS; WELLINGTON CENTREPIECES; GARDEN OF THE HESPERIDES CANDELABRUM; and MERCURY CANDELABRUM); by PHILIP RUNDELL (including the ACHILLES SHIELD); by JOHN BRIDGE (including the NATIONAL CUP); and by DIGBY SCOTT and BENJAMIN SMITH I (including the LLOYD'S PATRIOTIC FUND VASES). He modelled a few of his early designs, but most were modelled by WILLIAM THEED II or by EDWARD HODGES BAILY, who often departed from the Flaxman designs. His designs have influenced the work of later silversmiths both in England and in the United States. *See* David Bindman (ed.), *John Flaxman* (exhibition catalogue, 1979). *See* KEMBLE CUP.

Fletcher and Gardiner. A firm of silversmiths that is well known for having made in the United States, *c.* 1810–40, silverware in the EMPIRE STYLE. The partnership was formed by Thomas Fletcher (fl. 1809-50) and Sidney Gardiner (fl. 1809-38) in Boston and moved *c.* 1811 to Philadelphia. They specialized in presentation pieces in the form of two-handled cups, including several in the style of the WARWICK VASE (*see* FISHER CUP). A collection of designs by Fletcher is in the Metropolitan Museum of Art, New York. *See* Katherine Morrison McClinton, 'Fletcher and Gardiner' in *The Connoisseur*, March 1970, p. 211.

Fletcher Cup. An OSTRICH-EGG CUP having its bowl made of an ostrich egg, its cover of part of a different type of ostrich egg, and its silver stem in the form of a twisted and gnarled tree-trunk (similar to the stem of some GOURD-SHAPED 'STEEPLE CUPS'). It bears a London mark for 1592-3 and was bequeathed, in his will dated 15 October 1593, to Corpus Christi College, Cambridge, by Richard Fletcher, a Fellow of the college, 1569-73, and later successively Bishop of Bristol, Worcester, and London. The cup is called at the College 'The Gripe's Eye', the word *gripe* referring to a griffon-vulture, and the term being derived from *gripyshey*, vulture's egg. The cup is accompanied by its original boiled-leather, velvet-lined fitted case. The original *gripyshey* cup was given to the Guild of Corpus Christi by Henry Tangmere, *c.* 1350.

fleur de lis (French, lily flower). A decorative motif in the form of a stylized flower (said to have been suggested by the iris), having three vertical petals, the central one upright and the other two inclined outward, with the petals bound by a band midway or near the bottom and their lower ends similarly directed. It is an ancient emblem, since at least the year 527 when used on the crown of the Empress Theodora, and was chosen as the royal emblem of France by Charles V, 1364-80 (having been used there, sprinkled on the blue field of a coat of arms, since 1179). It is sometimes found on silverware, engraved or embossed. A variant with the heads of the petals divided like flowers is called *fleur-de-lis florencé*.

fluted-edge dish. *See* 'STRAWBERRY DISH'.

fluting. An ornamental concave decoration in the form of a series of parallel or converging grooves, of semi-circular, semi-elliptical, or rectangular section, and extending in a vertical, oblique, and sometimes curving direction.

flask. Leather bound, with electroplated silver mounts, James Dixon & Sons, Sheffield, *c.* 1870. Courtesy, Brand Inglis Ltd, London.

Fletcher Cup. Ostrich-egg cup, 1592-3, with original case. H. 38·2 cm. Corpus Christi College, Cambridge.

fluting. Dessert dish, fluted rim with scalloped edge, Paul de Lamerie, London, *c.* 1714. Courtesy, Asprey & Co. Ltd, London.

The grooves may be separated by a common arris (as on Doric columns). The opposite is REEDING or ribbing. Fluting is found on the body of some silver articles and also as a decoration on some handles, as well as on the rim of a 'STRAWBERRY DISH' and similar dessert dishes of circular or square shape, the shallow fluting being separated by thin arrises extending into the bottom of the piece. Sometimes a piece with vertical parallel fluting decoration is said to be 'cannelated'.

fly punching. A technique of making pierced decoration on SHEFFIELD PLATE to prevent the layer of copper from being seen in the pierced holes. The method involved using a 'fly punch' in the shape of the desired hole, then aligning the PLATED METAL over a steel plate previously pierced with the desired shape and driving the punch through into the steel hole, thus cutting the plated metal and dragging silver into the hole so as to conceal the copper edge.

flying scroll handle. A type of massive handle, in the form of a vertical SCROLL HANDLE or a DOUBLE-SCROLL HANDLE, the lower end of which is attached to the body of the object but the upper terminal (sometimes in the form of a figure, bust, bird or TERM) of which is unattached. Such a handle is found on some examples of a WINE COOLER, HELMET JUG, TWO-HANDLED CUP or CAKE-BASKET, or a smaller version on a SAUCE-BOAT or a CHAMBER CANDLE-STICK. *See* SUTHERLAND CISTERN.

Fogelberg, Andrew (*c.* 1732–1815). A silversmith, probably of Swedish birth and apprenticed to a Halmstad goldsmith, who settled in London in the early 1760s and became established there by 1770–1. He entered his mark 'AF' as a plateworker before 1773, and it is found on pieces made before 1777. He became from 1780 to 1793 a partner of Stephen Gilbert, who had been working from 1770 for the firm of JOHN PARKER and EDWARD WAKELIN in Panton St, Haymarket. They entered two joint marks 'AF/SG' in 1780 from 30 Church St, Soho, where Fogelberg had worked from 1773, and where he worked alone from 1793 until 1796, when he moved to Pond St, Hampstead, presumably to retire. Among his apprentices was PAUL STORR, *c.* 1785. Fogelberg specialized in making silver cameo-type MEDALLIONS, some adapted from the paste medallions of James Tassie (see TASSIE SILVER MEDALLIONS); his firm probably exported some to Sweden. *See* Charles C. Oman, 'Andrew Fogelberg' in *Apollo*, June 1947, p. 158.

flying scroll handle. Cake-basket, Paul de Lamerie, London, 1746–7. L. 35·5 cm. Ashmolean Museum, Oxford.

foil. (1) A very thin sheet of metal; *see* SILVER FOIL. (2) One of a series of connected similarly shaped arcs or lobes, three or more in number, forming a circular pattern: the resulting shapes are called trefoil, quatrefoil, cinquefoil, hexafoil, octofoil, decafoil, and multifoil. Some WAITERS, PLATTERS, TRAYS, SALVERS, etc. were made with rims in such shapes, as well as the spreading FOOT of some CANDLESTICKS and receptacles.

folding biscuit-box. A type of BISCUIT-BOX in the form of a stand having two (sometimes three) bowls hinged at the bottom so that, when closed, they rise to a vertical position and are fastened to the central column or ring but, when open, drop to a horizontal position. Each bowl has a hinged flap with pierced work in varied patterns, provided to help retain the warmth. The column has a loop carrying handle or an ornamental finial. Some rare examples were made in fantasy form, such as a cabin with a gable roof made so that

folding biscuit-box. Silver plated, three bowls shown open and closed. I. Freeman & Son Ltd, London (photo, courtesy James Hardy & Co. London).

the two sides of the roof open automatically when the piece is lifted by the centre handle. Sometimes called a 'biscuit warmer' although there is no warming device; also sometimes incorrectly called a MUFFINEER.

folding spoon. A type of SPOON that has a hinged stem, the hinge being midway along the stem or at the join of the stem and the bowl, so that the finial fits into the bowl. The earliest-known example, 15th century, was found in St Mary's churchyard, Scarborough, Yorkshire; records exist of examples made in the 17th century in England and the American Colonies. Such spoons were perhaps made, together with a folding knife and fork, as part of a TRAVELLER'S DINING SET. Some modern examples are made to fit into a narrow drinking cup.

font. A type of receptacle for holy water for baptizing by aspersion or affusion, being intended (unlike a BAPTISMAL BASIN) to be kept permanently in its accustomed place in a church. Few examples made of silver or silver gilt, used mainly for Royal baptisms until the 17th century, are extant. *See* LILY FONT; ROYAL FONT; STOUP; CHURCH PLATE.

'font-shaped' cup. A type of drinking vessel of GOTHIC STYLE, having a shallow circular vertical-sided bowl resting on a broad TRUMPET FOOT. Examples are known from the 15th and early 16th centuries, when the type was known as a 'flat-bowl cup'. The description 'font-shaped' has been applied by collectors and was not used in early inventories and records. The vessels have been said to have been probably intended for personal use as a drinking bowl, not as a ceremonial cup. Some examples are known from the Low Countries, but sixteen English ones were recorded in 1957. *See* CAMPION CUP; CHARLECOTE CUP; CRESSENER CUP; CORPUS CHRISTI COLLEGE (OXFORD) POMEGRANATE CUP; BODKIN CUP; DEANE CUP; HOWARD GRACE CUP; PETERSON CUP; SWAYTHLING CUP; WELFORD CUP. Other such cups are the Charsfield Cup, 1559-60, the Colaton Raleigh Cup, *c.* 1560, and the two Blennerhasset Cups, 1561-2. *See* Norman M. Penzer, 'Tudor "Font-shaped" Cups' in *Apollo,* December 1957, p. 174, February 1958, p. 44, and March 1958, p. 82.

foot. The support(s) of a vessel or utensil upon which it stands, being either (1) that part, usually circular, which broadens out from a stem (and may rest on a base or plinth), or (2) the bottom terminals of separate legs. Examples of the former type are the TRUMPET FOOT, STEPPED foot, and SKIRT FOOT. Examples of the latter type include the BALL FOOT, BUN FOOT, CLAW-AND-BALL FOOT, COLLET FOOT, PAW FOOT.

foot-ring. A slightly projecting ring, found on the bottom of a vessel, utensil or PLATE; it serves to raise the bottom of the piece from the surface on which it stands. It is sometimes called a 'foot-rim', 'basal ring', 'chime' or 'rim foot'. *See* SKIRT FOOT.

footbath. A receptacle designed for use when washing the feet. A silver example, possibly a travelling hand-basin, by PAUL CRESPIN, London, 1718-19 (formerly said to have been made for the King of Portugal, perhaps based on the fact that when sold at Christie's, London, in the late 19th century, it was listed as being owned by a Portuguese nobleman), is now in the British Museum, London.

footed salver. A type of SALVER supported by a short TRUMPET FOOT, COLLET FOOT or STEPPED foot, the foot being detachable in some examples. The salver was usually circular (rarely square or polygonal), with its rim (sometimes scalloped or multifoil) usually decorated with GADROONING, REEDING, EMBOSSING or BEADING, or with affixed MOUNTS. In some cases the salver was strengthened by having CUT CARD mounts affixed to the bottom around the stem. Some early salvers had a slightly depressed centre to position and retain an accompanying receptacle, such as a cup or bowl, or occasionally a tasting cup ('cup of assay') used for wine after it had been proved safe and potable. Later the central foot was dispensed with, and such pieces then became a type of WAITER with small feet affixed below the rim. Footed salvers for serving are often erroneously called a TAZZA, which is a drinking vessel. *See* G. Bernard Hughes, 'The Vogue for Footed Salvers' in *Country Life,* 21 October 1965, p. 1060.

footman's skirt-lifter. A long wooden staff used by a footman in former times, when a lady was descending from a carriage, to lift the edge of her skirt to prevent it from dragging and becoming soiled. A number of examples are at the Mansion House, London, having a silver cap at the tip and some with the cap surmounted by an ornamental silver-gilt finial. *See* HEM-LIFTER.

folding spoon. Fig-shaped bowl, 15th century. L. 12 cm. Rotunda Museum, Scarborough, Yorkshire (photo courtesy, Scarborough Borough Council).

Forbes Plateau. Detail of gallery with pierced decoration, John W. Forbes, New York, *c.* 1820–5. The White House, Washington, D.C.

Forbes. A family, of Scottish and Dutch ancestry, three generations of which were active as New York silversmiths. William Garret Forbes (1751–1840) was freed in 1770, and made much ware in the heavy Dutch style. His three sons, who worked with him at various times, and who had partnerships with him and with each other, working at several addresses in New York City, were: Colin van Gelder Forbes (1776–1859), John Wolfe Forbes (1781–1864), a leading silversmith of his day (*see* FORBES PLATEAU), and Garret Forbes (1785–1851). Their ware, in a variety of forms, was highly regarded; examples are now in several leading United States museums. Colin's son, William Forbes (1799–1835), continued the family business. *See* Rachel B. Crawford, 'The Forbes Family of Silversmiths' in *Antiques,* April 1975, p. 730.

Forbes Plateau. A PLATEAU of oval rectangular shape, made in three sections, each with a mirror bottom. Encircling the piece is a pierced GALLERY decorated with a series of winged lions facing an urn. At the juncture of the sections are four pedestals decorated with bas-relief figures of Flora (goddess of flowers) and Pomona (goddess of fruit trees), each surmounted by a figure of a spread-eagle. The plateau was made by John W. Forbes (*see* FORBES), New York, 1820–5, and was donated by Russell Hunter in 1962 to the White House, Washington, D.C. An identically shaped but smaller piece by Forbes, privately owned, is the only other known American plateau.

foreign origin mark. An extra HALLMARK, required in Great Britain from 1867 on imported articles of foreign-made silverware, in the form of a capital F within an oval ESCUTCHEON; from 1883 all imported foreign-made silverware was required to be submitted for ASSAYING at the Assay Office nearest to the port of entry, usually London or Chester. The F mark was discontinued in 1904, and a series of new ASSAY OFFICE HALLMARKS for imported silver was introduced, some of which were changed in 1906; *see* IMPORTED GOODS HALLMARKS. Since 1975 imported foreign-made ware has been admitted without further assaying if already stamped with the CONVENTION HALLMARKS. *See* BOUGET HALLMARK.

forgery. As applied to silverware, a close copy of valuable old silverware, made with the intent to deceive a prospective buyer and offered for sale usually at a high price, e.g., a copy of a silver article made by CASTING or ELECTROFORMING, where a piece is desired to make up an incomplete PAIR or SET (the copy is recognizable as such because the old hallmarks and decoration are less sharply defined, defects in the original are reproduced identically, and the position of the hallmarks is precisely the same). *See* Judith Banister, 'Forgers, Furbishers and Duty-Dodgers' in *Apollo,* October 1961, p. 104.

fork. A type of implement for serving and manipulating food, consisting of a straight handle attached to a shank terminating in two, three or four tines (prongs). Table forks were introduced *c.* 1600 in Italy as substitutes for eating with the fingers, and they were adopted in France and then in England (the earliest dated English example is from 1632). The first examples, intended for spearing food, have two tines (originally of steel, later of silver) with sharp points; later examples, made for lifting food, have three (from *c.* 1667) or four (from *c.* 1674) tines with rounded points. Forks have been made in many styles, with variations in the form and style of the handle and of the tines. They are often made as part of a pair with matching knives decorated EN SUITE to conform to other pieces of FLATWARE and sometimes as part of a DINNER SERVICE. Silver forks have been made in past centuries, and even more so in recent years, in a variety of forms depending on the particular use intended, including the DINNER FORK, ENTRÉE FORK, FISH FORK, POTATO FORK, SALAD FORK, OYSTER FORK, ICE-CREAM FORK, SERVING FORK, CARVING FORK, TOASTING FORK, PICKLE FORK, RUNCIBLE SPOON, and SUCKETT FORK. *See* G. Bernard Hughes, 'The Evolution of the Silver Table Fork' in *Country Life,* 24 September 1959, p. 364. *See* KNIFE AND FORK HANDLES.

forked handle. A type of HANDLE that is BIFURCATED near its top, the upper prong of the forked handle being affixed to the rim of a TEAPOT or other vessel and the lower prong curved downwards and affixed to the body. Examples also occur with the handle divided at the lower end.

Founder's Cup (or **Salt**). A term used at several colleges within the Universities of Oxford and Cambridge, referring to an important article of silverware given, or reputed to have been given, to the college in question by its founder (or foundress). *See* BEAUFORT CUP; MAGDALEN COLLEGE (OXFORD) MELON CUP; CORPUS CHRISTI COLLEGE (OXFORD) HOURGLASS SALT.

founding. The process of making and shaping an object by pouring molten metal into a mould. The same as CASTING.

fountain. *See* TABLE FOUNTAIN; WINE FOUNTAIN; CORONATION 'WINE FOUNTAIN'.

Fox, Charles. London silversmiths, presumed to be father and son. Charles Fox I (fl. 1801–22), of 3 Old St, Goswell St, and his sons and successors, C. T. & G. Fox, made most of their ware for the retailers Lambert & Rawlings, of Coventry St, Leicester Square, London; it included many objects of ruby glass with silver MOUNTS. Charles Fox II (fl. 1822–40) registered his first mark in 1822, address 139 Old St, and five other marks, the last in 1838. His numerous marks indicate that he had a large establishment, making various types of ware, executing personal handwork before the start of Victorian mass-production.

frame. A surround for a picture or a MIRROR; examples have been made of silver in many shapes, sizes, and styles. Some picture-frames have been adapted from a frame made for a mirror and, conversely, some mirror-frames have been converted from picture-frames.

Frances Jug. A mottled English TIGERWARE JUG with English silver MOUNTS (base, neck-band, and hinged lid) bearing the London hallmarks of 1580–1. It is said to have belonged in 1582 to Mrs Frances Jefferson, a servant of Elizabeth I, and to have been bequeathed by her with a condition restricting its descent to female descendants bearing the name Frances, and that it was inherited by Mrs Frances Pierce who, having no qualified descendants, sold it in 1801 to William Wilson, who resettled it on a similar trust. It was bought in 1908 by Crichton Bros., London, and it is said to be now in a private collection in the United States.
   A similar jug, with the marks 'WC' (for William Cocknidge) and London, 1576–7, was presented in 1965 from the Elizabeth B. Miles Collection to the Wadsworth Atheneum, Hartford, Connecticut, and another by the same maker is in the Metropolitan Museum of Art, New York.

Freake Posset Pot. An octagonal SMALL TWO-HANDLED CUP having on each of the panels on the bowl engraved depictions of exotic birds and plants, with on one panel the arms of Freake, probably Percy Freake, of Rathbarry Castle, Co. Cork, Ireland. The flat cover has a finial in the form of four upright leaves. It was made by John Cuthbert, Dublin, in 1685, and was acquired in 1959 by the Ulster Museum, Belfast.

Frederick, Prince of Wales, Service. A COMPOSITE SERVICE ordered by Frederick, Prince of Wales (1707–51), eldest son of George II (1683–1760), and now owned by the Crown. Some of the pieces were made by PAUL DE LAMERIE, as Goldsmith to the King, but many were ordered from other leading makers, including NICHOLAS SPRIMONT (some such articles bearing the marks of PAUL CRESPIN), GEORGE WICKES, and JOHN BRIDGE. The pieces were listed in an inventory of Royal plate made for William IV. *See* NEPTUNE CENTREPIECE.

fork. Three-tined, Hanoverian pattern, Pierre Platel, London, 1709. L. 19·8 cm. British Museum, London.

Frederick of Prussia Cup. A STANDING CUP of oxidized silver and parcel-gilt, made by R., J. & S. Garrard (*see* GARRARD & CO. LTD) as a christening gift, on 5 March 1859, from Queen Victoria and Prince Albert to their grandson and godchild Prince Frederick William Victor Albert of Prussia. The wide shallow bowl, enriched with coloured enamelling, gemstones, and pearls, and having on the rim groups of doves, rests on a spreading foot upon which is a figure of St George slaying the Dragon. The cover has a tall finial surmounted by a truncated column upon which sits a child, and is surrounded by allegorical figures of Faith, Hope, and Divine Love. The cup was exhibited at the London International Exhibition of 1862, and is shown in J. B. Waring, *Masterpieces of Industrial Art* (1863), vol. III, pl. 221.

freedom box. A type of BOX or CASKET, usually rectangular but sometimes circular or oval, made of silver (occasionally of gold) which is given to a recipient of the freedom of a city, town, corporation, college, or one of the Livery Companies, commemorating (together with the enclosed parchment, called a 'Freedom Paper') the occasion. A person so honoured by one of the Livery Companies, including the Goldsmiths' Company, was recognized as a FREEMAN of the Company. The box bears the engraved, chased or enamelled name or coat of arms of the recipient, together with the arms of the donor and an appropriate inscription. Such boxes were popular in the second half of the 19th century, and were a speciality of W. Benson, of Ludgate Hill, London. They were made especially in Ireland and presented to freed APPRENTICES and not only to eminent citizens but also to prominent visitors. Some unusual examples are in the form of crown-shaped ceremonial thimbles or a book. Such boxes were so designed that they could be used for snuff or tobacco. *See* Michael J. McAleer, 'The Gift of Freedom' in *The Connoisseur,* December 1981, p. 263. *See* BALFOUR FREEDOM BOX.

freeman. A person, usually an APPRENTICE, granted freedom by one of the Livery Companies, such as the Goldsmiths' Company. Such freedom was accompanied by certain privileges, e.g., the right to vote in a public election and to practise his trade, e.g., as a GOLDSMITH; but sometimes there were obligations, e.g., the payment of 'quarterage' as a condition to voting on Company affairs, unless excused by virtue of performing certain services.

French plating. A process of PLATING copper (also sometimes brass or iron) with SILVER LEAF, as used by French platers from the early 18th century, and later by English platers, to repair imperfectly plated copper pieces or to refinish exposed copper on worn pieces. The process involved affixing to the article, after heating it, two to four layers of silver leaf, then reheating, and repeating the process until a total of 30 to 60 leaves had been affixed, depending on the thickness of silver desired, and applying heavy pressure after each application of leaf, finally BURNISHING it to a smooth surface. The process ceased to be used after *c.* 1842 when ELECTROPLATING was developed. *See* CLOSE PLATING.

fret. A decorative border pattern in continuous repetitive form made by short lines meeting at 90° angles in various arrangements, and sometimes called a 'key-fret', 'Greek fret' or 'meander-fret' pattern. In cases where the lines are oblique and meet at acute and obtuse angles, the pattern is called a 'Japanese fret'.

Frith Apostle Spoons. A complete set of thirteen APOSTLE SPOONS, twelve bearing the maker's mark of William Cowdell and the London date mark for 1592–3 (the same marks as on the TICHBORNE SPOONS). The twelve spoons were owned by the Frith family, of Bank Hall, Derbyshire, from at least 1650 to 1893, when they were sold at auction. They were resold at Christie's, London, by order of the Executors of Mrs Alexander Mackay, on 14 December 1920, their subsequent whereabouts being unrecorded until they were acquired in 1930 from Coming of London by James B. Mahon, of New York. In 1929 the missing thirteenth spoon (St Andrew), by the same maker but dated 1593–4, was acquired by Mr Mahon, and the complete set was loaned by him from 1930 until 1937 to the Metropolitan Museum of Art, New York. The set was offered at auction in 1937 but was bought in. In 1967 it was given by Mr Mahon's son, James B. Mahon, Jr, and his wife, to the Metropolitan Museum of Art.

frosted silver. A silver ALLOY from which the copper on the surface has been removed by a chemical process, leaving a very thin surface film of pure silver that is brilliantly white. The process involves heating the alloy in air until a thin layer of copper oxide is formed on the surface; this layer is then removed by dipping the metal in hot dilute sulphuric acid. The matt 'frosted' result was popular in the period 1800–50 as a background for highly polished decoration of silver or silver gilt. The process is related to that of DEPLETION SILVERING.

frosting. A matt or slightly rough surface on a silver article; it is produced by the use of acid or a brush. *See* MATTING; FROSTED SILVER; SATIN FINISH.

fruit-basket. A type of large receptacle, for serving fresh fruit, in the form of a BASKET with everted rim and usually having four ornamental feet and decoration of PIERCED WORK.

fruit-bowl. A type of large BOWL for serving fresh fruit; it sometimes has an everted rim and stands on a high plinth, which may have pierced sides. However, there is no prescribed form or style for such bowls.

fruit-dish. A type of DISH, for serving fresh fruit, having a depressed centre or shallow well, and usually a wide ledge (MARLI) with EMBOSSED decoration. *See* FRUIT-PLATE; 'STRAWBERRY DISH'.

fruit fork. A type of small FORK, having usually three tines, used to hold a piece of fruit while it is being pared with a FRUIT KNIFE. It is usually made entirely of silver or silver gilt.

fruit knife. A type of small KNIFE, used for paring fruit, the blade being slightly curved and sharp-pointed. Such knives are often made with a mother-of-pearl, tortoise-shell or other ornamental HANDLE; the blade is usually of silver or silver gilt, not steel. Some examples have a folding blade, as on a penknife.

fruit-plate. A type of PLATE, of medium size, used when eating fresh fruit; such plates are usually decorated with fruit motifs and are often gilded.

fruit servers. A type of FORK and SPOON made as a pair and decorated EN SUITE, used for serving soft fruit. Such pairs are often ornately decorated; an example made by EDWARD FARRELL, 1816, has each handle in the form of a CANEPHOROS and the bowl modelled as a vine leaf. *See* FIGURAL FLATWARE.

funeral spoon. A type of SPOON, of no fixed form but often a HOOF SPOON, that was customarily given, as early as one example of 1684, in the American Colonies to the pall-bearers at a funeral; such spoons bear the name of the deceased and the date of death. Some were cast in one piece (those made in Boston), others had the bowl joined to the handle (those made in New York). *See* MEMORIAL SPOON.

funnel. A type of utensil shaped like an inverted hollow cone or a hemispherical or ogee-shaped bowl, having a tube at the bottom through which a liquid can be transferred to a receptacle with a narrow mouth. Miniature examples were made of silver for pharmaceutical use. Some funnels have a straight or ATTENUATED vertical tube (*see* PERFUME FUNNEL), but in others the tube is curved toward its lower end (*see* WINE FUNNEL).

Furber Service. A SERVICE consisting of 606 pieces of flatware and 132 pieces of hollow ware, some silver gilt or parcel gilt; it was made by the GORHAM COMPANY for Colonel Henry Jewett Furber (1840–1916), President of a New York insurance company, who placed the order in 1873. The pieces, some of which were designed – in HIGH VICTORIAN STYLE or with Japanese motifs – by THOMAS J. PAIRPOINT, bear the monogram 'EIF' (for Elvira Irwine Furber). The service was used by the Furbers for the last time in the 1890s at a dinner for Lillian Russell in Chicago. In 1949 it was sold by Furber's son to the Gorham Company.

furniture. (1) Actual usable articles of furniture made entirely of silver (very rare) or having a wooden core either overlaid completely (sheathed) with a layer of silver or decorated with silver mounts leaving the wood (often ebony or ebonized) exposed. Such pieces were usually made not for practical use but as background display in a formal interior. Secular furniture (as distinguished from CHURCH FURNISHINGS) has been classified by J.F.Hayward as (a) movable (BED, TABLE, TEAPOY, chair), (b) wall furniture (MIRROR, SCONCE), and (c) HEARTH FURNITURE (FIRE-DOGS, FIRE SCREEN). Such objects are usually found in the United Kingdom in Royal residences and in a few of the great country houses; one complete suite of silver furniture is now at Windsor Castle, including tables, mirrors, floor candelabra, sconces, and fire-dogs. Such silver furniture was made in England after the Restoration in 1660 (when many pieces were given by the Corporation of the City of London to Charles II) until the beginning of the 18th century. *See* Charles

fruit servers. Silver gilt, canephoros handles, Edward Farrell, London, 1816. L. 18 cm. Courtesy, Brand Inglis Ltd, London.

Furber Service. Ice-pail. W. 31·8 cm. Gorham Collection, Providence, R.I.

Oman, 'An XVIIIth-Century Record of Silver Furniture at Windsor Castle' in *The Connoisseur,* November 1934, p. 300; John F. Hayward, 'Silver Furniture' in *Apollo,* March 1958, p. 71, April 1958, p. 124, May 1958, p. 153, and June 1958, p. 220. *See* THRONE.

(2) Miniature articles of furniture made of silver; *see* MINIATURE SILVERWARE.

fusing. The process of combining or joining metals by the application of heat to cause melting, or surface melting, of the metals. The result is sometimes a homogeneous mass, as in the case of an ALLOY, and sometimes the metals retain their individual characteristics after being joined, as in the case of PLATED METAL.

G

gadrooning. Detail of rim of salver, Thomas Farren, London, 1730. Colonial Williamsburg, Va.

gadrooning. Ornamental convex decoration in the form of a continuous pattern of short, repetitive sections of REEDING ('gadroons'), set vertically, diagonally or twisted, and rounded at the extremities. It has the appearance of a round, encircling moulding with continuous regular notching. The style for silverware became popular in the late 17th century as a feature of the BAROQUE STYLE and continued into the 19th century. It is found encircling the base and the cover of many receptacles, such as TUREENS, and around the rim of PLATES, PLATTERS, CHARGERS, etc. Sometimes called 'nulling'. On some borders gadrooning alternates with FLUTING. *See* BAT-WING FLUTING.

Gainsborough Cup. A TWO-HANDLED CUP, urn-shaped and having two vertical handles squared at the top and curving down to the bottom of the bowl; the bowl and the cover are decorated with encircling ACANTHUS leaves. The cup was designed by Benjamin West, President of the Royal Academy of Arts, London, and was made by PAUL STORR in 1791. It was presented in 1800 to Margaret Gainsborough, daughter of the painter Thomas Gainsborough (1827–88), in appreciation of a painting donated by the artist to the Academy; it bears a palette-shaped plaque with an engraved donative inscription. The cup returned to the Academy in 1965, having been bequeathed to it by a descendant.

gallery. (1) A vertical retaining rim encircling an article, such as a TRAY or COASTER, being decorated with PIERCED WORK in a continuous pattern and topped by a wire edge. (2) A vertical pierced band encircling the rim of some articles as a decorative feature. When the pierced work is in the form of a series of adjacent arches, the pattern is sometimes called 'arcaded'.

Gainsborough Cup. Designed by Benjamin West, made by Paul Storr, London, 1791. H. 40·8 cm. Royal Academy of Arts, London.

Galloway Mazer. A STANDING MAZER having a silver-gilt band around the rim, the stem, and the spreading base, each ornately decorated with ENGRAVING and EMBOSSING. It bears the mark of James Gray, Edinburgh, 1569, and was formerly owned by the Earl of Galloway.

Galvanic Goblet. A silver GOBLET, made by PAUL STORR for RUNDELL, BRIDGE & RUNDELL, gilded (except for the outer rim of the lip) by a process which had been used experimentally in 1805 (*see* ELECTRO-GILDING). It bears the London mark of 1814–15, and was recorded in an inventory of Royal plate made in 1832 for William IV. The goblet has a hemispherical bowl, a straight stem, and a flat circular base. The bowl is decorated with an encircling frieze in low relief depicting the three floating figures of 'The Hours' linked by floral garlands, from a design by JOHN FLAXMAN II, made for Wedgwood. The foot bears the badge of the Prince of Wales, and is inscribed 'Galvanic Goblet', a designation derived from the name of Luigi Galvani (1737–98), the Bologna scientist. The goblet is now in the Royal Collection. Other versions of the goblet are known to have been made, one for the Duke of York (brother of George IV and William IV), and another, 1818, now in the City Museum and Art Gallery, Birmingham. *See* Charles C. Oman and Norman M. Penzer, 'The Galvanic Goblet' in *Country Life,* 4 March 1954, p. 606; Norman M. Penzer, 'The Galvanic Goblet: Paul Storr' in *The Connoisseur,* April 1954, Note, p. 188.

Garnier, Daniel (fl. 1696–1710). A London silversmith, of French Huguenot descent, who was made free of the Goldsmiths' Company by redemption
in 1696, and registered his mark *c.* 1697, address Pall Mall. It is said that he
was already probably a highly qualified silversmith upon arrival in England.
His best-known surviving pieces are a TOILET SERVICE at Melbury House,
Dorset, and the SNEYD CHANDELIER at Colonial Williamsburg, Virginia.

garnish. A set of dishes, sometimes extended to include other articles of
silverware used collectively, as for display on a sideboard.

garniture de cheminée (French). A set of ornaments to decorate the mantelshelf of a chimney-piece. Originally it was a set of Chinese export porcelain vases consisting of three, five or seven pieces, earlier examples being
composed of a central covered VASE, two smaller vases of the same form,
usually of BALUSTER shape, and two or four smaller vases of slender cylindrical or other shape, placed alternately, and all decorated EN SUITE. Some sets
included two GINGER-JARS. Later the term was applied to versions made of
silver in England and Holland. Many small vases and ginger-jars of the
period now found singly belonged originally to such a garniture. *See* GARNI-
TURE DE TABLE.

garniture de table (French). A set of VASES or other receptacles made for
ornamental (and sometimes also utilitarian) use on a table. Those intended
for a side-table in a reception hall, anteroom or salon were usually composed
of a set of vases similar to, but smaller than, a GARNITURE DE CHEMINÉE.
Those for a large serving table sometimes included a large CENTREPIECE with
accompanying DESSERT STANDS and other receptacles. An unusual example
made by ELKINGTON & CO., 1895, includes a centrepiece designed by
LÉONARD MOREL-LADEUIL, having a bowl supported by two fauns, and six
dessert stands and two salt-cellars, each with a bowl supported by *amorini.*

Garrard & Co. Ltd. A leading London manufacturing and retailing firm of
goldsmiths, silversmiths, and jewellers. Its founder was GEORGE WICKES, who
had a workshop in Threadneedle St. From 1730 to 1735 Wickes was in partnership with John Craig, and in 1735 he opened his own workshop at the
corner of Panton St and the Haymarket, from which date ledgers were kept
by him that survive today in the National Art Library at the Victoria and Albert Museum, London. In 1747 he took as a partner EDWARD WAKELIN, the
firm becoming Wickes and Wakelin; Wickes retired in 1759. Wakelin in the
early 1760s took as his partner JOHN PARKER (who in 1751 had been an apprentice to Wickes) and in 1766 Wakelin's son JOHN WAKELIN became an apprentice. In 1776 John Parker and Edward Wakelin retired, and John Wakelin and William Taylor registered their joint mark in the same year. They
operated the business until 1792, when ROBERT GARRARD I succeeded Taylor,
and a new mark, 'IW/RG', was registered for the firm of Wakelin & Garrard.
Later Garrard acquired a controlling interest and changed the name of the
firm to Garrard & Co. When Wakelin died or retired in 1802, Garrard became sole owner and registered his own mark, 'RG'. Upon Garrard's death
in 1818, he was succeeded by his sons, ROBERT GARRARD II, James, and Sebastian, and the firm's name became R., J. & S. Garrard from *c.* 1824 to 1832;
thereafter Robert dominated the firm, and when James became inactive before 1837 the name was changed to R. & S. Garrard & Co. The firm had prospered, and it succeeded RUNDELL, BRIDGE & RUNDELL in 1830 as Goldsmith to
the Crown and later, in 1843, as Crown Jewellers. It made many famous
HORSE-RACING TROPHIES (some modelled by EDMUND COTTERILL from *c.* 1831
to 1860) and yachting trophies, including the AMERICA'S CUP. Robert Garrard II was succeeded in 1881 by his nephew, James Mortimer Garrard (eldest son of Henry Garrard). He was followed in 1900 by his elder son, Sebastian Henry Garrard (1868–1946), who registered his mark, 'SH', in 1900.
(From 1822 to 1900 the firm's marks had been crowned, but in 1901 the
crown was omitted in deference to the objections of the SHEFFFIELD, ASSAY
OFFICE, which used a crown as its hallmark.) In 1911 the firm moved from
Panton St to 24 Albemarle St. In 1946, after 154 years of family control, there
was no Garrard male heir, and in 1952 the firm, as Garrard & Co. Ltd, was
amalgamated with the Goldsmiths' and Silversmiths' Co. Ltd (founded in
the 1880s by William Gibson and John Langman), and moved to its present
address at 112 Regent St, maintaining to the present time the name Garrard,
continuing to have the patronage of the Royal Family, and being responsible
for the maintenance of the Regalia and the Crown Jewels and their preparation for use at the Coronation. Since 1947 the Head Designer for silverware
has been ALEX STYLES. In 1963 the Company and MAPPIN & WEBB LTD, together with the silverware operation of ELKINGTON & CO., were joined to
form British Silverware Ltd, which is now owned by Sears Holdings Ltd.
Garrard designers and craftsmen continue to make sporting trophies and

gallery (2). Sugar-bowl with arcaded
rim, John Germon, Philadelphia, Pa, *c.*
1790–1800. H. 26·7 cm. Yale University
Art Gallery (Mabel Brady Garvan
Collection), New Haven, Conn.

Galvanic Goblet. Designed by John
Flaxman II, made by Paul Storr,
London, 1814–15. H. 12·7 cm. Royal
Collection; reproduced by gracious
permission of Her Majesty the Queen.

garniture de cheminée. Set of covered vases and ginger-jars with *repoussé* and chased decoration, Thomas Jenkins, London, 1675-6. Courtesy, Partridge (Fine Arts) Ltd, London.

commemorative pieces for prominent persons, firms, and Heads of State. *See* Christopher Lever, 'Garrard & Co.' in *The Connoisseur,* June 1974, p. 94; Will Allan, 'Garrard, the Crown Jewellers' in *The Connoisseur,* June 1980, p. 77.

Garrard, Robert (I) (1758-1818). A leading English silversmith in the early 19th century who acquired control of the firm that eventually became GAR-RARD & CO. LTD. He was apprenticed in 1773 to Stephen Unwin, a member of the Grocers' Company, and was freed in 1780, with address at Wakelin & Co., in Panton St, Haymarket. He became a partner of JOHN WAKELIN in 1792, and a joint mark, 'IW/RG', for the firm of Wakelin and Garrard was registered in 1792. Garrard gained sole control of the firm in 1802; he registered his own marks, 'RG', in 1801 and 1802. He was succeeded by his sons, ROBERT GARRARD II, James (1795-1870), and Sebastian (1798-1872), and their male descendants controlled the firm until 1946.

Garrard, Robert (II) (1793-1881). A son of ROBERT GARRARD I and the most renowned silversmith of the Garrard family, he was apprenticed to his father in 1809, freed by patrimony from the Grocers' Company in 1816, and entered his first mark in 1818, at Panton St, Haymarket, London. Upon the death of his father in 1818, he with his two brothers, James and Sebastian, formed the firm of R., J. & S. Garrard, and Robert assumed full control of the business until his death (*see* GARRARD & CO. LTD). He is reputed especially for his many large and imposing CENTREPIECES and trophies of FIGURAL SILVER-WARE, some modelled by EDMUND COTTERILL. *See* JOAN OF ARC STATUETTE; MOORISH CENTREPIECE; 'QUEEN VICTORIA'S DOGS' CENTREPIECE; TALISMAN CENTREPIECE.

garniture de table. Centrepiece, six dessert stands, and two salt-cellars, Elkington & Co., Birmingham, 1895. W. (of centrepiece) 89 cm. Courtesy, Christie's, London.

Garthorne, George (d. 1730). An English silversmith who was apprenticed in 1669 and freed in 1680, with address at Carey Lane, London. He made ware adapting the French style introduced into England by the Huguenots. As the Royal Goldsmith, he executed orders for William III and Queen Anne, including a silver CHANDELIER with twelve branches now at Hampton Court and two other silver chandeliers formerly at St James's Palace but now lost. He also made a WINE-BOTTLE, 1690, now in the Royal Collection, a WINE COOLER, 1694-5, owned by the Bank of England (*see* BANK OF ENGLAND WINE COOLER), and an ALTAR DISH now in the Tower of London (*see* GARTHORNE ALTAR DISH).

Garthorne Altar Dish. A circular silver-gilt ALTAR DISH made by GEORGE GARTHORNE, London, 1691, having a wide rim embossed with a floral frieze with four interspersed masks and having in the centre a medallion depicting, in relief, the scene of the Supper at Emmaus (Luke xxiv, 13ff.). It was made for Lord Lucas, then Constable of the Tower of London, and it is kept in the Jewel House of the Tower. It is placed on the altar of Westminster Abbey during the coronation service, and is displayed each year on the altar of the Tower's Chapel of St Peter ad Vincula at Christmas, Whitsun, and Easter. The dish is accompanied by a silver-gilt FLAGON which bears the mark 'SH'.

gauge. The measure of the diameter of WIRE or the thickness of sheet metal to be used to fabricate an article, referred to as 'heavy gauge' or 'light gauge' according to the thickness.

gauntlet. Strictly, a type of articulated metal glove worn as part of armour; but silver pieces in the form of a cylindrical CUFF were made in 1783 by Hester Bateman (*see* BATEMAN) and have been referred to as 'gauntlets'.

gem-decorated silverware. Articles of silverware that included in the original decoration various gemstones, these now being usually missing. Gemstones were used on medieval work, and the style was revived by the Arts and Crafts Movement of the 19th century. One early piece that still features gemstones is the HOWARD GRACE CUP, set with garnets and pearls. Other early examples, from which the gems are now missing from the settings, are the STONYHURST SALT, and a BEAKER, 1507, at Christ's College, Cambridge. Examples from the 19th century are the NATIONAL CUP, CORONATION CUP, PUGIN CHALICE, and the BURGES CLARET-JUGS. *See* RELIQUARY CROSS; LIMERICK CROSIER.

George III Statuette. A silver-gilt STATUETTE depicting a full-length standing figure of George III wearing the robes of the Order of the Garter, crowned and holding a sceptre. It was made in 1812 by PAUL STORR for RUNDELL, BRIDGE & RUNDELL, an early example of portrait modelling by English silversmiths. The figure rests on a three-tiered PLINTH bearing an engraved inscription. It is in the personal collection of Her Majesty the Queen.

Georgia silverware. Articles of silverware made in the state of Georgia from Colonial days, the earliest silversmiths having been in the cities of Augusta and Savannah, later ones in many inland communities. More than 58 marks have been identified of silversmiths working between 1790 and 1870. Many of the silversmiths were also engaged as jewellers and watchmakers, or as retailers selling imported ware. The local wares were mainly for domestic use, the earliest-known extant piece being TONGS, *c.* 1790. The best-known silversmith was Frederick Marquand. The ware has no regional characteristics, and much was brought from the north-east and overstamped locally by BACK-STAMPING. *See* G. B. Cutten, *The Silversmiths of Georgia* (1958); Katherine Gross Farnham and Callie Huger Efird, 'Early silversmiths and the silver trade in Georgia' in *Antiques,* March 1971, p. 380.

Georgian silverware. Articles of silverware made in England during the reigns of George I, 1714-27, George II, 1727-60, George III, 1760-1820, and George IV, 1820-30; but the term is also used loosely with respect to silverware made in the manner of ware produced throughout and after the 18th century. The term 'Early Georgian' generally refers to the period from *c.* 1710 to the 1720s, 'Middle Georgian' to the period from the 1720s to the 1770s; and 'Late Georgian' to the period from the 1770s to *c.* 1830. Silverware of the period embraced the ROCOCO STYLE, NEO-CLASSICAL STYLE, ADAM STYLE, REGENCY STYLE, and Gothic Revival style. Since there was no consistent style throughout the period, the term 'Georgian' is at best vague and its use should be discouraged.

German silver. *See* NICKEL SILVER.

Garthorne Altar Dish. Silver gilt, George Garthorne, London, 1691. Tower of London (Crown copyright, HMSO).

Gibbon Salt. Silver gilt and crystal, London, 1576-7. H. 30 cm. Goldsmiths' Company, London.

Gibbs Butter Dish. Silver gilt with 'frosted' cover, Paul Storr, for Rundell, Bridge & Rundell, London, 1817-18. H. 19 cm. Castle Museum, Nottingham.

Gibbon Salt. A large silver-gilt architectural PILLAR SALT, London, 1576-7, in the form of a baldachin standing on a square platform with four small vase-shaped feet and having at the centre of each side a free-standing Ionic column to support an elaborate tiered roof. In the centre of the piece, surrounded by the columns, there is a rock crystal pentagonal cylinder representing descending water and enclosing a silver-gilt standing figure of Neptune. The domed cover has an ornate finial in the form of an urn supporting a spice-box which has a pierced cover and supports a small vase; it covers a concealed receptacle for the salt. The piece was donated in 1632 to the Goldsmiths' Company by Simon Gibbon, a Cheapside goldsmith, perhaps to divert an annual search by the Company of goldsmiths' premises for ware of base metal; it bears a donative inscription.

Gibbs Butter Dish. A silver-gilt BUTTER-DISH in the form of a low circular bowl, the side of which is decorated with pierced vinework. It has a domed cover of coronet-style, with the dome of ungilded FROSTED SILVER, within six gilded vertical straps extending from the bottom rim upward to a flower finial. The bowl rests on a wider gilded stand with fluted decoration and four scrolled feet. The piece has a close-fitting silver-gilt liner. Made by PAUL STORR, 1817-18, for RUNDELL, BRIDGE & RUNDELL, it was in the collection of Richard Wagstaff, and was donated by his daughter in 1968 to the Castle Museum, Nottingham.

Gibbs Centrepiece. A massive, heavily decorated CENTREPIECE in the form of a covered bowl similar in shape to the WARWICK VASE, resting on a circular PLINTH. The bowl, which has a TRUMPET FOOT and two vertical loop handles decorated with vines, has decoration of rams' heads, fruit, and floral festoons; it is dated 1844 and was made by R. & S. Garrard (*see* GARRARD & CO. LTD). The cover is domed and surmounted by a finial in the form of three *putti* supporting a coronet and Prince of Wales's feathers; it is by R. & S. Garrard, 1858. The plinth is decorated EN SUITE with four figures of the infant Bacchus and vines; made by R. & S. Garrard, 1856, it bears an engraved donative inscription. The piece was presented by Edward VII, when Prince of Wales, to his tutor, Frederick Waymouth Gibbs, K.C., who bequeathed it to the Honourable Society of Lincoln's Inn, London.

Gibraltar Cup. A silver-gilt TWO-HANDLED CUP, having a cylindrical bowl with scroll handles and a domed cover. It was presented to Sir John Leake, Commander of the British Fleet at the relief of Gibraltar (1705) by Prince George of Hesse-Darmstadt, Commander-in-Chief of Gibraltar at the time. The cup, decorated with the arms of Leake, is marked London, 1707-8. It was bequeathed in 1953 by Col. A. Martin Leake, V.C., to the British Museum, London.

Gibson spoon. A type of MEDICAL SPOON having a hollow tubular stem and an elongated bowl which is covered by a hinged lid except at its extremity, left open for the administration of medicine. It was named after the London inventor, Charles Gibson, *c.* 1827. The medicine was administered by placing a finger over the end of the hollow stem and then removing the finger to permit the liquid to flow out and not (as suggested by an amusing but apocryphal explanation) by blowing through the tube. Sometimes called a 'castor-oil spoon'. *See* MEDICAL SILVERWARE.

gilding. The process of overlaying or covering an article with a thin layer of gold or gold ALLOY. The technique has been used since ancient times. The methods include: (1) oil gilding or water gilding, by attaching gold leaf by means of an adhesive (called a 'mordant'); (2) mercury gilding (fire gilding), by applying an amalgam of gold and mercury with a brush, then heating the object to cause the mercury to vaporize and to leave a thin film of gold; (3) friction gilding, by rubbing the surface with ashes of linen rags soaked in a solution of gold chloride, then burnishing and polishing; and (4) ELECTRO-GILDING, by depositing a layer of gold by an electric current, leaving a thin 'flash' of gold or a substantial covering, or leaving a more durable layer by 'hard gold plating'. Only methods (2) and (4) are used to gild silver. After certain gilding processes, the effect was enhanced by 'tooling', i.e., by incising the gold surface to create a design or a textured surface. As to certain articles of silver or of SHEFFIELD PLATE (e.g., SALT-CELLARS, EGG-CUPS, MUSTARD-POTS), it was necessary to gild the interior to prevent staining by certain foods (e.g., egg-yolks), but some silverware was gilded solely for decorative effect (e.g., MONTEITHS, CANDELABRA, EPERGNES, TEA SERVICES, CORONATION CUPS). In the case of mercury gilding done at high temperature, which would melt off soldered parts such as feet and handles, these were affixed after they and the piece itself had been gilded. Sheffield plate was very rarely gilded on the exterior. *See* PARCEL GILDING; VERMEIL.

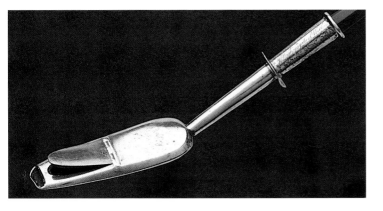

Gibson spoon. Maker's mark 'IJK', London, 1827. L. 14·7 cm. Wellcome Collection, Science Museum, London.

gimbal chamber candlestick. A type of CHAMBER CANDLESTICK, the stem of which is not attached to the base but is affixed to an arm that extends upward and inward from the rim, so that the weighted stem can swing (like a gimbal) and thus always remain vertical.

ginger-jar. A type of JAR, usually of oblate spheroid or of ovoid shape with flattened shoulders and an upright collar, over which fits a domed SLIP-ON COVER having an ornamental finial. Numerous silver examples are in the form of the Chinese porcelain prototypes from the reign of K'ang Hsi, 1662–1722. The silver jars are often decorated overall with ENGRAVING, EM-BOSSING, CHASING or REPOUSSÉ CHASING, often featuring CHINOISERIE motifs or flower-and-leaf patterns. Their height ranges from about 25 cm up to about 50 cm, as in the case of one example made by Thomas Jenkins, London, c. 1670, now in the Victoria and Albert Museum, London. They were often part of a GARNITURE DE CHEMINÉE or a GARNITURE DE TABLE.

girdle. A decorative raised band encircling an object, such as that encircling the bottom of the neck of a CLARET-JUG, to which is attached the lower end of the loop HANDLE.

girdle book. A small devotional book, often bound within elaborate silver (or gold) covers, carried in the 15th/17th centuries by women of rank or wealth, worn suspended from a chain attached to a girdle (an unbuckled looped belt). *See* BOOK COVER.

Gladstone Testimonial. A presentation piece in the form of a two-tiered square base surmounted by a bust of William Ewart Gladstone (1809–98), the British Prime Minister, with a figure of Liberty, holding a harp, standing on the lower base. It was acquired by a fund raised in 1886 by Joseph Pulitzer, publisher of the New York *World,* with over ten thousand subscribers, and presented on 9 July 1887 to Gladstone by 'his American Admirers' in recognition of his unsuccessful efforts to grant Home Rule to Ireland, which had been popularly supported in the United States. The piece, made by TIFFANY & CO. in 1887, is now owned by Sir William Gladstone, Bt, of Hawarden Castle, Deeside, Clwyd, Wales.

Gladstone Testimonial. Bust of W. E. Gladstone and figure of Liberty with harp, Tiffany & Co., New York, 1887. H. 93 cm. Courtesy, Sir William Gladstone, Bt.

Glasgow Assay Office. The ASSAY OFFICE established in Glasgow in the last quarter of the 17th century, and closed in 1964. Its ASSAY OFFICE HALLMARK used since 1681 depicts a tree having a bird perched on it and a bell in the branches, and across the trunk a fish. From 1819 until 1964 its STANDARD HALLMARK was a LION RAMPANT HALLMARK, and it was accompanied by a MAKER'S MARK. A DATE HALLMARK was used from 1681 to 1710, but was discontinued until 1819, from which date an alphabetical cycle remained in use until 1964. A DUTY MARK, with a Sovereign's head, was used from 1819 until 1896.

Glasgow Assay Office. Assay Office Hallmark in use until closure in 1964.

glass objects. Articles having an essential or an ornamental part made of glass, but (1) having a silver frame or silver MOUNTS, or (2) being a silver article with a glass LINER. The former group includes the VYVYAN SALT, the PARR POT, the BURGHLEY TANKARD, and the SUDELEY TANKARD, as well as various glass VASES, BOWLS (e.g., small bowls suspended from an EPERGNE), CRUETS, CLARET-JUGS, and SILVER-CASED BOTTLES. The latter group includes some CREAM-PAILS, SUGAR-BASKETS, BUTTER-DISHES, MUSTARD-POTS, SAUCE-BOATS, and especially SALT-CELLARS (which would become corroded if used without the liner). *See* CRYSTAL OBJECTS; MOUNTED OBJECTS.

Gleadowe, Reginald Yorke (1888–1944). An outstanding designer of silverware, who was Art Master at Winchester College, 1922–44, and Slade Professor of Fine Art at Oxford University, 1928–33. His work, although limited, was done mostly on commission. He worked closely with H. G. Murphy and with WAKELY & WHEELER LTD, who made pieces designed by him. He was the designer of the STALINGRAD SWORD and the JUBILEE BEAKERS.

Gleane Cup. A silver-gilt STANDING CUP having a tapering cylindrical bowl with a bulging bottom and an extended flat lip, a vase-shaped bracketed stem, a domed foot, and a cover with a vase-shaped finial surmounted by a bunch of flowers. The bowl is decorated with an embossed encircling frieze depicting Abigail before King David, with figures of gift-laden camels and asses; on the cover is a scene of David sending messengers to Nathan. An inscription records the cup as being a gift in 1633 from Sir Peter Gleane, Mayor of Norwich, 1615, and M.P. in 1628, to the church of St Peter Mancroft, Norwich. The maker's mark (thought possibly to be that of a German trained in Nuremberg) is not decipherable, but the vase is considered to be an example of Elizabethan secular plate, its date attributable probably to 1565. The earlier restored finial in the form of a pine-cone has been replaced in recent years by a floral finial, deliberately left ungilded to emphasize the substitution.

globe inkstand. An unusual type of INKSTAND that has the appearance of a globe set within a wire framework resting on a stemmed base (or on four curved legs) and surmounted by a tall finial. The hollow globe is composed of two sections, the lower hemisphere being fixed and enclosing articles of writing equipment, such as one, two or three INKPOTS, a pen, pencil, penknife, and ivory tablets; the upper hemisphere can be rotated, by pressure on the finial, to turn under the lower one. From a knop on the stem, curved arms rise to support the meridian circle and the vertical circle within which the globe is suspended. The height varies from 23 to 30 cm. The decoration includes swags around the globe, and occasionally masks and flowers. An ornate example has a figure of Atlas supporting the globe and an owl as the finial. Examples were made from *c.* 1770 to 1810. It was sometimes miscalled a 'Pitt's globe inkstand' due to having been so named in 1806 by the patentee after William Pitt the Younger, who had recently died.

Glynne Cup. A silver-gilt CUP (one of a pair) in fantasy form more commonly made by Continental silversmiths than in England, having upon a stemmed base a pierced basket-like ornament upon which stands a large figure in-the-round of a pelican 'in-her-piety' vulning (wounding) her breast to feed her young, the three small birds standing at her feet. The basket is supported by three brackets on a knopped stem that rests on a spreading foot engraved with a frieze depicting animals. The upper part of the pelican (the head, neck and wings) forms the cover, having as its handle the bird's curved neck. The body was originally made of a NAUTILUS SHELL, which was replaced in the late 17th century by gilded silver realistically engraved to simulate feathers; at the same time the piece was repaired and regilded. It bears the mark of a bird and the London hallmark for 1579–80. The cup was formerly owned by Sir Stephen Glynne, the 8th Baronet, then by his son, also Stephen, the 9th Baronet (d. 1874), and from him – he having died without issue – it passed to his sister Catherine, wife of the Prime Minister, William Ewart Gladstone (1809–98), and thereafter in the Gladstone family to the present owner, Sir William Gladstone, Bt, of Hawarden Castle, Deeside, Clwyd, Wales, from whom it has been on loan to the Victoria and Albert Museum, London.

Goat and Bee Jugs. Several silver versions of the well-known porcelain 'Goat and Bee Jugs' made at the Chelsea pottery from 1745, some white, some polychrome. The body is pear-shaped with an everted lip, and on each side there is at the bottom a figure of a recumbent goat and (on some examples) on the front, below the lip, a bee; the jugs have a crabstock handle and are decorated with applied flowers and foliage.

A similar silver-gilt jug was recorded by William Chaffers (*Marks and Monograms on Pottery and Porcelain,* 13th ed., 1912, p. 947) as being dated London 1724 and then owned by Mrs A. R. MacDonald. Another such jug was recorded by Sir Charles J. Jackson (*Illustrated History of English Plate,* 1911, p. 988) as bearing the mark of NICHOLAS SPRIMONT (who died in 1771) and London hallmarks for 1777–8 (six years after his death); there is no record of its whereabouts. Although the possibility of a silver prototype cannot be excluded, the four known extant silver examples are now regarded as having been made later than 1745, and probably cast from one of the Chelsea pieces (hence not prototypes, as once surmised). Of the four known silver examples two were acquired by the Victoria and Albert Museum, London, in

Gleane Cup. Silver gilt, London, 1565. H. 33 cm. Church of St Peter Mancroft, Norwich.

1944 and given by it in 1968 to the Goldsmiths' Company, London (now in its Spurious Plate Collection at Goldsmiths' Hall). These are: (a) one with a bee, gilded and bearing a transposed genuine London hallmark for 1724 (possibly the MacDonald example noted by Chaffers); and (b) one without a bee and bearing a forged London hallmark for 1760. Both pieces have been subjected to a spectrographic test for impurities in the silver, and the results indicate production in the early 19th century.

A third silver example, without a bee and dated 1737(?), and bearing the maker's mark 'EW' (for Edward Wood), was in the collection of Dr Bellamy Gardner and was shown by him at the Cheyne Exhibition at Chelsea Town Hall in 1924; but it was not included in the Sotheby's sale of his collection in June 1941. Such a jug, without a bee and bearing the London hallmarks for 1737 (perhaps the Gardner jug, its whereabouts in the interim being unrecorded), was bought in London by Mrs William B. Munro, of Pasadena, California, and was exhibited at the Los Angeles County Museum in 1958; it was bequeathed in 1969 by Mrs Munro to the Henry E. Huntington Library and Art Gallery, San Marino, California, where the date mark is now regarded as probably transposed or forged.

A fourth silver example, bearing the marks 'IW' (probably that of James Waters) and London, 1772-3, is in the Katz Collection at the Museum of Fine Arts, Boston, Massachusetts.

See Geoffrey Wills, '"Goat and Bee" Jugs' in *Apollo,* February 1958, p.58 (Mr Wills has informed the author that he never considered the Munro jug to be a prototype of the Chelsea jugs).

goblet. A type of drinking vessel having a bowl that is usually semi-ovoid, but that varies in shape, resting on a circular stemmed foot. The stem occurs in various forms and styles. The bowl is generally undecorated except for a CARTOUCHE bearing a coat of arms, but some examples have decoration of CHASING, ENGRAVING or EMBOSSING. When made in silver the type is usually called a WINE-CUP. *See* CHRISTENING GOBLET.

Godiva, Lady, Statuette. A silver-gilt STATUETTE of Lady Godiva (*c.* 1040-80) riding a fully caparisoned horse. The piece was designed and commissioned by Prince Albert as a gift to Queen Victoria on 26 August 1857. It was modelled by PIERRE-ÉMILE JEANNEST for ELKINGTON & CO., 1857, and was shown at the London International Exhibition of 1862. The statuette, resting on a rectangular stand of gilded bronze decorated with CHAMP-LEVÉ enamelling (the earliest-known use in England of such work), is in the Royal Collection.

Godman Tea Urn. A TEA-URN made at the Birmingham factory of MATTHEW BOULTON and John Fothergill, 1773, the significance of which is that it is the first piece of silver recorded in the Plate Register at the Birmingham Assay Office. The urn is in the form of a VASE resting on a square PLINTH with four feet and having a high-domed cover with a vase-shaped finial; the TAP is of silver and the SPIGOT of ivory. The urn is in the collection of Frederick du Cane Godman, since 1965 at the Birmingham Museum and Art Gallery.

gold plate. Strictly, articles made of gold; but the term is often incorrectly applied to articles of gilded silver, especially articles of gilded TABLEWARE. Articles of gold are naturally very scarce, only three English examples made before 1830 being in the Royal collections, and only a total of less than one hundred examples of surviving English gold ware were known to Arthur G. Grimwade in 1953. Such gold pieces are generally beyond the scope of this book. *See* PLATE; GILDING.

goldsmith. Strictly, a worker in gold, but long usage has applied the term to a worker also in silver, such as those who were Wardens of the Goldsmiths' Company (*see* GOLDSMITHS, WORSHIPFUL COMPANY OF) and were involved in the ASSAYING of silverware. For names and marks of many English goldsmiths (too numerous for entries here, except a few outstanding ones), *see* Sir Charles James Jackson, *English Goldsmiths and Their Marks* (2nd ed., 1921); Arthur G. Grimwade, *London Goldsmiths, 1697-1837* (2nd ed., 1982).

Goldsmiths, The Worshipful Company of. The successor to a guild of goldsmiths organized in England before 1180, and one of the oldest of the great City of London livery companies. By order of Henry III in 1238, six 'discreet goldsmiths' from its membership were to be selected by the Mayor and Aldermen of London to have the responsibility to set and enforce the standards for silver and gold, and from 1300, by order of Edward I, to mark pieces that had been approved, after ASSAYING, with the HALLMARK of a leopard's head (*see* LEOPARD'S HEAD HALLMARK). The company was incorporated in 1327 and has since greatly expanded its supervisory, educational,

globe inkstand. Three inkpots, silver mounted, Nathaniel Smith & Co., Sheffield. H. 20 cm. Courtesy, Sotheby's, London.

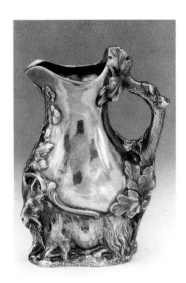

Goat and Bee Jug. Cream-jug (without bee), with marks for London, 1737, probably transposed or forged. H. 11·4 cm. Henry E. Huntington Library and Art Gallery, San Marino, Cal.

promotional, and charitable functions; a major function has been to operate the ASSAY OFFICE for London. Its main offices are in the Goldsmiths' Hall which has been rebuilt and enlarged several times, the present premises being in Foster Lane and its Assay Office in nearby Gutter Lane. *See* John Bodman Carrington and George Ravensworth Hughes, *The Plate of the Worshipful Company of Goldsmiths* (1926).

Goldsmiths' Company Candelabra. Three CANDELABRA commissioned by the Goldsmiths' Company, after the Great Exhibition of 1851, to encourage the art of silver-making in England, the design competition being won by Alfred Brown, who modelled the pieces for execution in 1854 by John Samuel Hunt for HUNT & ROSKELL. Each piece rests on a tripod base supporting a platform on the sides of which are the arms of the Company and upon which are attached twisting arms for the candle SOCKETS (ten arms for the smaller pair, twelve plus a central socket for the larger one). The figures on the three bases represent:

(1) The granting of the Charter of Incorporation of the Goldsmiths' Company in 1392 by Richard II, 1377-99, to the Prime Warden of the Company. To the right of the King stands Thomas d'Arundel, Chancellor and Archbishop of Canterbury. Seated at the left of the King is the Queen, Anne of Bohemia. Other figures are William Stonden, Mayor of London, the Chamberlain, and attendants. On the base are figures representing the processes of mining, refining and working precious metals.

(2) Benvenuto Cellini (1500-71), George Heriot (1563-1624, Scottish philanthropist), and Sir Martin Bowes (1497-1566, Lord Mayor of London, 1545-6, and Prime Warden, 1558, of the Goldsmiths' Company), each accompanied by a seated figure of his Genius.

(3) Michelangelo (1475-1564), Domenico Ghirlandaio (1449-94) kneeling to sketch a standing lady fitting on a garland, and Lorenzo de'Medici (1492-1519) inspecting some art work held by a page.

Goldsmiths' Company Centrepieces. Two CENTREPIECES, commissioned under the same circumstances as the GOLDSMITHS' COMPANY CANDELABRA, made by John Samuel Hunt for HUNT & ROSKELL, 1854-5. They are in the form of figure groups, each resting on a tripod base and representing the activities of the Company:

(1) Benevolence, having at the top of a pedestal a standing figure of Prudence, and kneeling at her side Benevolence distributing from her horn of

Goldsmiths' Company Candelabra. Three candelabra designed by Alfred Brown and made by John Samuel Hunt for Hunt & Roskell, London, 1854-5: (1) *above*, 'Granting the Charter', height 1·43 m; (2, 3) *right*, each 94 cm high. Goldsmiths' Company, London.

Goldsmiths' Company Centrepieces. Figure groups John Samuel Hunt for Hunt & Roskell, London, 1854–5: (1) *above*, 'Benevolence'; (2) *below*, 'Business Duties'. H. 66·2 cm. Goldsmiths' Company, London.

plenty to necessitous figures below: a scholar and his tutor, an invalid, a widow with her children, and an enfeebled artisan.

(2) Business Duties, having at the top of a pedestal a seated figure of Science pointing to the law upheld by Justice, with (on her left) Industry and (below) Mercury, representing Commerce, and consequent Prosperity with a horn of plenty, and on the other side Plutus, god of Wealth.

On both are medallions of Edward III, Henry VII, and James I, and at the angles are figures of two unicorns, the supporters of the Company.

Goldsmiths' Company Sideboard Dishes. (1) A SIDEBOARD DISH made for the Goldsmiths' Company in 1741 by PAUL DE LAMERIE. In the well are the arms of the Company in bold relief on a plain burnished ground. The border, 16·5 cm wide, has an edge of broken outline, and is decorated with four

Goldsmiths' Company Sideboard Dish (1). Paul de Lamerie, London, 1741. D. 78·8 cm. Goldsmiths' Company, London.

Goodricke Cup. Mounts 1563; silver (replacement) egg 1620. H. 34·3 cm. British Museum, London.

oval medallions depicting youthful figures representing Hercules with a club, Mercury with a cock, Vulcan with an anvil, and Minerva with an owl and serpent. Between the medallions are figures of an eagle, a hooded falcon, a lion, and a dolphin. (2) A pair of silver-gilt sideboard dishes commissioned by the Company for display on the buffet in its Livery Hall. Both were made by John Tapley for RUNDELL, BRIDGE & RUNDELL in 1840. One has, encircling a central boss decorated with the coat of arms of the Company, a scene depicting Richard II presenting the Charter of the Company to the Wardens in 1392, and the other a scene depicting the Triumph of Britannia.

golf trophy. A type of TROPHY, in the form of a silver golf club, often having attached by thin chains a silver replica of each winner's ball. The oldest extant example is one awarded by the City of Edinburgh. The most famous and second oldest is that awarded in 1754 by the Royal and Ancient Golf Club of St Andrews, Fife, Scotland, it being a replica of the wooden putter then used; it is unmarked, has engraved on the head a figure of St Andrew, and has attached 80 inscribed balls (balls of winners after 1834 having been attached to later silver replicas). The oldest-known Irish golf-club trophy is the Aughnacloy Putter made in 1889 of ebony and ivory with silver-gilt mounts and kept since 1956 at the Golf Club at Dungannon, Co. Tyrone; *see* T. C. H. Dickson, 'Ireland's Oldest Golf Trophy' in *Country Life,* 30 January 1964, p. 220.

Goodden, Robert Y. (1919–). An English designer who first trained as an architect, but gradually focused his attention on designing silverware. He was appointed a Professor at the Royal College of Art to create a separate school of silverware and jewelry, but retired in 1974 to devote himself to designing silverware, having previously designed pieces on commission for colleges and industry. In 1947 he was appointed Royal Designer for Industry. In 1953 he won the national competition for the design for a trophy to commemorate the coronation of Elizabeth II; *see* ELIZABETH II CORONATION CUP. He was appointed to the Livery of the Goldsmiths' Company in 1954 and served as its Prime Warden in 1966–7. He now maintains a studio at his home near Bath.

Goodricke Cup. A STANDING CUP, 1563, in the form of an OSTRICH-EGG CUP, having a silver bowl (replacing in 1620 the original ostrich-egg bowl), resting on a vase-shaped stem on a spreading foot. The everted rim and the stem are connected by three vertical silver straps cast as part-caryatids. The cover has embossing depicting running animals, and inside the cover is a medallion with the arms of Richard Goodricke (d. 1582), of Ribston, Yorkshire; its finial is a figure of a demi-lion. The replacement bowl is engraved with a human figure, birds, and flowers. Encircling its rim is the engraved inscription 'FARE/WEL/TIL/THEN' (the Goodricke motto), and on the rim are a monogram 'RG' and the date 1563. The cup was commissioned for Richard Goodricke by his wife Margaret. It was included in the Franks Bequest of 1897 to the British Museum, London.

Goodwood Cup. One of a series of HORSE-RACING TROPHIES awarded at Goodwood Racecourse, near Chichester, Sussex, the first in 1812, and annually from the 1820s. Individual trophies – usually referred to as a 'cup' – have varied in form, being generally a TWO-HANDLED CUP, but sometimes a VASE, a BOWL (*see* GOODWOOD 'CUP', 1829), a shield (*see* GOODWOOD 'CUP', 1833), a TEAPOT, or a figural group.

Goodwood 'Cup', 1829. A silver-gilt GOODWOOD CUP having a wide, flat-bottomed circular BOWL supported by three leonine legs resting on a triangular stand upon which is engraved 'Goodwood 1829'. The bowl is decorated with scenes in low relief depicting chariot races, and bears an inscription relating to its being awarded to George IV's mare in 1829. The cup, made by PAUL STORR in 1829, is based on an engraving by G. B. PIRANESI, inspired by an antique marble tripod vase of similar shape (but with a marine frieze) now in the Museo Nazionale, Rome.

Goodwood 'Cup', 1833. A GOODWOOD CUP in the form of a circular SHIELD having a centre decoration in high relief depicting a group of horsemen in combat with upraised swords. The design has been attributed to EDWARD HODGES BAILY; the piece was made by PAUL STORR for Storr & Mortimer, London, 1833. A plaque on the reverse relates the details of the race. The piece was in the collection of the Marquess of Anglesey, 1946, and was sold at Sotheby's, London, on 14 June 1984.

gorget. As to silverware: (1) A type of crescent-shaped badge worn by military personnel, suspended on the breast by a neck chain. It is derived from a

Goodwood 'Cup', 1829. Silver-gilt horse-racing trophy, Paul Storr, 1829. H. 44·5 cm. Royal Collection; reproduced by gracious permission of Her Majesty the Queen.

piece of armour worn around the neck to protect the throat. From *c.* 1650 until *c.* 1830 it was worn as a badge of rank in the British army. (2) One of several different types of object given during the 18th century by white traders to North American Indians in exchange for furs, and also given by officials when making peace treaties with the Indians. Such pieces were made mainly by silversmiths in the United States and Canada, but also, *c.* 1780–90, in England. Forty such gorgets were ordered by the Governor of Pennsylvania in 1757–8, to be issued upon the making of a peace treaty with the Delaware and Iroquois Indians, and others were made by Joseph Richardson, Sr (*see* RICHARDSON), for the Friendly Association for Regaining and Preserving Peace with the Indians by Pacific Means. *See* INDIAN-TRADE SILVERWARE.

Goodwood 'Cup', 1833. Shield, Paul Storr, 1833. D. 72·5 cm. Courtesy, Sotheby's, London.

Gorham Company. A leading American silverware firm, of Providence, Rhode Island. It was founded in 1831 by Jabez Gorham (1792–1869); he was an apprentice, 1806–13, to Nehemiah Dodge, a Providence silversmith, then from 1813 to 1831 a manufacturer and salesman of jewelry, and from 1831 a maker of COIN-SILVER SPOONS. He soon formed a partnership with Henry L. Webster, of Boston; it was named Gorham & Webster, and in 1837 became Gorham, Webster & Price. Gorham sold his interest and retired in 1841, but in the same year resumed silverware business, with his son John (1828–98), under the name J. Gorham & Son. John greatly expanded the business in the 1840s, adding new lines of silverware. In 1848 Jabez sold his interest to John, but the firm retained the name J. Gorham & Son until 1850. During the 1850s John further expanded the business, making HOLLOW WARE and using machinery to supplement handwork. To provide needed capital, John in 1850 took as a partner his cousin, Gorham Thurber, and the name became Gorham & Thurber. In 1852 a drop press was acquired, and thereafter many new patterns of spoons were produced, as well as new items of hollow ware. In 1852 the firm's name was changed to Gorham & Company. John made two trips to Europe, in 1852 and 1860, hiring in London and Paris skilled craftsmen and buying stock for his retail outlet. In 1857 George Wilkinson (1819–94) joined the firm as chief designer, continuing as such until succeeded in 1891 by WILLIAM CHRISTMAS CODMAN. In 1865 the firm was incorporated as Gorham Manufacturing Co., controlled equally by Gorham and Thurber, and retail stores were opened in New York City and elsewhere in the United States. During 1865 ELECTROPLATING was introduced. Much ware was made in HIGH VICTORIAN STYLE designed by THOMAS J. PAIRPOINT.

After the Civil War and the Panic of 1873, when sales had fallen off, the firm was forced to retrench; John had to dispose of his shares due to outside losses and went bankrupt in 1877, and in 1878 was ousted from the company. The company thereafter progressed with the times, making ware in NEO-CLASSICAL STYLE, Japanese style, COLONIAL REVIVAL STYLE, and Gothic Revival style. In 1881 F. ANTOINE HELLER, a French designer, joined the company and introduced new patterns for flatware and hollow ware in the ACADEMIC STYLE. During the 1890s MARTELÉ ware, in ART NOUVEAU STYLE, was introduced by Codman and the then President, Edward Holbrook. In 1925 ERIK MAGNUSSEN was brought from Denmark as special designer, creating designs in ART DECO STYLE. Production of silverware was curtailed during World War II while the company made war material. When business resumed, Burr Sebring, who had been chief designer since before 1965, designed in 1979 pieces in modernistic patterns. The present White House table service, with Gorham's King Charles pattern, totalling 3,434 pieces, was made in 1974–5. In 1967 the company was merged into the Textron Corporation, of Providence, since which time the manufacturing and sales departments have operated as the Gorham Division of Textron. *See* Charles H. Carpenter, Jr, *Gorham Silver 1831–1981* (1982). *See* BORG-WARNER TROPHY; CENTURY VASE; CHANTILLY PATTERN; COLUMBUS STATUE; DEWEY CUP; FURBER SERVICE; HIAWATHA'S BOAT.

gorget (2). Pendant, Joseph Richardson, Sr, Philadelphia, Pa, *c.* 1756–8. W. 13·5 cm. Historical Society of Pennsylvania, Philadelphia.

Gothic Style (English). The decorative style that prevailed in England during the reign of Henry VII, 1485–1509, founder of the House of Tudor. It was characterized by a boldness of form and an absence of ornamentation, as exemplified in silverware by some 'FONT-SHAPED' CUPS. The style was created by French architects to supersede the Romanesque style and it featured spires, pinnacles, and pointed arches, and in silverware ENAMELLING and jewels to echo the use of stained-glass windows, together with cast figures on finials of covers and on terminals of spoons. The term 'Gothic style' was first used by French artists before the Renaissance with regard to such medieval architecture, in contrast to classical, which they considered 'barbaric', as derived from the invading Gothic tribes. In England the word 'Gothick' was used in the 17th and 18th centuries to imply a tasteless style, but the pejorative meaning ceased when the Gothic Revival style developed in the mid-19th century, inspired by the Arts and Crafts Movement led by William Morris. In the United States it is found almost exclusively in ecclesiastical ware. *See* CRESSENER CUP; CAMPION CUP.

Gould, James (I) (fl. 1722–47). A London silversmith, apprenticed in 1714 and freed in 1722. Various marks were entered by him from 1722 until 1743, from Gutter Lane and Ave Maria Lane. His son, James Gould II, was apprenticed to him in 1744. Both were known as makers of CANDLESTICKS.

gourd-shaped standing cup. A type of STANDING CUP similar to the examples of the GOURD-SHAPED 'STEEPLE CUP' except that there is no steeple on the finial, but sometimes a figure. Nine such cups have been recorded as being in England, including the BANCKS CUP, the BERRY CUP (and its replica), and the FALSTAFF CUP.

gourd-shaped 'steeple cup'. A type of STANDING CUP related to the STEEPLE CUP and so called, having a bowl shaped like a gourd with its larger end upward (inverted pear-shaped) and having its stem in the form of a twisted and gnarled tree-trunk and having sometimes a steeple on the cover. The original design for such cups came from German designers in Augsburg and Nuremberg, 16th and early 17th centuries, but theirs had no steeple on the cover. Some such cups without a steeple were imported into England and were given English hallmarks; of these, seven are known to be now in Russia (some having the finial surmounted by a figure). Nine such cups without steeple (*see* GOURD-SHAPED STANDING CUP) have been recorded as being in England; four with steeple have been recorded in England. It has been suggested that the steeples were added later when a steeple became a popular form of finial in England; hence such cups strictly are not 'steeple cups'. *See* Norman M. Penzer, 'The Steeple Cup' in *Apollo,* April 1960, p. 103. *See* BERDEN CUP.

grace cup. A type of drinking vessel, occurring in various shapes and styles, that was used to drink a final health or grace drink after the saying of grace at the end of a meal, being passed around among those present. The earliest form was a large MAZER, then a deep handleless cup on a substantial stem that could be more securely held as it was passed along. Later the shape changed to that of a TWO-HANDLED CUP, with stem and spreading foot and with a domed or somewhat conical cover ornamented with a finial, and decorated with CUT CARD work or STRAPWORK, and essentially having two vertical side handles, usually of foliated scroll form. Such a cup became the symbol used on the trade card of many 18th-century silversmiths. The type of cup so used became known, from *c.* 1800, as a LOVING CUP. *See* HOWARD GRACE CUP; WARDEN'S GRACE CUP.

Grand Service. A COMPOSITE SERVICE owned by the Crown, comprising articles first ordered by George IV before and while he was Prince Regent, and also when King, and some by later Sovereigns. It includes a large number of silver-gilt articles, e.g., CANDELABRA (including the MERCURY CANDELABRUM and HESPERIDES, GARDEN OF THE, CANDELABRUM), SIDEBOARD DISHES, DESSERT STANDS, ICE-PAILS, SUGAR-VASES, WINE COOLERS, TUREENS, EWERS, etc., made by various silversmiths, among them PAUL STORR, JOHN BRIDGE, and PHILIP RUNDELL for RUNDELL, BRIDGE & RUNDELL.

Grant Tobacco Box. A TOBACCO-BOX, rectangular with rounded corners, with two compartments, each having a hinged lid and gilt interior, one of which is fitted with a rotating wheel. The box was made probably by George B. Sharp, Philadelphia, and has on the lids an engraved inscription 'President U.S. Grant from A.C. Borie', the latter, Alfred E. Borie, having been a Philadelphia businessman who was Secretary of the Navy in 1869. It is now in the White House Collection, Washington, D.C.

grape scissors. A dining implement used to cut the stems of a bunch of grapes; although made in the general form of a pair of SCISSORS, it has–instead of two cutting blades–two wide flat-faced blades, only one of which has a cutting edge. The handles are often decorated with vine foliage.

grapefruit spoon. A type of SPOON for eating fresh grapefruit cut in half; the bowl is somewhat elongated with a rounded point to aid in removing the segments. Silver examples have been made since *c.* 1900.

gravy-boat. *See* SAUCE-BOAT; DOUBLE-LIPPED SAUCE-BOAT; SAUCE-TUREEN; ARGYLL.

gravy ladle. The same as a SAUCE LADLE. *See* GRAVY SPOON.

gourd-shaped standing cup. Cup with figural finial, London, 1595. H. 38·7 cm. Courtesy, Brand Inglis Ltd, London.

Grant Tobacco Box. Two compartments, each with hinged lid, George B. Sharp, Philadelphia, Pa, *c.* 1869. L. 7 cm. The White House, Washington, D.C.

gravy spoon. A type of SPOON for serving gravy or sauce from a PLATTER or WELL PLATTER, as distinguished from a LADLE. It has usually a long handle and a deep bowl, circular or oval-shaped, and is similar to but longer than a BASTING SPOON. Some are in the form of a type of STRAINER SPOON.

great salt. A type of STANDING SALT that is large, massive, and lavishly ornamented, intended to be more ornamental than practical in view of the small amount of salt it contains. Such pieces were placed on the high table at ceremonial banquets, usually said to mark the division where important and less important guests were seated respectively 'above or below the salt'; but it has also been said that the great salt was placed before the principal guest seated on the right of the host, and other salts at the other end of the table. Most examples, particularly those made in the Elizabethan era, 1558–1603, are elaborately modelled, such as the PEDESTAL SALT, the HOURGLASS SALT, and the COVERED STANDING SALT, and especially those in architectural style (*see* ARCHITECTURAL SILVERWARE) or figural style (*see* HUNTSMAN SALT; MONKEY SALT). Some examples incorporate crystal in the body (*see* CRYSTAL ARTICLES) or glass panels (*see* GLASS ARTICLES). Some City of London Livery Companies possess examples of great salts, as do certain colleges of British universities, and some civic bodies. *See* CLOCK SALT; ELIZABETH I SALT; EXETER SALT.

Great Seal. Seal of William IV, engraved by Benjamin Wyon, 1831: *above*, obverse; *below*, reverse. D. 16·2 cm. British Museum, London.

Great Seal. The principal SEAL of the Sovereign or other Head of State. In Great Britain it is the seal of the Sovereign, made as a double seal with two intaglio faces so as to impress both sides of the wax (or, in modern times, plastic) facsimile that is affixed to the cords or ribbons on a formal document. The seal is kept in the custody of the Lord Chancellor and changed with each successive Sovereign, the old seal being defaced and the metal, weighing about 8 kg (18 lb), generally being used to make SEAL WARE; sometimes the Lord Chancellor made a gift of the seal or disposed of the metal. The seal of William IV, the earliest Great Seal known to have survived intact, was engraved by Benjamin Wyon, 1831, and shows the king on horseback (obverse) and enthroned (reverse); it is now in the British Museum, having been purchased at Sotheby's, London, in 1981. The first Great Seal of Northern Ireland, adopted in 1924, was formerly owned by the Duke of Abercorn; it was bought in 1985 by the Ulster Museum, Belfast.

Greek-vase silverware. Any receptacle made in the form of one of the types of ancient Greek pottery vases, e.g., a KRATER VASE (of the calyx type; *see* THEOCRITUS CUPS), a LEKANE VASE, an ASKOS JUG, an AMPHORA EWER or an OENOCHOE EWER. Such pieces have been made of silver in England. An ancient silver TWO-HANDLED CUP, Mycenaean, *c.* 1500 BC, in the form of a kantharos is at the National Museum, Athens, a copy being at the Victoria and Albert Museum, London. The silver replica of the PORTLAND VASE is related, as are the silver modified reproductions of the WARWICK VASE.

Green, Ward & Green. A London firm of retail jewellers and goldsmiths that was started as Green & Ward in 1799 at 1 Ludgate St by Thomas Abbott Green and John Ward; after being joined by Robert Green, it was called Green, Ward & Green, and later became Robert Green & Co. It moved in 1829 to 20 Cockspur St, Pall Mall, remaining there until the firm ceased trading in 1848. It was supplied by several London silversmiths, including PAUL STORR, and some important pieces of WELLINGTON PLATE were executed for the company by BENJAMIN SMITH I, such as the WELLINGTON CANDELABRA, and by BENJAMIN SMITH II, including the WELLINGTON SHIELD (the firm's name is on it) and the WATERLOO VASE. In the late 1830s and 1840s the bulk of their silver stock was supplied by James Charles Edington (much of whose work bears a Green & Ward label), such as the SLIGO CANDELABRA.

Grenadier Guardsman Statuette. One of a series of silver STATUETTES depicting soldiers of the senior British infantry regiment, the Grenadier Guards, raised in 1660. The regiment owns about thirty examples, showing uniforms ranging from 1660 to the present day and varying in height from 30·5 to 38 cm. The older examples were made by ELKINGTON & CO., and modern ones by Carrington & Co. Ltd, London. *See* REGIMENTAL SILVERWARE.

Greyhound Badge. The BADGE of office of the King's (Queen's) Messengers, the corps of diplomatic couriers (established by Charles II, 1660–85) attached to the British Foreign Office. Examples recorded in 1689 were made of painted vellum under a glass cover, such badges were painted until *c.* 1837, thereafter enamelled. The current badges, made by GARRARD & CO. LTD, are in the form of a silver-gilt oval with the raised cipher of the reigning Sovereign, surrounded by the Garter (which was omitted from *c.* 1905 to 1920) enamelled in blue with the motto in silver gilt; from the oval is sus-

Grenadier Guardsman Statuette. Soldier in uniform of private (1815), Elkington & Co. Ltd, Birmingham, 1924. H. 34·5 cm. Courtesy, Grenadier Guards.

pended a silver figure of a running greyhound. The badge is no longer used on missions, but is still worn on ceremonial occasions.

Gribelin, Simon (1661–1733). An engraver of silverware who, as a Huguenot, emigrated *c.* 1680 from Blois, France, to London, and in 1686 became a member of the Clockmakers' Company (having engraved many watch-cases), although he never registered as a goldsmith. He published two albums of his engravings, 1697 and 1700, made from pulls of his work. He did not always sign his work, but several pieces are known to have been engraved by him, and others are attributed to him based on stylistic grounds and his albums. He engraved heraldic devices on SALVERS of SEAL WARE, including the MONTAGU SALVER. His finest work is said to be the unsigned engraving on an oval dish made in 1695 by PIERRE HARACHE I and formerly in the Swaythling Collection. His son Samuel was the engraver of the EYRE SALVERS. *See* Charles C. Oman, 'English Engravers on Plate: Simon Gribelin' in *Apollo,* June 1957, p. 218; Yvonne Hackenbroch, 'Gribelin's Designs engraved on English Silver' in *The Connoisseur,* June 1968, p. 136.

griddle. A cooking utensil in the form of a gridiron, with a grating upon with to grill (broil) meat. Examples, having an extended wooden handle, were made of silver (presumably impracticable for heating) in the early 19th century. One example, 1820, with four small feet under the gridiron, has parallel concave ribs so that the drippings would flow from the ribs into a concave channel set at right-angles to the ribs, the channel having a pouring lip at one end.

Griffin Candelabra. A pair of silver-gilt CANDELABRA, each resting on a rectangular base supported by four scroll feet and having on each side of the wide, circular stem a figure of a seated griffin. The central stem is in the form of a fluted drum, surmounted by an ACANTHUS-decorated vase from which extends upward an extended stem having two lateral foliated scroll branches with sockets, then above them two more similar but smaller branches, the fifth candle socket being on the finial. In front of each stem is a tripod vase entwined by a serpent. Each bears on its plinth the Royal arms of George III and the badge of the Prince of Wales (later George IV). They were made by PAUL STORR, 1817–18, and are now in the Royal Collection.

Griffin Soup Tureen. A SOUP-TUREEN (originally one of a pair) with decoration of figures of griffins: a griffin passant as the finial on the cover, a griffin rampant as each of the two end handles, and two griffins rampant as the supporters of the escutcheon on the side of the bowl. The bowl is decorated with an encircling band of tied reeding, with four CLAW-AND-BALL FEET, with a lion's mask attachment above each foot, and with an escutcheon. The cover is decorated with floral and fruit swags. The piece was made by GEORGE WICKES, London, 1737–8, for Thomas Watson (1693–1750), Earl of Malton, later 1st Marquess of Rockingham, 1740, and was subsequently in the family of the Earls Fitzwilliam, at Wentworth House, Yorkshire, until it was sold by the 8th Earl in 1948 at Christie's, London. It is now at Colonial Williamsburg, Virginia.

grip. A small scroll protuberance on the top of the loop handle of some receptacles to afford a place for the user's thumb and provide a secure hold, as on some TANKARDS, CREAM-POTS, CANNS, PEPPER-BOXES, etc. Such grips are sometimes in the form of an applied ACANTHUS leaf. In some cases the handle has also a lower decorative protuberance and is termed a 'double grip'. Articles that have a THUMBPIECE do not generally have a grip on the handle.

grotesques (from Italian, *grotteschi*). Decorative motifs consisting of fanciful figures and half-figures that are partly human and animal and partly ACANTHUS foliage, used in conjunction with masks (based on the old classical theatrical masks) and such mythological figures as satyrs and sphinxes. They were originally inspired by mural decoration in the ruins of Nero's Golden House in Rome, and adapted by Raphael in the decoration of the *loggie* of the Vatican (hence sometimes called '*Raffaelesche*'). They continued to be popular in various guises and modifications until the beginning of the ROCOCO STYLE, *c.* 1730. They were principally used as decoration on walls and ceramic ware, and should not be confused with ARABESQUES (which are sometimes found on silverware) or with MORESQUES (rarely found on silverware).

Grotto Inkstand. A novelty INKSTAND made by Elkington, Mason & Co. (*see* ELKINGTON & CO.), and shown at the Great Exhibition of 1851. It depicted, alongside a beehive-shaped 'grotto' inkstand, a boy and girl waif begging for money, a London tradition, until the 1920s, called 'Please remember the grotto'.

group. (1) An assemblage of two or more objects of the same (or similar) form, suited to each other and intended to be used together, but not identical and not incomplete if the pieces are separated; examples are a GARNITURE DE CHEMINÉE and GARNITURE DE TABLE. (2) A single object that depicts two or more figures on a common base, such as the DRUID GROUP. *See* SET; PAIR; COMPANION PIECE.

guéridon (French). A type of table with a small top, used to support a decorative jar or other ornament, and usually placed in pairs, with one on each side of a mirror. Examples that are low and of wood often have, as the stem, the kneeling figure of a Negro or Moor, but silver examples, which are rare, have a plain or knopped stem. The term is derived from the name of the character Guéridon (a Moor) in a French play of the late 17th century. An English example, *c.* 1676, with a circular top and three legs, and about 1·12 m high, is at Knole House, Sevenoaks, Kent, and a similar example is at Windsor Castle. Such pieces should be distinguished from a TORCHÈRE, which is used singly or as one of a pair, but only to support a lamp, candelabrum or candlestick; that term was recognized only after 1696, i.e., later than the use of the term *guéridon,* already recognized in France.

guild spoon. A type of SPOON that was presented to a Livery Company by a new member upon his 'taking the livery', a practice of many such companies in the 16th century. Such spoons often have a finial or an inscription relevant to the particular company.

Guille Cruet. A parcel-gilt CRUET having a globular bowl resting on a wide stem and a spreading foot and having a long, slightly tapering neck, a recurving loop handle, and a long BRIDGE SPOUT; the cover, of CUSHION SHAPE, has a small finial. A band encircling the bowl is inscribed 'Sancta Paula Ora Pro Nobis', with roses separating the words. Within the handle is an upside-down figure of St James the Greater, and engraved on the top of the handle is the letter A for *Aqua,* indicating that it was one of a pair (the missing cruet would be marked V for *Vinum*). This is one of the only two known extant pre-Reformation cruets; it bears no hallmarks, but is attributed to London(?), *c.* 1530–5. It was dug up in St Saviour's Parish, Guernsey, Channel Islands, in 1831 and was given to John Guille; it was presented by a descendant in 1895 to the parish church of St Peter Port, Guernsey, and is on loan to the Candie Gardens Museum, St Peter Port.

guilloche. (1) A decorative pattern used as a border in the form of two or three bands twisted alternately over and under each other in a continuous manner in such a way as to leave openings that are sometimes filled in with rosettes or other ornamental motifs. It is sometimes used on silverware, as on the base or rim of an object. (2) An engraved decorative pattern made by

Griffin Candelabrum. One of a pair, silver gilt, Paul Storr, London, 1817–18. H. 82·5 cm. Royal Collection; reproduced by gracious permission of Her Majesty the Queen.

Griffin Soup Tureen. George Wickes, London, 1737–8. W. 45·7 cm. Colonial Williamsburg, Va.

the process of ENGINE-TURNING, sometimes referred to by the French terms *'guilloché'* and *'guillochage'*. When such engraving is covered with a transparent enamel that reveals the engine-turned pattern beneath, as on some BOXES by Carl Fabergé, it is called *tour à guillocher*.

gun furniture. Various silver articles that are functionally or decoratively attached to a gun or a pistol. *See* J.F.Hayward, 'Silver Mounts on Firearms' in *Proceedings of the Society of Silver Collectors,* London, 21 January 1963. *See* PISTOLS.

H

Hallamshire Bell. James Dixon & Co., Sheffield, 1965. H. 25·5 cm. Courtesy, the Company of Cutlers in Hallamshire, Sheffield.

Hallamshire Bell. A BELL of inverted krater shape suspended in a frame formed by three vertical curving flat arms extending upward from the circular base and inward to the finial which is surmounted by a white rose of York. It was made by JAMES DIXON & CO., Sheffield, in 1965, and was a gift in 1966 to the Company of Cutlers in Hallamshire, Sheffield, from Sir Eric Mensforth, Master Cutler, and Lady Mensforth, Mistress Cutler.

hallmark(s). Strictly, the punched mark(s) on an article of silver (or gold or platinum) to identify the Hall (in London, Goldsmiths' Hall, hence the term 'hallmark') or town ASSAY OFFICE where the article was assayed; but in general usage the term also embraces certain other marks, including in Great Britain, the STANDARD HALLMARK (to attest purity in compliance with standards legally established), the MAKER'S MARK, and the DATE HALLMARK (the code letter to show the year of assaying). Hallmarks on silver have been used in Great Britain since the reign of Edward I, 1272–1307 (*see* ENGLISH HALLMARKS), and in some countries on the Continent since the 14th century, but in the United States, where there is no government ASSAYING, there are now no official hallmarks (*see* UNITED STATES SILVER MARKS). As to silverware exported between countries that are members of or associated with the European Free Trade Association (EFTA) and have signed a hallmark convention, *see* CONVENTION HALLMARKS. After a hallmark has been punched on an article, no metallic additions may be legally made; but the piece may be polished and even decorated by various processes (e.g., ENGRAVING) that do not add metal, although EMBOSSING and CHASING are usually done before assaying. The hallmarks are punched in sequence, usually in a line, on any part of the article, and are sometimes conspicuously placed on the exterior of some HOLLOW WARE, although sometimes on the bottom. Before 1781 the various marks were individually punched, hence irregularly spaced. The hallmarks are punched so as to appear in relief, but some rare types are punched so that they appear in intaglio: *see* DRAWBACK MARK; DUTY MARK; INCUSE MARK. The number, grouping, and spacing of hallmarks on an article and on each of its parts, and their position on the article or the part, often indicate authenticity or alteration. *See* OWNERSHIP MARK; DESIGN REGISTRATION MARK.

ham stand. A sideboard accessory upon which to rest a whole ham for carving. It has a wire base and upright wire prongs to hold the ham, and is sometimes accompanied by a cylindrical piece to fit over the end bone of the ham to hold it while being carved. A silver example is at Goodwood House, West Sussex.

hammering. A process, used from ancient times until today, of shaping silver articles of HOLLOW WARE (using the methods of SINKING and RAISING) and flat articles (e.g., TRAYS, SALVERS, PLATTERS, which are formed by FLAT HAMMERING). The operation is done by hand, the silversmith using hammers of different sizes and having variously shaped heads to shape the metal over a wood block ('stake') or a leather pad ('saddle'). The hammering causes the metal to become hard and brittle, so that the work must be interrupted for periods of ANNEALING and QUENCHING to restore the metal to a MALLEABLE state. Great care and skill are required for hammering silver, for when the metal has once been extruded it cannot be restored to its former state. The tools must be kept immaculately clean so as to avoid marring the article. When the process is used for decorating, it is called EMBOSSING or REPOUSSÉ work. *See* PLANISHING.

hanap. An obsolete medieval Norman-French term for a covered drinking cup of GOBLET shape, akin to the Anglo-Saxon 'hnoep', a cup or goblet. *See* DEVIZES CUP.

Hanbury Cup. A silver-gilt STANDING CUP with cover, the bowl of which is almost cylindrical, being rounded toward the base and widening at the lip. The baluster stem rests on a low chased foot. The cover rises in a sharp curve to a cone which is surmounted by a figure of a demi-lion rampant (derived from the Hanbury crest). The decoration of chasing is highly raised, indicating the change of style from that of the mid-17th century Commonwealth period to the more florid style of the Restoration. An original cup (melted down in 1637) was a gift in 1608 from Richard Hanbury (1534–1608) to the Goldsmiths' Company (he was a goldsmith and a member of the Court of the Company), and an inscription on the cup recorded the gift. The present replacement cup, London, 1665, bears the maker's mark 'AM' (formerly ascribed to Andrew Moore, more recently to Arthur Mainwaring). For an almost identical cup, also melted down and replaced, *see* FEAKE CUP.

Hancocks. A London manufacturing and retailing silverware and jewelry firm founded in 1848 at 39 Bruton St by Charles Frederick Hancock (1808–91), of Birmingham, who had worked for HUNT & ROSKELL and registered his mark in 1849. In 1866 he partly retired and his eldest son, Charles (d. 1909) became a partner, the name becoming Hancock, Son & Co., and his brother Mortimer (d. 1901) became a partner in 1869. Hancock fully retired in 1870, when the name was changed to Hancocks & Co., and the firm is now known simply as Hancocks. It engaged as designers and modellers such artists as HENRY HUGH ARMSTEAD and the sculptor C. B. Birch. It featured PRESENTATION CUPS and HORSE-RACING TROPHIES, and important examples of SCULPTURAL SILVERWARE. In 1916 the firm moved its shop to Vigo St, and since 1970 it has been at 1 Burlington Gardens. *See* DRUID GROUP.

hand bell. A type of BELL that has an inverted cup-like shape and a straight vertical handle that is sometimes baluster-shaped with knops and collars near the crown; the waist is usually undecorated, unlike that of some TABLE BELLS. Such a bell sometimes served as a unit for an INKSTAND, but when the two are separated the purpose of the bell cannot be so identified. Some Victorian hand bells were made in sets of three, each different in size.

hand caddy spoon. A type of CADDY SPOON having its bowl in the form of an open hand, with the fingers made by DIE-STAMPING and with the handle in the form of a wrist or cuff. An earlier variety, called the 'fist-hand caddy spoon', has the fingers curled to form a deep bowl.

hand candlestick. The same as a CHAMBER CANDLESTICK.

hand-guard candlestick. A type of CANDLESTICK made in England *c.* 1630–5, having a wide DRIP-PAN that extends outward over a waisted section which rests on a wide spreading base, thus providing a place for a secure and safe hand-grip.

hand mirror. A type of MIRROR that is small and is set in a frame with a projecting handle, used mainly at a dressing table; mirror frames have been made in silver in many shapes and styles. Such a mirror is part of a TOILET SERVICE.

hand raising. *See* RAISING.

hand warmer. A type of calefactory (sometimes so called) in the form of a hollow sphere, to be filled with hot water or heated charcoal and used to warm the hands of a priest at the altar at Mass in cold weather. Such pieces are about 12·5 to 15 cm in diameter. A silver parcel-gilt example is recorded as having been used until the Reformation at St Paul's Cathedral, London (having been bequeathed to it by Bishop Fulk Basset, 1242–59), and another example as listed in a 1536 inventory of Lincoln Cathedral. A modern example, London, 1924–5, is in the Mancroft Heritage at the church of St Peter Mancroft, Norwich. Such pieces were introduced in Catholic churches at the end of the 19th century. Sometimes called a 'pome', from French *pomme,* apple. They are related to the ceramic hand-warmers, held in a lady's muff or pocket, made of Dutch or English delftware in the 17th century, sometimes in the form of a book. *See* CHURCH PLATE.

handle. (1) The part of a CUP, MUG, JUG, TEAPOT or other HOLLOW WARE by which the object is held when being used, usually with space for the fingers or hand to be passed through. Double handles are sometimes used, as on a TWO-HANDLED CUP, DOUBLE-LIPPED SAUCE-BOAT, etc. A handle may be either vertical or horizontal, simple or interlaced, at the side of a vessel or overhead (e.g., BAIL HANDLE), and in many shapes and styles, e.g., plain, scroll, foliated, wishbone-shaped, D-shaped, etc. The handle on some silverware is made of wood, bone or ivory, or is of two silver sections with some intervening heat-insulating material, or is wrapped in raffia or leather to protect the user's hand. *See* CARYATID HANDLE; HARP HANDLE; TAU HANDLE; FLYING SCROLL HANDLE; SQUARE HANDLE; DROP-RING HANDLE.

(2) The part of an article of FLATWARE or CUTLERY by which it is held when being used. Such handles, when made of silver, are decorated in a great variety of patterns, many of which are generally known by established names, such as ALBANY, BEAD, BRIGHT VINE, CHRYSANTHEMUM, COBURG, FEATHER EDGE, FIDDLE, HANOVERIAN, KINGS'S, OLD ENGLISH, ONSLOW, QUEEN'S, RAT-TAIL. Some such patterns were 'double-struck', i.e., with the pattern on both sides of the handle. The handle of certain flatware and cutlery is sometimes made of ivory or mother-of-pearl, especially pieces for eating fruit. *See* SELF HANDLE.

(3) The top end of a walking cane, walking stick or riding whip by which it is held by the user. Such handles were often made of silver, with decoration of ENGRAVING, CHASING or BRIGHT CUTTING.

handled beaker. A type of BEAKER that has a scroll handle. Such pieces are not often found.

Hannam, Thomas (fl. 1761–1808). A London silversmith apprenticed to JOHN CAFE in 1754 and later to William Cafe, and freed in 1761. He worked as a partner of Richard Mills in 1765 and of John Crouch, 1766–93; both firms are said to have had a virtual monopoly in making fine SALVERS and WAITERS.

'Hanover' silverware. Various articles of silverware that had been owned by George II, George III, George IV, and then William IV (upon whose death in 1837 and the accession of his niece, Queen Victoria, the throne of Hanover passed by the Salic law, which banned succession in the female line, to Ernest Augustus, Duke of Cumberland, the fifth and eldest surviving son of George III) and were claimed upon the latter's death by Ernest Augustus. He based his claim against Queen Victoria through the Electress Sophia of Celle who in 1658 had married the Elector of Hanover (from which marriage was derived the name and the claim) who later became in 1714 George I of England, the first Hanoverian king. After litigation and hearings before two commissions as to whether the articles of silver and also of jewelry belonged to the Royal Family (and hence had passed to Hanover) or to the Crown, most of the silverware was awarded in January 1858 to Hanover and was delivered by the Crown, including silver furniture purchased by George II, e.g., two large MIRRORS, two TABLES, two pairs of TORCHÈRES, and five chairs, all covered with silver. Some pieces were sold by a descendant in 1925–6 through a London firm and have been dispersed in England and the United States.

Hanoverian pattern. A pattern of FLATWARE and CUTLERY, in which the stem widens gradually toward the curved terminal and then turns upward (in contrast to the later OLD ENGLISH PATTERN, where the stem turns downward). The form was adopted because the spoon was laid on the table with the bottom of the bowl downward, in the French manner, enabling the pattern on the handle to be seen. It was so called as it was produced *c.* 1710–75, spanning the reigns of the first two Hanoverian kings, George I and George II.

Hanuk(k)a(h) lamp (1). Wall type, depicting Elijah and the ravens, designed by Elias Lindo, made by John Ruslen, London, 1709. H. 33·5 cm. Jewish Museum, London (photo courtesy, Warburg Institute, University of London).

Hanuk(k)a(h) lamp. A type of LAMP used in homes of the Jewish faith to commemorate the dedication of the altar in the purified Temple of Jerusalem after the victory of Judas Maccabaeus over the Syrians in 165 BC. It is used annually at the Festival of Lights *(Hanuka)*, which lasts eight days, usually in December. Such lamps have been made in several forms: (1) As a wall lamp, having a high flat back-plate, usually decorated with EMBOSSING or CHASING, and having near the bottom a horizontal row of eight projecting oil burners (one to be lit each night) and a wide horizontal projecting drip-pan; near the top of the back-plate there is a movable projecting ninth burner (the 'master light' or 'beadle') to be lit for illumination and used to light the other burners. Some such lamps are used in a synagogue on behalf of families that have none. (2) As a CANDELABRUM, to stand on a table, having a vertical column with eight oil burners or candlesticks in a horizontal row and with the ninth projecting slightly in front of the centre. (3) In various adaptations of the candelabrum type, sometimes with nine lights arranged on a flat, shaped base or in a line, as on a MENORAH. The earliest-known English silver example (of the wall type) was made by John Ruslen, 1709. *See* JEWISH RITUAL SILVERWARE.

Harache, Pierre (or **Peter**). Two London silversmiths, father and son, of Huguenot ancestry, whose registered marks, types of articles made, and styles of workmanship were so similar that it has been difficult for experts to determine which of the two was the maker of some pieces attributed to them.

Pierre Harache I (fl. 1682 – *c.* 1698), as a Huguenot, migrated from France – possibly from Rouen in 1681 – and was naturalized in England on 26 June 1682; on 21 July 1682 he was made a freeman of the City of London and was admitted by redemption to the Goldsmiths' Company (the first Huguenot immigrant to be admitted), and in 1687 was made a Liveryman of the Company. He registered a Sterling Standard Hallmark in 1683 and a BRITANNIA HALLMARK in 1697, with address in Suffolk St, near Charing Cross. Upon his retirement, *c.* 1698, he was succeeded by his son, Pierre Harache II (b. 1653; fl. 1698-1717), who was freed by redemption on 24 October 1698, and who registered three Britannia Hallmarks on 25 October 1698, with address in Compton St, Soho, until 1705 and in Grafton St, 1714-17.

The pieces attributed to one or the other are usually decorated with CHASING, EMBOSSING, CUT CARD work, GADROONING, PIERCED WORK, and cast mounts. The pieces attributed to the son, who acquired his father's moulds and designs, are usually said to be more numerous than the work of the father, and include many items, made *c.* 1700-5, of a high standard of design and execution. Some pieces attributed to Pierre Harache I, especially SALVERS, are finely engraved by SIMON GRIBELIN. *See* Judith Banister, 'The First Huguenot Silversmith' in *Country Life*, 10 June 1965, p. 1463; Margaret Holland, 'Pierre Harache and the Huguenots' in *Apollo*, July 1985, p. 57; Edward Wenham, 'Peter Harache' in *Antique Collector*, September–October 1985, p. 160.

Harbledown Mazers. A group of seven MAZERS, 13th and 14th centuries, at Harbledown Hospital, Kent, that includes some of the earliest-known examples. Some are without silver MOUNTS, and some have lost the silver footring.

harebell caddy spoon. A type of CADDY SPOON having its conical bowl in the form of a harebell (the Scottish bluebell) flower formed by the petals being hand-raised and REPOUSSÉ; the curved handle is a wire stem with a small stem leaf. A rare example made by Thomas Willmore, Birmingham, is dated 1791.

harebell candlestick. A type of CANDLESTICK having its stem and nozzle in the form of a harebell (the Scottish bluebell) flower, sometimes with a second flower along the stem. An example was made by E., E., J. & W. Barnard (*see* BARNARD, EDWARD, & SONS), 1840-1.

harp cup. A type of LOVING CUP having two HARP-SHAPED HANDLES, made in Ireland during the 18th century. The body is cylindrical and rests on a spreading foot. An example is in the National Museum of Ireland, Dublin.

harp-shaped handle. A type of vertical SCROLL HANDLE in the shape of the outline of a harp, as used on articles of IRISH SILVERWARE, especially the HARP CUP, and also on some English (also United States) HUGUENOT SILVERWARE, such as several TWO-HANDLED CUPS. The form was brought to England and Ireland by Huguenot silversmiths.

Harrods Replica. A silver replica (possibly on a wood core) of Harrods Store, London, made in 1927 and given to Sir Woodman Burbidge, then Managing Director of Harrods, by H. Gordon Selfridge, in settlement of a wager between them made in 1917 that within six years of the end of World War I the latter's London store would have greater gross annual revenue than Harrods. The piece, made by silversmiths at Harrods, is now owned by Lady Benita Burbidge and has been on display at Harrods, London. *See* ARCHITECTURAL SILVERWARE.

Harthill Candlesticks. A pair of silver-gilt CANDLESTICKS, 1675, of octagonal form, having an octagonal base, knops, and fluted stem, all decorated with ACANTHUS foliage. One bears on the base an inscription recording the gift by Peregrine, 2nd Duke of Leeds (1659-1729), to Harthill church, Yorkshire.

hash-dish. The same as an ENTRÉE-DISH.

harp-shaped handle. Silver-gilt covered jug, Charles Petit, London, 1674-5. H. 22 cm. Ashmolean Museum, Oxford.

Harthill Candlesticks. One of the pair, silver gilt, 1675. H. 35 cm. Harthill parish church, Yorkshire (photo courtesy, Historic Churches Preservation Trust, London).

Harrods Replica. Silver model showing Hans Crescent and main Brompton Road façades. W. 43·3 cm. Courtesy, Harrods Ltd, London.

Hastings, Warren, Cup. A TWO-HANDLED CUP having a short stem and a spreading foot, with a domed cover surmounted by a pineapple finial. The two vertical handles are each in the form of an elephant's head with a long proboscis (trunk). The body, foot, and cover are decorated with ACANTHUS leaves. The cup, with London date mark for 1785-6, bears a maker's mark 'IR' (probably for John Reily). It was sent to Westminster School, London, from Bengal, India, by Warren Hastings (1732-1818), the first Governor-General of British India, 1774-84, and Sir Elijah Impey, contemporaries in the 1740s at Westminster School (then known as St Peter's School), London, and by twenty others in India, all said to have been former pupils at the school. The cup is inscribed on one side with the twenty-two names and on the other side with the coat of arms of the school. It is gilded on the inside. *See* Jonathan Stone, 'The Warren Hastings Cup' in *The Connoisseur*, December 1960, p. 283.

hatching. A style of decoration with fine adjacent parallel lines to give the effect of shading. Sometimes two sets of equidistant parallel lines cross each other ('cross-hatching') at an oblique angle or at right-angles. It is sometimes found as part of the decoration of scrolls on early-17th-century BEAKERS. Sometimes other forms of hatching (different directions of the lines) were used to indicate various TINCTURES (colours) on heraldic ACHIEVEMENTS.

haunce (or **hanse**) **pot.** A type of silver FLAGON or JUG in the form of the TIGERWARE JUG, with a bulbous body and a long vertical neck, having one large scroll handle and a hinged lid with a THUMBPIECE. Such vessels of parcel-gilt silver are similar in form to the contemporary German stoneware jugs imported into England in the 16th century by the members of the Armourers and Brasiers' Company. *See* TYNDALE FLAGON.

havdalah candlestick. A type of CANDLESTICK used in certain Jewish communities at the services on the termination of the Sabbath. It was sometimes a vertical rectangular wire frame in which was enclosed a sliding candle NOZZLE, to be raised as the candle burned down.

hawking prize. A type of award for hawking, such as a cup, e.g., a large example 1781, made by John Wakelin and William Taylor (*see* GARRARD & CO. LTD), appropriately decorated with hawks' heads.

headband. An article of INDIAN-TRADE SILVERWARE made for and worn by North American Indians. Such pieces are usually in the form of a circular vertical band, decorated with encircling openwork and sometimes having circular or heart-shaped discs suspended from the lower rim; sometimes called a 'crown'. An example made for Chief Nicolas Vincent of the Huron tribe, who visited London in 1824-5 and was presented to George IV, bears the mark 'IT' and has been attributed to either Joseph Tison (1787-1869) or Jonathan Tyler (fl. 1817-28), c. 1824.

hearth furniture. Articles for use at a domestic fireplace, including FIRE-IRONS, FIRE-DOG (creeper), BELLOWS, FENDER, FIRE-PAN, and FIRE SCREEN. Some with silver MOUNTS are known from the period of Henry VIII,

Hastings, Warren, Cup. John Reily(?), London, 1785-6. H. 46·8 cm. Westminster School, London.

Helicon Vase. Centrepiece with plateau, oxidized silver and damascened steel, symbolizing the Apotheosis of Music and Poetry, designed by Léonard Morel-Ladeuil, made by Elkington & Co., Birmingham, completed 1871. Royal Collection; reproduced by gracious permission of Her Majesty the Queen.

1509–47, but they were more extensively used from the Restoration, 1660–88. A number recorded in inventories of Royal collections have disappeared, presumably melted down. Many used in early years in great manor houses have been preserved, especially large sets at Ham House, Richmond, and Knole House, Sevenoaks, Kent. *See* Norman M. Penzer, 'The Plate at Knole House' in *The Connoisseur*, March 1961, p. 84, and April 1961, p. 178.

Helicon Vase. A CENTREPIECE named after Mt Helicon, the mountain in Boeotia, Greece, that was sacred to the Muses. It symbolizes the Apotheosis of Music and Poetry. On the base there are two reclining draped female allegorical figures of Music and Poetry, and on the sides of the bowl are engraved scenes depicting the nine Muses with their attributes, four on one side, five on the other. On the pendent drapery handles there are escutcheons, one with portraits of the writers Homer, Shakespeare, Molière, and Byron, and the other with portraits of the composers Handel, Haydn, Beethoven, and Mozart. On the finial are figures of two youths, one holding aloft a lyre and the other, at his feet, holding a tuning fork. The piece rests on a PLATEAU decorated with bas-relief figures encircling the border. The piece, made of oxidized silver and DAMASCENED steel, was designed by LÉONARD MOREL-LADEUIL and was completed in 1871 (after six years' work) by ELKINGTON & CO. It was exhibited by Elkington in 1872 at the Society of Arts' Exhibition at the South Kensington Museum, London, in 1873 in Vienna, and in 1876 in Philadelphia. In 1887 it was presented to Queen Victoria as a Golden Jubilee gift, and is now in the Royal Collection.

Heller, F. Antoine (b. *c.* 1845, d. after 1894). A French silversmith and die-cutter, who was born at Saverne, Alsace, studied in Paris, and went to the United States in the late 1870s to work for TIFFANY & CO., where he developed the Olympian Pattern for FLATWARE. He left Tiffany in 1880 to return to Paris, and late in 1881 joined the GORHAM COMPANY, where his first work was to create in 1882 the Fontainebleau Pattern, in 1883 the Medici and Cluny Patterns, in 1884/5 the Old Masters and Nuremberg Patterns (the last having different animated sculptured figures on the handles), and in 1894 the Mythologique Pattern (featuring 24 subjects from mythology). His work in hollow ware followed the ACADEMIC STYLE.

helmet. A type of protective covering for the head. A parcel-gilt silver example in the form of an ancient Roman helmet was made by BENJAMIN SMITH I and his brother James, London, 1811. It is of burnished silver with a gilded figure of a wolf on the top. It was acquired in 1984 by the Victoria and Albert Museum, London.

helmet jug. A type of EWER shaped like an inverted helmet. The style was introduced into England by the Huguenots and is typical of their work. The form has a circular spreading base supporting a semi-ovoid bowl that is usually divided into sections by one or two horizontal encircling ribs. At the front there is a high pouring lip and at the rear a SCROLL HANDLE (in some cases a FLYING SCROLL HANDLE, but sometimes in the form of an arched CARYATID or mythological figure attached to the rim as well as to the body of the bowl). On some examples there is an applied mask or other ornament below

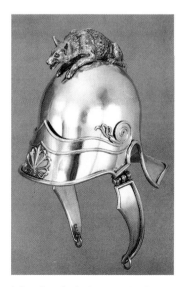

helmet. Parcel gilt, Benjamin Smith I and James Smith, London, 1811. Victoria and Albert Museum, London.

helmet jug. Silver gilt, Paul de Lamerie, London, 1741. H. 37·5 cm. Goldsmiths' Company, London.

the curve of the lip. A silver-gilt example made by PAUL DE LAMERIE, 1741, has its lower portion decorated with a winged mermaid with a double tail twisted around the stem and with the handle in the form of a marine god attached to the body at the top by a scroll held in his hands and at the bottom by a scroll attached to his tail; below the lip are the arms of the Goldsmiths' Company, for which the piece was made. Such jugs were generally used to hold rose-water for rinsing the hands after a meal; the type was often called a ROSE-WATER EWER, but sometimes a 'casque ewer'. They were made earlier in pottery, first in delftware, later in faience in France at Rouen and Moustiers. Small jugs in such form have been made for use as a MILK-JUG or a CREAM-JUG. *See* TREBY HELMET JUG.

hem holder. A small article having two thin adjacent arms joined in the manner of a pair of tweezers, with an encircling band to slide along the arms to loosen and tighten their grip, used by a lady to hold up the hem of a long flowing skirt. Attached to the joined end is a small ring to be placed on a finger. Sometimes called a 'train-lifter'. Examples are known from *c.* 1780. *See* FOOTMAN'S SKIRT-LIFTER.

Heming, George (fl. 1773-93). A London silversmith, son of THOMAS HEMING, who was apprenticed to his father in 1763 and entered his mark before 1773. He entered a joint mark with WILLIAM CHAWNER I in 1774, with address at King's Arms, New Bond St, from 1773 to 1781. A second mark was entered by them in 1781, with address in Old Bond St. In 1775 they received an order from Catherine the Great for two complete dinner services and two dessert services, and they employed 400 craftsmen for the work. From 1773 George, with William Chawner I, worked in the shop of Thomas Heming, using his marks until the early 1780s; in 1782 they succeeded to the business of Thomas Heming, and George continued alone from 1784 until 1793.

Heming, Thomas (fl. 1745-73). An outstanding London silversmith, son of Richard Heming. He was apprenticed in 1738 to Edmund Boddrington but was turned over on the same day to PETER ARCHAMBO I and freed in 1746. He entered his first mark in 1745 and opened his shop in Piccadilly, London, moving in 1765 to Bond St. In 1760 George III, upon his accession, appointed him Principal Goldsmith to the King, which position he held until 1782. He made many pieces of large and important silverware, including regalia and plate for the coronation of George III and plate for the Jewel House. In 1763 he made an ÉCUELLE (with a tray), surmounted by the Prince of Wales's feathers, for Queen Charlotte to give to her eldest son. In 1764 he made communion plate for Anglican churches in the American colonies, some now being at Trinity Church, New York City, and at Christ Church, Williamsburg, Virginia, and he later made communion plate for the private chapel at Windsor Castle. His pieces include thirty-eight CANDELABRA for the Russian Imperial Court, the SPEAKER'S WINE COOLER, the HEMING TWO-HANDLED CUPS, several TOILET SERVICES (including the CAROLINE MATHILDA TOILET SERVICE, the SOPHIA MAGDALENA TOILET SERVICE, and the WILLIAMS-WYNN TOILET SERVICE), and a DINNER SERVICE, 1761, for the Speaker of the House of Commons. His early work in the 1740s was in ROCOCO STYLE, inspired by French influence, but his later work was more restrained. He retired soon after 1773, but in the years 1773-82 his son, GEORGE HEMING, with WILLIAM CHAWNER I, worked at his shop, using his marks until the early 1780s; they succeeded to his business in 1782.

Heming Two-handled Cups. Cup with handles in the form of Bacchic figures, Thomas Heming, London, *c.* 1750. H. 38·5 cm. Cincinnati Art Museum (Gift of Mrs Robert McKay), Cincinnati, Ohio.

Heming Two-Handled Cups. Silver TWO-HANDLED CUPS made by or attributed, based on form and decoration, to THOMAS HEMING, *c.* 1750-71, of which seven examples are known. They all have a spreading foot and a short stem upon which rests a baluster-shaped or a vase-shaped bowl. The bowl has two vertical side handles, usually in the form of FLYING SCROLL HANDLES with TERM figures of twisting youthful Bacchantes facing in opposite directions. The cups are usually ornately embellished with cast and applied relief decoration in the form of encircling fruiting vines, the cover being surmounted by a decorative finial, sometimes the figure of an infant Bacchus holding a bunch of grapes in an upraised left hand. *See* TATTON CUP; POWLET CUP; SHAKERLEY CUP; CHATSWORTH CUP; TRINITY HALL CUP. An example, *c.* 1750, in the Cincinnati Art Museum, differs in that the handles are not of the flying scroll type, but are attached top and bottom to the bowl; each handle is decorated with a term of a youthful Bacchic figure. An example, 1753, almost identical with the Shakerley Cup, is in a private collection in Philadelphia, Pennsylvania (last recorded in 1971 as being owned by David H. H. Felix). In the case of some examples of such cups the cover bears the London mark of EMICK ROMER, with whom Heming collaborated and who used some of Heming's moulds, suggesting that Romer completed pieces started by Heming.

Hennell. A family of five generations of London silversmiths, including David Hennell I, and his two sons, Robert Hennell I (and his sons, David Hennell II and Samuel) and John (and his descendants, being his son Robert Hennell II, grandson Robert Hennell III, and great-grandsons, Robert Hennell IV and James Barclay Hennell).

David Hennell I (1712–85) was apprenticed in 1728 and freed in 1735. He entered his first mark in 1736, his address being King's Head Court, Gutter Lane. His second mark (presumably 1739) is not in the register. His third mark was entered in 1763 jointly with his son Robert, with address in Foster Lane, and another such mark was entered in 1768. He retired in 1773.

Robert Hennell I (1741–1811) was apprenticed in 1756 to his father and freed in 1763. He entered his first and second marks jointly with his father in 1763 and 1768, his third and fourth marks alone in 1772 and 1773, with address at 16 Foster Lane, a fifth mark jointly with his elder son David Hennell II in 1795, a sixth mark in 1802 jointly with David and his other son Samuel (who had joined the firm in 1802), and a seventh mark jointly with Samuel only later in 1802.

David Hennell II (1767–1829?), was apprenticed to his father in 1782 and freed in 1789. He entered his first mark jointly with his father in 1795, and his second mark jointly with his father and his younger brother Samuel in 1802.

Samuel Hennell (1778–1837) was freed by patrimony in 1800. He entered his first mark in 1802 jointly with his father, Robert Hennell I, and his brother David Hennell II, a second mark with his father later in 1802, a third mark alone in 1811, and a fourth mark in 1814 in partnership with John Terry (the firm terminating in 1816), all at different addresses. His descendants continued in the jewelry business.

Robert Hennell II (1763–1840), son of John Hennell (b. 1739), was apprenticed to his uncle Robert Hennell I in 1778 and freed in 1785. He entered his first mark, jointly with Henry Nutting, in 1808, at 38 Noble St, Foster Lane, a second mark alone in 1809, and third and fourth marks alone in 1820 and 1826 from 3 Lancaster Court, Strand. He retired in 1833, with his son Robert Hennell III taking over the business.

Robert Hennell III (1794–1868) was freed by patrimony in 1834. He entered his first mark in 1834 and a second in 1857.

Robert Hennell IV (1826–92), son of Robert Hennell III, was apprenticed to his father and freed in 1849. He entered marks in 1869 and 1870.

James Barclay Hennell (1828–99), son of Robert Hennell III, entered his mark in 1877. Upon his death in 1899, the family business ceased.

See Percy Hennell, 'The Hennells Identified' in *The Connoisseur*, December 1955, p.260; —, 'The Hennells' in *The Connoisseur*, February 1973, p.79.

Henslowe Ewer and Basin. Two conforming pieces made in London, 1562–3, and donated in 1563 to Winchester College by Randolph Henslowe, a local squire. (1) The EWER, of silver and parcel gilt having a thistle-shaped body resting on a reel-shaped stem and a decorated spreading base. It has a scroll handle and a WEDGE-SHAPED SPOUT. The centre of the bowl and the spout are encircled by a wide band engraved with ARABESQUE patterns. The low-domed lid is surmounted by a raised medallion bearing the enamelled arms of William of Wykeham (1324–1404), Bishop of Winchester and Lord High Chancellor of England, the founder of Winchester College. (2) A ROSE-WATER BASIN having on a central BOSS the enamelled arms of Winchester College; bands encircling the bottom and the rim bear a donative inscription.

herbal pot. A type of very small globular shaped pot, about 6 cm high, with an ATTENUATED spout and a scroll handle, similar to a BULLET TEAPOT; it is said to have been used to brew herbal beverages, such as camomile, to avoid brewing herbs in a pot normally used for tea. Sometimes called a 'tisane pot', from the French *tisane*, an infusion.

Hercules Candelabrum. A massive silver-gilt CANDELABRUM depicting a figure in-the-round of Hercules slaying the dragon Hydra, with a diminutive figure of his son Iolaus standing on the base. There is no central stem or branching arms, and the nine candle sockets rest on the heads of the dragon. The piece, by an unidentified modeller, was made in 1824 (the sockets in 1825) by EDWARD FARRELL on commission from Frederick, Duke of York (1763–1827), brother of George IV, through the retailer KENSINGTON LEWIS. It was sold at Christie's, London, from the Duke of York's Collection on 19 March 1827, and again at Christie's, London, on 18 October 1967, from the Collection of Lt-Col. Robert Milnes-Coates, DSO. *See* FIGURAL CANDELABRUM; FIGURAL SILVERWARE.

Hercules Salt. A silver-gilt COVERED STANDING SALT having an octagonal domed base and corresponding octagonal ribbed bands encircling the knop

Hercules Salt. Silver-gilt covered standing salt, London, 1542. H. 24·8 cm. Goldsmiths' Company, London.

Hesperides, Garden of the, Candelabrum (1). Silver-gilt twelve-branch candelabrum, Paul Storr, London, 1810-11. Royal Collection; reproduced by gracious permission of Her Majesty the Queen.

Hiawatha's Boat, Centrepiece, Gorham Company, Providence, R.I. 1871. L. 1·31 m. The White House Collection, Washington, D.C. (photo courtesy, Smithsonian Institution).

on the stem and the rim of the bowl. Above and below the knop on the stem are curved figural brackets, and S-shaped brackets are on the finial which is surmounted by a standing figure in-the-round of Hercules as a child holding a serpent and a shield. The piece, which bears the London hallmark for 1542, was acquired in 1914 by the Goldsmiths' Company, London. It was exhibited in 1983 at Sutton Place, Surrey.

Hercules Vase. A VASE in the form of a EWER that is decorated with motifs depicting the first seven of the twelve Labours of Hercules. The bowl is decorated with a sculptural figure of Hercules slaying the horses of Diomedes (the 7th Labour), and on the neck are the Stymphalian Birds (the 5th Labour), on the handle the Lernean Hydra (the 2nd Labour), and on the foot the Cleaning of the Augean Stables (the 6th Labour), with the other Labours also added. The piece was designed and modelled by EDMUND COTTERILL for R. & S. Garrard (*see* GARRARD & CO. LTD). It was awarded as a HORSE-RACING TROPHY at Ascot (called the Ascot Cup) in 1850, and was shown in London at the Great Exhibition of 1851, there called 'The Emperor of Russia's Vase'.

Hermitage Collection. Articles of English silverware now at the Hermitage Museum, Leningrad, acquired by Peter the Great, 1682-1725, Catherine I, 1725-27, and Catherine II, 1742-96. Some were sold by Charles I, 1625-49, or given by Charles II, 1660-85. The pieces include: (1) the great 'English Service' acquired by Catherine I, *c.* 1726-7, consisting originally of 36 silver-gilt pieces and over 300 silver pieces, all made to her order and bearing her cipher; (2) the THRONE by NICHOLAS CLAUSEN, 1713-14; (3) WINE COOLERS by, respectively, PHILIP ROLLOS I, 1705-6, Lewis Mettayer, 1712-13, and FREDERICK KANDLER, *c.* 1735 (the JERNINGHAM-KANDLER WINE COOLER); (4) TWO-HANDLED CUPS by PAUL CRESPIN, 1726-7, and by DAVID WILLAUME II, 1727-8; (5) a MONTEITH by GABRIEL SLEATH, 1710-11; (6) a WINE FOUNTAIN by PAUL DE LAMERIE, *c.* 1720; (7) a VASE by ANDREW FOGELBERG, 1770-1; (8) a CENTREPIECE by Samuel Wood and William Cripps, 1745-6; (9) a COFFEE-POT and a SHAVING BOWL by Samuel Courtauld I (*see* COURTAULD), 1757-8; (10) a toilet box by Augustin(e) Courtauld II, 1741-2; (11) CANDLESTICKS, a TEA-CADDY, and a covered STANDING CUP by THOMAS HEMING, *c.* 1750-78; (12) JUGS by William Fleming, 1725-6, and by Ann Tanqueray, *c.* 1725-7; and a great many other pieces. Those commissioned or bought by Catherine II bear the Imperial Arms. A number of pieces of English silverware are also in the State National Museum, in the Kremlin, Moscow. *See* Norman M. Penzer, 'English Plate in the Hermitage' in *The Connoisseur*, December 1958, p. 226, and February 1959, p. 14; Charles C. Oman, 'English Plate at the Hermitage, Leningrad, and the State National Museum, Moscow' in *The Connoisseur*, August 1958, p. 14; —, *The English Silver in the Kremlin* (1961). *See* LEOPARD POT.

Hesperides, Garden of the, Candelabrum. (1) A silver-gilt twelve-branch CANDELABRUM, made from a design partly by JOHN FLAXMAN II, modelled probably by WILLIAM THEED II, and executed by PAUL STORR for RUNDELL, BRIDGE & RUNDELL, 1810-11. Arising from an incurved tripod base is a short column, decorated at the top with acanthus leaves, attached to which are six foliated candle branches and above which there is a figural group depicting the dragon Ladon being offered a drinking bowl and an apple by three of the nymphs (sometimes erroneously called 'The Three Graces') who were the guardians of the Golden Apples of the Hesperides. The extension of the column above the group is an apple tree encircled by the twisting Ladon, and at the top are the other six foliated candle branches. On the tripod base are three seated figures of piping fauns, each having at his side a recumbent lion; the feet of the base are in the form of double lion's paws. The piece is one of a pair acquired by the Prince Regent (later, George IV, 1820-30) in June 1811, the other being the MERCURY CANDELABRUM; both are in the Royal Collection.

(2) A silver-gilt seven-branch candelabrum, with the same column and figural group as (1) above, made by PHILIP RUNDELL, 1821-2, with candle branches made by JOHN BRIDGE, 1830-1, but having on the base three figures of seated lionesses (based on the original design by Flaxman). The base bears two cartouches with the arms of the Goldsmiths' Company, London, added when it acquired the piece in 1880.

Hiawatha's Boat. A large CENTREPIECE in the form of a North American Indian canoe floating on calm water (a mirror PLATEAU, supported by figures of crouching bears and upon which are attached silver pieces depicting water-lilies, bulrushes, a turtle, and lizards). The canoe has a mast with a sail set, and in its stern Hiawatha reclines on robes of fur, holding a sword and a shield. On each side of the plateau are inscribed lines from Longfellow's poem *Hiawatha*. The piece was designed by THOMAS J. PAIRPOINT and made by Gorham (*see* GORHAM COMPANY), 1871. It was selected by the wife of

President U. S. Grant, at the Centennial Exposition held in Philadelphia in 1876, for the White House, Washington, D. C., where it was displayed on a sideboard in the Family Dining Room or for formal occasions on the State Dining Room table until *c.* 1970, when it was transferred to the Smithsonian Institution, Washington, D. C.

Hibernia Hallmark. A HALLMARK used by the DUBLIN ASSAY OFFICE, introduced on 25 March 1730 to indicate that duty had been paid. When in 1807 a new DUTY MARK was authorized (the Sovereign's head), the Hibernia mark continued in use as the Dublin Assay Office hallmark, along with the Crowned Harp Hallmark as the STANDARD HALLMARK. The mark depicts a seated female figure representing Hibernia, symbolic of Ireland, having at her left side a harp and in her upraised right hand a sheaf of wheat.

Hibernia Hallmark

High Victorian Style. A style of decoration that combines features of several other styles, the term having been applied in the United States to the fancy and elaborately decorated pieces that were popular there in the period 1850-76, reaching its apex in pieces shown at the Centennial Exposition held in Philadelphia in 1876. Among its leading exponents was THOMAS J. PAIRPOINT, who designed flamboyant pieces in such style for execution by Gorham (*see* GORHAM COMPANY). Few pieces were made in the style after 1876; it was succeeded in the 1870s by the NEO-CLASSICAL STYLE.

higher standard hallmarks. The BRITANNIA HALLMARK and the LION'S HEAD ERASED HALLMARK, which were required in England to be stamped on BRITANNIA SILVER between 30 May 1697 and 1 June 1720 while the FINENESS was fixed legally at 958·4, the former mark to attest compliance with the higher standard and the latter as proof that the assaying had been done at the LONDON ASSAY OFFICE.

hinge. A mechanism for joining two movable adjacent sections of an article and by which the article may be opened and closed (such as the LID and the body of a BOX, MUG or COFFEE-POT); it is composed of two small plates (leaves), sometimes shaped, which are affixed by screws to the two sections (the inside or outside) and has from 3 to 7 short tube-like contiguous projections (lugs) through which is passed a retaining pin upon which the plates rotate. Several types of hinge occur on silverware, e.g., (1) a BOOK HINGE; (2) a BLIND HINGE; and (3) a BOX HINGE. On some hinges of SHEFFIELD PLATE the caps, to conceal the copper in the ends of the pin, are of silver. Hinges on silverware may be up to 30 cm long, as on some CHEESE TOASTERS.

hoard. An article, or a group of articles, buried or hidden deliberately for concealment and safe-keeping and rediscovered at a date much later than the period of production, as distinguished from a TREASURE. Such items become treasure trove, in Great Britain, if made of gold or silver, and if hidden in the soil or a building by an unknown person, in which case the find becomes the property of the Crown, although in practice the finder is compensated; if not hidden, such objects belong to the finder. *See* STOKE PRIOR HOARD; NETHERHAMPTON HOARD; ARDAGH HOARD; CORBRIDGE LANX; DERRY-NAFLAN HOARD; TREWHIDDLE CHALICE.

hobnob waiter. One of a pair of WAITERS used to offer drinks to two persons drinking together ('hobnobbing'), sometimes so called in the late 18th century.

hock-bottle coaster. A type of WINE-BOTTLE COASTER, narrower than the standard type, used for a bottle of hock (white Rhine wine). Some examples have a spreading foot, to provide added stability.

Hogarth, William (1697-1764). The renowned English painter, satirist, and especially engraver who executed, *c.* 1718-35, decoration in ENGRAVING on articles of silverware made by others, including probably PAUL DE LAMERIE. He was an apprentice silversmith in 1716 and was freed in 1718, but is said not to have pursued that trade. He engraved book-plates and COATS OF ARMS, and preferred to engrave on copper for the production of printed work. His first success was 'The Harlot's Progress', followed some years later by the renowned 'The Rake's Progress'. Much of his early work was inspired by French pattern books, especially those of Jean Bérain. He did not sign his engravings on silver, but attributions have been made from documentary evidence. Engravings similar to those attributed to him are said to be in 'Hogarthian style', especially ornamental designs with two classical demi-figures symmetrically placed along the sides of a CARTOUCHE bearing a coat of arms. *See* Ann Forrester, 'Hogarth as an Engraver on Silver' in *The Connoisseur*, February 1963, p. 113. *See* WALPOLE SALVER.

Holbein Hourglass. A silver-gilt HOURGLASS, the design of which has been attributed possibly to Hans Holbein the Younger (1497-1543), the German artist and designer who settled in London in 1530, did work for Henry VIII, and designed for craftsmen in various fields. The hourglass, of the second quarter of the 16th century, but of unknown origin, has been attributed on stylistic grounds to England at the time when Holbein was designing there, and on the basis that the silver-gilt border mounts were made by STAMPING, a process more English than German. Unique in form, the piece consists of a horizontal frame having on each end a pendent strip terminating with a locking device, so that the hourglass can hang from one side, be swung across, and hang in reversed position on the other side. Its whereabouts today is not recorded. *See* L. G. G. Ramsey, 'A Holbein Hour-Glass?' in *The Connoisseur*, October 1954, p. 117.

hollow ware (or **holloware**). Articles of silverware that are hollow, such as BOWLS, pouring vessels, and drinking vessels, as distinguished from FLATWARE and CUTLERY.

honey-pot. A type of receptacle for serving honey, usually of cylindrical or beehive shape, having a cover and often a fixed saucer-like stand upon which to rest a small serving spoon; some have a cover with an indentation for the handle of the spoon, but it permits the entry of insects. In recent years such pieces are often made in cylindrical form with pierced work and provided with a glass liner. *See* G. Bernard Hughes, 'Honey for the Georgian Breakfast' in *Country Life*, 1 March 1973, p. 528. *See* BEEHIVE HONEY-POT; JAM-POT.

hoof spoon. Fig-shaped bowl and horse's-hoof finial, Ahasuerus Hendricks, New York, *c.* 1685. Yale University Art Gallery (Mabel Brady Garvan Collection), New Haven, Conn.

hoof spoon. A type of SPOON having either a curving stem widening toward the terminal or a straight stem with an ornamental design two-thirds toward the terminal, and having a finial in the form of a slanting horse's hoof, with its bottom in the same direction as the front of the FIG-SHAPED bowl of the spoon. Examples were made as early as *c.* 1595 in Germany, and later in Holland and the United States. *See* Helen Burr Smith, 'Four Hoof Spoons' in *Antiques*, June 1944, p. 292.

'Hooks and Lines' Punch Bowl. A PUNCH-BOWL of hemispherical form, having a low foot and two DROP-RING HANDLES. On each side there is an engraved scene in the manner of WILLIAM HOGARTH, one depicting a banquet table with eleven diners (below an inscription 'PROSPERITY TO HOOKS AND LINES'), the other depicting a procession on a quay (below an inscription 'AMICITIA PERPETVA'). Among the figures are Sir George Treby (d. 1742), M. P. for Dartmouth, and Arthur Holdsworth (d. 1696), Alderman and later Mayor of Dartmouth, who were members of a group interested in shipping to and fishing in Newfoundland, *c.* 1690, and whose coats of arms are engraved on the bowl. The bowl was made by PAUL DE LAMERIE, 1723-4, and was presented by Treby to Holdsworth; it is in the Farrar Collection at the Ashmolean Museum, Oxford. Sometimes called the 'Treby Punch-bowl'.

horn. The fibrous, pointed growth on the heads of some animals which, being tough, light, and easily worked, has for centuries been used in various forms and for many purposes. The horns principally employed were ox-

Hooks and Lines Punch Bowl. Hemispherical punch-bowl with engraved decoration, Paul de Lamerie, London, 1723-4. H. 21·6 cm. Ashmolean Museum, Oxford.

horns, ranging from white to dark brown, which have been used, with silver MOUNTS, to make a MUSICAL HORN, DRINKING HORN, and POWDER-HORN, as well as sometimes a HORN BEAKER. *See* WESTMINSTER TOBACCO-BOX; MOUNTED OBJECTS.

horn beaker. A type of BEAKER of which the body, of tapering cylindrical shape, is made of HORN, with silver MOUNTS in the form of a lip rim and a spreading base.

Hornick Ewer. A silver-gilt oval EWER of grotesque design, formed of a male and a female figure back-to-back with intertwined arms. The male figure has a fish tail and the head of a monster whose open mouth and protruding lower jaw form the pouring lip. The demi-figure of the female is under the tall handle made of two intertwined snakes. The piece is based on a 16th-century design of Erasmus Hornick (fl. 1640–85), a Flemish goldsmith and designer noted for his jewelry designs. It was made by J. Garrard & Co., (*see* GARRARD & CO. LTD) London, 1885, for James Mortimer Garrard, Prime Warden of the Goldsmiths' Company in 1896–7, and bears an inscription that it was presented by him to the Company in 1900.

Hornick Ewer. Silver gilt, Based on a 16th-century design by Erasmus Hornick, J. Garrard & Co., London, 1885, H. 40 cm. Goldsmiths' Company, London.

hors d'œuvres dish. A modern type of dish for serving a selection of hors d'œuvres, in the form of a silver platter with either a glass liner having several compartments or several small fitted glass dishes.

horse-racing cup. A type of HORSE-RACING TROPHY, in the form of a cup, awarded annually (usually as a new cup on each occasion rather than as a permanent trophy) as a prize for the winner of a particular race; hence, such cups differ in form and style periodically. Although some are called a 'Gold Cup' most are of silver gilt (the Ascot Gold Cup, inaugurated in 1807, is solid gold). The cups often have on the cover a finial in the form of a race horse and generally bear an engraved racing scene (sometimes an applied PLAQUE) and also an informative inscription. An unusual example, made by STEPHEN SMITH, London, 1868–9, has two horse's heads in-the-round on the lower part of the cup and a finial depicting St George slaying the Dragon. The oldest such cups known to have been awarded in England are the Frampton Moor Cup, 1666 (a TWO-HANDLED CUP of ogee shape), and the ASBY MASKE CUP, 1669. Today the most prestigious examples in England are those awarded annually at Aintree, Ascot (including the ROYAL HUNT CUP), Doncaster, Epsom, Goodwood (*see* GOODWOOD CUP), and Newmarket; those awarded in the the United States are for the Belmont, Kentucky Derby, and Preakness races. *See* Cyril E. Hunt, 'Souvenirs of Stuart Sportsmanship' in *Apollo*, November 1960, p. 142. *See* BRIGHTON CUP; DONCASTER CUP, 1828; GOODWOOD CUP, 1829; QUEEN'S CUP; RICHMOND RACE CUP; WANTAGE CUP.

horse-racing trophy. An article of silver or silver gilt awarded as a prize to the winner of a horse race. Early English examples were in the form of RACING BELLS, but from the Stuart period, *c.* 1600, awards were usually in the form of a BOWL or a TWO-HANDLED CUP. Later trophies – although in some cases referred to as a 'cup' – were often in the form of a VASE (e.g., the Queen's Vase, inaugurated by Queen Victoria at Ascot in 1838, and the HERCULES VASE), BOWL (*see* GOODWOOD 'CUP', 1829), PUNCH-BOWL, SALVER, SHIELD (*see* GOODWOOD 'CUP', 1833), or TEAPOT; some were made originally to be used as a CENTREPIECE. *See* A. G. Grimwade, 'The Wavertree Bequest of Racing Trophies' in *The Connoisseur*, August 1974, p. 238. *See* HORSE-RACING CUP; INDENTURE PLATE.

hot plate. A dinner-table or sideboard accessory upon which to keep warm a food receptacle by means of a burner (alcohol lamp) placed under a thin metal platform. The platform is usually rectangular, with four corner legs high enough to permit the burner to be placed under it in a frame. Some unusual examples are made as a 'double-decker', to hold receptacles in two tiers, each with its own burner, or with two burners for each tier if the platform is large enough to accommodate several receptacles.

hot-water urn. Urn with taps and spigots and lamp-stand, James Shruder, London, 1752. H. 56 cm. Folger's Coffee Collection, Procter & Gamble Co., Cincinnati, Ohio.

hot-water jug. A type of JUG midway in size between a large jug for beer or ale and a smaller jug for milk or cream. It was sometimes a unit of a TEA SERVICE, but less often than a KETTLE for hot water. The body is usually pear-shaped and of circular (sometimes of square or octagonal) section. Many resemble contemporary COFFEE-POTS, but have a pouring lip or a BEAK instead of a tubular SPOUT; they were more likely to have been made for hot water to dilute the strong tea made in the TEAPOT. The beak sometimes has on it a hinged flap (*see* SPOUT FLAP). The pot has a hinged lid, with a THUMBPIECE attached to the body. The loop or scroll handle is usually of wood, secured in FERRULES by pins, and generally opposite the lip or beak, but sometimes at

'hound sejant' goldsmith. Flagon, London, 1646–7. H. 25·4 cm. Victoria and Albert Museum, London.

hourglass salt. Hexafoil section (cover missing), 1516. H. 16·5 cm. Goldsmiths' Company, London

right-angles to it. Sometimes called a 'Turky coffee-pot' (*see* TURKISH COFFEE-POT).

hot-water plate. A double-walled PLATE having, between the upper and lower surfaces, a hollow space for hot water to keep food warm; the water is poured in through a small orifice at the rim.

hot-water stand. A shallow utensil to contain hot water and to be placed under a plate or dish to keep the contents warm. Such pieces, rectangular, circular or oval, usually have two side handles and either an orifice at the rim for filling or a removable overall cover.

hot-water urn. A type of URN for dispensing hot water in connection with the serving of tea or coffee. Examples have one or more TAPS and SPIGOTS, and rest on a stand provided with a heating device. *See* TEA-URN.

'hound sejant' goldsmith. An English silversmith of the mid-17th century, whose identity is unknown. His earliest pieces bear the London hallmark for 1646–7, and the latest for 1666, together with his maker's mark of a 'hound sejant' (sitting). Many of his pieces were made to order for ecclesiastical use and so bear no hallmark, but some fine marked examples (such as FLAGONS) were made for secular use by wealthy Royalists and Dutch merchants. His work is decorated with fine overall CHASING.

hourglass. A sandglass that measures time by the flow of sand from a glass receptacle into a connected similar receptacle and is reversible, the period of flow usually being one hour. Examples set into a silver frame are known to have been owned by Henry VIII, but none is known to have survived. *See* SPEECH TIMER.

hourglass salt. A type of STANDING SALT of which the body is in the form of two cones joined at their apexes to form an hourglass shape, the upper and lower parts being sometimes of hexagonal or hexafoil section, connected by a central knop of floral, architectural or other Gothic style. The cover is in the form of a cone of the same style as the body. The salt-bowl is circular, small, and shallow, fitting into the upper cone of the body. Some examples have on the cover a finial in the form of a standing figure, some an ornament similar to the knop joining the cones of the body, and some a flat horizontal disc. The term has been used by collectors but it is not found in early inventories or records. *See* CORPUS CHRISTI COLLEGE (OXFORD) HOURGLASS SALT; WARDEN HILL'S SALT.

hourglass spoon. A type of SPOON that is a variant form of a spoon with the KING'S PATTERN.

Howard Ewer. A silver-gilt EWER, accompanied by its BASIN, bearing the London hallmark for 1617–18, but said to have been made possibly on the Continent or by an immigrant silversmith in London. On the basin there is the pricked inscription 'The gift of the Right Honble Henry Howard, at the Guild, June Ye 16, 1663, in the Tyme of John Croshold, Major', and it has been surmised that the pieces were made for Henry Howard's grandfather, Thomas Howard, 2nd Earl of Arundel (1585–1646), adviser on art to Charles I. The relief decoration of tritons and mermaids depicts the Triumph of Neptune. The boss in the basin is engraved, depicting Mary Magdalen washing the feet of Christ, but this incongruous boss is affixed over another bearing a figure of Neptune in relief; the alteration was evidently made to raise the boss so as better to position the ewer. The pieces have been owned by the Corporation of Norwich since 1663.

Howard Grace Cup. An important 'FONT-SHAPED' CUP which, in its present form, is significant as showing the intrusion of Renaissance motifs in earlier GOTHIC STYLE. The original part of the piece was a 'font-shaped' cup, only 7·5 cm high, the bowl, base, and cover of which are made of elephant ivory; its date is uncertain. Later, in 1525, its capacity was increased by adding to the rim a tall silver-gilt band, and also adding the silver-gilt base and the cover with its high baluster-shaped finial topped by a standing figure in-the-round of St George slaying the Dragon. The lip band has, on a STIPPLED ground, an encircling inscription, in smooth Lombardic capitals, 'VINUM TUUM BIBE CUM GAUDIO' ('Drink thy wine with joy') and the cover is inscribed 'ESTOTE SOBRII'. It bears the London hallmark of 1525–6 and an unidentified maker's mark. The mounts are decorated with Gothic-style borders and with Renaissance bands, and are studded with garnets and pearls (many now missing). The early history of the piece is uncertain. On the band encircling the ivory cover are the engraved initials 'TB' and a mitre, which have given rise to the view that the piece had some association with Thomas à Becket (it has sometimes been called the 'Thomas à Becket Cup'), but this has been discredited, and the engraving has now been said to refer to a member of the Berkeley family whose crest was a mitre. The ivory cup has been said to have once belonged to Queen Catherine of Aragon, first wife of Henry VIII (based partly on the pomegranate, her emblem, in the decoration), but this has also been discredited. It has been suggested that there may have been another cup bearing the initials 'TB' and referred to as the 'Thomas à Becket Cup' in the 1438 will of John Stourton and as a bequest in 1513 of Sir Edward Howard (son of the 2nd Duke of Norfolk). It is now generally accepted that the known cup was once in the custody of Thomas Howard, 2nd Earl of Arundel (1585–1646), at Arundel House, London, and later, through Arundel and Stafford family heirs, came into the possession of Thomas Howard, of Corby Castle, Cumberland, who exhibited it in 1739–40 at the London Society of Antiquaries. Thereafter it descended through the Howard and Norfolk heirs, until it was sold by the 16th Duke of Norfolk at Christie's, London, on 12 May 1931, and then given by the buyer, Lord Wakefield, through the National Art-Collections Fund, to the Victoria and Albert Museum, London. *See* Norman M. Penzer, 'The Howard Grace Cup' in *The Connoisseur,* June 1946, p.87; —, 'Tudor "Font-shaped" Cups' in *Apollo,* February 1958, p.41, figs.I and II.

Huguenot silverware. Articles of silverware made in England by the French Protestant (Huguenot) silversmiths and apprentices who had fled from French provincial cities and towns when in 1685 the revocation by Louis XIV of the Edict of Nantes (1598) led to their persecution, as well as by their descendants born and apprenticed in England and by some English silversmiths who adopted their style and techniques. The workmanship and design were of the highest quality, hence soon led the local silversmiths to seek to exclude the Huguenots from the Goldsmiths' Company; this attempt failed, and many entered their own mark, but some sold their pieces under the mark of a friendly co-operating local silversmith (*see* SPONSOR'S MARK) or to a competing local silversmith who would then overstamp the work with his own mark. The Huguenot style was brought to England when French fashion was, in the Protestant reign of William and Mary, 1689–94, superseding the prior Dutch style in silverware; it was gradually incorporated by the 1720s into the native English styles, but it remained predominant, reflected in the design and workmanship of some of the finest English silverware, and it was continued by the descendants of the early refugees until after 1725 when the two styles merged. The Huguenot ware featured simplified forms in contrast to the BAROQUE style, with emphasis on STRAPWORK, CUT CARD work, and cast and applied ornaments, and decoration of elaborate ENGRAVING. Among the types of article that exemplify the style are the HELMET JUG, WINE COOLER, WINE-BOTTLE, TWO-HANDLED CUP, TEAPOTS, COFFEE-POTS, SALTS, and SALVERS. The leading first-generation Huguenot exponents of the style were PAUL CRESPIN, PIERRE HARACHE, SIMON PANTIN, PIERRE PLATEL, PHILIP ROLLOS I, DAVID WILLAUME I, and DANIEL GARNIER; sons of the original refugees who, having become English apprentices, continued the tradition, included especially PAUL DE LAMERIE and Augustin(e) Courtauld (*see* COURTAULD). The leading English silversmiths who adopted the style were ANTHONY NELME, BENJAMIN PYNE, and GEORGE GARTHORNE; the outstanding American was the New York silversmith BARTHOLOMEW LE ROUX. The leading engraver was SIMON GRIBELIN. *See* J.F.Haywood, *Huguenot Silverware in England, 1688–1727* (1959); Judith Banister, 'Home Bred or Huguenot?' in *Antiques,* September 1963, p.288; Hugh Tait, 'Huguenot Silver made in London (*c.* 1690–1723)' in *The Connoisseur,* August 1972, p.267, and September 1972, p.25.

Hukin & Heath. A firm of silversmiths, founded by J. W. Hukin and J. T. Heath, which registered its mark at the Birmingham Assay Office in November 1875. It purchased designs from CHRISTOPHER DRESSER after his first visit to Japan in 1877 and made pieces in the new Japanese style. A speciality of the firm was decorating objects of glass with silver MOUNTS.

Hull, John (1624–83). A leading Massachusetts silversmith who was born in England at Market Harborough, Leicestershire, and emigrated in November 1635 to Boston with his parents and a half-brother, a silversmith with whom John started to work, *c.* 1643-4. He was appointed in 1652 to make new coins for Massachusetts to replace the old clipped coinage, and at about this date took as his partner his friend ROBERT SANDERSON, the firm being known as HULL AND SANDERSON. *See* MASSACHUSETTS SILVERWARE.

Hull and Sanderson. The Massachusetts silversmith firm of JOHN HULL and ROBERT SANDERSON, formed *c.* 1652 or earlier. A silver two-handled DRAM-

Howard Grace Cup. Ivory and later silver-gilt additions, London, 1525-6. H. 32 cm. Victoria and Albert Museum, London.

CUP bearing the maiden initials of Ruth Brewer, who was married in 1651, and the mark of John Hull has been said consequently to be possibly the earliest-known example of silverware made in the American Colonies, but its date may be *c.* 1650-60. They made several STANDING CUPS for churches (*see* REHOBOTH CUP), and some important BEAKERS and SPOONS. Their work bears their individual marks 'IH' and 'RS' or the joint mark of the partnership. In 1659 the firm took as apprentices JEREMIAH DUMMER and Samuel Paddy. *See* MASSACHUSETTS SILVERWARE.

Hunt & Roskell. One of the most important London firms of silversmiths in the 19th century. The firm was founded by PAUL STORR (after he left RUNDELL, BRIDGE & RUNDELL in 1819) when in 1822 he joined John Mortimer, who three years before had acquired a silversmith business at 18 Harrison St, off Gray's Inn Road, London. The firm, called Storr & Mortimer, moved to New Bond St, and Storr in the mid-1830s brought in his nephew, John Samuel Hunt (d. 1865), who had worked as a chaser with Storr since 1810. EDWARD HODGES BAILY was in charge of the design studio from 1833 until 1857, and ANTOINE VECHTE was engaged in 1849-50. When Storr retired in 1839, the firm became Mortimer & Hunt, with its joint mark registered in 1839, and two other marks registered in 1843. Mortimer retired in 1844 and Hunt was joined by Robert Roskell, the firm, as Hunt & Roskell, becoming very successful. It employed young designers, e.g., Alfred Brown and the sculptor HENRY HUGH ARMSTEAD and bought models from the Rundell, Bridge & Rundell sales. The firm took as partners F. H. Hunt and R. H. Roskell, who made pieces for the London International Exhibition of 1862, imitating the style of Antoine Vechte and LÉONARD MOREL-LADEUIL. It employed G. A. Carter as a designer from *c.* 1870 until the late 1880s; he worked on the models for the ISMAY TESTIMONIAL. The firm continued until 1897, when it was bought by J. W. Benson.

hunting horn. A type of wind instrument, usually made of brass, having a coiled metal pipe terminating in a bell, used in hunting or riding to hounds. Examples have been made of silver. *See* MUSICAL WARE.

Huntsman Salt. A parcel-gilt multi-coloured GREAT SALT, *c.* 1460-80, having its stem in the form of a standing bearded huntsman with his left hand at his hip holding a hunting knife and with his right hand supporting on his head an oblate, globular, covered receptacle (the lower half made of rock crystal lined with a shallow silver tray and with silver mounts) for salt. The cover, made of glass, is probably a replacement for the original crystal cover. The base is encircled by a turreted battlement and on it are a very small figure of a boy with bagpipes and tiny figures of huntsmen with stags, hounds, etc. The finial is a bunch of leaves with a seeded berry at the top. The hands, feet, and clothing of the man, the base, the small figures, and the finial are all variously coloured, the colour possibly added at a later date. The piece was given to All Souls College, Oxford, but the details and date of the gift are unknown. C. H. Moffatt suggested in 1905 that the piece is 'probably German', others have suggested German or Flemish origin, Sir Charles J. Jackson has treated it as English, and Charles C. Oman has suggested that it was made by a German working in England or an Englishman influenced by German work. It is sometimes called the 'Giant Salt', and at All Souls College the 'Founder's Salt'.

Hurd, Jacob (1702/3-58). A leading silversmith of Boston, Massachusetts, many examples of whose work are still extant in museums and collections in the United States; these include several TWO-HANDLED CUPS in QUEEN ANNE STYLE (among them the TYNG CUP). After 1744 he incorporated in the decoration engraving in ROCOCO STYLE. He was succeeded by his sons, Nathaniel (1729-77) and Benjamin (1739-81), the former specializing in engraving inscriptions and heraldic ornaments and the latter being mainly an engraver. *See* Hollis French, *Jacob Hurd and his Sons, 1702-81* (1939).

hurricane candlestick. A type of CANDLESTICK having a glass chimney to protect the flame of the candle from the wind.

husk border. A border pattern of continuous wheat-husks. It was a feature of designs by ROBERT ADAM. The husks are occasionally festooned to form a SWAG pattern.

Hutton, Isaac (1767-1858). A silversmith of Albany, New York, who, with his brother George, produced silverware of conventional styles. *See* John Davis Hatch, Jr, 'Isaac Hutton' in *Antiques*, January 1945, p. 32.

Hutton Cup. The same as the ELIZABETH BOWES CUP.

Huntsman Salt. Parcel-gilt multi-coloured great salt, *c.* 1460-80. H. 44 cm. All Souls College, Oxford.

I

'I-Love-Liberty' spoon. A type of PICTURE-BACK SPOON having on the back of the bowl an inscription 'I love liberty' and a depiction of a bird escaping from an open birdcage, being an allusion to the outcry in the 1760s for the release of John Wilkes, a political leader and journalist who had been imprisoned for having criticized George III. *See* SONS OF LIBERTY BOWL; CROSBY CUP.

ice-pail. A type of receptacle for pieces of ice, usually of cylindrical shape tapering slightly inward to a flat base. Some early examples are BUCKET-SHAPED and are decorated with simulated staves and hoops, and have a BAIL HANDLE and no cover. Others are variously shaped and elaborately decorated with embossing and figures, e.g., one of silver gilt, now in the Royal Collection, made by JOHN BRIDGE, 1827, from a design of JOHN FLAXMAN II, decorated with a seated figure of Venus on the cover and a merman on each corner of the triangular base. Modern examples (usually called an 'ice-bucket') often have two opposed side handles instead of a bail handle, and generally have a cover (some a hinged lid that automatically drops into place when not held open) and a glass or thermos liner. The terms 'ice-bucket' and 'ice-pail' were formerly applied to a receptacle used to cool a bottle of wine, now called a WINE COOLER.

ice spade. A type of utensil in the shape of a spade, to be used for transferring shaved ice from one receptacle to another. *See* BUTTER TROWEL.

ice-cream dish. A type of dish for formally serving ice-cream. An example with a flat bottom and a raised inverted rim, and resting on four legs, was a part of the MACKAY SERVICE.

ice-cream fork. A type of dining FORK for eating ice-cream, sherbets, and some desserts, having a bifurcated somewhat spoon-like terminal.

ice tongs. A type of TONGS used for transferring a lump or cube of ice from an ICE-PAIL to a drinking vessel. It operates like a pair of scissors, having pivoting arms with ring handles and at the short end a pair of curved pincers with pointed ends that meet to grasp the piece of ice. *See* SUGAR TONGS; SUGAR NIPPERS.

iced-tea spoon. A modern type of SPOON having a small oval bowl and a stem about 20 cm long; it is used for stirring iced tea and other beverages served in a tall drinking-glass.

iconography. The art of representation by pictures or images, such as the depiction of Christian motifs that are found on some CHALICES and PATENS, frequent examples being the AGNUS DEI, Manus Dei (the right hand of God, usually shown palm down in the act of blessing), veronica (the impression of the face of Christ left on the alleged handkerchief of Veronica), sacred chrismon monogram (Chi-Rho or XP), Crucifixion, and the figure of Christ in various attitudes.

imbricated. Arranged to overlap in a regular pattern, in the manner of roof-tiles or fish-scales. Although the style is more often found in the scale-ground pattern enamelled on porcelain, it is also sometimes found in open-work on some silverware BASKETS and engraved on some FLAGONS and 'FONT-SHAPED' CUPS. Sometimes called 'scalework'. *See* CHARLECOTE CUP; MAGDALEN COLLEGE (OXFORD) POT; CASTING BOTTLE; FEATHERED FLAGON; BUTLEIGH SALT.

Imported Goods Hallmarks. The HALLMARKS required to be stamped in the United Kingdom on articles of silverware made abroad and imported into the country. From 1842 such articles were required to be assayed in the U.K. and from 1867 to be given a FOREIGN ORIGIN MARK, i.e., the letter 'F' in an oval ESCUTCHEON, in addition to the usual BRITISH HALLMARKS except articles made prior to 1800 and except, after 1939, articles more than 100 years old. From 1904 it was required that all foreign plate be marked with the decimal value of the FINENESS within a horizontal oval (STERLING SILVER with ·925 and BRITANNIA SILVER with ·9584), and also the DATE HALLMARK and the ASSAY OFFICE HALLMARK, but no longer the letter 'F'; and each Assay Office

ice-pail. One of a pair, simulated staves and hoops, and bail handle, Benjamin Laver, London, 1785. H. 17 cm. Courtesy, Partridge (Fine Arts) Ltd, London.

used a new Assay Office Hallmark for such imported ware, being from 1976, London, the zodiac sign for Leo; Sheffield, the zodiac sign for Libra; Birmingham, an equilateral triangle; and Edinburgh, St Andrew's cross. The MAKER'S MARK was replaced by the mark of a sponsor (usually the importer). The British Date Hallmark on such imported ware indicates the date of the British assaying rather than the date of production.

After 1975, with the introduction of CONVENTION HALLMARKS, a new system was established for imported silverware: (1) for plate imported from a Convention country, the established Convention Hallmarks are recognized without additional British marks (except that foreign standards for silver below ·925 are not recognized), but such ware not bearing the Convention Hallmarks must be assayed and stamped with the usual British Imported Goods Hallmarks; and (2) for plate imported from a non-Convention country, the British Imported Goods Halmarks are still in use, including the Assay Office Hallmarks that are different from those on articles made in the U.K., being one of the special Assay Office Hallmarks described above. After 1975 the millesimal marks indicating fineness omit the decimal point, but are still shown within a horizontal oval.

incense-boat. A boat-shaped receptacle, sometimes partly covered by a LID, for holding incense before it is placed in a CENSER. Such pieces are usually accompanied by a chained small SPOON and were used in connection with a censer. Numerous examples are found in CANADIAN SILVERWARE. *See* RAMSEY ABBEY CENSER.

incense-burner. A receptacle in which incense is burned for the purpose of scenting a room or (termed a CENSER) for ecclesiastical use. Such pieces are of no fixed form, but usually have a bulbous body resting on three or four feet and have pierced work to emit the scent. Some examples also have three attached rings for suspensory chains. English examples were made from the second half of the 17th century.

incuse. Strictly, an intaglio impression produced on the obverse (face) of a coin by a relief die. The term has been extended to apply to some infrequent marks on some British silverware (and gold) – an impression in intaglio produced by a punch having the mark on it in relief. Such marks were sometimes used by makers of SMALLWARE, and by a workman showing his initials or sign on pieces bearing his employer's MAKER'S MARK. The LONDON ASSAY OFFICE used such incuse marks for the DUTY MARK from 1784 to 1786 and for the Britannia DRAWBACK MARK from 1784 to 1785. As the die on such punches could be readily damaged, they were soon replaced by intaglio punches making relief (cameo) impressions, especially some that were made as a 'stub' which included several relief marks on the same punch.

Indenture plate. Articles of silverware made for and issued by the British Sovereign to ambassadors (*see* AMBASSADORIAL SILVERWARE) and to Speakers of the House of Commons, as well as christening gifts to godchildren of the Sovereign and a series of HORSE-RACING TROPHIES initiated by Queen Anne, all of which were issued through the Lord Chamberlain's Office and were recorded in his Day Books (still preserved in the Public Record Office). Such ware bears the Royal arms, but was not originally in the possession of the Crown; many such pieces have now been acquired by the Royal Collection, while others still remain in the possession of English families whose members have been given such ware or are now owned by museums. *See* ARMORIAL PLATE.

Indian (American) Spoon. One of a series of SPOONS having on the front of the terminal of large spoons sculptured figures depicting twelve American Indian dances and on the stem of small spoons figures in-the-round depicting twelve other Indian dances. Such spoons were made by TIFFANY & CO., based on designs first made by Charles T. Grosjean in 1884 and patented in 1885. They are not related to the SOUVENIR SPOONS made in the 1890s, some of which depicted Indian heads with feather head-dresses.

Indian (United States) silverware. Articles of silverware made by craftsmen of many tribes of American Indians who live on reservations widely distributed throughout the United States, including the Navajo, Hopi, Zuñi, and Santo Domingo (New Mexico and Arizona), Sioux (North Dakota), Choctaw (Mississippi), Seneca (New York), and Iroquois (north-eastern United States and Canada). The articles (apart from jewelry) – consisting of boxes, trays, picture-frames, vases, etc. – have traditionally been made of silver decorated with REPOUSSÉ work and turquoises. New styles and techniques are continually being developed both for expensive pieces that now have a thriving market and for tourist items.

incense-burner. Receptacle with three rings for suspensory chains, English, *c.* 1675. H. 35·6 cm. Toledo Museum of Art, Toledo, Ohio (photo courtesy, Brand Inglis Ltd, London).

Indian-trade silverware. Brooch by Pierre Huguet called Latour, Montreal, *c.* 1800–17. D. 19·8 cm Musée du Québec, Quebec.

ingot. Silver mined in Colorado, *c.* 1880. Yale University Art Gallery (American Arts Purchase Fund), New Haven, Conn.

Indian-trade silverware. Articles of silverware given in the 18th century to North American Indians; made by silversmiths in the United States and Canada, they were of two categories: (1) official pieces (e.g., MEDALS and penannular ARMBANDS) presented by the government for military or political reasons; and (2) ornamental ware sold to the Indians or given to them in exchange for furs. The latter group included jewelry, such as crescent-shaped GORGETS, HEADBANDS, brooches, sometimes bearing Masonic emblems (called 'shirt-buckles'), necklaces, heart-shaped ornaments, penannular wrist-bands, pendent plaques, and crosses (with two or three cross arms) – the crosses having no religious significance. The pieces were made by recognized silversmiths as well as by unknown Colonial craftsmen. Some such articles were given to the Indians by George Washington from 1789 and by later Presidents until 1843. Although the practice of making such gifts ended in the mid-19th century, such articles are today being reproduced by modern Indian craftsmen in Canada, such as Arthur Powless. *See* Arthur Woodward, 'Highlights in Indian Trade Silver' in *Antiques*, June 1945, p. 328; Charlotte Wilcoxen, 'Indian trade silver of the New York colonial frontier' in *Antiques*, December 1979, p. 1356; Conrad W. Graham, 'Trade Silver' in *Canadian Collector*, May/June 1985, p. 15.

inhaler. Mask in fitted case, made by Ferguson, London, *c.* 1851–60. H. 11·5 cm. Wellcome Collection, Science Museum, London.

ingot. A block of silver (or other metal) cast in a practicable shape (usually rectangular) and of weight convenient for storage, later to be either remelted for CASTING or flattened by ROLLING. Some ingots have been inscribed with the name of the mine of origin.

inhaler. An anaesthetic mask for administering chloroform. A silver example, *c.* 1851–60, has a covered protuberance for filling and a screened protuberance for inhaling. *See* MEDICAL SILVERWARE.

ink-box. A type of BOX to hold writing materials for use while travelling; the box, with a hinged lid, is rectangular and contains two smaller boxes (one for an INKPOT, the other for sand) and also space for quills.

inkpot. A receptacle for ink, now known as an 'ink-well'. Sometimes it was combined with a QUILL-POT, and usually it was a unit of an INKSTAND. Some small examples were made as a non-spilling travelling accessory; these have a SCREW COVER (with washer), a tight-fitting cap or glass stopper, and are usually furnished with a carrying case. A fantasy example was made in the form of a full-blown rose resting on its stem and spreading leaves.

inkstand. A desk stand for writing materials, made in numerous forms and styles, and supporting a variety of writing accessories, but the basic forms being as follows: (1) an oblong box, having a hinged lid, to hold an INKPOT, a POUNCE-POT, and sometimes a sealing-wax case and a wafer-box, and having a drawer at the bottom or a compartment at the back to hold quill pens; and (2) a TRAY upon which rests an inkpot, pounce-pot, SAND-BOX, QUILL-POT and wafer-box (some such articles being made of glass with silver mounts), with often a trough along the front for pens. On the tray type, the inkpot was sometimes surmounted by a TAPERSTICK for use with the sealing wax, along with a CANDLE EXTINGUISHER; and some also had a HAND BELL to ring for a messenger. The tray (triangular, rectangular, oval or canoe-shaped) was sometimes supported by four small feet and was sometimes fitted with guard-rings or recesses in which to place the inkpot and pounce-pot, and in the centre the bell or taperstick; it was sometimes bordered by a pierced gallery. In the mid-19th century some inkstands on trays were made in fanciful forms, as an ornamental piece for the desk. Early names for an inkstand were 'standish' and 'inkstandish'. *See* G. Bernard Hughes, 'Georgian Silver Inkstands' in *Country Life*, 7 February 1957, p. 230; Jonathan Stone, 'English Inkstands in Silver and Sheffield Plate' in *Antiques*, September 1966, p. 342. *See* TREASURY INKSTAND; GLOBE INKSTAND; LIBRARY SET; CASKET INKSTAND; BANK OF ENGLAND INKSTAND; CONYNGHAM INKSTAND; TEMPLE BAR INKSTAND; WALPOLE INKSTAND.

inkstand (1). Box with lidded compartments for pounce-pot, inkpot, and quill pens, John Ruslen, London, *c.* 1677. L. 16 cm. Courtesy, Asprey & Co. Ltd, London.

inscription. Words, names, and dates (other than a MAKER'S MARK or a HALL-MARK) on an article of silverware, to record ownership, date of production, information about the circumstances in which the piece was ordered, the purpose for which it was made, the name of the donor, e.g., inscriptions on commemorative ware. Some inscriptions are not contemporary with the making of the piece, so do not establish its date.

inscription plate. A small plate, of silver or heavily plated SHEFFIELD PLATE, that was used to provide a retailer with a method of inscribing on an article of Sheffield plate a customer's name, monogram, crest, coat of arms, inscription, etc., which the retailer could not ordinarily do by ENGRAVING (which

inkstand (2). Silver-gilt tray with two inkpots, two quill cleaners, and hand bell, Robert Hennell IV, London, 1881. L. 18 cm. Courtesy, Garrard & Co. Ltd, London.

would expose the copper layer below). The maker of the article cut out from the article an area of the size of the plate and soldered in the plate, which could then be engraved. An alternative method, employed after *c.* 1810, was for the silversmith to affix to the article by SWEATING a thin wafer of silver on which an inscription could be added by the retailer as required. Sometimes called a 'shield'.

insulator. A small ivory ring inserted in the vertical handle of some pieces of hollow ware, at the junction of a silver handle and silver PADS, to insulate the handle against heat. Sometimes such an insulator is inserted in a finial serving as a handle on a cover or lid.

Ireland, Great Seal of, Cup. *See* LOFTUS CUP.

Irish hallmarks. The Harp Crowned standard mark and the EEC entry commemorative mark, 1973.

Irish Hallmarks. The HALLMARKS punched on silverware in Ireland since 22 December 1637, when the Harp Crowned mark was introduced as the Irish STANDARD HALLMARK for silver of .925 fineness. On 25 March 1730 the HIBERNIA HALLMARK was introduced as a DUTY MARK; but it was superseded as duty mark by a Sovereign's head mark in 1807, and the Hibernia mark became the Dublin Assay Office 'Town Mark', to be used with the Harp Crowned as the Standard (Fineness) Mark. The standard mark introduced in 1637 was supplemented by a MAKER'S MARK, and also an annual 'Date Letter Mark', the use of which has continued, in alphabetical series, until today, changing on 1 June until 1931, thereafter on 1 January. For foreign silverware imported into Ireland without CONVENTION HALLMARKS the Dublin Assay Office Town mark is, since 1906, a BOUGET HALLMARK. For Irish silverware to be exported to a foreign country that accepts Convention Hallmarks, the Dublin Assay Office Town Mark is the Hibernia Hallmark on articles made in Ireland or the Bouget Hallmark on articles made outside Ireland; this is supplemented by the Maker's (Sponsor's) mark, arabic numerals denoting fineness, and the Common Control Mark (balance scales with 925). Irish silverware and hallmarks after 1921 are generally beyond the scope of this book, but two Irish COMMEMORATIVE MARKS have been used since that date, and they are described here so as to include a mention of all Irish marks to date: (1) in 1966, to commemorate the 50th Anniversary of the Rising of 1916, being in the form of the 'Sword of Light' (a flaming sword symbolizing the national desire for freedom, called 'An Claidheamh Solais'), with the dates 1916 and 1966; and (2) in 1973, to commemorate the Republic of Ireland's entry into the European Economic Community (EEC), being in the form of the Glenisheen collar (an Irish gold penannular collar dating from *c.* 700 BC), with the date 1973 encircled. For some provincial marks used locally, *see* LIMERICK SILVERWARE and CORK SILVERWARE.

Irish silverware. Articles of silverware made in Ireland (now Eire) from the 15th century (mainly pieces known by references in bequests as no examples are now known to survive), but principally from the mid-17th century to the late 19th century, made mainly at Dublin and Cork, but some also at Limerick and other provincial centres. Apart from Celtic ecclesiastical ware, mainly CHALICES, made from *c.* 1500 to *c.* 1650 and datable from engraved inscriptions, little early Irish silverware is extant, and such that survives follows English styles until *c.* 1660 when household silverware was produced and local forms and styles were introduced. These were influenced by Dutch silversmiths until *c.* 1685 when some immigrant Huguenot silversmiths brought new techniques and designs (featuring vertical FLUTING, CHINOISERIE and GADROONING), but local styles were retained into the 18th century, with little ornamentation and restrained decoration. During the early 18th century more opulent ware was made (especially TEAPOTS in Chinese form until superseded *c.* 1735 by ceramic ware) and also TWO-HANDLED CUPS, DISH RINGS, and various articles of domestic ware. Decoration from *c.* 1750 featured the Irish version of the ROCOCO STYLE, with elaborate CHASING and EMBOSSING, but there was introduced an Irish feature depicting farmyard and other genre scenes. In the period 1770–1810 the NEO-CLASSICAL STYLE (ADAM STYLE) prevailed, with much decoration in BRIGHT CUTTING. In the early 19th century quality lapsed, due to the duty-free importation from England of mass-produced MOUNTS to be assembled in Ireland, and many silversmiths ceased business or emigrated. Toward the 1850s interest was revived, and Irish motifs were popularized, such as harps, Celtic crosses, and shamrocks; articles especially identified with Ireland were produced, e.g., the HARP CUP, dish ring, and pointed-handle FLATWARE. In the following period of English REGENCY STYLE, Irish ware again deteriorated in quality and design. Little change resulted from the Arts and Crafts Movement, but in that period the Roman Catholic Church commissioned ecclesiastical ware; there was not much production in ART NOUVEAU STYLE or ART DECO STYLE. Many pieces of Irish silverware have been rechased after the original pro-

Issus, Battle of, Shield. Joseph Angell II for Rundell, Bridge & Rundell, London 1828. D. 74·5 cm. Courtesy, Sotheby's, London.

duction to suit later owners. A considerable quantity of Irish silverware was falsely marked by DUTY DODGERS (leading to the introduction of the HIBERNIA MARK) and was subject to forgery by many methods. *See* Francis Townshend 'The Irishness of Irish Silver' in *Apollo*, October 1966, p. 298; Douglas Bennett, *Irish Georgian Silver* (1973); Maureen T. Hillpot, 'Collection of Irish Silver' in *The Connoisseur*, November 1980, p. 176; John Teahan, 'Irish Silverware' in *Antiques*, October 1981, p. 915. *See* IRISH HALLMARKS; DUBLIN SILVERWARE; CORK SILVERWARE; LIMERICK SILVERWARE.

Ismay Testimonial. A sculptural CENTREPIECE which, together with four CANDELABRA and other silver articles, was made for presentation on 16 September 1885 to Thomas Henry Ismay, manager of the White Star Steamship Line, by the stockholders. The centrepiece, designed by G. A. Carter and made by HUNT & ROSKELL, has three figures seated on the base, depicting Vasco da Gama flanked by Captain Cook and Jason, and has behind them a large globe upon which is seated a figure of Commerce.

Issus, Battle of, Shield. One of several similar English SHIELDS having in the centre an embossed, chased, and cast medallion in high relief depicting a battle scene, with horsemen and a chariot, representing the Battle of Issus, in Asia Minor, 333 BC, in which Darius III, King of Persia, was defeated by Alexander the Great. The surrounding border includes four wide panels, within scrolled borders, depicting hunting and battle scenes, alternating with four smaller panels, each depicting a landscape; in the space between each pair of panels there is an animal-head mask. The original English shield was made by Joseph Angell II (*see* ANGELL), London, 1828, for RUNDELL, BRIDGE & RUNDELL. It is a copy of an unmarked shield in the Royal Collection, said by E. Alfred Jones to be probably Dutch, *c.* 1675, but which, in the Catalogue of the 1954 Exhibition of the Royal Plate at the Victoria and Albert Museum, London, has been attributed probably to Augsburg, early 18th century, in the manner of J. A. Thelot (1654-1734), of Augsburg. At least four examples of the Angell shield have been said to have been made in the Angell workshops, one of which, marked 1828, was sold at Sotheby's, London, on 22 November 1984, having on the reverse two suspension rings and the engraved badge of Hugh Percy, 3rd Duke of Northumberland (1785-1847), within the motto of the Order of the Garter and below a ducal coronet. Another example, which was a Doncaster Race Trophy in 1837, was exhibited in London at the Great Exhibition of 1851. A further example has

been said to have possibly been in the Royal Collection, but there is none recorded there today.

ivory objects. (1) Articles having the principal part made of ivory, the piece
also having silver MOUNTS, as in the case of some CUPS, VASES, and BOXES. An
ivory cylinder was incorporated into a TANKARD with silver-gilt mounts,
made by ROBERT GARRARD I, 1812, the ivory decorated with mythological
figures by a German carver, *c.* 1700. *See* HOWARD GRACE CUP; IVORY-SLEEVE
COVERED VASES; MOUNTED OBJECTS. (2) Mounts made of ivory, such as the
handles of some JUGS, TEAPOTS, COFFEE-POTS, PUNCH LADLES, etc., and the IN-
SULATOR rings inserted between two sections of some such silver handles,
and also the handles of some KNIVES and the finials on some covers. Sometimes ivory mounts were stained green.

Ivory-sleeve Covered Vases. A pair of covered VASES having their central
section made of carved ivory cylinders, and the other parts of silver gilt.
Above and below the ivory cylinders are bulging bands, each decorated with
GADROONING and masks; the stems are decorated with ACANTHUS leaves and
the feet with gadrooning. Each cover has a central dome surmounted by a
finial in the form of the figure of a bird. The ivory is decorated with an encircling carved frieze depicting at least thirty gambolling *putti*; it was carved
in the Low Countries, *c.* 1700, not by Il Fiammingo (François Duquesnoy,
1597–1643), as once attributed, but perhaps by François Langhemans, a
Flemish artist. The cylinders were probably brought to England from the
Low Countries and were mounted by DAVID WILLAUME I in 1711; the vases
were acquired in the Peter Wilding Bequest by the British Museum, London. The possible history of the pieces has been reported by Hugh Tait,
'Huguenot Silver made in London, *c.* 1690–1723: The Wilding Bequest' in
The Connoisseur, August 1972, p. 270.

J

Jacobite spoon. A type of PICTURE-BACK SPOON, with Jacobite motifs, made for the adherents of the royal House of Stuart to show loyalty to, or later in memory of, the exiled James II (1635-1701) after his abdication in 1698, and his descendants, James Edward Stuart, the 'Old Pretender' and his son Charles Edward Stuart (1720-88), 'Bonnie Prince Charlie' or the 'Young Pretender'. Some motifs were the rose of England representing the Crown, two rose buds emblematic of the two Pretenders, and an oak leaf alluding to the escape of Charles II by hiding in the Boscobel Oak in 1651.

jam-pot. A small receptacle for serving jam or preserves, usually having a cover with an indentation on the rim for the handle of a small serving spoon and often having a fixed saucer-like stand. *See* HONEY-POT.

Jamaica Service. A silver-gilt DINNER SERVICE purchased by the Crown with funds voted on 3 December 1801 to the Duke of Clarence (later William IV, 1830-7) by the Jamaica Assembly in recognition of his support of their opposition to the anti-slavery campaign. The pieces, made by DIGBY SCOTT and BENJAMIN SMITH I, London, 1803-4, for RUNDELL, BRIDGE & RUNDELL, bear the arms of Jamaica and of George III, then reigning, and are generally decorated with engraved marine and military trophies. The service includes two pairs of elaborate SOUP-TUREENS (one circular and one oval), eight SAUCE-TUREENS, and six ICE-PAILS. It is now in the Royal Collection. The tureens closely resemble two silver-gilt tureens made by Henri Auguste, the French Court Goldsmith, in Paris in 1787, that were bought by Rundell, Bridge & Rundell, *c.* 1800, and sold by them (with the Royal arms applied in 1801) to George III; they are also in the Royal Collection.

Jamaica silverware. Articles of silverware made in the island of Jamaica. Records indicate the presence of goldsmiths there from the 1620s, but no marked piece is known attributed to before *c.* 1715. A law providing for assaying and marking silver was enacted in the 1740s. Two silversmiths are known from the period 1747-65, Charles Wood and Anthony Danver, who made cast silverware probably from London prototypes. From 1745 to 1760 more than twenty silversmiths were recorded, but the industry diminished during a local revolution and did not revive until the 19th century.

Janus finial. A type of FINIAL that is Janus-faced, having two heads facing in opposite directions. The heads are sometimes masks depicting comedy and tragedy, and sometimes lion and unicorn motifs are so used.

jar. A deep wide-mouthed vessel, usually without handles and generally cylindrical, although sometimes of BALUSTER, ovoid or other shapes, They vary greatly in size and have many different uses. *See* GINGER-JAR.

jardinière. A large type of BOWL used as a receptacle for plants or flowers. Such pieces are circular or occasionally oval, and sometimes have BOMBÉ sides. Examples in silver are known from the late 18th century onward. Some examples made in recent years are in fantasy shape, such as one in the shape of a swan, *c.* 1971.

Jarvie, Robert R. (1865-1941). A silversmith born in Schenectady, New York, who moved to Chicago before 1893. In 1905 he started his workshop, making mainly CANDLESTICKS in the style of PAUL REVERE II. Later he did much work in contemporary style, but was not listed as a silversmith until 1912. He made many trophies, executing pieces designed by the architect George Grant Elmslie. *See* David A. Hanks, 'Robert R. Jarvie' in *Antiques*, September 1976, p. 522.

Jasmine Vase. A VASE made of silver with DAMASCENED steel panels, designed by AUGUSTE ADOLPHE WILLMS and made by Frederick Elkington for ELKINGTON & CO., 1883-4. The ovoid body, the neck, and the spreading foot are formed of steel damascened with gold and silver, the body being decorated front and back with panels depicting birds and floral sprays. Silver ornaments are affixed in the form of Cupids and jasmine sprays (a relatively minor feature) on the side handles, squirrels on the foot, an eagle atop the cover, and a mask on the neck. It is in the Victoria and Albert Museum, London.

jardinière. Oval bowl with *bombé* sides, William Frisbee, London, 1799. Courtesy, Partridge (Fine Arts) Ltd. London.

Jerningham-Kandler Wine Cooler.
Electroform copy, 1880, of the original,
c. 1735, by Charles Kandler, in the
Hermitage, Leningrad, L. 1·60 m.
Victoria and Albert Museum, London.

Jeannest, Pierre-Emile (1813-57). A silversmith who was born in Paris, came to England in 1845/6, was employed to model ceramic ware at Mintons, Stoke-on-Trent, and by 1849-50 had become head of the fine art department of ELKINGTON & CO., which position he held until his death. His early work was in BAROQUE STYLE, but later in RENAISSANCE STYLE and classical style. He specialized in making sculptural ware, the subjects including Lady Godiva (*see* GODIVA, LADY, STATUETTE), the equestrian ELIZABETH I STATUETTE, 1850-1, and the group of Elizabeth I with the Earl of Leicester. He developed the technique of oxidizing silver to produce a matt surface (*see* OXIDIZED SILVERWARE) and also the use of ENAMELLING on silverware.

Jenkins, Thomas (fl. 1668-1705/6). A London silversmith who entered his mark, the initials 'TI' between scallop shells, for BRITANNIA SILVER in 1697, with address at Essex St, Strand. He was freed of the Butchers' Company, of which he was an official from 1685 to 1702. He was a prolific silversmith, more than 100 pieces made by him having been identified. His work covered a wide range of secular and church ware, including pieces with CHINOISERIE decoration. Until recent years his mark had been mistakenly attributed to Thomas Issod, who had entered a mark 'TI' in 1697, but who is known for making mainly spoons. *See* Judith Banister, 'Thomas Jenkins, 17th Century Master Goldsmith' in *Goldsmiths' Company Review, 1976-7*, p. 28; Arthur Grimwade and Judith Banister, 'Thomas Jenkins unveiled' in *The Connoisseur*, July 1977, p. 173. *See* PEACOCK CUP.

Jerningham-Kandler Wine Cooler. A WINE COOLER, one of the most elaborate pieces of decorative silver plate, conceived and ordered by Henry Jerningham (or Jernegan; d. 1761), a goldsmith (once an apprentice, 1706-13, of ANTHONY NELME) of Russell St, Covent Garden, London, and also a banker. He selected as designer George Vertue (1684-1756), the engraver and antiquary, and had the animal figures that form the stand modelled in wax by the Antwerp sculptor John Michael Rysbrack (1694-1770), who had settled in England, and made by CHARLES KANDLER. When, after four years, the piece was finished, *c.* 1735, no buyer could be found, and it was offered in 1735 as a prize in a lottery to raise funds to build a bridge over the Thames at Westminster. It was won by William Battine (1683-1770), of East Marden, Sussex, who exhibited it and later sold it probably through Jerningham and Kandler, in 1738 to Biron (Bühren), Duke of Courland, favourite of Empress Anne of Russia, 1730-40; it is now in the Hermitage Museum, Leningrad. It was forgotten until rediscovered in 1880, and several silver-plated facsimiles were made by ELECTROFORMING in 1880 by ELKINGTON & CO.; one of these is in the Victoria and Albert Museum, London, and another in the Metropolitan Museum of Art, New York.

The wine cooler is oval with a flat bottom, and it rests on a quadrangular stand formed by figures in-the-round of four chained and crouching panthers (or leopards?). On each side of the cooler are groups, in high relief, of *putti* in Bacchanalian attitudes. The rim is everted and bordered by intertwined foliage. The two handles are in the form of TERMS, one male and one female, each holding bunches of grapes, emerging from hollow scrolls and

Joan of Arc Statuette. Robert Garrard II, London, 1863. H. 54·5 cm. Photo courtesy, Sir Christopher Lever.

supported by bifurcated volutes attached to the rim of the cooler. The piece bears the maker's mark 'KA' and the date mark 'T' for 1734–5; it is overall 1·79 m long and its capacity is about 275 litres (60 gallons). It is sometimes referred to as the 'Westminster Bridge Cistern'. *See* Norman M. Penzer, 'The Jerningham-Kandler Wine Cooler' in *Apollo*, September 1956, p. 80, and October 1956, p. 111.

jewel-box. A type of BOX, often part of a TOILET SERVICE, for holding jewels. Such boxes are of no fixed shape or style, and are decorated in many styles. Sometimes called a CASKET.

jewelled decoration. Decoration of some outstanding articles of silverware by the affixing of gemstones to enhance the piece, such as the ELECTION CUP and the HOWARD GRACE CUP. Some silverware articles feature, as an integral part of the piece, an element of rock crystal; *see* CRYSTAL ARTICLES.

jewel(le)ry. Various articles of jewelry made of silver and worn on the person, such as finger-rings, brooches, pendants, chains, necklaces, bracelets, etc., which are not generally treated as PLATE, are not within the scope of this book; but certain articles of silver jewelry (sometimes considered as objects of vertu) are usually discussed in books on silverware, and hence are the subject of entries here, e.g., VINAIGRETTES, CHATELAINES, SEALS, WATCH-CASES, SNUFF-BOXES, and other types of BOX, as well as a few articles of jewelry often made of SHEFFIELD PLATE, e.g., BUTTONS and BUCKLES. *See* Harold Newman, *An Illustrated Dictionary of Jewelry* (1981).

Jewish ritual silverware. Articles of silverware used in synagogues and Jewish household ceremonies, especially in the Orthodox ritual; some English examples date from the founding in 1701 of the Bevis Marks Synagogue in London. Apart from such pieces made in London by ABRAHAM DE OLIVEYRA (and like ware made in New York by MYER MYERS), most of such pieces were the work of non-Jewish silversmiths; since *c.* 1965 almost all types of such ware have been made in modern style by GERALD BENNEY. Among such articles made in England are TORAH BELLS *(Rimmonim)*, TORAH BREASTPLATE, TORAH POINTER, SABBATH LAMP, HANUK(K)A(H) LAMP, MENORAH, KIDDUSH CUP, ETHROG-BOX, and SPICE-BOX, as well as the MEGILLAH-CASE, Havdalah Box, Mezuzah, Seder Plate, Bread Tray, and Bread Knife. Such articles are sometimes referred to collectively as 'Judaica'. *See* Cecil Roth, 'The Jewish Museum' in *The Connoisseur*, September 1933, p. 15, and October 1933, p. 228; Arthur G. Grimwade, 'The Ritual Silver of Bevis Marks Synagogue' in *Apollo*, April 1950, p. 103, and May 1950, p. 130; Jonathan Stone, 'Anglo-Jewish Silver' in *The Antique Collector*, February 1985, p. 64. *See* DOUCEUR.

Joan of Arc Statuette. A silver equestrian STATUETTE made by ROBERT GARRARD II in 1863, depicting Joan of Arc astride a prancing horse and holding a banner aloft. Its present whereabouts is unknown.

jockey-cap caddy spoon. A type of CADDY SPOON having the bowl in the form of a jockey-cap, the handle being the peak (visor) of the cap. Such spoons were made in five principal varieties: (1) with the cap marked into segments, sometimes with a star or snowdrop motif on the top of the crown; (2) with the cap and peak ribbed; (3) with the cap and peak plain or lightly engraved; (4) with the cap decorated with DIE-STAMPING of various motifs; and (5) with the cap decorated with FILIGREE or FALSE FILIGREE work. Early examples have the hallmarks on the peak, later ones on the back of the cap. Such caddy spoons were made in great quantity and in recent years forgeries have been produced, in some cases by adding a peak to a Georgian WATCH-CASE.

joint handle. An implement to assist a person carving a joint, being a handle to be placed over the bone, and secured by a thumbscrew, so that the joint could be held firmly. Sometimes called a 'leg-of-mutton holder'.

jolly-boat decanter wagon. A type of DECANTER WAGON that is unlike conventional forms, being in the shape of a wooden naval jolly-boat resting on four wheels (or small rollers) and having sometimes a pulling shaft; in the boat there are two large circular recesses for decanters, and sometimes two small ones alongside for stoppers. Such pieces are about 30 cm long, excluding the shaft; some are additionally decorated with an anchor at the stern and a coil of rope at the bow to serve as a pulling ring.

jorum. The same as a PUNCH-BOWL. The term is said to be derived probably from Joram (2 Sam., viii, 10), who brought vessels of silver, gold, and brass.

Jewish ritual silverware. Sabbath lamp, Abraham de Oliveyra, London, 1734. H. 75 cm. Jewish Museum, London (photo courtesy, Warburg Institute, University of London).

Jubilee Centrepiece. Parcel gilt, Sir Alfred Gilbert, 1887. W. 1·12 m. Royal Collection; reproduced by gracious permission of Her Majesty the Queen.

Judgment of Solomon Sconces. One of the surviving six examples, silver gilt, with reflector plate depicting the Judgment of Solomon, Charles Shelley, London, *c.* 1689–94; sockets by Paul Storr, 1816. H. 52 cm. Royal Collection; reproduced by gracious permission of Her Majesty the Queen.

Justice Centrepiece. Colonnade centrepiece (without plateau), William Pitts I and Joseph Preedy, London, 1795–6. H. 64·cm. York City Council (photo courtesy, Castle Museum, York).

Jubilee Beakers. A pair of silver-gilt covered BEAKERS of tapering shape, having a stepped cover with a mother-of-pearl finial and a spreading foot. They are decorated with engraved figures of mermaids. The pieces were designed by REGINALD YORKE GLEADOWE, made by WAKELY & WHEELER LTD, and engraved by G. T. Friend, and were presented (to commemorate the Silver Jubilee, 1935, of George V) by the Goldsmiths' Company to the City of London. They are now at the Mansion House, London.

Jubilee Centrepiece. An elaborate CENTREPIECE (sometimes called an EPERGNE) intended to represent 'Britannia's Realm'. It has a tall central column formed by a silver-mounted crystal ball surmounted by a twisting female figure whose serpentine tail is set with blue-green mother-of-pearl; at the top is a bowl supporting a standing figure depicting Britannia. Extending from each side is a large bowl terminating in the figure of a flying dragon (a Chinese symbol of the Emperor); between the dragons there are two black metal standing figures, one representing Queen Victoria holding a sceptre and an orb, and the other St George holding the head of the slain dragon. On the ebony plinth (square with indented corners) are silver plaques engraved, respectively, '1837', '1887', 'Victoria Queen Empress', and one recording the piece as having been presented to Victoria by 'The Officers of her combined Military forces' to commemorate the 50th anniversary of her accession. The piece was designed by Sir Alfred Gilbert (1854–1934) and made by him and his assistants in 1887, later gilded (but now worn off) except the two standing figures. The piece is in the Royal Collection, and is now on loan by Her Majesty the Queen to the Victoria and Albert Museum, London.

Jubilee Cup. A silver-gilt TWO-HANDLED CUP having a cylindrical bowl resting on a stemmed foot, two vertical dolphin handles, and a cover surmounted by a finial in the form of a standing figure of Queen Victoria. On the bowl are four medallions of India, Canada, Australia, and Africa. It was made by E., J. & W. Barnard, 1886, and bears the arms of Sir Reginald Hanson, Lord Mayor of London, who donated it to the City of London to commemorate the Golden Jubilee of Queen Victoria in 1887. It is now at the Mansion House, London.

Judgment of Solomon Sconces. Six silver-gilt two-branch WALL-SCONCES (originally there were eight), each having on the shield-shaped reflector plate an embossed medallion depicting 'The Judgment of Solomon' and at the top a Royal crown above the cipher of William and Mary, 1689–94, and on the shoulders two Royal crowns (all the crowns being of a later date). Each piece has, on its wide embossed rim, emblematic motifs of a rose, a thistle, an Irish harp, and a fleur de lis. The set is now attributed to CHARLES SHELLEY, London. The pieces were restored in 1812 by RUNDELL, BRIDGE & RUNDELL, and new sockets were made by PAUL STORR in 1816. The six sconces are in the Royal Collection at Windsor Castle.

jug. A vessel for holding and pouring a liquid. Jugs have been made in many forms, styles, and sizes, but generally the shape is globular, baluster-shaped, cylindrical, ovoid or helmet-shaped. Most examples have a vertical loop or scroll handle. Some have a wide mouth with a BEAK or a pouring lip, and some, of baluster shape, have a tall narrow neck and a pouring lip. Those having a hinged lid and a thumbpiece are usually drinking vessels (preferably termed a TANKARD or a MUG), but small uncovered jugs are usually a MILK-JUG or a CREAM-JUG. Some glass jugs have silver MOUNTS; *see* CLARET-JUG. Jugs may be decorated simply or ornately, some elaborately with cast applied figures. In the United States, a jug is usually called a 'pitcher'. *See* COVERED JUG; BEER-JUG; WINE-JUG; COFFEE-JUG; HOT-WATER JUG; HELMET JUG; STONEWARE JUG; TIGERWARE JUG; EWER; FLAGON.

julep-cup. A type of BEAKER, so called in the United States, and mainly in Kentucky, used for drinking a mint julep; generally made in sets, such cups are cylindrical, usually undecorated, but sometimes with a band encircling the rim and another around the base.

Justice Centrepiece. A two-part COLONNADE CENTREPIECE consisting of (1) a mirrored hexagonal PLATEAU having along the rim a low GALLERY pierced with PALES, and resting on six CLAW-AND-BALL FEET; and (2) an oval temple-like structure supported by four tall legs upon which rests a galleried oval platform from which extend upward six columns supporting a fluted dome with a finial in the form of a standing winged male figure, said to depict Fame, sounding a trumpet; on the platform there is a square plinth supporting a figure of Justice. It was made by WILLIAM PITTS I and JOSEPH PREEDY, 1795–6, and was the gift of an anonymous donor to be used at the York assizes and mayoral banquets. It is now owned by the York City Council, and is exhibited at the Castle Museum, York.

An earlier comparable centrepiece, made by the same silversmiths, 1794, was presented in that year to the Mercers' Company, London, and was sold at Christie's, London, on 22 May 1974. It had an oval plateau with scroll feet, no figure on the platform, a different figure on the finial, and two plaques with the crest of the Mercers' Company, but was basically of similar form.

K

Kandler, Charles (Frederick) (fl. 1727–50). A highly regarded London silversmith, having no record of apprenticeship or freedom, whose identity has not been established; nor have some of the marks attributed to him been positively confirmed as his, rather than those of another silversmith of the same name. It has been suggested that he may have been related to Johann Joachim Kändler (fl. 1731–74), the renowned Meissen porcelain modeller. He probably came in 1726 from Germany to London, where he formed a partnership with James Murray (d. c. 1730), entering two joint marks in 1727, with address in St Martin's Lane; by 1735 he had moved to work alone in St James's, Westminster, where he was possibly joined by a nephew (or cousin), also named Charles Frederick Kandler, who had come from Germany. A mark for Charles Frederick Kandler alone was entered in 1735. Several apprentices are recorded with the master's name variously shown as: Charles (two in 1735); Charles Frederick (1743); and Frederick (1748 and 1760). It has been suggested by Norman M. Penzer that the last two names, and the 1735 mark, are those of the nephew, Charles Frederick Kandler, who may have dropped his first name in order to be distinguished from Charles Kandler.

Charles Kandler made few, but important and highly decorated, pieces (mainly in ROCOCO STYLE), some of which are in the Hermitage, Leningrad; Frederick was more prolific. *See*, for pieces made by Charles, JERNINGHAM-KANDLER WINE COOLER; KANDLER MIRROR; KANDLER TEA-KETTLE.

Another Charles Kandler (fl. 1778–93), with no record of apprenticeship or freedom, but with address at 100 Jermyn St, London, entered a mark 'CK' in 1778; Dr Penzer has suggested that he may have been a son of Frederick, but nothing definite is known of him.

Kandler Mirror. A MIRROR in a cast silver-gilt frame formed by connected scrolls in late BAROQUE STYLE. It rests on four scroll feet decorated with heads of Mercury and Apollo in low-relief and is surmounted by four eagles holding in their beaks branches with leaves and berries. It is decorated with many applied branches of non-gilded silver upon which are many insects, and in the middle of the rim are two frogs and a lizard; the flowers and insects are naturalistically coloured. At the top there is a Russian Imperial Eagle surmounted by a crown. The piece was made by CHARLES KANDLER; the date letter is illegible, but the piece bears the London Assay Office hallmark of 1697–1719. The piece is said to have belonged to Tsar Peter III of Russia (1728–62), having come from the palace of Oranienbaum, his residence in the 18th century. It is now in the Hermitage Museum, Leningrad. *See* Paul Derwis, 'Some English Silver Plate at the Hermitage' in *Burlington Magazine*, July 1935, p. 35.

Kandler Tea Kettle. A TEA-KETTLE WITH STAND, extravagantly decorated with EMBOSSING and cast figures in-the-round, made by CHARLES KANDLER, c. 1735. The kettle is of oblate spherical form, having a BAIL HANDLE and a SPOUT. The handle has two arms in the form of female figures facing outward, their upraised arms holding the wicker-covered silver grip. The spout is the torso of a Siren blowing a horn (the mouth of the kettle). The cover is flush with the top of the kettle and has a figure finial. The kettle rests on a circular STAND supported by three figures of mermen on a rocky base, and the stand rests on a triangular TRAY with moulded rim and three claw feet. The kettle and stand are connected by two chains so that they may be lifted together.

Kandler Tea Kettle. Tea-kettle with stand, Charles Kandler, London, c. 1735. H. 33·5 cm. Victoria and Albert Museum, London.

Kent Epergne. Epergne candelabrum (without base-plate, dishes, and casters), designed by William Kent and made by George Wickes, London, 1745-6. Royal Collection; reproduced by gracious permission of Her Majesty the Queen.

Kiddush Cup. Goblet with Hebrew inscriptions, Pierre Gillois, London, 1769. H. 19 cm. Jewish Museum, London (photo courtesy, Warburg Institute, University of London).

Kean Testimonial. A group of nine pieces of silverware presented in 1862 to the English actor, Charles John Kean (1811-68), by Fellows at Eton College and by other friends and admirers as a tribute to his acting. The principal-piece is a vase of oxidized parcel-gilt silver, having on the body figures in low relief depicting Kean and his wife (Ellen Tree) in various Shakespearean roles. On the neck are medallion portraits of Elizabeth I and Queen Victoria, and on the foot are the elfin attendants of Queen Mab supporting medallions with portraits of Mr and Mrs Kean. On the PLINTH are depicted three views of Eton College, together with a plaque bearing an inscription. The group, designed and executed by HENRY HUGH ARMSTEAD for HUNT & ROSKELL, were shown in the London International Exhibition of 1862. The vase is illustrated in J. B. Waring, *Masterpieces of Industrial Art* (1863), vol. II, pl. 129.

Keith Chalice. A silver-gilt CHALICE with pierced, engraved, and applied decoration, set with gemstones; it has a TRUMPET FOOT resting on an eight-lobed base, and the short stem has a large knop. On the underside there is an inscription 'Given by E. M. Fox for use of the Chapel of the House of Mercy, Clewer, June 1856'. It was designed by William Butterfield for the Ecclesiological Society, and made by John Keith, London, 1850; it was shown at the Great Exhibition of 1851, and is now in the Victoria and Albert Museum, London.

Kemble Cup. An imposing STANDING CUP designed by JOHN FLAXMAN II, modelled by his pupil EDWARD HODGES BAILY, and executed by RUNDELL, BRIDGE & RUNDELL. It was presented to the actor John Philip Kemble (1757-1823) upon his retirement in 1817.

Ken Brazier. A BRAZIER (termed by the owner a CHAFING DISH) of typical form, with a bowl resting on three feet and having a long horizontal handle. It was made in London, 1686-7, and is engraved with the arms of Thomas Ken, Bishop of Bath and Wells, 1685-90, and a Fellow of Winchester College, and was donated to the college by a descendant of Rev. John Jenkyns, Vicar of Frome, Somerset, who had received it from Ken; it is still owned by Winchester College.

Kent, William (1685-1748). An English architect, painter, landscape gardener, and furniture designer, who also designed silverware, especially articles intended for the homes that he planned. Fourteen of his designs for silverware are shown in a book by John Vardy (1744). *See* J. F. Hayward, 'Silver made from designs of William Kent' in *The Connoisseur*, June 1970, p. 106; Charles C. Oman, 'Silver Designs by William Kent' in *Apollo*, January 1972, p. 22. *See* KENT EPERGNE; PELHAM CUP.

Kent Epergne. A large EPERGNE-CANDELABRUM designed by WILLIAM KENT and made originally by GEORGE WICKES in 1745-6 as part of the FREDERICK, PRINCE OF WALES, SERVICE. It is a two-tiered piece with eight legs, standing on a base-plate and having at the top an openwork canopy. Surmounting the canopy now are the Prince of Wales's feathers which were substituted, when the piece was made, for the small tureen shown in the original design. The piece now includes six candle sockets, four large dishes, four small dishes, and four casters. Various alterations were made to the original piece: in 1829 by RUNDELL, BRIDGE & RUNDELL, by substituting on the base-plate four large scroll feet for eight small ball feet, and by adding at the ends of the base-plate figures of a lion and a unicorn, and at each side a Triton blowing a conch shell; and in 1847 by GARRARD & CO., by adding swags between the feet of the base-plate and adding the detachable candle sockets. On the bottom of the base-plate are the engraved arms of Frederick as Prince of Wales. The piece is now in the Royal Collection.

Kentucky silverware. Articles of silverware made in Kentucky, especially in the early and middle decades of the 19th century, until faced with Eastern competition in the 1860s. The early ware consisted mainly of articles made of COIN SILVER, particularly pitchers (JUGS), and the popular JULEP-CUPS. The first recorded silversmith was John Fitch, *c.* 1780, but the best known was Asa Blanchard, *c.* 1808-38. Others included Eli Garner, Daniel Franklin Winchester, John G. Schwing, and John Kitts. Silverware was made mainly in Louisville, Frankfort, and Lexington, and featured principally trophies made for horse-racing and county fairs, as well as objects for domestic use. *See* Noble W. and Lucie F. Hiatt, *The Silversmiths of Kentucky, 1785-1850* (1954); Lockwood Barr, 'Kentucky Silver and its Makers' in *Antiques*, July 1945, p. 25; William Barrow Floyd, 'Kentucky Coin-silver Pitchers' in *Antiques*, March 1974, p. 576; Henry H. Harned, 'Ante-bellum Kentucky Silver' in *Antiques*, April 1974, p. 818.

kettle. A large flat-bottomed utensil employed for heating liquids, having a SPOUT, a BAIL HANDLE, and a COVER. Kettles occur in many shapes and styles: they may be globular, pear-shaped, oblate, bullet-shaped, baluster-shaped or melon-shaped; they are usually of circular section, but some are polygonal. The handle is either fixed or swivelling, and is all metal or consists of two metal arms connected at the top by a wooden, ivory, ceramic or wicker-covered hand-grip. The spout is in various styles, some being a BEAK SPOUT and others having applied decoration; some have a SPOUT FLAP or a SPOUT CAP. Some kettles rest on a STAND having a heating device for keeping the contents warm. *See* TEA-KETTLE; TEA-KETTLE WITH STAND; PUNCH-POT; RUM-KETTLE.

kettle-drum. A type of percussion instrument in the form of a hemispherical drum; although such drums are usually made of brass or copper, examples have been made of silver, these being intended for use on state occasions. They include a set made in 1804 by P., A. and W. Bateman (*see* BATEMAN) and presented by George III to the Household Cavalry, and a pair presented by William IV to the Life Guards and still used on ceremonial occasions. *See* REGIMENTAL SILVERWARE.

key-fret border. A type of border pattern in the form of one straight line (sometimes two lines intertwined) turning at right-angles in a continuous, repetitive labyrinthine design suggestive of the wards of a key. It is found on some ware in the NEO-CLASSICAL STYLE or ADAM STYLE. It is derived from Greek architecture, *c.*1000–700 BC. Sometimes called merely 'fret'; also called 'Greek-fret border' and 'meander border'.

keyhole pattern. A type of pattern of pierced work found on the flat horizontal handle of some PORRINGERS, having at the terminal an aperture suggestive of the form of a keyhole with, usually, four to ten other apertures. It superseded, *c.*1730, the so-called 'geometric pattern' which included apertures of various shapes, some open at the sides.

Kiddush cup. A GOBLET used for drinking wine in Jewish religious ceremonies, on special occasions such as a wedding or in the benediction before the evening meal preceding each Sabbath or a holy festival. An English example, 1832, is an exact copy of a Dutch prototype of *c.*1730; it was probably ordered by Sir Moses Montefiore (1784–1885) when he had his own private synagogue built in the grounds of his London home. Ordinarily, there is no special form for such cups, and any type of WINE-CUP may be used, but usually one with some engraved Hebrew inscription. *See* JEWISH RITUAL SILVERWARE.

Kidney Cup. Silver gilt, William Kidney, London, 1740. H. 36·2 cm. Goldsmiths' Company, London.

Kidney Cup. A silver-gilt TWO-HANDLED CUP having an inverted-bell-shaped bowl with decoration of an embossed and chased ROCOCO STYLE heraldic cartouche on each side supported by a satyr and a running ass against a background of wheat-sheaves, aquatic foliage, and shells. Each handle is in the form of a TERM, one male, holding a bowl and a bunch of grapes, the other a Bacchante holding a sickle; the handles are attached, top and bottom, to the body by animal masks. The band encircling the base is decorated with satyr masks and shells. The low-domed cover has a finial surmounted by a bust of Silenus. The piece was made by William Kidney, London, 1740.

Kimpton Bowl. A silver-gilt BOWL, *c.*1480, of hemispherical shape, resting on a wide stem supported by a spreading base. It is undecorated except for a band of square piercing encircling the base. It was used as a CHALICE at Kimpton Church, Hampshire, until acquired in 1931 by the Victoria and Albert Museum, London.

King John's Cup. A silver-gilt STANDING CUP, *c.* 1325, the oldest-known surviving piece of English secular medieval plate, owned since before 1548 by King's Lynn, Norfolk (hence sometimes called the 'King's Lynn Cup' or the 'Lynn Cup'). Its circular base has a spreading flat extension with a curved pentagonal edge. The cup is supported by a knopped Gothic column formed by five attached pillars. The bowl is of inverted bell shape and, having a BAYONET JOINT, is detachable for use as a separate cup. The flat cover has an edge of CRESTING and a high pointed finial (a replacement). The cup, base, cover, and knop are all divided by foliate straps with relief ornaments into five panels, each decorated with CHAMPLEVÉ enamelling as the ground for applied figures of courtiers (one male and one female), one above the other, of engraved and enamelled silver on a blue and green field with stars, together with foliate decoration in colours. On the bottom of the base there are four inscriptions that refer to repairing and re-enamelling from 1692 to 1782. It is not known why the cup has been called since 1548 the 'King

Kimpton Bowl. Silver gilt, *c.* 1480. H. 10·4 cm. Victoria and Albert Museum, London.

King John's Cup. Silver gilt, with enamelled decoration, *c.* 1325. H. 37 cm. Detail of foot. King's Lynn Museum and Art Gallery.

John's Cup'; one theory, deemed by Norman M. Penzer to be the most reasonable explanation, is that it was donated to the town for use at annual festivals to celebrate privileges granted to the town in the 13th century by King John, 1199-1216, its patron, the donor possibly having been a wealthy inhabitant, Robert Braunch, Mayor of Lynn in 1350 and 1360. The cup weighs 76 oz. 4½ drams, not 40 oz. as misstated in some early writings. *See* Norman M. Penzer, 'The King's Lynn Cup' in *The Connoisseur*, September 1946, p.12, and December 1946, p.79; Herbert Maryon, 'The King John Cup at King's Lynn' in *The Connoisseur*, May 1953, p.88.

King's mark. The same as the LEOPARD'S HEAD HALLMARK.

King's pattern. A pattern for the handle of FLATWARE and CUTLERY which is fiddle-shaped with scrolled and threaded edges, having at the end (on both sides) a scallop-shell and along the stem a pair of ANTHEMION motifs in relief. The pattern, developed in the REGENCY STYLE, is more massive than the comparable QUEEN'S PATTERN. A rare variant form is called the King's Husk pattern. *See* HOURGLASS SPOON.

Kirk Stieff Co. The leading firm of silversmiths in Baltimore, Maryland, and the oldest such firm with a continuous history in the United States. The present company was formed in 1979, when the Stieff Company acquired Samuel Kirk & Sons, Inc. The latter was founded by Samuel Kirk (1793-1872), who was born in Doylestown, Pennsylvania, served his apprenticeship in Philadelphia, and in 1815 opened his own silversmith shop in Baltimore, with John Smith as partner until 1821. In 1846 Kirk's son, Henry Child Kirk, became a partner, the firm's name becoming S.Kirk & Son. Two other sons joined the firm in 1861, and thereafter minor changes in the name were made. The firm's work featured REPOUSSÉ decoration (which it introduced in the United States before 1822) but it also made ware in NEO-CLASSICAL STYLE and with CHINOISERIE motifs. The Stieff Company was founded in Baltimore in 1892 by Charles Stieff, and the present company is controlled by the third and fourth generations of Stieffs. The Company does a nationwide business, including making authentic reproductions of museum silverware. *See* Louise Durbin, 'Samuel Kirk, 19th-century silversmith' in *Antiques*, December 1968, p.868.

kitchen pepper-pot. A type of CASTER that is of simple undecorated form, or sparsely decorated, and is usually cylindrical (but sometimes octagonal, sloping inward toward the top), with a flat base and characterized by having a vertical SCROLL HANDLE and a low-domed cover with large pierced holes. The cover is either a SCREW COVER, a SLIP-ON COVER (liable to fall off during sprinkling) or a BAYONET COVER (for secure fastening). Such pieces were made for sprinkling coarse ground black pepper or spices. Some were made as pairs (for spice and pepper – the covers being marked respectively 'S' and 'P'); in order that the covers would have similar decorative piercing with holes of the same size externally, some pots intended for pepper were fitted with a small-hole liner under the cover. These casters (sometimes called a 'spice dredger') succeeded the BELL SALT with its pierced ball-shaped finial.

Kirk Stieff Co. Cream-jug with *repoussé* decoration, Samuel Kirk & Sons, Inc., Baltimore, Md, 1828. Kirk Museum Silver Collection.

As such pieces are of small size and usually well made and sometimes decorated, it has been said that they were more likely for dinner-table use rather than for kitchens. *See* G. Bernard Hughes, 'Silver Spice Dredgers' in *Country Life*, 28 September 1951, p. 974. *See* PEPPER CASTER.

kitchen silverware. Various articles for use in the kitchen, hence seldom made of silver except occasionally for wealthy users. Examples include the CORER, LARDING NEEDLE, PASTRY CUTTER, SKEWER, KITCHEN PEPPER-POT, and SKILLET.

Knesworth Chandelier. A CHANDELIER designed in ROCOCO STYLE, having a baluster form with twelve scroll arms for candle SOCKETS, the arms, sockets and nozzles being chased with foliage and scrollwork. The upper part is entwined by three large dolphins and chased with bulrushes. Above is a vase surmounted by a large gilt pine-cone masking the suspension hook. It was donated to the Fishmongers' Company, London, in 1752 by Sir Thomas Knesworth, and it bears the arms of the Company and of the donor, with a donative inscription. It bears the mark of William Alexander, 1752, but was made by his workman, William Gould, a maker of candlesticks.

knife. An implement for carving or cutting food, consisting of a straight handle (haft) attached to a thin straight blade of sharp-edged steel on some types, but of silver or other hard metal on ordinary table knives. Knives have been made in many styles and sizes, with variations in the form and style of the handle, but table knives (originally made in pairs, one to cut, the other to convey food to the mouth) are now made usually in sets decorated EN SUITE to conform to the other pieces of the FLATWARE. Some types of handle (e.g., a PISTOL HANDLE) are made of thin metal and are hollow, filled with resin or shellac. Examples of knives made with silver handles include the DINNER KNIFE, ENTRÉE KNIFE, FISH KNIFE, STEAK KNIFE, BUTTER SPREADER, FRUIT KNIFE, CHEESE KNIFE, and CARVING KNIFE. Other types of knife include the paper knife (letter opener) and WEDDING KNIFE.

Table knives for individual use are said to have been introduced in the 14th century. The blade, originally pointed to spear food, became rounded in the late 15th century, except that some steak knives, carving knives, and fruit knives are still pointed, and some are serrated. Some early knives with a steel blade and a non-metal haft (e.g., of ivory or porcelain) have a silver FERRULE to connect them, and also a silver finial at the terminal of the haft. *See* G. Bernard Hughes, 'Old English Table Knives and Forks' in *Country Life*, 17 February 1950, p. 450. *See* COMMUNION-BREAD KNIFE.

knife and fork handles. Silver HANDLES into which are inserted the steel or silver knife blade or fork. Such handles, usually made EN SUITE, have been made in many shapes and styles of decoration, such as a PISTOL HANDLE.

knife-box. A sideboard receptacle for holding a set of DINNER KNIVES (usually twelve) and sometimes DINNER FORKS, having its interior fitted with partitions for the individual knives (and forks) holding them in an upright position (blades down) and apart from each other so as to protect the sharp blades. The box is usually square (sometimes semicircular) with a BOMBÉ front and has a lid hinged on the rear side and sloping downward toward the lower front. Such boxes were usually made of wood, sometimes covered with shagreen and lined with plush or velvet, and having silver (or SHEFFIELD PLATE) handles and decorative mounts (including, sometimes on fine examples, silver edging along the top of the partitions); but one example made entirely of silver is known, the work of Peter and Ann Bateman (*see* BATEMAN), 1797. Some examples have spaces also for several other articles of FLATWARE. Sometimes called a 'cutlery-box'. *See* Peer Philip, 'Knife Boxes' in *Collector's Guide*, July 1983, p. 54. *See* CUTLERY-URN.

knife-rest. A small, low utensil for supporting the blade of a KNIFE at the dinner table, sometimes made as part of a SERVICE. They were made mainly in two forms: (1) a short rod joining the centre of two X-shaped ends that acted as supports for the piece; and (2) two triangular ends joined at each angle by parallel rods. Some examples were made in fantasy style, the ends being in the form of figures of children, animals, etc.

knop. (1) The same as a FINIAL. (2) A protruding ornament, usually globular but of various shapes and styles of decoration, occurring midway on the stem of a CHALICE, CANDLESTICK, STANDING CUP, etc.; sometimes called a 'knot'.

(k)nurling. A decorative pattern in the form of a series of adjacent, oblong protuberances, singly or in pairs of different widths, such as made by

kitchen pepper-pot. Caster, Johannes Roseboom, New York, c. 1760–70. Yale University Art Gallery (Mabel Brady Garvan Collection), New Haven, Conn.

knife-box. Wood with Sheffield plate fittings, holding set of twelve knives and forks, Edward Fox, Sheffield, c. 1780. H. 28 cm. City Museum, Sheffield.

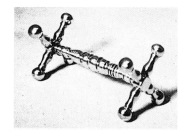

knife-rest (1). X-shaped ends, London, 1930. L. 7·5 cm. The Mansion House, London.

grooves crossing a convex moulding at varying intervals and comparable to oblong beading on a BEAD-AND REEL-PATTERN. It is sometimes used on silverware as an edging, and is related to, but differs from, GADROONING.

krater vase. A type of receptacle, made of silver in the form of a Greek pottery krater of the calyx type, to be used as a WINE COOLER. Such pieces have a thistle-shaped bowl with an everted rim and a spreading base, and two horizontal uplifted, loop handles extending from the lower part of the bowl. A silver-gilt pair, decorated with Bacchante figures, were made as wine coolers by PAUL STORR, 1810, and another single example was made by Henry Harland, of New Orleans, Louisiana, *c.* 1830. Some receptacles, made as wine coolers and similar in form to the WARWICK VASE, are comparable but are wider and lower. *See* LIEVEN CUP; THEOCRITUS CUPS; GREEK-VASE SILVERWARE.

L

lace-back spoon. A type of SPOON having on the back of the bowl relief decoration in the form of patterns suggestive of needlework or scrolling designs such as vine-leaf motifs. *See* PICTURE-BACK SPOON; TRIFID SPOON.

Lacock Cup. A parcel-gilt STANDING CUP having a hemispherical bowl, a spreading foot, and a tall tapering conical cover topped with a ball finial. It was probably originally a late-medieval secular cup, but after the Reformation was adapted as a COMMUNION CUP. It has, encircling the base, the top of the stem, and the rim of the bowl, gilt CRESTING of Gothic foliage and corded ribs. It has no marks, but has been attributed to *c.* 1450. It is owned by the parish church of Lacock, Wiltshire, but has been on loan at the British Museum, London. A somewhat similar piece, *c.* 1440, is the Founder's Cup at Christ's College, Cambridge, but its bowl is less rounded and it is decorated with bands of foliage.

ladle. A type of SPOON, having a deep cup-like bowl and a long handle, used for transferring a liquid from one receptacle to another. The length and angle of the handle and the size and shape of the bowl vary, depending on the intended use of the piece. Examples such as a SOUP LADLE or SAUCE LADLE were often made EN SUITE with a TUREEN or a SAUCE-BOAT, and some form part of a DINNER SERVICE. Some have a long straight handle of turned wood or twisted whalebone, others have a silver handle, either tubular or, more often, flat and gently curved. The bowl is circular, oval or ovoid; some have a single pouring lip on one side, while others have a lip on both sides. Some have on the handle a small hook for suspension from the side of a receptacle. Some ladles were made from melted-down silver coins, and occasionally have a coin set into the bowl. *See* PUNCH LADLE; TODDY LADLE; CREAM LADLE; SUGAR LADLE.

Lambert Apostle Spoons. A complete set of thirteen silver-gilt APOSTLE SPOONS, each with original gilding and bearing the maker's mark 'BY' (attributed to Benjamin Yates) and the London marks for 1626-7. The figures appear to have been cast from six different models, with ten of the attributes cast separately. On the head of each figure is a circular horizontal nimbus on which is depicted a dove (the Holy Spirit), and on the back of the bowl of each spoon are the pricked initials, 'P' over 'IE', of the original owner. The set was given in 1887 to the Goldsmiths' Company, London, by George Lambert, its Prime Warden in that year.

lambrequin. A decorative pattern in the form of an ornamental pendent drapery, derived from the mantle or drapery around a COAT OF ARMS. The form was developed on some French faience into a BAROQUE STYLE scalloped border pattern of pendent drapery, lacework, leaves, and scrollwork, usually with alternate large and small motifs. The simple lambrequin is found as decoration on some English silver TWO-HANDLED CUPS, sometimes as a 'reversed lambrequin', with the direction reversed. The same as MANTLING.

Lamerie, Paul de (1688-1751). The most highly reputed London silversmith of his time, producing much ware in gradually changing styles. He was born in Holland, brought by his Huguenot parents (named 'de la Marie') to

Lacock Cup. Parcel gilt, London, *c.* 1450(?). H. 35 cm. Lacock parish church, Wiltshire (photo courtesy, British Museum, London).

London in 1689, and was apprenticed in 1703 to PIERRE PLATEL and freed in 1713, with address at Windmill St, near Haymarket, and then registered his first mark. In 1733 he registered a new mark when he changed to using STERLING SILVER after having voluntarily continued to use BRITANNIA SILVER from 1697. In 1738 he moved to Gerrard St and in 1739 registered his third mark, when required by law to register a mark with different characters. His early work was in restrained QUEEN ANNE STYLE and HUGUENOT STYLE, but by the 1730s he had become the leading exponent of the ROCOCO STYLE, especially in large and extravagant pieces, such as several WINE COOLERS, EWERS, BASKETS, and TWO-HANDLED CUPS, while also making many articles of domestic ware of good design and craftsmanship. Some of his work was made from designs by WILLIAM THEED I. He was appointed Goldsmith to the King in 1716, and made many pieces for the Russian Imperial Court, and also for the Rt. Hon. George Treby, M.P. By the 1740s his work was more sparsely decorated. Many of his original invoices survive. Having no sons or colleagues to succeed him, he ordered his large stock to be sold at auction, indicating that he had worked not only on commission but also for stock, hence making much ware in conservative forms, decorated mainly by outside engravers. *See* Philip A. S. Phillips, *Paul de Lamerie, A Study of his Life and Works* (1935).

lamp. A utensil for producing artificial light, originally by means of a burning wick in oil or by a candle. Some silver examples of oil lamps are made to stand on a flat surface, such as that resembling a Roman terracotta oil lamp or a table lamp, while others are for suspension by chains, such as a SANCTUARY LAMP or SABBATH LAMP. *See* OIL LAMP; ARGAND LAMP; HANUK(K)A(H) LAMP; MENORAH.

lamp-stand. A type of STAND, for a TEAPOT, TEA-KETTLE, TUREEN, etc., which supports a spirit lamp under the receptacle.

lanceolate. Lance-shaped like a lanceolate leaf, with a point at the apex and swelling on both sides toward the bottom, having there sometimes another point. The motif has been used, as vertical relief decoration, in a series encircling the lower part of the bowl and also the cover, alternating with SPOON-HANDLE STRAPS, of some TWO-HANDLED CUPS, such as those made by PIERRE PLATEL and Augustin(e) Courtauld II (*see* COURTAULD).

lantern. A portable or hanging enclosure for a light, usually with surrounding glass panels to protect the flame. One type has a metal frame of square or polygonal section holding four or more vertical panels, and with an interior candle socket or provision for some other source of light. An example is known made of SHEFFIELD PLATE, 1795, having four glass panels and a hinged door, with a flat base fitted with a candle socket; at the back there is a vertical loop handle and the air vent on top is partially covered by a leaf.

Laub- und Bandelwerk. *See* STRAPWORK.

launching silverware. Articles of silverware, of various types, e.g., a TANKARD, CANDLESTICK, etc., that were presented in the early 18th century to Master Shipwrights at the time of the launching of a British Naval vessel. Many such presentation pieces are known since 1708, and some examples are at the National Maritime Museum, Greenwich. The pieces were usually engraved with a device or an inscription and with the Royal Arms of Queen Anne, George I or George II, but rarely with the names of the recipients. *See* E. Alfred Jones, 'Some Builders of Ships for the Royal Navy and their Gifts of Plate, from 1708 to 1731' in *Burlington Magazine*, September 1920, p.130.

lay plate. The same as a PLACE PLATE; also called a 'service plate'.

Lazy Susan. A popular name for a rotating self-service server used on a sideboard or dining table, usually for a SUPPER SET, and being in the form of a wide shallow circular covered basin which could be filled with hot water to keep warm the contents of the receptacles placed on it. It has been made in various sizes, to accommodate different numbers of receptacles; one known silver-plated example supports three covered VEGETABLE-DISHES alternating with three SAUCE-BOATS, surrounding a central SOUP-TUREEN and having among these pieces six CASTERS.

leaf caddy spoon. A type of CADDY SPOON having its bowl in the form of a leaf, and an intertwined twisted handle, sometimes in the form of a tendril, terminating in a small loop. An example was made by PAUL STORR, *c.*1820, in the form of a strawberry leaf. Other examples are in the form of a vine leaf or tea leaf.

Lee Cup. Silver gilt, London, 1590. H. 40 cm. City of Portsmouth, Hampshire.

Leigh Cup (1). Silver gilt with enamelled decoration, London, 1499–1500(?). H. 41 cm. Mercers' Company, London.

lekane vase. Vase with engraved decoration of Roman warriors, Louisa Courtauld and George Cowles, London, 1771. Courtesy, Courtaulds plc, London.

Leake Salt. A silver-gilt COVERED STANDING SALT, made by Francis Leake, 1660, that stands on a spreading foot and has a waisted body topped by a bowl (for the salt), from the rim of which project three vertical scrolled BRACKETS supporting a cover upon which is a figure of St George. The entire surface is decorated with EMBOSSING and CHASING. It is now in the Jewel House at the Tower of London.

leather objects. Articles made of leather and having silver MOUNTS, such as a FLASK, TANKARD, JUG or POWDER-HORN. *See* BLACKJACK; MOUNTED OBJECTS.

Lee Cup. A silver-gilt STANDING CUP having a thistle-shaped bowl resting on a knopped stem and a domed base. The low-domed cover has a vase-shaped finial surmounted by a standing female figure; its rim bears the inscription 'AMICORUM BENEFICIA NON PERIBUNT' (The good deeds of friends shall not perish). The bowl is engraved with floral sprays surrounding three roundels engraved, respectively, with: (1) the arms of Portsmouth; (2) the coat of arms of the Merchant Taylors' Company, surrounded by an inscription 'THE GYFTE OF ROBERT LEE OF LONDON, MARCHANT TAYLER'; and (3) Lee's monogram surrounded by the inscription 'TO THE TOVNE OF PORTESMOVTH'. The cup bears the maker's mark 'PW/IN' and the London hallmark for 1590. The cup was given by Lee as Mayor of Portsmouth and has been used by successive mayors. *See* DUCIE CUP.

Leigh Cup. (1) A silver-gilt STANDING CUP reputed to be the second earliest HANAP (covered cup) known with an English hallmark; it bears a maker's mark and the date mark for 1499–1500(?). The circular base rests on three small bottle-shaped (*see* PILGRIM FLASK) feet. The stem, bowl (of inverted bell shape), and cover are decorated with raised cross-bands, and within the diamond-shaped spaces formed by the bands are alternately relief replicas of flagons and busts of maidens (being the badges of the Worshipful Company of Mercers). The cup was bequeathed to the Company in 1571 by Sir Thomas Leigh. On the cover there is a hexagonal boss with panels bearing enamelled coats of arms; it is surmounted by a figure of a seated maiden with, reposing on her lap, a unicorn with the word 'DESYR' engraved on its side. Some of the decoration, including the bands, the busts, and the flagons, has been said to have been added after 1499 but before 1571. Encircling the bowl and cover are blue enamelled bands bearing in gold letters the couplet 'TO ELECT THE MASTER OF THE MERCERIE, HITHER AM I SENT / AND BY SIR THOMAS LEIGH FOR THE SAME ENTENT', with busts of maidens between the words. The cup is now used only at the election of a new Master of the Mercers' Company. It is traditionally said to have belonged to the Hospital of St Thomas of Acon, which stood on the site of the present Mercers' Hall. There are three copies of it in existence, one in the Victoria and Albert Museum, London, one at the Hall of the Grocers' Company, London, and one in a Berlin museum.

(2) A TWO-HANDLED CUP having a tall slender vase-shaped body and a tall neck, with two lateral vertical handles extending from the shoulder to above the rim and curving downward to the bottom of the bowl. It was made by Hester Bateman (*see* BATEMAN) in 1784. It was donated by Theophilus Leigh in 1785 to Balliol College, Oxford, where he had been Master.

Leinster Service. An important DINNER SERVICE made by GEORGE WICKES, London, from 1745 to 1747 for James Fitzgerald, Earl of Kildare (created Duke of Leinster in 1766). It consists of 170 surviving pieces, including dishes, plates, fish plates (mazarines), waiters, salts, scallop shells, bread baskets, dish ring, and epergne with plateau. The common motif is a serpentine threaded border bound with STRAPWORK and having shells at intervals. It is owned by Mohammed Mahdi Al-Tajir, the Ambassador of the United Arab Emirates in London, who has in recent years acquired much of the important silverware sold at auction there. *See* Elaine Barr, *George Wickes* (1980), p. 197. *See* THANET SERVICE.

lekane vase. A type of VASE in the form of a lekane (a so-called Greek pottery vase made in southern Italy), having an ovoid body resting on a stemmed base and two upright loop handles extending above the rim and having a cover with a high finial. An example, made by Louisa Courtauld (*see* COURTAULD) and George Cowles, 1771, is decorated with engraved figures of Roman warriors in an encircling landscape, and with GADROONING, ACANTHUS leaves, and KEY-FRET BORDER. *See* GREEK-VASE SILVERWARE.

Lennard Cup. A STANDING CUP that is composed of a Chinese greenish-blue celadon porcelain bowl set in silver-gilt MOUNTS bearing a maker's mark 'RF' conjoined (recently attributed to Roger Flynt) and the London date mark for 1569–70; the bowl dates from the Jia Jing (Chia Ching) period, 1522–66, and is one of the earliest known examples of a Chinese ceramic object with mounts bearing an English hallmark. The bowl is hemispherical and is decorated on the exterior with a faintly incised pattern of chrysanthemum scrolls on a greenish-blue ground and on the interior with an incised medallion depicting a hare. The silver-gilt mounts include a wide low stem on a domed foot, a deep everted mouth rim engraved with a frieze depicting animals and having along its bottom an inverted CRESTING (but without vertical straps connecting it to the stem), and a low-domed cover with embossed decoration and a small finial. The piece is named after its former owner, Samuel Lennard (1553–1618), and was sold in 1932 at Sotheby's, London, by Sir Stephen Lennard, Bt, to Percival David; it is now in the Percival David Foundation of Chinese Art, London University. *See* CELADON OBJECTS.

Leopard Pot. One of a pair of massive silver-gilt LIVERY POTS, each in the form of a leopard sejant (sitting) holding a shield and having a detachable head. Although designed as flagons, their size – 91·5 cm high – indicates that they were meant for show only. The pair, made in 1601, were sold in 1627 from the Jewel House of Elizabeth I to Peter the Great, and are now in the Kremlin, Moscow. A pair of copies made by ELECTROFORMING are in the Victoria and Albert Museum, London.

Leopard's Head Hallmark. The English HALLMARK (taken from the Royal Arms) for silver (and gold), established by Edward I in 1300 and directed to be applied by the 'gardiens of the Craft' of London goldsmiths (later the successive Wardens of the Goldsmiths' Company) to articles meeting the established standards of quality. Later the mark was referred to as the 'King's (Queen's) mark'. In 1544 the LION PASSANT GUARDANT HALLMARK was adopted as the STANDARD HALLMARK for silver, and the Leopard's Head Hallmark became, and has since (except during the 1697–1720 period of BRITANNIA SILVER) been, the ASSAY OFFICE HALLMARK of the London Assay Office. The head, full face, is within a shield; the shape of the shield has varied at different periods. The early leopard's head, from *c.* 1478, wore a beard and later a crown, but by 1821 both were eliminated and there was substituted a new-style full-face lion's head, although it continued to be called a 'leopard's head'.

Since the British Hallmarking Act of 1973, this mark is used as the London Assay Office Hallmark for all silver (and other metals) assayed there, including Britannia Silver. The Leopard's Head Mark was also used, together with the local mark, by some former provincial Assay Offices (Chester, Exeter, Newcastle, York).

Le Roux, Bartholomew (1668–1713). A Huguenot silversmith who emigrated to New York and who is best known for having made several massive two-handled PUNCH-BOWLS.

Le Sage. A family of Huguenot silversmiths working in London. John (Hugh) Le Sage, born probably in Alençon, France, emigrated to England and was apprenticed to Lewis Cuny in 1708; he entered his first mark in 1718, a second one in 1722, and his third and fourth marks in 1739, at various addresses, the last being Great Suffolk St, Charing Cross. He became Subordinate Goldsmith to the King. He is known as a prolific maker of MINIATURE SILVERWARE, but he also retailed many such articles made by others. Simon Le Sage, his elder son, was apprenticed to his father in 1742 and freed in 1755, registering two marks in 1754 from his father's address; he retired in 1761, having been Subordinate Goldsmith to the King. Augustin Le Sage (b. after 1718), the younger son, was freed by patrimony as a jeweller in 1782, having previously worked as a goldsmith at Great Suffolk St.

letter-finial spoon. A type of SPOON having on the front and reverse of the finial a capital letter. A rare example, London, 1494, has the gilt letters B and W on a matt ground.

letter-rack. A type of desk or table utensil with openwork partitions for holding upright several letters, sometimes having a central vertical handle for carrying. *See* BANNOCK-RACK; TOAST-RACK.

Lewis, Kensington (*c.*1790–1854). A London silversmith known principally as a prominent and very active retailer of silverware. Born Lewis Kensington Solomon, he changed his name in or before 1811. Before his partnership with his father, Samuel Solomon (d. 1822), was dissolved in 1821, he had achieved some notoriety by buying a cup, salver, and tankard at the executor's sale in May 1816 at Christie's, London, of the collection of the 11th Duke of Norfolk (d. 1815). In 1822 he opened his own retail shop at 22 St James's St, specializing in antique ware and in modern versions of such

Leopard's Head Hallmark.

Le Sage, John. Silver-gilt ewer with merman handles, London, 1725. H. 41·5 cm. Toledo Museum of Art, Toledo, Ohio (photo courtesy, Brand Inglis Ltd, London).

lighthouse caster. One of a pair, Robert Goode, London, *c.* 1690. H. 15·2 cm. Courtesy, Sotheby's, London.

style. Thanks to the patronage of the Duke of York, he prospered, and in 1825-6 opened another shop at 146 Regent St. He was the retailer of almost all the silverware made by EDWARD FARRELL from *c.* 1815 until their relationship ended in the mid-1830s. Upon the death of York in 1827, he closed the Regent St shop, auctioning its stock. He became associated in 1834-5 with Benjamin Preston at 41 Coppice Row, Clerkenwell. In 1838 he retired, disposed of the shop in St James's St, and moved to Oxford, engaging in property deals until he became insolvent in 1845. *See* John Culme, 'Kensington Lewis' in *The Connoisseur*, September 1975, p. 26.

Liberty Punch Bowl. *See* SONS OF LIBERTY BOWL.

Liberty silverware. Articles of silverware made for Liberty & Co., London, founded in 1875 by Arthur Lazenby Liberty, initially to dispose of a stock of Japanese ware. The silverware was in ART NOUVEAU STYLE, and was made for the company by outside suppliers, mainly William Hutton & Sons, Sheffield, and W. H. Haseler & Co., Birmingham. Liberty used many designers, among whom was BERNARD CUZNER, but in order to promote the name Liberty did not disclose their names; it registered its mark in 1894. The silver was sold under the trade name 'Cymric', being made by a company, jointly owned with W. H. Haseler & Co., which was dissolved in 1927. *See* CYMRIC SILVERWARE.

library set. A group of writing utensils for use at a desk, including usually an INK-POT, PEN-TRAY, POUNCE-POT, and sometimes a TAPERSTICK, often accompanied by a TRAY. Also called a 'desk set'.

lid. A covering for closing a BOX or the mouth of a MUG, TANKARD or other open-topped object, usually attached to the body of the piece by a metal hinge. *See* COVER.

Lieven Cup. A silver-gilt cup in the form of a Greek krater of the calyx type, having a cover with a finial in the form of the Royal crown. On the front of the cup is a relief scene depicting a girl playing pipes alongside a child, and on the back an inscription recording it as a gift from George IV to the Count and Countess de Lieven; the Count was Russian Ambassador to Britain, 1812-34, and his wife, Princess Dorothea (1785-1857), a Russian noblewoman. The cup stands on a square plinth having on two sides the Royal arms. It was made by PHILIP RUNDELL, 1821, and is now at the Mansion House, London. *See* GREEK-VASE SILVERWARE.

lighthouse caster. A type of CASTER of which the entire body and the cover are of cylindrical shape; the whole piece has straight vertical sides and rests on a slightly spreading base. Some examples have on the base and on the BAYONET COVER decoration of GADROONING, and the pierced patterned holes for sprinkling usually occur only on the cylindrical part of the cover, below the low-domed top with its small finial. Sometimes called a 'cylindrical caster'.

Lily Font. A silver-gilt CHRISTENING BOWL in the form of a trumpet lily, having fluted sides and – along the lip – decoration of applied water-lilies, and having a tripod base upon which are three figures of seated *amorini*, each playing a lyre. The piece, hallmarked 1840-1, was made by E., J. & W. Barnard (*see* BARNARD, EDWARD, & SONS) for the christening on 10 February 1841 of Victoria (1840-1901), Princess Royal (eldest daughter of Queen Victoria; she later married Emperor Frederick III of Germany), and it has since been generally used for all christenings in the Royal Family, the latest that of Prince Henry on 21 December 1984. It bears the joint arms of Queen Victoria, Prince Albert, and the Princess Royal. The piece is kept in the Jewel House of the Tower of London. *See* ROYAL FONT.

Lily Font. Silver gilt, E., J. & W. Barnard, London, 1840. H. 43·2 cm. Tower of London (Crown copyright, HMSO).

Limerick Crosier. A silver-gilt CROSIER made in Ireland in 1418 for Conor (Cornelius) O'Dea (d. 1434), Bishop of Limerick. The staff is encircled by a hexagonal band upon which rests a knob set with gemstones and a band with six Gothic niches, enamelled blue and green, in which are standing biblical figures, and above it are six smaller niches in which are standing figures of saints. The crook is decorated with foliated CRESTING and its head (supported by a symbolic pelican in-her-piety) encloses an Annunciation group of figures. It is owned by St John's Cathedral, Limerick, accompanied by the LIMERICK MITRE. *See* Robert Wyse Jackson, 'The Mitre and Crozier of Bishop Cornelius O'Dea' in *The Connoisseur*, July 1969, p. 149.

Limerick Mitre. A silver-gilt MITRE (of the precious-mitre type) made in Ireland, *c.* 1418, for Conor (Cornelius) O'Dea (d. 1434), Bishop of Limerick.

It is composed of two conoidal silver plates, hinged together, with leather backing, ornamented with gemstones and pearls and with crystal crosses pattée decorated with black-letter (Old English) characters; attached are embroidered orphreys and two 19th-century infulae. It bears an enamelled inscription stating that it was made by Thomas D. Carry. *See* LIMERICK CROSIER.

Limerick silverware. Articles of silver made in Limerick, Ireland. Although goldsmiths worked in Limerick from *c.* 700 BC, the local makers there were never granted their own ASSAY OFFICE, and from 1711 the work was sent to Dublin for assaying and hallmarking. The earliest-known dated piece of Limerick silverware is a CHALICE of 1663, Early local marks included a depiction of a gateway between two towers and a star; from *c.* 1710 the word 'Sterling' was used to denote the standard, along with a maker's mark. Some twenty-five silversmiths have been recorded there, Limerick being the most important Irish centre after Dublin and Cork (*see* IRISH SILVERWARE). The ware included spoons, buttons, and FREEDOM-BOXES, as well as some CHURCH PLATE.

Lincoln Tea and Coffee Service. A seven-piece SERVICE for tea and coffee made by the GORHAM COMPANY and acquired in 1861 by Mrs Abraham Lincoln for the White House (said by her to have been given by friends). The service consists of: (1) a HOT-WATER URN with one TAP and SPIGOT, and having two DROP-RING HANDLES suspended from goat-head masks; (2) a TEAPOT; (3) a COFFEE-POT; (4) a pot for hot milk (curiously, identical with the teapot); (5) a CREAM-JUG; (6) a SUGAR-BOWL; and (7) a SLOP-BOWL. It was not specially made for Mrs Lincoln, but was acquired from a retailer. It is accompanied by a TRAY made by J. Marquand. The pieces are engraved with the crest and initials 'MTL' of Mary Todd Lincoln. In 1869 Mrs Lincoln confirmed that the set had been given to her daughter-in-law, Mrs Robert Todd Lincoln; however, after Robert Todd Lincoln had his wife declared insane and confined, she subsequently repudiated the gift following her release. The set was donated in 1957 by Mr Lincoln Isham, great-grandson of President and Mrs Lincoln, to the Smithsonian Institution, Washington, D.C.

Lincoln Tête-à-Tête Set. A TÊTE-À-TÊTE SET made by the GORHAM COMPANY, *c.* 1860, for Mrs Abraham Lincoln. The COFFEE-POT, SUGAR-BOWL, and CREAM-JUG are engine-turned globular pieces, engraved with the monogram 'MTL' (for Mary Todd Lincoln) and with the Todd family crest. The set was given in 1972 to the Smithsonian Institution, Washington, D. C., from the estate of Mr Lincoln Isham, great-grandson of President and Mrs Lincoln. The legs of the three pieces are in the form of chicken legs, hence the set was referred to in Mr Isham's will as 'Mrs Abraham Lincoln's chicken-leg coffee set'.

liner. An accessory that fits closely within some silver articles and acts as a container (e.g., a glass liner in a SALT-CELLAR, MUSTARD-JAR, BUTTER-DISH, SUGAR-BOWL or WINE COOLER, or a silver TUREEN LINER in some SOUP-TUREENS), to avoid contact between the contents and the metal article itself. Liners were often made of blue, or sometimes ruby-coloured glass, and served to emphasize the PIERCED WORK decoration of a metal receptacle. Occasionally a liner for a silver object was made of SHEFFIELD PLATE for economy, while also providing a massive appearance.

lion couchant. The depiction of a lion lying down with its head raised. Various receptacles have feet in the form of such figures in-the-round, and the THUMBPIECE on the hinge of some TANKARDS also takes this form.

Lion Passant Guardant Hallmark. The English STANDARD HALLMARK (taken from the Royal Arms) in general use from 1544 to 1821–2, depicting a lion walking dexter (toward the viewer's left) with its dexter (right) forepaw raised and its head turned facing the viewer. It was adopted by the Goldsmiths' Company in 1544 as the Standard Hallmark for STERLING SILVER in the reign of Henry VIII, believed to be the result of the fact that the coinage had been debased to contain less silver than Sterling Silver plate, to show the superiority of plate. Originally the lion was crowned but from 1550 until 1821 it was uncrowned. Except during the period from 1697 to 1720 (when it was suppressed while the HIGHER STANDARD HALLMARKS for BRITANNIA SILVER were used), it continued in general use as the Standard Hallmark until, in 1822, following the accession of George IV, the London Assay Office introduced the LION PASSANT HALLMARK. Although the same mark was used by the other Assay Offices in England at various times, there were differences of detail in the designs. The mark remained in use at Birmingham until 1873–4 and at Sheffield until 1974, but since 1 January 1975 all three English Assay Offices have used the same Lion Passant Hallmark. *See* LION RAMPANT HALLMARK; LION'S HEAD ERASED HALLMARK; LEOPARD'S HEAD HALLMARK.

Limerick Crosier. Silver-gilt head, decorated with gemstones and enamelling, Irish, 1418. H. (overall) 2 m. St John's Cathedral, Limerick.

Lion Passant Guardant Hallmark. Style as used by the Birmingham Assay Office from 1773.

Lincoln Tea and Coffee Service. Gorham Company, Providence, R.I., *c.* 1860. Smithsonian Institution, Washington, D.C.

Lincoln Tête-à-Tête Set. Gorham Company, Providence, R.I., *c.* 1860. H. (of coffee-pot) 14 cm. Smithsonian Institution, Washington, D.C.

Lion Passant Hallmark. Sterling standard mark in general use (with slight variations) until 1821–2.

Lion Rampant Hallmark. Style as used by Edinburgh Assay Office from 1 January 1975.

Lion's Head Erased Hallmark.

Lion Passant Hallmark. The English STANDARD HALLMARK depicting an uncrowned lion walking dexter (toward the viewer's left) with its dexter (right) forepaw raised and its head in profile. It was introduced at the London Assay Office in 1822 as the Standard Hallmark for STERLING SILVER, superseding the LION PASSANT GUARDANT HALLMARK, and has since remained in continuous use there. The designs of the same mark, used at various times at other English Assay Offices to attest Sterling silver, have varied slightly, but since 1 January 1975 a uniform style has been adopted.

Lion Rampant Hallmark. The STANDARD HALLMARK used at the EDINBURGH ASSAY OFFICE since the British Hallmarking Act of 1973, when in 1975 it replaced the THISTLE HALLMARK. The mark depicts the lion standing and rearing up, with its head in profile facing the dexter (viewer's left) side of the shield and with its dexter (right) forepaw raised higher than the other paw. It was the Standard Hallmark used at the Glasgow Assay Office from 1819 until its closure in 1964.

lion sejant spoon. A type of SPOON having a straight stem terminating in a finial in the form of a lion sitting upright with straight forelegs, sometimes with a shield in front of its body, and usually facing left, but in some examples facing front (lion sejant affronté). The term 'sejant' is derived from Old French, *seiant*, sitting. Such spoons are known from the early 15th century and were produced into the 17th century. *See* Norman Gask, 'Lion Sejant Spoons' in *The Connoisseur*, August 1929, p. 91.

Lion's Head Erased Hallmark. The English ASSAY OFFICE HALLMARK required on BRITANNIA SILVER from 30 May 1697 (after the standard for silver had been raised to stop the melting down of silver coins) until 1 June 1720 and which continued to be used on it thereafter, along with the BRITANNIA HALLMARK. It depicted a lion's head in profile, facing the viewer's left, with its neck jagged as if torn off. Since the British Hallmarking Act of 1973 this mark is no longer used on any British silverware.

Lion's Head Hallmark. *See* LEOPARD'S HEAD HALLMARK.

lip. The everted pouring projection at the front edge of the mouth of a JUG (pitcher) or SAUCE-BOAT, or of a SPOUT. *See* BEAK; LIP SPOUT; BEAK SPOUT.

lip spout. A type of SPOUT that has a pouring LIP rather than a cut-off end, called a 'snip spout'.

liqueur frame. A receptacle, functionally comparable to a DECANTER FRAME or CRUET STAND, having a flat base supporting two circular rings in which to rest decorated bottles for liqueurs and having a central vertical handle for carrying the frame. Such pieces made in the Victorian period were often elaborately modelled with ROCOCO STYLE scrolls and curving brackets to support the rings, and the glass bottles were partially encased in silver openwork and had a silver collar below the neck and a silver stopper.

liqueur set. A group of articles for serving a liqueur, often consisting of a SALVER and small GOBLETS, together with a DECANTER (often of glass with silver mounts).

Liverpool jug. A type of JUG having a bulging body, a flat bottom, a BEAK SPOUT, and a loop handle. Examples, including two made by PAUL REVERE II, are in the same form as a ceramic jug.

livery pot. A term, formerly applied to a large pouring receptacle resembling a FLAGON, used preferably for 16th-century examples of English silverware, of which the early type, *c.* 1572–3, weighed about 20–30 oz., and later smaller ones, *c.* 1576–7, about 15–20 oz. The term is derived from the 'livery' (ration) of wine served from it. *See* MAGDALEN COLLEGE (OXFORD) POT; LEOPARD POT; WESTWELL FLAGONS.

Lloyd's Patriotic Fund Vases. A group of 73 similar (but not identical) VASES paid for from a fund solicited on 20 July 1803 by Lloyd's underwriters to encourage and reward military and naval officers for valour. Fifteen were awarded to commemorate services at the British naval victory under Nelson at Trafalgar on 21 October 1805 (hence they are sometimes called 'Trafalgar Vases'). The vases are in the form of a Greek pottery krater of the volute type, resting on a circular base and having two upright handles extending from oak-spray terminals near the shoulder of the bowl and terminating, level with the finial, in a volute enclosing a patera. On the front of the vase there is seated figure of Britannia in low relief, depicted holding in her right hand a statuette of Victory and in her left hand a palm frond, sometimes accompanied by an inscription 'Britannia Triumphant' or 'A grateful country to her brave defender'; on the back there is a figure of Hercules slaying the Hydra, sometimes with an inscription, either 'For our King, our Country, and our God' or 'Britons Strike Home'. On the cover there is a finial in the form of a standing lion in-the-round. The vases were made from a prize-winning design by Edward Edwards and John Shaw, and a finial design by JOHN FLAXMAN II; the 73 examples were made for RUNDELL, BRIDGE & RUNDELL in 1804–9 by BENJAMIN SMITH I and DIGBY SCOTT and by PAUL STORR. The bases are stamped with the Latin signature of Rundell, Bridge & Rundell. Each of the 66 vases presented between 4 May 1804 and January 1809 bears an inscription with the name of the recipient and a recital of his deeds; the other seven, with no inscription, were never presented (one of these, 1805–6, made by Smith and Scott, is in the Victoria and Albert Museum). *See* Roger M. Berkowitz, 'The Patriotic Fund Vases' in *Apollo*, February 1981, p. 104.

loaded. Filled, as in the case of some hollow CANDLESTICKS, with resin or other heavy substance to provide stability.

lobed. Shaped with projections of rounded form, horizontally (as the rim of some PLATES, PLATTERS, SALVERS, etc.) or vertically (as on the bodies and covers of some BOWLS, TUREENS, etc.); in the latter the lobes are often of different sizes and are crossed by vertical spaced RIBBING. *See* FOIL (2).

lobster crack. A type of implement for cracking the claws of a lobster (or crab), being made in two forms: (1) Two arms hinged to each other at one end and having the upper half of the arms recessed or multi-pronged so as to hold the claw in position when pressure is applied; some have a swivel hinge which is reversible to allow the width of the space between the arms to be adjusted. (2) Two arms that swivel on a central pin, like SCISSORS, having the incurved handles usually provided with a clasp and the other ends curved and attenuated to a point (for use as a pick) with the interior sides roughened and having an oval recessed section to hold the claw in position when pressure is applied. *See* NUTCRACKER; LOBSTER PICK.

liqueur frame. Silver-gilt frame with silver-encased glass bottles, Robert Garrard II, London, 1845. H. 32·8 cm. Courtesy, Garrard & Co. Ltd, London.

liqueur set. Silver-gilt salver, maker's mark 'HH', 1868, six goblets made by T. Smiley, 1870, and amber-coloured glass decanter with silver mounts, 1900. H. (of decanter) 21·6 cm. Courtesy, Garrard & Co. Ltd, London

livery pot. London, 1578. H. 19·4 cm. British Museum, London.

Lloyd's Patriotic Fund Vase. Vase made by Benjamin Smith I and Digby Scott, London, 1805-6, presented to Samuel Pym. H. 38·5 cm. Courtesy, S. J. Phillips Ltd, London.

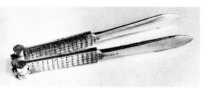

lobster crack (1). Close plate, 19th century. L. 24 cm. City Museum, Sheffield.

lobster pick. A type of dining implement for extracting the meat from a lobster shell, being about 20 cm long and very thin, having as one half a rod of square section terminating in a curved two-pointed claw and as the other half a flat extension in the form of a scoop; between the two sections is a widened thumbpiece, usually decorated on both sides with a representation in relief of a lobster. Examples are made in sterling silver and silver-plated ware. *See* LOBSTER CRACK.

locket. A small case, usually with a hinged lid, to contain a memento. A silver example, 1656, having its two covers decorated with FILIGREE motifs on a flat plate, was acquired by purchase in 1969 by the British Museum, London.

Loftus Cup. (1) A covered silver-gilt SEAL CUP, in the form of a STANDING CUP, made from the GREAT SEAL of Ireland (hence sometimes called the 'Great Seal of Ireland Cup'), for Adam Loftus (1533-1607), Archbishop of Dublin, 1567, and from 1581 Lord Chancellor of Ireland. It was made by an unidentified goldsmith with mark 'HL', and is dated London, 1593. The seal, which had been used for all state papers since the accession of Elizabeth I, 1558, was then worn out and had to be replaced, and Loftus had the old seal, as a perquisite of office, melted down and made into a cup; the cup remained in the Loftus family until 1960, when it was acquired from the estate of a direct descendant, the Marquess of Ely, by the Ulster Museum, Belfast. The cup has a cylindrical bowl resting on a knopped and bracketed stem on a waisted TRUMPET FOOT; the stepped CUSHION SHAPE cover has a finial topped by two tiers of brackets surmounted by two tiny figures of angels. Affixed to the bowl is a plate with an engraved inscription reciting the facts. *See* SEAL WARE.

(2) Another seal cup (mark: 'WI') made for Loftus in 1604 from the later Great Seal of Ireland, destroyed upon the death of Elizabeth I, 1603, when Loftus was still Lord Chancellor of Ireland. It was acquired at Christie's, London, on 29 April 1902 by J. Pierpont Morgan, and was sold by the Trustees of the Morgan Library, New York, at Christie's, London, on 2 December 1981; it is now reported to be in a New York private collection. It is a silver-gilt standing cup that differs from (1) above in that it has an ovoid bowl, a bell-shaped foot, and a low-domed cover surmounted by three brackets. It too bears a plate with an engraved inscription.

London Assay Office. The ASSAY OFFICE, established in 1544 by Henry VIII, which has used, and still does use, as its ASSAY OFFICE HALLMARK for silverware (and other precious metals) the LEOPARD'S HEAD HALLMARK, except on BRITANNIA SILVER before 1975, when the LION'S HEAD ERASED HALLMARK together with the BRITANNIA HALLMARK were required (*see* HIGHER STANDARD HALLMARKS). The use of the DATE HALLMARK in London commenced in 1478; also punched are the MAKER'S MARK and the STANDARD MARK. When a piece is submitted for ASSAYING by a firm or person not registered as a silversmith, such as a commercial silver-casting firm, the letters 'LAO' for London Assay Office are punched in lieu of a maker's mark; *see* ELIZABETH, PRINCESS, STATUETTE. In London the hallmarks are punched at the Assay Office at Goldsmiths' Hall (hence the use of the term 'hallmark'; see GOLDSMITHS, WORSHIP-

locket. Open case showing external filigree decoration, London, 1656. H. 8·5 cm. British Museum, London.

FUL COMPANY OF), which was originally the only such office in Britain and which today maintains a record of most London hallmarks. *See* Susan M. Hare, *Touching Gold and Silver* (1978).

Lord Mayor's Cup. A DOUCEUR in the form of a TWO-HANDLED CUP. One example, presented to Sir Richard Hoare, has each handle in the form of a gnarled tree-trunk and a cover decorated with vine leaves and a rococo scroll finial; the bowl is decorated with a scene, emblematic of London and the Thames, adapted from the pediment of the Mansion House, and depicting a seated figure of Britannia holding a cartouche-shaped shield engraved with the arms of Judah. Made by George Boothby, London, 1744-5, it is owned by the Spanish and Portuguese Jews Congregation of the Bevis Marks Synagogue, London, and is on loan to the Jewish Museum, London.

Lord Mayor's Salver. One of a group of DOUCEURS, each in the form of a SALVER. Five basically similar examples were made between 1697 and 1710 by John Ruslen, of the Golden Cup, St Swithin's Lane, London, and two in 1716 and 1728 by Robert Hill, London; all are oval and have a depressed centre with a large embossed medallion, a wide sloping border decorated with embossed flowers and foliage, and a narrow level rim. The earliest,

Lord Mayor's Cup Two-handled cup, George Boothby, London, 1744-5. H. 40·7 cm. Spanish and Portuguese Jews Congregation, London (photo courtesy, the Jewish Museum, London).

Lord Mayor's Salver. John Ruslen, London, 1701-2. W. 81 cm. Private collection; on loan to the Jewish Museum, London (photo courtesy, Warburg Institute, University of London).

1697, has four foliated loop handles, and the central medallion depicts a scene with Abraham entertaining Angels outside the house of Sara; it bears an engraved inscription recording its being a gift from Grace Lloyd Barnes, of Redland Hall, to the church of St Michael, Bristol, which still owns it. On the six other examples – five of which have simpler handles and one is without handles – the medallion depicts the shield of the Bevis Marks Synagogue, London, displaying the arms of Judah, being the 'Tent of Meeting' in the wilderness (Exodus, xxxiii, 7), under clouds and guarded by a warrior. In 1935 it was reported that, of the other four Ruslen pieces, one, 1699, was owned by Lord Jersey; one, 1701-2, by the 1st Baron Swaythling (perhaps the one now in a private collection and on loan to the Jewish Museum, London); one, 1708, by Stuart Wortley; and one, 1710, by Lord Ancaster. Of the two Hill pieces, one was reported to be in the Spencer Churchill Collection, and the other (without handles) as having been acquired by the Bevis Marks Synagogue. An example in different form was made by Jonathan Swift, 1731; it is rectangular and, except for an engraved central medallion depicting the arms of Judah, is undecorated. *See* Cecil Roth, 'The Lord Mayor's Salvers' in *The Connoisseur*, May 1935, p. 296.

loving cup. A broad term for a large drinking vessel, passed among guests for shared drinking at a banquet or other festive gathering, having two (or sometimes three) vertical side handles for convenience in handing the vessel from person to person. The body is usually semi-ovoid or vase-shaped and rests on a spreading foot. Such vessels were so called only from *c.* 1800, and were the successors to the GRACE CUP, but came to be used for a wider range of occasions. *See* G.Bernard Hughes, '400 Years of Silver Loving-Cups' in *Country Life*, 28 December 1972, p.198. *See* THREE-HANDLED CUP.

Luck of Woodsome Hall, The. A brass TRUMPET with silver mounts around the tube and the bell (mouth). It was made by Simon Beale (the State Trumpeter to Cromwell and Charles II), signed and dated 1667, and is 78 cm long. Formerly owned by the family of the Earls of Dartmouth, at their seat at Woodsome Hall, Yorkshire, it was sold first in 1922 by the 7th Earl of Dartmouth (d.1958), then at Christie's in 1939 as part of the Percival Griffiths Collection, and again at Christie's in 1968. It was called a 'luck' (an object on which the prosperity of a family, etc., is supposed to depend) because of the tradition that failure to sound the trumpet on important occasions would bring ill-luck to the owner. Its present whereabouts is unknown.

Lumley Cup. A silver-gilt TWO-HANDLED CUP of inverted bell shape, with two loop handles extending from the rim to the upper part of the bowl. The bowl is encircled by a low-relief frieze depicting a procession with Bacchus conducting Ariadne standing in a quadriga. It was made by PAUL STORR for Storr & Mortimer, 1837, and rests on a silver-gilt cube-shaped plinth made by Samuel Hunt for HUNT & ROSKELL, 1845. The cup and plinth were presented on 18 July 1845 to Benjamin Lumley (1811?–1875), an operatic impresario, by the performers to commemorate his first successful season at Her Majesty's Theatre, London, as set forth in an inscription on the plinth. The piece was bequeathed by Miss Grace Lumley to the Victoria and Albert Museum, London.

lustre (luster). The appearance of the smooth surface of a mineral (e.g., silver) produced by the reflection of light striking the surface. There are several grades of lustre, depending on its intensity, that of polished silver being the highest, known as 'metallic lustre'. Lustre is seen on a smooth surface (where no ridges are present to reflect the light in many directions), and is achieved on silver by POLISHING, BUFFING, and BURNISHING. *See* PATINA; TARNISH.

Lynn Cup. The same as KING JOHN'S CUP.

M

mace. A heavy STAFF (derived from a medieval knight's weapon used for breaking an opponent's armour) still used in modern times as a symbol of authority or dignity by some public bodies and officials. Early examples (from the mid-13th century) were fitted with four or more metal blades with serrated edges and a plain haft with a terminal silver decoration bearing a coat of arms. Later, *c.*1500, the method of carrying a mace was reversed, so that the war-head was held downward and modified to a shaped knop, and the other end enriched until it gradually took the form of four brackets, later a cup-like ornament, surmounted by a monde. English examples usually have a straight handle with three knops and the cup-shaped elaborate head with four brackets topped by an orb or a monde. Examples have been made of silver or of silver-gilt, but some have a wooden core sheathed with silver. More than 100 maces dating from the 17th to 20th centuries are extant, most

mace. Silver-gilt Great Mace of the former Irish House of Lords, Dublin, *c.* 1766. National Museum of Ireland, Dublin.

of them still owned by the bodies for which they were originally made. There are four basic types: (1) Sergeants' maces, for sergeants-at-arms and local law-enforcing authorities; (2) Civic maces, for mayors; (3) Faculty maces, for universities, colleges, faculties, and courts; and (4) Great Maces, such as the ten examples in the Jewel House of the Tower of London, those of the House of Commons, the House of Lords, and the Lord Chancellor, and, in the United States, that of the House of Representatives. The Great Maces, up to 1·60 m long, are carried by a mace-bearer as a symbol of dignity. *See* G. Bernard Hughes, 'The Story of the English Mace' in *Country Life*, 8 August 1952, p. 406. *See* NORWICH MACE; DEVIZES MACES; SMITHSONIAN MACE; BATON; OAR.

machine stamping. The process of DIE STAMPING silver (or other metal) by the use of mechanical presses to produce uniformly shaped blanks to be assembled by hand in making mass-produced articles, such as buttons or the sections of CANDLESTICKS made of SHEFFIELD PLATE, or some examples of HOLLOW WARE, such as some small inexpensive TEAPOTS.

Mackay Service. A combined DINNER SERVICE and DESSERT SERVICE, consisting of 1,250 pieces to provide service for 24, made by TIFFANY & CO. in 1877–8; it was presented to his wife by John W. Mackay (1831–1902) who had sent the required half-ton of silver bullion to Tiffany from his Comstock Lode Mine in Virginia City, Nevada. The service was exhibited in the American Pavilion at the Paris Exposition of 1878, and was used in the Mackay homes in Paris and London. It included almost every type of HOLLOW WARE and FLATWARE, and bore the monogram 'MLM' (for Marie Louise Mackay) and a coat of arms designed for her for the service; many of the pieces were decorated with an engraved Irish shamrock and Scottish thistle symbolizing her ancestry. The service, though highly praised for its design and workmanship, was criticized for being ostentatious. The service was provided with nine fitted chests, and a leather-bound album with silver mounts contained photographs of the pieces, which are now dispersed in public and private collections. *See* Charles H. Carpenter, Jr, 'The Mackay Service made by Tiffany & Co.' in *Antiques*, October 1978, p. 794.

Macready Testimonial. An elaborate CENTREPIECE resting on a tripod base supporting a group of six figures, having at each corner an *amorino* and being surmounted by a standing figure of Shakespeare. It was designed by Charles Grant and made by BENJAMIN SMITH II, London, 1841, as a testimonial to William Charles Macready (1792–1873), the English tragedian, and presented to him on 19 June 1843. It has been lent anonymously to the Victoria and Albert Museum, London.

Magdalen College (Oxford) Melon Cup. A silver-gilt STANDING CUP, the bowl and cover together being in globular form with melon-type vertical ridges and one segment completely dotted (seeds?); it has a stem in the form of an urn atop a bell-shaped section, resting on a domed spreading base. The finial is a tiny standing figure (of later date) of Mary Magdalen(e). The piece is owned by Magdalen College, Oxford, and has for some years been called there 'The Founder's Cup', but John F. Hayward has established, based on recently discovered documents: (a) that the cup, bearing London marks for 1601–2, could not have been donated by the College's founder, William Waynflete, Bishop of Winchester (d. 1486); (b) that it was the cup mentioned in a 17th-century inventory that was sent in 1642 by Dr Accepted Frewen, then President of Magdalen, to the Mint, pursuant to the orders of Charles I, to be melted down, but in fact was redeemed by Frewen for his personal ownership and restored by him in 1660 to the College; (c) that thereafter it appeared in College inventories from 1672; and (d) that the College owned an earlier cup, called the 'Magdalen Box', that was presumably sold or melted down except for its finial, a figure of Mary Magdalen(e), which was saved as a relic and probably affixed as the finial on the later cup. *See* John F. Hayward, 'The Tudor Plate of Magdalen College, Oxford' in *Burlington Magazine*, May 1983, p. 260, figs. 2, 3. *See* MELON CUP.

Magdalen College (Oxford) Pot. A silver-gilt FLAGON having a pear-shaped body with a narrow neck and a spreading foot, and having one vertical loop handle; the finial is a small seeded berry. The piece is decorated overall with chasing in an IMBRICATED pattern. Its probable origin was attributed to Germany by H. C. Moffatt in 1906 and by E. Alfred Jones in 1940, but John F. Hayward, in *Burlington Magazine*, May 1983, p. 260, has cited records and comparable pieces to establish that it is of English make, early 16th century. Owned by Magdalen College, Oxford, and known there as the 'Magdalen Pot', it is regarded as the earliest-known example of the English Tudor silver LIVERY POT.

Magdalen College (Oxford) Melon Cup. Silver gilt, London 1601–2. H. 24 cm.

Magdalen College (Oxford) Pot. Silvergilt flagon, English, early 16th century. H. 35·5 cm.

Magdalen cup. Silver gilt covered beaker, London, 1573–4. H. 19·3 cm. City Art Gallery, Manchester.

Magdalen cup. A type of covered BEAKER, so called in some mid-16th-century inventories because it is in the same form as the covered pot containing ointment that Mary Magdalen(e) is seen holding in her hand in certain paintings of the late 15th and early 16th centuries. The only known surviving silver-gilt example is one, London, 1573–4, formerly belonging for many years to the Byrom family of Manchester, England, and now owned by the City Art Gallery, Manchester (having been acquired at the Byrom sale at Sotheby's, 26 April 1956); it is of cylindrical shape with a pulley- or spool-shaped base and finial, the body decorated overall with encircling, engraved birds, beasts, and flowers (attributed to the Huguenot engraver Niçaise Roussel); the low-domed cover, with overall embossing of fruit and flowers, has a tall knopped finial. The only other known surviving Magdalen cup (in a private collection) has a cylindrical body of engraved crystal, and the finial is surmounted by a figure of a warrior holding a shield and spear; it is attributed to Thomas Bampton, 1572–3. *See* Charles C. Oman, 'Magdalen Cups' in *Apollo*, August 1938, p. 83.

Magnolia Vase. A circular VASE with sloping sides and a low vertical neck (the form having been suggested by pottery relics of the Pueblo cliff-dwellers of south-western United States), to which are attached ten vertical loop, so-called 'Toltec' (Mexican Indian), handles. The overall decoration consists of REPOUSSÉ American flowers and leaves on the body, swirls in ART NOUVEAU STYLE on the base, and insets of enamelling, gold, and gemstones. It was designed by John T. Curran, Chief Designer, and made by TIFFANY & CO., 1892. It was shown by Tiffany at the World's Columbian Exposition, Chicago, 1893, and is now owned by the Metropolitan Museum of Art, New York (gift of Mrs Winthrop Atwell, 1899).

Magnussen, Erik (1884–1961). A designer and maker of modernistic silverware, born in Denmark where he was apprenticed from 1898 to 1901, worked as a chaser from 1902 to 1909, and had his own studio from 1909. His hollow ware and jewelry were exhibited in Denmark and elsewhere. In 1925 he was engaged by the GORHAM COMPANY to work in the United States and was provided with a special studio where he designed and executed his ware, originally in ART DECO STYLE but after 1927 in his CUBIC STYLE. He left Gorham in 1929, had a workshop in Chicago, and from 1932 to 1938 worked in Los Angeles, returning in 1939 to Denmark. His work is characterized by geometric shapes and faceted surfaces, with a minimum of decoration but occasional use of gemstones, ivory or ebony.

maidenhead spoon. A type of SPOON having a straight stem terminating in a finial in the form of a female bust emerging from the calyx of a flower (sometimes ACANTHUS leaves) and having flowing straight hair or sometimes plaited hair. The figure has been said to represent the Virgin Mary (*see* VIRGIN SPOON), but as to the rare examples depicting a figure with plaited hair, the term 'Virgin spoon' is a misnomer, for sacred iconography allows such a hairstyle only to married women. Such spoons are known from *c*. 1450, but date mainly from the 16th century, and they were discontinued *c*. 1650; they were made by silversmiths in London and in provincial centres. The term has been applied by collectors, but is not found in early inventories or records. *See* Norman Gask, 'Rare Maidenhead Spoons' in *Apollo*, December 1950, p. 169.

maker's mark. The mark, punched on an article of silverware for the purpose of identifying the maker. It is included as a HALLMARK, being punched by the silversmith before the piece is submitted to the ASSAY OFFICE for ASSAYING. The use of a maker's mark (and of a date mark) was introduced at Montpellier, France, in 1355. In Great Britain it has always been permitted for such a mark to be registered at any Assay Office (*see* MARK PLATE) by any maker, even by a maker not a member of the Goldsmiths' Company, including foreigners (as in the case of the Huguenots who registered their marks in the early 18th century). The mark was originally, from 1363, either a pictorial symbol selected by the maker or his two initials; from 1697 to 1719 the first two letters of his surname were used; from 1720 to 1739 it could be any one of the prior forms; and since 1739 it is the initials of the maker's first name and surname in a style of lettering not previously used by another maker. There is at Goldsmiths' Hall, London, an almost complete record of maker's marks from 1765 (and some from as early as 1697). Although hundreds of such marks have been identified, many have not been, and articles bearing such an unidentified mark, e.g., those by the 'HOUND SEJANT' GOLDSMITH, must be referred to by the relevant initials or symbol. Occasionally from *c*. 1772 on, a piece bears the maker's mark and is inscribed with the name and address of the retailer for whom it was made; and in modern times articles made expressly for a retailer occasionally bear the retailer's mark

Magnolia Vase. Designed by John T. Curran for Tiffany & Co., New York, 1892. H. 70·8 cm. Metropolitan Museum of Art, New York.

rather than that of the maker, e.g., LIBERTY SILVERWARE; TIFFANY SILVERWARE. *See* SPONSOR'S MARK. Other instances where a piece may bear a maker's mark other than that of the actual silversmith who made it are: (1) where a foreign maker in London had, for any of several reasons, another silversmith present it to the Assay Office and to 'sponsor' the piece to avoid resentment by local competitors; (2) an imported article, which had to be assayed locally (*see* IMPORTED GOODS HALLMARKS); (3) a piece made to private order and without a hallmark when made, but which if later resold by a goldsmith had to be assayed and was then struck with the mark of that goldsmith; and (4) a piece marked 'LAO' (*see* LONDON ASSAY OFFICE).

In some cases an article has no maker's mark at all, e.g.: (1) when the maker was evading the regulations to avoid paying the tax that at the time had to be paid to the Assay Office (*see* DUTY DODGER) or because he was an alien not entitled to have his work assayed and marked; or (2) when the piece was made to private order and the buyer did not require the mark, especially when old articles that had already been assayed were later refashioned.

For photographic reproductions of the marks of many London silversmiths, *see* Charles J. Jackson, *English Goldsmiths and their marks, 1479–1919* (1949); Arthur G. Grimwade, *London Goldsmiths, 1697–1837* (1976).

Magnussen, Erik. Candlesticks designed for the Gorham Company, *c.* 1928. H. 35 cm. Gorham Collection, Providence, R.I.

malleable. Susceptible of being extended or beaten into a desired shape by HAMMERING or by pressure of ROLLING. Silver is the second most malleable metal (after gold). *See* DUCTILE.

Malling jug. A type of 16th-century English tin-glazed earthenware JUG with a cylindrical neck and globular body on a spreading base (the shape inspired by Rhenish TIGERWARE JUGS), usually with a mottled glaze (predominantly blue or brown), and often having silver or silver-gilt MOUNTS (sometimes a band encircling the shoulder). The type is so called because the first specimen to be discovered was excavated in the churchyard at West Malling, Kent; but there is no evidence that such jugs were made there, London being said to be the most likely place of origin. There are three jugs in the British Museum, London, dating from the mid-16th century, of which the bodies are coloured, respectively, brown, speckled purple, and speckled black-and-white. An example, coloured green, orange, purple, and other hues, and having silver-gilt mounts (comprising a neck-band, body-straps, handle FERRULES, foot-ring, and cover) and bearing a MAKER'S MARK of a fleur de lis and the London marks for 1581–2, was sold at Christie's, London, in 1903.

mancerina (Mexican). The same as a TREMBLEUSE. Such a piece, in the form of a saucer with a central gallery, was developed for Antonio Sebastián de Toledo, Marques de Mancera, who suffered from Parkinson's disease and needed such a cup for his unsteady hand.

Mancroft Thistle Cup. A silver-gilt STANDING CUP having a bowl of thistle shape resting on a bracketed vase-shaped stem supported by a spreading foot. The decoration on the lower half of the bowl, on the base, and on the cover is of foliage, and the cover has a high bracketed vase-shaped finial surmounted with a standing figure of a man holding a large scroll. The piece, bearing a London date mark for 1543, was originally a secular cup, and is reputed to be the oldest piece of church plate in Norwich, where it is traditionally used by a priest at the church of St Peter Mancroft when celebrating his first Communion there.

Mannerist Style. A style of decoration involving an excessive adherence to a particular style, especially that of the Renaissance. It originated in Italy, spread to northern Europe, and was brought in the late 16th century to England by German and Dutch craftsmen, as well as through the importation of books of engravings; it had less appeal in England and only few examples are known. The style featured the use of antique materials to embellish articles of silverware, the ignoring of function in relation to design, the use of enamelling and gemstones along with rock crystal, and the complete covering of available space with ornamentation. Examples of the style are the BOOTH CUP and the RUTLAND EWER. *See* J. F. Hayward, 'The Mannerist Goldsmiths: England' in *The Connoisseur*, May 1965, p. 80, June 1966, p. 90, and January 1967, p. 19.

Mansfield, John (1601–74). The earliest-known silversmith in Massachusetts; having emigrated from London, he is recorded as having been working in 1634 in Charleston, near Boston. A SWEETMEAT-DISH, *c.* 1630–50?, bearing a mark 'IM', has been attributed possibly to him: *See* MASSACHUSETTS SILVERWARE.

Mancroft Thistle Cup. Silver gilt, London, 1543. H. 29·8 cm. Church of St Peter Mancroft, Norwich.

mantling. A decorative motif, in heraldry, in the form of a mantle or drapery around a COAT OF ARMS. The same as LAMBREQUIN.

Mappin & Webb Ltd. A leading London firm of silversmiths and retailers of jewelry and quality giftware. It was founded in 1774 by Jonathan Mappin, who opened a small silver workshop in Sheffield and entered his first mark there in 1775. His business prospered, and in 1849 his descendants opened several shops in London as Joseph Mappin & Son, and later as Mappin Brothers. The latter firm exhibited at the Great Exhibition of 1851. The elder brother, Frederick Mappin, left the firm *c.* 1858 to engage in steel production, and his brother, John Newton Mappin, joined with George Webb to form Mappin & Webb. It opened its first shop in London in 1862, followed by several others. In 1900 the firm became Mappin & Webb Ltd. In 1904 it opened a branch in Paris, and in 1909 moved to its present address there at 1 rue de la Paix. The company's main London address is at 170 Regent St, and it has branches in London and many cities in the United Kingdom, as well several abroad. In 1963 the company and GARRARD & CO. LTD, together with the silverware operation of ELKINGTON & CO., were combined to form British Silverware Ltd.

marine rococo ware. Articles of silverware in ROCOCO STYLE that are decorated with marine motifs, usually including figures of Tritons. An example is a SALVER designed by NICHOLAS SPRIMONT for Frederick, Prince of Wales, but bearing the mark of PAUL CRESPIN, 1742. Others are a set of four DESSERT STANDS, each in the form of a shell supported by two Tritons, bearing the mark of PAUL STORR, 1812, and made for RUNDELL, BRIDGE & RUNDELL, and each having an added base made by PHILIP RUNDELL, 1820; the set is in the Royal Collection.

mark plate. (1) A copper plate used by an ASSAY OFFICE, to be struck with the various maker's marks registered there. Such plates were required from 1676 (except when discontinued in the period 1696-1773) by the Goldsmiths' Company, and one from 1676 is at Goldsmiths' Hall, London. An example, 1702, owned by the Goldsmiths' Company of Newcastle-upon-Tyne, has a series of concentric scratched circles to position the marks and has, at the top, a hole by which to suspend it. (2) A plate, kept by an Assay Office, to be struck with HALLMARKS (but not maker's marks) at the end of each year before they are defaced.

Marks, Gilbert (Leigh) (1861-1905). A London silversmith whose career started with Johnson, Walder & Tolhurst, manufacturing silversmiths, of 80 Aldersgate St, where pieces executed by him were shown in the firm's exhibitions. He became interested in the Arts and Crafts Movement, and started his own workshop after *c.* 1885, working only part-time, and entering his first mark in 1896. He was a designer and craftsman, and his work was made entirely by hand, featuring REPOUSSÉ decoration, in high and low relief, of flowers and fruit of the variety appropriate to the function of the ware. His work was executed with botanical realism and generally in ART NOUVEAU STYLE. Much of his work was done in response to official commissions. His work in the 1890s tended to be more elaborate and stylized. *See* Katherine Harlow, 'Gilbert Marks, Forgotten Silversmith' in *Antique Collector*, July 1984, p. 42.

Marlborough Centrepiece. A CENTREPIECE (an example of FIGURAL SILVERWARE) having an elaborate PLINTH supporting a group scene depicting the 1st Duke of Marlborough (1650-1722) on horseback writing a despatch after the victory in 1704 at Blenheim in the War of the Spanish Succession. The piece was designed by EDMUND COTTERILL and executed in 1846 by ROBERT GARRARD II for R. & S. Garrard & Co., London. It was made as part of a set of plate for the 6th Duke of Marlborough; it is still in the Blenheim Collection and is normally on display to visitors in the Saloon. There are, on the interior of the rim of the plinth, square apertures indicating that originally detachable candlesticks were to be inserted.

Marlborough Pilgrim Bottles. A pair of PILGRIM BOTTLES, each having a tall thin neck and a suspensory chain attached to masks at the base of the neck. Both are engraved with the arms of the 1st Duke of Marlborough (1650-1722) and his wife (*née* Mary Gould; m. 1702). Although having no hallmark, the pieces bear the maker's mark of PIERRE PLATEL, and date from *c.* 1702-14.

marli (or **marly**). The border of a PLATE or DISH which extends from the WELL to the rim and is often almost parallel with the bottom of the well. Also called a 'ledge' or 'bouge'.

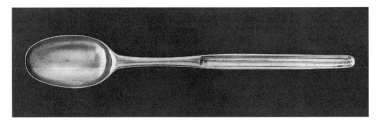

marrow spoon. London, *c.* 1718. L. 15·5 cm. Colonial Williamsburg, Va.

marrow scoop. A long thin implement used to extract marrow from a marrow-bone, having one end channelled in the form of a long narrow scoop, but sometimes having both ends channelled and of two widths so as to fit bones of different sizes. It succeeded the MARROW SPOON. Some examples are used today as a stirrer for a long cold drink or as a SWIZZLE STICK. *See* CHEESE SCOOP; CORER.

marrow spoon. A type of SPOON, having a conventional bowl and a handle channelled in the form of a long narrow scoop, used to extract marrow from a marrow-bone. It was the precursor of the MARROW SCOOP.

Marston Wine Cup. A parcel-gilt WINE-CUP having a plain hemispherical bowl and TRUMPET FOOT, the latter supported by three feet in the form of talbots standing on plinths. Scratched under the base is the name 'G Skydmor', presumably that of the original owner, a wealthy bailiff and butcher of Oxford in 1455. The cup, unmarked, dates from *c.* 1450; originally a secular piece, it is now owned by the parish church of Marston, near Oxford, where it is used as a COMMUNION CUP.

Martelé. The trade name for articles of silverware, produced by the GORHAM COMPANY, that were formed by HAMMERING (*martelé* being the French term for 'hammered') and CHASING, the decoration usually being in ART NOUVEAU STYLE. The ware was introduced in 1897 by WILLIAM CHRISTMAS CODMAN and by Edward Holbrook, who held office as President of Gorham, 1894–1919. The pieces were designed by various artists and made by different silversmiths and chasers, all working closely in conjunction with Codman. Early examples were made of STERLING SILVER (·925 fine), but from 1898 until 1905 a more MALLEABLE alloy (·950 fine), was used, and from 1905 an alloy ·9584 fine (the same as BRITANNIA SILVER). There was no uniform surface, as hammer marks were sometimes left untouched, but often were PLANISHED to give a smooth, although fragile, appearance. No mechanical process was used to supplement the hand work. Most pieces were oxidized, by use of a sulphide compound, to leave a black deposit in order to accent the details of the chasing; today, the black deposit has usually disappeared as a result of repeated polishing (or worse, buffing) in ignorance of, or without regard to, the maker's original intention. A few pieces received added decoration of enamelling. The range of articles was very wide, including many items of tableware and such large pieces as CANDELABRA; some 4,800 pieces (of almost 100 types of objects) were made between 1897 and 1912. Production diminished after 1909, regular production ended in 1912, and the last piece was made in 1930. Various marks were used on the ware, including the word 'Martelé' from 1900; some pieces bear special code numbers or letters. *See* Charles H. Carpenter, Jr, 'Gorham's Martelé Silver' in *Antiques*, December 1982, p. 1256.

Maryland silverware. Articles of silverware made at Baltimore, Maryland, originally by immigrant silversmiths from England, Ireland, and Germany (whose work reflected foreign styles), and later wares by local makers who became influenced by the silversmiths of nearby Philadelphia (*see* PHILADELPHIA SILVERWARE). There was an ASSAY OFFICE from 1814 to 1830 which established the only official hallmarks used in the United States and enforced a standard of fineness of ·917, higher than that of the usual local COIN SILVER (·892) which provided the main source of the metal, but this was abandoned in order to compete with the ·925 standard of Philadelphia silverware. A leading silversmith was Samuel Kirk (1793–1872), who is said to have introduced into the United States the REPOUSSÉ technique, hence it is often called there 'Kirk Style' or 'Baltimore Style' (*see* KIRK STIEFF CO.). Other Baltimore silversmiths included William Ball (1763–1815), Richard Rutter (fl. 1790–8), and Charles Louis Boehm (1774–1868). A characteristic of local ware from 1818 is the use of an animal-head decoration on spouts, and there was a preference for large pieces of good workmanship and design rather than those with much ornamentation. *See* J. Hall Pleasants and Howard Sill,

Marston Wine Cup. Parcel gilt, English, *c.* 1450. H. 15 cm. Parish church, Marston, Oxfordshire (photo courtesy, Historic Churches Preservation Trust).

Martelé. Rose-water basin in Art Nouveau style. Gorham Collection, Providence, R.I.

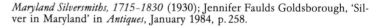

matched service. Coffee service of octagonal section: (*left*) cream-jug, Augustine Courtauld I(?), London, 1720; (*centre*) coffee-pot, John Newton, London, 1722; (*right*) sugar-bowl, Thomas Mason, London, 1728. Folger's Coffee Collection, Procter & Gamble Co., Cincinnati, Ohio.

Maryland Silversmiths, 1715–1830 (1930); Jennifer Faulds Goldsborough, 'Silver in Maryland' in *Antiques*, January 1984, p. 258.

mask. A decorative motif in the form of a representation, usually in relief, of a face. Masks were originally derived from ancient Greek and Roman sources; often grotesque, they depict faces of human beings, satyrs, and animals. Masks occur on MUGS and JUGS, being generally placed below the pouring lip, and on BOWLS, WINE COOLERS, etc., being placed on the side.

Masonic badge. A type of BADGE worn by the fraternal order of Freemasons, made of silver with decoration of PIERCED WORK, ENAMELLING, and ENGRAVING, and depicting symbols of the order. Such badges date generally from *c.*1750, and many were made by Thomas Harper, *c.*1784–95.

Massachusetts silverware. Articles of silverware made in Massachusetts, principally in Boston, from Colonial days. The work was influenced by the Puritans and others who emigrated from England from 1629, and the forms of the pieces, usually household ware (mainly MUGS, TANKARDS, PORRINGERS, CREAM-JUGS, CHAFING DISHES), were those popular in England during the reign of Charles I, 1625–49, and the Commonwealth, 1649–60, featuring simplicity in design and an absence of applied decoration. The earliest silversmith was JOHN MANSFIELD, and other prominent makers included BENJAMIN BURT, JOHN BURT, JOHN CONEY, JEREMIAH DUMMER, JOHN HULL, JACOB HURD, PAUL REVERE I, PAUL REVERE II, OBADIAH RICH, ROBERT SANDERSON, and EDWARD WINSLOW. More than 400 silversmiths are said to have been active in Massachusetts in Colonial days. *See* Edward Wenham, 'Early Massachusetts Silversmiths' in *The Connoisseur*, January 1934, p. 165.

masterpiece. A piece of silverware required to be made by an APPRENTICE, after his years of training and learning various techniques, to qualify as a Master Silversmith. It may be any type of article of his own choosing, but it must receive no assistance in its execution. If the piece is approved, he is accepted and may register his own mark. No English example in the form of a COLUMBINE CUP has been identified (*see* RICHMOND, JOHN, CUP).

matched service. A SERVICE comprising assembled pieces made EN SUITE in identical style of decoration, but including articles made by different silversmiths, and hence bearing different MAKER'S MARKS and HALLMARKS. Many identical DINNER FORKS and DINNER KNIVES of a service were made by different silversmiths, hence can form a part of a matched service. Some COFFEE SERVICES and TEA SERVICES are matched services, especially those dating from early years of the 18th century. A service that includes articles of identical

Massachusetts silverware. Cann with double-scroll handle, Benjamin Burt, Boston, Mass., *c.* 1860–85. H. 14 cm. Yale University Art Gallery (Mabel Brady Garvan Collection), New Haven, Conn.

style and decorated *en suite* and all having the same maker's mark but different date marks is considered to be a 'true service'. *See* COMPOSITE SERVICE.

matt-chased. A surface decoration having, on a background of MATTING, a design made by FLAT CHASING. It is found on some BELL SALTS and WINE-CUPS.

matting. Decoration in the form of dull, lustreless, matt surface, produced by PUNCHING, with a burred or round-headed tool, on the front of the piece an overall pattern of small closely packed indentations or dots. It is found in a wide band encircling some WINE-CUPS, TWO-HANDLED CUPS, TUMBLERS, TANKARDS, and other drinking vessels to reduce the risk of their slipping from the drinker's hand. Sometimes called 'pinking'. The converse is PEBBLED. *See* MATT-CHASED; PRICKING; FROSTING; POUNCE; DOT REPOUSSÉ.

Maundy Dish. A silver-gilt DISH, bearing an unidentified maker's mark and a London date mark for 1660, and – in the centre – the arms and cipher (added later) of William and Mary, 1689–94, of the period between 13 February and 11 April 1689. The dish is still used every year to hold the Maundy Money distributed by the British Sovereign on Maundy Thursday (the Thursday in Holy Week) to a selected group of elderly men and women equal in number to the years of the Sovereign's age. The ceremony is based on the ancient custom of washing the feet of the poor on that day, following Christ's example in washing the feet of his disciples (John, xiii, 5–17). Each year's Maundy Money consists of specially struck and dated silver coins (in the denominations 1*d*, 2*d*, 3*d*, and 4*d*), the total number of pence presented to each recipient also being equal to the Sovereign's age; it is now supplemented by a small gift in today's currency.

Maundy Dish. London, 1660, with arms and cipher (added later) of William and Mary. D. 65·3 cm. Tower of London (Crown copyright, HMSO).

mazarine. A drainer in the form of an oval (rarely circular) pierced plate that rests in a deeper and wider serving dish. Some examples were made in two parts, with a shallow dish to hold hot water supporting a slightly depressed pierced plate. More usual examples were flat, and it was intended that fish, cooked in the kitchen and brought to the dining room in the pot, would there be transferred to the pierced plate to drain; the term mazarine was then applied to only the pierced plate. The pierced work occurs in a great variety of holes and patterns, sometimes depicting a net holding fish. Such drainers range in length from about 30 to 60 cm. The origin of the term is uncertain, but is generally said not to be derived from Cardinal Mazarin, who died in 1661 before such pieces were used; Norman M. Penzer suggested the theory that the term was derived as a diminutive of the word 'MAZER', but another explanation is that proposed by G. Bernard Hughes, that the name was first applied by Charles de Marguetel de St Denis, Seigneur de St-Evremonde (1613–1703), in honour of his friend Hortense Mancini (1646–99), Duchess of Mazarin and a niece of the Cardinal. Of the silver examples extant today, many were made by PAUL STORR. At the Mansion House, London, there are three of different sizes made by William Bateman (*see* BATEMAN), 1815. Designs in early Sheffield pattern books referred to

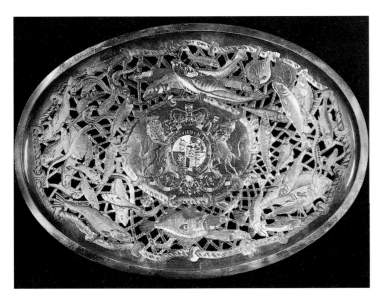

mazarine. Drainer with decoration depicting a net holding fish, George Hunter, 1762. L. 44·5 cm. Royal Collection; reproduced by gracious permission of Her Majesty the Queen.

mazarine. Serving dish and drainer, Paul Storr, London, 1818. L. 56 cm. Courtesy, Partridge (Fine Arts) Ltd, London.

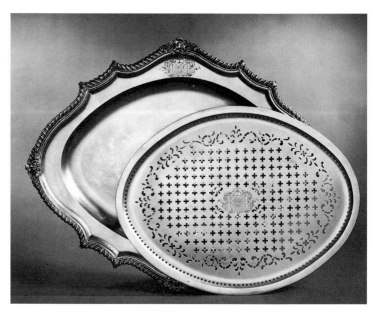

medal (American Indian). 'Happy Warrior Medal', Daniel C. Fuetter, New York, 1764. D. 5·4 cm. Yale University Art Gallery (Mabel Brady Garvan Collection), New Haven, Conn.

such pieces as a 'fish plate'. There are many ceramic examples, known as 'fish drainers'. *See* Norman M. Penzer, 'What is a Mazarine?' in *The Connoisseur*, April 1955, p. 104; G. Bernard Hughes, 'The Mazarine for Elegance' in *Country Life*, 14 March 1968, p. 602.

mazer. A type of drinking vessel, made of turned hard close-grained wood (usually of the excrescences that form on the trunk of the English burr-maple tree, not bird's-eye maple, as often said), usually in the form of a wide flat-bottomed shallow bowl, some early ones being entirely of wood (*see* HARBLEDOWN MAZERS), but most examples having a wide rim-band and some a foot-rim of silver or silver gilt. Many have on the interior of the bottom a central PRINT (known in the 15th century as a 'founce') decorated with EN-GRAVING and sometimes ENAMELLING; this has been said to be possibly to simulate the BOSS on a Greek *patera*, but is more probably merely a form of decoration employing the natural shape of the excrescence. A few late examples have two silver handles affixed to straps that connect the rim to the base. The diameter of the bowl ranges from about 9 to 28 cm, the miniature ones to be used with one hand and usually to drink the health of an infant (*see* THOMAS MAZER), the size and shape depending on that of the wood. Some mazers rest on a stemmed foot (*see* STANDING MAZER), and some are small cups (*see* MAZER CUP). The rim-band sometimes bears an engraved decoration or a religious or secular inscription. Examples are known from the 14th century, but few were made after the 16th century. Large numbers were in use in the 14th and 15th centuries, Canterbury Cathedral having owned 182 in 1328, Battle Abbey 32 in 1437, and Westminster Abbey 51 in the mid-16th century. The name is said to be derived from the Middle English word *maser*, maple. *See* Edwin H. Pinto, 'Mazers and their Wood' in *The Connoisseur*, March 1949, p. 33. *See* BANNATYNE (BUTE) MAZER; CROMWELL MAZER; SAFFRON WALDEN MAZER; SCROPE MAZER; SWAN MAZER; THREE KINGS MAZER; BRIDAL CUP.

mazer cup. A type of MAZER in the form of a CUP that, in the 17th century, superseded the usual type of MAZER, being made of beech or pear wood instead of maple and having a deeper and narrower bowl. Such pieces were sometimes without the silver rim-band of the usual mazer.

meat-dish. A type of DISH for serving the roast or main dish at a meal. It is oval and has a RIM variously decorated, e.g., with GADROONING, BEADING, REED-AND-TIE BORDER, etc. Such dishes vary from about 25 to 50 cm in length. *See* SECOND-COURSE DISH.

medal, American Indian. A type of medal given in the Colonial era to North American Indians as an official evidence of friendship, and after the Revolution given to Indian chiefs who visited the U. S. President or who signed a treaty of peace. The earliest-known medal made in the American Colonies was given in 1661 by Virginia to Indians, to be worn by them when visiting the settlements; the medals measured 15 × 10 cm, and bore elaborate designs, including the words 'King of Potomac' (hence called 'Potomac Medals'). The earliest-known 'Indian Peace medal' was awarded by the Quakers at Philadelphia, having been made in 1757 by Joseph Richardson, Sr (*see* RICHARDSON). A medal called 'The Happy Warrior Medal' was awarded by the British to friendly chiefs; it was made in 1764 by Daniel C. Fuetter, a New York die-maker. Medals known as 'The Washington Indian Peace Medals' were oval silver plaques, having a suspension ring, engraved with a scene depicting President Washington with an Indian chief and, on the reverse, the seal of the United States; these were made from 1789 to 1795 by Joseph Richardson, Jr. Later 'Presidential Medals', made by the Philadelphia Mint until 1840, bore on one side an engraved bust of the incumbent President, and on the reverse a tomahawk and a calumet, with two clasped hands. *See* Harrold E. Gillingham, 'Early American Indian Medals' in *Antiques*, December 1924, p. 312. *See* INDIAN-TRADE SILVERWARE.

medallion. A thin flat ornamental tablet, usually circular or oval, bearing a portrait, design or inscription, often as a memorial. Some examples made of silver, such as three in the British Museum made by CHRISTIAN VAN VIANEN, *c.* 1630–44, feature a portrait in low relief.

medical label. A type of BOTTLE TICKET formerly used on some bottles of medical lotion (such as *eau de miel* and *arquebuzarde*, used to heal gun-shot wounds).

medicine cup. Silver gilt, London, 1789. H. 6·3 cm. Wellcome Collection, Science Museum, London.

medical silverware. Articles of silverware related to medical practice, including (1) surgical and diagnostic instruments (e.g., forceps, scalpels, catheters, lancets, probes, needles, tongue depressors) and prosthetic appliances – all outside the scope of this book; (2) phlebotomy ware (BLEEDING BOWL); (3) feeding utensils for infants and invalids (e.g., GIBSON SPOON, MEDICAL SPOONS, FEEDING BOTTLE, FEEDING CUP, FEEDING BOWL, PAP BOWL, and SPOUT CUP); (4) aids to personal health and hygiene (e.g., TOOTHBRUSH SET, TONGUE SCRAPER, NIPPLE SHIELD, EAR-TRUMPET, EYE BATH, and pill-box). Some BOTTLE TICKETS were made for receptacles for medicinal preparations (*see* MEDICAL LABEL). Some medical articles were decorated with ENGRAVING or EMBOSSING. Surgical instruments were sometimes provided with a fitted case, occasionally made of silver but more often of shagreen, tortoise-shell or *cuir bouilli*. A large variety of silver medical ware is in the Wellcome Collection at the Science Museum, London, and silver surgical instruments are owned by the Royal College of Surgeons, London. *See* Eric Delieb, 'Medical Silver' in *Apollo*, June 1961, p. 194. *See* MORTAR; DISPENSARY; INHALER; BALANCE SCALE; FUNNEL; SPECULUM; MEDICINE CUP.

medical spoons. Various types of SPOON used to administer medicine or to feed an infant. *See* MEDICINE SPOON; GIBSON SPOON; FEEDING SPOON; PAP SPOON.

medicine cup. A type of medical vessel in the form of two semi-ovoid cups joined at their bases, one larger than the other, similar in shape to, but smaller than, a double EGG-CUP. Silver examples are known from 1789. *See* MEDICAL SILVERWARE.

medicine spoon. A type of MEDICAL SPOON used to administer medicine, made in three forms: (1) a short spoon with a vertical ring handle and no stem; (2) a stemmed spoon of usual shape but having the front end of the bowl covered except for a small aperture; and (3) a long spoon that is double-ended, having a bowl of different size at each end. Some examples of the third type have a hinged stem, so that one bowl swivels to fit inside the other.

medicine-spoon caddy spoon. A type of CADDY SPOON in the form of a MEDICINE SPOON (type 1), having an oval bowl and a short handle. It is said to have been the earliest type of caddy spoon when, *c.* 1755–60, the medicine spoon was adapted to measure and dispense tea.

megillah-case. A small cylindrical (sometimes octagonal) case, appropriately decorated and inscribed, to enclose the scroll upon which is handwritten the Book of Esther, read at the Jewish Festival of Purim while the congregation follow the reading on small scrolls of their own. The case usually has a spreading foot and a pomegranate finial, but some are shaped like a fish (symbolic of the month of Purim). Examples in silver, 18th/19th centuries, are known from Continental and Oriental countries, but none of silver is at the Jewish Museum, London. *See* SCROLL CONTAINER; JEWISH RITUAL SILVERWARE.

medicine spoon (1). Silver gilt, with graduated markings; length 11·2 cm. (2) Partially covered bowl; length 14·4 cm. (3) Double-ended; length 13 cm. Wellcome Collection, Science Museum, London.

Menzies Memorial Trophy. Cricket trophy, Stuart Devlin, London, 1980. H. 28 cm. Courtesy, Stuart Devlin.

melon cup. A type of STANDING CUP of which the combined bowl and low-domed cover are of MELON SHAPE, the bowl resting on a stemmed foot. *See* MAGDALEN COLLEGE (OXFORD) MELON CUP; 'POMEGRANATE' CUP.

melon shape. A shape, resembling that of a muskmelon or canteloupe, often used for the body of a MELON TEAPOT and other pieces of a TEA SERVICE, as well as for some STANDING CUPS (*see* MELON CUP), being globular with vertical bands dividing the surface of the piece.

melon teapot. A type of TEAPOT that has a body of MELON SHAPE. Such pieces were made in the 1730s and again in the 19th century, such as an example by Charles Fox, 1837.

memento mori (Latin). Literally, remember you must die. A motif used as decoration on various articles of silverware in the form of a reminder of mortality, e.g., a coffin, a death's head or a skeleton. Such pieces were ordinarily not in remembrance of a deceased person, but were intended as an abstract reminder of death, especially in the 16th and 17th centuries. They include finger-rings, brooches, pomanders, and other types of article. Some articles with such motifs were presented to chief mourners and ministers at funerals, especially finger-rings with, inscribed on the interior, the name, age, and date of death of a deceased person. A pair of silver spoons, with a York hallmark of the period 1660–85, were engraved with *memento mori* inscriptions. *See* SKELETON STATUETTE.

memorial spoon. A type of SPOON that is inscribed with the name of a deceased person, sometimes given to the bereaved family by custom in England and the United States. *See* FUNERAL SPOON.

Menorah. A type of seven-nozzle CANDELABRUM used in the Jewish faith on the Sabbath and Holy Days as an ancient Symbol of Judaism but of no ritualistic significance. It has a horizontal row of three concentric semi-circular branches to hold six candles, with one more in the centre (Exodus, xxxvii, 18); the seven are said to symbolize the seven days of the Creation. It is said to copy the seven-nozzle candelabrum carried off in triumph from the Temple in Jerusalem by the Roman Emperor Titus, AD 70, and depicted in relief on the Arch of Titus in Rome. Sometimes called a 'Synagogue Lamp'. *See* HANUK(K)A(H) LAMP; SABBATH LAMP; SANCTUARY LAMP; JEWISH RITUAL SILVERWARE.

menu-card holder. A type of decorative CARD HOLDER having a slot for holding vertically a menu card; it is used at formal dinners, and is usually similar to, but slightly larger than, a PLACE-CARD HOLDER. It has a flat base, sometimes with a supporting scroll at the back.

Mercury Candelabrum. Silver gilt, twelve-branched, made by Paul Storr for Rundell, Bridge & Rundell, London. (1) 1809–10, height 1·03 m. Royal Collection; reproduced by gracious permission of Her Majesty the Queen. (2) 1816, height 1·02 m. (with branches by Philip Rundell, 1819). Courtesy, Christie's, London.

Menzies Memorial Trophy. A cricket TROPHY awarded periodically as the prize in the competition between a specially selected Australian side (the Prime Minister's Eleven) and the visiting team representing England. It was made by STUART DEVLIN in 1980, having been commissioned as a memorial to Sir Robert Menzies, Prime Minister of Australia, 1949–66, and depicts eleven cricketers in different playing attitudes (batting, bowling, and fielding).

Mercury Candelabrum. (1) A silver-gilt twelve-branch CANDELABRUM made from a design partly by JOHN FLAXMAN II, modelled probably by WILLIAM THEED, and executed by PAUL STORR for RUNDELL, BRIDGE & RUNDELL, 1809–10. Rising from an incurved tripod base is a short column attached to which are six curving foliated candle branches and above which there is a figural group depicting Mercury descending to present to the Nysiades (the three Nymphs of Mount Nysa) the infant Bacchus, whose care had been entrusted to them by his father, Zeus. The extension of the column above the group is fluted and decorated with grape-vines, and supports the upside-down figure of Mercury. At the top of the column are the other six candle branches. On the tripod base are three seated piping fauns, each having at its side a figure of a recumbent lion; the feet of the base are in the form of double lion's paws. The piece is one of a pair made by Storr and acquired by the Prince Regent (later George IV, 1820–30) in June 1811, the other being the GARDEN OF THE HESPERIDES CANDELABRUM; both are in the Royal Collection.

(2) A silver-gilt twelve-branch candelabrum comparable to (1) above, with a similar figure group, except that (a) on the base – similar to that of the seven-branch Garden of the Hesperides Candelabrum owned by the Goldsmiths' Company – there are three seated lionesses instead of piping fauns, (b) its twelve branches are all at the top of the column, (c) the figures of the group are compressed, (d) the branches are scroll, not foliated, and (e) the feet of the base are scrolled shells. It was made by Paul Storr for Rundell, Bridge & Rundell in 1816, the branches being by PHILIP RUNDELL, 1819. It was sold at Christie's, London, on 31 March 1976.

Mermaid Ewer. A EWER in the form of a mermaid, the enclosed bowl being her horizontal torso, between her upright bust and her elevated tail (the handle); in her upraised right hand she holds a comb, and formerly held in her left hand a mirror (now missing). The tail, engraved with fish-scales, has a detachable end that can be unscrewed to permit the body to be filled with water which pours out through the figure's nipples. The figure rests on a spreading foot and is engraved on the body with an escutcheon. The accompanying large BASIN is in the form of a scallop shell, and is embossed with marine motifs and an escutcheon. Both pieces are by an unidentified silversmith (mark 'TB'). Only two examples of such ewers and basins are known to survive; one, London, 1610–11, is in the Victoria and Albert Museum, London, and the other, London, 1616–17 (with the comb missing and the mirror probably a modern replacement) was acquired in 1976 by the Toledo Museum of Art, Toledo, Ohio.

Mermaid Ewer. Ewer, London, 1610-11. H. 31·7 cm. Victoria and Albert Museum, London.

mermaid spoon. A type of SPOON having a straight stem terminating in a finial in the form of a figure in-the-round of a mermaid.

Merry plate. A type of COMPOSITE METAL consisting of a layer of STERLING SILVER fused directly on to refined NICKEL SILVER, without any under-layer of copper. The process was patented in March 1836 by Anthony Merry, of Birmingham; however, because it had been anticipated by Thomas Nicholson, the patent was invalidated. It superseded ROBERTS PLATE and was later replaced by BRITISH PLATE.

mether. A type of Irish drinking CUP said to have been used for drinking mead (a fermented drink made of water and honey, with malt and yeast), the Irish term being a *meader*. Silver examples, based on early wooden prototypes found in bogs, have been made in Ireland with a four-sided mouth rising slightly at the corners and tapering down to a circular or square base, and with two (sometimes one or three) vertical square loop handles, sometimes extending down to the level of the base. The height ranges from 12·5 to 30 cm. An example, called a 'mead cup', made by Richard Williams, Dublin, 1772, is in the Untermyer Collection at the Metropolitan Museum of Art, New York, and a modern version, with applied decorative bands, was made by Edmond Johnson, 1901.

mether. Square section and handles, Richard Williams, Dublin, 1772. H. 12·7 cm. Metropolitan Museum of Art (Gift of Irwin Untermyer, 1968), New York.

Methuen Cup. A STANDING CUP having a silver-gilt bowl, cover, and base, with a circular rock-crystal stem set in silver-gilt circular mounts. The bowl and cover are of oblate spherical form, and each bears a lengthy encircling, engraved, secular inscription. The finial of the cover is crystal, surmounted by a vertical ring. The cup bears the unidentified mark 'Vh' and has been presumed to be of Scottish origin, mid-16th century. It descended in the Methuen family and is one of the earliest surviving examples of Scottish secular plate. It was donated in 1949 by William Randolph Hearst to the Los Angeles County Museum of Art.

Mexican silverware. Articles of silverware made in Mexico, mainly from the mid-16th century on (i.e., later than articles made in the pre-Columbian era by native Indian craftsmen, none of which is known to be extant). The early silversmiths came from Spain with the *Conquistadores*; they organized guilds and worked under strict legal regulations. Due to the large amount of silver locally available (more than was produced in the United States and Canada together or in all of Europe), the making of silverware was extensive. The first pieces were SEALS, but soon the principal production, reflecting the coming of Christianity to Mexico, became ecclesiastical ware for the churches and the many private chapels of the wealthy; such ware included almost all types of CHURCH FURNISHINGS and CHURCH PLATE, even such large pieces as altar antependia. Later, secular silverware, associated with the period of the Mexican Revolution, *c.* 1821, was made in many types of domestic ware. Most Mexican silverware is hand-crafted, inspired by the motifs of the pre-Columbian Maya, Toltec, Aztec, Mixtec, and Zapotec cultures, and ranges in style from abstract and fantastic to realistic. In recent years mass-production has been introduced, with factories superseding the individual craftsmen. There are no national HALLMARKS, but a great number of MAKER'S MARKS and local assay marks have been used. Some genuine Colonial period ware has forged marks, and a large number of copies of Colonial ware bear marks that have been forged. Since the second quarter of the 20th century, pieces have been made in modernistic style, as well as much ware produced for the tourist trade, in centres such as Taxco. *See* Lawrence Anderson, *The Art of the Silversmith in Mexico, 1519–1936,* (1941, 1975); Joseph Vilner, 'Mexican Silver' in *The Connoisseur,* October 1965, p. 841.

Meyrick Cup. A silver-gilt covered STANDING CUP (a copy of the Oriel College, Oxford, Founder's Cup made in France, late-15th century) made by Crichton Bros., London, 1911. It is owned by the Meyrick Society, a London society of collectors of arms and armour, founded in 1890, and named after Sir Samuel Bush Meyrick (d. 1848), the noted authority on arms and armour. It was donated to the Society in 1913 by its then Vice-President, Guy Francis Laking, and is used as a LOVING CUP at meetings of the Society. The cup is engraved with the arms of the Society and the cover with the names of its members from 1890 to the present day; on the back of the cover there is soldered a small box containing discs engraved with the names and coats of arms of the successive presidents of the Society.

Mildenhall Treasure. A TREASURE, discovered in the 1940s, comprising 34 pieces of tableware of 4th-century Romano-British silver hidden at Mildenhall, Suffolk, England, probably having been owned by a high-ranking imperial official. The major piece is the NEPTUNE DISH; the other pieces include two platters, four flanged bowls, one covered bowl, two goblets, eight spoons (some with Christian symbols), and five small ladles with detachable handles. The treasure, found in a field that was being ploughed, was kept by the owner of the land for some years, but in 1946 was declared treasure trove and was acquired by the British Museum. It is mentioned here because of its significance as an important example of Roman silverware found in England. *See* K. S. Painter, *The Mildenhall Treasure* (1977).

milk-jug. A type of JUG (pitcher) for serving milk with tea, being of medium size, about 7·5 cm high, larger than a CREAM-JUG but smaller that a HOT-WATER JUG. When tea was first introduced in England, it was drunk without milk, but *c.* 1720 the jug for cold milk was first used. The form was often similar to that of the hot-water jug, but some examples were pear-shaped, ewer-shaped or a miniature version of the HELMET JUG. The style varied, matching the current styles of TEAPOTS and COFFEE-POTS, such jugs usually being made EN SUITE. Early examples have a stemmed foot, but later, for better stability, such jugs have a flat bottom, a narrow foot-rim, a spreading base, or three or four small feet. The everted pouring lip (sometimes a BEAK) was usually opposite the handle, which was often a scroll or DOUBLE SCROLL HANDLE, with some small ornament at the top, or a TAU HANDLE. Later, when hot milk was served with tea, the milk-jugs were provided with a cover. The decoration was in various styles, including ENGRAVING, CHASING, GADROONING, REEDING, and – in the ROCOCO STYLE – much EMBOSSING. The milk-jug was often a unit of the TEA SERVICE. *See* Charles C. Oman, 'English Silver Milk Jugs in the Eighteenth Century' in *Apollo,* July 1931, p. 14; G. Bernard

Methuen Cup. Silver gilt and rock crystal, Scottish, mid-16th century. H. 17·8 cm. Los Angeles County Museum of Art (William Randolph Hearst Collection), Los Angeles, Cal.

milk-jug. Jug with tau handle and ball feet, from a tea service by Salomon Marion, Quebec, *c.* 1820-30. Musée du Québec, Quebec.

Hughes, 'Georgian Silver Milk Jugs' in *Country Life*, 15 September 1955, p. 562; —, 'Georgian Milk and Cream Jugs' in *Apollo*, June 1956, p. 199.

Milton Shield. An oval SHIELD made of embossed silver plaques set within surrounds made of decorative bands of iron DAMASCENED with gold. The plaques depict in low relief numerous figures in incidents from Milton's *Paradise Lost*. The central plaque depicts the Archangel Raphael telling Adam and Eve of the war in Heaven (Canto V). In the plaque on the left the army of the rebel angels march to the combat, and in that on the right they are seen in defeat, while between them and below the central plaque the Archangel Michael defeats Satan (Canto VI). Above the central plaque is God the Father. In the upper part of the surround is Raphael's story of the Creation (Canto VII); in the lower part are allegories of Death and Sin (Canto I). The shield was designed and (except for the bands) executed by LÉONARD MOREL-LADEUIL for ELKINGTON & CO. in the style of ANTOINE VECHTE, and is inscribed 'Morel Ladeuil Fecit 1866'; it is not hallmarked as it is made of mixed materials. The shield was awarded a gold medal at the Paris Exposition of 1867 and was purchased in that year by the South Kensington Museum (now the Victoria and Albert Museum), London. Several copies were made by Elkington by ELECTROFORMING for loans by the museum to provincial museums and some for sale to the public, and some were made (with the museum's name inscribed) for sale by Elkington. *See* BUNYAN SHIELD.

Milton Shield. Plaques with embossed scenes based on *Paradise Lost*, Léonard Morel-Ladeuil for Elkington & Co., Birmingham, 1866. W. 67·5 cm. Victoria and Albert Museum, London.

miniature silverware. Tiny versions of articles of various types that, when full-size, have a functional or ornamental use (including parts of a SERVICE, FURNITURE, MUGS, VASES, PORRINGERS, etc.), as distinguished from SMALL-WARE, and often referred to as TOYS. The earliest known hallmarked example made in England is a SWEETMEAT-DISH of 1653; most of the known English pieces date from the 18th century. Such ware includes two groups: (1) very small pieces, about 4 cm. high, made for display in a doll's house (formerly called a 'Baby House'), it being uncertain whether they were intended for adults or children; and (2) somewhat larger pieces made as playthings for young girls. Some were made by apprentice silversmiths to demonstrate their skills, but the maker's mark present on many examples proves that such pieces were made mainly by established silversmiths, some of them specialists in making miniature ware. It has been seriously doubted whether such miniatures (with possibly a few exceptions, apparently not fully decorated) were made, as sometimes averred, as SALESMAN'S SAMPLES.

Hallmarks were required on miniature silverware until exemption was granted by the Act of 1738 for articles weighing less than 10 dwt, but thereafter some silversmiths continued to punch a maker's mark, and sometimes the pieces – especially those made of BRITANNIA SILVER – were submitted for ASSAYING.

The most noted English makers of such ware were: George Manjoy (fl. 1684–1713), his marks being 'GM' (not for George Middleton, as has often been stated) and 'MA' (not for Isaac Malyn, as sometimes stated); David Clayton (fl. 1697–1735), his marks having often been confused with those of Augustin(e) Courtauld II (*see* COURTAULD); and JOHN HUGH LE SAGE.

See G. Bernard Hughes, *Small Antique Silverware* (1957); —, 'Old English Silver Toys' in *Country Life*, 31 March 1950, p. 870; John D. Kernan, 'American Miniature Silver' in *Antiques*, December 1961, p. 567; Victor Houart, *Miniature Silver Toys* (English translation, 1981), pp. 157, 228 (for British ware); Miranda Poliakoff, 'Silver Toys' in *V & A Album 4* (1985), p. 165.

mirror. A looking-glass made in various shapes, sizes, and styles. Examples made with a silver FRAME include large WALL MIRRORS, TOILET MIRRORS, HAND MIRRORS, and shaving mirrors, as well as the mirror in a silver PLATEAU to support a CENTREPIECE. Some wall mirrors and toilet mirrors have detachable silver CRESTING. *See* KANDLER MIRROR.

mirror sconce. A type of SCONCE, usually of the pilaster type with one branch, that is found affixed at each side of a WALL MIRROR or a TOILET MIRROR so that the light from the candles will add to reflectivity. Many such pieces have been recorded in the Royal plate, but most have apparently been melted down.

missal cover. The front cover of a missal or other devotional book that was sometimes made of silver or silver gilt, ornately decorated with enamelling and set with gemstones. *See* BOOK COVER.

mitre (miter). A liturgical head-dress worn by bishops and abbots, formed, since the 18th century, by front and back sections of conoidal shape, having hanging at the back two embroidered lappets (*infulae*) and, encircling the bottom, an embroidered band (orphrey). Examples of 'precious mitres' are

mitre. Silver conoidal sections, English, *c.* 1660. H. 29·8 cm. Pembroke College, Cambridge.

molinet. Chocolate-pot with protruding rod, Paul Crespin II, London, 1738-9. H. 24 cm. Ashmolean Museum, Oxford.

known with the conoidal sections made of silver, e.g., one (unmarked) now at Pembroke College, Cambridge, said to have been made in the early 17th century for Matthew Wren (d. 1667), Bishop of Ely, 1638–67; it has decoration of bands with REPOUSSÉ ornament and, at the top of each peak, a foliated cross pattée. A silver mitre of William of Wykeham (1324–1404), Bishop of Winchester and founder of New College, Oxford, bequeathed by him to the College, is still extant; it has been twice reconstructed in this century. *See* LIMERICK MITRE.

modern silverware. Articles of silverware made from *c*. 1880 until *c*. 1945 (for the period since 1945, *see* CONTEMPORARY SILVERWARE); in this period silversmiths began to depart from methods and forms of the past and, with the introduction of the ART NOUVEAU STYLE, began to create original forms of their own conception, until in the 20th century mass-production led to the introduction of new techniques based on the need for functionalism and efficient production methods. The changes paralleled the rise of the Arts and Crafts Movement, and its urge for individual handwork and the departure from uniformity, and merged into the later practice of combining the use of machines with creative handwork. New materials came into general use, such as stainless steel and modern alloys, especially for household ware and tableware, but such articles are beyond the scope of this book, which is concerned only with silver articles. Among the outstanding British designers and makers of silverware of the period *c*. 1930–45 are OMAR RAMSDEN and EDWARD SPENCER. Modern articles classified as works of art and exempt from British purchase tax (VAT) are usually engraved with the designer's signature. *See* G. Bernard Hughes, 'British Modern Silver' in *Country Life*, 24 August 1951, p. 580; Graham Hughes, *Modern Silver throughout the World, 1880–1967* (1967). *See* CUBIC STYLE.

molinet. A type of rod (muddler) to be inserted into a CHOCOLATE-POT through an aperture in the LID or COVER, and to be twirled so as to stir and froth the beverage. Examples made of silver, hardwood or glass were about 25 to 30 cm long. Some have a protruding silver flange (plain or pierced) on the lower end of a wooden rod. Often called a 'mill'. The name is derived from the French *moulinet*, a small mill.

money holder. An article for carrying money, being of two forms: (1) a COIN HOLDER; and (2) a clip for paper money, made in a great variety of forms, often in novelty designs. *See* PURSE MOUNT.

monkey mustard-pot. A fantasy type of MUSTARD-POT having, standing on a flat base beside the pot, a figure of a monkey repelled by the escaping fumes.

Monkey Salt. A silver-gilt GREAT SALT, early 16th century (repaired in the 18th), having its stem in the form of a monkey with ruby eyes, seated on a cushion and balancing on its head a hemispherical crystal bowl in which rests the silver receptacle for salt. The circular base rests on three feet in the form of tiny figures in-the-round of 'wodewoses' (wild men), each seated on a cushion and holding a club. Inside the salt receptacle is a mask depicting a lion's head. The cover is missing. The form, it has been suggested, may have some affinity with Goldsmiths' Row, built in 1500 and carved with depictions of wild men and wild beasts. The piece is owned by New College, Oxford, to which it was given in 1516 by Archbishop William Warham (1450–1532), who had been a member of the College between 1473 and 1488 and who was appointed Archbishop of Canterbury in 1504.

monogram. A character composed of two or more initial letters, usually representing a name, and employed as an identifying ornament. A monogram was often engraved on articles of a silver SERVICE; sometimes a monogram was obliterated or cut out (and replaced by a silver disc) in order to facilitate the sale of a piece.

monstrance. Originally, any receptacle in which a sacred relic was exposed to public view; now, a standing footed vessel in which the consecrated Host, enclosed in crystal, is exposed to be venerated by the faithful. Early examples were large and imposing, and were sometimes combined with a RELIQUARY. Later examples, in the 17th to early 19th centuries, have two layers of crystal which enclose the Host, supported by a stemmed base and surrounded by the rays of a Gloria, sometimes surmounted by a cross or a crown (e.g., one of silver gilt, 1693, in the National Museum of Ireland, Dublin) and sometimes having the crystals secured together by a chain and padlock. Sometimes the base of the piece, when reversed, serves as a CHALICE, e.g., one of silver gilt, *c*. 1670, at Sizergh Castle, Kendal, Cumbria. Also called an 'ostensorium'. *See* WESTMINSTER MONSTRANCE; CHURCH PLATE.

Monkey Salt. Silver gilt with crystal bowl, early 16th century. H. 25·5 cm. New College, Oxford.

Montagu Salver. A silver-gilt SEAL SALVER, the earliest-known extant example, made for Charles Montagu (1661–1715), Earl of Halifax and Chancellor of the Exchequer, from the Exchequer Seal that had become obsolete upon the death in 1694 of Mary I, Queen Regnant with William III. It was made in 1694–5 or 1695–6, bearing the maker's mark 'BB', probably for Benjamin Bathurst, and engraved *c.* 1695 by SIMON GRIBELIN, The salver, with a border of GADROONING, depicts the obverse and the reverse of the seal, above the arms of the Chancellor, on a ground of drapery. A short foot is joined to the tray by CUT CARD work. A replica was made by DAVID WILLAUME, 1726, and both salvers were sold from the collection of the Duke of Sussex at Christie's, London, on 24 June 1843. The original was resold in 1929 (incorrectly attributed to 1687), and was bought by Sir William Burrell and bequeathed by him in 1944 to the City of Glasgow, being now in the Burrell Museum there; the replica was donated by F. P. Schiller to the Honourable Society of the Inner Temple, London.

Montagu Salver. Silver gilt, Benjamin Bathurst(?), London, *c.* 1695, with engraved decoration by Simon Gribelin. D. 34 cm. Burrell Museum, Glasgow.

Montefiore Candelabrum. A tall fantasy CANDELABRUM, with silver matt finish, in the form of a desert scene, with a central palm tree having ten arms for candle sockets, and around its base figures in-the-round of two camels, one donkey, and several native riders. At the top of the palm tree there is a bowl as a finial. The piece, London, 1858, was a gift from H. H. Tousson Pacha to Sir Moses Haim Montefiore (1784–1885) and his wife in recognition of their philanthropic acts. Owned by the Montefiore Endowment Fund, London, it is on loan to the Victoria and Albert Museum, London.

Montefiore Centrepiece. A large massive sculptural CENTREPIECE presented by his admirers to Sir Moses Haim Montefiore (1784–1885), English philanthropist, to commemorate his mission to the Middle East in 1840. It rests on a tiered base having four incurved sides and supported by corner figures of sphinxes. At the corners of the base are four seated figures in-the-round depicting on the front corners Moses holding the Ten Commandments and Ezra the Scribe (440 BC), and at the rear corners one Oriental Jew enchained and another liberated. Between the figures are plaques, of which three depict in low relief scenes related to the 1840 mission, while the one at the front has a donative inscription engraved in Hebrew and English. Behind the four figures are tall grape vines. At the top is a figure in-the-round of David slaying a lion. The piece was designed by Sir George Hayter (1792–1871), modelled by EDWARD HODGES BAILY, and made by Mortimer & Hunt (*see* HUNT & ROSKELL). Owned by the Montefiore Endowment Fund, it was included in a 1956 exhibition at the Victoria and Albert Museum, London, where it is now on loan.

Montefiore Centrepiece. Designed by Sir George Hayter, modelled by Edward Hodges Baily, and made by Mortimer & Hunt, London, 1840. H. 1·04 m. Montefiore Endowment Fund, London.

monteith. A type of large circular or oval BOWL having a rim with a continuous series of SCALLOPS, vertical or sometimes bent outward, so that six or eight wine glasses can be suspended by the foot, allowing the bowl of each to be cooled by immersion in iced water before use. Originally monteiths were made of silver, English examples being known from 1666, and some were made in the United States and Dublin. (Later they were made of porcelain or glazed earthenware, as well as of glass.) The width ranges from 23 to 28 cm. Some have, around the rim, BAROQUE STYLE scrollwork in relief or cast cherubs' heads, and almost all have a pair of DROP-RING HANDLES. The bowl generally rests on a FOOT-RING (sometimes detachable) or a SPLAYED foot, and is usually decorated with GADROONING, EMBOSSING or vertical FLUTING. Later examples, *c.* 1690–1710, were in the form of (and served as) a PUNCH-BOWL with a detachable scalloped rim (known as the 'collar') which, when attached, converted the piece into a monteith. It has been said that the 17th-century Oxford diarist Anthony à Wood (and often repeated, but with no other basis) that the term was derived from the name of a Scotsman – Monteith (Monteigh) – who, at Oxford in the reign of Charles II, 1660–85, used to wear a cloak or coat scalloped at the bottom. *See* Jessie McNab, 'The Legacy of a Fantastical Scot' in *The Metropolitan Museum of Art Bulletin*, February 1961, p. 172; G. Bernard Hughes, 'Bowls for Cooling Wine Glasses' in *Country Life*, 20 September 1962, p. 668; Georgina E. Lee, *British and American Monteith Bowls* (1978). *See* COLMAN MONTEITH; COVERED MONTEITH.

monument candlestick. A type of CANDLESTICK similar to a COLUMN CANDLESTICK but without a capital such as is found on classical Greek and Roman columns.

Monymusk Reliquary. A Celtic portable SHRINE in the form of a rectangular carved solid wood box with a hinged lid, resembling a small stone oratory with a hipped roof. The front and lid are sheathed with silver plates (the back, bottom, and ends with bronze), lightly incised with depictions of in-

monument candlestick. One of a pair, maker's mark 'TD', London, 1682. H. 25·4 cm. Ashmolean Museum, Oxford.

Monymusk Reliquary. Portable shrine, Scottish, 7th/8th century. L. 9 cm. National Museum of Antiquities of Scotland, Edinburgh.

Moody Salt. Scroll salt with cut-card decoration, London, 1664-5. H. 19 cm. Victoria and Albert Museum, London.

mortar. Miniature mortar and pestle for pharmaceutical use, London, 1901. H. 2·5 cm. Wellcome Collection, Science Museum, London.

tertwined animals. It is decorated with gilt-bronze medallions bordered in red. A hinged latch extends upward on one end to the bottom of the ridge-pole, which has an extended tag at each end for a carrying strap or chain. It was formerly called the *Brechannoch* of St Columba (521–97) and was found in Scotland, attributed to the 7th/8th century. It is said to have been presented *c.* 1211 by William the Lion (1143–1214), King of Scotland, 1165–1214, to the Abbot of Arbroath, with certain lands and duties, pursuant to which a later Abbot appeared with it at the battle of Bannockburn, 1314, to bless the Scottish army. Thereafter it, with the lands and duties, was transferred to the de Monymusk family, of Aberdeenshire, until transferred to the Irvines of Drum as Custodians, but was kept at Monymusk by Augustinian monks in a priory which in 1534 was partly destroyed by fire; the reliquary was then removed to the House of Monymusk and kept there until 1933, when it was sold to the National Museum of Antiquities of Scotland, Edinburgh.

Moody Salt. A SCROLL SALT having a square base and a smaller square upper platform in which there is a depression for holding salt. From the platform rise four scroll-terminal BRACKETS (one at each corner) to support a plate. The salt has overall decoration of embossed leaves. It is one of the late examples of such scroll salts which were becoming obsolete as the significance of the GREAT SALTS diminished. On the base are the pricked initials 'A' over 'VM'; the piece came into the Moody family *c.*1750, but it is unlikely that the initials, so arranged, have any connection with the family. The piece bears an unidentified maker's mark 'WH' and a London hallmark of 1664–5. It was bequeathed in 1912 by Frances Reubell Bryan to the Victoria and Albert Museum, London.

Moore, Andrew (fl. *c.* 1690–1700). A London silversmith, freed by patrimony in 1664. Little is known of him except that his mark appears on silver FURNITURE, 1690, in the Royal Collection, such as a large TABLE and a WALL MIRROR, and on a set of eight FIRE-DOGS, 1697, owned by the Duke of Buccleuch and Queensberry.

Moor's-head spoon. A type of SPOON having a straight stem surmounted by a finial, on early examples, in the form of a child's head (sometimes said to represent the Holy Child), and later a Moor's head. Such spoons are usually of small size, apparently intended for a child's use. *See* SARACEN'S-HEAD SPOON.

Morel-Ladeuil, Léonard (1820–88). A French designer and maker of silverware, born at Clermont-Ferrand, who achieved his first recognition in Paris, having been from *c.* 1835 a pupil of ANTOINE VECHTE and later his assistant. In 1852 a SHIELD made by him, of silver and DAMASCENED iron, was shown at the Paris Exhibition of Fine Arts, as a result of which he became recognized as an artist in REPOUSSÉ work. He was employed and brought to England in 1859 by Henry Elkington to design and execute prestigious pieces for ELKINGTON & CO., and was provided from 1862 with a studio above the firm's showrooms in Regent St, London. He achieved public recognition with his 'SLEEP' TABLE, shown at the 1862 London International Exhibition, along with two TAZZE with *repoussé* decoration depicting Night and Morning. He adopted and used RENAISSANCE STYLE motifs in the manner revived by Vechte, and his work included mainly elaborately embossed presentation and exhibition pieces, of which (out of the 42 known examples of his work) several were shown in international exhibitions. Among his best-known works are the HELICON VASE, completed in 1871, and the MILTON SHIELD, which latter piece he tried unsuccessfully to emulate with the BUNYAN SHIELD shown in Paris in 1878. The whereabouts of the Invention Vase, designed by him in 1863, is unknown. In 1885 he retired to France, but continued to work for Elkington & Co. until his death.

Moresques. Decorative motifs of intertwined flowers, leaves, and scrolls, used in the 16th–18th centuries and so termed in England, similar to ARAB-ESQUES, especially those derived from Moorish sources in Spain and Sicily, both of which were at one time under Saracen domination. The term is also sometimes applied to a decorative style of Roman motifs which are more properly termed GROTESQUES and which are less frequently found on silverware. There are twenty-eight Moresque patterns engraved by Thomas Geminus in his book, *Morysee and Dansshime* (London 1548), intended for use by goldsmiths.

mortar. A circular vessel in which various materials are triturated with a pestle. Miniature silver examples bearing English hallmarks (but said to have possibly been imported) are about 3·5 cm wide, and have concave sides and two horizontal knob handles. They were intended for pharmaceutical use and also for pulverizing small lumps of sugar broken from a sugar-loaf.

Mostyn Salt. A GREAT SALT of the PEDESTAL SALT type, having a spool-shaped body resting on three CLAW-AND-BALL FEET and having a domed STEPPED cover sumounted by an urn-shaped finial (from which the small figure that was at its top is now missing). This imposing piece of TUDOR SILVERWARE, London, 1586–7, has elaborate overall decoration featuring birds, animals, and half-figures surrounded by floral and foliate motifs. It was at one time part of the plate of Lord Mostyn, of Mostyn Hall, Flintshire, and was bought from him in 1886 for the Victoria and Albert Museum, London. An ELECTROFORM copy is in the Assay Office of the Goldsmiths' Company, London.

mote skimmer (or **spoon**). A type of SPOON having a bowl with a pierced pattern of small holes, used to skim off floating particles of tea leaves and motes (tea dust) from a cup of tea. The handle is thin and tapering, with a sharpened (sometimes barbed) point, perhaps to be used to remove particles of tea leaves clogging the spout of a teapot, although its use is uncertain. Some bowls have pierced work in patterned designs with large openings, probably because in the early days of tea-drinking the particles of tea were coarser than those of today. On some examples the bowl has, on the underside, decoration in relief (*see* PICTURE-BACK SPOON). The terms 'mulberry spoon' and 'olive spoon' have sometimes been used (but without satisfactory explanation) for spoons of this type; the so-called French olive spoons do not have a pointed handle.

mother-of-pearl objects. Articles of which an essential part is made of mother-of-pearl, with silver or silver-gilt MOUNTS, as in the case of some STANDING CUPS and TWO-HANDLED CUPS (with the bowl of mother-of-pearl), and also some BOWLS, BASINS, CASKETS, FLAGONS, and SALTS. *See* MOUNTED OBJECTS.

motto. In heraldry, a word, phrase or sentence that forms part of an ACHIEVEMENT or of a COAT OF ARMS, often found on ARMORIAL PLATE.

mo(u)lding. A band or section applied to an article either as decoration or to conceal a joint, being made with contours varying in section and named by reference to the pattern, such as cyma, ovolo, etc. *See* BILLET; ROPE MOULDING.

Mostyn Salt. Great salt, London, 1586–7. H. 41 cm. Victoria and Albert Museum, London.

mote skimmer. Spoon with foliated pierced work on bowl, London, *c.* 1720. L. 14·7 cm. Wadsworth Atheneum (Elizabeth B. Miles Collection), Hartford, Conn.

mount. (1) A decorative silver ornament attached to an article of glass, or sometimes porcelain, such as the silver FOOT-RING or neck ornament on a CLARET-JUG or a vase. (2) A narrow band affixed to the edge of an article of SHEFFIELD PLATE to conceal the copper at the edge. Mounts varied in type as the technique developed in the period 1750–1825 until they were made of SOLID SILVER, being cast in various patterns. Sometimes mounts of silver WIRE were used to conceal and strengthen the joints of Sheffield plate, as well as mounts made by STAMPING. (3) A silver attachment added to some natural object to make it into a serviceable article, as in the case of the mounts on a COCONUT CUP, a sauce-boat made of COWRIE SHELL, a crystal MARRIAGE CASKET, etc.

mounted objects. A variety of articles, usually a JUG or CUP, embellished with silver or silver-gilt MOUNTS affixed to an object of unrelated material, frequently some natural substance; *see* MOUNTED SPOON. Many such mounted objects made in England in the medieval and Tudor periods, *c.* 1375–1600, survived the melting-pot of the Civil War years, *c.* 1650–60, because the low silver content did not justify their destruction. *See* AGATE OBJECTS; COCONUT CUP; CRYSTAL ARTICLES; GLASS OBJECTS; HORN; IVORY OBJECTS; LEATHER OBJECTS; MOTHER-OF-PEARL OBJECTS; NAUTILUS SHELL; OSTRICH-EGG CUP; CELA-

mother-of-pearl objects. Parcel-gilt dish with mother-of-pearl lining in well, English, 17th century. Victoria and Albert Museum, London.

DON OBJECTS; PORCELAIN OBJECTS; POTTERY OBJECTS; SERPENTINE OBJECTS; STONEWARE OBJECTS; TIGERWARE JUG; WOOD OBJECTS; SKULL CUP.

muffin-dish. Matt silver set with chrysoprases, C. R. Ashbee, London, 1900. D. 22 cm. Victoria and Albert Museum, London.

mounted spoon. A type of SPOON of which the bowl or part of the stem is made of some material unrelated to the silver of the handle, such as a bowl of coconut shell, mother-of-pearl, crystal, agate, etc.

m(o)ustache spoon. A type of SPOON made with a guard on one side of the bowl to protect the user's m(o)ustache, said to have been patented in 1875 by E. B. A. Mitchelson, of Philadelphia, and produced in the United States and England. Examples were made in right-hand and left-hand versions.

mouth. The orifice of a JAR or JUG (pitcher), sometimes having a LIP or a BEAK SPOUT to facilitate pouring.

mouth wire. A band of strengthening silver WIRE applied by SOLDERING around the edge of the mouth of an article after the piece has been shaped by HAMMERING and RAISING.

muffin-dish. A covered DISH with a deep WELL for serving hot muffins, biscuits or tea-cakes. *See* FOLDING BISCUIT-BOX.

muffineer. (1) A type of small CASTER intended primarily for sprinkling tiny grains, such as some ground spices and black pepper, although sometimes said to have been used for salt, sugar, and various spices to be sprinkled on hot muffins. Such casters are usually vase-shaped or pyriform and without any handle; they have a domed cover that is pierced with small circular holes rather than the ornamental pierced work on most casters. The surface is usually smooth, with no decoration except on the cover, but some examples have embossing or engraving. The lower part sometimes has pierced decoration and is provided with a blue-glass liner, and a few are gilded. *See* G. Bernard Hughes, 'Cinnamon for the Muffin' in *Country Life*, 22 October 1959, p. 636. (2) A term sometimes incorrectly applied to a type of receptacle for keeping muffins and biscuits warm, properly known as a FOLDING BISCUIT-BOX.

muffineer. Caster with bands of pierced decoration on body and blue-glass liner, Nathaniel Smith & Co., Sheffield, 1783. H. 11 cm. City Museum, Sheffield.

mug. A drinking vessel in the form of a small TANKARD, having a vertical loop handle, a SCROLL HANDLE or a DOUBLE-SCROLL HANDLE, and a rim without a pouring lip. Only a few have a hinged LID, and these are without the THUMBPIECE such as is found on the lid of a tankard. Mugs may have a flat bottom, a FOOT-RING or a COLLET FOOT. They have been made in various forms, usually cylindrical or tapering cylindrical, but sometimes waisted, barrel-shaped, polygonal, inverted bell-shaped or occasionally 'square' (i.e., cylindrical but having the same measurement for both diameter and height, so as to show a square silhouette), and sometimes having a bulbous lower half and a cylindrical neck. They were decorated with ENGRAVING, FLAT CHASING or EMBOSSING; on some examples the lower third of the body is decorated with encircling lobed fluting. The usual capacity is about a half-pint or one pint. A mug of small size sometimes formed part of a child's CHRISTENING SET. *See* BEAKER; CANN; STEIN.

mull. A Scottish type of SNUFF-BOX, usually made from HORN (the end part of cattle or ram's horns), but sometimes made of silver, or of lignum vitae (a hard wood) or hardstone with silver mounts. The hinged LID on some examples is often set with a cairngorm. A large version is the table mull, to be passed along from one diner to the next (as done with port); some such pieces are made of the horn tips set with cairngorms and equipped with chained implements, such as a snuff-spoon (for applying the snuff to the nose), a rake and spike (for blending the snuff), and a hare's foot (for wiping the upper lip). The term 'mull' is the local dialect for 'mill', as some such boxes also had an apparatus for pulverizing the snuff.

mullet. In heraldry, a small star; sometimes used by a silversmith along with his initials as a part of his registered MAKER'S MARK.

Munro Apostle Spoons. The earliest known complete set of APOSTLE SPOONS with all thirteen bearing the same maker's mark (a fringed 'S') and date mark (London 1527). Each spoon has a silver-gilt finial (the figure having a horizontal nimbus). Eight of the set are recorded as having been owned by Bishop Whyte of Winchester (1511–60), and were purchased in 1890 by the Marquess of Breadalbane, who had the name 'Breadalbane' stamped on the back of each stem; they were acquired on 12 May 1926 by Charles G. Rupert. The remaining five were located in the 1930s in various private collections. The set was donated in 1966 by Mrs W. B. Munro to the

Henry E. Huntington Gallery, San Marino, California. It is not certain whether the thirteen spoons form an original set, as one other such spoon (St Thomas) with the same maker's and date marks is known.

musical horn. A type of wind instrument made of silver in the shape of an ox horn; early examples were made of natural HORN with silver MOUNTS. Such horns have served as a 'horn of tenure' (a token of land rights), an archery prize, or a 'moot horn' (to summon local meetings). *See* DRINKING HORN; HUNTING HORN; POWDER-HORN; MUSICAL WARE.

musical ware. (1) Musical instruments made of silver or having silver mounts, such as a WHISTLE, BELL, MUSICAL HORN, TRUMPET, BUGLE, DRUM. (2) Ornamental pieces in the form of musical instruments, such as a violin.

mustard 'caster'. An early form, *c.* 1670s, of receptacle for serving dry unprepared mustard. It is similar in form to the usual SUGAR CASTER, but the domed cover is either unpierced ('blind') or is blocked with an interior sleeve (now often missing), as the mustard was in the form of a ball of compressed powder, to be scraped or ground by an individual diner and mixed on his plate with vinegar. Sometimes called a 'blind caster' or a 'dry-mustard jar'. *See* MUSTARD-POT.

mustard-pot. A type of small receptacle for serving prepared (wet) mustard. The usual form is the DRUM-SHAPED MUSTARD-POT, but some are vase-shaped (*see* VASE-SHAPED MUSTARD-POT), or occasionally rectangular with rounded corners. Some are of novelty shape, such as one with an ovoid pot and cover or one including an animal figure (*see* MONKEY MUSTARD-POT), and some are OGEE-shaped with ROCOCO STYLE decoration. The hinged LID has a THUMB-PIECE and usually an indentation for the stem of the MUSTARD SPOON. The finial is sometimes in the form of a figure of a monkey grimacing from the strong fumes, sometimes the head of a different animal. Some pots, especially those in cylinder form, are pierced and have a glass LINER (or a gilded interior) to prevent corrosion of the silver by the vinegar in the mustard and to facilitate cleaning. Some are made in sets of three for three varieties of mustard. *See* Norman M. Penzer, 'Mustard and the First Silver Mustard Pots' in *Antique Collector*, October 1957, p. 186, and December 1957, p. 225; Honour Godfrey, 'Silver Mustard Pots – Colman Collection at Cooper Hewitt Museum' in *The Connoisseur*, October 1980, p. 140. *See* MUSTARD 'CASTER'.

mustard spoon. A type of small SPOON for serving prepared (wet) mustard from a MUSTARD-POT. It usually has a slightly curved stem and elongated deep bowl, and rests in the pot, the LID of which is provided with an indentation for the stem. Such silver spoons were used with ceramic mustard-pots as well as with silver pots. Sometimes called a 'mustard ladle'.

Myddleton Cup. A silver-gilt STANDING CUP, the bowl of which is of ovoid shape, having a vase-shaped stem resting on a TRUMPET FOOT and decorated with ACANTHUS leaves. The stem has three brackets, each in the form of a winged female TERM, and on a knop there is, between each pair of brackets, an applied female bust. The bowl is decorated by FLAT CHASING with large scallop shells surrounded by scrollwork and four medallions, one of which shows the arms of Sir Hugh Myddleton, Bt (1555–1631). The cup bears the maker's mark 'RS' and date letter for 1599–1600. Myddleton was a London

mustard-pot. (*Left*) Drum-shaped, Paul Revere II, Boston, Mass., *c.* 1800. H. 6·3 cm. Yale University Art Gallery (Mabel Brady Garvan Collection), New Haven, Conn. (*Centre*) Vase-shaped, Edward Wakelin, London, undated. H. 15 cm. Ashmolean Museum, Oxford. (*Right*). Novelty shape, with goat's-head finial, Paul Storr, 1836. Colman Collection. Courtesy, Garrard & Co. Ltd, London.

Myddleton Cup. Silver gilt, maker's mark 'RS', 1599–1600. H. 27·5 cm. Goldsmiths' Company, London.

goldsmith and banker, with many business activities; in 1610 he was Prime Warden of the Goldsmiths' Company. The cup was given to him in 1613 by the Company in recognition of his work in connection with the New River Project to supply water to London; he presented the cup, *c*.1617, to the head of his family residing near Denbigh, North Wales. Later Robert Myddleton gave it to Sir Hugh's grand-nephew, Hugh M. Peacock, of Stamford, and it remained in the family until the end of the 19th century. It was purchased in 1922 by the Goldsmiths' Company.

Myddleton was lessee of a silver mine in Wales, and three cups made of silver from his mine were donated by him in 1617 to, respectively, the towns of Denbigh, Ruthin, and Oswestry; each cup was inscribed with the name of the town, together with the donor's name, arms, and motto, and bore the London date mark for 1616–17 and the maker's mark 'FS'.

Myers, Myer (1723–95). A leading New York silversmith, of Dutch descent, who was freed from apprenticeship in 1746, and in 1754 was trading in Philadelphia and New York City. During the Revolution he resided in Connecticut, but in 1784 returned to New York. He is best known for having made JEWISH RITUAL SILVERWARE, including pieces commissioned by the Synagogues of Philadelphia and of Newport, Rhode Island, but he also made articles of domestic ware, including BASKETS, CANDLESTICKS, etc. His work was mainly in ROCOCO STYLE, but later he made ware in the FEDERAL STYLE. His marks are 'MM' and 'Myers', and also 'H&M' for Halsted & Myers in 1763–4. *See* Jeanette W. Rosenbaum, *Myer Myers, Goldsmith, 1723–1795* (1954). *See* TORAH BELLS.

N

Nanny Statuette. A drinking cup in the form of a standing figure of a milkmaid, her left hand upraised to support on her head a cylindrical cup in the form of a milk-pail. The plinth is engraved with the name 'NANNY'. The piece was made by FREDERICK KANDLER, 1777, and was formerly in the collection of the Earl of Ducie. *See* STATUETTE.

napkin clip. A type of fastener in the form of a clip, used instead of a NAPKIN RING. Enamelled examples in the form of butterflies, their movable wings operating the clip, were included in the MACKAY SERVICE.

napkin hook. A C-shaped wire hook used to suspend a napkin from the collar or cravat, or with a ring to fit over a waistcoat button. Such pieces were sometimes found in a TRAVELLING SET. Sometimes called a 'napkin claw'.

napkin ring. A circular, elliptical or hexagonal band used to enclose a rolled table napkin and identify the user of the napkin. Such rings are variously decorated, and sometimes bear the engraved name, initials or monogram of the user.

National Cup. A silver-gilt STANDING CUP designed in Gothic Revival style in 1819 by JOHN FLAXMAN II and executed by JOHN BRIDGE for RUNDELL, BRIDGE & RUNDELL in 1824–5. Its compressed pear-shaped bowl, resting on a straight reeded stem with a small central knop, is decorated with three narrow niches, in each of which is the figure of a patron saint (St George of England, St Andrew of Scotland, and St Patrick of Ireland) standing under a Gothic arch; between the niches are wide panels in which are a large rose, a thistle and St Andrew's cross, and a shamrock, all set with gemstones (not in the Flaxman design). The low-domed cover has a finial surmounted by an equestrian figure of St George slaying the Dragon. The cup, sold to George IV on 21 June 1825, is in the Royal Collection. Two later versions of the cup have been recorded; one of 1826–7, set with gemstones, is in a private collection.

native silver. Specimen from Guanexuato, Mexico. W. 5 cm. Geological Museum, London.

native silver. Silver metal occurring naturally, sometimes as crystals, but usually in elongated, reticulated, arborescent, and wiry form, and often combined with small amounts of gold, mercury, and other elements. Superb specimens have been found in Kongsberg, Norway, and some in Peru, Spain, and Mexico.

nautilus shell. The shell of a cephalopod mollusc native to the South Pacific and Indian Oceans; it is a spiral chambered shell of two layers, the outer one porcellaneous and the inner one pearly (hence the name 'pearly nautilus'). Such shells, after having the outer surface decoratively carved, (first done by the Chinese and later by the Dutch), were used as drinking vessels, the flaring lip being cut away and replaced by a smooth silver rim; a carved shell, when encased in an elaborate silver MOUNT, served as a GOBLET, with a foot resting on a spreading base. Among other uses was the incorporation of a shell into a large covered SALT, such as the BURGHLEY NEF. *See* GLYNNE CUP; MOUNTED OBJECTS.

nef. A dinner-table ornamental or utilitarian article in the form of a fanciful model of a ship, with masts, sails, rigging, poop, an ornamental bowsprit, and sometimes canopies on the deck, and with various figures aboard; the hull rests on a ornamental base. The earliest examples, 13th–16th century (in the form of a three-masted carrack, such as the renowned silver-gilt Schlüsselfelder Ship made in Nuremberg, 1503), were drinking cups, but were impracticable; later ones were receptacles for dining implements and napkins. Some included a SALT-CELLAR, and were placed on the table near the host at a banquet as a type of GREAT SALT. No extant English silver example is known, but a copy of a treatise of *c.* 1326–7, at the British Museum, depicts one used in England. Such pieces were used in France, Germany, the Low Countries, Italy, and Spain, and some were imported into England, being mentioned in a 14th-century list of Royal plate; the best known is the BURGHLEY NEF. *See* Charles C. Oman, *Medieval Silver Nefs* (1963).

Nelme, Anthony (fl. 1681–1722). A leading London silversmith, apprenticed in 1672 and freed in 1679, who established his business *c.* 1689. His work, produced in great quantity and variety, was done first in the style of RESTORATION SILVERWARE, and later in the style of HUGUENOT SILVERWARE and in QUEEN ANNE STYLE, pieces in the last two categories perhaps made either by himself or by Huguenot journeymen employed by him. He registered his first mark before 1697, working from *c.* 1685 until his death in 1722 at the Golden Bottle, Amen Corner, Ave Maria Lane, near St Paul's, but also having another shop in Foster Lane in 1691. He made pieces commissioned by Queen Anne soon after 1702, and some for members of the nobility. He took his son, FRANCIS NELME, as a partner in 1721 and was succeeded by him in the following year. His work included a SOUP-TUREEN, 1703 (said to be the first made in England), TEAPOTS, CANDLESTICKS, PILGRIM BOTTLES, and also less pretentious pieces. He had a large establishment, and the work was recognized for the high quality of his technical skill and artistry of design.

Nelme, Francis (fl. 1719–39). The son of ANTHONY NELME, apprenticed to his father in 1712 and freed in 1719. He became a partner of his father in 1721 and succeeded to the business in 1722, working from the same address until 1727. He entered his first mark (his father's pre-1697 mark) in 1723 and a second in 1739. He moved in 1727 to St Martin's Lane, Ludgate, and had a London address in the years 1739–59. He continued to use his father's models, but is best known for his own patterns in more elaborate style. Fewer of his pieces survive than those of his father. His business was taken over in 1739 by Thomas Whipham, a silversmith who had moved from Foster Lane. Whipham took as a partner in 1756 Charles Wright (d. 1815), who managed the business from 1775 to 1783, when it passed to THOMAS CHAWNER, at nearby Amen Corner, Paternoster Row.

Nelson Cup. A TWO-HANDLED CUP bearing an inscription 'To Admiral Lord Nelson / from / Thomas Hardy / 15th June 1804.' The cup is cylindrical, with the bowl tapering inward to a stem that rests on a spreading foot; it has two scroll handles, and is undecorated except for an encircling wire band. It was made by Peter and Ann Bateman (*see* BATEMAN), 1791. The cup was donated in 1924 to the Monmouth Museum, which considers the inscription to be 'dubious'.

neo-classical style. A style of decoration that was a revival, in the second half of the 18th century, of classical decoration (hence sometimes called 'Classical Revival'), based on that of ancient Greece and Rome; it followed the ROCOCO STYLE. Neo-classicism was to some extent a product of the archaeological excavations of Herculaneum and Pompeii in the 1750s, and the term, in its early phases, is more or less interchangeable with the term ADAM STYLE in England, *c.* 1765–95. In France it is often called *Louis Seize* style. It is notable for its employment of SWAGS, wreaths, ANTHEMIONS, PALMETTES,

National Cup. Silver gilt, set with gemstones, John Bridge, London, 1824–5, Royal Collection; reproduced by gracious permission of Her Majesty the Queen.

nautilus shell. Salt in the form of a gamecock, the bowl being a natural shell in silver-gilt mounts, London, *c.* 1570. H. 20·5 cm. Victoria and Albert Museum, London.

Neptune Centrepiece. Silver gilt, maker's mark of Paul Crespin, 1741. H. 68·5 cm. Royal Collection; reproduced by gracious permission of Her Majesty the Queen.

PATERAE, ram's-heads, and similar classical motifs, as well as the frequent use of DROP-RING HANDLES. After the Revolution of 1789 in France, the early neo-classical style developed into the DIRECTOIRE STYLE (principally a furniture style) and then into the EMPIRE STYLE; the latter was contemporary with the English REGENCY STYLE, which owes much to it. During the neo-classical period, mass-production was developed at Birmingham and Sheffield and much ware of SHEFFIELD PLATE was made economically by STAMPING and FLY-PUNCHING, competition being provided by silver articles made of metal of thin GAUGE and having simple designs and ornamentation, such as shallow FLUTING, BEADING, and later BRIGHT CUTTING.

Neptune Centrepiece. A very ornate silver-gilt sculptural CENTREPIECE bearing the mark of PAUL CRESPIN, 1741, but which has been said possibly to have been made by NICHOLAS SPRIMONT and marked for him by Crespin. The elaborate stand is replete with emblems of the sea, shells, and sea-foam; the upraised tails of four dolphins are entwined around scrolls which, together with four mermen, support the tureen-shaped bowl, upon the cover of which sits a figure of Neptune holding a trident. The ROCOCO STYLE piece was made for Frederick, Prince of Wales (eldest son of George II), and is in the Royal Collection. *See* Arthur G. Grimwade, 'Crespin or Sprimont' in *Apollo*, August 1969, p. 126. The bowl and stand are supported by an open-work PLATEAU having four legs in the form of rearing sea-horses joined by festoons and shells, and with a crossed trident and oar upright at each side and end; the plateau was made by RUNDELL, BRIDGE & RUNDELL, but errone-ously attributed by E. Alfred Jones 'probably' to Augustin(e) Courtauld (*see* COURTAULD). A similar silver-gilt two-tiered centrepiece, London, 1780, has been reported to be in the collection of the Duke of Rutland.

Neptune Dish. A large circular DISH (weighing 8·40 kg) of Romano-British silverware, possibly 4th century, found in the 1940s – as part of the MILDEN-HALL TREASURE – covering other pieces of silverware. It has a beaded rim and overall EMBOSSING depicting in the centre a mask of Neptune with dolphins in his hair and beard, encircled by a narrow frieze depicting sea creatures and a wider outer frieze depicting a Dionysian revelry with Bacchus, Her-cules, Pan, and Silenus, and dancing satyrs and maenads.

nest. A group of identical articles that, when stacked one above the other, fit together to give the appearance of a straight-sided composite article, such as a nest of almost cylindrical TUMBLERS or TUMBLER CUPS. Sometimes there is a supporting stand that serves also as a cover for the topmost article, or occa-sionally a spreading base on the lowest one and a separate cover to complete the group. Articles so stacked should have sides that are almost vertical, with no extended FOOT-RING or everted lip which would preclude such stacking. Although most BEAKERS, having a tapering shape, would not form a nest, one set of six made by JOHN BRIDGE, 1828, each with a short stem and a circular foot, but with an almost cylindrical bowl, can be stacked as a nest. *See* CAMP CUP.

Netherhampton Hoard. A HOARD, including seven SEAL-TOP SPOONS (the earliest dated 1596 and the latest 1632) found at Netherhampton, Wiltshire, having been deposited there after 1632. The spoons, which were probably made at Salisbury, have silver stems and silver-gilt seal-top finials. They have been at the British Museum since 1907.

New College (Oxford) Pax. A silver-gilt rectangular PAX depicting the Crucifixion, with cast and chased figures of Christ, the Virgin Mary, and St John the Evangelist (John, xix, 26–7). The scene is within a frame surmounted by a CRESTING of trefoils and delicately engraved with a bird at the top, a dragon-like creature at the bottom, and surrounding branches, foliage, and flowers (including a Tudor rose). The piece has no hallmarks; the pax has been attributed, on stylistic grounds, to English origin, *c.* 1520–30, but the frame has been attributed, on the basis of the Tudor rose, to probably a different craftsman and a slightly later date.

New Orleans silverware. Cake-basket, Adolph Himmel, *c.* 1863–4. W. 33·5 cm. Anglo-American Art Museum, Louisiana State University, Baton Rouge, La.

New Orleans silverware. Articles of silverware made at New Orleans, Louisiana. The earliest pieces were made by French immigrants or their descendants, then after 1812 by English immigrants, and in the 1840s–50s by Germans, including Adolphe Himmel (1826–77; born at Zweibrücken, Germany, he lived in New Orleans from 1851) and Christoph Küchler (fl. 1852–9). The leading firm of silversmiths was Hyde & Goodrich (founded 1829), which – while making some silverware – mainly sold pieces made by Himmel and Küchler, as well as the work of other local, northern, and foreign silversmiths; the firm, after many changes of partners and name, became A. B. Griswold & Co., which continued until 1924. Many New Orleans pieces are at the Anglo-American Art Museum, Baton Rouge, Louisiana. *See* Carey T. Mackie, H. Parrott Bacot, and Charles L. Mackie, *Crescent City Silver* (1980); —, 'Hyde and Goodrich: New Orleans silver manufacturers' in *Antiques*, August 1982, p. 293; Carey T. Mackie, 'New Orleans Silver' in *The Connoisseur*, May 1981, p. 57.

New York bowl. A type of uncovered BOWL, made *c.* 1680–1740, only in New York State (inspired by Dutch BRANDY-BOWLS used on festive occasions and possibly based on a North European type of bowl), being of shallow hemispherical shape, with a diameter of about 14 to 25·5 cm, and resting on

Neptune Dish. Part of the Mildenhall Treasure, Romano-British, 4th century(?). W. 60·5 cm. British Museum, London

Newdigate Centrepiece. Paul de Lamerie, London, 1743-4. H. 23 cm. Victoria and Albert Museum, London.

New York bowl. Benjamin Wynkook, *c.* 1707. Courtesy, Sotheby's, Inc., New York.

nipple shield. David Hennell II and Robert Hennell I, London, 1799. D. 6·5 cm. Wellcome Collection, Science Museum, London.

a low cylindrical FOOT-RING with a flanged lower edge. Such bowls have two opposed vertical cast, S-shaped foliated handles, each usually with a small ball near the top (a debased CARYATID HANDLE). The bowls are decoratively divided into six segments or lobes by chased vertical lines, having within each segment a chased curving outline framing an embossed stylized floral motif. They were made by Dutch and Huguenot silversmiths. An example made by Benjamin Wynkook, *c.* 1707, was sold at Sotheby's, New York, on 17 November 1981. In 1961 eighteen examples, extant or recorded, were listed. Such bowls should be distinguished from similarly shaped bowls of smaller diameter and having a WIRE HANDLE or a cut-steel handle rather than a cast handle. A bowl (called a PUNCH-BOWL), similar in size, form, and decoration to the New York bowls, but without handles, was made in New Haven, Connecticut, *c.* 1745, by Cornelius Kierstede (1675–1757), formerly of New York; it is at the Yale University Art Gallery, New Haven, Connecticut. *See* John N. Pearce, 'New York's two-handled paneled silver bowls' in *Antiques*, October 1961, p. 341. *See* NEW YORK SILVERWARE.

New York silverware. No silverware of local make is known from the period of Dutch control from 1610 until 1664, when the colony came under British control. With the acquisition of silver coins by the privateers in the last quarter of the 17th century, Dutch and Huguenot silversmiths had the material to start their work, making pieces of heavy gauge, especially BEAKERS, BRANDY-BOWLS, PORRINGERS, TANKARDS, MUGS, and TEAPOTS. Among the leading silversmiths were MYER MYERS, the TEN EYCK family, Peter Van Dyck (1684–1751), Simeon Soumain (1685–1750), Nicholas Roosevelt (1715–71), and the FORBES family. *See* NEW YORK BOWL.

Newcastle silverware. Articles of silverware made at Newcastle-upon-Tyne, in north-east England, from the mid-17th century. A cup made by John Wilkerson, 1664, may be the first piece made there. An ASSAY OFFICE was established in 1423, but was closed from 1687 to 1701, re-opened in 1702, and terminated in 1884. A Town Mark was prescribed in 1685 in the form of a single castle, which in 1672 was changed to three towers, two above one; the shape and the size of the shield has varied. The STANDARD HALLMARKS were changed from time to time. Most of the local pieces were domestic ware, including many TANKARDS and TWO-HANDLED CUPS. Among the leading silversmiths were William Ramsey (fl. 1656–70), Eli Bilton (fl. 1682–1703), Isaac Cooksan (d. 1754), John Langlands (d. 1793), and Thomas Watson (fl. 1793–1845). *See* Christopher Lever, 'Two Centuries of Newcastle Silver' in *Country Life*, 14 March 1974, p. 596.

Newdigate Centrepiece. A CENTREPIECE made by PAUL DE LAMERIE, 1743–4. It is in the form of a central bowl resting on a separate circular base, from which extend four curved branches that support detachable circular silver dishes (replaceable by knobs) with borders decorated with flower and shell motifs; the dishes are from the same mould as the dishes on an EPERGNE made by de Lamerie and now in the Royal Collection. The piece is inscribed to record its being a wedding gift to Sir Roger and Lady Newdigate in 1743, and it remained in the family until it was sold in 1919 at Sotheby's, London, and was acquired by the Victoria and Albert Museum, London.

nickel silver. A silver-white ALLOY of copper, nickel, and zinc (no silver) in varying proportions, but usually 2:1:1 to 3:1:1. It is similar to PAKTONG, imported from Canton, China, before nickel became commercially available. It was first produced at Hildburghausen, in Saxe-Meiningen, Germany, *c*.1824, and in Berlin, and was imported in INGOT form into England *c*.1830 and there refined by Percival Norton Johnson, founder of Johnson, Mathey & Co.; it became the principal base used by ELKINGTON & CO. for ware made by ELECTROPLATING. It was also imported into the United States. It is hard and tough, but DUCTILE and MALLEABLE, and not affected by exposure to air, hence was used for tableware and commercial objects. The British platers of Birmingham and Sheffield advertised it from *c*. 1835 as 'Argentan' or 'Berlin Metal', and distinguished it from 'plated German silver' (*see* PLATED METAL). It was also used to make BRITISH PLATE. Until World War I it was called 'German silver'. Sometimes it was called, in the United States, 'Nevada silver'. When electroplated, such wares were sometimes called 'EPGS' (electroplated German silver) or 'EPNS' (electroplated nickel silver).

niello. An inlay used in decorating in black on silver (infrequently on gold) that is somewhat related to CHAMPLEVÉ work except that the effect is metallic rather than vitreous. The process involved engraving (or, for large areas, using other indenting processes) the design into a metal plate, then filling the indented portions with a powdered black matt ALLOY made of metallic sulphides (sulphur with silver, copper, and lead) according to various formulae, together with a flux, after which the piece was heated until the alloy melted (at 1200° C.) and became fused in the grooves and depressions of the design; the piece, when cooled, was scraped and polished until the niello was removed except in the then contrasting design. In the 11th century new niello formulae were developed, and it was used on some pieces made during the Renaissance. The technique was revived in the 19th century and it was used in London by S. H. and D. Gass. In recent years it has been simulated by painting on the surface with a niello preparation as a background or a design.

Noble Chalice. Parcel gilt, English, mid-13th century. H. 14 cm. British Museum, London.

Nile, Battle of the, Cup. A TWO-HANDLED CUP having a semi-ovoid bowl resting on a spreading foot, and having two handles in the form of winged figures of Victory, extending from the rim down to the bottom of the bowl. It was made by PAUL STORR, 1799, and was presented to Admiral Lord Nelson by the Governor and Company of the Merchants of England Trading in the Levant Seas, to commemorate his victory at the Battle of the Nile in 1798. The cover has a finial in the form of a seated figure of Neptune holding a trident, and decoration of dolphins and crocodiles. On one side of the cup is the coat of arms of Nelson, on the other side a donative inscription. Bequeathed by Nelson to his sister, Susannah Bolton, the cup was subsequently inherited by Nelson's nephew, Thomas Bolton, 2nd Earl Nelson, and was acquired with the Trafalgar House Collection by the National Maritime Museum, Greenwich. It is sometimes called 'The Nile Turkey Cup'.

nipple shield. A small protective object to be placed over a nursing woman's nipple during infant feeding. It is a circular, slightly convex, disc having either (1) a central hole that encircles the nipple, or (2) a conical protuberance that fits over the nipple, having a varying number of small pierced holes. Silver examples are numerous from the first decade of the 18th century, and a few earlier. The diameter of the disc ranges from 4·5 to 6·7 cm. *See* MEDICAL SILVERWARE.

Noble Chalice. A mid-13th-century CHALICE, having a wide hemispherical bowl, a stem with a large knop, and a spreading foot, partially decorated with a close HATCHING pattern, and the knop heavily WRITHEN. The outside of the rim, the knop, and the moulding on the foot are gilded, with gilding (renewed at a later date) also on the inside of the bowl. The piece was formerly in the collection of Sir John Noble, Bt, of Ardkinglas, Argyllshire, and was acquired in 1968 by the British Museum, London.

Noble Salt. A silver-gilt STANDING SALT having a shallow bowl, a stem of vase shape with brackets, and a low-domed cover, all completely decorated with scrolls and foliage. The piece, *c*.1610, was for many years in the collection of Sir John Noble, Bt, of Ardkinglas, Argyllshire, and was acquired in 1976 by the British Museum, London.

Norfolk Toilet Service. A TOILET SERVICE of 32 pieces made in 1708 by BENJAMIN PYNE, London, for the 8th Duke of Norfolk; the pieces bear the arms of Howard, in which family the dukedom has remained continuously since 1483.

North American silverware. A broad term sometimes confined to silverware of the United States, sometimes also that of Canada, but rarely includ-

Noble Salt. Silver gilt, maker's mark 'TYL', London, *c*. 1610. H. 21·2 cm. British Museum, London.

Northampton Cup. Ox-eye cup, *c.* 1616. H. 21·7 cm. Trinity Hospital, Greenwich (photo courtesy, the Mercers' Company, London).

ing that of Mexico. *See* CANADIAN SILVERWARE; MEXICAN SILVERWARE; UNITED STATES SILVERWARE.

Northampton Cup. An OX-EYE CUP (COLLEGE CUP) owned by Trinity Hospital, Greenwich (founded in 1615 by the will of Henry Howard, Earl of Northampton), the cup having been donated to it in 1616 by Thomas, Earl of Arundel and Surrey, a grand-nephew of the Earl of Northampton; it is held for the Hospital by the Mercers' Company, London. A replica of the cup was made in 1919 by GARRARD & CO, LTD for Prince Albert (later George VI) upon his taking the freedom of the Mercers' Company.

Norwich Mace. A MACE of which the handle is composed of seven graduated crystal prisms set in silver-gilt mounts and joined together by crystal and silver-gilt bands; its head is in the form of a crown topped by a cross. Both handle and head are studded with cabochon gemstones and pearls. It was made by Augustine Stywards, a goldsmith of Norwich, in 1549–50, and was presented to the City of Norwich on 4 June 1550.

Norwich silverware. Aricles of English silverware made at Norwich, in Norfolk. Goldsmiths were recorded there from 1142, but marked pieces are known only from 1565, when an ASSAY OFFICE was established; it continued until 1697, and date letters were established during the periods 1565–71, 1624–42, and 1688–97. The Town Mark was originally a castle surmounting a lion passant; in the 17th century it was a crowned rose and later a rose with a stem; and after 1701 a variant of the earliest mark was used. The ware was principally CHURCH PLATE, but extant pieces include BEAKERS, FLAGONS, TANKARDS, and SPOONS. The leading local silversmith was long thought to have been Peter Peterson, but pieces thought to bear his mark have recently been attributed to William Cobbold (1530–86). Other leading silversmiths were Timothy Scottowe (1595–1645) and Arthur Haselwood (1593–1671). *See* G. N. Barrett, *Norwich Silver and its Marks, 1565–72* (1981); George Levine, 'Silver made in Norwich' in *The Connoisseur*, November 1973, p. 199; Margaret Holland, 'Norwich Silver' in *Antiques*, June 1984, p. 1374.

Nottingham Butter Dish. A silver-gilt BUTTER-DISH in the form of a low circular bowl of which the side is decorated with pierced vinework. It has a domed cover in coronet style, with the dome of 'frosted' ungilded silver, within six gilded vertical straps extending from the bottom rim upward to a flower finial. The bowl, which rests on a wider gilded stand with fluted decoration and four scrolled feet, has a close-fitting silver-gilt LINER. Made by PAUL STORR, 1817–18, for RUNDELL, BRIDGE & RUNDELL, the piece is owned by the Castle Museum, Nottingham.

nozzle. A cylindrical candle-holder that fits within the SOCKET of a CANDLESTICK or CANDELABRUM and is detachable. It usually has a wide rim to serve as a DRIP-PAN (*bobêche*), but not when it is elaborately decorated in relief or with GADROONING or is otherwise embellished. It is sometimes ambiguously called a 'socket' and erroneously called a SCONCE.

nutcracker. A type of implement for cracking nuts, consisting of two arms joined to each other at one end by a hinge, the arms being recessed or multi-pronged so as to hold a nut in position when pressure is applied to it. The arms are usually connected by a swivel hinge that is reversible to allow use with nuts of different sizes. As silver would be too soft for the intended use, most nutcrackers are of SILVER-PLATED WARE, while some have silver handles with steel ends and hinge. *See* LOBSTER CRACK.

nutmeg grater. An implement for grating nutmeg (to be sprinkled on punch, toddy or other hot beverages, or on meat or other food), used principally during the period 1780–1840. There were two types: (1) portable,

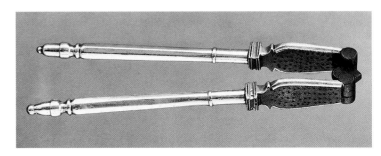

nutcracker. Silver handles, London(?), *c.* 1770. L. 14·5 cm. Colonial Williamsburg, Va.

made in a variety of shapes, such as a cylindrical tube, a circular, oval or rectangular box, a teardrop, heart, egg, urn, or rum-keg; and (2) table type, half-cylindrical or canoe-shaped. Inside there was a space for the whole nutmeg, an iron or steel grater, and sometimes space for storing grated nutmeg. Many examples bear a monogram, but few a crest. The pieces, which had one or more hinged LIDS or SLIP-ON COVERS, were usually plain, though some were decorated with BRIGHT CUTTING. *See* G. Bernard Hughes, 'Silver Nutmeg-graters' in *Country Life*, 30 December 1954, p. 2306; Judith Banister, 'Silver Nutmeg Graters' in *Antique Dealer and Collectors Guide*, October 1965, p. 51; Elizabeth B. Miles, *The English Silver Pocket Nutmeg Grater* (1966). *See* TOBACCO RASPER.

O

oar. A silver replica of an oar, for many years a symbol primarily of Admiralty jurisdiction, usually decorated with an engraved or relief depiction of a foul anchor. The shape resembles a steering oar more than a rowing oar. In England there have been two types: (1) an oar combined with a MACE, which is a symbol of the jurisdiction of the Admiralty Division of the High Court to arrest on the high seas, and which is placed before the Court when in session and carried in processions by the Admiralty Marshal; and (2) simpler forms (called a 'Water Bailiff's Oar') that serve as the symbols of suthority granted to various ports over local waters and are carried by local water-

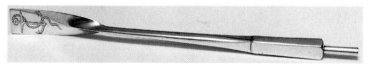

oar. Admiralty oar with engraved foul anchor, L. 61 cm. Courtesy, Massachusetts Historical Society, Boston, Mass.

bailiffs. In England an oar was formerly carried before a criminal convicted in the Admiralty Court and being led to execution. Sixty oars (out of 67 known examples) were shown in 1966 at an exhibition at the National Maritime Museum, London, the earliest ones dating from 1485 and 1559. Some examples were kept in a cylindrical case, on the top of which the oar could be screwed. Sometimes a TIPSTAFF conceals a miniature oar, to be screwed on the top to evidence the right of a water-bailiff to make an arrest on a ship. In the American Colonies the oar symbolized the authority granted by the English Crown to arrest persons and vessels on the high seas; it was placed before a sitting judge and carried before a condemned pirate on his way to execution. Such oars usually have inscribed on the handle the name of the Court and on the blade on one side the Royal arms and on the other side the foul anchor. Some are of silver, some of silver on an iron core. In modern times silver oars have been awarded as rowing prizes. *See* G. Bernard Hughes, 'Silver Oars of the Admiralty' in *Country Life*, 10 August 1958, p. 748; Judith Banister, 'The Right to Bear a Silver Oar' in *Country Life*, 16 June 1966, p. 1602; Joan Woollambe, 'The Silver Oar: Symbol of Admiralty Jurisdiction' in *Apollo*, April 1967, p. 288.

oenochoe ewer. A type of EWER made of silver in the form of an ancient Greek pottery oenochoe. An example in the Victoria and Albert Museum, London, was made in London, 1840–1, by Charles Reily and George Storer, closely adapted as to form, but with different decoration, from a pottery ewer in the collection of Sir William Hamilton, illustrated in the 1766–7 catalogue by d'Hancarville, pl. 23; the piece has, on a ground of HATCHING, an encircling frieze of classical figures. *See* OENOCHOE-TYPE SILVERWARE; GREEK-VASE SILVERWARE.

oenochoe-type silverware. Articles of silverware made in the 1850s–70s based in general on the form of the ancient Greek pottery oenochoe, but varying in several particulars. A number of such pieces were made. One example is a HOT-WATER JUG that forms part of a COFFEE SERVICE/TEA SERVICE in so-called Etruscan style made by TIFFANY & CO., 1858–73, the service also including a COFFEE-POT, TEAPOT, MILK-JUG, CREAM-JUG, SLOP-BOWL, and

oenochoe ewer. Frieze of classical figures on hatched ground, Charles Reily and George Storer, London, 1840-1, H. 30·5 cm. Victoria and Albert Museum, London.

SUGAR-BOWL, all once owned by William Slocum Groesbeck (1815–97), of Ohio, and now in the Yale University Art Gallery. The hot-water jug has a hemispherical bowl, an elongated cylindrical neck, a hinged lid upon which rests a replica of a Greek helmet, and a SQUARE HANDLE that rises above the top of the lid and has a female mask at the top corner; the bowl is decorated with an encircling low-relief frieze depicting classical figures and horsemen on a ground of HATCHING, and with engraved ANTHEMION motifs on the neck and applied ACANTHUS leaves on the lower part of the bowl. A silver-gilt hot-water jug of similar form, but with different surface decoration, was made by Edward Moore, for Tiffany & Co., c. 1861, and was presented to President Lincoln upon his first inauguration, 1861; it is now in the Smithsonian Institution, Washington, D.C. A hot-water jug and a teapot of basically the same form and decoration were made in 1867 by Roberts & Belk, of Sheffield. A very similarly shaped and decorated jug was made in 1857–8 by Thomas Bradbury & Sons, Sheffield (it is now in the Victoria and Albert Museum, London) and another was made by EDWARD BARNARD & SONS, 1861. *See* OENOCHOE EWER; GREEK-VASE SILVERWARE.

oenochoe-type silverware. Hot-water jug, Tiffany & Co., New York, c. 1860. H. 24 cm. Yale University Art Gallery (gift of George Pierson in honour of Charles C. Montgomery), New Haven, Conn.

officer's mess-kit. A set of eating implements in a fitted case for use by an army officer; it normally includes a KNIFE (sometimes with a corkscrew attached), FORK, and SPOON. The implements, often of silver, were usually made with a hinge to allow them to be folded in half; the HANDLES were often made of ivory, Such kits became popular among British officers at the time of the Boer War, 1899–1902.

ogee. A curve with a double or S-shaped form, one curve convex extending into one concave. It occurs as the sectional form of a MOULDING on some silverware.

oil-and-vinegar cruets. A pair of matching CRUETS for oil and vinegar. Some have as the finial on the LID a cut-out capital letter 'O' or 'V'.

oil-and-vinegar stand. A type of STAND or frame with provision for holding two CRUETS, usually in the form of a flat platform resting on small feet and having two galleried rings or two wire frames to hold the cruets in place. Some examples have two small rings at the side for the stoppers of glass cruets, and sometimes a ring for a CASTER. The glass cruets usually have a silver handle and neck with pouring lip and lid, or merely a silver stopper. *See* CRUET STAND; SOY STAND.

oil lamp. A type of LAMP that provides artificial light by combustion of oil, usually by means of a lighted wick. Some silver examples are in the form of the Roman terracotta oil lamp, such as one made in 1806–7 by DIGBY SCOTT and BENJAMIN SMITH I. Another type, sometimes called an 'oil candlestick', is in the form of a CHAMBER CANDLESTICK, with a central oil reservoir surmounted by a globular glass chimney, and has, rising from the base, a tall vertical carrying handle. *See* ARGAND LAMP; SANCTUARY LAMP.

oil lamp. Digby Scott and Benjamin Smith I, London 1806–7. H. 5·7 cm. Victoria and Albert Museum, London.

oil stock. The same as a CHRISMATORY.

Old English pattern. A pattern of FLATWARE, in which the undecorated stem of the handle widens gradually toward the curved-end terminal and then turns downward (in contrast to the earlier HANOVERIAN PATTERN, where the handle turns upward); the terminal is raised and has a central inward point. It is the pattern found on the earliest English SPOON having its stem curving in the opposite direction to the bowl. The pattern was popular from c. 1760 to c. 1820. Spoons of such form were in the 1770s embellished with the FEATHER-EDGE PATTERN and in the 1780s with BRIGHT CUTTING or THREADING.

Old Sheffield Plate. *See* SHEFFIELD PLATE.

Oliveyra, Abraham Lopes de (1657–1750). Probably the earliest Jewish silversmith in London. He was born in Amsterdam, came to London in 1697, and entered his first mark c. 1724–5, with address at St Helen's, Bishopsgate, and a second mark in 1739, with address at 112 Houndsditch (near the Bevis Marks Synagogue). He did work for several London synagogues from c. 1719, making JEWISH RITUAL SILVERWARE, but he also made secular ware, and was, in addition, an accomplished engraver. His earliest-known extant work is a pair of TORAH BELLS, 1716–17, bearing the unregistered maker's mark 'AO' (then illegal, for it did not consist of the first two letters of his surname, as required since 1697); he made other Torah bells from 1725 to 1737, and also in 1737 a DOUCEUR (Lord Mayor's Salver) which has not survived. *See* Jonathan Stone, 'Anglo-Jewish Silver …' in *Antique Collector*, February 1985, p. 64.

Olympic Torch, The. A TROPHY made in Birmingham, 1948, from a design by BERNARD CUZNER and executed by Cuzner and Stanley G.Morris, with engraving by William Biddle; it was commissioned by the Goldsmiths' Company on the occasion of the XIVth Olympiad, held in London in 1948. The torch has an octagonal stem narrowing down to a WRITHEN ball and a rounded terminal; at the upper end there is an octagonal ornament decorated with panels of oak leaves and flowers, above which is a nozzle for the flame, the nozzle being decorated with four crowned leopard's heads alternating with flat-chased decoration. Rising from the nozzle is a silver-gilt openwork flame. The stem bears an engraved inscription 'This torch was made for the Worshipful Company of Goldsmiths'.

Onslow pattern. A decorative pattern on the handle of FLATWARE and CUT-LERY, mainly on SERVING SPOONS and LADLES, having a stem that widens toward the ribbed scroll terminal which curves downward. It was named after Sir Arthur Onslow (1691-1768), who was six times Speaker of the House of Commons, 1728-61. Such pieces were first made *c.*1745-75, and the pattern is still popular.

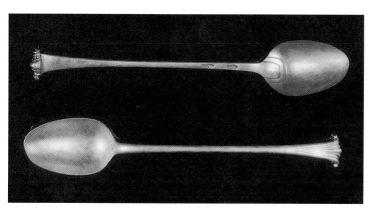

Onslow pattern. Serving spoons, Myer Myers, New York, *c.* 1760-75. L. 29 cm. Yale University Art Gallery (Mabel Brady Garvan Collection), New Haven, Conn.

openwork. A style of reticulated decoration on silver articles, featuring openings in the body of the piece which permit the passage of light. The work is executed by (1) PIERCING, (2) SAW CUTTING, or (3) WIREWORK. It is found on some HOLLOW WARE, such as a BREAD-BASKET, FRUIT-BOWL or SALT-CELLAR, and on some FLATWARE, such as a FISH SLICE or the rim of a SALVER. Sometimes the openwork is more utilitarian than decorative, as on a MAZA-RINE, TEA STRAINER or SIFTER SPOON, as well as the COVER of various types of CASTER. *See* FRET; SHEATHED WARE.

orange-and-lemon strainer. A type of STRAINER used in the mid-17th and 18th centuries for straining the juice of oranges or lemons, used for flavouring punch. Most examples have two horizontal side handles or rests, either flat pierced handles or shaped wire handles; others have one tubular handle, one flat handle, or one vertical ring handle. The flat bottom of the shallow bowl of the strainer is extensively pierced (sometimes by drilling or SAW-CUTTING), the perforations being simple dots placed in circular or geometric patterns or being decorative patterned arrangements of variously shaped holes. Some examples with one handle have, on the rim opposite the handle, a hook to allow the piece to be hung on the rim of the receptacle when not in use. The usual width ranges from about 6·5 to 11·5 cm. Large strainers, about 30 to 60 cm wide, for straining juice directly into a PUNCH-BOWL, are PUNCH STRAINERS. *See* Bernard Chewdson, 'Silver Strainers' in *The Connoisseur*, May 1950, p. 106; G. Bernard Hughes, 'Evolution of the Orange Strainer' in *Country Life*, 9 May 1968, p.1240. *See* TEA STRAINER; WINE FUNNEL.

order. The BADGE or insigne worn by a member of various types of orders, such as the orders of Royalty, nobility, chivalry or merit, e.g., the British Order of the Garter. The badges were sometimes made of silver or silver gilt (or gold), usually ornately enamelled and set with gemstones. Such badges, as well as the badges of guilds and other bodies, are generally beyond the scope of this book. *See* MASONIC BADGE.

Ormside Bowl. A BOWL composed of two joined shells – an outer silver-gilt shell ornamented with REPOUSSÉ decoration of cursive interlacing of Celtic character, and an inner shell of plain gilded bronze – held together by rivets that are concealed on both shells by applied bosses, some of which are set

Ortolan Basket. Wickerwork basket with 'wheatear' nests, Robert Hennell IV, London, 1850. L. 70·5 cm. Goldsmiths' Company, London.

with glass paste. The bottom of the inner shell is depressed, and above it a raised medallion is affixed by five rivets and encircled by plaited silver-gilt wire. A similar medallion is on the outer shell, and the bosses on the rivets serve as feet for the bowl. The bowl dates from the Anglo-Saxon period, late 8th century, and was found in the churchyard at Ormside (Ormshead), Westmorland (now Cumbria). It is owned by the Yorkshire Museum, York.

Ortolan Basket. A WICKERWORK BASKET made for serving ortolans, small passage-migrant birds (a species of bunting sometimes called, incorrectly, a wheatear – the wheatear being a smaller species) that were netted, fattened, and served as a delicacy. The embossed interior of the basket is made to simulate twelve adjacent bird's nests formed of woven stalks and ears of wheat (probably symbolic of the erroneous appellation 'wheatear'), with the tips of ten ears projecting slightly over the rim of the basket. The piece has a BAIL HANDLE surmounted by a coronet. The group of nests is removable (to facilitate cleaning) and is attached to the raised bottom of the basket by six wing-head screws. The basket, made by Robert Hennell IV (*see* HENNELL), is marked London, 1850; it is owned by the Goldsmiths' Company, London. For a similar type of basket, having six nests composed of stalks and ears of wheat, but made of English earthenware, *see* R. F. Johnson, 'English Ortolans: A Gastronomic Bygone' in *Country Life*, 18 November 1954, p. 1751, where it is stated that wheatears were tiny birds found in great numbers on the Sussex Downs, snared by shepherds for sale to city epicures (they were a favourite dish of Charles II), and even extolled in poetry; the species has, however, been protected since 1947.

Osgood Cup. A STANDING CUP having a cylindrical bowl resting on a stem with three knops and a flat base. The cover is surmounted by two upraised arms holding a heart and bears an inscription in Greek and Latin. The cup, made in London, 1680-1, was given to Winchester College by Dr Richard Osgood (d. 1693), a Fellow of the College.

Osman, Louis (1914–). An English architect, designer, and maker of silver articles, producing some pieces by ELECTROFORMING. He has made ecclesiastical pieces for several English cathedrals. *See* RADNOR CENTREPIECE.

Ostrich Cup, The. An OSTRICH-EGG CUP, of which the bowl is mounted in encircling horizontal bands at the top and bottom, joined by three hinged vertical straps, and rests on a stem in the form of three ostrich legs standing on a capstan-shaped base. The cover, completing the egg shape, is surmounted by a figure of an ostrich standing on three ostrich feathers. The MOUNTS are of silver gilt. The unmarked piece, 1610, has been owned since at least 1618 by Exeter College, Oxford, and was held back when silver plate was ordered to be handed over to Charles I in 1642.

ostrich-egg cup. A type of STANDING CUP of which the bowl (and sometimes also the cover) is made from the shell of an ostrich egg. Such pieces have a silver stem and base, and have ornamented hinged vertical straps of silver or silver gilt to hold the shell in place. In some early records, the term 'gryphon-egg cup' was used to designate such cups, perhaps in the belief that the eggs were those of the large griffon-vulture. The shell of an ostrich egg has also been used to make a EWER and a TANKARD (*see* ASTON TANKARD). *See* OSTRICH CUP, THE; DUCIE CUP; FLETCHER CUP; GOODRICKE CUP; MOUNTED OBJECTS.

Outram Shield. A SHIELD having a central medallion depicting in relief the transfer by Lt-Gen. Sir James Outram (1803–63), the British general of the Bombay Army in India, and Chief Commissioner of Oudh, of his command to General Henry Havelock for the relief of Lucknow in the Indian Mutiny. The medallion is encircled by a narrow band decorated with foliage, interspersed with eight small relief medallions with heads of his friends and comrades, then by a wide border with a frieze depicting events in his career, and then by a narrow band; the shield is made of OXIDIZED SILVER and the two bands of steel are decorated with DAMASCENED gold. The shield was designed and modelled by HENRY HUGH ARMSTEAD, adapting the style of ANTOINE VECHTE, and was made for HUNT & ROSKELL, bearing the maker's mark of John Samuel Hunt and Robert Roskell, with the London date mark for 1862-3. It was made for presentation to Outram by his friends in the Bombay Presidency to commemorate the relief of Lucknow in 1858. It was shown at the London International Exhibition of 1862 and at the Paris Exposition of 1867. It is owned by Outram's great-great-grandson, Sir Alan Outram, Bt, and is on loan to the Victoria and Albert Museum, London.

ovoid cup. A type of STANDING CUP, with cover, of Grecian form (adapted from a Wedgwood pottery design), the shape of the bowl and cover together

Ostrich Cup. Ostrich-egg bowl in silver-gilt mounts, unmarked, 1610. H. 25·5 cm. Exeter College, Oxford.

being ovoid, with the bowl resting on a small TRUMPET FOOT. A silver-gilt example, with the mark of Francis Boone Thomas, London, 1873, is decorated with vertical ATTENUATED ribbing, alternately raised (plain) and sunken (matt), and midway with an encircling band of drapery SWAGS and, encircling the base, a KEY-FRET BORDER; it has two handles in the form of bearded satyrs with ram's horns and a finial in the form of an acorn. A comparable piece, marked 'JBC' (for JOHN BODMAN CARRINGTON), London, 1902, is similar except that the decorative centre band is of olives and the band encircling the foot is floral. Both pieces are owned by the Goldsmiths' Company, London. A similar piece, but with the finial in the form of a nude *putto*, was made by John Arnell, London, 1772–3; it is in the Victoria and Albert Museum, London. (Two Wedgwood examples, of black basaltes, *c.* 1775, have acorn finials, as does a modified version, 1920, and an example with a chocolate-coloured glaze, 1875, has a vase-shaped finial.)

owl silverware. Articles of silverware, made by CASTING, in the form of a standing owl. Large examples were made to hold a wine-bottle and had a detachable head; small examples were made as an INKPOT, the owl's head being a hinged LID. Occasionally a CASTER or PEPPERETTE was made in the form of an owl, with pierced sprinkling holes in the detachable head, as well as a MUSTARD-POT with a removable head. *See* OWL SPOON.

owl spoon. A type of SPOON having a straight stem terminating in a finial in the form of a figure in-the-round depicting an owl. Examples made in England are known, one set being dated 1506.

ownership mark. A type of mark (not a HALLMARK) intended to provide evidence of ownership, it is found engraved on some early English silverware, e.g., on the BERMONDSEY DISH.

ox-eye cup. A type of CUP having a pear-shaped body and a slightly flaring mouth, and characteristically having two opposed ring-shaped vertical handles at the neck, hence called an 'ox-eye cup'. The capacity is about two-thirds of a pint. Such cups were used at some English colleges (hence sometimes called a 'college cup'), especially at Oxford University, and also at Eton College, the Inns of Court, and some of the Livery Companies, but none is known from Cambridge University. The earliest recorded example dates from 1616; others are known from the early 18th to the late 19th century. Such cups have been presented to several Oxford colleges, where various names have been applied to them, e.g., 'ox-eye' (at Merton, Corpus Christi, New College, and St John's), 'tun' (at Magdalen, which owns nearly 50, and at Brasenose), 'zegadine' (so called since 1642 at Balliol); at Eton College the term 'Strangers' Cup' is used. Examples are sometimes called merely a 'silver pot with ears'. A modern version, made by JOHN DONALD, is at Balliol College. *See* NORTHAMPTON CUP.

Oxford Colleges Plate. Articles of silverware owned by individual colleges of the University of Oxford. *See* H. C. Moffatt, *Old English Plate* (1906), with photographs of over 150 articles, made at various dates between *c.* 1350 and 1815, owned by eighteen of the colleges.

oxidized silverware. Articles of silverware that have been given a matt, greyish surface, by the process of oxidation (combination with oxygen). After being introduced into England from France and Germany in the 1850s, such ware soon came to be preferred to FROSTED SILVER with its brilliant surface finish. The technique was developed by PIERRE-ÉMILE JEANNEST and used also by HENRY HUGH ARMSTEAD. Other silversmiths extended its use by combining it with other techniques, such as PARCEL GILDING. *See* TARNISH.

oyster fork. A type of dining FORK for eating raw oysters or clams from the half-shell; it is smaller than other table table forks and has three (sometimes four) pointed tines. Early examples have long straight tines of equal length, but modern ones have short tines, the outer two being wide, flat, and curved.

ovoid cup. Silver gilt, Francis Boone Thomas, London, 1873. H. 25·5 cm. Goldsmiths' Company, London.

oyster fork. Hester Bateman, London, 1790. L. 13·5 cm. Holburne of Menstrie Museum (University of Bath).

P

pad. A small metal connection sometimes found at the juncture of a handle, or the FERRULE for a handle, with the body of an object, such as a COFFEE-POT; it may vary in form and thickness.

pagoda epergne. A type of EPERGNE which has, in addition to several curving arms that support various sorts of dishes or bowls, a decorative canopy at the top in the form of a pagoda roof from which small bells are suspended, and which is usually surmounted by a finial, sometimes in the form of a figure in-the-round. Some rare examples have a double canopy, one above the other.

pail. A type of receptacle for holding and carrying a liquid or other substance, such as ice. It is usually cylindrical, tapering slightly inward toward the base and having a flat bottom and a swinging BAIL HANDLE. Sometimes called a 'bucket'. *See* CREAM-PAIL; ICE-PAIL.

pair. Two objects of the same kind and form, suited to each other and intended to be used together as a unit or to stand together as related figures; they are more sought after when bearing the same maker's marks and date marks. Objects forming a pair are not necessarily identical. *See* COMPANION PIECE; SET; GROUP.

Pairpoint, Thomas J. (fl. 1860–80). An English designer of silverware, initially specializing in designing and executing SHIELDS, examples having been made for Lambert & Rawlings, London, and for Joseph Angell III (*see* ANGELL) which won awards in 1862, and another for HARRY EMANUEL, that was exhibited in Paris in 1867. He went to the United States in 1868 to design for the GORHAM COMPANY; his designs there include the CENTURY VASE, and among other notable items attributed to him are HIAWATHA'S BOAT, pieces in the FURBER SERVICE, and most of the articles of HIGH VICTORIAN STYLE made by Gorham. He made a competition design in 1875 for the BRYANT VASE, but it was not selected. After he left Gorham in 1877, he joined the Meriden Britannia Company, Meriden, Connecticut, and in the 1880s he helped form the Pairpoint Manufacturing Co. *See* EPERGNE-CANDELABRUM

paktong (from Chinese *pai-t'ung*, white copper). An ALLOY of nickel, copper, and zinc, resembling NICKEL SILVER. It is white with a yellowish tinge, hard and tough. It was made in China before 1597 at Canton, and was imported into England in the 18th century as a private venture by officers of

pagoda epergne. Thomas Pitts, London, 1761. L. 102·5 cm. Folger's Coffee Collection, Procter & Gamble Co., Cincinnati, Ohio.

the East India Company. It was made into various articles (erroneously termed 'tutenag', a related zinc alloy), such as CANDLESTICKS (sometimes silver-plated), fire-grates, and fenders. It was first produced in England by Edward Thomason, of Birmingham, in 1823, and later developed in Germany as nickel silver.

pale. A narrow vertical strip; usually such strips are arranged in rows to form an openwork pattern, occuring as decoration either on some pieces having a glass LINER or as a GALLERY on trays, etc.

palmette. A decorative motif in the form of a stylized palm leaf resembling a spread fan. It consists of an odd number of stylized leaves of diminishing size and radiating outward from a tall central leaf. In appearance, it is not unlike the Greek ANTHEMION but is derived from the fronds of the date palm. It has been used repetitively in a row to form a border pattern encircling the base of some CUPS and TANKARDS or the rim of some DISHES.

palm-tree candlestick. A type of TABLE CANDLESTICK in the form of a palm tree, the stem – representing the trunk – being surmounted by palm fronds; on a pair made by TIFFANY & CO. the fronds are detachable.

pan. A type of cooking utensil that is broad and shallow, having a flat bottom and a single long horizontal handle. Such utensils are not generally made of silver except as an accessory to a CHAFING DISH; but *see* PRESERVING PAN.

palm-tree candlestick. Pair, with detachable fronds. Courtesy, Tiffany & Co., New York.

Pantin. A family of five generations of English silversmiths. Simon Pantin I (fl. *c.* 1694–1728), a Huguenot from a Rouen family, emigrated to London and was apprenticed to PIERRE HARACHE I from *c.* 1694 and freed in 1701. He established himself in St Martin's Lane, 1699–1701, and entered his first mark from there in 1701, moving to St Martin's in the Fields in 1709–11; he entered a second mark in 1717 and a third in 1720, both with address at Castle St, Leicester Fields. He had a wide clientele and produced many important pieces now in major collections and museums.

Simon Pantin II (died 1733), became his father's apprentice in 1717; he entered his first mark in 1729 and his second in 1731. Mary Pantin, widow of Simon Pantin II, entered her mark in 1733, address Green St, Leicester Fields, until 1735. Lewis Pantin I, presumably a son of Simon Pantin II, with no record of apprenticeship or freedom, entered his first mark in 1734 and a second in 1739; he is said to have been the successor of Simon Pantin II in the period 1733–44. His son, Lewis Pantin II, entered a number of marks at various addresses between 1768 and 1802, and his son, Lewis Pantin III, freed by patrimony in 1799, with address at St Martin's Le Grand, entered marks in 1788 and 1798. *See* Edward Wenham, 'The Pantin Family' in *Antique Collector*, March–April 1945, p. 58.

pap-boat. A small receptacle for feeding pap (a soft food made of bread cooked in milk) to infants and invalids. The typical form is boat-shaped, having the feeding end shaped as a short lip or an extended tapering lip to be placed to the mouth of the person being fed, and the holding end somewhat incurved, and usually without a handle. Some examples are circular, and some have a fixed cover extending over either the holding or the feeding half. Occasionally there is a flat handle or a vertical loop handle, and sometimes a long, straight, stem handle; those without a handle may in some cases have a flat and pointed projection extending level with the rim on the holding end. Silver examples are sparsely decorated, usually with only a reeded or narrow embossed rim; however, a few have a rim with scalloped edge or GADROONING, and some have decoration on the bowl of REPOUSSÉ work. A few have a coin embedded in the interior of the bowl. The length ranges from 7 to 14 cm. *See* SPOUT CUP; MEDICAL SILVERWARE.

pap-boat. Hester Bateman, London, 1785. L. 11·8 cm. Wellcome Collection, Science Museum, London.

parapet teapot. The same as a CAPE TEAPOT.

parcel gilding. A style of decoration on silverware where only a part of the article is covered with GILDING, e.g., a design in relief gilded to contrast with its smooth silver background. Sometimes called 'party-gilt'.

Parker, John (fl. 1758–77). A London silversmith, apprenticed in 1751 to GEORGE WICKES and freed in 1762. He entered his first mark sometime after 1758 with EDWARD WAKELIN, successor to Wickes, with address at Panton St, Haymarket, presumably making a substantial cash contribution. In 1766 JOHN WAKELIN, son of Edward, became an apprentice, and the firm continued until 1776 when Parker and Edward Wakelin retired, to be succeeded in 1777 by John Wakelin and William Taylor, which firm made some important

Parker Salt. Silver-gilt pedestal salt, Robert Danbe(?), London, 1562-3. H. 29·3 cm. Corpus Christi College, Cambridge.

pieces, e.g., the BOLTON CENTREPIECE. In 1792 Wakelin took as a partner ROBERT GARRARD I, and the firm subsequently became GARRARD & CO. LTD. (Another London silversmith named John Parker appears to have been not related.)

Parker Ewer. A silver-gilt EWER 1545-6, of octagonal section and resting on a circular base, the eight vertical panels of the bowl being alternately plain or decorated with engraved ARABESQUE patterns. The handle is an angular loop, and the bowl has a WEDGE-SHAPED SPOUT. The lid has a vertical thumbpiece with a central medallion enamelled with the arms of Matthew Parker, Master of Corpus Christi College, Cambridge, 1544-53, and Archbishop of Canterbury, 1559-75, who donated the piece, with the companion ROSE-WATER BOWL and other plate, on 1 September 1570 to Corpus Christi College. It is the earliest-known example of a rose-water ewer of such form made in England and is similar in outline to a design by Hans Holbein the Younger. The interior of the accompanying bowl is decorated with widening spiral fluting, within which is a central disc bearing the arms of Parker as Archbishop, added after 1559.

Parker Salt. A silver-gilt PEDESTAL SALT having its body of drum shape, decorated with three embossed satyr masks, and having a tiered cover decorated with three embossed heads of cherubs, and topped by a high flask-shaped finial supported by three projecting sea-horses. The base rests on three feet in the form of forequarters of monsters. The piece bears the mark 'RD', probably for Robert Danbe, London 1562-3, and was donated by Archbishop Matthew Parker on 1 September 1570, with other plate, to Corpus Christi College, Cambridge. *See* PARKER EWER.

Parker Standing Cup. A silver-gilt STANDING CUP, *c.*1565, having a spool-shaped body resting on a vase-shaped stem supported by a spreading foot, and having a cover with a bracketed finial surmounted by a figure of Cupid holding a shield and a staff. It was donated on 1 January 1569 by Matthew Parker (Archbishop of Canterbury, 1559-75) to Gonville and Caius College, Cambridge. A standing cup, *c.*1565, of similar shape but differing in decoration (and lacking its finial), was donated by him at the same time to Trinity Hall, Cambridge. Inside the cover of both pieces there is an engraved inscription.

Parr Pot. A glass JUG with a hinged lid, having wide vertical bands of opaque white *(lattimo)* Venetian-style *(façon de Venise)* glass, separated by narrow stripes of clear glass and having silver-gilt MOUNTS (the base, collar neck-band, and lid) hallmarked London, 1546-7. The lid bears the enamelled coat of arms of William, Lord Parr of Horton (d. 1546), uncle and Chamberlain of Henry VIII's sixth wife, Katherine Parr. Inside the lid are the engraved initials 'ML', which may be for Maud Lane (eldest daughter of Lord Parr), the wife of Sir Ralph Lane. The jug was, in 1774, in the collection of Horace Walpole (1717-97) at Strawberry Hill, and after the sale of that collection in 1842 it was bought by John Dent for Sudeley Castle, at Winchcombe, Gloucestershire (formerly the home of Katherine Parr who, following the death of Henry VIII, had in 1547 married Baron Seymour of Sudeley), and hence it is sometimes called the 'Sudeley Tankard'. It was acquired by the Museum of London in 1967 (after an export licence had been refused to the Boston Museum of Fine Arts) from the collection of Mrs Dent-Brocklehurst at Sudeley Castle. A lidded jug of identical glass and shape (but with slightly different mounts) is in the British Museum, the glass being attributed there probably to the Netherlands, *c.*1540 (as possibly also was the Parr glass); its mounts are hallmarked London, 1548-9. It has been said that a similar piece is listed in the 1559 and 1574 inventories of Elizabeth I. *See* Philippa Fox-Robinson, 'The Parr Pot' in *Burlington Magazine*, January 1968, p. 45, fig. 59. *See* GLASS OBJECTS.

pastille burner. A utensil for scenting a room by means of a smouldering scented pastille, without a separate heating device. (The pastille, often pyramidal in shape, was made of compressed powdered charcoal combined with an aromatic substance.) Although many pieces for such purpose were made of porcelain in highly decorative form, the few known silver examples are very simply made: one, made by ROBERT GARRARD I in 1812, is in the form of a shallow pan resting on three ball feet and having a single projecting boxwood handle. *See* PERFUME BURNER; CASSOLETTE; POT-POURRI BOWL; POT-POURRI VASE.

pastry cutter. A kitchen utensil having at one end a wheel with a crimped edge and at the other end, at right-angles to the handle, a crimped blade. Silver examples are known from 1683.

Parr Pot. Opaque white glass (probably Netherlands, *c.* 1540), with silver-gilt mounts. London, 1546-7. Museum of London.

patch line. A line visible on a silver object, revealing where a patch has been inserted; it is emphasized when the surface is breathed upon or if the piece is tarnished. It results from the transfer of an ARMORIAL, the substitution of a blank for a monogram or substitution of a HALLMARK, or from some types of repair; often attempts are made to conceal such lines by means of superimposed decoration. *See* FAKE.

paten. A small PLATE or shallow DISH used for bearing the Communion bread in the Eucharist service. The early form in England was flat, but later examples have a shallow well and *c.*1684 a central foot was added. The paten in the Roman Catholic service is used for the bread that is offered at the Mass and upon which, after the breaking of the bread, the consecrated Host is placed; in the Anglican service it is the vessel upon which the bread is consecrated and later carried for distribution to the communicants. When, in the Elizabethan era, the pre-Reformation paten was discarded, a paten sometimes served as a COVER for a COMMUNION CUP. Early examples generally have engraved decoration, usually of Christian motifs (*see* ICONOGRAPHY), but some are undecorated. Later patens rest on a stem and have a spreading base, somewhat like a footed SALVER. Footed patens were made with a cover, often domed. *See* CHURCH PLATE.

patera. A circular low-relief ornament, derived from the Greek libation *phiale* and the Roman *patera*, resembling a shallow dish. It is found on pieces of silverware made in the NEO-CLASSICAL STYLE and ADAM STYLE. It is sometimes embellished with FLUTING and foliage patterns, and sometimes encloses a rosette.

patina. A thin, greenish film or discoloration that forms, after long exposure to the atmosphere, on bronze and copper, adding a prized artistic effect. The natural patina is a carbonate of copper that forms to protect the metal from further OXIDATION. By extension of the term, it has been applied to a reddish patina-effect on ancient gold and to the so-called patina on silver that is a permanent surface blur resulting from numerous shallow scratches. An artificial patina can be produced with acids, but can usually be detected by the even irregularities, as contrasted with the uneven surface of natural patina; artificial patina can also be produced by ELECTROPLATING, but it shows slight bubbling or flaking. *See* TARNISH; LUSTRE; BUFFING.

paw foot. A type of FOOT in the form of a clawed paw.

pax. An osculatory, or ecclesiastical tablet, sometimes made of silver, bearing a Christian religious representation (usually depicting the Crucifixion, the Agnus Dei, the head of Christ, or the Virgin and Child), which is kissed first by the priest and then successively by members of the congregation. A pax was often an upright rectangular, or sometimes circular, piece, occasionally with a loop or projecting scroll handle on the back to enable it to be held out by the priest to members of the congregation or with a handle on each side to enable it to be handed from one person to the next. A TRIPTYCH appropriately decorated may have been used as a pax. It is sometimes called by the Old English term *Paxbrede* (peace board). The name is derived from the Latin phrase *pax vobiscum* (peace be with you) spoken by each user in turn when the pax was passed on. A pax, usually not of silver, was generally used in every English parish church before the Reformation and in every recusant chapel, but few English examples, especially silver ones, have survived; *see* NEW COLLEGE (OXFORD) PAX. Two Canadian silver examples, Montreal, *c.* 1790, are in the Henry Birks Collection, Montreal: one, depicting the Crucifixion and the Holy Dove, made by Pierre Huguet called Latour; and one, depicting the Virgin and Child, made by Paul Lambert. *See* CHURCH PLATE.

Peahen Cup. A silver CUP in the form of a peahen in-the-round with three chicks, all standing on an oval base with chased decoration depicting reptiles, snails, etc. The head and neck of the peahen form the cover of the cup. The cup, which is not hallmarked, is inscribed to show that it was given in 1642 by Mary, the widow of James Peacock, to the Skinners' Company, London.

pear-shaped. (1) Pyriform, as in the case of a VASE or TEAPOT made in the form of a pear; the term 'inverted pyriform' is used when the greatest diameter of the piece is nearer the top. *See* BALUSTER. (2) The shape of a DISH if its outline conforms to the vertical section of a pear.

pebbled. Decoration having a grainy relief surface suggestive of small pebbles. The converse is MATTING.

Peahen Cup. Removable cover (the head and neck), unmarked, given to the Skinners' Company, London, 1642. H. 42 cm.

pedestal salt. Two examples, each with figural finial: with spreading base, London, 1566–7 (cover, 1571–2), height 14·3 cm; and with four feet, London, 1563–4. height 15·3 Both Victoria and Albert Museum, London.

peg tankard. Interior showing pegs, Marmaduke Best, York, 1670. H. 17·8 cm. Goldsmiths' Company, London.

Pelham Cup. Silver-gilt copy, John Jacobs, London, 1755, Private collection.

pectoral cross. A type of CROSS that is worn suspended on the breast, usually by bishops and abbots, and sometimes by canons and laymen.

pedestal salt. A type of STANDING SALT that is massive, but smaller than a GREAT SALT, and elaborately decorated, usually about 30 to 38·5 cm high, but in the case of some small examples only about 15 cm high. Such salts have a circular (occasionally square or hexagonal) or spool-shaped body with a depression at the top for the salt, and have a domed cover with an elaborate finial (sometimes a steeple or a figure); they rest on a spreading base or on four feet. Examples were made in England *c.* 1560–1600 (*see* TUDOR SILVER-WARE), and have ornate decoration of EMBOSSING encircling the base and on the dome of the cover. Two examples – including the MOSTYN SALT – were purchased in 1886 for the Victoria and Albert Museum, London. A small pedestal salt was made *c.* 1910 by OSCAR RAMSDEN and ALWYN CARR. Sometimes called a 'drum salt'. *See* PARKER SALT; READE SALT; ROGERS SALT.

peg tankard. A type of TANKARD, for use by a group of drinkers, having on the interior a vertical row of up to eight equidistant pegs to measure the amount that each person was to drink as the tankard was passed around (comparable both to the glass *Passglas* used in Germany, Bohemia, and the Netherlands in the 16th to 18th centuries, and to the ancient drinking vessels having a vertical row of pegs on the outside). English examples, 1656–70, are known from York and Newcastle-upon-Tyne. Such tankards usually rest on pomegranate-shaped ball feet and have a THUMBPIECE formed by two pomegranates. *See* SCANDINAVIAN-TYPE TANKARD.

Pelham Cup. A TWO-HANDLED CUP, the original (for some silver-gilt versions, see below) having been made of gold, *c.* 1736, from a design by WILLIAM KENT, without any maker's mark or hallmark. The design is included in a design book published by John Vardy, 1744. The cup has a thistle-shaped body, resting on a stemmed base and having two vertical scroll handles and a domed cover with a finial in the form of the Prince of Wales's feathers. It was commissioned by Col. James Pelham (*c.* 1690–1761) when he was Private Secretary, 1728–37, to Frederick Louis, Prince of Wales (1707–51), eldest son of George II, either for himself or possibly intended as a gift for the Prince, but it was given instead in 1755 to the 9th Earl of Lincoln. The cup was made from the metal of Pelham's gold snuff-boxes. It was sold at Christie's, London, on 7 July 1921 by Lincoln descendants, and in 1969 was in a private collection. Numerous silver-gilt cups based on the Kent design have been made, with different finials and other changes, including:

(1) One made by John Jacobs, London, 1755, probably commissioned by Pelham for himself; in 1969 it was in the same private collection as the gold cup.

(2) A pair, made by THOMAS HEMING, each with a crown finial: one, London, 1763–4, for a christening gift from George III to George Ferdinand

Fitzroy (b. 1761), and in 1969 in a London private collection; the other, 1764, for Frederick Wyndham, Earl of Egremont, and owned today by Lord Egremont, at Petworth House, West Sussex.

(3) A pair, made by John Swift, 1769-70, with a leaf-and-bud finial; one is in the Bristol Art Gallery and Museum, the other was in 1969 in a London private collection (probably the same piece as that sold at Christie's, London, on 28 March 1984).

(4) A larger cup, mark 'RG', 1771, having a griffin finial and decorated with the arms of William, 2nd Earl of Lonsdale; in 1969 it was on loan to the Victoria and Albert Museum, London.

(5) A pair, made by WILLIAM PITTS I and JOSEPH PREEDY, 1797, presented to the Hon. W. F. Wyndham and owned today by Lord Egremont, at Petworth House, West Sussex.

(6) A version (considerably varied from the original) made by D. and J. Wellby, 1915-16, and privately owned in 1969.
See John F. Hayward, 'The Pelham gold cup' in *The Connoisseur*, July 1969, p. 162.

pellet. A small disk or boss, sometimes used, either singly or in a group arranged in a circle, by a silversmith along with his initials as a part of his registered MAKER'S MARK.

pen tray. A type of TRAY, often forming part of a LIBRARY SET, on which to rest quill pens. It is larger than a SPOON TRAY and similar to a SNUFFER TRAY except that it is usually without decoration.

penner. A type of tubular case for quill pens, sometimes worn in Scotland attached to a girdle. Some examples from the 17th century have compartments for pens and an ink-well, and have one end engraved as a SEAL. *See* QUILL-CASE.

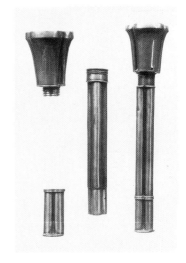

penner. Holder shown (*left*) in three parts, and (*right*) when assembled; 17th century. L. 15 cm. Ashmolean Museum (Ashmole Bequest), Oxford.

pennyweight. A measure (abbreviated as dwt) used in expressing the WEIGHT of silverware, equal to 1/20th of a troy ounce or 24 grains. Originally, it was the weight of a silver penny, hence the name. It is used for amounts less than, and for fractions of, an ounce.

pepper-box. A type of BOX, small and polygonal, used for ground pepper; it sometimes has a pierced cover.

pepper caster. A type of CASTER for sprinkling ground pepper, similar to a SALT CASTER but having smaller holes in the cover. It is sometimes made as one of a pair with a salt caster or as one of a set with a salt caster and a MUSTARD 'CASTER' (blind caster). Sometimes two pepper casters were made as a pair, one for black pepper, the other for stronger cayenne; later, when such casters were not used for cayenne, some were converted for use as a mustard 'caster' by the insertion of a sleeve to block the holes. Sometimes called a 'pepper-canister' or 'pepper-pot'. *See* PEPPERETTE; KITCHEN PEPPER-POT; BUN PEPPER; PEPPER-BOX.

pepper mill. A utensil for grinding peppercorns. Examples made of silver are usually of capstan shape, tall or compressed.

pepperette. A small PEPPER CASTER such as is included in a CONDIMENT SET.

Pepys Cup. A parcel-gilt STANDING CUP, presented *c.* 1677 by Samuel Pepys (1633-1707) to the Clothworkers' Company, London, of which he was elected Master in 1677. It has a silver bowl pierced and chased with foliage, griffins, and symbols associated with the Company; the bowl encases and reveals a detachable silver-gilt bell-shaped LINER that extends to slightly above the rim of the bowl. The quatrefoil foot has applied silver plaques bearing the Pepys monogram 'SP' and coats of arms of Pepys and the Company, respectively. The bowl rests on a baluster stem. The cover, also pierced and chased, has a finial surmounted by a cast figure of a ram couchant, the emblem of the Company. The cup bears an unidentified maker's mark 'JG', but no hallmarks. *See* SHEATHED WARE; CAGEWORK.

Pepys Cup. Silver bowl with pierced and chased decoration, and silver-gilt liner, maker's mark 'JG', presented *c.* 1677 to the Clothworkers' Company, London.

perfume-bottle. *See* SCENT-BOTTLE.

perfume burner. A utensil for vaporizing liquid perfume so that scent is emitted through openwork in the cover. Such articles were used in English homes, especially during the Caroline period, mid-17th century. Known silver examples are of two main types: (1) 17th-century examples that include a BRAZIER, having a base to contain burning charcoal, with pierced work, a long horizontal handle, and three short legs, and a receptacle for the per-

fume, with a pierced cover; and (2) 18th-century examples that have a stand which supports a spirit lamp and a receptacle for the perfume with a pierced ornament on the cover. *See* PASTILLE BURNER; CASSOLETTE; POT-POURRI BOWL; POT-POURRI VASE; CORONATION WINE FOUNTAIN.

perfume funnel. A small FUNNEL used to transfer perfume from a bottle into a small SCENT-BOTTLE. Unlike a WINE FUNNEL, it is made in one piece, has a straight tube, and has no interior strainer. Some have decoration on the bowl. A similar, but larger, funnel was used to decant spirits into a glass decanter.

Peterson Cup. A silver-gilt 'FONT-SHAPED' CUP having a bowl with low vertical sides and a broad, short baluster stem with a spreading foot. Encircling the bowl is an engraved inscription 'THE+MOST+HERE+OF+IS+DVNE+BY+PETER+PETERSON'. The cup, probably made at Norwich, bears no date mark, but it has been attributed to a year post-1574, when date marks ceased to be used there. It has a maker's mark which was formerly believed to be that of Peter Peterson, a local silversmith, but it is now regarded as that of William Cobbold (*see* NORWICH SILVERWARE). The name Peterson on the cup derives from the facts that Peterson agreed in 1574 to present a silver cup to the City of Norwich in return for being excused from certain duties, that he did give a cup made in 1567–8 (formerly called the 'Ranson Cup') which was later melted down, and a substitute cup, larger than the original, was made in part with the metal (hence 'The most ...'). The new cup is very similar to two cups made in London, 1561–2, known as the Blennerhasset Cups, also owned by Norwich (thus providing three similar cups for the three chief city officials). *See* Norman M. Penzer, 'Tudor "Font-shaped" Cups', in *Apollo*, March 1958, p.82; George J. Levine, 'Silver made in Norwich' in *The Connoisseur*, November 1973, p. 199, fig. 4.

Philadelphia silverware. Articles of silverware made at Philadelphia, Pennsylvania, from the 1690s by various silversmiths, including two Huguenots, Cesar Ghiselin (1670–1734) and Johannis Nys (1671–1734). Among the other leading silversmiths in the 18th/19th centuries were the RICHARDSON family and PHILIP SYNG, JR, as well as Edmund Milne (1724–1822), who specialized in INDIAN-TRADE SILVERWARE and CAMP CUPS, Richard Humphreys (1750–1832), and Joseph Anthony, Jr (1760–1814). The ware included many examples of TEA SERVICES and COFFEE SERVICES. A characteristic of local design is found, on some TEAPOTS and BOWLS, in the form of a GALLERY around the opening at the top; others are the finial in the form of a pineapple and the BEADING of small size along the edge of some pieces. *See* Edward Wenham, 'Philadelphia Silversmiths' in *The Connoisseur*, January 1936, p. 31; *Philadelphia Silver, 1682–1800* (Philadelphia Museum of Art exhibition catalogue, 1975).

photographic etching. A modern process of decorating silverware with an intricate design by transferring it photographically to a flat, or nearly flat, surface.

piano candlestick. A type of CANDLESTICK made with a wide base and a short stem from which extends a single long branch to overhang the front of a piano (or the edge of a mantelpiece).

Pickering Cup. A silver-gilt Tudor STANDING CUP, the bowl and cover of which are of oblate globular form. The hemispherical bowl is supported by two curved brackets resting on a baluster-knopped stem with a trumpet-shaped foot. The cover is surmounted by a steeple topped by a finial in the form of a winged figure of Peace. The cup was made and engraved in 1604, but the original cover disappeared and the present one is a replacement, based on old records, made in 1677. It is the earliest-known globular STEEPLE

perfume burner.
(1) With brazier, English, 1628–9, height 22·2 cm. Los Angeles County Museum of Art (William Randolph Hearst Collection), Los Angeles, Cal.
(2) With spirit lamp and stand, Andrew Fogelberg and Stephen Gilbert, London, 1784–5, height 18·7 cm. Courtesy, Brand Inglis Ltd, London.

Peterson Cup. Silver-gilt 'font-shaped' cup (*centre*), probably Norwich, post-1574, height 14 cm (flanked by the two Blennerhasset Cups, London, 1561–2). City of Norwich.

CUP. Both sections are decorated with engraved Tudor roses and daisies (marguerites), the badge of Margaret Beaufort, mother of Henry VII (the first Tudor Sovereign). The makers are unidentified; the mark on the cup is 'IA' and that on the cover 'IH'. The original cup was bequeathed in 1604 by Maurice Pickering, a Burgess (councillor) of the City of Westminster, as a gift from him and his wife Joane to the Court of Burgesses of Westminster, to be used as a LOVING CUP; the arms of the Burgesses, and the testator's directions as to the use of the cup (inexplicably dated 1558), are engraved on the bowl. The identity of the donor of the replacement cover is unknown. The entire piece is furnished with a shaped leather-covered wooden case. *See* Norman M. Penzer, 'The Pickering Cup' in *Apollo*, February 1960, p. 37, and March 1960, p. 64.

Pickett, William (fl. 1758-85). A London silversmith, his origins and apprenticeship being unknown, who entered his mark in 1769, address 32 Ludgate Hill, London. He was a partner, 1758-72, of WILLIAM THEED I (both being former shopmen of Henry Hurt) and married into the Theed family. The firm was mainly in the retail jewelry business, and Pickett devoted most of his time to his duties as an Alderman of London. In 1772, upon the death of Theed, Pickett formed with PHILIP RUNDELL a partnership called Pickett and Rundell, which continued until 1785 when Rundell, while Pickett was suffering from depression, purchased his interest in the firm, and continued it with JOHN BRIDGE, who had joined the firm in 1777. Pickett became Lord Mayor of London in 1789. *See* RUNDELL, BRIDGE & RUNDELL.

pickle-dish. A type of small DISH of no prescribed form but often of leaf shape or in the shape of a SCALLOP or pecten shell, and generally with three small feet or a slight FOOT-RING. *See* PICKLE FORK.

pickle fork. A type of small FORK for use with a PICKLE-DISH, having three (or sometimes four) tines, the outer two generally having barbed points.

picture-back spoon. A type of TEASPOON having on the back of the bowl relief decoration depicting a great variety of motifs, some of political (*see* JACOBITE SPOON) or commemorative significance, others of decorative or esoteric character, such as a hen with chicks, a stork holding a serpent in its beak, a dove with an olive branch, harvest motifs, a pyriform teapot, a scallop shell, a rigged galleon, a double-headed eagle, a flower-basket, etc. Early examples had the design made by ENGRAVING or ETCHING, but later less expensive pieces were made by STAMPING. Sometimes called a 'fancy-back spoon'. *See* 'I-LOVE-LIBERTY' SPOON.

Pickering Cup. Silver-gilt cup, 1604, with replacement cover, 1677. H. 71 cm. Westminster City Council, London.

picture-back spoon. Back of bowl showing relief decoration. Ashmolean Museum, Oxford.

pierced work. Soap-box with decorative pattern on lid. H. 9·5 cm. Ashmolean Museum, Oxford.

picture sconce. A type of WALL SCONCE, so called in Royal inventories, the back-plate of which has ornate decoration of EMBOSSING that suggests a picture within an elaborate frame. *See* JUDGMENT OF SOLOMON SCONCES.

piecrust rim. The same as a CHIPPENDALE RIM.

pierced work. A type of OPENWORK made by piercing the metal to make a pattern of small holes; the holes are usually circular, but are sometimes square or of other shapes. Sometimes the holes are in rows, but often they are arranged into a decorative pattern of various styles, interspersed with ENGRAVING and CHASING. The early technique involved the punching of the holes with chisels, but in the 1770s the method of SAW-CUTTING was introduced. The most frequent examples are STRAINERS and the covers of CASTERS, but such work is also found on pieces having a glass LINER, such as a MUSTARD-POT or a SALT-CELLAR, and on larger pieces such as a BASKET, a DISH RING or a WINE-BOTTLE STAND, or on the seldom seen cradle type of CHEESE STAND. *See* SHEATHED WARE; CAGEWORK.

piggin. James Fray, Dublin, 1830. H. 15 cm. National Museum of Ireland, Dublin.

piggin. A type of small receptacle in the form of a wooden pail with one upright stave handle, used as a dipper or for serving milk or cream. An Irish example decorated with pierced openwork has a glass liner. Some later Scottish examples were made with two flat handles extending horizontally from the rim.

pilgrim bottle. An adaptation of the PILGRIM FLASK, made in silver in the form of a bottle with a globular body (sometimes compressed) having a tall narrow neck and a decorated stopper, and having a suspensory chain (or two such chains) from the stopper to the neck or shoulder. Such bottles (often about 75 to 90 cm high) were too large for carrying, and were made as ornaments for wealthy homes. Sometimes they were made in pairs. *See* MARLBOROUGH PILGRIM BOTTLES.

pilgrim flask. Originally, a bottle of compressed gourd shape, made of leather, porcelain or pottery, having on its sides one or two pairs of lugs through which passed a long strap or chain whereby it could be carried slung over the shoulder. Of Roman origin, and also found of Chinese porcelain, such bottles were used in the 12th to 16th centuries by pilgrims to carry drinking water. An adaptation of such flasks, variously called a WINE-BOTTLE, a PILGRIM BOTTLE or a 'costrel', was made of silver in the 17th and 18th centuries, as well as the earlier CASTING BOTTLE of the 16th century. *See* FLASK.

pillar candlestick. The same as a COLUMN CANDLESTICK.

pillar salt. A type of GREAT SALT having a central hollow cylindrical (sometimes pentagonal) column (pillar) of rock crystal which encloses a silver standing figure. *See* GIBBON SALT; WALKER SALT; CRYSTAL ARTICLES.

'pineapple' cup. A rare and misnamed type of STANDING CUP having its bowl and cover together of inverted ovoid shape and decorated overall with REPOUSSÉ lobes (scales) and said to resemble a pineapple (hence so called) but actually resembling a pine cone. Such cups were made in England *c.* 1600–10, before pineapples were first imported into the country in 1632. Three (possibly four) examples are known with English marks:

(1) One, originally gilded, owned by the church of St Mary the Virgin, Farnham, Essex, having been acquired by it between 1686 and 1708, bears the unidentified maker's mark 'TC' and has been attributed to English make, 1612; it has a baluster stem, a circular foot chased with petals, and a cover surmounted by a snake ring finial (possibly a later addition). *See* William James Pressey (ed.), *Church Plate of the County of Essex* (1926), p.244, pl.XIV.

(2) Another such gilded cup, in the Hermitage, Leningrad, differs from the Farnham cup in that it is taller, its stem is in the form of a standing figure of a youthful Bacchus, and its finial is in the form of a cluster of ungilded flowers. It bears the unidentified maker's mark 'RS' and an English date mark 1607–8, together with other marks. It has been attributed by Norman M. Penzer (*The Connoisseur*, December 1958, p.226) to English make 'for the export market or perhaps for a direct order', but by Charles Oman (*The Connoisseur*, August 1959, p.14, fig.2) to German make in the style of Hans Petzolt – both writers identifying the additional marks as Moscow control marks (required after Catherine II ordered in 1762 that all plate be collected at St Petersburg).

(3) A silver-gilt cup, with mark 'S/W', London, 1608, that has been owned by S. J. Shrubsole Ltd, London (*see* advertisement in *Antiques*, October 1983, p.655); it has a stem in the form of a gnarled tree being held by a woodcutter, and has a flower-bud finial.

(4) A silver-gilt cup formerly owned by S. J. Phillips Ltd, London, has a maker's mark 'IK' and the London date mark for 1610; its stem is in the form of a tree-trunk with cut-off stumps of branches, above which is a knop in the form of a ball secured top and bottom by foliated mounts, and its finial is in the form of a flower bud.

The Farnham cup is 22·5 cm high, the Shrubsole cup 26·7 cm, and the Phillips cup 38·5 cm. A fifth such cup, in the Kremlin, Moscow, is of German make. Such cups have been said to be basically in the form of the German type made at Nuremberg in the 17th century and known there as an *Ananaspokal*; however, the bowls are very similar to the German 16th/17th-century type of glass receptacle in pine-cone form (called a *Pinienzapfenflasche*).

pilgrim bottle. Parcel gilt, compressed body with teardrop motifs and cast foliage, C. T. & G. Fox for Lambert & Rawlings, London, 1850. H. 61·6 cm. Victoria and Albert Museum, London.

pipe, tobacco. A slender tube with a small bowl at one end, for smoking tobacco. The type with a long stem and small bowl – usually of clay, although several examples of silver are known – is called a 'church-warden pipe'. Both short and long pipes have been made of silver; one example, 38 cm long, is in four sections. In the American Colonies, silver pipes were given to the

Indians. *See* Eclecticus, 'A Rare James I Silver Pipe, *c*. 1610-1620' in *Apollo*. March 1955, p. 66, and December 1955, p. 27. *See* CALUMET.

pipe lighter. A household smoking accessory for lighting a tobacco pipe by the use of smokeless charcoal before the introduction of matches. It is in the form of a BRAZIER except that it is smaller and the hemispherical basin has no pierced work. It often has an accompanying tray, with a pair of tongs (used to lift a piece of burning charcoal) and sometimes also a small blow-pipe.

pipkin. The same as a BRANDY-SAUCEPAN.

Piranesi, Giovanni Battista (1720-78). An Italian engraver, etcher, and architect, educated in Venice, who settled in Rome in 1740 and made many etchings of buildings, both real and imaginary, and views of Rome. He also made designs for articles of silverware, which were usually based on antique prototypes and were closely adapted by leading silversmiths, including: (1) an early example of such pieces, a pair of silver-gilt covered vases made by PAUL STORR, 1800, for Francis Russell, 5th Duke of Bedford, in the Bedford Collection at Woburn Abbey, Bedfordshire; (2) eight WINE COOLERS in krater shape, the form based on the Medici Krater at the Uffizi Gallery, Florence, but with the frieze based on the frieze on the Borghese Krater; they were made in 1805 for the Prince of Wales (later George IV) – some by Storr and some by BENJAMIN SMITH I and James Smith – and are in the Royal Collection; (3) eight wine coolers decorated with low-relief scenes depicting the 'Birth of Bacchus', made for the Prince of Wales in 1811-12; (4) the DONCASTER CUP, 1828; (5) the GOODWOOD 'CUP', 1829; and (6) the silver-gilt WARWICK VASE. *See* David Udy, 'Piranesi's "Vasi", the English Silversmith and his Patrons' in *Burlington Magazine*, December 1978, p. 820.

'pineapple' cup (4). Silver gilt, maker's mark 'IK', London, 1610. H. 38·5 cm. Courtesy, S. J. Phillips Ltd, London.

piscatorial caddy spoon. A type of CADDY SPOON that has a bowl suggestive of a fish, there being two varieties: (1) the 'salmon' variety, having an elliptical bowl with a fish-tail handle, decorated with overall fish-scale (IMBRICATED) engraving and with an eye and a slit mouth; (2) the 'carp' variety, having an elliptical bowl with a fish-tail handle and dorsal fins on each side of the bowl, together with an eye and a slit mouth, decorated overall with REPOUSSÉ fish-scale motifs (one example is elliptical but entirely undecorated). There are FAKES of such caddy spoons with the scales later embossed and obliterating the marks, or with the fins soldered on.

pistol handle. A type of HANDLE for a KNIFE or FORK made in the form of an 18th-century pistol-grip. The style varies, some examples being oval in section, some octagonal. Such handles were made mainly at Sheffield, *c*. 1775, having been first made by STAMPING with a machine patented in 1769 by John Pickering and improved by Richard Ford, of Birmingham. Each handle was struck as two halves, soldered together, and filled with resin or shellac. *See* KNIFE AND FORK HANDLES.

pistols. Some examples have been made with silver decoration, applied by affixing a silver handle, by encasing the grip in openwork silver, or by inserting silver decorative inlays in the barrel and handle. Examples of the last type, with steel barrels and handles having ornate silver inlays, were made by H. W. Mortimer & Co., London, 1794, with the inlay work done by Moses Brent, a specialist haft-maker. *See* Judith Banister, 'Silver and the Chase' in *The Connoisseur*, December 1977, pp. 264-5, 267. *See* GUN FURNITURE.

pipe lighter. Basin for charcoal, Thomas Hammersley, New York, *c*. 1750-70. H. 5·4 cm. Yale University Art Gallery (Mabel Brady Garvan Collection), New Haven, Conn.

Pistrucci, Benedetto (1784-1855). An Italian engraver and a designer of coins and medals. He was born in Rome, where he achieved great success. He went to Paris in 1814 and settled in London in 1815. There he was commissioned to execute the cameo of St George and the Dragon which appears on British coinage. After becoming Chief Engraver for the Royal Mint, he executed dies for the new coinage and the coronation medals for George IV in 1820 and for Queen Victoria in 1838. He made the design for the ST GEORGE SHIELD.

pitcher. The same as a JUG; a term used in the United States.

Pitts, Thomas (fl. 1757-87). A London silversmith who was apprenticed to Charles Halfield in 1737, but turned over to DAVID WILLAUME II in 1742, and freed in 1744. He did not register his mark until after 1758. His son WILLIAM PITTS I was apprenticed to him. He is best known for several EPERGNES made in ROCOCO STYLE, 1759-67; some have baskets suspended from or supported by branching arms, as well as a large central basket, and some are PAGODA EPERGNES. Eight epergnes in United States museums (and some in private collections there) have formerly been attributed to Thomas Powell and one to Thomas Potts (his marks were registered in 1728 and 1758), based on the letters 'TP' in the maker's mark, but as such letters are shown with a PELLET in an oblong escutcheon, the mark of Pitts, all these pieces have since 1965–7 been attributed to Pitts, from whom a predecessor of GARRARD & CO. LTD purchased in 1766–75 'nothing but epergnes', as stated in its records. *See* Edith Gaines, 'Powell? Potts? Pitts!–the T. P. Epergnes', in *Antiques*, April 1965, p. 462; —, 'More by–and about–Pitts of the epergnes', in *Antiques*, June 1967, p. 748.

Pitts, William (I) (fl. 1781–1806). A London silversmith, son of THOMAS PITTS, who was apprenticed in 1769 and freed in 1784. His first mark was entered in 1781, with address at 17 St Martin's St, Leicester Fields, and a second mark in 1786 from 26 Litchfield St, St Anne's, Soho. He entered a third mark jointly with JOSEPH PREEDY in 1791, and moved to 8 Newport St, St Anne's, in 1795 and later, when the firm was terminated in 1799, fourth and fifth marks alone in 1800 and 1806. The firm with Preedy made pierced BASKETS and EPERGNES of silver gilt, but later, when alone, Pitts produced cast ornate CANDELABRA made in ROCOCO STYLE.

Pitts, William (II) (1790–1840). A London silversmith, son of a silver chaser and sculptor, to whom he was apprenticed. In the 1820s he began to design as well as doing CHASING and EMBOSSING on silverware, and in the 1830s he did sculptural work. He worked as a chaser for RUNDELL, BRIDGE & RUNDELL, *c.* 1810–36 (examples of his work in this period, 1810–13, are in the Royal Collection), and for the firm of PAUL STORR, John Mortimer, and John Hunt in 1837. He did part of the chasing and embossing for GREEN, WARD & GREEN on the WELLINGTON SHIELD and all such work for Rundell, Bridge & Rundell on the ACHILLES SHIELD. In later life he made, in imitation of those shields, a design and a plaster model for the AENEAS SHIELD (but it remained partially unexecuted when he committed suicide in 1840) and a design and model for the Hercules Shield. He made many designs for epergnes and candelabra.

place-card holder. A type of decorative CARD HOLDER having a slot for holding vertically a place card; it is usually similar to, but smaller than, a MENU-CARD HOLDER.

plate (3). Set, silver gilt, Edward Wakelin, London, 1759. W. 23·5 cm. Courtesy, Spink & Son Ltd, London.

place mat. A type of dinner-table accessory in the form of a flat mat, to be set on a table under a dinner plate, a meat-dish, or a heated receptacle to protect the surface of the table from the heat. Such mats are usually circular and of varying sizes. Examples, made in sets, are of silver or more usually of SILVER-PLATED WARE, and have a baize-covered weighted flat bottom and the top decorated with ENGRAVING, CHASING or ETCHING to avoid showing scratches from use.

place plate. A type of PLATE, larger than a DINNER PLATE, and usually more decorative, that is set at the place of each diner when a dinner table is laid before a meal and that is removed with the first-course plate; it is not used to serve food. Sometimes called a 'service plate', and generally known in the United States as a 'lay plate'.

place setting. The group of different dining implements in a DINNER SERVICE that are for use by each diner, including FORKS, KNIVES, and SPOONS, the usual place setting consisting of six or eight or more types of implement, even though all are not generally for use at the same meal.

planishing. The process of toughening, smoothing, and polishing an article of silverware by lightly hammering it with a smooth-faced slightly convex hammer, particularly to remove the marks left by the various other hammers after the piece has been shaped by HAMMERING. Planishing also serves to assure an overall uniform thickness of the silver. It leaves tiny irregular indentations on the surface which characterize hand-raised silverware. The piece is finished by POLISHING, i.e., by being buffed (today on an electrically powered wheel) and polished with jeweller's rouge.

plaque. A flat object made to be (1) used as an ornament, (2) inserted decoratively in a larger article, or (3) hung on a wall as a decoration. Such plaques, made in large numbers in continental Europe, were often mounted in silver articles made in England in the 17th and early 18th centuries, e.g., large BASINS and DISHES, of which usually only the border was hallmarked in England. Small plaques depicting topographical subjects were mounted in VINAIGRETTES and in the covers of SNUFF-BOXES (*see* CASTLE-TOP WARE) and in some HORSE-RACING CUPS. Some plaques were made as a memorial, with embossed figures and an inscription. Plaques were usually decorated by EM-BOSSING or CHASING to depict biblical or classical subjects; sometimes a plaque is embellished by having attached to it a protruding feature, such as the extended arm of a figure. Large wall plaques were made by ELKINGTON & CO. by ELECTROFORMING and ELECTROPLATING.

plate. (1) Generically, articles of silver (or gold), such as TABLEWARE, CANDLESTICKS, drinking vessels, and ornaments treated collectively, but not including objects of SMALLWARE. *See* GOLD PLATE. (2) Articles of PLATED METAL. (3) A table utensil from which food is eaten, usually circular (sometimes polygonal) and usually with a LEDGE (MARLI) and a shallow WELL; some modern examples are flat with a low upturned rim and no well. The size ranges from about 15 to 28 cm in diameter. Depending upon their size and use, plates are known as a PLACE PLATE, DINNER PLATE, SOUP PLATE, SALAD PLATE, FRUIT PLATE, DESSERT PLATE, BUTTER PLATE. *See* DISH; PLATTER; PRÉSENTOIR.

plate rack. A type of stand for supporting and carrying a number of PLATES. A rare silver example, made by DAVID WILLAUME II, 1744, rests on four curved legs with hoof feet, and has divisions for the plates. It was in the William Randolph Hearst Collection, disposed of at auction in 1958.

plate warmer. A type of utensil for warming plates to be used for serving a hot meal; it is in the form of a cylindrical receptacle having a large aperture on one side for inserting and stacking the plates inside before exposing the open side to the fire. An unusual example of SHEFFIELD PLATE, *c.* 1810, is bucket-shaped, rests on three legs, and has a BAIL HANDLE so placed that it causes the receptacle to tilt backwards when being carried, thus preventing the plates from slipping out; it is in the Sheffield collection of Dr Lowry Dale Kirby, Nashville, Tennessee.

plateau. A large flat table ornament, usually a horizontal framed mirror, upon which are stood a CENTREPIECE or EPERGNE, as well as CANDLESTICKS, SALTS, CRUETS, CASTERS, etc., and sometimes small ornamental pieces. Some were made in several sections, to extend along the length of a large dining table, and especially a banquet table. There is usually an encircling low silver or silver-gilt GALLERY, and on some examples figures are interspersed along the rim. *See* WELLINGTON PORTUGUESE SERVICE; ETON COLLEGE CHAPEL REPLICA; FORBES PLATEAU.

Platel, Pierre. Vase-shaped caster, London, 1708–9. H. 24 cm. Ashmolean Museum, Oxford.

plateau. Silver gilt, in three sections, Rundell & Bridge, London, 1834. L. 2·06 m. Goldsmiths' Company, London.

plated metal. Two or more layers of different metals joined to each other by PLATING and without being fused into a homogeneous mass as is an ALLOY. It is also called 'composite metal', and includes SHEFFIELD PLATE, BRITISH PLATE, ROBERTS PLATE, and MERRY PLATE. *See* NICKEL SILVER; ELECTROPLATING.

plated wire. Any WIRE that is entirely covered with a thin coating of silver. It was made first in England *c.* 1760 from a thin strip of copper over which a film of silver was fused and then wrought by hand to form a tube having a seam along the join. The hollow wire was filled with lead-tin solder and shaped by hand. Later it was made under a process patented in 1768 by George Whateley pursuant to which a rod, 4 ft (1·22 m) long and 1 in. (2·5 cm) in diameter, made of an ALLOY of copper and brass, was encased in a strip of rolled silver and the metals fused; it was then drawn through a series of holes gradually decreasing in diameter until the desired GAUGE was reached. This process was improved in the early 1790s and again in 1800 by substituting for the drawing by manpower a power-operated winch which drew the wire to the constantly decreasing gauge. Firms in Sheffield and Birmingham have specialized in making plated wire.

Platel, Pierre (or **Peter**) (*c.* 1664–1719). A London silversmith, from a Huguenot family from Lille, France, who arrived in England in 1688 and was naturalized in 1697. His mark was entered in 1699, address Pall Mall. He made some important pieces now in major collections. He took PAUL DE LAMERIE as an apprentice, 1703–13.

plating. The process of covering or overlaying a base metal with silver so as to give an article the appearance of SOLID SILVER. Techniques include FRENCH PLATING, CLOSE PLATING, and ELECTROPLATING. The process is called by platers 'charging'. *See* SHEFFIELD PLATE.

platter. A large shallow DISH, usually oval, for serving food. Such pieces usually have a LEDGE (or MARLI) and a WELL. *See* CHARGER; TREE PLATTER; WELL PLATTER.

platter tilter. A rectangular, sloping slab to be placed under one end of a PLATTER, so causing the gravy to flow to the opposite end.

Plimsoll Cup. An ornamental PRESENTATION CUP having a globular body, a TRUMPET FOOT, a tall narrow neck, and a cover with a finial in the form of a standing sailor with his arms folded. The two handles, extending from the top of the body to the neck, are angular, each in the form of a broken mast with torn sails and rigging. The bowl is decorated with a scene of a ship being wrecked in a storm, and the base is inscribed 'ENGLAND EXPECTS EVERY MAN TO DO HIS DUTY'. The cup was presented to Samuel Plimsoll, M.P. (1824–98), 'The Sailors' Friend', by the Liverpool Branch of the Firemens's and Seamen's Union to celebrate the passing of the Merchant Shipping Act (1876), a measure which he had advocated in the House of Commons and which led to the introduction of the ship's load line (the Plimsoll line). The cup bears the Sheffield Assay Office mark for 1875–6 and the maker's mark 'IEB'. It is in the Liverpool City Museum.

plinth. Strictly the lowest, usually square, part of the base of a column; correspondingly, the base of a figure or VASE similarly designed. By extension, the term is used to refer to a separate stand upon which a figure or article rests.

Plummer, John (fl. 1648–72). An English silversmith, the son of James Plummer (d. 1663), a silversmith of York. He made SCANDINAVIAN-TYPE TANKARDS, some with engraved decoration of flowers in a style inspired by contemporary herbals and flowers, the identity of the engraver being unknown.

Plummer, William (fl. 1755–91). A London silversmith, apprenticed in 1746 and freed in 1755. His first mark was entered in 1755, address Foster Lane. He moved to Gutter Lane in 1757. His second and third marks were entered in 1774 and 1789. He had a large establishment, and specialized in making, by SAW-CUTTING, pierced CAKE-BASKETS, SUGAR-BASKETS, SWEETMEAT-BASKETS, and CREAM-BASKETS, many of which survive.

Plunkett Spoons. A group of SPOONS (five APOSTLE SPOONS, including a Master Spoon, and one St Christopher Spoon) that were once owned by John Plunkett (1518–83) and his wife Katherine Lutrell, who were married in 1538. The spoons are not hallmarked. The St Christopher Spoon is engraved 'CP/IP', said to be for Sir Christopher Plunkett and his son John Plunkett, as donor/donee, and the bowl bears the date 1518 (the year of John Plunkett's birth). The Apostle Spoons are marked 'IP/KL', said to be for John Plunkett and Katherine Lutrell, as donor/donee, and the bowls bear the date 1538 (the year of their marriage). It is believed that the initials, being engraved rather than punched, are not joint maker's marks. The spoons were inherited by Mary Plunkett, of Dunshaughlin, Co. Meath, Ireland, who married Michael Grace, and they then descended through the Grace family to Mrs Lachlan White (Frances Mary Grace), of Dublin. The spoons, attributed by G. E. P. How (based on their form, the modelling of the figures, and the method by which the finials are joined to the stems) to London manufacture, were originally gilded, and on the head of each Apostle is a horizontal pierced nimbus. The group was presented in 1974 to the Wadsworth Atheneum, Hartford, Connecticut. *See* G. E. P. How, 'The Plunkett St Christopher and Apostle Spoons' in *The Connoisseur*, September 1943, p. 13.

polishing. The process of finishing a silver article, after it has been formed and rubbed with any of various abrasives to give it its preliminary finishing, so as to remove its dull and lustreless appearance resulting from the processes of fabrication. It is done by machine, using a polishing lathe fitted with various polishing brushes charged with emery powder and oil or with tripoli, and then by lathe or hand, using a polishing mop charged with tripoli or rouge, after which the piece is finished by BUFFING with a buff stick.

Plimsoll Cup. Presentation cup, maker's mark 'IEB', Sheffield, 1875–6. H. 66 cm. Merseyside County Museums, Liverpool.

'Pomegranate' Cup. Silver gilt, London, 1563. H. 26·5 cm. Inner Temple, London (photo courtesy, Goldsmiths' Company, London).

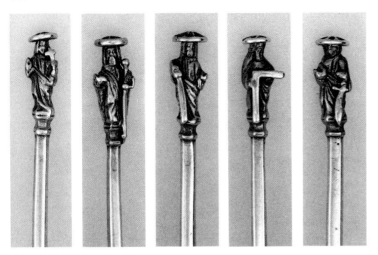

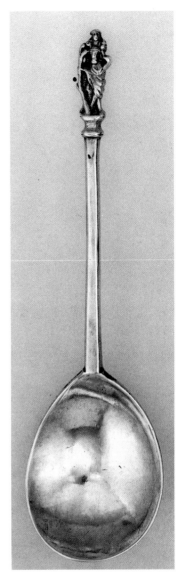

Small areas and corners are polished by BURNISHING. Excessive polishing results in a 'mirror finish' that is not desirable, and when done on antique silverware it removes the PATINA.

pomander. Originally, a mixture of highly scented spices and perfumes, made into a ball in medieval times and carried in a perforated box or bag to counteract offensive odours, and also supposedly to protect against infection. Later the term was applied to the receptacle, often shaped like an apple or a pear, that was worn like a pendant during the 14th–17th centuries. This was usually a perforated metal globular case, opening midway, to contain the ball, but some examples were made with from four to sixteen hinged compartments *(loculi)*, each with a sliding cover, that opened out like the segments of an orange; each of these contained a different scent, the name of which (or an identifying numeral) was inscribed on the separate lids (some without any pierced walls were primarily for storage of scents rather than being a true pomander). The segmented type often had an enclosed VINAIGRETTE as the core of the fruit. Examples in the form of a human skull were worn as a MEMENTO MORI. Articles made similarly were sometimes also devotional jewelry, with inscribed names of saints and with a religious figure in the centre. Women wore pomanders suspended from a girdle or a CHATELAINE, and men by suspending them from a chain around the neck. Pomanders were made of silver, silver-gilt, gold or other metal, decorated with enamelling and sometimes gemstones. They were sometimes called a 'scent ball', a 'musk ball' or a *'pomme d'ambre'*. See W. Turner, 'Pomanders' in *The Connoisseur*, March 1912, p. 151; Edward Wenham, 'Pomanders' in *The Connoisseur*, April 1934, p. 228. *See* TABLE POMANDER; SCENT-BOTTLE.

Plunkett Spoons. St Christopher spoon, 1518 (*above*), and details showing finials of five Apostle spoons, 1538. Wadsworth Atheneum, Hartford, Conn.

'Pomegranate' Cup. A silver-gilt STANDING CUP sometimes erroneously so called on the basis of the supposed resemblance of its combined bowl and cover to a pomegranate. It has vertically ribbed sides (unlike the smooth surface of a pomegranate), and the tiny seeds depicted on one segment are unlike those of a pomegranate; the stem is in the form of a vine, whereas pomegranates grow on trees; and the seeded finial in a leafy calyx does not resemble any part of a pomegranate or a melon, and may have been intended to be decorative rather than realistic. The cup bears an unidentified maker's mark and a London date mark for 1563, and is owned by the Honourable Society of the Inner Temple, London. *See* MELON CUP; MAGDALEN COLLEGE (OXFORD) MELON CUP.

pome. *See* HAND WARMER.

poppy spoon. A type of SPOON having a hexagonal stem and knop, surmounted by a finial suggestive of a poppy. A rare example was made in London, 1538.

porcelain objects. Articles of which an essential part is made of porcelain but which have English silver or silver-gilt MOUNTS (comparable to many porcelain articles with mounts of gilded bronze or ormolu), including some Chinese porcelain vases (converted into *kendi* by the mounts), STANDING CUPS (converted by mounts attached to a cup), BOWLS, BASINS, and BOXES, Among them are: (1) several Ming blue-and-white pieces of the Wan-Li

pomander. Six hinged compartments, English(?), *c.* 1620. Colonial Williamsburg, Va.

porcelain objects. Chinese porcelain jar, Ming dynasty (reign of Wan-Li, 1573–1619), with English mounts, *c.* 1665. Victoria and Albert Museum, London.

porringer (2). Single handle with pierced geometric pattern, London, 1683–4. D. (of bowl) 12·5 cm. Colonial Williamsburg, Va.

porter's badge. Silver badge, with identification number. H. 15 cm. Bank of England, London.

period (1573–1619); (2) some Ming polychrome EWERS; (3) the BURGHLEY HOUSE PORCELAIN OBJECTS; (4) the LENNARD CUP; (5) the TRENCHARD BOWL; and (6) the original ROBINSON BOWL. Examples made of Continental or English porcelain having English silver mounts have not been found. *See* S. W. Bushell and E. Alfred Jones, 'Ming Bowl with a Silver Mount of the Tudor Period' in *Burlington Magazine*, November 1908, p. 257; E. Alfred Jones, 'A Ming Bowl in the Hearst Collection' in *The Connoisseur*, December 1929, p. 345; Edward Wenham, 'Silver-mounted Porcelain' in *The Connoisseur*, April 1936, p. 199; Yvonne Hackenbroch, 'Chinese Porcelain in European Silver Mounts' in *The Connoisseur*, June 1955, p. 22; Philippa Glanville, 'Chinese Porcelain and English Goldsmiths *c.* 1560 to *c.* 1660' in *V&A Album*, 3 (1984). *See* CELADON OBJECTS; POTTERY OBJECTS; STONEWARE JUG.

porringer. (1) A term usually applied in England to the unspouted SMALL TWO-HANDLED CUP sometimes called there a POSSET-POT. The word is derived from the French *potager*, a soup-bowl, and its early English adaptations, 'pottager' and 'pottanger', were terms for a bowl used for drinking broth. (2) A type of shallow flat-bottomed BOWL having straight or convex vertical sides and one flat horizontal curvilinear (usually triangular-shaped and pierced) side handle extending from (or near) the rim. Such pieces were possibly used to serve hot porridge. A 1702 list in the Jewel House at the Tower of London refers to a 'Porridge Pot', and the English delftware pieces so shaped are called 'porringers'. The bowl is usually without a cover (although some American examples have a cover with a finial), which is not essential to maintain the heat of the porridge. The handle is usually pierced with an intricate pattern of holes, such as circles, quatrefoils, cinquefoils, crescents, hearts, etc. (sometimes termed 'geometric shapes') and occasionally the KEY-HOLE PATTERN. A bowl so shaped but slightly larger, and usually having a cover, is called an ÉCUELLE; smaller versions have been called, especially in England, a BLEEDING BOWL or, incorrectly, a CUPPING BOWL, and sometimes a 'child's porringer'. *See* QUAICH.

In British usage the term 'porringer' is usually applied to type (1), but in the United States it is always applied to type (2) as a feeding bowl for children, which is preferable nomenclature, as it distinguishes such a receptacle from the 'posset-pot' described above, which is so called in the United States as well as in England, or sometimes called a CAUDLE-CUP. Moreover, the *Oxford English Dictionary* defines a 'porringer' as a 'small basin' and alternatively as a type of head-dress so shaped, citing such use by Shakespeare, thus supporting the use of the term for the utensil described as type (2).

Porte-Dieu. The term used in French-speaking provinces of Canada for a CIBORIUM.

porter's badge. A type of BADGE, such as those worn by porters of the Bank of England, being of oval shape, bearing the name of the Bank and the identifying number of the porter. Some such pieces have in recent years been mounted as NAPKIN RINGS.

porter's cup. A type of GOBLET given to wine porters of the Vintners' Company; a number of 17th-century examples are still owned by the Company.

porter's staff. A type of STAFF such as those carried by porters of the Bank of England, having a silver FERRULE surmounted by a ball-shaped finial engraved with the name of the Bank and a year date (sometimes the date of assaying, which was probably the same as the year in which an individual staff came into the Bank's possession). The ferrule is usually divided midway by a narrow raised band, the part below it being cylindrical, and the part above decagonal in section. Examples are extant from 1749. *See* BEADLE'S STAFF; TIPSTAFF; VERGE.

Portland Vase. In silverware: a silver-gilt VASE made as a replica of the cased-glass Portland Vase (reproduced in 1790 by Josiah Wedgwood in jasperware, and by others in ceramic wares and in glass). Two examples were made by PHILIP RUNDELL, 1820 and 1823, for RUNDELL, BRIDGE & RUNDELL. The one dated 1820 was sold at Sotheby's, New York, on 17 June 1981, for $35,000 (£16,900).

portrait statuette. A type of STATUETTE (or statue) that depicts the likeness in-the-round of a known person, as distinguished from the pieces that depict literary or mythological characters. *See* COLUMBUS STATUE; GEORGE III STATUETTE; ELIZABETH, PRINCESS, STATUETTE; VICTORIA STATUETTE.

posset-pot (or **posset-cup**). A type of SMALL TWO-HANDLED CUP having bulging sides that are BALUSTER- or OGEE-shaped, or sometimes having sides that are almost vertical but slightly curved inward toward the base; such cups rest on a flat bottom, a spreading foot, a FOOT-RING or four feet, and characteristically have two vertical side handles, usually scrolled CARYATID HANDLES (sometimes simplified or debased). Some have a flat or low-domed cover, usually with a finial (some baluster-shaped, some spool-shaped), but the cover is often missing (probably lost). The height ranges from 10 to 18 cm. Such cups are decorated in various styles, such as with EMBOSSING, ENGRAVING, CHASING, GADROONING or CUT CARD work, and they sometimes have, extending upward from the base, an encircling band of REEDING or of ACANTHUS leaves. They do not have an upcurved spout, as does a SPOUT CUP. Rare examples have an accompanying small tray. They were used for, and are suitable for, serving a clear soup, such as bouillon. *See* G. Bernard Hughes, 'The True Nature of the Porringer' in *Country Life*, 9 April 1964, p. 826. *See* STERNE CUP; FREAKE POSSET POT; DOPPING POSSET POT.

The terms 'posset-pot' and 'posset-cup' have long, and now probably irreversibly, been applied by English writers and the English silver trade to such cups without a spout, just as they have been applied in England to cups of tin-glazed earthenware or glass that have one or more vertical side handles but no spout (*see* Phelps Warren, 'The English Posset Pot' in *Antiques*, April 1983, p. 835). The terms seem to be misnomers, as these cups do not have the upcurved spout such as is characteristic of the traditional ceramic posset-pot, formerly used for drinking posset (a beverage formerly popular in England and the United States, made of hot milk curdled by an infusion of ale or wine, with bread-crumbs, sugar, and spices) and which are provided with the spout so as to avoid drinking the curdled milk on the surface of the beverage. The terms 'posset-pot' and 'posset-cup' have, as a result of long usage, come to be generally accepted; but a preferable term would be 'small two-handled cup' (Norman M. Penzer, in 1961, referred to a 'small two-handled cup, formerly known as a posset cup or porringer'), and any such cup with a spout should be differentiated by being termed a 'spout cup', as should also the similar type used for caudle, sometimes now termed a CAUDLE-CUP. Moreover, such unspouted cups have frequently been called in England (though not in the United States) a 'PORRINGER', but it is recommended that the use of that term should be restricted – as it is in the United States – to the type of shallow bowl, with one side handle, that is more suitable for use in eating warm porridge.

postal scale. A type of counter scale having a graduated dial and a rotating pointer; small silver examples were made by the GORHAM COMPANY from 1897. *See* BALANCE SCALE.

posy holder. A type of small funnel-shaped container for holding a posy (a flower or a nosegay), basically intended to be worn attached to a dress. Such pieces are usually vertical and trumpet-shaped or cornucopia-shaped (with a terminal loop), having a funnel of silver (or glass or other material) – in which was placed a moistened sponge – to hold the posy; the funnel is deep if intended for flower stems, shallow for flower heads. The handle may be of ivory, amber, porcelain, mother-of-pearl, etc. The posy is secured by a pin across the mouth of the funnel or by an internal grip, and the holder is attached to the dress by a pin or hook. Some examples have, attached by a chain, a finger-ring for use when held by hand, and some are made as a brooch. Occasional examples were made with a folding tripod stand (released by a terminal knob). Such pieces, of silver or silver-gilt, have been decorated lavishly, some with gemstones, pearls or enamelling, and some have been made of FILIGREE. They have been called a *porte-fleur*, a *porte-bouquet* or a *bouquetier*. *See* G. Bernard Hughes and Therle Hughes, 'Old English Posy-Holders' in *Country Life*, 5 August 1949, p. 398.

pot. A type of vessel, made in many shapes, sizes, and styles of decoration, but generally of circular section, and employed for a variety of domestic purposes. It usually has a HANDLE and is provided with a COVER. *See* TEAPOT; CHOCOLATE-POT; COFFEE-POT; HONEY-POT; JAM-POT; POUNCE-POT; MUSTARD-POT; LIVERY POT.

pot-pourri bowl. A type of BOWL, usually circular, having pierced decoration on the cover or on the shoulder, or on both; it is used, in the same way as a POT-POURRI VASE, to scent a room, but only with dry *pot-pourri* (a mixture of dried flower petals and spices), which is more often used in England than the liquid kind used in France.

pot-pourri vase. A type of ceramic vase, sometimes having silver MOUNTS, characterized by having pierced decoration on the shoulder or cover, or on both. Its purpose is the same as that of a POT-POURRI BOWL, but it is used only with a liquid *pot-pourri*.

porter's staff. Silver ferrule and finial engraved with name and date. H. (of ferrule) *c.* 20 cm. Bank of England, London.

Portland Vase. Silver-gilt replica, Philip Rundell for Rundell, Bridge & Rundell, London, 1820. H. 24·5 cm. Courtesy, Sotheby's, New York.

potato fork. Six tines, Joseph Walley, Liverpool, 1778–9. L. 31 cm. Grosvenor Museum, Chester.

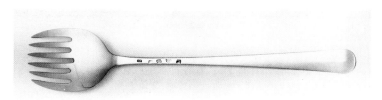

potato fork. A type of FORK having a wide bowl with six TINES. An example made by Joseph Walley of Liverpool, with a Chester date mark for 1778–9, is in the Grosvenor Museum, Chester; other examples, made in Dublin and London, are known. Such forks were sometimes made by altering a spoon to form the tines.

potato patty-pan. A type of kitchen utensil in the form of a large deep circular pan with slanting sides and provided with an inserted flat pierced lifter having a tall central handle. One example, 1801, sometimes said to have been called a 'fish kettle', is engraved with the arms of the Duke of Kent, father of Queen Victoria.

potato ring. A misnomer sometimes applied to a DISH RING on the erroneous assumption that such pieces were to support a wooden bowl in which were served a heap of hot baked potatoes. Not only is it preferable to serve hot baked potatoes in a folded napkin to help retain the heat, rather than in an open bowl, but most of those in Ireland who served baked potatoes would have been unlikely to own an ornate silver dish ring. It is possible that the type of article in the form of a wire stand, composed of two horizontal rings joined by four vertical wire supports, may sometimes have been used to serve potatoes wrapped in a napkin; if so, then such a piece might justifiably be designated a 'potato ring' rather than a 'dish ring'. The term 'potato ring' has not been used at the DUBLIN ASSAY OFFICE.

pottery objects. Articles of which an essential part is made of glazed earthenware but which have English silver or silver-gilt MOUNTS. Examples include JUGS made of Turkish (Iznik) earthenware (formerly erroneously called 'Rhodian pottery') mounted in England, *c.* 1580–92 (*see* RHODIAN JUG). Other examples of silver mounted pottery include imported Rhenish STONEWARE JUGS and some jugs of English make (*see* MALLING JUG), including examples of Fulham ware. *See* Edward Wenham, 'Silver Mounted Pottery' in *The Connoisseur,* May 1931, p. 251; Judith Banister, 'Pottery Garnished with Silver' in *Antique Dealer & Collectors Guide,* June 1966, p. 76. *See* PORCELAIN OBJECTS; MOUNTED OBJECTS.

pounce. (1) n. A fine powder made of pulverized gum sandarach or cuttle-fish-bone, formerly used on parchment or absorbent writing paper to make it smooth for writing, or to restore the smooth surface after erasure and so prevent ink from spreading. Pounce is to be distinguished from pumice or other powders or sand used instead of blotting paper to dry ink after writing. (2) v. To make a design by hammering on the reverse side of silver, or other metal, as in EMBOSSING or in REPOUSSÉ work, so as to create an overall pattern of small relief dots suggesting the appearance of sprinkled sand or pounce. *See* MATTING; PRICKING; PUNCHING; STIPPLED.

pounce-pot. A type of small POT having a perforated COVER, used for sprinkling POUNCE. After pounce was no longer needed, such pots were used for sprinkling fine sand to blot the ink. A pounce-pot was sometimes a unit of an INKSTAND or of a LIBRARY SET. Sometimes called a 'pounce dredger'. *See* SAND-BOX.

pounced work. Decoration made by pouncing (*see* POUNCE).

pouncet pot. A type of small box to contain a scented vinegar, having a pierced lid to emit the scent. The term, an early name for a VINAIGRETTE, may have been originally a misspelling for a 'pounced pot'; it was used by Shakespeare and also by Sir Walter Scott.

powder-flask. A type of flask-shaped receptacle used for the storage of gunpowder and having a cap for measuring the charge. *See* POWDER-HORN.

powder-horn. A type of small horn-shaped receptacle for the storage of gunpowder and for measuring the charge. Some examples are made entirely of

249 POWL-PRIC

silver, but others are of natural HORN, leather or porcelain, the receptacle being fitted with silver MOUNTS. *See* MUSICAL HORN; DRINKING HORN; POWDER-FLASK.

Powlet Cup. A silver-gilt TWO-HANDLED CUP generally similar to the TATTON CUP, except that the finial on the cover is in the form of a figure of a youthful Bacchus. Although unmarked, the cup has been attributed to THOMAS HEMING, *c.* 1761, based on its form and style of decoration. It bears the engraved arms of Charles Powlet, 4th Duke of Bolton, who was the bearer of the Queen Consort's crown at the coronation of George III and Queen Charlotte in 1761, and it has been suggested that the cup was a Royal gift made for the occasion by Heming in his capacity as Principal Goldsmith to the King. The cup was purchased in 1970 by the Victoria and Albert Museum, London. *See* HEMING TWO-HANDLED CUPS.

Preedy, Joseph (fl. 1777-1800). A London silversmith, apprenticed to Thomas Whipham in 1765 and turned over to William Plummer in 1766. He entered his first mark in 1777 at Westmoreland Buildings, Aldersgate St. He became a partner of WILLIAM PITTS I in 1791 at 26 Litchfield St, St Anne's, Soho, and moved in 1795 to 8 Great Newport St, St Anne's. When the firm terminated in 1799, he entered his separate mark in 1800 at 8 Great Newport St. The firm specialized in making ornate pierced BASKETS and EPERGNES of silver gilt.

presentation cup. Any CUP that is presented to a person to commemorate a special occasion, hence usually inscribed with the recipient's name, the date, and relevant data. Such cups were usually in the form of a VASE-SHAPED STANDING CUP or a TWO-HANDLED CUP; they were a speciality of the COURTAULD family.

presentation sword. A type of SWORD made expressly for presentation to military officers for dress wear, the silver-hilt and the scabbard usually being ornately decorated with silver MOUNTS. In the United States such swords were a speciality of TIFFANY & CO. from *c* 1860, and particularly during the period of the American Civil War, although a few were also made in the period 1870-80 and some during the Spanish-American War, 1898. *See* Philip Medicus, 'American silver-hilted swords' in *Antiques,* November 1941, p. 244, and December 1941, p. 342; A. V. B. Norman, 'British Presentation Swords' in *The Connoisseur,* December 1967, p. 232.

preserving pan. A type of PAN that has a large, wide and deep bowl, cylindrical but slightly incurved, and two vertical loop lifting handles. Examples in silver are rare.

price. As to silverware: the price of an article, which may vary considerably, depending on its age (usually shown by the HALLMARKS), maker (whether highly reputed, currently in vogue or little known), rarity as to type, style or origin, any ARMORIALS it bears (whether or not contemporary), and its condition (whether it or any part is a FAKE or has been repaired, and whether the piece or any mark on it has been altered), as well as the circumstances of the particular sale, i.e., whether from an urban or provincial dealer or at auction (the latter always influenced by the bidders present at a particular sale and the extent of competition). The basic price (often quoted on the basis of the mere WEIGHT of the piece in ounces) is dependent primarily on the current market price of silver bullion, but prices for collectible silverware include an increment for FASHION, a factor based on several of the above-mentioned elements. Some books give guidance as to estimated price ranges; *see* Peter Waldron, *The Price Guide to Antique Silver* (1985).

pricket candlestick. A type of CANDLESTICK having at the top of its shaft, instead of a NOZZLE or SOCKET, a vertical metal spike on which to impale a thick candle. Sometimes called an 'altar candlestick', as it is the type used on church altars, usually large and having a baluster stem resting on a tripod base, a style adapted from the design on candlesticks used in France and Flanders.

pricking. The technique of decorating the surface of silverware by making, from the front, a design using a series of small dots, as was done in the 16th and 17th centuries for marking initials, monograms, ARMORIALS, or dates on the handles of some SPOONS, or on some small CUPS and DISHES made as a wedding or christening gift. The work is said to have been done by needlepoint by persons who were unskilled in ENGRAVING. More recently, the method was used for inscriptions on some work by C. R. ASHBEE. *See* PUNCHING; MATTING; POUNCE; STIPPLED.

print. The Watson Mazer, Scottish, mid-16th century, showing boss and print. D. (of bowl) 19 cm. Royal Scottish Museum, Edinburgh.

processional cross. Crucifix cross with fleur-de-lis terminals, Ignace-François Ranvoyzé, Quebec, *c.* 1800. H. 65 cm. National Museum of Man, Ottawa.

print. A silver circular decorative plaque set on the BOSS in the bottom of the interior of some wooden MAZERS, QUAICHES, and WASSAIL BOWLS; the print is engraved with a decorative symbol, the head of a person, or a COAT OF ARMS.

processional cross. A type of large CROSS that is carried in a church procession, usually bearing figures on both sides. The tubular base of such a cross is often fitted over a wooden staff. Few examples made of silver in England have survived (*see* CANTERBURY PROCESSIONAL CROSS), but two very similar Canadian processional crucifix crosses, both with fleur-de-lis terminals on the arms, are extant: one made by Ignace-François Ranvoyzé, Quebec, *c.* 1800, in the National Museum of Man, Ottawa, and another made by Pierre Huguet called Latour, Quebec, late 18th century, in the City Art Museum, St Louis, Missouri. *See* QUEBEC SILVERWARE; CHURCH FURNISHINGS.

provenance (sometimes **provenience**). The source of an object; strictly, the term refers to the known record of prior ownership as distinguished from the place of production.

pseudo-hallmark. A mark resembling, but not conflicting with, a British HALLMARK, such as any mark that has been applied in a country other than the United Kingdom, and may imply by its appearance that it, or a part of it, is a British hallmark. Such marks are punched by a silversmith, not by an ASSAY OFFICE, and include some marks used in the United States, Canada, Australia, South Africa, and India, as well as marks on so-called China-trade ware made in Canton for export. Such marks would not normally deceive persons familiar with silverware as, unless they have become worn, they are usually clearly distinguishable from genuine hallmarks. Since 1 January 1975, although it is legal in the United Kingdom to own silverware with such marks, any such article must, before being sold, be submitted to an Assay Office for verification that the mark does not conflict with a British hallmark. *See* Martin C. B. Gubbins, 'Pseudo-hallmarks on Silver' in *The Connoisseur,* August 1974, p. 256.

pudding slicer. A serving utensil in the form of a flat rectangular FISH SLICE but having a low vertical band along one side.

Pudsey Spoon. A SEAL-TOP SPOON, marked London, 1525–6, having a FIG-SHAPED bowl and having engraved on the seal a five-petal rose. It was formerly thought, perhaps based on the rose, that it was the spoon said to have been given by Henry VI (d. 1471), of the House of Lancaster, to Sir Ralph Pudsey, of Bolton Hall, where the king, in the Wars of the Roses, concealed himself after the battle of Hexham, 1464; however, the present view, based on the marked date letter (originally misread as 1445, but correctly recorded in an 1869 catalogue), is that it is not the original spoon and that the rose is not the red rose sometimes used as a badge by the House of Lancaster, but a later badge of Henry VII, 1485–1509, the first Tudor king. The spoon is owned by the City Museum, Liverpool.

Pugin, A(ugustus) W(elby) N(orthmore) (1812–52). An English architect and designer, of French descent, who was born in London. By 1826 he worked in the Print Room of the British Museum and became employed by RUNDELL, BRIDGE & RUNDELL. He made designs in many fields, and especially for metalware. Most were executed by Rundell, Bridge & Rundell and after 1840 by John Hardman & Co., Birmingham – the firm founded by Pugin and his close associate, John Hardman II (1811–67). His designs were influenced by Gothic sources, which is apparent both in the ecclesiastical and domestic silverware that he designed and in the architecture of his many English churches. He revived interest in medieval styles and techniques, was opposed to mechanical processes, and was an advocate of the artist-craftsman. His principal patron was the 16th Earl of Shrewsbury. Five of his designs for silverware for Rundell, Bridge & Rundell, signed by him and dated 1827, countersigned by John Gawler Bridge, are in the Victoria and Albert Museum, London. *See* Shirley Bury, 'In Search of Pugin's Church Plate' in *The Connoisseur,* May 1967, p. 29; Alexandra Wedgwood, *The Pugin Family* (1977). *See* PUGIN CHALICE; PUGIN FLAGON; CORONATION CUP.

Pugin Chalice. A parcel-gilt CHALICE having a hemispherical bowl, a straight stem, and a six-lobed base, with the stem having one knop midway with decoration of amethysts and garnets. On the base are plaques decorated with CHAMPLEVÉ enamelling. Designed by A. W. N. PUGIN, the piece was made by John Hardman & Co., Birmingham, and bears the Birmingham mark for 1849–50. It was shown at the Great Exhibition of 1851, and is now in the Victoria and Albert Museum, London.

Pugin Flagon. A silver-gilt and glass FLAGON formed of a pear-shaped ruby-glass bottle with silver mounts. The glass bottle rests in a calyx-type silver band having CRESTING encircling the top and supported by a wide four-lobed base. The silver mount encircling the neck has a BEAK SPOUT, and descends to a pierced band with inverted cresting. The SCROLL HANDLE surrounds at the top a circular ornament with a swirling openwork pattern, and extends down to the lower part of the glass bottle. The hinged lid has a band surmounted by a nest-like ornament upon which is a figure of a vulning pelican. A circular plaque is on the front of the glass bottle. The band around the neck bears an engraved inscription. The glass was made by Thomas Willemont (1786–1871) and the mounts by John Hardman & Co., Birmingham, the piece being executed from a design by A. W. N. PUGIN. The flagon was donated on 25 March 1849 by Katherine Willemont to Davington Priory, and is now owned by the vicar and churchwardens of the priory church of St Mary Magdalene and St Lawrence, Davington, Kent. A similar piece is in the parish church of Tamsworth, near Lichfield, Staffordshire.

A glass-and-silver version, in the Victoria and Albert Museum, London, was made in 1858–9, also by John Hardman & Co., but from a design by John Hardman Powell (1827–95), and was shown in the 1862 International Exhibition. It is of basically similar form, except that: (1) the base is ten-lobed, (2) the handle does not have the circular ornament at the top, (3) the bottle does not have a plaque at the front but has four silver vertical straps connecting the base and the neckband, each having midway a blue-enamelled disc set with a cabochon, and (4) the neckband is set with cabochons.

pulley salt. The same as a SCROLL SALT.

punch. (1) A tool (short form of 'puncheon') used by silversmiths to impress a shape, pattern, hole, or letter or numerical character into silver, usually by tapping or hammering it against the metal. There are various types of punch; the 'repoussé punch', for making REPOUSSÉ decoration, has a blunt rounded head; 'tracer', for CHASING, has a flatter head; 'matting tool', for making a textured surface, has ends with various patterns to make a hatched, grained or other decorative surface; 'doming punch', to form a hemispherical depression, has a globular head; 'perloir' or 'beading tool', to make BEADING; 'letter punch', to impress a letter, numeral, or symbol, such as a HALLMARK, has the mark in intaglio; and 'centre punch', to start a hole, has a pointed end. All types are made in a range of sizes. *See* PUNCHING.

(2) A beverage, varying in composition, but usually having a base of wine or distilled spirit, together with other ingredients such as milk, water, sugar, spices, fruit juice, etc., and usually served hot. (The term 'punch' is derived from the Hindi word *'pac'* meaning 'five', due to the five ingredients used originally in India.) *See* PUNCH-BOWL; PUNCH-CUP; PUNCH LADLE; PUNCH-POT; PUNCH STRAINER.

punch-bowl. A large circular BOWL, at least 23 cm wide, originally for serving PUNCH (later, iced beverages or eggnog), and sometimes having a cover. The decoration on early English examples was usually limited to engraved

punch-bowl. Bowl in form of monteith, with cups and ladle, Asprey & Co., London, 1977. W. (of bowl) 33 cm. Courtesy, Asprey & Co. Ltd.

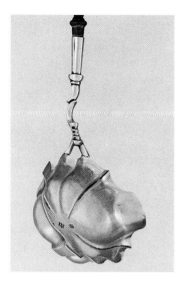

punch ladle. Silver bowl and ferrule, Robert Innes, London, 1751–2. L. 34·5 cm. Colonial Williamsburg, Va.

punch strainer. John Clarke, Providence, R.I. L. 32 cm. Yale University Art Gallery (Mabel Brady Garvan Collection), New Haven, Conn.

punching. Wine taster with punched decoration, London, 1642–3. W. 9·2 cm. Victoria and Albert Museum, London.

ARMORIALS, but some, of HUGUENOT SILVERWARE, have applied SPOON-HANDLE STRAPS. Unlike the comparably shaped MONTEITH, such a bowl usually has no handles and often rests on a SPLAYED foot. Some exceptionally large examples have a capacity of three to four gallons (13·5 to 18 litres). Some are accompanied by a number of PUNCH-CUPS. Sometimes called a JORUM. Examples of FAKE punch-bowls are known, raised from a PLATE or DISH and bearing a false or altered HALLMARK. *See* Judith Banister, 'Noble Silver: Punch Bowls and Monteiths' in *Antique Dealer & Collectors Guide,* May 1967, p. 60. *See* CODRINGTON PUNCH BOWL; SONS OF LIBERTY BOWL; PUNCH LADLE; ROSE-WATER BOWL; WASSAIL BOWL.

punch-cup. A type of CUP for drinking PUNCH (or other beverage served from a PUNCH-BOWL), being a small flat-bottomed or stem-footed cup with one loop handle. Examples accompanying some punch-bowls have a small hook for suspension on the rim of the bowl.

punch ladle. A type of LADLE used for serving PUNCH (or other beverages) from a PUNCH-BOWL into individual PUNCH-CUPS or drinking glasses. The handle, varying in length, is usually straight but sometimes slightly curved, and is attached to the bowl of the ladle at right-angles to its greatest width. The handle in early examples is made of silver, later ones being of turned wood set in a long silver FERRULE attached to the bowl of the ladle; in the late-18th century the wood handle was sometimes superseded by one of ivory or whalebone, of circular or square section near the ferrule but having the upper part twisted to afford a firm grip. The bowl of the ladle may be circular, oval, ovoid, scalloped or shell-shaped, and is sometimes pointed or tapering at one end or both ends to facilitate pouring; sometimes it is tilted at a 135° angle. Sometimes a coin is set into the bowl of the ladle or has been hammered to form the bowl. *See* G. Bernard Hughes, 'Silver Punch-Ladles' in *Country Life,* 17 November 1950, p. 1690. See TODDY LADLE.

punch-pot. A type of KETTLE resembling the TEA-KETTLE in a TEA SERVICE, but usually smaller and of oblate globular shape, having a curved SPOUT and a single HANDLE. The handle is usually overhead (a BAIL HANDLE) but on some early examples it was on the side, as on a contemporary TEAPOT. Such kettles usually lack the interior strainer at the base of the spout, such as is invariably present in a teapot. English silver examples are known from *c.* 1750, and were used for brewing and serving hot punch. Some examples rest on a STAND that has an aperture for inserting a spirit lamp. Sometimes called a 'punch-kettle'. *See* RUM-KETTLE.

punch stirrer. A utensil for stirring the contents of a PUNCH-BOWL, having a long handle to which are attached two wide flat blades crossed at right-angles, to be rotated in the PUNCH, in the same manner as a SWIZZLE STICK. Sometimes called a 'punch whisk'.

punch strainer. A utensil for straining orange or lemon juice squeezed directly into a PUNCH-BOWL. It has a deep hemispherical pierced bowl with two long side handles to extend across the punch-bowl and rest on its rim; the length varies from about 30 to 60 cm. The handles are flat and horizontal, and are usually ornately decorated with ENGRAVING, CHASING or PIERCED WORK, and the perforations in the bowl of the strainer form a dot pattern or are shaped holes arranged in elaborate patterns. Some early examples have a long handle on one side only, and on the other side a hook to be clipped to the rim of the punch-bowl. The bowl of the strainer extends down into the punch, to allow the squeezed oranges (including peel) to be placed there to impart added flavour to the punch. *See* ORANGE-AND-LEMON STRAINER.

puncherie. A term used in the 18th century for a complete silver equipage for serving punch, including a PUNCH-BOWL, PUNCH LADLE, PUNCH-CUPS (or glass goblets), SPICE-BOX, SUGAR-BOWL, and NUTMEG GRATER.

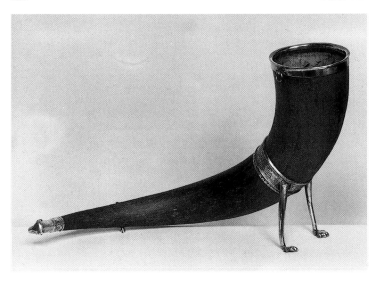

Pusey Drinking Horn. Natural horn with silver-gilt mounts, early 15th century. H. 25·5 cm. Victoria and Albert Museum, London.

punching. The technique of decorating by handwork the front surface of silverware (or other metal) by use of a PUNCH so as to make a pattern consisting of small depressions or dots, each made by a single stroke of the punch, rather than a continuous line as produced by CHASING. It is sometimes used to make, either as a border design or an overall pattern, a decoration consisting of depressions of varying sizes. *See* POUNCE; PRICKING; MATTING.

Puritan spoon. A type of SPOON that has a plain flat stem, widening from an oval bowl toward the top and having the terminal cut off at right-angles to the stem (of rectangular section), thus having no finial. The type was later developed in England into the TRIFID SPOON, and some examples were made in the United States. Some such spoons have one or two small notches cut in the terminal. The name is perhaps derived from the austerity of the form, favoured by the 16th/17th-century Puritans.

purse mount. A decorative mount attached to a purse and closed by hinges along its top. Examples made of silver survive, including one for a sporran.

Pyne, Benjamin. Silver-gilt dessert plate with engraved armorial, London, 1698. W. 21·5 cm. Victoria and Albert Museum, London.

Pusey Drinking Horn. A DRINKING HORN embellished with silver-gilt MOUNTS, including a lip rim, tip ornament (an animal head), and a central band (bearing a donative inscription) to which are attached two legs to support the horn in a standing position, the mounts having been added in the 15th century. According to tradition, the horn was given, together with the manor of Pusey, Berkshire, by King Canute, 1017–35, to William Pusey, one of his officers who reported news of an impending Saxon attack. The piece remained associated with the manor of Pusey until 1922, and was donated in 1938 by the widow of Philip Bouverie-Pusey, of Pusey, to the Victoria and Albert Museum, London.

push piece. A small projecting device concealing a spring, sometimes found on the rim of a BOX, such as a SNUFF-BOX, which is to be pressed to release a catch and thus allow the LID to be opened.

Pyne, Benjamin (1653?–1732). A leading London silversmith, apprenticed in 1667 and freed in 1676. He entered his mark in 1697, with address at St Martin's Le Grand. From 1685 he did work for Sir Richard Hoare, banker, and received orders for MACES, regalia, and CHURCH PLATE. He was at one time employed by Queen Anne, 1702-14, and was Subordinate Goldsmith to George I in 1714. His work was in traditional English style, but also in the style of HUGUENOT SILVERWARE, the latter perhaps made by himself or by employing Huguenot journeymen. Among the pieces he made are the NORFOLK TOILET SERVICE, a TWO-HANDLED CUP now at the Mansion House, London, and ornate DISHES, SAUCE-BOATS, and CANDLESTICKS. *See* CODRINGTON PUNCH BOWL.

pyriform. The same as PEAR-SHAPED.

pyx. In the Christian Church, a receptacle in which the Host (the Eucharist wafer) is reserved for veneration in church, for carrying it in procession, and

pyx. Altar type, parcel gilt, Roland Paradis, Montreal, 1739. H. 8·6 cm. Musée du Québec, Quebec.

pyx. Viaticum type, François Sasseville, Quebec, *c.* 1845. W. 4·8 cm. Musée du Québec, Quebec.

for bringing it to the sick *(viaticum)* to administer the sacrament. The *viaticum* type of pyx was usually a small box *(pyxis),* sometimes in the form of a WATCH-CASE, but some intended for altar use were in the form of a covered cup *(cuppa)*; some, to be suspended over the altar, were in the form of a dove (the Holy Spirit) or other religious image. Sometimes the Host was kept in an inner case *(capsula)* within the pyx. The pyx was required to have a securely fastened cover to prevent accidental opening, especially in the case of the type that was suspended above the altar. Some examples were made of crystal so that the Host was visible, and when made as a standing pyx it was closely related to a CIBORIUM. *See* SWINBURNE PYX; CHURCH PLATE.

pyx chest. A locked strong-box, used by the Royal Mint, in which to deposit sample coins of each striking (including coins of silver and all other metals) until they have been formally assayed at 'The trial of the pyx', held annually at Goldsmiths' Hall from 1870 until the present day to confirm that the coins are of the proper standard as to weight and FINENESS.

Q

quaich (or **quaigh**). A Scottish type of shallow uncovered drinking vessel, generally in the form of the shallow PORRINGER. Those of small size were for individual use, larger ones to be passed around on ceremonial occasions in the same way as a LOVING CUP. It has two (rarely, three or four) flat horizontal handles (termed 'lugs' in Scotland) extending level from the rim of the bowl; the handles are unpierced and usually droop downward at the extremities (the downward curves were to secure the cup when fastened by a leather thong to the owner's leg while travelling, as the kilt had no pocket and the sporran insufficient space). Early examples are of wood, bone or horn, being made sometimes with silver MOUNTS, and later ones entirely of silver. Those with a wooden bowl were often made of vertical staves (sometimes of alternating contrasting woods) bound horizontally with two bands of withies; some silver examples are decorated to simulate this form. Some examples have in the interior a decorative PRINT on the bottom (originally made to cover the junction of the wooden staves). The width is usually in the range of 9·5 to 25 cm. Modern examples are made in many sizes. *See* J. Milne-Davidson, 'The Scottish Quaich', in *The Antique Collector,* 1 September 1938, p. 23; Richard L. McClenahan, 'Some Scottish Quaiches', in *Antiques,* September 1969, p. 402.

Quarter Seal. A SEAL composed of the upper half of obverse and reverse sides of the Great Seal of Scotland (each piece being one quarter of the whole seal), used there for certain types of document. An example is at the British Museum, London. The National Museum of Antiquities of Scotland owns silver matrices for the Quarter Seals of George IV and William IV.

Quebec silverware. Articles of silverware made in the Province of Quebec, Canada, from the early 18th century. The first silversmiths were Catholics

quaich. James Penman, Edinburgh, 1685. W. 24·8 cm. Royal Scottish Museum, Edinburgh.

who came from France and trained local apprentices. The leading makers of the early French period, *c.* 1730-50, producing mainly CHURCH PLATE, were, in Quebec City, Paul Lambert called Saint-Paul (1691-1749) and Jean-François Landron (1686-1759), and in Montreal, Roland Paradis (1696-1754). During the early years of English control the leaders were Ignace-François Ranvoyzé (1739-1819) in Quebec City, ROBERT CRUICKSHANK in Montreal, and Ignace-François Delzenne (1717-80) in Quebec City and Montreal. In the 19th century the leading silversmith in Quebec City was Laurent Amyot (1764-1838) who, after a trip to France in 1787, introduced the Louis XVI style; he was followed in Montreal by Pierre Huguet called Latour (1749-1817) and Salomon Marion (1782-1832) and in Quebec City by François Sasseville (1797-1864). *See* Ramsey Traquair, *The Old Silver of Quebec* (1940); Ian C. Morgan, 'Silversmiths of French Canada', in *Antiques,* March 1957, p. 251; W. E. Greening, 'Silversmiths of French Canada' in *The Connoisseur,* July 1966, p. 213; Jean Trudel, 'Silver in New France' in *The Connoisseur,* February 1974, p. 147. *See* CANADIAN SILVERWARE.

Quebec silverware. Monstrance, crystal within Gloria, Jean-François Landron, Quebec, *c.* 1730. Musée du Québec, Quebec.

Queen Anne Alms Dishes. Two silver-gilt circular ALMS DISHES, both attributed probably to CHARLES SHELLEY, *c.* 1660, and bearing the initials A and R (for Queen Anne, 1702-14), probably substituted for the cipher 'CR' (for Charles II, 1660-85). One has a wide rim embossed with figures of a stag, boar, bull, and horse between embossed tulips and leafage, and in the well a crowned rose flanked by the initials; it is in the Jewel House of the Tower of London. The other dish has an almost identical rim, but the animals on it are a lion, unicorn, running dog, and stag, and the initials are smaller and placed alongside the rose within a circular surround; it is in the Royal Collection. According to an inventory made during the reign of William IV, the latter was part of the Communion Plate used during the coronation service.

Queen Anne Style. In the decorative arts, the style of decoration named after the reign of Queen Anne, 1702-14, but which prevailed in England from *c.* 1688 until *c.* 1720 and, with increased ornament, until *c.* 1730; as to silverware, it was influenced by the softness of BRITANNIA SILVER made in the period 1697-1720. The emphasis was on good design and fine workmanship rather than the flamboyance of the preceding BAROQUE STYLE, with less use of EMBOSSING and an absence of applied ornaments. The ware, much of it executed by CASTING, was made increasingly in the style of HUGUENOT SILVERWARE but was also influenced by local styles. Among the leading native English silversmiths of the period were ANTHONY NELME and BENJAMIN PYNE. The style became popular also in the United States, especially in the period 1720-50.

Queen's College (Oxford) Drinking Horn, The. A DRINKING HORN of buffalo horn with silver-gilt MOUNTS of two encircling bands supported by three eagle's-claw feet, an encircling band at the open end, a recurving mouthpiece (a monster's head), and a cover with a silver-gilt finial in the form of a standing eagle. On the bands and the cover is engraved the word 'Wacceyl' (wassail), repeated three times. The horn has been cut in recent times into three sections and has a silver-gilt lining. The original parts date from the 14th century, but some of the silver mounts are attributed to the 17th century. According to tradition, the horn was given to The Queen's College, Oxford, by Robert de Eglesfield (d. 1349), founder of the College in 1341 and chaplain to Queen Philippa (wife of Edward III), in whose honour it was named.

Queen's Cup, The. A silver-gilt STANDING CUP, an example of SCULPTURAL SILVERWARE, the bowl and cover being of oblate globular shape resting on a bracketed wide stem on a domed foot. On the cover is a cast group of figures depicting a scene at Oatlands Park, Surrey, with the huntsman John Selwyn, under-keeper at Oatlands Park, slaying a stag while being watched from above by an equestrian figure of Queen Victoria. The cup was designed and modelled by EDMUND COTTERILL and was made in 1846 by ROBERT GARRARD II for R. & S. Garrard. It was presented by Queen Victoria in 1847 as the prize for the Ascot Cup race, and it is uncertain how it reached the Bedford Collection at Woburn Abbey, as the Duke of Bedford's horse ran second.

Queen Anne Alms Dishes. One of two attributed to Charles Shelley, silver gilt, London, *c.* 1660. D. 61 cm. Tower of London (Crown copyright, HMSO).

Queen's pattern. A pattern for the handle of FLATWARE and CUTLERY that is comparable to the KING'S PATTERN, having at the terminal (on both sides) a SCALLOP shell, but the stem being less curved and having at the juncture with the bowl a stylized floral pattern.

Queen's Tankard, The. A TANKARD having its body decorated with pierced work and having on its lid figures depicting two dogs killing a wild boar. It

'Queen Victoria's Dogs' Centrepiece. Silver gilt, designed by Prince Albert and made by Robert Garrard II, 1842–3. H. 76·5 cm. Royal Collection; reproduced by gracious permission of Her Majesty the Queen.

was made by ROBERT GARRARD II in 1827 from a design by EDMUND COTTER-ILL. On the base is the word 'Ascot', the piece having been the prize for the Ascot Cup race in 1857.

'Queen Victoria's Dogs' Centrepiece. A silver-gilt CENTREPIECE designed by Prince Albert in 1842, soon after his marriage to Queen Victoria, and made in 1842–3 by ROBERT GARRARD II for R. & S. Garrard & Co. It has a central pedestal supporting a shallow quatrefoil dish and rising from a square plinth upon which are, around the pedestal, naturalistic standing figures (modelled by EDMUND COTTERILL) in-the-round depicting four of the Queen's favourite dogs – a greyhound, a Skye terrier, a rough-haired terrier, and a dachshund. On the plinth are the Royal arms of Victoria and Albert. The piece was shown at the Great Exhibition of 1851. It is now in the Royal Collection.

quenching. The cooling of silver (or other metal), during the process of AN-NEALING, by immersing it in water, oil or other liquid after it has been heated; the liquid is called a 'quenching bath'. *See* TEMPERING.

quill-case. A writing accessory in the form of a vertical container divided into sections for holding writing quills. *See* PENNER.

quill-pot. A type of receptacle used to contain small lead shot for cleaning the ink from the nib of quill pens, having a COVER pierced with holes (from three to five) through which quills could be inserted and kept upright. Sometimes it was combined with an INKPOT in the form of a receptacle containing a glass liner for ink, surrounded by lead shot; the cover of the receptacle has a central hole for using the ink and surrounding holes giving access to the shot. Also called a 'quill cleaner'.

quilting. An ornamental overall decoration having the appearance of quilted work, made by CHASING the surface with depressed lines which form a chequered pattern of squares and lozenges. In silverware it is found on some TUREENS, including a pair made by EDWARD WAKELIN, 1755. Also called 'matelassé', from the French word *matelas,* mattress.

R

racing bell. A type of BELL in the form of a hollow perforated sphere containing a loose ball that causes it to emit a ringing sound when shaken; it has a small suspensory ring, and is similar to the bell attached to a baby's RATTLE. Such bells were awarded as prizes for horse races in the 16th and 17th centuries, often in Scotland and the north of England. The earliest-known example was awarded at Chester in 1522, and in 1588 Elizabeth I gave a gold bell as a prize for a race on Salisbury Plain. Two extant Scottish examples are the Lanark Bell and the Paisley Bell. *See* HORSE-RACING TROPHIES.

Radnor Centrepiece. A CENTREPIECE made by LOUIS OSMAN, 1968, composed of three parts, to be placed together to form one pattern. The largest part is in the form of three oak leaves, with the stem surmounted by a vertical acorn, and the other two parts are single oak leaves. The piece was commissioned by the Dowager Countess of Radnor as a gift to her son, each part bearing his coat of arms (enamelled by Dilys Osman), incorporating the arms of Oakley (for his mother) and of Radnor (for his father, who was Chairman of the Forestry Commission), hence the oak-leaf motif. The piece has been on loan to the Goldsmiths' Company, London.

raising. A process of shaping a silver article of HOLLOW WARE that is too deep or too narrow to be formed by SINKING. It is a type of HAMMERING where the article is raised from a flat plate by blows working, in a series of concentric rings, from the centre or from a flat base toward the rim, extruding the metal outward and curving it upward while holding it over a shaped metal stake or 'anvil'. When the top has been reached, the edge is made stronger by hammering it so as to overlap and thus thicken it (called 'caulking' or 'corking'). The process requires repeating blows and ANNEALING, es-

Radnor Centrepiece. Two of the three parts, Louis Osman, London, 1968. Private Collection (photo courtesy, Goldsmiths' Company, London).

pecially to raise a tall object. Some articles of hollow ware that are tall (e.g., a TANKARD or COFFEE-POT) are shaped, not by raising, but by turning a flat plate of silver into a cylindrical or conical shape and, after SOLDERING the edges into a seam, soldering on to it a flat base. The process is sometimes called 'hand raising'.

Ramsden, Omar (1873–1939). A leading English designer of silverware, born in Sheffield (his baptismal name was Omer), who received his early training there from his father and studied designing. He was apprenticed in 1887 to a Sheffield silversmith. In 1898 he registered his first mark jointly with ALWYN CARR, his friend and thereafter his collaborator and partner until 1919. They first worked in Sheffield, but soon moved to London, with a workshop at Albert Bridge, Battersea. Before long, they transferred their activities to their long-time studio-workshop (and Ramsden's home) at St Dunstan's, Seymour Place, off Fulham Road, South Kensington. An early work was a MACE made from a prize-winning design and commissioned by the Duke of Norfolk for the City of Sheffield. Success soon followed, and they employed a large staff of silversmiths, designers, chasers, engravers, and enamellers, including Walter Andrews and Leonard Moss as silversmiths, A. E. Ulyett as chaser (he also modelled finials and bosses), Robert Massey (succeeded by Ernest Wright) as engraver, Jeanne Etève (succeeded by Henri de Konigh) as enameller, and Robert Hewlett, L. W. Burt, and LESLIE DURBIN as modellers. Ramsden was mainly the entrepreneur, and never executed any piece; Carr was the designer and financial supporter. They were followers of the Arts and Crafts Movement, and did some work in ART NOUVEAU STYLE. After they had been apart during World War I, the firm was dissolved in 1919, and Ramsden then registered his own well-known mark 'O R Me Fecit' that subsequently appeared, in several variations, and sometimes with his signature, on all the work, even though it was not actually made by him. The style of the work shows Celtic influence and is characterized by using, as a form of decoration, HAMMERING marks that were not removed by PLANISHING. The workshop produced much ecclesiastical ware and many presentation pieces, including a series of MAZERS in modified medieval style, and also many WINE-CUPS. In his last period, the workshop made domestic ware emphasizing line, undecorated except for hammering marks. In 1973 a travelling exhibition of his work was shown in Sheffield, Birmingham, Bristol, and London. *See* Judith Banister, 'An Exhibitionist on Exhibition' in *Country Life,* 8 February 1973, p. 321; Peter Cannon-Brookes, 'Omar Ramsden – Artist-Goldsmith' in *The Connoisseur,* April 1974, p.250. *See* THREE KINGS MAZER; WESTMINSTER MONSTRANCE.

Ramsey Abbey Censer. A silver-gilt cast CENSER, second quarter of the 14th century, in the form of an undecorated shallow bowl surmounted by a hexagonal chapter house or chapel with ogival arches and a pointed roof, topped by a final in the form of a ram emerging from waves (a rebus for Ramsey

Ramsey Abbey Censer and Incense Boat.
Silver-gilt censer and parcel-gilt
incense-boat. Both second quarter of
14th century. Victoria and Albert
Museum, London.

Abbey, a Benedictine house in Huntingdonshire); it has long suspensory
chains. The censer is accompanied by a parcel-gilt INCENSE-BOAT, last quarter
of the 14th century, that rests on a hexafoil base and is half-closed, having a
hinged lid extending over the other half of the boat and having a ram's head
at each end. Both pieces were found in the bed of Whittlesea Mere, Huntingdonshire, when it was drained in 1850, and are now in the Victoria and
Albert Museum, London.

rat-tail. A decorative pattern found on the handle of some FLATWARE and
CUTLERY, in the form of a slender tapering and raised ridge running lengthwise, suggestive of the shape of a rat's tail. *See* RAT-TAIL HANDLE. It is found
also on some SPOONS; *see* RAT-TAIL SPOON. Such rat-tails are found also on the
handles of some TANKARDS, extending down from the hinge of the lid and
sometimes down the rear of the piece under the handle. The pattern was
used mainly until *c.* 1725, but later examples are found.

rat-tail handle. A type of handle on some FLATWARE and CUTLERY having a
raised pattern in the form of a RAT-TAIL, extending down along the stem,
from the point of a double-curved raised motif at the top. On some HANO-
VERIAN PATTERN ware, the rat-tail is on the front of the handle and extends
along almost its full length.

rat-tail spoon. Any of several types of SPOON characterized by having on the
back of the bowl, extending from the join to the stem, a RAT-TAIL pattern,
which sometimes extends halfway down the bowl (as on a TRIFID SPOON) but
on later examples almost the whole length of the bowl. The rat-tail is found
in three styles: (1) plain, (2) with a raised ridge down the centre, and (3)
with such a ridge decorated with a line of BEADING. Originally the purpose
of the rat-tail was to strengthen the join, but later it was struck in a die also
as decoration. *See* DOG-NOSE SPOON.

rattle. A type of instrument which produces a rattling sound when shaken.
It is an infant's toy, often made of silver, containing a number of hard objects to produce the sound. Most have hollow spherical BELLS attached, and
occasionally a teething device at one end, such as a coral stalk, and a WHISTLE
in the handle end. Rattles are known from *c.* 1700, but most extant examples
date from after *c.* 1760. See TEETHING STICK.

razor set. A set of 'cut-throat' razors, made with silver mounts and sometimes tortoise-shell handles, and kept, sometimes with accompanying accessories, in a fitted case. Some complete sets included several folding razors,
several razor strops, and such SMALLWARE as scissors, button-hook, tweezers,
etc. Some large cases, rectangular and vertical, had a hinged LID that was cut
diagonally at the sides so that, when opened, it revealed the contents (like a
KNIFE-BOX); the cases were made of wood, covered with leather or shagreen,
and often had silver MOUNTS. Sometimes called a 'Field Companion'. *See*
SHAVING SET.

Reade Salt. A silver-gilt PEDESTAL SALT having a cylindrical spool-shaped
body resting on a spreading base and having a tiered cover with an urn-
shaped finial upon which stands a figure of a Roman warrior holding a
shield and a spear. It is decorated overall with EMBOSSING and on the body

rattle. Silver rattle with whistle and
bells and coral handle, English, *c.* 1810.
Victoria and Albert Museum, London.

are three CARTOUCHES framing coats of arms which were originally enamelled. It bears the maker's mark of William Cobbold (1530–86), of Norwich, 1568–9, and was regilded in 1735 by Nathaniel Roe. The salt was purchased in 1568 for the City of Norwich from a cash bequest by Peter Reade (d. 1568), Alderman in 1562, to purchase a piece for use by successive mayors, and bears a pricked inscription recording the gift. It is reputed to be the finest known example of English provincial silverware.

recusant plate. Articles of silverware which were owned from *c.* 1550 by Catholics in Britain who refused to attend the service of the Established Church (which refusal was, for about two centuries after *c.* 1570, a statutory offence punishable by fine). Despite the practice being an offence, recusant chapels were maintained at many Catholic manor houses and many recusant articles were retained or were made to order in England and Scotland until *c.* 1790. The articles included pieces of CHURCH PLATE, such as a CHALICE, PATEN, PYX, RELIQUARY, CENSER, and other objects usual in a Catholic church. Much recusant plate was not sent to Goldsmiths' Hall for hallmarking – on the ground that it was not offered for sale – and hence is unmarked, but many pieces do bear the mark of the maker.

Reed & Barton. A large firm, in Taunton, Massachusetts, known originally for its ware of BRITANNIA METAL and its PLATED METAL, but which from the 1850s also made objects of STERLING SILVER. It was founded by Henry Gooding Reed (1810–1901) who was born in Taunton and became an apprentice to the firm of Isaac Babbit and William Crossman, which produced the first Britannia metal made in the United States. In 1834, when the firm ceased production, Reed, with Charles E. Barton and Horatio Leonard, took over the plant, under the name of The Taunton Britannia Manufacturing Company, changed in 1840 to Reed & Barton. The firm followed English styles and techniques, soon producing mainly plated ware, but from 1889 making much ware of sterling silver, especially tableware and wedding gifts. When Reed died, he left his shares to his daughter and control passed to his son-in-law, William Dowse, who was succeeded in 1923 by his son-in-law, Sinclair Weeks. *See* George S. Gibb, *The Whitesmiths of Taunton* (1946).

reed-and-tie rim. A decorative RIM pattern in the form of REEDING, but with crossed straps at intervals to simulate ribbons that tie the reeding together. It was popular in the NEO-CLASSICAL STYLE and the ADAM STYLE.

reeded rim. A decorative type of RIM in the form of continuous encircling REEDING. *See* REED-AND-TIE RIM.

reeding. Relief ornamentation in the form of a series of contiguous parallel, narrow convex reeds. It was used sometimes to form a border pattern, sometimes to encircle the neck or the body of a TANKARD, MUG or CUP. The opposite is FLUTING. Also called 'ribbing'.

Reform Cup. A silver-gilt TWO-HANDLED CUP of vase shape, having a bowl of bell *(campana)* shape, embossed and chased with oak branches and having handles in the form of twisted oak branches. It is decorated with engravings of the rose, thistle, and shamrock (symbolic of England, Scotland, and Ireland). The cover has an engraved scroll with the words 'Reform Bill', and a finial in the form of the Royal crown and sceptre. The cup was presented by the Metropolitan Districts of London, from a penny subscription, to John Russell (1792–1878), 1st Earl Russell and 6th Duke of Bedford, who introduced the Reform Bill of 1832. It was made by J & J. Angell (*see* ANGELL) in 1832–3. The cup, which is engraved with the coat of arms of the Dukes of Bedford, is at Woburn Abbey, Bedfordshire, the Bedford ancestral home.

Régence style. A French decorative style that was transitional between the style of Louis XIV, 1643–1715, and that of Louis XV, 1715–74, being named after the Regency of Philip II of Orléans, 1715–23, although in practice it prevailed from *c.* 1700 until *c.* 1720–30, when the ROCOCO STYLE was introduced. It featured classicism and symmetry, with trelliswork, scrolls, shells, foliage, and other naturalistic subjects, with examples of CUT CARD technique. The style, which was more restrained than the following rococo style, was introduced into England by Huguenot silversmiths fleeing France after the revocation in 1685 of the Edict of Nantes (*see* HUGUENOT SILVERWARE).

Regency silverware. Articles of silverware made in England during the period of the Regency (*see* REGENCY STYLE) when the demand for such ware was greatly increasing and the improvement in the methods of making ware of PLATED METAL was leading to mass-production. Many large and imposing pieces of SCULPTURAL SILVERWARE and presentation ware, such as the

Reade Salt. Silver-gilt pedestal salt, William Cobbold, Norwich, 1568–9. H. 38·5 cm. City of Norwich.

Reform Cup. Silver gilt, J. & J. Angell, London, 1832–3. H. 39·5 cm. Woburn Abbey (reproduced by permission of the Trustees of the Bedford Estate).

Regency Sugar Vases. Silver-gilt covered vase from the Wellington Ambassadorial Service, Benjamin Smith I and James Smith, London, 1810–11. H. 20·3 cm. Wellington Museum, Apsley House, London (photo, Victoria and Albert Museum).

WELLINGTON PLATE and AMBASSADORIAL SILVERWARE, were made, especially articles designed by THOMAS STOTHARD and JOHN FLAXMAN II which were executed by PAUL STORR for RUNDELL, BRIDGE & RUNDELL and by BENJAMIN SMITH I and DIGBY SCOTT. Much household ware was also produced, generally following the style of the highly ornamented services. *See* Judith Banister, 'Design in Regency Silver' in *Antiques,* September 1964, p. 299. *See* REGENCY SUGAR-VASES.

Regency style. The English decorative style which prevailed, strictly speaking, from 1811 to 1820, during the latter part of the reign of George III when the affairs of the country were in the hands of the Prince Regent, afterwards George IV, whose interest in antique silver plate and whose patronage of contemporary silversmiths greatly influenced the development of the style of domestic silverware. In common parlance, the term is extended both before and after those dates to embrace the period from the 1780s to the late 1830s (including the reigns of George IV and William IV). The Regency style in England is a version of the French EMPIRE STYLE with some modifications. Generally, the rendering of classical subjects lacks the lightness of the preceding NEO-CLASSICAL STYLE and ADAM STYLE, and is inclined to be pompous, opulent, and heavy. The use of Egyptian motifs is a feature of the period and marks the revival of interest in ancient Egypt which followed Napoleon's campaign there in 1798; and, under the influence of the designs for silver plate published in 1806 by Charles Heathcote Tatham, the style of Roman Imperial art superseded the Greco-Roman style. In silverware grandeur was sought by the use of a great quantity of metal. The work featured presentation pieces, centrepieces, and trophies having sculptural decoration, made from designs by outstanding sculptors unfamiliar with silver-making techniques, resulting in excessive detail and often tasteless ware.

Regency Sugar Vases. A group of silver-gilt covered SUGAR-VASES of which several examples have been made by different silversmiths. The bowl is of global shape with an incurved neck, rests on a short stem supported by a spreading base having four scroll feet, and has two horizontal uplifted loop handles. The bowl has overall decoration of EMBOSSING and CHASING in the form of a band of ACANTHUS leaves on the neck, below which, encircling the bowl, is a wider band with a foliated double-volute pattern and then a calyx of vertical GADROONING. The form is based in general on a Roman marble-covered funerary urn formerly in the collection of William, 1st Marquess of Lansdowne, and now in a private collection; the silver examples have a slightly modified silhouette, but the decoration is similar. The original set was made by BENJAMIN SMITH I and DIGBY SCOTT for RUNDELL, BRIDGE & RUNDELL, London, 1805. After 1805 Smith, with his brother James, made copies, including the group of eight made in 1809–10 for the Prince of Wales (later George IV) that is now in the Royal Collection (each cover having a hole to accommodate the handle of the accompanying LADLE), and four, 1808–9 (without ladles), that were formerly owned by the 6th Marquess of Ormonde (d. 1971), of which three are now in the Victoria and Albert Museum, London, and one is in the Bowes Museum, Barnard Castle, Co. Durham; another example is in the Wellington Museum, Apsley House, London, as part of the WELLINGTON AMBASSADORIAL SERVICE.

Regency tankard. A type of TANKARD made in England during the Regency, 1811–20, having very elaborate ornamentation in the form of low-relief figures around the body and on the handle.

regimental silverware. Articles of silverware owned by military regiments for display, usually in the officers' mess, often being STATUETTES (sometimes equestrian) of officers or men, or depictions of weapons (e.g., cannon or airplanes), but sometimes ware for utilitarian use. Such pieces have generally been donated to a regiment by a retiring officer or given as a testimonial to an officer, and are taken with the regiment wherever stationed (except on combat duty). They include CENTREPIECES, TWO-HANDLED CUPS, TUREENS, and ROSE-WATER BASINS. *See Souvenir of Loan Collection of Regimental Plate,* London, 1915; Julian Saunders, 'Regimental Silver' in *Antique Collector,* September 1985, p. 86. *See* GRENADIER GUARDSMAN STATUETTE; CAMP KETTLE; COLOUR-PIKE FINIAL; DRUM.

Registry Mark. *See* DESIGN REGISTRATION MARK.

Rehoboth Cup. A STANDING CUP having a tapering cylindrical bowl resting on a knopped stem and having a spreading foot. Although engraved with the inscription 'Capt. Willets' *[sic]* donation to/ye Ch. of Rehoboth, 1674', evidencing a money bequest by Capt. Thomas Willet (1610–74) which was used to purchase the cup, the cup may have been made earlier and pur-

Rehoboth Cup. Standing cup, John Hull and Robert Sanderson, Boston, Mass., *c.* 1674. H. 18·5 cm. Yale University Art Gallery (Mabel Brady Garvan Collection), New Haven, Conn.

chased in 1674 or possibly made later; hence its date, *c.* 1674, is indetermi-
nate. It may have been used for secular purposes and later as a COMMUNION
CUP. The cup bears the makers' marks of the partners JOHN HULL and ROBERT
SANDERSON.

reliquary. A small CASKET, pendant, pectoral cross or other receptacle for
keeping or displaying a religious relic. Some, especially those made to contain an important relic such as the bones of a saint, were often very highly
decorated and ornamented with gemstones, but less pretentious types were
made of silver or silver gilt to contain relics of less importance. Some examples were in the form of the part of the human body that was said to be
the enclosed relic, e.g., a head, foot, finger, etc. *See* RELIQUARY CROSS; SHRINE.

reliquary cross. A type of RELIQUARY in the form of a CROSS, usually a Latin
cross but sometimes a patriarchal or other form of cross. Some were decorated with gemstones, now generally missing. Some examples were made to
be worn, suspended from a chain; others are large, to be kept standing on an
altar in a church. *See* ALTAR CROSS.

Renaissance style. The decorative style that prevailed during the period of
the Renaissance, from the 15th century until the early 17th century, originat-
ing in northern Italy and spreading throughout Europe, but to a much lesser
extent in England. It reflected the cultural and artistic revolution that
flowed from the transition from medieval to modern times, with the contemporary study of antiquity and the consequent rebirth of classicism after the
period of the Gothic style. The style featured the use of sculptured human
and animal figures, ARABESQUES, and GROTESQUES, as well as SWAGS, SCROLLS,
ACANTHUS leaves, MASKS, and classical mouldings. In English silverware, its
use was influenced in practice by the presence of foreign artists, such as
Hans Holbein the Younger, and by the importation of engraved designs
made by silversmiths in Germany and the Low Countries, more often imitated than simply copied, and with a single piece frequently embodying
several motifs taken from engravings by different artists. It is found in England mainly in the GREAT SALTS and the STANDING CUPS (many incorporating
the use of crystal and the placing of steeples on covers), in the flat-chased
BELL SALTS, in the restrained decoration of floral patterns, and in the frequent use of GILDING. The period recognized the importance of the artist as
replacing the craftsman. The style persisted until the introduction of the
BAROQUE STYLE.

replated ware. Articles of SHEFFIELD PLATE which, due to the silver surface
having worn off (thus revealing the copper), have been given a later coating
of silver, occasionally done in the mid-Victorian period, by the process of
ELECTROPLATING. When aged, the result is difficult to detect, but it appears
somewhat whitish in contrast to the faintly bluish hue of the original fused
silver.

repoussé. A long-established and universally used technique (often called
EMBOSSING) of producing relief decoration on a metal plate by punching
(pouncing) and hammering thin metal from the back in order to raise the
design on the front. The metal plate is sometimes turned over so that some
embossing can be done on the front to enhance the desired relief design.
The work is done by means of hand PUNCHES and hammers, or sometimes by
mechanical means by the use of metal or stone dies (called 'embossing
dies'). The metal to be decorated is laid on a bed of a yielding material (e.g.,
wood, lead, a leather sand-filled bag, or usually pitch) after the design has
been scratched on with a tracer, and then the design is punched and hammered in (with periodic ANNEALING to prevent the metal from becoming
brittle). On some examples the relief design is refined by CHASING on the
front (sometimes called 'REPOUSSÉ CHASING') or ENGRAVING, or sometimes
embellished by additional metal soldered to the front. Sometimes, in imitation of true *repoussé* work, the decorative design is not beaten from the reverse but pieces of metal are cut out separately, embossed, and affixed to the
front. The process must be distinguished from STAMPING. *See* DOT REPOUSSÉ,
STAMPED REPOUSSÉ.

repoussé chasing. A style of decoration produced by EMBOSSING from the
back and refined by CHASING from the front of the piece, sharpening the details and giving highlights. *See* ST MARTIN'S SALVER.

reproduction. A reasonably close copy of a genuine old article of silverware,
but one made without any intent to deceive and so usually having, apart
from the different HALLMARKS, some other identifiable difference, as in the
case of the reproductions of the silver replica of the WARWICK VASE.

reliquary cross. Patriarchal cross set with
gemstones, Irish, *c.* 1633. Holy Cross
Abbey, Co. Tipperary.

Revere, Paul. Tea service by Paul
Revere II, Boston, Mass., after 1785.
Metropolitan Museum of Art (bequest
of A. T. Clearwater, 1933), New York.

Restoration silverware. Articles of CAROLINE SILVERWARE made in England
during the Restoration when the monarchy was re-established under
Charles II, 1660–85, following the death of Oliver Cromwell in 1658, and
continuing until the fall of James II in 1688. As a result of the destruction of
much silverware during the Protectorate from 1653 to 1658, there arose a demand for new ware for the Royal regalia for the monarchy, and also new
plate – especially large and important pieces – to refurbish palaces and houses
of the nobility; much ware of earlier date had to be altered to comply with
the new styles or to have Royal insignia added. The new ware of the period
featured extravagant ornament and enamelling. *See* Charles C. Oman, 'Restoration Silver at the Royal Academy' in *Burlington Magazine*, February 1961,
p. 44; —, 'After the Republican Interlude – Silver at the Restoration' in *The
Connoisseur*, February 1961, p. 9.

Revere, Paul (I) (1702–54). A silversmith of Boston, Massachusetts; he was
a French Huguenot who in 1730 anglicized his name, Apollos Rivoire. He
had emigrated from Guernsey in 1715 and settled in Massachusetts where,
after serving as an apprentice under JOHN CONEY, he established himself as a
silversmith *c.* 1729, using as his mark the initials 'PR'; however, some pieces
bear the stamped mark 'P Revere' used by him, *c.* 1740–50, and after his death
used in the 1760s by his son, PAUL REVERE II, creating doubt in some cases as
to who was the maker.

Revere, Paul (II) (1735–1818). A Boston silversmith, son of PAUL REVERE I
and famed as an American Revolutionary patriot, especially for his midnight
ride on 18/19 April 1775 to warn the colonists of the advance of British
troops. He learned the silversmith trade from his father, and became a very
prolific, and the best-known, American silversmith; but he had other
skills – being also an engraver, designer, printer, and owner of a copper
mill – and became very prosperous. His most famous pieces are the SONS OF
LIBERTY BOWL and the Templeman Tea Service, but he is reputed also for his
TANKARDS, PITCHERS, and other household plate. Before the Revolution his
work was in Georgian style, but thereafter he followed the latest English
styles. His mark was his surname in various rectangular punches; but some
pieces presumably made by him in the 1760s are stamped with a mark 'P Revere' in a style previously used by his father, *c.* 1740–50, so creating doubt as
to who was the maker.

Rhode Island silverware. Articles of silverware made in Rhode Island during the early Colonial period at Newport (on the island of Aquidneck) and
in King's County (on the mainland) by a number of silversmiths who produced various types of ware of high quality, numerous examples of which
survive today. Among such silversmiths were: at Newport, Samuel Vernon
(1683–1737), Daniel Russell (*c.* 1698–*c.* 1771), Arnold Collins (d. 1735), and
Benjamin Brenton (1695–1749); at Little Rest (now Kingston), Samuel
Casey (1724–70); and, at Providence, Joshua Doane (d. 1753), Nehemiah
Dodge (fl. 1794–1826), and Jabez Gorham (1792–1869), founder of the GOR-
HAM COMPANY. *See* Ralph E. Carpenter, Jr. *The Arts and Crafts of Newport,
Rhode Island* (1954); Margaret Ballard, 'Early Silver in Trinity Church, New-
port, Rhode Island' in *Antiques*, October 1981, p. 922.

Rhodian jug. Iznik pottery, with English
silver-gilt mounts, *c.* 1580. H. 26 cm.
Victoria and Albert Museum, London.

Rhodes, Benjamin (fl. 1694–1723). An English engraver who worked for
goldsmiths making plate for Sir William Hoare, a banker who became also a

retailer of silverware. He kept account books from 1 January 1694 to 6 January 1698, still extant, which list engravings that he made for such goldsmiths. Only a few pieces engraved by him have been identified, such as some items made in 1697 by John Bodington. *See* Charles C. Oman, 'Benjamin Rhodes' in *Apollo*, May 1957, p. 173.

Rhodian jug. A misnomer for a type of JUG of Turkish (Iznik) pottery with English 16th-century silver-gilt MOUNTS. It was so called in the 19th century as a result of a mistaken belief – based on the fact that fragments of such Iznik pottery had been excavated at Lindos, on the island of Rhodes – that the ware was made locally. An example is a jug made of such pottery with mounts (the base ring, the lip ring, and the hinged lid) of *c.* 1580; the jug is decorated with underglaze blue ENAMELLING with reserved white leaves having red dots. *See* POTTERY OBJECTS.

ribbing. The same as REEDING.

Rich, Obadiah (1809–88). A silversmith born in Charlestown, Massachusetts, and apprenticed to Moses Morse; he opened his own workshop in 1830 at 69 Washington St, Boston. From 1832 to 1835 he was a partner of Samuel L. Ward in Boston. In 1850 he moved to Woburn, Massachusetts, where he became a partner in the firm of Brackett & Crosby; despite becoming blind soon afterwards, he continued his association with the firm. In his twenty active years he made the WEBSTER VASE, two tripod INKSTANDS (one in the Fogg Art Museum, Cambridge, Massachusetts; one in the Yale University Art Gallery, New Haven, Connecticut), a pair of important pitchers and salvers, and other ware, all in ROCOCO STYLE. *See* Martha Gandy Fales, 'Obadiah Rich, Boston Silversmith' in *Antiques*, October 1968, p. 565. *See* BRITANNIA CUP.

Richmond, John, Cup. Silver gilt, unmarked, *c.* 1525–35. H. 31·5 cm. Armourers' and Brasiers' Company, London (photo courtesy, the Goldsmiths' Company, London).

Richardson. A family of three generations of American silversmiths working in Philadelphia, Pennsylvania. Francis Richardson I (1681–1730), born in New York City, made few known pieces (mark: 'FR'). His elder son, Francis Richardson II (1706–82), worked as a silversmith until 1742, but few of his pieces survive. The second son, Joseph Richardson, Sr (1711–84), who inherited and continued his father's business, was more prolific (mark: 'IR'), having made coffee-pots, tea-kettles, sauce-boats, etc., as well as ARMBANDS and GORGETS used as gifts to the Indians. Joseph's sons – Joseph, Jr (1752-1831), and Nathaniel (1754-1827) – were freed from apprenticeship in 1775 and worked together as a firm of silversmiths (mark: 'INR') at 50 Front St from 1785 to 1791. Nathaniel is best known for his 19-piece tea-and-coffee service, *c.* 1790, now at the Henry Francis du Pont Winterthur Museum, Wilmington, Delaware. The firm bought ware from John Masterson, London, which they resold or copied. Nathaniel retired in 1791 and became an ironmonger; his brother continued as a silversmith until 1808, making many important pieces (mark: 'JR'). *See* Martha Gandy Fales, 'Some forged Richardson silver' in *Antiques*, May 1961, p. 466; —, *Joseph Richardson and Family, Philadelphia Silversmiths* (1974); Robert S. Stuart, 'The Richardsons – A Family of Silversmiths' in *The Connoisseur*, November 1978, p. 202.

Richmond, John, Cup. A silver-gilt STANDING CUP, of so-called COLUMBINE CUP form, having the bowl and the cover embossed with encircling wide lobes terminating in a calyx-shaped ornament; the stem is also decorated with such lobes. The cover has a globular lobed finial. The cup, by an unidentified maker and without hallmark, has been attributed to *c.* 1525–35. It was given to the Armourers' and Brasiers' Company in 1557 by John Richmond (d. 1559), three times Master of the Company, to be used upon the choosing of each new Master and is still so used. The cup bears a posthumous inscription asking prayers for Richmond and his two wives. It has been said that such cups, made in England in the 16th century, had been one of the three patterns from which every German apprentice goldsmith could choose when executing his MASTERPIECE. *See* BOLEYN CUP.

Richmond Race Cup. Adapted from a design by Robert Adam and made by Daniel Smith and Robert Sharp, London, 1770. The Marquess of Zetland (photo courtesy, Bowes Museum, Barnard Castle, Co. Durham).

Richmond Race Cup. A HORSE-RACING CUP in the form of an elaborate TWO-HANDLED CUP of urn shape, adapted from a design by ROBERT ADAM and made in ADAM STYLE by Daniel Smith and Robert Sharp, London, 1770. It has two vertical handles in the form of winged female figures and, encircling the lip of the bowl, a low-relief frieze of racing horses and jockeys; on the front and reverse there are oval plaques (from a stock model) with racing horses and their jockeys depicted in low relief. The lower part of the bowl and the high waisted cover are decorated with ACANTHUS leaves, and there is a flower finial. The cup is owned by the Marquess of Zetland. A similar cup, from the same design, was made by the same silversmiths in 1764 for Hugh Percy, Earl of Northumberland, Lord Lieutenant of Ireland.

Robinson Bowl. Walnut bowl (replacing Chinese porcelain original) with silver-gilt mounts, London, 1596–7. Victoria and Albert Museum, London.

Rochester Cathedral Tazze. The two surviving examples, silver gilt: London, 1528, with cover, 1532, height 24·8 cm; and London, 1531 or 1532. British Museum, London.

riding equipment. Articles used by a horse rider, or horse-harness trappings, sometimes made entirely or partially of silver or silver-plated, such as SPURS, STIRRUPS, BOOT HOOKS, bridle bits, saddle buttons, crops, and buckles. Sometimes saddlery equipment, including some horse-brasses, was silvered by CLOSE PLATING to protect it from corrosion. Such ware was a speciality of Philip Antrobus Ltd, at its workshop in Birmingham, established in 1815, before the firm moved *c.* 1900 to London, where it is still a manufacturer and retailer of silverware. *See* Judith Banister, 'Silver and the Chase' in *The Connoisseur*, December 1977, p. 262.

rim. With respect to silverware, the narrow area bordering the edge of such objects as a TRAY, WAITER, SALVER, PLATE or BOWL; many different decorative styles are used. *See* BATH RIM; CHIPPENDALE RIM; REEDED RIM; REED-AND-TIE RIM; SCROLL-AND-SHELL RIM.

Roberts Plate. A COMPOSITE METAL consisting of NICKEL SILVER fused between layers of copper and STERLING SILVER. The process was patented in July 1830 by Samuel Roberts, of Sheffield, and antedated the introduction of BRITISH PLATE, *c.* 1835, and of MERRY PLATE in 1836. The process involved either first fusing the copper with nickel silver and then the nickel silver with sterling silver, or simultaneously fusing all three constituents; thus, if the silver layer became worn, the under-layer of copper would not become visible, there being an intermediate layer of white metal. Other makers, licensed by Roberts, made much use of the process, but due to the brittle nature of nickel silver, few examples have survived. It was superseded by Merry Plate.

Robinson Bowl. A carved walnut bowl with silver-gilt MOUNTS, London, 1596–7. The bowl is said to be a replacement (provided before 1879, by an antique dealer, Durlacher) for a Chinese Ming porcelain bowl of the reign of Wan Li, 1578–1619, that had been broken. It is decagonal–an unusual shape for bowls of Chinese export porcelain of that period. The bowl has mounts bearing an unidentified maker's mark 'IH' (the same as that on the mounts of the TRENCHARD BOWL); these consist of a band encircling the rim and another around the base connected by four vertical decorative straps (attached at top and bottom by hinges similar to those securing the straps on some TIGERWARE JUGS), each in the form of a female figure. The piece was acquired in 1879 from the J. C. Robinson Collection by the Victoria and Albert Museum, London. *See* Philippa Glanville, 'Chinese Porcelain and English Goldsmiths *c.* 1560 to *c.* 1660' in *V&A Album 3* (1984), p. 253 and fig. 10. *See* PORCELAIN OBJECTS.

rocaille caddy spoon. A type of CADDY SPOON having its bowl in the form of *rocaille* (rockwork), including a sea-shell (SCALLOP, mussel or limpet).

Rochester Cathedral Tazze. Two silver-gilt TAZZE, one 1528 (with cover, 1532, having an openwork finial) and one 1531 or 1532, being the sole survivors of a set of twelve or more pieces, all of the same design and quality but the work of different makers and made at different dates. Each tazza has a wide stem, a spreading foot, and a shallow bowl with its interior having a DIAPER PATTERN of circular depressions; there is a Latin inscription around the interior of the rim. The form of the pieces is repeated in a drawing by Hans Holbein the Younger (1497–1543), now in the Kunstmuseum, Basel, said to date from the time of his return to England in 1532. The tazze were made in London, probably for secular use, and were presented to Rochester Cathedral by an unknown benefactor after the Reformation, perhaps in the reign of Elizabeth I, 1558–1603, to replace medieval CHALICES that had been melted down. They were purchased in 1971 from the Cathedral chapter by the British Museum, London. *See* ARLINGTON TAZZA.

Rochester Mazer. A MAZER with silver mounts, London, 1532; the wooden bowl has, around its rim, a silver band with a scalloped lower edge, and also has an enamelled silver PRINT, with a similar scalloped edge, depicting St Benedict (the name inscribed as 'ST BENIT') on a ground of flowers (the black, green, and amber-coloured enamelling being now almost worn away). Encircling the band is an inscription in Tudor capital letters, 'CIPHUS/REFECTORII/ROFENSIS/PER/FRATREM/ROBERTUM/PECHAM'. The piece was originally in the Benedictine Priory at Rochester, Kent, and is now in the British Museum, London.

rococo silverware. Articles of silverware made in England in the ROCOCO STYLE in the period *c.* 1730–60 and for a few years thereafter, in a wide range of domestic articles, including SOUP-TUREENS, CENTREPIECES, EPERGNES, TWO-HANDLED CUPS, EWERS, PUNCH-BOWLS, WINE COOLERS, SALVERS, SAUCE-BOATS,

Rochester Mazer. Wooden bowl with silver mounts, London, 1532. D. 18·5 cm. British Museum, London.

BASKETS, TEA-KETTLES, CANDLESTICKS, and INKSTANDS. The leading exponents of the style in England were the renowned PAUL DE LAMERIE, along with PAUL CRESPIN, THOMAS HEMING, CHARLES KANDLER, FREDERICK KANDLER, NICHOLAS SPRIMONT, EDWARD WAKELIN, and GEORGE WICKES. The ware was ornately decorated, featuring heavy cast ornamentation and undulations of outline, and later much REPOUSSÉ work and pierced decoration. *See* Arthur G. Grimwade, *Rococo Silver, 1727 to 1765* (1974); *Rococo* (Victoria and Albert Museum exhibition catalogue, 1984), pp. 99–125.

rococo style. A style of decoration that in France followed the BAROQUE STYLE, and particularly the RÉGENCE STYLE (where it was often called 'rocaille'), the principal features of which are asymmetry of ornament and flowing lines, with a repertoire consisting to a considerable extent of rockwork, shells, flowers, foliage, scrollwork, and C- and S-curves. It was developed in France under Louis XV, 1715–74, and was imitated in Italy, Germany, Austria, and to a lesser extent in England, *c.* 1730–60. In England it followed the QUEEN ANNE STYLE, and was succeeded by the NEO-CLASSICAL STYLE and the REGENCY STYLE. It became popular in the American Colonies *c.* 1750. In the first quarter of the 19th century, there was in England a period of 'revived rococo style', but it lost popularity in mid-century as the asymmetrical scrollwork was too often badly reproduced by unskilled artisans. *See* ROCOCO SILVERWARE.

Rogers, Daniel (1735–1816). A silversmith of Ipswich, Massachusetts, apprenticed in 1749 and freed in 1756, who used the mark 'D. Rogers' or 'DR'. Owing to the fact that there was another silversmith named Daniel Rogers – of Newport, Rhode Island – who lived from 1753 to 1792, many of the known marked pieces, especially spoons, had been attributed to him, but subsequent research has revealed that many such examples – some being at the Henry Francis du Pont Winterthur Museum, near Wilmington, Delaware – have a family association with Ipswich, and hence such pieces are now considered to be by the Ipswich Rogers. A third Daniel Rogers is recorded from New York (fl. 1836), but no mark has been identified either with him or with the Newport Rogers. *See* Martha Gandy Fales, 'Daniel Rogers, Silversmiths' in *Antiques*, April 1967, p. 487.

Rogers Salt. A silver-gilt GREAT SALT of the PEDESTAL SALT type, having a spool-shaped body formed by a rock-crystal cylinder held in position by silver-gilt encircling bands around the foot and the top of the cylinder, the bands being decorated with ACANTHUS leaves on a matt ground. The cylinder encloses a parchment roll that displays the coloured arms of the Goldsmiths' Company, an escutcheon inscribed 'Ric Rogers Comptroller of the Mint', and scrollwork with figures of unicorns, toads, and birds. In one side of the crystal cylinder is sunk a circular engraved silver-gilt disc. The base rests on three CLAW-AND-BALL FEET, and the high-domed cover rises to three curving brackets which enclose a faceted crystal ball that is surmounted by a three-sided steeple, as on later STEEPLE SALTS. The receptacle for the salt is larger than usual and is sunk in a band above the upper rim on the cylinder. The piece bears the London mark of 1601, and was donated in 1652 to the Goldsmiths' Company by Richard Rogers, a member of the Court of the Company, *c.* 1600–35, and Comptroller of the Mint; on the rim is an engraved inscription recording the gift.

rolling. The process of flattening an unheated INGOT of silver, to produce sheets of desired thickness, by passing it in a rolling mill repeatedly through

Rogers Salt. Silver gilt and rock-crystal cylinder with enclosed parchment, London, 1601. H. 56 cm. Goldsmiths' Company, London.

rollers of decreasing gap. The process, developed in the late 17th century, superseded the earlier method of flattening silver by HAMMERING, and lowered the cost of silverware both by reducing the man-hours required and by producing sheets of lower GAUGE.

Rollos, Philip (I) (fl. 1697-1710). A Huguenot silversmith of unknown birthplace who emigrated to London, was naturalized in 1690/1, freed by redemption in 1697, and became a Liveryman in 1698. He registered his mark in 1697. He made imposing and elaborate pieces, including several WINE COOLERS (one, 1699, now in the Hermitage, Leningrad; one, 1701, at Althorp; and one, 1710, at Burghley House), as well as TWO-HANDLED CUPS, ICE-PAILS, SCONCES, and FIRE-DOGS. He was Subordinate Goldsmith to William III and to Queen Anne, being succeeded by his son, PHILIP ROLLOS II. *See* BURGHLEY WINE COOLER.

Rollos, Philip (II) (fl. 1705-21). A London silversmith, son of PHILIP ROLLOS I; he was apprenticed in 1692, turned over to his father, freed in 1705, and became a Liveryman in 1712. He registered his first mark in 1705, with address Heath Cock Court, Strand, and a second mark in 1720. He succeeded his father as Subordinate Goldsmith to Queen Anne. He made a number of important pieces now in private collections, some of greater richness than those of his father.

Roman leaf caddy spoon. A type of CADDY SPOON having its bowl in the shape of an irregular ellipse suggestive of a leaf shape, but more like an ancient Roman oil lamp, and having its handle curling upward in a helical shape.

Romer, Emick (1724-99). A silversmith, born at Halden, Norway, who in 1749 was living at Bragernaes and in 1751 at nearby Stromso; he was apprenticed in Norway in 1749. He migrated to London, and worked there from the late 1750s to the early 1790s (from *c.* 1770 to *c.* 1773 at 123 High Holborn). He returned to Norway by May 1795. He presumably registered a mark in London by 1759, but there is no surviving record of his having done so. He specialized in PIERCED WORK and CHASING as decoration for BASKETS, SWEETMEAT-DISHES, SALTS, and EPERGNES, and made many COLUMN CANDLESTICKS. His mark appears on pieces in the CAROLINE MATHILDA TOILET SERVICE and in the WILLIAMS-WYNN TOILET SERVICE, as well as on the cover of the CHATSWORTH CUP, all made by THOMAS HEMING (with whom he collaborated and some of whose moulds he used). A BRAZIER, London 1763-4, now at Colonial Williamsburg, Virginia, has been attributed to him. *See* Judith Banister, 'Emick Romer: A Norwegian Silversmith in 18th-century London' in *Antique Dealer & Collectors Guide*, October 1966, p. 61.

Romsey Candlesticks. A pair of CANDLESTICKS of unique form, each having three scroll legs that support an octagonal faceted stem; on each leg there is an applied shield engraved, respectively, with the arms of the See of Bristol, the arms of John Romsey (d. 1721) and the depiction of two ships, these engravings commemorating the gift of the candlesticks to Bristol Cathedral by Romsey, the owner of two ships, as a thank-offering following a successful privateering expedition in 1711 to the West Indies. The pair was made by GABRIEL SLEATH, 1712.

rope handle. A type of handle in the form of a continuous length of rope, found on some BASKETS and other receptacles. Sometimes called a 'cable handle'.

rope moulding. A type of MOULDING in the form of a continuous twisting band of rope-like appearance, found around the rim of various receptacles and executed by CASTING, EMBOSSING or applying twisted wire. Sometimes called 'cable moulding', especially when thick.

rosary cross. A type of CROSS, small but varying in size, which is worn at the end of a rosary, as a gaud. Silver examples are probably of Irish or Canadian origin. *See* Edward A. McGuire, 'Old Irish Rosaries and Rosary Crosses' in *The Connoisseur*, September 1947, p. 85.

rose-bowl. A type of BOWL, used as a receptacle for cut flowers, having a pierced cover or being provided with a removable wire mesh through which to insert the flower stems. Such pieces are today sometimes called a 'flower-bowl'; for a modern example, *see* FESTIVAL OF BRITAIN ROSE-BOWL. Sometimes a bowl which was not originally intended to hold cut flowers has subsequently been provided with a mesh cover and offered for sale described as a rose-bowl.

Romer, Emick. Brazier with three hinged flaps as supports for a receptacle. London, 1763-4. D (of bowl) 17·8 cm. Colonial Williamsburg, Va.

Romsey Candlesticks. One of the pair, Gabriel Sleath, London, 1712. H. 53·2 cm. Bristol Cathedral (photo courtesy, Historic Churches Preservation Trust, London).

Rose Hallmark. The ASSAY OFFICE HALLMARK used from 1 January 1975 at the SHEFFIELD ASSAY OFFICE.

rose-water basin. A large ABLUTION BASIN with a WELL and usually a wide ornately decorated rim, used as a receptacle for rose-water poured from a ROSE-WATER EWER for diners to rinse their fingers at the table. The rim is often decorated with engraved ARABESQUES or with FLAT CHASING of STRAP-WORK, and there is a central BOSS upon which to rest the ewer; late-16th-century examples are ornately decorated with EMBOSSING, often depicting mythological motifs, but 17th-century pieces are simpler, often with only bands of REEDING. Such pieces are usually decorated EN SUITE with the ewer. Sets are known from the 16th century and were used until the early Victorian period, but their use generally ceased in Western countries after the introduction of the FINGER BOWL, although such sets are still used in the Middle East and North Africa. Sometimes a deep BOWL, occasionally a MONTEITH, is loosely referred to as a 'rose-water bowl', *See* ALMS DISH.

rose-water ewer. A EWER used in the 16th to early-19th centuries to pour rose-water into a ROSE-WATER BASIN to be used at a dinner table. Such a ewer was usually decorated EN SUITE with the basin.

rosette. A decorative motif of circular shape composed of a series of adjacent and symmetrically placed ornaments in the form of naturalistic or stylized leaves, having a varying number of divisions. Its use dates from antiquity, and it is found on silverware in the NEO-CLASSICAL STYLE or the ADAM STYLE.

Royal Academy Cigar Lighter. A cigar lighter for table use, made in the form of a bear taking honey from a skep beehive. Designed by Sir Joseph Edgar Boehm (1834–90), the English sculptor, and executed by Alexander Crichton, it was donated by the former to the Royal Academy of Arts,'London, upon his being elected a member, in accordance with the tradition that each new member should donate a 'handsome present'.

Royal Collection. As to silverware, *see* CROWN SILVERWARE.

Royal Dish Warmers. A pair of silver-gilt DISH WARMERS, each composed of: (1) a large oval stand supported by four feet in the form of eagles with spread wings, having two horizontal loop handles, and having attached to its bottom two removable spirit lamps; (2) a large oval shallow liner; (3) an oval high-domed cover with a vertical loop handle in the form of intertwined snakes. The lower rim of the cover is decorated with an encircling VITRUVIAN SCROLL and the shoulder with a band of ACANTHUS leaves. The cover of one was made by DIGBY SCOTT and BENJAMIN SMITH I, 1806, and of the other by Smith, 1807; the stands and liners were made by ROBERT GARRARD II, 1843; and the spirit lamps were made by H. Frazer, 1903. The pair are in the Jewel House at the Tower of London.

Royal Academy Cigar Lighter. Flame in the lantern (left), wick on the removable pole, designed by T. E. Boehm and made by Alexander Crichton, London, 1888. H. 15·2 cm. Royal Academy of Arts, London.

Royal Dish Warmers. One of the pair, silver gilt, the cover made by Benjamin Smith I, 1807, the stand and liner by Robert Garrard II, 1843. L. 67 cm. Tower of London (Crown copyright, HMSO).

Royal Font. Silver gilt, maker's mark 'RF', 1660–1. H. 80 cm. Tower of London (Crown copyright, HMSO).

Royal Font. A silver-gilt CHRISTENING BOWL, 1660–1, having a hemispherical bowl supported by a narrow cylindrical stem with a thin knop midway, resting on a cushion-shaped base; the low-domed STEPPED cover is surmounted by a figure group said to depict the Apostle Philip baptizing the eunuch of Queen Candace of Ethiopia (Acts, viii, 38). The bowl and cover have embossing of foliage and *putti*; both bear the unidentified maker's mark 'RF' and were regilded in 1702, 1727, and 1761. The piece was first used at the christening of a future Sovereign when George III's eldest son (later George IV) was baptized in 1762. The font is accompanied by a silver-gilt dish, which formerly served as its base (*see* CHARLES II ALTAR DISHES). Both pieces are kept in the Jewel House at the Tower of London. *See* LILY FONT.

Royal Hunt Cup. One of a series of silver-gilt HORSE-RACING CUPS, a different one having been awarded annually at Ascot since 1843 to the winner of a one-mile handicap race; each is decorated with the Royal arms.

Royal Oak Cup. a silver-gilt STANDING CUP presented by Charles II to the Barber-Surgeons' Company in 1676 to commemorate his hiding in the Boscobel Oak when he was fleeing the country after his defeat by Cromwell at Worcester in 1651. The silver-gilt bowl and cover are of SHEATHED WARE with EMBOSSING to represent oak leaves. The bowl rests on a stem in the form of a tree-trunk, at the foot of which are figures of lizards and snails. An embossed CARTOUCHE with a commemorative inscription is flanked by oak leaves, and suspended from the branches are four bells in the form of acorns. The cover has a finial in the form of a Royal crown. The cup is marked London, 1676.

Royal Wedding Collection. A group of pieces, made of STERLING SILVER, some with PARCEL GILDING, to commemorate the wedding of H.R.H. The Prince of Wales and Lady Diana Spencer on 29 July 1981, including a CENTREPIECE bowl (having four corner feet in the form of griffins and an encircling floral band), a JUG, a pair of CANDLESTICKS, two BONBONNIÈRES, six GOBLETS, and a CANTEEN with PLACE SETTINGS of FLATWARE and CUTLERY. The applied gilt ornaments include the Prince-of-Wales's feathers motif and the initials 'C' and 'D' linked by a lovers' knot. The group was designed and made by GARRARD & CO. LTD, with each piece bearing the engraved number of the set and on some an appropriate engraved inscription. *See* CROWN SILVERWARE.

Royal Wine Cooler. An oval silver-gilt WINE COOLER, designed probably by JOHN FLAXMAN II and made by JOHN BRIDGE for RUNDELL, BRIDGE & RUNDELL, 1829–30, on the order of George IV. It is a massive receptacle in ROCOCO STYLE, having the lower part of the bowl formed as giant SCALLOP shells, and the upper part as sea caves with figures of children and animals in a grape harvest. The bowl (which is provided with a plain oval liner) rests on a wide stem decorated with seaweed, supported by an elaborate base of coral and shells embedded in rock and having four scroll feet in the form of volutes that conceal castors. On each side of the bowl are two figures representing–based on their attributes–Dionysus (Bacchus) and Ariadne (the pair

Royal Wine Cooler. Silver gilt, John Bridge for Rundell, Bridge & Rundell, London, 1829–30. L. 1·38 cm. Tower of London (Crown copyright, HMSO).

sometimes said to be Venus and Adonis), and at the ends of the bowl are handles in a form derived from the Royal supporters, one the head of the crowned lion and the other the head of the unicorn. The piece is 1·38 m. long and weighs almost 8,000 oz.; it is said to hold 144 bottles. The accompanying LADLE, 1841, has a long straight handle made of ivory with silver-gilt bands and a bowl in the form of a large silver-gilt snail shell.

The piece was used: (1) perhaps first by William IV at his 65th birthday dinner, 31 August 1830, and at his coronation banquet on 8 September 1831; (2) on the occasion of the christening of the future Edward VII on 26 January 1842 at St George's Chapel, Windsor Castle, being used then with its accompanying ladle as a PUNCH-BOWL; and (3) in 1844 for the christening reception of Alfred, second son of Queen Victoria. *See* Norman M. Penzer, 'The Royal Wine-Cooler of John Bridge' in *Apollo*, November 1955, p. 131.

rum-kettle. A type of KETTLE used for serving heated rum drinks. It is usually smaller than a TEA-KETTLE or a PUNCH-POT, and often has a beak-shaped pouring LIP instead of a spout.

runcible spoon. A type of FORK having three wide tines or prongs, one of which has a sharp edge and is curved like a spoon; said to have been used for pickles. (The word 'runcible' was coined as a nonsense term by Edward Lear in 'The Owl and the Pussy Cat' published in 1871).

Rundell, Philip (1743-1827). A leading London silversmith, who was born in Bath, Somerset, and apprenticed in 1760 to William Rogers, a jeweller of Bath. He went to London in 1767 as a shopman in the silversmith firm of WILLIAM THEED I and WILLIAM PICKETT, formed in 1758, at 32 Ludgate Hill, and upon the death of Theed in 1772 he became a partner of Pickett, and sole owner of the firm, Pickett & Rundell, by purchase in 1785. In 1788 he took as partner JOHN BRIDGE, who had joined the firm in 1777, and by 1805 took as partner his nephew, Edmund Waller Rundell, the firm then becoming RUNDELL, BRIDGE & RUNDELL. When PAUL STORR ended his working arrangement with the firm in 1819, Rundell entered his first mark, with address in Dean St, Soho, and a second and a third mark in 1819 and 1822. He retired in 1823. He was an eccentric but astute and successful businessman, and left a fortune.

Rundell, Bridge & Rundell. The most prestigious London firm of silversmiths of the first half of the 19th century. Its origin can be traced to a goldsmith, Henry Hurt, who had a retail jewelry business, *c.* 1745, at 32 Ludgate Hill, London, and who succeeded to a like business of Thomas Chesson, formerly of Cheapside. That business was acquired in 1758 by Hurt's shopman, WILLIAM THEED I, who became joint owner with WILLIAM PICKETT, another shopman. Theed retired in 1768 and died in 1772, and Pickett became sole owner. The firm had been joined in 1767/9 by PHILIP RUNDELL, who became a partner in 1777 – the name of the firm being changed to Pickett & Rundell – and then sole owner by purchase from Pickett in 1785. JOHN BRIDGE, who had joined the firm in 1777, became a partner of Rundell in 1785, the firm, still at 32 Ludgate Hill, being called from 1788 until 1805 Rundell & Bridge. It achieved great success and was recognized as the leading London silversmith; in 1804 it was appointed Goldsmith in Ordinary to George III. By 1805 Rundell's nephew, Edmund Waller Rundell, became a partner, the firm then becoming Rundell, Bridge & Rundell (with Bridge in charge of the silverwork). Its reputation grew, thanks to the patronage of the Prince of Wales (later as Prince Regent) and of his brother, the Duke of York, and its success continued throughout the Regency, 1811-20. Its appointment as Goldsmith in Ordinary was renewed in the succeeding reign of George IV, 1820-30 (after which GARRARD & CO. was appointed CROWN GOLDSMITH). From 1803 the firm employed the sculptor WILLIAM THEED II as designer; he became a partner and, in 1808, head of the design department and also chief modeller until his death in 1817. He was succeeded by JOHN FLAXMAN II (who had done design work for the firm since 1805) until 1826. The firm engaged PAUL STORR, *c.* 1807, to manage its workshop at 53 Dean St, Soho, London. It established another workshop at Lime Kiln Lane, Greenwich. From 1802 it engaged DIGBY SCOTT and BENJAMIN SMITH I as managers to provide important silverware; they entered a joint mark in 1802 and, after the firm was dissolved in 1807, Smith continued to produce prestigious pieces until 1813-14. In 1807 Paul Storr formed a partnership (known as Storr & Co.) with Philip Rundell, John Bridge, Edmund Rundell, and William Theed II; from its workshop at 53 Dean St, Soho, it produced – under the Storr mark – much important ware for the firm until Storr withdrew in 1819. Pieces made during this period were engraved with the name of the firm and the Latin phrase *Aurifices Regis et Principis Walliae Londini Fecerunt*. The firm then had an international clientele and reputation, and in the early

Rundell, Bridge & Rundell. Wash bowl (ordered by Queen Adelaide as a birthday gift for William IV), John Bridge, London, 1833. D. 37 cm. Courtesy, Sotheby's, London.

decades of the 19th century it employed over 1,000 people, including prominent designers such as EDWARD HODGES BAILY, EDMUND COTTERILL, Charles Cotton (1756–1819), Sir Francis Chantrey (1781–1814), and Charles Heathcote Tatham (1772–1842). It also obtained designs from leading artists and sculptors such as John Flaxman II, A. W. N. PUGIN, THOMAS STOTHARD, and BENEDETTO PISTRUCCI, as well as employing silversmiths of repute, including WILLIAM PITTS I and WILLIAM PITTS II.

Philip Rundell, having entered three marks after 1819 without becoming active as a silversmith, retired in 1823; John Bridge then entered five marks, likewise not becoming an active silversmith, and became head of the firm. Edmund Rundell retired in 1830, and the firm became Rundell, Bridge & Co. After the death of Bridge in 1834, the firm closed the Dean St workshop, but continued at Ludgate Hill, where it accepted commissions but farmed out the work to other silversmiths, including William Bateman I (*see* BATEMAN), EDWARD BARNARD & SONS, and John Tapley, Many of the products were adaptations of pieces previously made by or for the firm, using parts of earlier designs and combining the work of different designers to meet contemporary demands and taste, The firm's work continued to influence that of other silversmiths throughout the Victorian era. Until its dissolution in 1842, the company also held the appointment as Crown Jewellers, being succeeded as such in 1843 by Garrard & Co.

See Shirley Bury, 'The Lengthening Shadow of Rundell's' in *The Connoisseur*, February 1966, p.79, March 1966, p.152, and April 1966, p.218; Charles C. Oman, 'A Problem of Artistic Responsibility' in *Apollo*, March 1966, p.174; John F. Hayward, 'Rundell, Bridge & Rundell' in *Antiques*, June 1971, p.860, and July 1971, p.110.

Ruslen Salver. One of several DOUCEURS, in the form of a four-handled oval SALVER, of which five very similar surviving examples were made by John Ruslen, London, between 1697 and 1710. *See* LORD MAYOR'S SALVER.

Rutland Ewer. A EWER of which the tall ovoid-shaped body is made of three cylindrical pieces of agate, one above the other, joined by horizontal silver-gilt bands and also by vertical brackets attached to the bands. The neck is made of a fourth agate cylinder, with silver-gilt mounts. The handle, extending upward from the rim and curving down to the shoulder, is decorated with a reclining figure of a merman with a twisting bifurcated tail, and on his back there is a large snail with, on its back, another, smaller snail. On the vertical brackets there are collets for gemstones (now missing). The ewer, with a London mark for 1579, is accompanied by a basin with an agate BOSS, decorated with embossing of dolphins, turtles, lobsters, and crayfish. The piece, which is owned by the Duke of Rutland, is an example of the MANNERIST STYLE.

S

S-scroll. A decorative pattern basically in the form of the capital letter S, but variously proportioned. It is the shape of some HANDLES, especially those on some examples of a TWO-HANDLED CUP.

Sabbath lamp. A type of CHANDELIER found in certain Jewish homes as a source of light on the Sabbath eve, having seven oil lamps. Made in various forms, it often consists of six parts, one suspended above the other, such as (1) a suspension hook, (2) pierced crown, (3) a ball-, oval- or baluster-shaped ornament, (4) a star-shaped seven-well oil lamp (the Sephardic type from lands where oil was plentiful having a deep bowl, the Ashkenazic type having an economical shallow bowl), (5) a circular drip pan, and (6) a pendant of acorn, cone or other ornamental shape. An English example, made by Hester Bateman (*see* BATEMAN), 1781, was sold at Christie's, London, in December 1963. *See* MENORAH; HANUK(K)A(H) LAMP; SANCTUARY LAMP; JEWISH RITUAL SILVERWARE.

sacring bell. A small BELL, in the form of a HAND BELL, used during the celebration of Mass in the Catholic Church. It is rung at the Elevation, when the priest raises the consecrated Eucharistic elements – the Host and the chalice;

it may also be rung at the last part of the Preface – the Sanctus – and is hence sometimes loosely called a 'Sanctus bell'. The bell is indistinguishable in form from the usual hand bell accompanying an INKSTAND. *See* CHURCH PLATE.

Saffron Walden Mazer. A MAZER made in 1507 and kept in the almshouses in Saffron Walden, Essex, until 1929. Samuel Pepys recorded that he drank from it on a visit there in 1659, noting that on the bottom of the interior was a PRINT depicting the Virgin and Child. It was sold at Christie's, London, in 1929 and again in 1971.

St Agnes Tazza. A parcel-gilt TAZZA having a shallow bowl supported by a spool-shaped stem resting on a domed foot. It is decorated with stylized scrollwork, foliage, and bunches of fruit, and has a central PRINT depicting a female bust. It was made in London, 1579-80, and was given in 1711 to the parish church of the village of St Agnes, Cornwall, by John Worth, Sheriff of Cornwall. The church, needing funds for repairs, sold the tazza at Christie's, London, in 1972, and the dealer who acquired it resold it to an American buyer; an export licence was refused, and in March 1973 the piece was bought by the Cecil Higgins Art Gallery, Bedford.

St Agnes Tazza. Parcel gilt, London, 1579-80. H. 12 cm. Cecil Higgins Art Gallery, Bedford.

St Dunstan Cup. A STANDING CUP having on the finial a figure of St Dunstan (patron saint of goldsmiths), Archbishop of Canterbury from 959 until his death in 988. The cup, owned by the Goldsmiths' Company, London, was used by members of the Company on St Dunstan's eve and day, until broken up on 14 November 1547 pursuant to orders of Edward VI.

St George Shield. A SHIELD having a central medallion depicting in low relief a figure of St George on horseback slaying the Dragon, surrounded by a circle of GADROONING and an outer border of a low-relief frieze, adapted from a frieze of the Parthenon, depicting warrior horsemen. It was made by PHILIP RUNDELL in 1822-3 for RUNDELL, BRIDGE & RUNDELL from a design by BENEDETTO PISTRUCCI.

St Louis silverware. Articles of silverware made in St Louis, Missouri. The earliest examples, early 19th century, were trinkets of INDIAN-TRADE SILVERWARE and also spoons. Among the many active silversmiths was Charles Billon (fl.1817-22). The leading firm was founded in 1829 by Louis Jaccard, an émigré from Switzerland who settled in St Louis and made some silver articles but mainly purchased from Eastern manufacturers whose ware he marked by BACK-STAMPING; he produced ware for several exhibitions from the 1880s. The firm he founded became E.Jaccard & Co., and is now Jaccard Jewelry Co. In the 1880s it had absorbed the business of Freeman A.Durgin, established in 1855. *See* Deborah J. Binder, 'St Louis Silver' in *Antiques*, December 1981, p.402.

St George Shield. Philip Rundell for Rundell, Bridge & Rundell, London, 1822-3. D. 71 cm. Victoria and Albert Museum, London.

St Martin's Salver. A circular SALVER, 1662, with a broad border of REPOUSSÉ CHASING depicting four *putti* among large flowers and foliage, with the centre engraved with a coat of arms and an inscription recording the gift in 1686 by Mrs Alice Denham to the parish church of St Martin, New Sarum, Salisbury.

St Michael's Bowl. A parcel-gilt unmarked circular BOWL, *c.*1480-1530, having curved sides with a wide border decorated with REPOUSSÉ spiral lobes surrounding a central dome decorated with wavy flames on a matt ground and having a PRINT engraved with a group of carnations, formerly enamelled. The moulded foot is stamped with an encircling band of flowers and foliage. On the rim is a pricked inscription 'St Michaell Bristoll 1684', referring to the church of St Michael the Archangel, Bristol, which owns the piece (it having been listed in an inventory of 1575). The bowl has been on loan to the City Museum and Art Gallery, Bristol, and kept at the church of St Nicholas, Bristol.

saint spoon. A type of SPOON having a straight stem terminating in a finial in the form of a figure in-the-round of a saint, the figure being identifiable – as in the case of APOSTLE SPOONS – by the attribute associated with the saint depicted. Such spoons made in England, differing from most Continental examples, usually depict the saint with a nimbus; the nimbus is sometimes placed vertically at the back of the head, sometimes, perhaps on later examples, horizontally on the head. Some London Livery Companies own such spoons depicting their patron saint.

salad fork. A type of dining FORK for eating salad, of medium length and having three or four flat tines.

St Martin's Salver. Border decoration of *putti* among flowers and foliage, English, 1662. D. 45·8 cm. Church of St Martin, Salisbury (photo courtesy, Historic Churches Preservation Trust, London).

salad-plate. A type of PLATE for salad, for use by an individual diner at a dinner table. In the mid-18th century certain dishes so designated were in the form of circular, fluted, shallow bowls having a scalloped rim and three scroll feet; but other forms may well have been used for salad. A salad-plate of fan shape was made by THOMAS HEMING in 1780. In recent years a crescent-shaped salad-plate has become customary, designed to be placed on the table fitted alongside the dinner plate.

salad servers. A PAIR of implements, to be used together for serving a salad, consisting of (1) a SPOON with a somewhat flattened bowl, and (2) a FORK having a shape like that of the spoon except that the bowl is cut to produce three flat prongs.

salesman's sample. A tiny silver article, in the same form as a full-size functional piece, that was made for and carried by a travelling salesman to avoid bulky luggage with its temptation to highwaymen. Such pieces, usually bearing only the MAKER'S MARK, were a small portion of the many pieces of MINIATURE SILVERWARE. *See* TOY.

Salisbury Tazza. A silver COVERED TAZZA having a baluster-shaped stem resting on a circular base; the low-domed cover, which conforms to the shape of the bowl, has a finial topped by a bunch of tied arrows surmounted by a helmet, which appears in the coat of arms of Robert Cecil (1563–1612), 1st Earl of Salisbury. The bottom of the bowl is decorated in intaglio (appearing on the interior in relief) with a concentric pattern of flower and fruit motifs of sizes diminishing toward the centre, said to have been inspired by designs on Elizabethan embroidery. The piece is owned by the Church of Our Lady, Trondheim, Norway, having been presented to it in 1762 by Thomas Albrigtsen Angell (1692–1767), a local philanthropist, who had probably inherited it from his maternal grandparents who owned it before 1662; its presence in Trondheim then is confirmed by a *tazza* there, dated 1662, which was copied from it. It bears the unidentified maker's mark 'LM', and the London mark for 1603–4; its history between 1603 and 1662 is speculative, but it has been surmised that it came to Norway from England through some Royal or diplomatic connection. *See* Thorvald Krohn-Hansen, 'The Salisbury Tazza' in *The Connoisseur*, April 1965, p. 232.

salt. A receptacle for holding table salt. Such pieces were made in a great variety of shapes, styles, and sizes, from the large elaborate STANDING SALTS and especially the ceremonial GREAT SALTS to the more frequently seen SALT-CELLARS, TRENCHER SALTS, and SALT CASTERS (salt shakers). Salts made of silver or of SHEFFIELD PLATE often have the interior protected by TINNING or GILDING, but those of better quality are provided with a glass LINER to protect the metal from being corroded through contact with damp salt. The trencher salt and the salt-cellar are often accompanied by a small SALT SPOON. *See* SCROLL SALT; BOX SALT; NAUTILUS SHELL.

salt caster. A type of SALT in the form of a CASTER, to be used for holding and sprinkling table salt; it is smaller than a SUGAR CASTER. Although salt in early times was coarse and hydrous (so not practical for use in a caster), such casters were sometimes made then, and also in recent times, for salt that is finer and specially prepared for sprinkling. Salt casters are often made as one of a pair with a PEPPER CASTER. Early examples were in the form of a cylindrical box with a detachable cover having pierced holes of various shapes; later ones are pear-shaped or of waisted cylindrical form and have a hemispherical lower part, tapering inward and upward to a cylindrical neck. The pierced holes were sometimes arranged in various decorative patterns. Some examples of a PEDESTAL SALT have a pierced cover to permit sprinkling. Also called a 'salt shaker'. *See* CHURCH SALT.

salt-cellar. A type of SALT in the form of a small shallow bowl to hold salt for individual use at the dinner table. It has been made in a great variety of shapes and styles, usually circular or oval, but sometimes rectangular, triangular, polygonal, boat-shaped, tureen-shaped, or oblate. It rests either on a footed base or on three or four decorative feet. Usually there is no handle, but a few of boat-shape have uplifted end handles or a BAIL HANDLE. Only very rarely is there a cover. Decoration varies, some examples having a rim with REEDING or GADROONING, and some overall EMBOSSING or applied decoration. A few are of fantasy shape (e.g., one in the form of a conch shell supported by a dragon, or a SET made by PAUL STORR depicting a Triton holding an upturned snail shell). Salt-cellars often have a gilded interior (as protection against corrosion by damp salt) or are accompanied by a LINER of clear or coloured (usually blue) glass (sometimes with a shaped rim), in which cases the silver receptacle has decoration of PIERCED WORK or SAW-

CUTTING to reveal the enclosed glass. A variant modern type is made of glass that rests in a silver receptacle, EN SUITE with a CASTER and a MUSTARD-POT. Some are made in PAIRS or in sets of four or more. Some are accompanied by a conforming small tray and some by a conforming tiny SALT SPOON. The addition, *c.* 1820, of the word 'cellar' resulted from a corruption of the French word *salière*, salt-box. *See* G. Bernard Hughes, 'Silver Salt Cellars' in *Country Life*, 13 October 1955, p. 804. *See* TRENCHER SALT; CAPSTAN SALT; CAULDRON SALT; BOX SALT; FIGURAL SALT-CELLAR, DOUBLE SALT.

salt spoon. A small SPOON for serving salt from a SALT-CELLAR, usually in the form of a small LADLE with an oval bowl or a spoon with a small circular bowl; but the scoop may be of various shapes, such as a shallow hemisphere, shell, heart or flat shovel. Its introduction ended the custom of the early 18th century of taking salt with the tip of a knife. Three examples made by Charles A. Burnett (1785-1849), of Alexandria, Virginia, are the earliest surviving pieces of American silver specifically ordered for the White House, Washington, D. C.; they are inscribed 'President's House'.

salver. A type of flat serving utensil, without a handle, upon which was placed, originally, a drinking vessel and, later, letters, visiting cards, newspapers, etc., for formal presentation by a servant. Some have a FOOT-RING, four decorative feet, or a spreading foot, and some a detachable TRUMPET FOOT; the last-mentioned type, however, should not be, but sometimes erroneously is, confused with and called a TAZZA (*see* FOOTED SALVER). Salvers occur in various sizes (ranging from 25 cm to 55 cm wide) and shapes, being basically circular but in some cases square or polygonal with rounded corners, while some large ones are oval or rectangular. Styles of decoration vary, the flat surface sometimes being decorated with overall ENGRAVING or CHASING, occasionally with CHINOISERIES, ARMORIALS, foliage, flowers or birds. The rim is often edged with GADROONING, REEDING, BEADING or PIERCED WORK, or is irregularly shaped in various styles, e.g., scalloped or lobed, or a BATH RIM, CHIPPENDALE RIM or PIECRUST BORDER, or a border having indented corners. Salvers have often been presented as a gift on a special occasion, appropriately engraved with a COAT OF ARMS or an inscription to commemorate the occasion; some were donated to a church for use as an ALMS DISH. The comparable flat server of smaller size is usually called a WAITER or sometimes a 'presenter'; an early term was a 'table'. In the 1730s-50s silversmiths specialized in making elaborately decorated salvers which required great skill; such examples have been used merely for display as a SIDEBOARD DISH. *See* G. Bernard Hughes, 'Silver Salvers, Waiters and Trays' in *Country Life*, 29 September 1950, p. 996; Helen Comstock, '18th-century English Salvers' in *Antiques*, November 1959, p. 450. *See* LORD MAYOR'S SALVER; ST MARTIN'S SALVER; WALPOLE SALVER; TEA-KETTLE SALVER; TRAY; SEAL WARE.

salver. Upcurved rim, four scroll feet, Paul de Lamerie, London, 1750-1. W. 24·8 cm. Ashmolean Museum, Oxford.

sanctuary lamp. A type of OIL LAMP, hung in a High Anglican or Catholic church, being in the form of a deep hemispherical bowl with three suspensory chains attached to the rim and rising to a cover-like domed piece which in turn was suspended by a ring at its top. An example made by CHARLES KANDLER *c.* 1727 is now in the Victoria and Albert Museum, London. Two other examples, 1700 and 1789, respectively, are at Arundel Castle, Sussex.

sand-box. A small BOX, CASTER or other receptacle formerly used to contain fine sand to be sprinkled on wet ink to blot it; it is sometimes a unit of an INKSTAND. *See* POUNCE-POT.

sand casting. A process of CASTING an object by pouring molten metal into a sand mould, a technique used for many years by silversmiths for many types of small articles. It involves using two adjacent iron boxes which are filled with tightly packed, wet sand ('marl') so as to enclose a model of the desired object; after the boxes are separated and the model removed, the mould of sand is dried hard, dusted with powdered charcoal (to form a parting surface), and clamped together, then filled with molten metal. Several such sand moulds can be made in one operation and joined by narrow channels, so that a number of silver objects can be made by one pouring.

Sanderson, Robert (1608-93). A silversmith, born in London, who was apprenticed there in 1623 to William Rawlins for nine years, and freed in 1632; he emigrated after 1635 (having been in trouble for using some substandard plate), and his presence in New England was recorded in 1638. He settled first in Hampton, New Hampshire, and *c.* 1652 may have lived in Watertown, Massachusetts. When JOHN HULL was selected in 1652 to mint the first coins in Massachusetts (or possibly sooner), he took Sanderson as his partner, the firm being known as HULL AND SANDERSON. They had a shop in Boston. Surviving examples of work by Sanderson are mainly ecclesiastical plate. His sons, Benjamin and Robert, also became silversmiths. *See* MASSACHUSETTS SILVERWARE.

Saracen's-head spoon. A type of SPOON having a thin straight stem with a finial in the form of a bust of a male figure said to represent a Saracen. Such spoons are known from the 16th century. *See* MOOR'S-HEAD SPOON.

satin finish. A dull surface on a silver article produced by a rotating wire wheel that makes many tiny scratches. It is sometimes called 'butler's finish'. *See* FROSTING.

sauce-boat. Griffin handle, unmarked, London, *c.* 1740(?), H. 20·3 cm. Ashmolean Museum, Oxford.

sauce-boat. A boat-shaped receptacle for serving sauce. Early examples have a pouring lip at each end and two side handles (*see* DOUBLE-LIPPED SAUCE-BOAT); these were impracticable for pouring and are more suitable for serving hot gravy with a LADLE, and hence are preferably called a GRAVY-BOAT. Later sauce-boats have at one end a long everted pouring lip (even when accompanied by a sauce ladle) and at the other end a curved or scroll handle (sometimes a FLYING SCROLL HANDLE in the form of a bird, griffin or animal) rising above the rim. The rim usually dips midway on the sides. Such pieces usually stand on a spreading foot, but sometimes on four short legs (occasionally decorated with masks) or on three feet (one under the lipped end and two near the back end, or vice versa). Only rarely is there a cover (*see* COVERED SAUCE-BOAT). The fact that some sauce-boats were often used when serving fish is evidenced by the fish and sea-shell motifs in the decoration of many examples. Sauce-boats are often accompanied by a small ladle made EN SUITE, but the handle at the end and the pouring lip suggest that the usual method of use was pouring. Occasionally, there is a conforming oval supporting dish, known in French as a *présentoir*. Some rare examples have a double wall to be filled with hot water to keep the sauce warm. Some are made in fantasy shape, with animal forms having an open-mouth pouring orifice. A few have been made as a small circular bowl with one lip and one side handle. Sauce-boats are generally sold in pairs. *See* G. Bernard Hughes, 'Saucers and Sauce-boats' in *Country Life*, 2 December 1954, p. 2015. *See* BUTTER-BOAT; CREAM-BOAT; SAUCE-TUREEN; BOURDALOU.

sauce ladle. A type of LADLE similar to, but smaller than, a SOUP LADLE, for use with a SAUCE-BOAT, a GRAVY-BOAT or a SAUCE-TUREEN. It has a curved handle, and its style often conforms with that of the owner's FLATWARE; some examples are decorative, however, having a shaped bowl and an ornamented handle. It is the same as a gravy ladle.

sauce-tureen. A type of TUREEN, similar to but smaller than a SOUP-TUREEN, for serving sauce or hot gravy. The bowl usually is of oval or CANOE SHAPE, having at each end a vertical curved loop handle rising above the rim and having a domed cover with a finial, sometimes in the form of a lifting ring. The bowl usually rests on an oval spreading foot, but occasionally has four short legs with decorative feet. Late examples, after *c.* 1800, sometimes have elaborate mounts and sometimes horizontal handles or DROP-RING HANDLES. A sauce-tureen is sometimes accompanied by a matching stand with a raised centre, to protect the table from the heat of the contents and also to serve as a rest for the LADLE, unless there is a notch in the cover to allow the bowl of the ladle to be placed inside the tureen. The decoration is frequently of GA-DROONING, ENGRAVING, CHASING or BRIGHT CUTTING. Such tureens were sometimes made as a pair, or as a set of four (one to be placed at each corner of a formal dinner table).

saucepan. (1) A culinary utensil for making sauces, melting butter, or heating liquids such as milk. Examples were made of silver in the early 18th century in substitution for pans of brass or copper (which involved health risks and impaired flavours). It is a flat-bottomed vessel with vertical, bulging or ogee-shaped sides, and often has a pouring lip; it has a long, straight handle, of ivory, ebony, or turned wood, set at right-angles to the lip and projecting from a long attenuated FERRULE. The capacity varies from $\frac{1}{4}$ pint to $1\frac{1}{2}$ pints. It sometimes has a hinged domed lid or a detachable cover with a finial. It is often accompanied by a supporting stand, having three legs within which there is a frame that holds a heating device (a spirit lamp or a mortar light made of beeswax with a flax wick). *See* G. Bernard Hughes, 'Silver Sauce Pans' in *Country Life*, 26 July 1956, p. 185. *See* BRANDY-SAUCEPAN; SKILLET. (2) A modern large utensil in the form of a kitchen saucepan with a cover and a long handle; as a heat-conductive silver saucepan is not practicable for cooking, such a piece must be intended for use as a serving receptacle.

saucer. A small shallow DISH, usually circular, either for serving food or as a stand for a drinking CUP. Generally those for use with a cup have in the centre a slight depression in which to position the cup. The name is derived from the fact that some early examples, *c*.1728, were made to hold sauce; but ornate examples, even from the 17th century, were more probably for serving sweetmeats. The width usually ranges from 12·5 to 15 cm.

saucer-dish. A type of shallow DISH without a WELL or MARLI, such as the Chinese ceramic saucer-dish which differed from the European form. Examples in English silver were made in the 1630s, being about 12·5 cm in diameter and of low GAUGE due to the shortage of silver at the time. Many such saucer-dishes were made by William Maundy. The style has been revived in recent years.

Savannah silverware. Articles of silverware made in Savannah, Georgia. Before the Revolution in 1776 eight silversmiths were recorded there, and a list names over sixty between 1733 and 1856, the first being William Parker who arrived in 1733. The output was small and only a few pieces from the 18th and early 19th centuries survive. Most of the pieces were FLATWARE, but some was HOLLOW WARE of simple form and decoration. *See* James A. Williams, 'Savannah Silver and Silversmiths' in *Antiques*, March 1967, p. 347.

save-all. A type of pan having in the centre a spike on which a candle-end can be placed for burning; the melted tallow that collects in the pan can then be removed for re-use.

saw-cutting. A type of OPENWORK made by cutting, with a piercing saw, holes of irregular and decorative shapes. It is usually found on articles such as a SUGAR-BOWL, CREAM-PAIL, DECANTER STAND, on MOUNTS for a CLARET-JUG or on flat FISH SLICES; but often it is found on smaller articles, such as some SALT-CELLARS having a glass LINER. The technique involves the use of a piercing saw having a very thin blade; first, a hole is drilled into the silver plate, then the saw, held vertically, is inserted and the plate brought against the saw to cut the design. Its early use was revived for making pieces in the NEO-CLASSICAL STYLE designed by ROBERT ADAM.

scales. A weighing implement, of which an example of the beam type, made of silver, is known, having been used to weigh coins when coin clipping was practised before the introduction of the milled-edge coin. *See* BALANCE SCALE; POSTAL SCALE.

scallop (rarely, **escallop**). A type of receptacle in the form of the shell of a scallop (a marine bivalve mollusc), sometimes made of silver by CASTING from nature, being radially ribbed (15 to 19 ribs of diminishing width and length) and having a slightly undulating rim. Such receptacles made of silver have been used for many purposes: (1) a vessel used at a baptismal service for pouring (affusion) of the holy water, emblematic of St James; (2) an uncovered serving DISH, usually containing seafood baked in the oven in the dish, and usually having three feet, sometimes with a rim edged with GADROONING or BEADING, and sometimes accompanied by a LADLE; (3) a BASKET for fruit or bread, with a FLYING SCROLL HANDLE topped with an ornate finial and resting on three feet; (4) a BUTTER-SHELL; (5) a SAUCE-BOAT, generally for use with a fish course, and accompanied by a stand and a ladle; (6) a SALT-CELLAR or PICKLE-DISH resting on three scroll- or shell-shaped feet; and (7) a type of BOX having a hinged lid shaped like a scallop shell, such boxes having been used for sugar (*see* SCALLOP-SHELL SUGAR-BOX) or as a SPICE-BOX. *See* Judith Banister, 'Scallop Shells in English Silver', in *Antique Dealer & Collectors Guide*, June 1967, p. 68; G. Bernard Hughes, 'The Escallop Shell in Silver' in *Country Life*, 6 November 1969, p. 1180. *See* SCALLOP-SHELL CADDY SPOON; COCKLE SHELL.

scallop-shell caddy spoon. A type of CADDY-SPOON having its bowl in the form of a SCALLOP shell, the handle being the small flat end of the shell. These were developed from the scallop shells that the Chinese packed in tea-chests for use as ladles to dispense and measure tea. A great variety of such spoons were produced, over sixty examples having been shown in an exhibition in 1965.

scallop-shell sugar-box. A type of SUGAR-BOX having a lid in the form of a SCALLOP shell and low vertical sides following the outline of the shell, the lid being hinged to the straight side; it has four feet, sometimes in the form of scallop shells, winkles, snails or dolphins. Some examples are provided with, at the front, a small ring or shell for lifting the lid. Some such boxes have, mounted as the lid, an actual scallop shell. Sometimes called a 'scallop-shell spice-box'.

scallop-shell sugar-box. Silver, maker's mark 'TI', English, 1620, width 16·5 cm; and silver with lid of natural shell, English, late 16th–early 17th century, width 16·8 cm. Both Ashmolean Museum, Oxford.

scalloped teapot. Oval section (with conforming stand), fluted attenuated spout, bands of bright-cut decoration, Henry Chawner, London, 1790. H. 16 cm. Courtesy, Partridge (Fine Arts) Ltd, London.

scent-bottle. Silver gilt, unmarked, English, *c.* 1695. H. 12·7 cm. Courtesy, Brand Inglis Ltd, London.

scalloped. Having a continuous series of segments of a circle, resembling the edge of a SCALLOP shell; often a RIM is so shaped, with twelve such segments. *See* SCALLOPED TEAPOT.

scalloped teapot. A type of TEAPOT that is oval-shaped and has sides in the form of a continuous band of vertical scallops, i.e., of SCALLOP section. The spout, which is usually straight and ATTENUATED, is sometimes fluted.

Scandinavian-type tankard. A type of PEG TANKARD made in Scandinavia but also at several centres in England. It has a cylindrical body resting on three ball or pomegranate feet, above which are applied cast ACANTHUS leaves. The hinged LID is almost flat and is turned down vertically over the rim of the body. The handle is either scroll-shaped, widening towards the top, or a DOUBLE-SCROLL HANDLE, and has a THUMBPIECE. The characteristic feature is a vertical row of equidistant small pegs on the interior along the line of the handle, to serve as markers to measure the amount to be drunk by successive drinkers. Such tankards were made in England from 1656, mainly at York (some by JOHN PLUMMER) and Hull.

scent-bottle. A type of receptacle for perfume. Such pieces have been made in many forms and styles since the mid-17th century, when they became popular for use instead of a POMANDER. Some were part of a TOILET SERVICE (occasionally made of glass encased in an openwork silver pattern), and some (made in a variety of materials, including silver and gold) were smaller and portable. Sometimes called a 'perfume-bottle'. *See* Kate Foster, *Scent Bottles* (1966). *See* SCENT-FLASK.

scent-flask. A type of SCENT-BOTTLE in the shape of a PILGRIM FLASK with pendent chains. Examples are known from the 16th and early 17th centuries.

sceptre. A staff or baton carried by a Sovereign or other official as a ceremonial emblem of authority. The British Royal Sceptre is of gold, but silver examples are known, e.g., one at Gonville and Caius College, Cambridge, originally given to the College of Physicians by Dr John Caius (1510–73) when elected to membership in the reign of Edward VI, and reclaimed by him and donated in 1557 to the College at the time when he endowed Gonville Hall and renamed it Gonville and Caius College; it is a silver-gilt rod with an enamelled BOSS at each end and the head supported by four serpents taken from the Caius coat of arms.

Sc(h)ofield, John (fl. 1776–96). A London silversmith, with no record of apprenticeship or freedom, who entered his first mark in 1776, in partnership with Robert Jones, address 40 Bartholomew Close, a second mark alone in 1778 at 29 Bell Yard, Temple Bar, and a third mark in 1787. He has been said to have been one of the finest designers and craftsmen of the period, specializing in making CANDLESTICKS and CANDELABRA and excelling in mounting glass. He may have worked for Jeffreys, Jones and Gilbert, then Goldsmiths to the Crown, and have made silverware for Carlton House, a London residence of Royalty.

scientific instruments. Many examples of scientific instruments have been made of silver or with silver mounts, such as surgical, astronomical (e.g., orrery, armillary sphere, telescope, equatorial dial), navigational (astrolabe, compass, sextant), drawing (protractor), etc. Some instruments made of brass have silver dials due to the fact that markings could be engraved on them with accuracy. Such instruments are beyond the scope of this book. *See* MEDICAL SILVERWARE; VISION AIDS.

scimitar blade. ·A type of knife blade that is curved on both edges, being sharp on the convex edge; its shape is suggestive of a scimitar, except that it has a rounded end. It is contrasted with the usual knife blade with parallel edges.

scissors. A type of cutting instrument consisting of two blades, each having a ring handle, that pivot on a pin; similar to but smaller than shears. Examples made of silver are found in an ÉTUI with other SEWING ACCESSORIES, on a CHATELAINE, in a manicure set, or as a surgical instrument. A pair of scissors is sometimes provided with a fitted SCISSORS-CASE. *See* GRAPE SCISSORS; STORK SCISSORS; SNUFFER.

scissors-case. A small container to hold a pair of SCISSORS, usually having a wide upper part to conform to the shape of the scissors and often having a suspensory ring for hanging on a CHATELAINE. Examples have been made of silver (or gold) decorated with CHAMPLEVÉ enamelling. English examples are known from the 17th century.

sconce. (1) A CANDLESTICK (or a group of candlesticks) that projects on a curving arm from a back-plate, the most usual type being a WALL SCONCE, but some are made as a MIRROR SCONCE. *See* ARM SCONCE; PICTURE SCONCE. Some were intended to magnify the light from the candle(s) by reflecting it from the mirror or other type of back-plate, but some having no reflector were made solely as an ornamental wall illuminator, especially those with elaborate EMBOSSING and CHASING. They were often made in large sets for a sizable room; many exist at Knole House and other manor houses. Sometimes formerly called a 'hanging candlestick' or 'candlestick plate'. (2) The term 'sconce' has sometimes been applied to the SOCKET for a candle on a CANDLESTICK, CANDELABRUM or CHANDELIER, or to a CHAMBER CANDLESTICK, but this obsolete usage should be discouraged. (3) The term 'sconce' has been erroneously applied to a small projecting wall-plate or shelf used to support an ornament. *See* ARGAND LAMP; FURNITURE.

scorification. A process of separating silver (or gold) from an ore or from sweepings containing waste silver (or gold) by oxidizing it in a scorifier (furnace) with lead, borax, etc. to produce a slag of lead oxide and leave the silver (or gold) in a lead button from which the lead can then be removed by CUPELLATION.

Scorton Arrow. An archery TROPHY in the form of a silver arrow, 64 cm long, having three fletchings (vanes). It has been awarded annually since 1663 by the Scorton Archers, and is named after the town of Scorton, near Richmond, Yorkshire, near which the annual contests are held. It is said to be the oldest extant English sporting trophy. It bears no hallmarks, but has been attributed to *c.*1670; its origin is unknown, and the story about its having been awarded by Elizabeth I and won by Roger Ascham (d. 1568) has been doubted.

Scott, Digby (fl. 1802-7). A silversmith from Birmingham(?) with no record of apprenticeship or being freed, but who probably worked in Birmingham for MATTHEW BOULTON. In 1802 he joined BENJAMIN SMITH I in London at Lime Kiln Lane, Greenwich, entering a joint mark in 1802 and a second joint mark in 1803. They produced pieces mainly for RUNDELL, BRIDGE & RUNDELL. The partnership with Smith was dissolved in 1807, after which time Smith entered separate marks and continued as a principal silversmith for Rundell, Bridge & Rundell until 1813/14.

Scottish Hallmarks. The HALLMARKS punched on silverware in Scotland, since 1552 in Edinburgh (*see* EDINBURGH ASSAY OFFICE) and in Glasgow from the last quarter of the 17th century until 1964 (*see* GLASGOW ASSAY OFFICE). Other Scottish cities and towns formerly assayed silver, each having its own Town Marks.

Scottish silverware. Articles of silverware made in Scotland (mainly in Edinburgh, Aberdeen, Dundee, and Glasgow) from the 15th century onwards, and assayed at a large number of cities and towns, but principally Edinburgh (now the only one with an ASSAY OFFICE) and Glasgow. The articles, especially in the period 1690-1740, were of high quality, good craftsmanship, and elegant line without ornate decoration. Among the pieces especially identified with Scotland are the QUAICH, the THISTLE CUP, the BARREL TEAPOT, the BULLET TEAPOT, and the KITCHEN PEPPER-POT; but after *c.*1700 a wide range of articles was produced, almost as extensive as the ware from London, but often made with characteristic local design features. Among the leading silversmiths were Alexander Kincaid (fl. 1690s) and Patrick Robertson (fl. 1770s). *See* Edward Wenham, 'The Gipsy Silversmiths of Scotland' in *Antique Collector*, March–April 1947, p. 58; Ian Finlay, *Scottish Gold and Silver Work* (1958); —, 'Scottish Ceremonial Plate' in *Apollo*, January 1956, p. 6, and February 1956, p. 48; —, 'The Finest Age of Scottish Silver' in *Country Life*, 27 August 1959, p. 130; —, 'Masterpieces of Scottish Silver' in *Country Life*, 22 August 1963, p. 443.

scrape mark. The mark (sometimes a long gouge) on a piece of silverware where the ASSAY OFFICE has scraped away a small sample of the metal for testing (ASSAYING). Such marks are usually eradicated by the silversmith by POLISHING when a piece has been returned after assaying, but they are sometimes still seen on the bottom of some TRAYS, WAITERS, and other articles.

scratch mark. A mark made by scratching or engraving on the bottom of an article a numeral to indicate a model number or the weight of the piece.

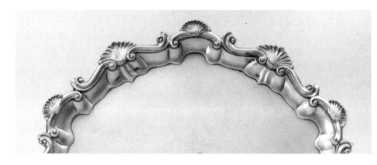

scroll-and-shell rim. Detail of salver, William Bennett, London, 1816. Courtesy, Sotheby's, London.

screw cover. A type of circular COVER with interior threading to fit securely over the upright threaded collar of a receptacle, as on a FLAGON, FLASK or some types of SALT or CASTER. *See* DOME COVER; SLIP-ON COVER; BAYONET COVER.

scroll. A decorative pattern in the form of a spiral or convoluted curve, re-entrant or continuous, including relief ornament in this form which is based on the curve made by a parchment scroll. *See* SCROLL HANDLE; DOUBLE SCROLL HANDLE.

scroll-and-shell rim. A decorative RIM found on some TRAYS, WAITERS, and SALVERS in the basic form (subject to variations in detail) of a series of S-shaped scrolls alternating in direction, separated by alternating large and small relief SCALLOP shells. Between the rim and the flat bottom of the piece is a band of scrolled fluting. *See* BATH RIM; CHIPPENDALE RIM.

scroll container. A cylindrical container for preserving a scroll, sometimes inscribed as a presentation piece and accompanied by an ornamental wooden box. *See* MEGILLAH-CASE.

scroll handle. A type of HANDLE in the form of a single SCROLL, found on some MUGS, CANNS, and TWO-HANDLED CUPS; sometimes called an 'S-scroll handle'. *See* DOUBLE SCROLL HANDLE.

scroll salt. A type of STANDING SALT having a circular, square or polygonal body with a wide base and an equally wide platform on top of the central support, the support being vertical with straight or waisted sides so that the shape of the piece resembles a spool or a pulley-wheel (hence sometimes called a 'pulley-salt'). In the centre of the platform is an uncovered depression for salt, and around it are three (if made before *c.* 1660) or four (after *c.* 1660) vertical scroll brackets curving upward and outward from the rim. Early examples are undecorated but later ones are elaborately formed. They were made in England and the American Colonies in the 17th and early 18th centuries, the earliest-known example (*see* WROTHE SALT) dating from 1633. They are usually about 15 cm high but ornate examples range up to 30 cm. The vertical brackets (whose purpose has been disputed) were to support a dish or an after-dinner bowl of fruit, as shown on some Dutch engravings and still-life paintings, and as mentioned by Samuel Pepys in describing the SEYMOUR SALT; they were not to support a napkin to cover the salt, as has sometimes been supposed. The hollow central part is known as the 'coffin' which, in the case of one dishonest maker, was clogged with solder to falsify the weight. *See* Norman M. Penzer, 'Scroll Salts' in *Apollo Annual*, 1949. *See* DETHICK SALT; MOODY SALT; SWORD BEARER'S SALT.

scroll handle. Detail of tankard, John Coney, Boston, Mass., *c.* 1805. H. 15·2 cm. Wadsworth Atheneum, Hartford, Conn.

scrolling foliage. A decorative pattern in the form of a continuous band of spiralling scrolls with foliated lines, the adjacent connected scrolls curving in opposite directions. It is found on some CUPS and SUGAR-VASES from the 16th to the 19th century. Sometimes referred to as 'foliated scrolls'.

Scrope Mazer. A MAZER, *c.* 1400, that was at a later date raised so as to rest on three feet cast as female masks. It is in York Minster. *See* STANDING MAZER.

seal. A device bearing a monogram or design in INTAGLIO for imparting an impression in relief on a soft tenacious substance, e.g. clay or wax or a wafer (a thin disc of dried paste). Seals have been made from ancient times, of clay and later of various substances, e.g., silver, gold, cornelian and other gem-stones, coral, glass, etc. The earliest forms were flat (called a 'stamp seal'), then on the outside of a cylinder (called a 'cylinder seal'), and later they were mounted on signet rings and also on a shank, usually about 3 to 5 cm in height, made of gold, silver, enamelled ware, or steel, as well as of porcelain. From the 16th century seals were worn suspended from a neck chain, girdle or CHATELAINE, and from the 17th century men wore seals dangling from a watch chain. Large 'table seals' were used by corporations and cities, and in England each Sovereign has a distinctive GREAT SEAL (*see* SEAL WARE). The term 'seal' is also applied to the wax or other substance upon which the design has been impressed, and the seal is sometimes referred to as the 'matrix'. The former term for seal was a 'sphragis'.

seal-box. A type of BOX that is used to contain and preserve a wax impression of a SEAL, especially a GREAT SEAL, for later authentication of sealed documents. Such impressions were formerly preserved by wrapping them in silk, but later a circular box was introduced, early examples often being of tin or other metal, but after the mid-18th century they were generally made of silver, bearing an engraved, later REPOUSSÉ-CHASED, depiction of the seal. A silver-gilt engraved circular example, for a seal on a commission granted in 1604 by James VI of Scotland to the 3rd Earl of Montrose, is owned by the 7th Duke of Montrose, having been on loan to the Royal Scottish Museum, Edinburgh. Such boxes were also used for seals of British universities; these were oval and engraved, e.g., one made in 1745 by James Glen for the University of Glasgow, one made in 1740 for the University of Cambridge, and three made in 1809 and one in 1814 by Peter and William Bateman (*see* BATEMAN) for the University of Oxford. When the wax seal preserved in the box is still attached to a document, the box is called a SKIPPET. *See* Judith Banister, 'Preserving a Good Impression – Some Silver Seal Boxes' in *Country Life*, 4 June 1981, p. 1608.

seal cup. A type of STANDING CUP made as SEAL WARE from an obsolete and defaced SEAL. The earliest examples are the BACON CUPS, 1573-4. *See* LOFTUS CUP.

seal salver. A type of SALVER that has been made as SEAL WARE from the metal of an obsolete and defaced GREAT SEAL or sometimes a lesser seal, e.g., an Exchequer Seal, Privy Seal, or a Judicial Seal. Such pieces are usually decorated with an engraved central medallion that depicts the obverse and reverse of the seal. The earliest-known extant example is the MONTAGU SALVER, and the reputed finest example is the WALPOLE SALVER. *See* EYRE SALVERS.

seal-top spoon. A type of SPOON having at the top of the straight stem an ornament of BALUSTER shape supporting a flat-top finial shaped like a seal (hexagonal, circular or oval). The seal was sometimes pricked with the name or monogram of the owner or a date. Such spoons were made from the early 15th century until the mid-17th century. The Scottish version has a thinner and flatter stem, and the finial is smaller and oblong. *See* PUDSEY SPOON.

seal ware. Articles, such as a commemorative CUP or SALVER, made from the metal of an obsolete and defaced GREAT SEAL of England (or of Ireland) which, since the reign of Elizabeth I until recent times, has been given as a perquisite of office, upon the death of the Sovereign or a change of the seal, to the Lord Chancellor and Keeper of the Seal who became responsible for the new seal. (Previously, the obsolete seal was cut into pieces after an impression of it had been preserved in a SEAL-BOX.) Each article so made was usually engraved with a representation of the obverse and reverse of the obsolete seal and an appropriate inscription. In the early 17th century the new article was a cup, but from the reign of William III, 1695-1702, it was usually a salver. Not all the British Great Seals were made into seal ware. From the time of George IV some were divided into the obverse and reverse parts, and each part given to a different recipient or sometimes set in a salver or a dish; a counterseal of a seal of Queen Victoria was left intact and was purchased in 1977 by the British Museum. Comparable seal ware was sometimes made from the obsolete seals of the Chancellor of the Exchequer or other state officials. *See* Judith Banister, 'Rewards of High Office' in *Country Life*, 29 January 1981, p. 278, and 5 February 1981, p. 334. *See* SEAL CUP; SEAL SALVER.

seamed. With respect to silver HOLLOW WARE: made from a flat sheet of metal bent to form a tube and having the edges joined by SOLDERING.

second-course dish. A type of DISH used at a formal dinner for serving a course preceding the main course. Such dishes are similar to a MEAT-DISH in form and decoration, but are somewhat smaller, ranging from 25 to 36 cm in diameter.

seal-top spoon. Silver-gilt, London, 1635. Courtesy, Asprey & Co. Ltd, London.

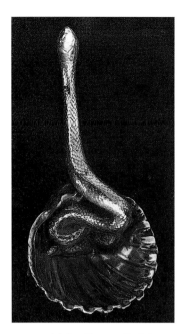

serpent-and-shell caddy spoon. English, *c.* 1820(?). L. 7·5 cm. Colchester & Essex Museum (Lewer Collection), Colchester.

serpentine objects. Tankard with silver mounts, *c.* 1620. H. 20·2 cm. Victoria and Albert Museum, London.

sewing accessories. Pin-cushion set in silver frame, Richard Cooper, London, *c.* 1670. L. 15·3 cm. Courtesy, Brand Inglis Ltd, London.

self base. The bottom of a vessel, such as a BEAKER, a MUG or a TRENCHER SALT, upon which it directly rests, i.e., having no FOOT-RING nor any supporting legs or feet.

self handle. A type of HANDLE to a receptacle, e.g., a SUGAR-BASKET, which is merely an upward extension of the ends of the receptacle forming an overhead loop, as distinguished from an applied handle.

serpent-and-shell caddy spoon. A type of CADDY SPOON having the bowl in the shape of a sea-shell, from which a serpent rears in convolutions to form a handle that fits the thumb and finger of the user. An example – said by the owner, the Colchester & Essex Museum, Colchester, to be the only one known – bears an unidentified mark; it has been attributed, based on the engraving on the back of the bowl, to *c.* 1820.

serpentine objects. Articles of which an essential part is made of serpentine (a type of rock of many varieties and characteristics, including marble), having MOUNTS of silver; among such pieces the most usual are TANKARDS, FLAGONS, VASES, and BOWLS. One such tankard, *c.* 1620, is in the Victoria and Albert Museum, London. *See* MOUNTED OBJECTS; SWAYTHLING BOWL.

server. A type of dining implement, made in a variety of shapes, sizes, and styles, for serving food; *see* FISH SERVER; SALAD SERVERS; SERVING FORK; SERVING KNIFE; SERVING SPOON; SERVING TONGS.

service. Various articles of TABLEWARE intended for use collectively for a particular meal or purpose, such as a DINNER SERVICE, COFFEE SERVICE, TEA SERVICE or DESSERT SERVICE, all of the articles being made of silver, silver gilt, PLATED METAL or SILVER-PLATED WARE, and decorated EN SUITE with the same pattern. A complete service usually includes pouring vessels, BOWLS, DISHES, PLATES, FLATWARE, CUTLERY, and accessories. If the pieces are all by the same maker, with the same MAKER'S MARKS and same HALLMARKS (but possibly different date marks), they constitute a 'true service'; but *see* COMPOSITE SERVICE; MATCHED SERVICE; SET.

service plate. The same as a PLACE PLATE.

serving fork. A type of FORK for serving food from a PLATTER or BOWL, being longer than a DINNER FORK and having three or four wide flat tines, the outer two being sometimes curved and tapering to a point. It was sometimes made EN SUITE with a SERVING SPOON, to be used for serving salad from a salad-bowl; *see* SALAD SERVERS.

serving knife. A type of implement for serving food from a PLATTER or large PLATE, having a flat blade like a spatula and no cutting edge, and occurring in various sizes, shapes, and styles. Also called simply a 'server'.

serving spoon. A type of SPOON of medium-large size, between a TABLESPOON and a STUFFING SPOON, used for serving food from a BOWL or DISH; sometimes made EN SUITE with a SERVING FORK, to be used for serving salad from a salad-bowl. The length of such spoons ranges from 33 to 38 cm.

serving tongs. A type of serving implement in the form of U-shaped TONGS having on the end of one arm the TINES of a fork, and on the end of the other arm the bowl of a spoon.

set. More than two objects (an extension of a PAIR) of the same or similar form, suited to each other and intended to be used together in a definite number as a unit, incomplete if separated, but not essentially identical; examples are APOSTLE SPOONS and CHESSMEN. Sometimes the term is applied loosely to a group of articles related to each other and intended to be used together, but capable of individual use and being of indeterminate number, e.g., a set of knives, forks, etc., or such articles of different forms, e.g., a BLACK-COFFEE SET, COMMUNION SET, CONDIMENT SET, TÊTE-À-TÊTE SET, TRAVELLER'S DINING SET, TRAVELLER'S TEA SET, TOOTHBRUSH SET. *See* GROUP; COMPANION PIECE; SERVICE.

sewing accessories. Various articles used in connection with sewing and needlework, made of or mounted with silver, such as SCISSORS, shears, THIMBLES, bodkins, needle-cases, pin-cushions, shuttles, and crochet hooks.

Seymour Salt. An elaborate silver-gilt GREAT SALT that is basically in the form of a SCROLL SALT. It rests on an octagonal base with eight corner feet in the form of small lions couchant, the base being in two tiers, having at each corner of the upper and lower tiers the head of a winged cherub. From the base rises a four-panel rock-crystal cylinder which supports a wide octagonal flat plate having a central circular depression for salt. The four crystal plates are joined by four vertical straps connected at the top and bottom by bands of CRESTING and each having at its base a figure of a ram; in the centre of each panel are alternating figures of the Archangel Michael and groups representing Abraham's sacrifice. On the rim of the plate are four large figures of eagles standing on mondes and with outspread wings (their heads serving as supports for a dish, as do the upright scrolls on a scroll salt), alternating with four small mondes upon each of which is a figure of a sitting greyhound; the eight mondes rest on openwork bases.

The piece was made c. 1662 (and described by Samuel Pepys on 27 April 1662) upon order from the Portsmouth Corporation for presentation to Catherine of Braganza (daughter of John IV of Portugal) at the time of her marriage to Charles II. When the Queen returned to Portugal in March 1692, she sold the salt to Thomas Seymour (d. 1698), a London businessman, of Lombard St, who had it inscribed and donated it in 1693 to the Goldsmiths' Company (which still owns it) in return for his being excused from serving as a warden. The piece bears no hallmarks, probably because Royal gifts were exempt from ASSAYING.

Seymour Salt. Silver-gilt scroll salt, crystal central cylinder, English, c. 1662. H. 26·8 cm. Goldsmiths' Company, London.

shaftesbury. A type of receptacle for containing and dispensing wine, being a long horizontal, cylindrical glass receptacle in the form of a tun (cask), resting on supporting feet and having at one end a TAP and SPIGOT. The only known example, c. 1740, has a silver stand and mounts, and has a figure of Bacchus astride it. The term appears in a dictionary of c. 1770, which referred to a capacity of one gallon; the known example (holding much less than a gallon), which was acquired in 1749 by the Vintners' Company, London, was referred to as a 'shaftesbury' at a meeting of the Company on 25 May 1749. No explanation of the term is known.

Shakerley Cup. A silver-gilt TWO-HANDLED CUP having a vase-shaped bowl resting on a spreading base and having two FLYING SCROLL HANDLES similar to the handles on the TATTON CUP except that the figures, emerging from scrolls, are vertical rather than twisting, and there is no engraved armorial on the tabor held by the figure of Pan. The decoration differs in that the bowl has swirling fluting, but the bowl and cover are decorated overall with applied fruiting vine stalks, bunches of grapes, and insects. The cover has a finial in the form of an infant Bacchus. The cup bears the mark of THOMAS HEMING, 1759–60. It was engraved c. 1790 with the arms of Charles Shakerley (1767–1834). The cup was donated in 1959 by the Esso Petroleum Company to the Victoria and Albert Museum, London. *See* HEMING TWO-HANDLED CUPS.

Shakespeare Vase. An oxidized silver VASE, made as a memorial to Shakespeare, designed and modelled by the sculptor Rafaelle Monti and made by Charles F. Hancock (*see* HANCOCKS), c. 1860. The finial is a seated figure of Shakespeare writing. On the bowl are two medallions with figures in low relief depicting Othello and Miranda, and between the medallions are figures in-the-round of other Shakespearean characters; on the base are figures of Hamlet, Lear, Ophelia, and Lady Macbeth, and below them small medallions with heads of the monarchs in the history plays, with in the centre a head of Elizabeth I. The vase was shown at the London International Exhibition of 1862, and is illustrated in J. B. Waring, *Masterpieces of Industrial Art* (1863), vol. III, plate 232.

shaftesbury. Glass barrel, silver mounts and stand, c. 1740. H. 40·5 cm. Vintners' Company, London.

shaving bowl. A large, wide-rimmed, circular or oval BOWL with a large shallow well, characterized by an arc-shaped indentation in the rim to allow the bowl to be fitted snugly under the chin of the person being shaved. It is usually undecorated except for a coat of arms or a cipher. Such bowls were sometimes accompanied by a conforming SHAVING JUG and SOAP-BOX (see SHAVING SET); also called a 'barber's bowl' and, especially such bowls in ceramic ware, 'Mambrino's helmet' (the name given by Don Quixote to the barber's bowl which he appropriated and wore in place of a helmet). It has been said traditionally that the shaving bowl was also used as a BLEEDING BOWL before 1774 (perhaps based on the dual role of barber-surgeons), but this seems unlikely.

shaving jug. A type of JUG that sometimes accompanied a SHAVING BOWL. It is usually pear-shaped with a vertical handle (sometimes scroll or double-scroll), a hinged LID, and sometimes a BEAK SPOUT. Some examples have decoration of GADROONING along the base and the rim of the mouth, but generally no other decoration except a coat of arms or a cipher. It forms part of a SHAVING SET.

Shakerley Cup. Silver gilt, Thomas Heming, London, 1759–60. H. 39 cm. Victoria and Albert Museum, London.

shaving bowl. Robert Cooper, London, 1712. D. 31·2 cm. Courtesy, Asprey & Co. Ltd, London.

shaving jug. Anthony Nelme, London, 1710–11. H. 19 cm. Ashmolean Museum, Oxford.

sheathed ware (1). Brown earthenware jug encased in silver-gilt openwork, and with engraved neck and lid, English, *c.* 1550. H. 15·3 cm. Victoria and Albert Museum, London.

Sheffield Assay Office. Assay Office Hallmarks: crown (in use from 1773); and rose (in use from 1 January 1975).

shaving set. A set of articles for personal use when shaving or for use by a barber, comprising a SHAVING BOWL, SHAVING JUG, and SOAP-BOX, and sometimes a silver-mounted cut-throat razor, a silver-mounted razor-strop, and a silver-handled shaving brush, all sometimes provided with a silver-mounted fitted case. A set, made by EDWARD WAKELIN in 1751, is owned by the Royal College of Surgeons of England, London. *See* RAZOR SET.

sheathed ware. (1) A type of ware, of silver, glass or earthenware, that is encased in a sheath of silver having OPENWORK decoration that reveals the inner body. The inner body, when of silver, is usually of SILVER GILT, the gilt being visible through the pierced decoration to provide a contrasting effect; *see* CAGEWORK; CAGEWORK CUPS; PEPYS CUP. In some cases the interior piece is made of glazed earthenware, similar to the TIGERWARE JUG, and the entire body and neck are encased in a hinged openwork silver sheathing. Some glass toilet-table bottles have a silver sheath extending over the body (the glass having been blown into the sheath). The piercing was usually in an elaborate pattern, depicting flowers, foliage, birds, animals, *amorini*, etc. The style may have been derived from the silver-encased glassware, known as *opus interrasile*, made of Roman glass in the 1st century AD. (2) Articles of wood or base metal that are completely encased with silver, such as some TABLES and other pieces of FURNITURE, as well as some HEARTH FURNITURE.

Sheffield Assay Office. The ASSAY OFFICE opened in Sheffield in 1773, its first marks being struck on 20 September; until 1975 it used as its ASSAY OFFICE HALLMARK on silverware a crown, this mark being accompanied by a STANDARD HALLMARK and a MAKER'S MARK, with a DATE HALLMARK (from 1773 until 1824 date letters were used not alphabetically in series, but at random). Between 1780 and 1853 the crown mark and the date mark were usually joined on one punch. Since 1975 its mark has been a rose (also used there on gold since 1904).

Sheffield plate. A PLATED METAL (COMPOSITE METAL) made by FUSING a thin silver plate on to a thicker plate of a base metal (usually copper), and then rolling the bimetallic mass, in ingot form, into sheets; the resulting metal retains the original proportions throughout, expanding in unity when rolled under pressure to the desired thickness. The basic method had been used since antiquity but became practicable only after the modern process was discovered in 1742 by THOMAS BOLSOVER, of Sheffield (who called the metal 'Copper Rolled Plate'). The process was not used commercially until the 1750s when manufacturing was started by Joseph Hancock. The term 'Sheffield Plate' has been recorded since 1771. Although more time and skill were required for the shaping of articles made of Sheffield plate than for those made of silver, the former were less costly due to the tax (enacted in 1784, and raised in 1797, 1804, and 1815) levied on articles of SOLID SILVER, and so the industry grew and thrived, especially in Sheffield and Birmingham (*see* MATTHEW BOULTON). The Sheffield plate was of excellent quality and, when new, distinguishable in appearance from solid silver only by its colour in bright daylight, when it reveals a faint bluish tinge; but after the piece has become well worn, the copper shows through, especially along the edges. On early ware, the base metal was covered with silver on one side only (SINGLE-PLATED), the other side being covered with tin; but later ware, especially HOLLOW WARE, was DOUBLE-PLATED. When the composite plate was cut, the base metal was revealed along the edge and this the platers concealed by various methods (*see* EDGING) or by affixing, by SOLDERING, decorative cast bands of BEADING or other patterns; such mountings were usually made of hollow silver filled with lead (in which case they were affixed by soft soldering to prevent the lead from melting). Sheffield plate was largely superseded *c.* 1835 by BRITISH PLATE, and more so *c.* 1840 by the much cheaper process of ELECTROPLATING. Sheffield plate has usually been thereafter referred to as 'Old Sheffield Plate' to distinguish it from the cheaper electroplated ware; however, there are several technical methods employed to differentiate it from electroplated ware. There is no legal requirement for a HALLMARK on Sheffield plate (*see* SHEFFIELD PLATE MARKS). Sheffield plate was decorated by a great variety of methods, including EMBOSSING, CHASING, FLAT CHASING, REEDING, FLUTING, STAMPING, BRIGHT CUTTING, HAMMERING, and GILDING, as well as the affixing of MOUNTS, borders, etc., made of STERLING SILVER, but rarely by ENGRAVING (which would reveal the under-layer of copper). Sheffield plate was sometimes called 'fused silver plate'; it must be distinguished from SHEFFIELD SILVERWARE, made of solid silver and bearing the hallmark of the SHEFFIELD ASSAY OFFICE. *See* Frederick Bradbury, *History of Old Sheffield Plate* (1912, 1968); Helen Comstock, 'Sheffield Plate' in *Antiques*, February 1964, p. 209; G. Bernard Hughes, 'Identifying Old Sheffield Plate' in *Country Life*, 10 April 1969, p. 850; —, *Antique Sheffield Plate* (1970); Peter Wallage, 'Sheffield Plate or electro-plate?', in *Collectors Guide*, January 1986, p. 64.

Sheffield plate. Tray, *c.* 1810. Courtesy, Garrard & Co. Ltd, London.

Sheffield Plate marks. Although there is no legal requirement now for a MAKER'S MARK on SHEFFIELD PLATE, such marks have been used since 1755 and some are still used. Some early marks from 1755 closely resembled London maker's marks on silver, so the London silversmiths agitated to have the use of such marks terminated and it was prohibited in 1772. No such marks were registered between 1773 and 1783. By Act of 1784 a maker of Sheffield Plate or of a ware that resembled silver, and who was working within 100 miles of Sheffield (and by Act of 1834 a maker working near Birmingham) was permitted to register at the ASSAY OFFICE a mark associated with his name, provided that it did not resemble a mark used on SOLID SILVER; but many marks not associated with a maker's name were registered and used. Such provision as to Sheffield plate and close-plated ware (*see* CLOSE PLATING) was terminated in 1836, and no such marks were registered after that date, although marks continued to be used. Some platers from 1765 added to their mark a crown, with the intent of distinguishing their work from inferior imitations imported from France and Austria; however, as the crown was the HALLMARK of the SHEFFIELD ASSAY OFFICE, such use was prohibited from 1825. There never has been any requirement for a DATE HALLMARK on Sheffield plate, so it is difficult to fix the date of some marked pieces except by considering the date of registration of the maker's mark.

Sheffield plated. Any SILVER-PLATED WARE that has been made in Sheffield by ELECTROPLATING and which cannot in Great Britain be legally called SHEFFIELD PLATE (which term is restricted to copper with a covering of silver), the 'd' being added deceptively in order to keep strictly within the law.

Sheffield silverware. Articles made of silver at Sheffield, other than the vast quantity of SHEFFIELD PLATE and related similar ware and pieces made by ELECTROPLATING. A great variety of wares, for domestic and decorative purposes, was made, but especially CANDLESTICKS, many of which were purchased by silversmiths of London and Edinburgh who over-struck them (*see* BACK-STAMPING) with their local mark. *See* SHEFFIELD ASSAY OFFICE.

shell-back spoon. A type of SPOON having on the back, at the juncture of the stem and the bowl, a SCALLOP shell in relief.

Shelley, Charles (fl. 1663–89). An English silversmith who was Royal Goldsmith to Charles II. He made a number of articles now in the Royal Collection (*see* FEATHERED FLAGON; JUDGMENT OF SOLOMON SCONCES).

shellfish silverware. A type of article in the form of a realistic representation of a species of shellfish, for use as an ornament or as a receptacle, such as a pair of SALTS in the form of, respectively, a crab and a lobster, made by NICHOLAS SPRIMONT and now in the Royal Collection. *See* SCALLOP; TURTLE TUREEN.

shield. (1) An imposing and massive piece made in the form of a circular shield, often of SILVER GILT, decorated with a central medallion depicting in high relief some historical or mythological event, and having in the back two rings to suspend it on a wall, e.g., ACHILLES SHIELD; AENEAS SHIELD; ISSUS,

BATTLE OF, SHIELD; MILTON SHIELD; OUTRAM SHIELD; ST GEORGE SHIELD; VECHTE SHIELD; WELLINGTON SHIELD. Comparable pieces, without suspension rings, were also made in the 19th century, including those intended to be used as a SIDEBOARD DISH (e.g., AGINCOURT SIDEBOARD DISH; CRÉCY SIDE-BOARD DISH), and others made as HORSE-RACING TROPHIES. (2) A term sometimes applied to an INSCRIPTION PLATE.

shoulder. The bulge just below the NECK of a VASE, BOTTLE or similar hollow vessel.

shoulder-belt plate. A military emblem or BADGE worn on the chest to ensure that a soldier's sword-belt and pouch-belt slung across his shoulders would cross at the centre of his chest. Some were made of silver, decorated with the name or badge of his regiment. *See* Major H. G. Parkyn, 'Shoulder-belt Plates' in *The Connoisseur*, November 1920, p. 147. *See* BELT PLATE.

shrine. A type of Christian RELIQUARY; examples were made from the 8th to the 11th centuries, in a variety of forms and of various materials, some having silver MOUNTS. A form associated with Ireland, but made throughout the Western Christian world, is the so-called 'house-shaped shrine', sometimes called 'tomb-shaped' or 'church-shaped', being in the form of a small stone oratory having a gabled roof, such as the MONYMUSK RELIQUARY. Another famed Irish example is the CATHACH SHRINE, in the form of a book; others are in the form of a bell (the Shrine of St Patrick's Bell) and a hinged metal belt (the Moylough Belt Shrine).

sideboard dish. A type of large, massive, and highly ornamented dish, circular or oval, made for display rather than use. Some examples are decorated merely with ARMORIALS, often within a decorative border, but a number are decorated in relief with battle scenes (*see* AGINCOURT SIDEBOARD DISH; CRÉCY SIDEBOARD DISH) or with scenes featuring mythological characters (*see* BACCHUS AND ARIADNE SIDEBOARD DISH). Such pieces with relief decoration are sometimes called a SHIELD or, erroneously, a SALVER or a CHARGER. *See* GOLDSMITHS' COMPANY SIDEBOARD DISH.

sideboard service. A type of SERVICE for use on a dining-room sideboard; it includes receptacles from which diners can serve themselves, such as large TUREENS, CHAFING DISHES, VEGETABLE-DISHES, and BOWLS, as well as SERVERS.

sifter spoon. A type of SPOON of medium size, having the bowl pierced with small holes, usually in a pattern, for sprinkling sugar. *See* STRAINER SPOON.

silver. A metallic element that is medium heavy, DUCTILE, and MALLEABLE. It is generally used in an ALLOY with copper to increase its hardness; *see* SILVER ALLOY; STERLING SILVER; BRITANNIA SILVER. It has a melting point of 961 °C. (1 762 °F.) It acquires an attractive PATINA, and can take a high degree of polish (reflecting 95 % of the incident light falling on its surface), but is subject to TARNISH by contact with sulphurous fumes in the air. Silver can be processed and decorated by HAMMERING (in shaping it or in making REPOUSSÉ decoration), ROLLING, CASTING, SPINNING, ENGRAVING, CHISELLING, and EMBOSSING. It can be used to make more durable and decorative an article made of copper; *see* ELECTROPLATING. Silver has been used from ancient times for a great variety of articles, principally jewelry and drinking vessels, but in the Middle Ages, when living standards declined, mainly for ecclesiastical ware (*see* CHURCH FURNISHINGS and CHURCH PLATE). After the 16th century, when the supply of silver became plentiful from New World sources, quantities of fine SILVERWARE were made in all European countries, especially England and France.

The principal sources of silver are alloys occurring in nature (e.g., electrum) and ARGENTIFEROUS ores, together with a small amount of NATIVE SILVER. Silver ores have been known since the First Metal Age, and have been worked since the third and second millennia BC. Silver mines have long been known in Spain, and since the 10th century in Germany and the 16th century in Austria and Hungary; but only small amounts occur in Britain. The great increase in the supply of silver came with the discoveries in the New World (in Mexico and the north-west coast of South America) in the early 16th century, especially the Potosi Mines in Peru. In the mid-19th century huge deposits were found in the United States (in Nevada and Colorado), then in Australia and elsewhere. Silver is extracted from ores by CUPELLATION or SCORIFICATION, is refined by many modern processes, and is tested by ASSAYING. *See* ANNEALING; ARGENT.

silver alloy. An alloy of SILVER and copper to produce a metal hard enough to be workable. In the United Kingdom the legal standard (STERLING SILVER)

is 92·5 % silver (FINENESS of 0·925), but for BRITANNIA SILVER (no longer generally made) it was 95·84 %. The standard in the United States is 92·1 %.

silver-cased bottle. A type of glass BOTTLE, often a SCENT-BOTTLE of a TOILET
SERVICE, that has an openwork decorative silver covering, the molten glass
having been blown into the silver casing. *See* GLASS OBJECTS; SHEATHED WARE.

silver depositing. The technique of decorating with silver the surface of an
article of glass or ceramic ware. As glass and ceramics are non-conductors of
electricity, they cannot be silvered by ELECTROPLATING, so the article is transformed into an electrical conductor by coating it completely with a composition containing graphite or other conductive substance, then immersing it in
a plating bath, with the result that the entire surface is plated with silver.
The desired design is then painted on the surface with a non-conductive
resist varnish, and the piece is returned to the plating bath under opposite
conditions, with the plating current reversed. Thus, the silver, except in the
areas covered by the varnish, is dissolved, leaving the design. The varnish
is then removed by an organic solvent, leaving the silver design on the glass
or ceramic article. The process has been applied by the GORHAM COMPANY to
pieces of Rockwood pottery.

silver foil. A paper-thin sheet of silver made by hammering sheet silver and
used by beating it on to a metal object or securing it by means of a fixative.
Although thicker than SILVER LEAF, it is too thin to be used satisfactorily in
making silverware. *See* FRENCH PLATING.

silver gilt. Silver that has a thin covering of gold, applied by a process of
GILDING. Various articles of silverware, including some large EPERGNES, TEA
SERVICES, SIDEBOARD DISHES, and HORSE-RACING TROPHIES, have been gilded,
not merely to prevent TARNISH, but as decoration. Such ware has sometimes
been loosely referred to as 'gilt' or even as 'gold'.

silver-lapped edging. The method of EDGING pieces of SHEFFIELD PLATE by a
process which involved first making a fine-bore tube from a narrow ribbon
of very thin silver, then opening the seam of the tube and drawing it along a
plate of the required thickness so as to form a U-shaped WIRE which was soldered over the edge of the object. Sometimes called a 'silver-lapped mount'.
See SINGLE-LAPPED EDGING; DOUBLE-LAPPED EDGING.

silver leaf. A very thin sheet of silver (usually 0·005 mm thick), thinner than
SILVER FOIL, that is made by hammering a silver sheet placed between plates
of copper or sheets of parchment. It is too thin and fragile to be used ordinarily in making silverware. *See* CLOSE PLATING.

silver-plated ware. Ware made of a base metal that has been given a silver
surface by the process of CLOSE PLATING or of ELECTROPLATING, as distinguished from PLATED METAL which is composed of two or more different
metals joined by FUSING, such as SHEFFIELD PLATE.

silver shape. The form of a piece of porcelain or pottery that is copied or
adapted from an article of silverware, e.g., some pieces made at the Chelsea
pottery by NICHOLAS SPRIMONT. Sometimes a moulding had been adapted
from a silver prototype or a piece has been decorated with a pattern previously used on silverware. Some 18th-century porcelain was designed by
silversmiths. Conversely, some silver articles have been made in the form of
ceramic prototypes; *see* CERAMIC-STYLE SILVERWARE. *See* Richard Ormond,
'Silver Shapes in Chelsea Porcelain' in *Country Life*, 1 February 1968, p. 224;
Judith Banister, 'Pottery and porcelain of "silver-shape"', in *The Antique
Dealer and Collectors Guide*, February 1983, p 26.

silversmith. A worker in silver, but also in gold, the term GOLDSMITH often
being applied without distinction to those who worked in either field; however, those who specialized in ENGRAVING were usually regarded apart and
designated as engravers. Silversmiths have been classified according to the
type of pieces that they made, the main groups being the largeworkers and
the smallworkers, but specialists were appropriately classified as a candle-
stick-maker, spoon-maker, salt-maker, snuffer-maker, hilt-maker, and even
spectacle-maker and buckle-maker. For the biographies (2,553) and marks of
many early London silversmiths, *see* Arthur G. Grimwade, *London Goldsmiths,
1697–1837* (2nd ed., 1982). *See* WOMEN SILVERSMITHS; APPRENTICE.

silversmithing. The various processes used in shaping WROUGHT articles of
silverware and in decorating the metal, such as by EMBOSSING, CHASING, EN-
GRAVING. *See* Robert Goodden and Philip Popham, *Silversmithing* (1971).

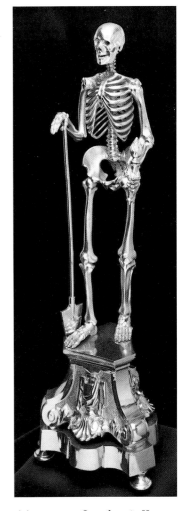

skeleton statuette. One of a pair. H.
45·5 cm. Wellcome Collection, Science
Museum, London.

silverware. Collectively, articles made of silver, SHEFFIELD PLATE or SILVER-PLATED WARE, including articles generally classified as HOLLOW WARE, FLATWARE, CUTLERY, and SMALLWARE, and being mainly articles of TABLEWARE, articles for domestic use, and domestic lighting equipment, as well as CHURCH FURNISHINGS and CHURCH PLATE, but excluding, for purposes of this book, JEWELRY and many personal utilitarian articles; but *see* WRITING ACCESSORIES, TOILET ACCESSORIES, SEWING ACCESSORIES, SMOKING ACCESSORIES, RIDING EQUIPMENT, GUN FURNITURE, SCIENTIFIC INSTRUMENTS, and VISION AIDS.

single-lapped edging. An early method of EDGING articles made of SHEFFIELD PLATE so as to conceal the copper line at the edge. The process, introduced by Joseph Hancock in 1758, involved the application of a thicker coating of silver than was usual and then cutting the edge of the plated copper with a blunt tool in such a manner that the silver layer extended beyond the copper and could then be lapped over to conceal the raw edge. *See* DOUBLE-LAPPED EDGING; SILVER-LAPPED EDGING.

single-plated. The type of PLATED METAL that has a layer of silver on one side only, and hence is used only on articles the underside of which is not intended to show. *See* DOUBLE-PLATED.

sinking. A process of shaping a shallow silver article (e.g., a SAUCER) by hand by HAMMERING a sheet of flat metal (usually circular) first into a depression in a wooden block and then in a sand-filled leather pad ('saddle'). The hammering must begin at the outer edge, and as each blow affects only a small area, the process is continued to form a row, and then other rows, moving toward the centre until a bowl shape is formed, or far enough to leave a flat bottom for the article. The tool used is a ball-ended 'sinking hammer'. *See* RAISING.

skeleton statuette. A STATUETTE depicting in-the-round a human skeleton standing on a plinth, presumably made as a MEMENTO MORI. A silver-plated pair–with one skeleton holding a scythe and a torch, the other holding a spade and a torch–is in the Wellcome Collection at the Science Museum, London.

skewer. A culinary implement used originally for fastening a joint of meat to a spit, but later smaller ones were used to retain the shape of meat or game while being roasted. It is generally in the form of a long, flat, tapering implement, pointed at one end and having at the other end usually a ring to facilitate withdrawal and by which to hang the skewer on a hook, but some have a decorative terminal. The length ranges from about 15 to 38 cm, the shorter ones being generally called a 'poultry skewer' or a 'game skewer'. They were sometimes made in sets of varying sizes. Those with sharp edges have frequently been used as a paper knife. *See* CARVING SKEWER.

skillet. A type of culinary utensil, somewhat similar to a BRANDY-SAUCEPAN, having a cylindrical or slightly curved bowl, but differing in that it has three or four short legs attached to the flat bottom, and is without a lip. The skillet has either one vertical scroll metal handle or a long horizontal wooden handle, and has a cover, either flat or in the form of an upside-down PORRINGER. A few silver examples are known from the 17th century, including one made by Nicholas Wollaston, London, 1653, and one by William Rouse (1639–1705), of Boston, Massachusetts. *See* Graham Hood, 'A new form in American 17th-century silverware' in *Antiques*, December 1968, p. 879.

skimmer. *See* STRAINER SPOON.

skinker-pot. A type of vessel used from *c.*1340 to *c.*1640, by a servant called a 'skinker', to bring wine from the barrels in the cellar and from which the wine was poured into a FLAGON or served into WINE-CUPS. The piece was of BEAKER shape, but with an attached curved SPOUT. Such pieces were made in four sizes.

skippet. A type of small, flat circular BOX used to enclose and protect the wax SEAL impression attached to a formal document; it is found mainly accompanying a treaty, which is usually bound in leather covers, the seal being attached to the binding by tasselled cords. The cover is usually engraved with a facsimile of the seal. An early Scottish example, *c.*1667, made by Thomas Kirkwood, Edinburgh, engraved with the arms of Scotland before the Union (1707), has an attached document bestowing a baronetcy. Others, with the arms of George II, were made by Mordecai Fox, one in 1752 and one in 1761. Skippets have been used also in the United States, the first used for

skippet. Protective box attached to the British ratification of the Treaty of Paris, 1783. National Archives & Records Service, Washington, D.C.

skull cup. Human cranium in silver mounts, W. & G. Sissons, Sheffield, 1864. H. 17 cm. City Museum, Sheffield.

the Treaty of Ghent, 1812; five U.S. examples are known attached to treaties. *See* Joan Sayers Brown, 'Skippets' in *Antiques*, July 1978, p. 140. *See* SEAL-BOX.

skirt foot. A type of wide FOOT-RING that slopes outward from near the bottom of an article (e.g., on some TANKARDS), providing the piece with added stability.

skull cup. A type of STANDING CUP of which the bowl is made of a human skull-cap. One example includes a skull picked up, *c.* 1860-4, on Flodden Field, in Northumberland, the scene of the 1513 battle. The cup has silver mounts in the form of a spreading foot with applied vines, a stem with a knop bearing four cast masks, and a rim with an inscription in Greek letters. It has a silver lining and two applied silver plaques with armorials. The piece bears the maker's mark of W. & G. Sissons, Sheffield, and is dated 1864.

Sleath, Gabriel (1674-1756). A London silversmith who was apprenticed in 1691 and freed in 1701, and entered his first mark in 1707, with address in Gutter Lane. After a second and a third mark, he entered a fourth in 1730 in partnership with Francis Crump. His surviving pieces include a variety of ware, the most important being WINE COOLERS.

'Sleep' Table. A silver TABLE designed and modelled by LÉONARD MOREL-LADEUIL for ELKINGTON & CO., and donated by the City of Birmingham to the then Prince and Princess of Wales (later Edward VII and Queen Alexandra) as a wedding gift in 1863. The design depicts the dreams of three sleeping figures. The table has a circular top, slightly depressed within the rim, resting on a leg supported by a tripod base with three feet in the form of poppies. On the base are seated reclining figures of, respectively, a farmer, a soldier, and a minstrel. A column on the table is surmounted by a standing semi-nude figure of the goddess of Sleep strewing poppies (which are also shown along the table leg). There are on the table three chased groups of allegorical figures representing the dreams of the figures: for the farmer, Peace, Plenty, and Mirth; for the soldier, Victory, Glory, and Fame; for the minstrel, Love, Music, and Fortuna. It has been reported that the table is not in the Royal Collection, and its whereabouts – if it still exists – is unknown. It was shown at the London International Exhibition, 1862, and the only known extant record of it is a description and chromolithograph in J. B. Waring, *Masterpieces of Industrial Art* (1863), vol. II, fig. 1.

Sligo Candelabra. Pair, with palm-tree stems, James Charles Edington, London, 1837 (*above*) and 1838 (*below*). Courtesy, Sotheby's, London.

Sligo Candelabra. A pair of CANDELABRA, each having a triform base and a palm-tree stem with six candle sockets and a central finial surmounted by a pine cone; on the base and around the stem is a group of Negroes in idealized plantation attire symbolizing Freedom. Each candelabrum bears the arms of Howe Peter (1788-1845), 2nd Marquess of Sligo, and an inscription recording the gift of the two pieces to him – in 1837 and 1838, respectively – by the Negroes of Jamaica and the inhabitants of the town of Westport there, in appreciation of his efforts to aid them during his governorship. The pieces were made by James Charles Edington, London, 1837 and 1838, but both are engraved 'Green & Ward', the retail firm (*see* GREEN, WARD & GREEN) that marketed Edington's ware. The donee was the only son of John Denis, Earl of Altamont, and, from 1800, 1st Marquess of Sligo, and had succeeded to the titles in 1809. The pair was sold at Sotheby's, London, on 13 June 1983 by the Trustees of the Sligo Settled Estates on the instructions of the then Earl of Altamont, son and heir of the 10th Marquess of Sligo.

slip-on cover. A type of cylindrical COVER that fits closely around an upright smooth cylindrical collar at the top of the body of a JAR, CASTER, etc., the lower part of the cover that extends down over the collar being sometimes called the 'bezel'. It is held in place by friction (resulting from the closeness of the fit) and is not firmly secured as is a SCREW COVER or a BAYONET COVER. Some examples obtain a firmer fit by having a sleeve of springy metal that fits inside the top of the body. Sometimes called a 'cap cover' or a 'pull-off cover'. *See* DOME COVER; DROP-IN COVER.

slipped-stalk spoon. A type of SPOON without an ornamental finial and having the top of its straight stem cut off transversally and sloping down toward the back. The stem of such spoons widens slightly away from the bowl. They were popular between *c.* 1620 and *c.* 1650 in England and were the earliest type of spoon known to have been made in the American Colonies, *c.* 1670-80. Some examples have the owner's initials on the bowl or on the slipped end. Also called a 'slip-top spoon', a 'slip-end spoon', and a 'slipped-in-the-stalk spoon'.

small two-handled cup. Cup and cover with embossed floral decoration and debased caryatid handles, London, *c.* 1660-70. Wadsworth Atheneum (Elizabeth B. Miles Collection), Hartford, Conn.

Smelt Cup. Cup, London, 1599-1600, replacement cover with pierced steeple, 1617. H. 37·5 cm. Victoria and Albert Museum, London.

sloke-pot. A term used in Ireland for a SAUCEPAN, employed there to cook at table stewed sloke (seaweed).

slop-bowl. A type of BOWL, used at a tea table, into which are poured the rinsings of the TEACUPS; often part of a TEA SERVICE, it may range from about 10 to 17·5 cm in diameter. Also called a 'slop-basin' or, rarely, a 'voiding bowl' (*see* VOIDER).

slot wine label. A type of BOTTLE TICKET (wine label) that is without a wine name but is made instead with a slot at the back to permit the insertion of an appropriate label.

small sword. A type of SWORD used for duelling or fencing; it is light in weight and has a tapering steel blade, sometimes with a silver hilt. Such swords were worn by well-to-do gentlemen in the American Colonies.

small two-handled cup. A type of circular cup that is of small size (about 10 to 18 cm high) and that has baluster- or ogee-shaped sides, two opposed vertical handles that are thin and usually in the form of a debased CARYATID HANDLE, and generally no cover. Such cups, occurring frequently in England, are often called there a POSSET-POT, a CAUDLE-CUP or a PORRINGER, but those terms are preferably applied to articles of completely different form. *See* TWO-HANDLED CUP.

smallware. Various small articles of silverware that fall outside the categories of HOLLOW WARE, CUTLERY, and TABLEWARE, such as TOILET ACCESSORIES, SEWING ACCESSORIES, SMOKING ACCESSORIES, WRITING ACCESSORIES, SNUFF-BOXES, WATCH-CASES, and VISION AIDS, but excluding articles of MINIATURE SILVERWARE. Such articles are generally beyond the scope of this book.

Smelt Cup. A silver-gilt STANDING CUP having a bowl of inverted bell shape resting on a plain unknopped stem with a spreading foot. The cover (a replacement added in 1617) is decorated with a pierced steeple; but the stem has no BRACKETS such as are often found on a STEEPLE CUP. The cup has a maker's mark 'BL' and London date mark, 1599-1600. It is inscribed to show its having been given by Leonard Smelt in 1619 to his grandson and ward Leonard. It is in the Victoria and Albert Museum, London.

Smith, Benjamin (I) (1764-1823). A prominent London silversmith who was employed first by MATTHEW BOULTON at Soho, Birmingham, in 1790. He and his brother James became partners of Boulton until 1802, when Benjamin left Birmingham to go to London. (James formed a new partnership with Boulton until he joined Benjamin in London in 1809.) Benjamin, whose London workshop was at Lime Kiln Lane, Greenwich, took as his partner DIGBY SCOTT, and they entered their first and second joint marks in 1802 and 1803. They made important pieces, almost exclusively from 1802 to 1807, for RUNDELL, BRIDGE & RUNDELL. The firm was dissolved in 1807, and Smith then entered alone his third and fourth marks in 1807, and in 1809 his fifth mark jointly with James, then his sixth and seventh marks alone in 1812 and 1814 (continuing until then to do work for Rundell, Bridge & Rundell), when he moved to Camberwell. In 1816 he entered his eighth mark jointly with his son BENJAMIN SMITH II (who succeeded him in 1822), followed by a ninth mark alone in 1818. Smith made several pieces for GREEN, WARD & GREEN for presentation to the Duke of Wellington (including the WELLINGTON WATERLOO CANDELABRA in 1816-17) and also the JAMAICA SERVICE.

Smith, Benjamin (II) (1793-1850). The eldest son of BENJAMIN SMITH I, he was apprenticed to his father in 1808 and freed in 1815(?), and entered his first mark jointly with his father in 1816, with address in Camberwell, and his second mark alone in 1818. In 1822 he moved his workshop to 12 Duke St, Lincoln's Inn Fields, and entered his third and fourth marks, very similar to those of his father, in 1822 and 1837. He supplied models to ELKINGTON & CO, to be copied or made by ELECTROPLATING, and was in charge of electroplating for Elkington at Moorgate in the 1840s until he was dismissed in 1849. He then resumed working in Duke St and, under the influence of Henry Cole, featured organic naturalistic motifs and created pieces by ELECTROFORMING from flowers, leaves, and other natural objects. His best-known pieces are the WATERLOO VASE and the WELLINGTON SHIELD, both made on order from GREEN, WARD & GREEN. Control of the firm passed in 1850 to his son, STEPHEN SMITH.

Smith, Stephen (fl. 1850-86). The son of BENJAMIN SMITH II who continued the silversmith business at 12 Duke St, Lincoln's Inn Fields, and took as a partner his father's employee, William Nicholson, registering their joint mark in 1850 as Smith, Nicholson & Co. He abandoned the naturalistic styles used by his father and grandfather, producing more restrained work, and became interested in making HORSE-RACING CUPS (notably one parcel-gilt example, 1868–9, now in the Victoria and Albert Museum, London) and TESTIMONIAL SILVERWARE. Nicholson left the firm in 1864, and Smith continued it with his son, Stephen Smith II, registering a mark for Stephen Smith & Son, and other marks from 1865 until 1884. Smith sold out in 1886 to Martin Goldstein, and died in 1890.

Smithsonian Mace. A parcel-gilt MACE made in 1965 by LESLIE G. DURBIN for and on commission from the Smithsonian Institution, Washington, D.C. The head is composed of three elements: the finial as a figure of a demi-lion holding a gilded sun, taken from the arms of Sir Hugh Smithson (later the 1st Duke of Northumberland), over a 'wavy bordure' which is a mark of bastardy, acknowledging the fact that James L. M. Smithson (1765–1829), the English physician who was the founder and benefactor of the Smithsonian Institution, was the illegitimate son of Sir Hugh; below the finial, six shields relating to aspects of James Smithson's life; and below them an astrolabe encircled by the motto of the Institution. Encircling the shaft is a gold ribbon engraved with the names of former Secretaries of the Institution, and set in the foot is a piece of the mineral smithsonite.

smoking accessories. Articles used by smokers of cigars, cigarettes, and PIPES, often made entirely or partially of silver, such as: (1) lighters; (2) cigar holders, clippers, piercers, cases, and boxes; (3) cigarette holders, snuffers, cases and boxes; and (4) telescopic church-warden's pipes, pipe tampers, stem-cleaners, reamers, pipe-rests, and pipe-trays. Such articles are generally beyond the scope of this book. *See* CIGAR LIGHTER; CIGAR-BOX; CIGARETTE-BOX; PIPE LIGHTER.

Smythier Flagon. *See* FEATHERED FLAGON (3).

snarling iron. A tool used in EMBOSSING metal articles of HOLLOW WARE. The curved tool has a domed beak which is placed inside the piece and the process involves holding the other end of the tool in a vice and striking the shank with a hammer, which by repercussion causes the beak to produce the desired decorative relief work, as the piece is rotated and the operation repeated in order to make the design.

Sneyd Chandelier. A CHANDELIER with ten arms, made for William III by DANIEL GARNIER, *c.* 1694/7. It bears the maker's mark, but no HALLMARK, as ASSAYING was not required for pieces made for the Crown. It was listed in the Royal Inventory for 1721, and was for many years owned by the Sneyd family, at Keele Hall, Staffordshire, until sold at Christie's, London, in 1924

Smithsonian Mace. Parcel-gilt head, Leslie Durbin, London, 1965. Smithsonian Institution, Washington, D.C. (photo courtesy, Leslie Durbin).

Sneyd Chandelier. Daniel Garnier, London, *c.* 1694/7. H. 68·5 cm. Colonial Williamsburg, Va.

snuffer. Length 20·5 cm. Victoria and Albert Museum, London.

snuffer stand (1). Stand with snuffer, Thomas Merry, London, 1715. Courtesy, Brand Inglis Ltd, London.

to William Randolph Hearst; since 1938 it has been at Colonial Williamsburg, Virginia.

snuff-box. A small BOX, usually having a hinged LID, for holding snuff (pulverized tobacco). The bottom part is usually made in one piece, the lid being attached by means of a hinged metal frame fitted to both parts. Some examples have two compartments, with a hinged lid at the top and another at the bottom. Some frames, which enclosed porcelain parts, were made of silver, silver gilt, or PLATED WARE. Decoration included ENGRAVING, CHASING, EMBOSSING, ENGINE-TURNING, or ENAMELLING, setting with gemstones, or ornate cast lids. The box is usually rectangular, but there are also many in a vast variety of fanciful shapes. Some have a tortoise-shell liner decorated with various types of piqué work. Some plated examples have a copper penny soldered to the lid. Boxes for ladies were accompanied by a SNUFF SPOON. Although most were portable, some boxes were large, to be passed after dinner with the port or stood on the mantelshelf; these had a lift-off cover and a scoop to replenish small boxes. In view of the great variety of snuff-boxes, most of which were made of material other than silver, they are beyond the scope of this book. *See* H. McCausland, *Snuff and Snuff-boxes* (1951); C. Le Corbeiller, *European and American Snuff-boxes* (1966). *See* MULL; CASTLE-TOP WARE.

snuff spoon. A type of SPOON to be used to take snuff from a SNUFF-BOX; its characteristic feature is its tiny size, but it is of no special form. Some examples included in a snuff-box may originally have been made merely as toy spoons.

snuffer (usually referred to as a pair of snuffers). A scissors-like implement used: (1) to cut off a candle's snuff (the charred end of the wick that had not burned down – before the use *c.* 1825 of paraffin candles with a self-consuming wick) and thus prevent the candle from smoking (the process being known as 'candle snitting'); or (2) to trim the snuff of a burning candle to prevent the wick from curling and dipping into the melted wax on the top of the candle. It is in the form of a pair of scissors, to the top of the longer blade of which is attached a small open-sided box, and to the end of the shorter blade a flat plate by which the snuff is impelled into the box. The snuffer has a pointed end to be used to remove a candle stub from the NOZZLE or the SOCKET of a CANDLESTICK. In early examples the snuff fell from the box when the blades were opened, but later examples had a spring device to keep the box closed until intentionally manually opened, thus rendering a SNUFFER DISH obsolete. There are two types of snuffer: the STANDING SNUFFER and the TRAY SNUFFER. In 1749 Benjamin Cartwright patented a type of mechanical snuffer which had a coiled spring to control the action of the flat plate. Snuffers are still used today. *See* G. Bernard Hughes, 'Old English Candle Snuffers' in *Antiques*, November 1946, p. 316; —, 'Snuffing of the Georgian Candle' in *Country Life*, 13 March 1969, p. 619. *See* BAINBRIDGE SNUFFER; WICK TRIMMER; CANDLE EXTINGUISHER; DOUTER.

snuffer dish. A type of DISH into which the snuff (the charred part of a wick) after being clipped by a SNUFFER, was dropped for safety. It was usually rectangular, having a flat base and sides deep enough to contain the snuffer, and sometimes four small feet and a handle (varying in form); some later examples also have a THUMBPIECE. They were popular in the period 1740-60.

snuffer stand. (1) A stand for a SNUFFER, in the form of an upright rectangular box, open at the top, supported by a short leg on a flat base (the snuffer being kept standing upright, handles up, in the box). At the back of the box there is a loop handle. Sometimes at the front of the box there is a hook to support a CANDLE EXTINGUISHER. (2) An unusual type combines a CHAMBER CANDLESTICK with a snuffer stand, the handle of the candlestick being attached to a socket on the side of the box of the snuffer stand. *See* SNUFFER TRAY.

snuffer tray. A small shallow TRAY upon which to rest a SNUFFER. Such trays are variously shaped and decorated, some having four feet, a vertical RIM (decorated with REEDING, PIERCED WORK or GADROONING), and sometimes two small side handles (on the short ends) or a single back-handle (on the long side). Later examples are oval, of CANOE SHAPE or hourglass-shape, or shaped to conform to the shape of the snuffer, and some are ornamented with relief MASKS. A large type was made to hold both a snuffer and a pair of CANDLE EXTINGUISHERS. After the development of the large-size tray and the TABLE SNUFFER, the small snuffer was designated a 'chamber snuffer' and kept with a CHAMBER CANDLESTICK (*see* SNUFFER STAND). *See* SPOON TRAY; PEN TRAY.

soap-box. (1). A spherical receptacle for a scented wash ball (a ball of hard coloured toilet soap, usually bearing the impressed trademark of the maker). The box is divided midway horizontally, the lower half being the receptacle resting on a spreading foot and the upper half being a hinged lid or a BAY-ONET COVER, in either case having a lifting knob or a finial. The upper half, and sometimes part of the lower half, has a pattern of pierced decoration to permit the soap to dry and the scent to escape. Some examples have a small lifting knob on the front of the lid. The interior is often gilded. Examples for use with a SHAVING SET have no pierced work. Such boxes range in width from about 6·5 to 10 cm. *See* G. Bernard Hughes, 'Silver Boxes for Scented Soap' in *Country Life*, 13 September 1973, p. 723. *See* SPONGE-BOX. (2) A flat box, circular, oval or rectangular, to hold a flat piece of soap, the cover sometimes being pierced. Such a box is often a unit of a TOILET SERVICE.

socket. (1) A cylindrical holder for a candle in a CANDLESTICK, CANDELABRUM or CHANDELIER, attached to the stem or to an arm, and sometimes having a slide with slits on each side which, when pressed by a protruding collet, per-mits the candle to be raised or lowered. Often there is fitted into the socket a detachable NOZZLE to hold the candle, having attached to it a protruding rim to act as a DRIP-PAN *(bobêche)*. Sometimes a candle socket is referred to as a SCONCE, an obsolete term in this sense. (2) The same as a FERRULE, into which is inserted the end of a HANDLE made of boxwood, ebony or ivory.

solder. The metal or metallic ALLOY that is used in molten form to join pieces of silver (or other metal). Various solders are produced commercially for use in different types of SOLDERING, each having an appropriate melting point for use in 'hard soldering' or 'soft soldering'. Solders used for objects of gold or silver must have the same proportion of the precious metal as the pieces to be joined; such solders are now made by refiners in the pre-scribed proportions. Solders that melt readily are 'soft solders'; those that fuse only at red heat are 'hard solders'. The solder used to join silver was for-merly an alloy of silver and bronze (hence detectable by its colour), but modern solder is an alloy of silver and zinc (white and less easy to detect) which combines the qualities of hard soldering with the advantages of a lower melting point.

soldering. The process of joining pieces of metal by the use of SOLDER hav-ing a melting point lower than that of the metals to be joined. The technique is used in making and repairing silverware. Solders of decreasing melting points are employed to permit further soldering without damaging a piece that has already been soldered. If the solder has a melting point only slightly below that of the metal pieces, it penetrates the metal and makes a firm join (called 'hard soldering' or sometimes 'brazing'); if its melting point is much lower, a weaker join results ('soft soldering'). Pieces to be joined must have clean surfaces and be coated with a flux to dissolve the oxide film which would impede the join, and after fusing (by the use of a gas or oxygen blow-pipe) the piece must be dipped in pickle (an acid bath) to remove the flux. Soldering was used in Mesopotamia from the 3rd millennium BC and in the Minoan civilization from the 2nd millennium BC; the ancient process in-volved binding the pieces together with a metal wire and applying heat which would cause the base metal of the wire to oxidize, and so it required that the surface of the wire be coated with a flux (e.g., wine lees or natron) to prevent oxidation.

snuffer stand (1). Stand with snuffer and candle extinguisher, John Laughton, London, 1697. H. 17·8 cm. Courtesy, Brand Inglis Ltd, London.

snuffer stand (2). Stand with snuffer and candle extinguisher and removable chamber candlestick, 1688–9. City Art Gallery, Manchester.

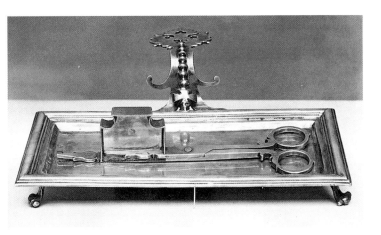

snuffer tray. Tray and snuffer, length 23 cm. Victoria and Albert Museum, London.

Sons of Liberty Bowl. Punch-bowl, Paul Revere II, Boston, 1768. W. 28 cm. Museum of Fine Arts, Boston, Mass.

solid silver. Metal consisting entirely of silver or a silver alloy (of any specified FINENESS), not of a base metal mechanically fused with silver (such as PLATED METAL) or SILVER-PLATED WARE.

solitaire service. A type of CABARET SERVICE for one person, often accompanied by a contemporary fitted travelling case. *See* TÊTE-À-TÊTE SERVICE.

Sons of Liberty Bowl. A PUNCH-BOWL of hemispherical shape with a slightly everted rim, resting on a two-tiered low circular base, undecorated except for engraved symbols and inscriptions, and known also as the 'Liberty Punch Bowl' and 'The Rescinders Bowl'. It was made by PAUL REVERE II in 1768, on order of the fifteen fellow-members of the Sons of Liberty, to commemorate the defiance of George III, on the eve of the American Revolution, by the 92 members of the Massachusetts Bay House of Representatives who had voted on 30 June 1768 against rescinding a letter hostile to the king (the vote resulting in the dissolution of the body), and affirming their support for John Wilkes (1727–97), English political leader and journalist, and the 45th issue, published in 1763, of his paper (the *North Briton*), which had attacked the royal policy of suppressing Colonial government (as a result of which Wilkes was imprisoned, although later elected to Parliament). The bowl weighs 45 oz. and holds 45 gills (the number being symbolic of the 45th issue). The bowl is engraved on one side with an inscription dedicating it to the 92 members, and on the obverse with a circle in which is engraved 'No. 45' and 'Wilkes and Liberty', and a torn General Warrant (the illegal warrant of 1765 that led to the imprisonment of Wilkes), with attached to the circle flags inscribed 'Magna Carta' and 'Bill of Rights', slogans of Wilkes's fight; encircling the rim of the bowl are the engraved names of the fifteen members. The bowl, 28 cm wide, is in the Museum of Fine Arts, Boston, Massachusetts, and has a donative inscription encircling the base just below the bowl. A number of copies have been made. *See* CROSBY CUP; 'I-LOVE-LIBERTY' SPOON.

Sophia Magdalena Toilet Service. A silver-gilt TOILET SERVICE made in London by Daniel Smith and Robert Sharp, 1779, consisting of seventeen pieces decorated in ADAM STYLE. It has been traditionally said (but not established) that it was made for Queen Sophia Magdalena of Sweden, wife of Gustavus III, 1771–92, and eldest sister of Christian VII of Denmark (1749–1818), hence the sister-in-law of Caroline Mathilda, for whom the CAROLINE MATHILDA TOILET SERVICE had been made in 1760. The service is in the local Gustavian style (similar to the French Louis XVI style). It is now in the Livrustkammaren (Royal Armoury) of the Nordiska Museum, Stockholm.

soufflé-dish. A type of DISH in which to serve a soufflé, being circular with vertical sides. A silver example, 1851, having a glass liner (in which the soufflé was cooked) to be inserted into the serving dish, is among the plate of the Honourable Society of Lincoln's Inn, London.

soup-bowl. (1) A type of shallow BOWL for serving a thick soup, such as a cream soup or bisque. It is either without handles or has small lug handles; it is usually accompanied by a matching SAUCER, and some examples have a

COVER. *See* SOUP-CUP; SOUP-PLATE; ÉCUELLE. (2) A circular type of SOUP-TUREEN, not often found; a rare known example rests on a stand equipped with a heating lamp.

soup-cup. A type of CUP for serving bouillon or consommé. It is shallow, without a COVER, and has two vertical side handles, and is usually accompanied by a matching SAUCER. Sometimes called a 'bouillon-cup'. *See* SOUP-PLATE; SOUP-BOWL; ÉCUELLE.

soup ladle. A type of LADLE used for serving soup from a SOUP-TUREEN and usually decorated EN SUITE. It has a circular bowl and a long handle, that is slightly curved and widens toward the top. The style of the handle varies, often conforming to the FLATWARE (e.g., the ONSLOW PATTERN), but luxurious examples have an ornamental terminal, sometimes in the form of the head of a bird or animal.

soup-plate. A type of circular PLATE having a shallow WELL, usually surrounded by a MARLI (ledge). The diameter is about 25 cm. Such plates are used for serving individual portions of various types of soup; but *see* SOUP-CUP; SOUP-BOWL; ÉCUELLE.

soup spoon. A type of SPOON, having a circular bowl, used with a SOUP-PLATE; a smaller spoon, called a BOUILLON SPOON, is used with a SOUP-BOWL or SOUP-CUP.

soup-tureen. A type of large TUREEN from which to serve soup into a SOUP-PLATE. It is usually oval or circular, sometimes CANOE-SHAPED (a few American examples are rectangular), having a domed cover with an ornamental or ring FINIAL (often held in place by a nut-and-bolt rather than affixed by SOLDERING). It generally rests on a spreading foot or on four short legs with ornamental feet, and is sometimes accompanied by a supporting stand (*see* SOUP-TUREEN WITH STAND). There are usually two horizontal handles, but sometimes there are vertical loop handles, and occasionally DROP-RING HANDLES, figural handles or scroll handles, always affixed at the narrow ends of the tureen. The rim is usually level, but sometimes is dipped or curved. Some such tureens are provided with a TUREEN LINER. A few examples are of great weight, being decorated with massive applied mounts and masks. Some silver tureens are gilded, and some are decorated with applied figures of marine forms to suggest the intended use for fish soup (*see* FISH-SOUP TUREEN) or with appropriate motifs for game soup. Rare examples are in fantasy shape to suggest the use (*see* TURTLE TUREEN). Soup-tureens have been made in pairs. The earliest-known English piece is said to be one by ANTHONY NELME, 1703. An important collection of soup-tureens is in the Campbell Museum, Camden, New Jersey. *See* Catalogue, *Selections from the Campbell Museum Collection* (4th ed., 1978). *See* GRIFFIN SOUP-TUREEN; SOUP LADLE.

soup-tureen with stand. (1) A type of SOUP-TUREEN that rests on an accompanying flat-bottomed stand, usually of conforming shape and style of decoration. The stand usually has two loop handles at the narrow ends. An unusual example has in the centre a STEPPED circular plinth to support the tureen, the base of which fits securely over the top of the plinth. (2) A type of soup-tureen that rests on a stand in which there is a heating device such as a spirit lamp. Such tureens were generally of the circular rather than the oval form so as to rest on a circular stand, usually supported by three legs. *See* YORK, DUKE OF, SOUP-TUREENS.

Southampton Tazza. A silver-gilt TAZZA, said to be the finest known example bearing an English hallmark. The interior of the bowl is completely decorated, within a narrow border of STRAPWORK and ARABESQUES, with a REPOUSSÉ and chased scene depicting the meeting of Isaac and Rebecca; the exterior is chased with bunches of fruit, and has an engraved border with depictions of animals, insects, and fish. The vase-shaped stem is chased with fruit, and the domed foot is decorated with marine monsters. The piece, by an unidentified maker, bears an English date mark for 1567. It has been said that the workmanship shows Dutch or German influence; the piece was probably made by an immigrant worker, or the central plaque may have been imported and mounted in England. It is owned by St Michael's church, Southampton.

souvenir spoon. A type of SPOON made in innumerable forms, styles, and sizes, mainly to satisfy a souvenir-collecting craze that raged in the United States in the 1890s. The terminal (and sometimes the interior of the bowl) usually featured some state, city, geographical landmark or public building,

soup-tureen. Tureen and ladle from the Thanet Service, Paul de Lamerie, London, 1743. W. (of tureen) 40 cm. Courtesy, Sotheby's, London.

soup-tureen with stand (1). Tureen and stand with central plinth, Paul Storr, London, 1816–17. W. (of stand) 48·5 cm. Campbell Museum, Camden, N.J.

but some featured regional events, exhibitions, holidays, fraternal organizations, actors, prominent persons, Apostles, the Salem witch, American Indians, flowers, as well as a limitless variety of other motifs. Only earlier souvenir spoons, such as those made to commemorate the wedding or the 1689 coronation of William and Mary, are of interest to serious collectors. But thousands of collectors seek varieties of those made in the 1890s, and some varieties in the 20th century. There were early United States examples from the period 1850–70, but the fad developed *c.* 1890, when examples were made in great number and variety by the GORHAM COMPANY and TIFFANY & CO., as well as dozens of smaller manufacturers. The spoons were made of silver or were SILVER-PLATED WARE, with plain or gilded bowls, and some with decoration of enamelling or engraving; they were produced by DIE-STAMPING, SAND CASTING or CIRE PERDUE casting. The same kind of terminal was used on various types of spoon, and sometimes bowls and handles were joined interchangeably, all adding to the choice available to collectors. Some handles were made with the entire stem, not merely the terminal, in fantasy form. *See* Dorothy T. Rainwater and Danna H. Felger, *American Spoons: Souvenir and Historical* (1977). *See* INDIAN (AMERICAN) SPOONS.

Sovereign's Head Mark. The same as the DUTY MARK.

soy-bottle. A type of small bottle for serving soy (an oriental sauce made from soy beans and other ingredients) or other pungent sauce. It was usually made of faceted glass, having a narrow neck and a glass stopper, but some have silver MOUNTS. Such bottles are sometimes accompanied by a CRUET LABEL bearing the name of one of the ten or more varieties of such sauces, but some have engraved on them the name of the contents, e.g., catsup, anchovy, kyan, quin, chilivin, lemon, etc. They were made in PAIRS or SETS, and were usually provided with a SOY STAND.

soy stand. A type of stand or frame used to hold a number of SOY-BOTTLES, from six to ten, each containing a different sauce, including soy. It has a wire frame (with rings to hold the individual bottles in place) standing on a footed platform (varying in shape) and having a tall central pillar topped by a loop or a ring for carrying. A variant type had provision for three bottles in a row on an oval platform. Some frames were made of heavy wood, topped and edged with a silver plate. The frames often provided, in addition to the bottle-rings, rings for a MUSTARD-POT or other receptacles, and sometimes rings for the stoppers when removed. Some are provided with faceted glass bottles, each having a CRUET LABEL or the engraved name of the contents. *See* G. Bernard Hughes, 'Soy Frames for Georgian Sauce' in *Country Life*, 1 August 1968, p. 296. *See* CRUET STAND; CRUET STAND/SOY STAND.

soy stand. Stand and glass soy-bottles with silver mounts and labels, London, 1808. L. 20·5 cm. Goldsmiths' Company, London.

Speaker's Plate. Articles of silverware furnished to the Speaker of the House of Commons and traditionally retained by him after retirement as an allowance and a perquisite of office, the amount retained being up to a specified maximum in weight. *See* SPEAKER'S WINE COOLER.

Speaker's Wine Cooler. A very large WINE COOLER of the type sometimes called a 'cistern'. The body, of oval BOMBÉ shape, has a dipped gadrooned rim, and is supported by four scroll feet; it has two horizontal loop handles. Standing with fore feet on the rim of the bowl and hind feet on the handles

Speaker's Wine Cooler. Oval *bombé* shape, Thomas Heming, London, 1770. L. 1·38 m. Courtesy, Christie's, London.

are figures in-the-round of the Royal Supporters (the crowned lion and the unicorn). On one side of the bowl, above a band of grapes, leaves, and scroll ornaments, is engraved the Royal Arms of George III with the Garter motto and crown, flanked by the initials 'GR', and on the other side the arms of Sir John Cust, the intended recipient of the piece (who died before it was completed), for whom it was to have been part of his allowance as retiring Speaker of the House of Commons (*see* SPEAKER'S PLATE). The piece, made by THOMAS HEMING, 1770, was loaned by descendants of Cust to the House of Commons Dining Room in 1951, then returned to the owner, Lord Brownlow, who kept it at his seat, Belton House, Grantham, Lincolnshire (hence it is sometimes called the 'Belton Wine Cooler'); it was sold at Christie's, London, on 29 May 1963.

spectroscopic emission. A process used in ASSAYING articles containing silver (or gold) of high purity where the methods of CUPELLATION or SCORIFICATION are not suitable. It involves the use of an electric current, known as 'arc excitation', a technique developed in 1874 by Lockyer and Roberts.

speculum (aural). A medical instrument (auriscope) used for dilating and examining the ear. Examples of the Brunton type, *c.* 1862–1900, were made in silver with several alternative ear-pieces. *See* MEDICAL SILVERWARE.

speech stand. A device used by a speaker or lecturer to hold before him the manuscript of his speech while he reads it. An example in the form of a square of glass set in a silver-gilt frame and supported by a stand (its height being adjustable to suit the speaker) is at the Mansion House, London.

speech timer. A type of HOURGLASS used to indicate the end of the time allotted to a speechmaker. An example at the Mansion House, London, is in the form of a silver frame supporting three hourglasses, each having sand of a different colour and timed for 10, 20, and 30 minutes, respectively, for use on varying occasions.

Spencer, Edward (1873–1938) A London designer of many forms of silverware. He founded the Artificers Guild, with headquarters in Conduit St, London, and a branch in Kings Parade, Cambridge. His work combined with silver many other materials, such as ivory, mother-of-pearl, shagreen, wood, and nuts. He had at one time a staff of forty. His work bears the mark of the Artificers Guild. Much of it is in ART NOUVEAU STYLE, although made towards the end of the period in which that style was in vogue.

spice-box. (1) A type of dining-table accessory in the form of a BOX, varying in shape and style, intended to hold spices. It is usually of oval or rectangular shape, with two or more compartments, having a centrally hinged lid or slides as covers. Some early examples (sometimes called and used as a SUGAR-BOX) have an outline in the shape of a scallop shell (*see* SCALLOP-SHELL SUGAR-BOX); the sides are vertical and the box rests on small scallop-shell feet, its hinged lid also being in the form of a scallop shell. Later examples include a large rectangular box, made of ivory or wood, that contains several rectangular spice-boxes. Some examples include a NUTMEG GRATER. A small spice-box was sometimes a part of a TRAVELLER'S DINING SET, used perhaps for salt and pepper. *See* DOUBLE-LIDDED BOX; BOX SALT. (2) An article used in Jewish ritual, in the form of a small box to contain spices and used in the home, not in a synagogue, on the evening of the Sabbath, to give out pleasant scent as an augury for the coming week. Often an ordinary CASTER was used for the purpose, but there are some such articles made in the form of a steeple with a pierced roof, at the top of which is a pennant or a ball. *See* JEWISH RITUAL SILVERWARE.

spigot. A type of valve or cock used to control the flow of liquid through a TAP, as found on some COFFEE-URNS, TEA-URNS, and WINE FOUNTAINS. They are often made of silver except that the handle is sometimes made of wood or ivory. *See* BARREL TAP; CHAMPAGNE SPIGOT.

spinning. A process of shaping silver HOLLOW WARE; the technique, employed since ancient times, was first used at Sheffield *c.* 1820. It involves holding a piece of flat sheet silver firmly with a smooth hand tool or roller and pressing it against a wooden form (chuck) having the inside dimensions of the intended article, while the piece rotates on a lathe. The metal is worked upward from the base to the top edge of the desired article. If the metal is not of sufficiently heavy GAUGE to produce a thick edge, then either the top edge may be lapped or WIRE may be soldered on to it to form a rim. This method has been used for silverware more than hollow casting (*see* CASTING), and also when the number of articles required did not justify the

speculum. Auriscope with ear-pieces, second half of 19th century. H. 10 cm. Wellcome Collection, Science Museum, London.

spice-box (1). Double box with nutmeg grater under handle, David Tanqueray, London, 1715. L. 17·5 cm. British Museum, London.

cost of making dies for STAMPING. Some articles made in England by spinning were produced from thin-gauge PLATED METAL imported in the 1820s-30s from France; in such ware the larger proportion of copper imparts a slightly pinkish hue to the silver surface.

spit post. A type of culinary accessory in the form of a post, used as one of a pair to support a horizontal roasting spit. Each post is supported by scrolls on a circular base and has at the top a horseshoe-shaped bracket upon which to rest the spit; slots, grips, and thumbpieces are on the post to support a carving dish. An example made by THOMAS HEMING, 1770, was sold at Sotheby's, New York, on 14 February 1985. A pair made in 1784 by Aldridge & Green, London, were referred to, in contemporary ledgers of PARKER & WAKELIN (*see* JOHN PARKER), as a 'beef machine', this term being used also in 1971 when the pieces were shown by Asprey & Co. at the Grosvenor House Antiques Fair, London. Sometimes called a 'joint holder'.

spittoon. A cuspidor (sometimes called a 'spitting bowl'), usually globular with a wide flaring rim or a high funnel-shaped mouth, and generally with one side handle. A few examples from the 18th century, of silver or silver gilt, are known. Two examples were recorded by Samuel Pepys in June 1685 as being owned by him. Bowls of other shape and style may have been used for the same purpose, but are not usually so designated.

splayd. A type of eating implement developed in recent years that combines the functions of a knife, fork, and spoon and is intended for casual meals, such as at buffets and picnics, and while watching television. Shaped like a spoon, it has three tines and at the right-hand side a vertical blade. They were originally made of stainless steel, but examples are also being made in plated silver. Also called a 'party fork'.

splayed. Flared or spreading, as in the case of the FOOT of a CANDLESTICK or a VASE which has a diameter larger at the base than above.

sponge-box. A type of receptacle for a toilet sponge, being about 10 cm in diameter, in the form of a sphere divided horizontally midway, the lower half resting on a spreading base and the upper half being a hinged lid having a pattern of pierced work. *See* SOAP-BOX.

sponsor's mark. (1) In the United Kingdom, a MAKER'S MARK punched on a piece of silverware, not by its maker, but by a friendly silversmith who, when the maker was a foreigner not entitled to submit his work, sponsored the piece by presenting it to the ASSAY OFFICE for the necessary HALLMARKS to be added. (2) Under the system of CONVENTION HALLMARKS, the mark of the maker or of a firm which engaged him to produce a piece and placed its own mark on it instead of the maker's mark.

spoon. A type of household implement used (depending on the form and size) for serving, stirring, basting, eating, etc., and consisting of a shallow bowl (usually oval, sometimes circular) and a handle (varying in length, curvature, and style of decoration). From about the 1660s to the 1760s the stem curved in the same direction as the bowl, but thereafter, with the advent of spoons made in the OLD ENGLISH PATTERN, the stem curved in the opposite direction to the bowl, so that when the spoon is laid on a table both the bottom of the bowl and the terminal of the stem are in contact with the surface and the spoon is in a balanced position; hence on later spoons the decoration is on the front of the handle. Depending on the shape, size, and use, spoons include the types known as BASTING SPOON, BOUILLON SPOON, CADDY SPOON, COFFEE SPOON, DESSERT SPOON, EGG SPOON, GRAVY SPOON, ICED-TEA SPOON, MARROW SPOON, SALT SPOON, SERVING SPOON, SIFTER SPOON, SOUP SPOON, STUFFING SPOON, TABLESPOON, TEASPOON, LADLE, MOTE SKIMMER, TEA STRAINER. The styles of spoons vary tremendously, especially in the shape of the stem, the decoration on the bowl, and the form of the terminal. A great many styles have been given special names, including the ACORN SPOON, APOSTLE SPOON, BALUSTER-TOP SPOON, BERRY SPOON, BUDDHA SPOON, COFFIN-END SPOON, DIAMOND-POINT SPOON, DISC-END SPOON, DOG-NOSE SPOON, DROP SPOON, FANCY-BACK SPOON, HOOF SPOON, LACE-BACK SPOON, LETTER-FINIAL SPOON, LION-SEJANT SPOON, MAIDENHEAD SPOON, MOOR'S-HEAD SPOON, OWL SPOON, PICTURE-BACK SPOON, POPPY SPOON, PURITAN SPOON, RAT-TAIL SPOON, SAINT SPOON, SARACEN'S-HEAD SPOON, SEAL-TOP SPOON, SHELL-BACK SPOON, SLIPPED-STALK SPOON, STUMP-TOP SPOON, TICHBORNE SPOON, TRIFID SPOON, VIRGIN SPOON, WAVY-END SPOON, WODEWOSE SPOON. Spoons were sometimes related to a special occasion, such as a CORONATION SPOON, GUILD SPOON, FUNERAL SPOON, MEMORIAL SPOON, or SOUVENIR SPOON, and some, not distinguishable by their form, were for a special use, such as an ecclesiastical

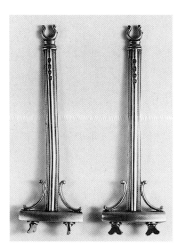
spit post. Pair of posts, Thomas Heming, London, 1770. H. 20·3 cm. Courtesy, Sotheby's, New York.

spoon-handle straps. Two-handled cup, Pierre Platel, London, 1705. H. 25·5 cm. Ashmolean Museum, Oxford.

spout cap. Teapot with cap connected to finial, Benjamin Pyne, London, *c.* 1690. H. 16·4 cm. Ashmolean Museum, Oxford.

STRAINER SPOON or a CHALICE SPOON. The patterns of some spoons have distinctive names, based on the shape and style of the handle, e.g., FIDDLE PATTERN, Old English Pattern, ONSLOW PATTERN, and dozens of others, both old and modern. *See* FIG-SHAPED; HANDLE; MEDICAL SPOON; FOLDING SPOON; M(O)USTACHE SPOON. *See* G. E. P. How and J. P. How, *English and Scottish Silver Spoons* (3 vols., 1952–7); Michael Snodin, *English Silver Spoons* (1974); Victor Houart, *Antique Spoons* (1982).

spoon-handle straps. Relief decorative motifs in the form of spoon handles applied vertically in a row encircling the lower part of the body of some EWERS, HELMET JUGS, TWO-HANDLED CUPS, and STANDING CUPS. Frequently the motifs are alternately large and small, and sometimes the larger ones have varying decoration.

spoon stand. A footed BOWL in the centre of which is a column with a pierced gallery in which to suspend spoons.

spoon tray. A type of small oblong TRAY, oval or rectangular, used as a receptacle for TEASPOONS (especially before TEACUPS were accompanied by a SAUCER) or for a MOTE SKIMMER. Such trays resemble a SNUFFER TRAY, but usually have less ornate decoration, ordinarily only a moulded rim.

spoon warmer. A type of dinner-table utensil for keeping warm the bowl of a STUFFING SPOON or a SERVING SPOON, being in the form of a hollow receptacle with a shaped opening, the bowl of the spoon to be inserted through the opening into hot water in the receptacle. Some silver examples are in the form of a barrel having an opening at one end and resting on a rock-shaped base.

spout. The tubular protuberance through which the liquid contents of a pot is poured or sometimes drunk. Spouts occur in many forms, including those that are straight, ATTENUATED, curved or swan-necked. Sometimes the LIP of the spout has a somewhat animalistic form, e.g., DUCK'S-HEAD SPOUT. *See* LIP SPOUT; SWAN-NECK SPOUT; SPOUT FLAP; SPOUT CUP.

spout cap. A small covering for the mouth of the SPOUT on some TEAPOTS and COFFEE-POTS to prevent the loss of heat. It is removable manually but is safeguarded against loss by being connected by a chain to the finial on the lid of the pot. *See* SPOUT FLAP.

spout cup (or **spout pot**). A type of drinking vessel that usually has a cylindrical or pear-shaped body resting on a FOOT-RING, a flat base or a splayed foot, and characterized by having a thin, swan-neck, tapering SPOUT extending upward and outward from near the base and rising to slightly above the rim (similar to glazed-earthenware or glass cups with such spouts). The spout was so placed to enable a person to drink the posset (*see* POSSET-CUP) or the caudle (*see* CAUDLE-CUP) in the lower part of the vessel. Rare examples have a SPOUT CAP. Such cups usually have a single SCROLL HANDLE, set at right-angles to the spout, but some have two side handles. They usually have a hinged lid or removable cover, flat or high-domed, with a small finial. The type with a fixed cover extending over only the front half of the mouth is usually called a FEEDING CUP. One known example has an interior strainer at the base of the spout, confirming its intended use for drinking posset or caudle. *See* V. Isabelle Miller, 'American Silver Spout Cups' in *Antiques*, August 1943, p. 73; G. Bernard Hughes, 'Old English Spout Cups' in *Country Life*, 17 January 1957, p. 98. *See* SPOUT TANKARD; MEDICAL SILVERWARE.

spout flap. A small swinging flap, hinged at the top of the SPOUT of some TEAPOTS and COFFEE-POTS, which opens automatically during pouring but when the pot is not tilted it remains closed to prevent the loss of heat. *See* SPOUT CAP.

spout tankard. An unusual type of TANKARD having a thin curved SPOUT similar to that of a SPOUT CUP, and having one scroll handle and a hinged lid. An example bearing the mark of Timothy Skottowe, Norwich, 1642–3, is in the Victoria and Albert Museum, London.

Sprimont, Nicholas (1716–71). Known principally as a founder (with Charles Gouyn), *c.*1745, of the porcelain factory at Chelsea, London, and as a modeller there, he was also a silversmith and made silverware that anticipated his work as a porcelain modeller. He was a Huguenot, born in Liège, Belgium, and was apprenticed to his uncle, Nicholas Joseph Sprimont, a silversmith there; he emigrated before November 1742 to England, and became a resident of Chelsea. In 1743 he registered his only mark, his address

spout cup. Pear-shaped body, Benjamin Hiller, Boston, Mass., *c.* 1725–35. H. 14·5 cm. Yale University Art Gallery (Mabel Brady Garvan Collection), New Haven, Conn.

spout flap. Coffee-pot with hinged lid and cut-card decoration, William Lukin, London, 1702. H. 23·5 cm. Folger's Coffee Collection, Procter & Gamble Co., Cincinnati, Ohio.

Sprimont, Nicholas. Cake-basket, fixed bail handle, London, 1745. L. 44·5 cm. Ashmolean Museum, Oxford.

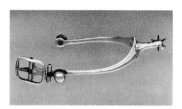

spur. Steel, close plated, with small rowel, Benjamin Cartwright, London, 1772–3. Colonial Williamsburg, Va.

square coffee-pot. Pouring beak and removable handle, George Wickes, London, 1745. H. 20 cm. Folger's Coffee Collection, Procter & Gamble Co., Cincinnati, Ohio.

being a house and shop that he rented in Compton St, Soho, from 1743 to 1748, but by 1747 he lived at Monmouth House, Lawrence St, Chelsea. By 1745 the porcelain factory had started and he was proprietor, *c.* 1745–71; *c.* 1748 he apparently ceased working as a silversmith. A few surviving large and imposing pieces of silverware in ROCOCO STYLE are attributed to him, e.g., the NEPTUNE CENTREPIECE, a pair of marine-decorated SALTS, 1742, dishes, and SAUCE-BOATS, 1743–4, all in the Royal Collection; the ASHBURN-HAM CENTREPIECE and the CRESPIN TUREEN; and a TEA KETTLE, 1745, in the Hermitage, Leningrad. Several of his silver pieces are decorated with naturalistic motifs, such as reptiles and shells, in the style of Bernard Palissy; and some silver pieces were copied in porcelain at the Chelsea pottery. He was sponsored (*see* SPONSOR'S MARK) by PAUL CRESPIN, his friend and neighbour, who may have worked on some pieces that Sprimont made. *See* Arthur G. Grimwade, 'Crespin or Sprimont? An unsolved problem of Rococo silver' in *Apollo*, August 1969, p. 126.

spur. An article of RIDING EQUIPMENT, fitted with a small wheel (rowel), to be secured to the heel of a horseman. Examples made of silver are known from days of knighthood until the mid-19th century; some are of steel with CLOSE PLATING of silver, with the rowels (of various sizes) made of steel, and with leather straps and cradle, and with silver chains and BUCKLES. Such spurs were a speciality of Walsall, Staffordshire, a town noted for making harness hardware. Small-size spurs were made for women. (A pair of gold spurs, made for Charles II in 1661, are in the Royal Regalia.) *See* COCK-FIGHTING SPURS.

square coffee-pot. A type of COFFEE-POT having a square horizontal section. A rare example was made by GEORGE WICKES, London, 1745; it has a BEAK instead of a SPOUT, and the handle is removable, being held in place by two pins attached by short chains to the FERRULES.

square handle. A type of HANDLE found on some TEAPOTS, SUGAR-BOWLS, etc.; it has three straight sides and a short upper vertical section, all meeting at right-angles. The upper vertical section and the lower horizontal side are affixed separately to the body of the piece, with the horizontal side terminating in an outward curve extending below the point where it is affixed. *See* TAU HANDLE.

Stabler, Harold (1872–1945). A London silversmith and industrial designer, well known for the ceramic tiles he designed for London Transport. He was a leading exponent of the ART DECO STYLE in silverware. He featured the application of coloured enamels to CASKETS, using especially opaque blue enamel in connection with interwoven patterns of NIELLO work or ENGRAVING. He designed many pieces, including PRESENTATION CUPS, executed by WAKELY & WHEELER LTD for the Goldsmiths' & Silversmiths' Co., London, and worked in association with their craftsmen, such as the eminent chaser, B.J. Colson. He joined Llewellyn Rathbone in Liverpool and later taught in London. His late work revealed Chinese influence. He designed prototypes for pieces of stainless steel for Firth Vickers, but they were not produced commercially. *See* EDWARD VIII CUP.

staff. A type of pole (wand or rod), usually of wood with a silver FERRULE surmounted by a silver ornament bearing an inscription or emblematic decoration and carried by a church, university or corporate functionary as a symbol of office. Such a staff is carried in an upright position and is long enough to touch the ground, unlike the shorter MACE, BATON, and SCEPTRE. *See* BEADLE'S STAFF; CROSIER; PORTER'S STAFF; TIPSTAFF; VERGE.

Stalingrad Sword. The SWORD presented on behalf of George VI to the citizens of Stalingrad (now Volgograd) to commemorate the Russian defeat of the German forces there in World War II. It is in the form of a two-handed crusader's sword, 1·26 m long, with a dedication in English and Russian engraved on its two-edged steel blade. The grip is bound with 18-carat gold wire, with ferrules of red-enamelled silver. The pommel is a carved crystal secured by a gold rose. The quillon is of wrought silver terminating with leopard's heads. The chape (point) has a gilt flame motif. The scabbard is of red morocco leather, bound with silver lockets, between which are three red stars set in silver-gilt frames radiating gold rays. The sword resulted from collaboration of a team, co-ordinated by the Goldsmiths' Company, London, headed by eighteen craftsmen, including REGINALD Y. GLEADOWE (winner of the design competition) as designer and LESLIE G. DURBIN (who made the quillons and scabbard fittings). The design was approved by George VI and the sword, after being displayed in many British cities, was presented by Churchill to Stalin, at the Teheran Conference, on 29 November 1943, and was delivered in Moscow on 2 February 1944 to a deputation from the city of Stalingrad.

stamped repoussé. A type of relief decoration executed by STAMPING, the result having the appearance of EMBOSSING or REPOUSSÉ work.

stamping. The process of making a complete relief pattern on silver or other metal by forcing, by a blow of a hammer, a PUNCH with the desired pattern in relief (cameo or male) into a metal sheet placed over a corresponding depressed (intaglio or female) mould, or vice versa. This process, unlike the hand-done REPOUSSÉ process, permits the making of a number of identical objects, and was an early method of mass-production. The process was used in ancient Greece for metalwork, and also during the Renaissance period in the 16th century; it was highly developed in the 19th century to make mass-produced articles. It is now done by DIE STAMPING or by a mechanical process of MACHINE STAMPING. It was introduced in England for silver in the third quarter of the 18th century, first for making decorated buttons, then other articles, and particularly for candlesticks of SHEFFIELD PLATE which were stamped in several parts, soldered together, and then loaded with resin to provide stability. *See* STAMPED REPOUSSÉ.

stand. (1) A type of dinner-table or sideboard accessory that serves as a support for a BOWL, TEAPOT, COFFEE-POT, TEA-KETTLE, TEA-URN, SOUP-TUREEN or other receptacle for heated contents; it serves to protect the surface on which it stands from the heat of the contents. *See* DISH STAND; DISH RING; DISH CROSS. Although a flat WAITER was probably often so used, some stands were made expressly for the purpose, usually EN SUITE with the receptacle. Some such stands have, extending inward from their legs, arms for holding a warming device, e.g., a spirit lamp. *See* COFFEE-POT WITH STAND; TEA-KETTLE WITH STAND; SOUP-TUREEN WITH STAND; CHAFING DISH. (2) A tall floor pedestal upon which to rest a VASE or other ornamental object; an example, 1 m high, made of solid silver, 1665, is in the Royal Collection. Examples in some manor houses are made with a wooden core covered with silver.

standard hallmark. The HALLMARK punched on articles ot silver (or of gold) to attest the purity of the metal. In England the standard hallmark for STERLING SILVER was, from 1544 until 1822, the LION PASSANT GUARDANT HALLMARK (except for BRITANNIA SILVER from 1697 to 1720, when the BRITANNIA HALLMARK, being the HIGHER STANDARD HALLMARK, was used); in 1822 the LION PASSANT HALLMARK was introduced. The lion was crowned in the period 1544–49. The CONVENTION HALLMARK to attest standard is the numeral '925'. In Scotland, the Standard Hallmark at Edinburgh was the thistle from 1759 to 1975, when it was changed to the LION RAMPANT HALLMARK, and at Glasgow the Lion Rampant was used from 1819 to 1964. In Ireland the Harp Crowned has been used since 1637.

standing bowl. A type of BOWL that is supported by a stem and a FOOT. *See* SWAYTHLING BOWL.

square handle. Sugar-bowl, William B. Meyer, New York, *c.* 1820–8. H. 26·5 cm. Yale University Art Gallery (gift of Mrs William Crozier and William Williams), New Haven, Conn.

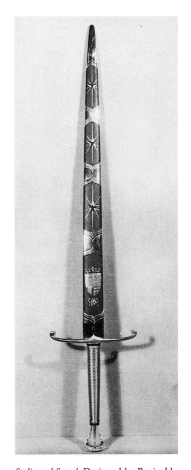

Stalingrad Sword. Designed by Reginald Y. Gleadowe, silver fittings made by Leslie Durbin, London, 1943. L. 1·26 m. Photo courtesy, Leslie Durbin.

standing cup. A type of tall CUP, usually about 40 to 75 cm high, having a bowl resting on a knopped or BALUSTER stem supported by a spreading or domed foot; the bowl is often cylindrical, but sometimes semi-ovoid, vase-shaped, inverted bell-shaped, or ogee-shaped, and usually has an elaborate decorated cover often with a figural finial. The lower part of the bowl is sometimes encircled by CALYX decoration or with applied SPOON-HANDLE STRAPS. Such cups, made in England from the 14th century, have traditionally been used for special ceremonial occasions, and many are owned by the London Livery Companies and by colleges. See GOURD-SHAPED 'STEEPLE CUP'; STEEPLE CUP; MELON CUP.

standing dish. A term sometimes used, incorrectly, in England to refer to a TAZZA (a drinking vessel and not a type of dish).

standing mazer. A type of MAZER of which the bowl rests upon a wide and usually plain stem (some are shaped and decorated) with a spreading base; the stem is sometimes detachable to allow the piece to be used as a bowl or a cup (sometimes called a MAZER CUP). Examples are the GALLOWAY MAZER, Craigievar Mazer, St Mary's Mazer, Fergusson Mazer, Tulloch Mazer, and the so-called St Leonard's Mazer (having a silver bowl). Such pieces were a speciality of 16th-century Scotland. See G. E. P. How, 'Scottish Standing Mazers' in *The Connoisseur*, May 1934, p. 313, and in *Proceedings of the Society of Antiquaries of Scotland*, lxviii, 1933-4.

standing salt. A tall and imposing receptacle for table salt. It is usually supported by several feet or legs or by a spreading foot, as distinguished from a low SALT-CELLAR which rests on small feet, a low TRENCHER SALT which rests flat on a SELF BASE, and a SALT CASTER which has a pierced COVER for sprinkling. The term includes examples of the massive and elaborate GREAT SALT and the more austere SCROLL SALT. See HOURGLASS SALT; STEEPLE SALT; CLOCK SALT; PEDESTAL SALT; COVERED STANDING SALT; ELIZABETH I SALT; DOUBLE SALT.

standing snuffer. A type of SNUFFER that rests vertically, ring-shaped handles upward, in a SNUFFER STAND. It has no supporting feet, unlike the usual TRAY SNUFFER.

standish (or **inkstandish**). The name, used before the 19th century, for an INKSTAND.

Stapley, Jack E. (1925–). A silverware designer and craftsman who attended the Royal College of Art, London, and taught at the Gravesend School of Art, Essex. He has a studio at Gravesend where he has made MACES and other ceremonial ware. See FESTIVAL OF BRITAIN ROSE-BOWL.

statuette. A type of ornament in the form of a free-standing full-length figure in-the-round, usually a PORTRAIT STATUETTE depicting royalty or a prominent historical character; some are standing figures (e.g., CHARLES II STATUETTE; GEORGE III STATUETTE; APOSTLE STATUETTES), and some equestrian (e.g., VICTORIA STATUETTE; ELIZABETH, PRINCESS, STATUETTE; GODIVA, LADY, STATUETTE; JOAN OF ARC STATUETTE; and WELLINGTON STATUETTE). Some such ornaments depict animals (see ANIMAL SILVERWARE) or birds (see BIRD SILVERWARE). A statuette is made as a complete article, unlike the attached figures that are part of the decoration of FIGURAL SILVERWARE. See GRENADIER GUARDSMAN STATUETTE; NANNY STATUETTE; SKELETON STATUETTE; COLUMBUS STATUE.

steak knife. A type of DINNER KNIFE that has a very sharp, slightly curved, and pointed steel blade.

steeple cup. A type of STANDING CUP having a domed cover surmounted by a tall finial in the form of a 3- or 4-sided pyramidal steeple with pierced or solid sides. Such cups, exclusively of English make, c. 1600–50, and not copied on the Continent, are often of silver gilt; they average about 45 cm in height, but range up to 90 cm. Although they are known in a great variety of styles of decoration (including overall ENGRAVING, CHASING, and EMBOSSING, as well as with SPOON-HANDLE STRAPS), they have been said (in an exhaustive review by Norman M. Penzer) to have four basic characteristics in common: (1) the bowl is of inverted conical or bell shape and, with the cover, forms an ovoid shape; (2) the cover is of low-domed shape with three (rarely, four) scrolled and cusped brackets, often decorated with a griffin's head, which support the pyramidal steeple that has at its peak a ball or spike, but sometimes a figure of a Roman soldier with a shield and spear or of St George and the Dragon; (3) the stem is short and of baluster shape with a central

steeple cup. Cup of typical form with three-sided pyramidal steeple finial, T. C. Mostyn, London, 1613. Wadsworth Atheneum (Elizabeth B. Miles Collection), Hartford, Conn.

knop, above and below which are collars; and (4) there is a high TRUMPET FOOT. Two groups of cups are said to be variations of the basic form: (1) those having a slender stem without a knop; and (2) those having a slender baluster stem, and also a bowl and cover that together are globe-shaped; the latter were perhaps originally WINE-CUPS with a cover added later. For another group including some examples with a steeple on the cover – not strictly steeple cups – *see* GOURD-SHAPED 'STEEPLE CUP'. It has been suggested that the steeple on all these cups, made principally in the late Elizabethan period and early years of James I's reign, symbolized the stable rule of such years; but a more likely source, according to Dr Penzer, is the steeple which, like early obelisks, had its basis in ancient symbolism and church architecture. The term 'pinnacle cup' was used for early examples of such cups, and the term 'steeple cup' was first recorded in 1909. An Index of 135 steeple, cups, prepared by Dr Penzer, was published in 1965 by the Society of Silver Collectors, London; about 150 are said to be extant today (including 16 in the Kremlin), despite the melting down of much silverware in the pre-Restoration period, 1650–60. A modern version of a steeple cup was made by C. R. ASHBEE in 1900. *See* Cyril G. E. Bunt, 'Note on English Steeple Cups' in *The Connoisseur*, March 1946, p. 17; Norman M. Penzer, 'The Steeple Cup' in *Apollo*, December 1959, p. 161, April 1960, p. 103, June 1960, p. 165, October 1960, p. 105, December 1960, p. 173, and July 1964, p. 44. *See* CHARING CUP; BODMIN CUP; CHESTER, RICHARD, CUP.

stepped. Jug with stepped foot, Henry Brind, London, 1743. H. 22·2 cm. Courtesy, Brand Inglis Ltd, London.

steeple double-salt. A type of STEEPLE SALT that has two salt-cellars, one above the other, supported by brackets. One such piece, London, 1599, is recorded. Two known extant examples each have an undecorated cylindrical spool-shaped body resting on three CLAW-AND-BALL FEET and a four-sided pyramidal-steeple finial supported by four brackets; one, London, 1620, is in the Irwin Untermyer Collection, at the Metropolitan Museum of Art, New York. *See* BEESTON SALT.

steeple salt. A type of COVERED STANDING SALT of which the cover has a finial in the form of a tall pyramidal steeple, in some cases resting on BRACKET supports; some rare examples have two tiers of such supports (*see* STEEPLE DOUBLE SALT). It was one of the last types of GREAT SALT to be made before such forms became obsolete *c.* 1625–50.

stepped. Having a series of adjacent graduated tiers, each diminishing in size as the tiers ascend, as in the case of a 'stepped foot', 'stepped lid' or 'stepped cover'. Sometimes called 'tiered' or 'terraced'. *See* GREAT SEAL OF IRELAND CUP; MOSTYN SALT; SOUP-TUREEN WITH STAND.

sterling silver. An ALLOY of silver and copper that in the United Kingdom has a FINENESS of 0·925 parts of silver and 0·075 parts of copper (in WEIGHT, 11·1 troy oz. of silver to 0·9 oz. copper). It was established as the legal standard for wrought silver in 1238, and in 1300 the requirement for the use of a HALLMARK was introduced by Edward I in order to prevent fraud on the part of unscrupulous goldsmiths, the mark being the LEOPARD'S HEAD HALLMARK. In the United States the legal standard for sterling silver, introduced by Charles Tiffany in 1852 for silverware sold by TIFFANY & CO., and later adopted by the Government, is 0·921 parts of silver; but no hallmarks are legally required. The word 'sterling' is said to be derived from the name enacted in 1343 for the English silver penny, called formerly an 'e(a)sterling' after the Germans ('Easterlings') who, early in the 13th century, had been brought in by King John to refine silver for coins.

Sterne Cup. Silver gilt, London, 1673–4. H. 19·7 cm. Victoria and Albert Museum, London.

Sterne Cup. A silver-gilt SMALL TWO-HANDLED CUP (sometimes called a POSSET-POT or a PORRINGER) of BALUSTER form, with two debased CARYATID HANDLES and a flat low-domed cover having a turned finial. It is inscribed 'The Gift of King Charles the Second to Arch-Bishop Sterne Lord Almoner', and bears the London mark for 1673–4. It was purchased in 1925 for the Victoria and Albert Museum, London.

stew pan. A type of culinary utensil in the form of a shallow circular pan, sometimes with two lateral uplifted handles. Such pans were usually made of a base metal for kitchen use, but a silver example made by SIMON PANTIN I, 1716, is at Ickworth Lodge, Bury St Edmunds, Suffolk.

stick. A type of BATON, carried as a symbol of office, e.g., those carried on formal occasions by the officers of the Royal Household known as Gold-Stick-in-Waiting and Silver-Stick-in-Waiting (offices instituted in 1678 by Charles II with responsibility for the daytime safety of the Sovereign). Such Sticks are made of ebony, with a long gold or silver FERRULE on the foot and a short gold or silver head with the cipher of the reigning Sovereign: Gold

stirrup cup. Head of fox, Asprey & Co., London, 1977. L. 15·4 cm. Courtesy, Asprey & Co. Ltd, London.

Sticks are 1·12 m in length, and Silver Sticks 91·5 cm. New Sticks were issued in each successive reign until that of Queen Victoria, 1837–1901 (hence, each of the Sticks is use today bears the monogram of a previous Sovereign).

One example of a Silver Stick, with London hallmark for 1820–1, was issued in 1821 (in the reign of George IV) to Sir Robert Hill, Lt-Colonel of the Household Cavalry; in 1953, a descendant, Miss Emily C. Hill, presented it to the Household Cavalry. Another silver example, used in the reign of George II, 1727–60, and a Gold Stick from the reign of William IV, 1830–7, made by John Linnet, 1831, for GARRARD & CO., were in the art collection of Urban Hanlon Broughton (1857–1929), who moved it in 1926 to Anglesey Abbey, near Cambridge; following the death of his elder son, the 1st Baron Fairhaven (1896–1966), the Abbey, together with the art collection, were acquired by the National Trust, and the two Sticks were donated to the Household Cavalry (which also owns several others). The three examples noted above are kept at the Household Cavalry Museum, Windsor; they are still carried on formal occasions.

stippled. A form of decoration made by engraving a pattern of massed dots as distinguished from lines, often serving on silverware as a ground for an inscription, the letters of which form a plain reserve. *See* WELFORD CUP; HOWARD GRACE CUP; PRICKING; POUNCE; MATTING.

stirrup. A horseman's foot-rest, used as an aid in mounting and a support while riding. A silver example in the Royal Collection may have been made as a HORSE-RACING TROPHY rather than for actual use. *See* RIDING EQUIPMENT.

stirrup cup. A type of drinking vessel in the form of an animal head, an adaptation of the ancient Greek rhyton. It is without a handle and has no foot, hence cannot be stood except when inverted to rest on its rim when not in use (unless placed in a STIRRUP-CUP FRAME). Such cups usually have at the closed end the head (mask) in-the-round of a fox (with ears laid back or pricked), but sometimes the head of a different animal. (Strictly, the term refers to the final drink taken by a mounted rider to hounds about to depart for the chase, but by extension it has come to apply also to the special type of drinking vessel which is sometimes used on such occasions.) The term was first recorded in the 1760s, but such cups have later sometimes been called a 'fox-head drinking cup'. The size varies, small for a dram and larger for punch. The mid-19th-century examples are more realistically modelled than earlier ones. Some bear on the neckband an appropriate inscription. Similar cups have been made, sometimes as a sporting TROPHY, in the form of the head of, e.g., a boar (by John S. Hunt, 1846), a bulldog or foxhound (by James Barclay, 1877–80), a hare (by William Simmons, 1777, and by Emes and Barnard, 1809), a greyhound (by Edward Thompson, 1820), a horse (for Thomas & Co., London, 1924), and a stag (by John S. Hunt, 1864, and by Paul Storr, 1834). An unusual set of such cups, in the form of stag hoofs, was made by John Robins, London, 1802. *See* G. Bernard Hughes, 'Silver Stirrup Cups' in *Country Life*, 19 January 1956, p. 106; Judith Banister, 'Cups of the Chase' in *Country Life*, 1 December 1977, p. 1613.

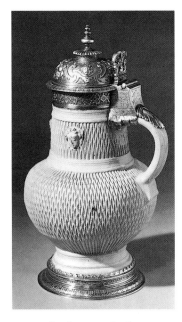

stoneware jug. Stoneware jug from Siegburg with English mounts, *c.* 1580. H. 23·2 cm. Courtesy, Asprey & Co. Ltd, London.

stirrup-cup frame. A type of floor-standing rack in the form of a central pole, with a tripod base, from which extend a number of tiers of branching arms terminating in circular holders; in each holder can be suspended upright a glass STIRRUP CUP of the type that has a ball base and hence can be stood up only when inverted. An example with a silver rack, 58·5 cm high, with four tiers of rings to hold up to thirty-one cups, was made by Edward Aldridge & Co., London, 1760. The form may have been suggested by the Dutch polycandelon (made to be hung from the ceiling and having rings in which to suspend up to twelve point-tipped glass cone-beakers that serve as oil lamps). Sometimes called a 'tumbler frame', but tumblers can be stood upright on a flat surface and need not be so suspended.

Stoke Prior Hoard. A HOARD comprising seven pieces of English silver, consisting of STANDING CUPS and TRENCHER SALTS, found in 1893 in a rabbit burrow at Stoke Prior, Worcestershire. The pieces, variously dated between 1578 and 1740, are believed to have been hidden after a theft. Some are now in the Victoria and Albert Museum, London.

stoneware jug. A type of JUG, made of stoneware, that has MOUNTS of English silver or silver gilt. Such pieces, which are generally in the form of TIGERWARE JUGS, include: (1) jugs from Siegburg, Germany, imported into England in the 16th century by Protestant refugees from the Rhineland, having a white body decorated with an overall relief DIAPER PATTERN of network, sometimes extending upward to cover the neck, and having on the neck relief female masks (two very similar examples, both *c.*1580, are known, one in the Victoria and Albert Museum, London, and the other, silver gilt, in the Untermyer Collection in the Metropolitan Museum of Art, New York, differing mainly in the diaper pattern on the body and in the engraving on the mounts, especially the engraved birds on the BOX HINGES for the lids); and (2) jugs made in England at Wrotham and elsewhere in Kent, and at Nottingham, similar to the Siegburg jugs, having a body with comparable network decoration or having a shorter and plain-coloured body. *See* MALLING JUG; POTTERY OBJECTS; MOUNTED OBJECTS.

Stonyhurst Salt. A GREAT SALT having a domed circular base from which extend upward four jewelled silver-gilt scroll brackets (two surmounted by crystal rods) surrounding an octagonal crystal cylinder which encloses a silver rod. The cylinder is surmounted by the domed crystal base upon which rests the covered silver receptacle for salt, the cover having a high knopped finial resting on another crystal. The piece originally included in its decoration ten crystals (four now missing) and 52 rubies and carbuncles, said to have been salvaged from a reliquary of *c.* 1200; it was probably made from melted-down silver parts left over from some 15th-century ecclesiastical plate that had been transformed into parts for a secular piece at the time of the Reformation. It bears on several of the silver parts the London hallmark of 1577 and the maker's mark 'IR' (probably for John Robinson, d. 1591) with, between them, flowers in a shaped shield (an unidentified mark not elsewhere recorded). There has been a long-standing tradition, now discredited, that in 1794 the salt was at Stonyhurst, Lancashire (a Jesuit college, founded at St Omer, France, moved to Bruges in 1762, to Liège in 1773, and to Stonyhurst in 1794), when the house there was given to the Society of Jesus by a Catholic former St Omer pupil, Thomas Weld of Lulworth, a descendant of the family that had built Stonyhurst; however, a 1914 letter mentions a letter (now missing) from the unknown donor of the salt stating that he was a Protestant, hence he was not Weld. There are no extant records to establish when or how Stonyhurst acquired the salt except a mention, in another 1914 letter, of a now missing document that referred to the college's acquisition of the salt at least 100 years previously. The salt was unrecorded until it appeared in the catalogue of the Park Lane, London, Exposition of 1929. Being regarded as secular plate, it was sold by the Rector of Stonyhurst on 3 June 1914, and came into the possession of Sir John Noble, Bt; it was sold by Noble at Christie's, London, on 19 June 1957, and was purchased in 1958 by the British Museum. *See* Hugh Tait, 'The "Stonyhurst" Salt' in *Apollo*, April 1964, p. 270.

stork scissors. A type of small SCISSORS having the handles shaped like the body of a stork (with finger-loops attached to the feet) and the blades (pivoting on a pin set in the eye) as its beak; used today as embroidery scissors, they were made in the 19th century and sometimes said (possibly based on the stork-like form) to have been used as a medical instrument for cutting the umbilical cord. Such scissors are about 10 cm long, but miniature examples, 4 cm long, have also been made. *See* SUGAR NIPPERS.

Storr, Paul (1771-1844). One of the most outstanding English silversmiths, born in London and apprenticed in 1785 to ANDREW FOGELBERG. In 1792 he was freed and formed a partnership with William Frisbee (registering their joint mark, with address at Cock Lane, Snow Hill), but he had his own workshop at 30 Church St, Soho, London. In 1793 he registered his own mark and in 1796 he dissolved the firm and moved to 20 Air St, Soho; there, in 1797, he made - for the christening of the grandson of the 3rd Duke of Portland - the gold Portland Font, which was sold at Christie's, London, on 11 July 1985 for £950,000 ($1,300,000). He moved again 1807 to 53 Dean St, Soho, working mainly for PHILIP RUNDELL. In the period 1811-19 he was associated with RUNDELL, BRIDGE & RUNDELL, managing their large workshop (although he also kept his own workshop and mark) and making pieces that were sold to George IV. Upon leaving that firm he established a new workshop in Harrison St, off Gray's Inn Road, making some pieces for GREEN, WARD & GREEN. In 1822 he joined with John Mortimer to form the firm of Storr and Mortimer in New Bond St. The firm became over-extended, however, and took as a partner John Hunt, the nephew of Storr's wife, the firm becoming Storr, Mortimer & Hunt. In 1838 Storr and Mortimer quarrelled, and in 1839 Storr retired (the firm becoming HUNT & ROSKELL). Storr was very prolific, making numerous examples of important domestic ware in simple form as well as in elaborate sculptural style (much of it for large manor houses), and also many presentation and ecclesiastical pieces. His early work was in NEO-CLASSICAL STYLE, later work being in ROCOCO STYLE. He often made pieces less from his own designs than from designs by artists in other

Stonyhurst Salt. Great Salt with crystal elements and jewelled silver mounts, London, 1577. H. 26·3 cm. British Museum, London.

stoup. Portable type, Ignace-François Ranvoyzé, Quebec, 1780. H. 13·8 cm. Musée du Québec, Quebec.

strainer. Thomas Allen, London, 1719. L. 15·3 cm. Courtesy, Partridge (Fine Arts) Ltd, London.

media, such as JOHN FLAXMAN II, THOMAS STOTHARD, and WILLIAM THEED II, and the Italian engraver GIOVANNI BATTISTA PIRANESI. His execution was of the highest order, although sometimes excessively florid. He made a number of pieces to supplement the work of PAUL DE LAMERIE, including some additional pieces made in 1814 for the Mansion House, London, and also some PLINTHS for use with EPERGNES made by others. *See* Alfred E. Jones, 'Paul Storr, Royal Goldsmith' in *The Connoisseur*, July 1942, p. 14; Norman M. Penzer, *Paul Storr, the last of the Goldsmiths* (1954, 1971). *See* THEOCRITUS CUPS; NILE, BATTLE OF THE, CUP.

Stothard, Thomas (1755–1834). A London illustrator and painter who became a leading designer of silverware. He was a friend of JOHN FLAXMAN II and a fellow-designer at RUNDELL, BRIDGE & RUNDELL. Among his best-known pieces are the WELLINGTON SHIELD, the BACCHUS AND ARIADNE SIDEBOARD DISH, and the WATERLOO VASE; the last was modelled by his son, Alfred Joseph Stothard (1793–1864), medallist. *See* Ann Eliza Bray, *The Life of Thomas Stothard* (1851).

Stoughton Cup. A TWO-HANDLED CUP, with cover, made by JOHN CONEY, 1695, engraved with the arms of Stoughton and donated by William Stoughton (d. 1701) to Harvard College in 1701. The lower part of the bowl and the cover are decorated with applied ACANTHUS leaves. It is now owned by the Fogg Art Museum, Cambridge, Massachusetts.

stoup. A receptacle *(bénitier)* for holy water. Usually a stoup (often called a FONT) is affixed to the wall of a Catholic church, near its entrance, so that persons entering the church may dip their fingers in the water before blessing themselves. Some rare wall examples have been made of silver or silver gilt. A portable receptacle for holy water, called an 'aspersorium', is generally in the form of a receptacle with a BAIL HANDLE; examples have been made of silver, especially in Mexico.

strainer. An implement, made in many shapes, styles and sizes, all having PIERCED WORK and used to strain various liquids; the different types include a TEA STRAINER, ORANGE-AND-LEMON STRAINER, PUNCH STRAINER, STRAINER SPOON, MOTE SKIMMER; and SUGAR SKIMMER.

strainer spoon. A type of SPOON having pierced decoration in the bowl, for use in straining a liquid. There are three forms of such spoons: (1) A spoon with overall pierced holes in the bowl. Some are for secular use, while others are for ecclesiastical use (to strain impurities from the Communion wine), but the latter are identifiable as such only if they have a religious inscription or a revealing engraved design. (2) A spoon with pierced holes on only one half of the bowl. Such spoons were used to strain seeds from a PUNCH-BOWL, to remove floating tea leaves from a teacup or to skim boiling sugar water; sometimes called a 'skimmer' (*see* SUGAR SKIMMER). (3) A spoon having in its bowl a vertical divider with vertical slits, designed to permit thick gravy to be scooped up on one half of the bowl and strained into the other half. *See* SIFTER SPOON.

strapwork. A decorative pattern in the form of interlaced straight or curved bands resembling straps. It was used on metalware in the 16th century, notably during the Renaissance period, continuing into the 17th century; in the period of the BAROQUE STYLE it became more voluted and was often accompanied by leafy ornaments (then called *Laub- und Bandelwerk*, German for 'leaf- and strapwork'). It is found on some silver PEDESTAL SALTS made in the Elizabethan era, late 16th century, and also on TRAYS made in the mid-18th century. The term has sometimes been applied to the decorative motif of applied vertical straps generally known more specifically as SPOON-HANDLE STRAPS, and sometimes the term is qualified to denote the particular style of the design.

'strawberry dish'. A long-established trade name for a type of shallow DISH with a flat base and of circular or square shape, having an upcurved SCALLOPED, REEDED, and FLUTED rim with from 12 to 32 lobes. Usually the narrow ribs between the fluting extend into the flat base, but on some examples these ribs fade out at the bottom of the curved rim. A few have a scalloped rim without fluting, and on some examples the top of the fluting is bent outward horizontally. Such dishes are known from 1699 and were a popular article of HUGUENOT SILVERWARE, but later they were made by many English silversmiths. They occur in various sizes, from 18 to 25 cm in diameter, and are often undecorated or have decoration merely of CHASING or ENGRAVING, occasionally only an ARMORIAL. Rare examples have a cover, sometimes with a hinged ring finial as a handle. Such dishes were always made of silver,

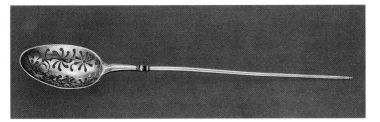

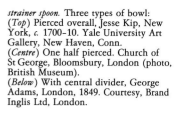

strainer spoon. Three types of bowl: (*Top*) Pierced overall, Jesse Kip, New York, *c.* 1700–10. Yale University Art Gallery, New Haven, Conn. (*Centre*) One half pierced. Church of St George, Bloomsbury, London (photo, British Museum). (*Below*) With central divider, George Adams, London, 1849. Courtesy, Brand Inglis Ltd, London.

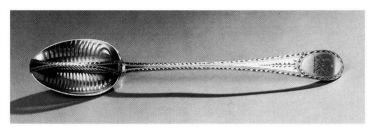

as a base metal was thought to impart an unpleasant taste. Occasionally a larger companion dish was made from which the strawberries would be served into the smaller individual dishes. Such dishes were obviously used for various purposes, usually as a DESSERT DISH but not necessarily for strawberries, so the usual trade name is unjustified and a preferable name would be a 'flute-edged dish'. *See* G. Bernard Hughes, 'Strawberries from a silver dish' in *Country Life*, 3 June 1965, p. 1375.

Stuart Altar Dish. A circular silver-gilt ALTAR DISH having the well completely decorated with an embossed scene depicting the Last Supper (on the wall of the room is the embossed Stuart arms enclosed within the Garter) and having a wide rim decorated with four oval medallions depicting biblical scenes, separated by large grotesque masks within scroll work. The dish bears the unidentified mark 'HG', and the London mark for 1664–5. The dish, which is placed on the high altar of Westminster Abbey during the coronation service and used for the administration of the Sacraments, is kept in the Jewel House at the Tower of London.

Studley Bowl. A silver-gilt, circular BOWL with sides slanting outward from a vertical pierced FOOT-RING; the cover is low-domed, rising to a flattened globular finial. The engraved and chased decoration consists of overall lettering in black-letter (Old English) script of the late 14th century, interspersed with foliage, with on the bowl a contracted form of the word 'Festeyinge' (feasting) and on the bowl and on the cover the letters of the alphabet (except J, U, and W). The piece, which dates from *c.* 1390, was intended originally for secular use, probably as a child's porridge bowl and primer, but was used *c.* 1814 as an ALMS-DISH in the church at Studley Royal, near Ripon, Yorkshire. (It was originally known as a 'collock', a term formerly used to refer to a pot without a foot or a handle employed as a child's feeding bowl.) It was given to the Victoria and Albert Museum, London, in 1914 by Harvey Haddon.

stuffing spoon. A type of SPOON with a large bowl and a long handle, used for serving the stuffing (dressing) from a stuffed roasted fowl, e.g., a turkey. Also called a 'ragout spoon' or 'turkey spoon', and – in Scotland and Ireland – a 'hash spoon'. The term 'dressing spoon' is generally used in the United States.

stumer. A British slang term for a FAKE.

Studley Bowl. Silver gilt, with black-letter inscription, English, late 14th century. H. 14 cm. Victoria and Albert Museum, London.

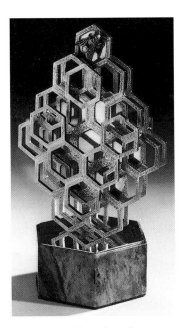

Styles, Alex G. Silver-gilt trophy ('Women Mean Business' Award), 1983. Courtesy, Garrard & Co. Ltd, London.

stump-top spoon. A type of SPOON having a heavy straight stem of octagonal section, terminating in a finial formed by extending the sides of the stem into an octagonal pyramid.

Styles, Alex G. (1922–). An internationally recognized designer of silverware who has been with, and designed exclusively for, GARRARD & CO. LTD, since 1947. His designs range from maces and trophies to domestic ware and presentation pieces, such as his 1983 trophy for the 'Women Mean Business' Award. He was made a Freeman of the GOLDSMITHS' COMPANY in 1964 and a Liveryman in 1974. He has produced important pieces by the process of ELECTROFORMING, having developed a new process involving the use of plastic moulds. In 1988 he was given a one-man retrospective exhibition at Goldsmiths' Hall, London.

subscription box. A type of entirely closed receptacle (sometimes egg-shaped, resting on four feet) having an open slit in the top, through which coins can be dropped; it was intended for collecting subscriptions at meetings or for tips, the coins being removed by turning the box upside down. Such boxes were made of SHEFFIELD PLATE, but no example is known made of silver.

suckett fork. A type of implement, sometimes called a 'suckett spoon', combining the functions of a FORK and a SPOON, having at one end of the stem (which is sometimes of rectangular section and twisted in the middle) a fork with two–in later examples, three–long tines and at the other end a hemispherical or semi-ovoid bowl. Such implements are known from the first half of the 16th century, but most surviving examples date from the late-17th and early-18th centuries. They were used to pick up candied fruits (succades, as then called) and stem ginger. A separate fork and a matching spoon were sometimes made for the purpose.

Sudeley Tankard. The same as the PARR POT.

sugar-basket. A type of receptacle for holding and serving sugar, usually urn-shaped, CANOE-SHAPED or eggcup-shaped, with a stemmed foot, or sometimes BUCKET-SHAPED on a flat base, and generally having a BAIL HANDLE. Many are decorated with PIERCED WORK and have a glass LINER, and in some cases the interior is electro-gilded. Only rarely is there a cover. Sometimes called a 'sugar-basin'. Examples were made EN SUITE with a CREAM-BASKET. *See* G. Bernard Hughes, 'Silver Baskets for Fine Sugar' in *Country Life*, 16 July 1964, p. 182.

sugar-bowl. A type of BOWL for holding and serving sugar, originally made as an individual piece but later made EN SUITE as part of a TEA SERVICE or a COFFEE SERVICE. Such bowls occur in many shapes, styles, and sizes, but usually are of circular, oval or polygonal section, although some are hemispherical, pear-shaped, vase-shaped or urn-shaped. They may rest on a flat bottom, a FOOT-RING, a spreading base or on small feet, and a few have side handles. Some, of globular shape resting on a circular foot, have a low-domed reversible cover surmounted by a narrow horizontal ring, being an inverted small replica of the bowl; such a cover, when inverted and placed on the table, served as a receptacle for used tea leaves or as a SPOON-TRAY. Occasionally a sugar-bowl and two conforming TEA-CADDIES were kept together in a fitted chest. Sometimes called a 'sugar-dish' or a 'sugar-basin' or, when vase-shaped, a 'SUGAR-VASE' or 'sugar-urn', or, when BUCKET-SHAPED with a bail handle, a 'sugar-pail'. *See* G. Bernard Hughes, 'Silver Sugar-Boxes and Bowls' in *Country Life*, 5 April 1956, p. 690. *See* SUGAR-BOX.

sugar-box. A type of BOX for holding sugar, usually circular, oval or rectangular with chamfered corners and having a slightly domed hinged lid (often with a hinged hasp to fasten it). Early examples are sparsely decorated, usually merely with encircling bands, but some later ones are ornate, with four feet and decoration of REPOUSSÉ or CUT CARD work and having a finial as a handle on the lid. In some cases the lid is in the form of a SCALLOP shell; *see* SCALLOP-SHELL SUGAR-BOX. Some oval or oblong examples have a central interior division to form two compartments to hold two varieties of sugar; each has a hinged lid with a knop handle and there is sometimes space for a SUGAR SPOON. A sugar-box was often made EN SUITE with one or two TEA-CADDIES; but such a box was sometimes used alone to serve lump sugar with a glass of brandy or liqueur. *See* Kathryn Buhler, 'The nine colonial sugar boxes' in *Antiques*, January 1964, p. 88.

sugar caster. A type of CASTER used to sprinkle table-sugar; it is similar to, but larger than, a SALT CASTER. Sometimes called a 'sugar sifter'.

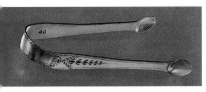

sugar tongs. Three forms:
(1) Bow tongs, Stephen Adams, London, *c.* 1785, length 14 cm.;
(2) Fire tongs, London, *c.* 1700, length 14 cm.;
(3) Scissors tongs, London, *c.* 1750, length 11·5 cm.
All Wadsworth Atheneum (Elizabeth B. Miles Collection), Hartford, Conn.

suckett fork. Combined fork and spoon, London, 1674–5. L. 17·3 cm. Colonial Williamsburg, Va.

sugar chopper. A type of implement with a blade, formerly used to cut lumps of sugar from a sugar loaf (a moulded conical mass about 60 cm high). *See* SUGAR CRUSHER.

sugar crusher. An implement in the form of a straight rod (sometimes of twisted wire) with a vertical ring handle and, at the other end, a flat circular disc; it was formerly used to crush a lump of sugar previously cut from a sugar loaf. *See* SUGAR CHOPPER.

sugar dredger. The same as a SUGAR CASTER.

sugar ladle. A small type of LADLE, for use with a SUGAR-BOWL or SUGAR-BASKET, having a pierced bowl for sprinkling sugar over fruit, etc. Also called a 'sugar sifter'.

sugar nip(per)s. A type of SUGAR TONGS in the form of a pair of scissors or pincers with ring handles; its pivoting arms (the pivot is enclosed in a box-like case) each terminate in curved and pointed pincers (like ICE TONGS) instead of concave grips. (The term is sometimes also applied to the type with concave grips). The form is the same as the larger nippers with steel pincers that were used to break a lump of sugar from a sugar loaf. Some Victorian examples were made in fantasy forms, such as a harlequin hanging from two rings (his feet the nippers), or a STORK SCISSORS in which the bird's feet are attached to the finger-rings and its long horizontal beak, with grips attached, serves as the nippers.

sugar scoop. A type of dinner-table accessory for serving loose sugar, being in the form of a cylindrical, partially open, scoop set at an angle of 45° on a stemmed foot. Some examples have, suspended from the HANDLE, a tiny replica for taking individual helpings from the scoop.

sugar skimmer. A type of implement used for removing the scum from boiling sugar water, having a straight handle and a flat circular blade-like extension with pierced holes in half of the surface. An example, *c.* 1745, is at Chatsworth and one, *c.* 1835, is in the National Museum of Ireland, Dublin. *See* STRAINER SPOON.

sugar spoon. A type of SPOON for serving powdered sugar, having the bowl pierced with holes in various sizes and patterns. Also called a 'sifter spoon' or a 'sugar sifter'.

sugar tongs. A type of TONGS, made in several forms and sizes, used for lifting a lump of sugar from a SUGAR-BOWL. They have been made in three basic forms: (1) bow tongs, of one piece of metal bent in U-shape forming two spring arms that resume their parallel position when hand pressure is released (sometimes called 'spring tongs'); (2) fire tongs, of two arms joined at one end by a pivot and having a handle extending above the pivot; and (3) scissors tongs, of two arms pivoting at the centre, in the form of a pair of scissors, with ring grips on the two handles (sometimes called 'scissors tongs' or 'SUGAR NIPPERS'). A rare version of the fire-tongs type has, at the junction of the two arms, a steel spring enclosed within a ring that joins the two arms, opening by the pressure of the spring and closing by the user's fingers and thumb. The length of sugar tongs ranges from 10 to 15 cm. The arms are decorated in various styles, with EMBOSSING, ENGRAVING, CHASING, PIERCED WORK or BRIGHT CUTTING, and are made in many shapes and styles. The small concave grips at the end of the arms are also variously decorated, some being oval, scallop-shaped, leaf-shaped, etc. Many sugar tongs were made EN SUITE with other units of the TEA EQUIPAGE. Some Regency examples, *c.* 1810–20, were made with arms of tortoise-shell, mother-of-pearl or ivory, riveted to the metal spring arch. *See* George B. Cutten, 'American Silver Sugar Tongs' in *Antiques*, February 1946, p. 112; G. Bernard Hughes, 'Silver Sugar Tongs' in *Country Life*, 24 October 1952, p. 1329; Francis Townshend, 'Irish Silver Sugar Tongs' in *Country Life*, 11 June 1964, p. 1510.

sugar-bowl. (*Above*) Embossed and chased decoration, three feet, William Thompson, Dublin, *c.* 1760–70. Victoria and Albert Museum, London. (*Below*) Bowl with reversible cover, Simon Soumain, New York, *c.* 1738–45. H. 10·5 cm. Yale University Art Gallery (Mabel Brady Garvan Collection), New Haven, Conn.

sugar-vase. A type of receptacle for sugar, shaped in the form of a vase with two vertical or horizontal side handles and sometimes a domed cover. *See* REGENCY SUGAR VASES; WELLINGTON AMBASSADORIAL SERVICE.

suite, en (French). Shaped and decorated in identical fashion, so as to form a SET, as a DINNER SERVICE or a TEA SERVICE.

Sulhamstead Apostle Spoons. A complete set of thirteen silver-gilt APOSTLE SPOONS, all bearing the maker's mark 'IS' and the London date mark for 1617. Each figure has a nimbus chased with a depiction of a dove (the Holy Spirit). Twelve of the set were owned by Col. Newman Thoyts, of Sulhamstead House, near Reading, Berkshire, and were sold at Christie's, London, on 28 April 1910; the Scottish purchaser sold them later to Henry Ford, who subsequently acquired the thirteenth spoon (St James the Less). The set is now owned by the Edison Institute of the Henry Ford Museum, Dearborn, Michigan.

Summerly Art Manufactures. The name used by Sir Henry Cole (1808–82), whose pseudonym as a painter from the 1840s had been Felix Summerly, to market articles of everyday use made of ceramic ware, glass, silver, etc., produced under his programme by various prominent British designers assembled *c.* 1846 and intended for exhibitions in London. The designers included John Colcott Horsley, John Bell, Richard Redgrave, and Daniel Maclise. Among the firms that executed silverware from the designs were that of BENJAMIN SMITH II and DIGBY SCOTT, and also HUNT & ROSKELL, as well as several plateworkers in Sheffield. An example was 'The Vintagers', three DECANTER STOPPERS, designed by Horsley, 1847. The project soon failed because the designers did not understand the practical problems of the silversmiths, and it was abandoned in 1849. Some copies of the silver pieces were made in the 1850s and 1860s, and are now in the Victoria and Albert Museum, London. Cole became, in 1852, the first Director of the Museum of Manufactures (the collection which formed the nucleus of the Victoria and Albert Museum). *See* Shirley Bury, 'Felix Summerly's Art Manufactures' in *Apollo*, January 1967, p. 28.

sugar-vase. Silver gilt, Digby Scott and Benjamin Smith I for Rundell, Bridge & Rundell, London, 1805-6. H. 17·3 cm. Victoria and Albert Museum, London.

sundial (pocket). A miniature type of sundial. An example from the Saxon period, 10th century, was unearthed in July 1939 at Canterbury Cathedral and a replica in silver was made for the Science Museum, London, by LESLIE DURBIN. It is in the form of a rectangular silver tablet with a gold cap and suspension chain, with a gnomon in the form of a gold pin to be inserted in the appropriate hole for the month of use and with three columns bearing the names of the months.

sunken-base candlestick. A type of CANDLESTICK having a base, usually square, with the area near the stem recessed below the level of the border of the base.

supper set. A group of DISHES for sideboard self-service, usually consisting of four fan-shaped dishes which, when placed together, form a circle or oval. Sometimes the four dishes are made so as to leave a central space in which is placed a circular dish or SOUP-TUREEN, or sometimes a SOY STAND. The pieces sometimes rest on a mahogany tray, a rotating hot-water warmer, or a stand with a heating device. The individual dishes generally have no cover. *See* LAZY SUSAN.

surgical-instruments case. A type of small case for surgical instruments. A parcel-gilt example, decorated with coloured enamelling, including the arms of Henry VIII, and having an attached carrying chain, was donated between 1509 and 1525 by Henry VIII to the Barber-Surgeons' Company, London, and is now owned by the Barbers' Company.

surgical-instruments case. Silver with enamelling (and carrying case, left). H. 18·3 cm. Barbers' Company, London (photo courtesy, Goldsmiths' Company, London).

surtout (de table). *See* EPERGNE. An epergne, called a 'surtoute', was made by GEORGE WICKES, 1745-6, from a design by WILLIAM KENT, for Frederick, Prince of Wales (1707-51), the separate base being engraved with his arms and having at the top, in the Kent design, a canopy surmounted by a small tureen. It was altered twice (apart from the deviations from the design, by – among other things – eliminating the tureen and substituting the Prince of Wales's feathers): first, in 1829, to make it conform to the pieces of 'The Grand Service' made on the order of George IV, by JOHN BRIDGE, for RUNDELL, BRIDGE & RUNDELL; and, in 1847, by GARRARD & CO., by adding swags between the four feet (changed from eight feet in the Kent design). It is now in the Royal Collection.

See J. F. Hayward, 'A "Surtoute" designed by William Kent' in *The Connoisseur*, March 1959, p. 82.

Sutherland Wine Cooler. Oval, with flying scroll handles, Paul de Lamerie, London, 1719. L. 96·5 cm. Minneapolis Institute of Arts, Minn.

Sutherland Wine Cooler. A WINE COOLER made by PAUL DE LAMERIE, 1719, for the 1st Earl Gower (1694-1754), bearing the arms (engraved 1771/86) of the 2nd Earl Gower, and being in the collection of his descendants, the 1st to 4th Dukes of Sutherland, until 1961. It is oval, standing on a high base of three receding bands decorated with REPOUSSÉ strapwork, rosettes, and husks. The bowl is convex, plain at its base, above which there is a matted band decorated with eight grotesque masks alternating with shells, each surmounted by strapwork; above the band on each side is a bearded mask. The two massive FLYING SCROLL HANDLES are in the form of DOUBLE SCROLLS with mask terminals rising above the rim of the bowl. It was sold at Christie's, London, on 29 November 1961, and is now owned by the Minneapolis Institute of Arts.

swag. A decorative motif in the form of garlands of flowers, fruit, leaves, ribbons or drapery, suspended from the two ends and hanging in a natural curve. It is found on silverware of the 16th century and also ware in the NEO-CLASSICAL STYLE and ADAM STYLE, executed by ENGRAVING, CHASING, or STAMPING. Also called a 'festoon'.

swaging. The process of shaping the edge of a piece of silver or other metal by holding it on a swage block – a shaped metal tool, invented in 1792, consisting of a pair of hinged metal jaws (swages), one jaw having a design in relief, and the other jaw, the 'face', having the design recessed (intaglio) – and then hammering or pressing the jaws together. When making a border pattern on a flat piece, the complete continuous design was raised in stages by pushing the object progressively forward and repeating the operation. The process was used mainly for FLATWARE and handles of CUTLERY, and is still employed in making hand-forged spoons. After the operation, the rough edges of the piece must be filed smooth.

Swan Automaton. A silver swan that appears to float on 'water' simulated by rotating glass rods. It contains an intricate mechanism that causes the neck to bend down and give the impression of taking a fish from the 'water' (actually ejecting it from its beak). The swan was first recorded as being in James Cox's Museum, London, in 1774 and was transferred in succession to several private museums in London and Paris. It was shown by HARRY EMANUEL at the Paris Exposition of 1867, where it was seen, and later described, by Mark Twain. In 1872 it was acquired by John Bowes and transferred by him in 1877 to the Bowes Museum, Barnard Castle, Co. Durham. The only mark is 'ET', said to be the mark introduced in France in 1864 for imported precious metalware, hence the swan is presumed to have been made in England *c.* 1770.

Swan Mazer. A MAZER, late 14th century, with silver-gilt mounts, having, in lieu of the usual BOSS with a PRINT in the bottom of the bowl, a hexagonal pillar, pierced at the bottom, surmounted by a battlemented lip (almost level with the rim of the bowl), upon which rests a silver-gilt swan with a downturned neck. Within the pillar there is a hollow tube, open at both ends, so that a liquid, when poured into the bowl, rises in the space between the pillar and the tube; on reaching the level of the lip (slightly higher than the swan's bill), the liquid flows into and down the tube (giving the appearance of being drunk by the swan) and is siphoned out through the pierced holes

Swan Automaton. Silver swan, *c.* 1770. H. 80 cm. Bowes Museum, Barnard Castle, Co. Durham.

Swan Mazer. Silver-gilt swan and mounts, English, late 14th century. W. (of swan) 7 cm. Corpus Christi College, Cambridge.

swan-neck spout. Coffee-pot with rococo-style spout, Guernsey, *c.* 1775–80. H. 28 cm. Courtesy, Brand Inglis Ltd, London.

and a hole in the bottom of the bowl – thus preventing the bowl from over-flowing – unless the holes are closed with a finger. The piece is owned by Corpus Christi College, Cambridge, having been donated *c.* 1385 by John Northwode, formerly a Fellow of the College. Four other mazers with such a swan, but not the siphon, are recorded, three at Harbledown Hospital, Kent (*see* HARBLEDOWN MAZERS), and one at St James's Hospital, Canterbury.

swan-neck spout. A type of SPOUT with an S-shaped curve in the form of a swan's neck, found on some TEAPOTS and COFFEE-POTS (mainly dating from the period of the ROCOCO STYLE), and often decorated along its entire length, but especially near the lower end.

Swaythling Apostle Spoons. A set of twelve APOSTLE SPOONS (without the Master Spoon), composed of two groups of six dated, respectively, London 1524 and London 1553, each spoon having engraved on the front of the stem the name of the Apostle (the only known set with names so engraved), though some of the names are said to be incorrect. Each bowl bears on the back the engraved initials 'MC' for Martha Clayton, the wife of Sir Robert Clayton, Bt, Lord Mayor of London, 1679–80, to whom the set is reputed to have been given by Charles II. The first modern record of the set occurred when it was sold at Christie's, London, on 28 March 1892, after which it was in the collection of the 1st Baron Swaythling (1832–1911). It was offered for sale at Christie's, London, on 7 May 1924, but was withdrawn; it was sold by the 3rd Baron Swaythling at Christie's, London, on 17 July 1946. Its present whereabouts is unknown.

Swaythling Bowl. A circular STANDING BOWL having curved sides, the body being of serpentine marble, with a silver-gilt everted rim and a wide footed base decorated with REPOUSSÉ vertical lobes. It is unmarked, *c.* 1490–1510, and is one of the earliest examples of such silver-mounted bowls. It was acquired in 1924 from the Swaythling Collection by the Victoria and Albert Museum, London. *See* SERPENTINE OBJECTS.

Swaythling Cup. A FONT-SHAPED CUP, *c.* 1500, having a shallow vertical-sided bowl supported by a wide stem resting on a wide base. The cover has a finial in the form of a cup-shaped ornament with its rim edged with CREST-ING. The piece is entirely undecorated. It was in the Swaythling Collection and is now in the Victoria and Albert Museum, London. *See* Norman M. Penzer, 'The Swaythling Cup' in *The Connoisseur*, March 1946, p. 88.

sweating (on). The process of joining to an article of silver or SHEFFIELD PLATE or one made by ELECTROPLATING some ancillary silver part, such as a small shield bearing an engraved coat of arms, or an INSCRIPTION PLATE. The process involves heating the basic piece, placing on it the small part, and rubbing vigorously with a steel tool until they adhere to each other. After BURNISHING, the join is difficult to detect except by warming the piece; this reveals a difference in colour between the two parts. Also called 'rubbing in'.

sweetmeat-basket. A type of BASKET that is smaller than, but similar to, a CAKE-BASKET or a FRUIT-BASKET, and intended to hold sweetmeats (candied confections). It is usually circular, oval or of CANOE SHAPE, and is either placed on a table or suspended on an EPERGNE. It has an everted rim and is usually decorated with PIERCED WORK or with bands of vertical PALES on the rim and the lower part of the bowl, but undecorated on its flat bottom. Such baskets usually have four legs, sometimes joined to a descending apron at the bottom of the bowl. Some are made of WIREWORK, with applied decorative mounts. Some are gilded. *See* G. Bernard Hughes, 'Sweetmeat Baskets of the Georgians' in *Country Life*, 7 December 1967, p. 1514.

sweetmeat-dish. A type of DISH of various forms, styles, and sizes, used, among other presumed purposes, for serving sweetmeats. Some examples have handles in the form of horizontal SCALLOP shells or in fantasy shape. *See* 'STRAWBERRY' DISH; FLUTED DISH.

Swettenham-Morgan Apostle Spoons. A complete set of thirteen silver APOSTLE SPOONS, all bearing the maker's mark of a mallet within a crescent and the London date mark for 1617. The name of each Apostle is engraved on the pedestal upon which the figure stands, and although each of the attributes is intact, in some cases the nimbus, bearing a chased depiction of a dove (the Holy Spirit) is broken or missing. The set was owned from 1787 by Thomas Willis-Swettenham, of Swettenham Hall, Cheshire, and Swettenham descendants. When offered for sale at Christie's, London, on 27 March 1901, from the collection of Col. Warren-Swettenham, it was withdrawn, and was sold that day to J. Pierpont Morgan.

The set remained in the Morgan family collection (on loan to the Metropolitan Museum of Art, New York) until sold by the executors of the Morgan estate at Parke-Bernet Galleries, Inc., New York, on 1 November 1947, the buyer being Francis E. Fowler; it has been donated by Francis E. Fowler, Jr, to the Fowler Museum of Cultural History at the University of California, Los Angeles.

Swinburne Pyx. A parcel-gilt PYX, English, *c.* 1310, in the form of a low cylindrical box with a flat cover secured by a BAYONET JOINT. The side is decorated with an engraved encircling arcade enclosing subjects now not identifiable. The cover and the bottom are each formed of two plaques joined together, the cover having on the top a depiction of the Virgin and Child, on its back the Nativity, and the bottom having on the inside a depiction of the head of Christ, on the outside an Agnus Dei; all are engraved on varying diaper grounds. The piece was originally decorated with translucent *basse taille* enamel, now worn off. It was owned by the Swinburne family of Pontop, Co. Durham, from the 14th century until it was acquired in 1950 by the Victoria and Albert Museum, London. *See* Charles Oman, 'The Swinburne Pyx' in *Burlington Magazine*, December 1950, p. 337.

Swinburne Pyx. Parcel gilt, *c.* 1310. D. 5·7 cm. Victoria and Albert Museum, London.

swizzle stick. A type of small implement for stirring a beverage; originally used for swizzle (a drink made of rum or other spirit, sugar, bitters, and ice), it is now used for stirring champagne (albeit deprecated by champagne connoisseurs who deplore the dissipation of the bubbles). It is made in various forms, some having several blades attached to the end of a straight stem handle (sometimes silver, sometimes wood). Inexpensive types may be merely a thin glass or wooden rod with some type of enlarged head, but some examples, made of silver or gold, consist of a small case (sometimes provided with a suspensory ring for attaching to a watch-chain) containing three tipped curved wires that the user can release to project from the case. It is a small version of a PUNCH STIRRER.

sword. A long-bladed weapon, ornately decorated examples of which were often primarily a symbol of authority or an article of ceremonial attire. In England, the right of a city to possess a civic sword was granted by the King, and in the 14th century only seven are recorded. *See* PRESENTATION SWORD; SMALL SWORD; STALINGRAD SWORD; SWORD-HILT.

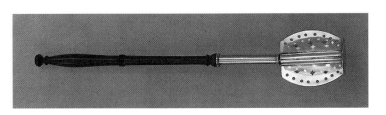

swizzle stick. Five rounded pierced blades, London, *c.* 1770. L. 33·2 cm. Wadsworth Atheneum (Elizabeth B. Miles Collection), Hartford, Conn.

Sword Bearer's Salt. An elaborate SCROLL SALT made by Augustin(e) Courtauld II (*see* COURTAULD) in 1730 for Edward Gestlin Carver, and given by Carver to Thomas Carbennel, who in 1741 presented it to William Dormer, the Sword Bearer of the Corporation of the City of London, and his successors for use at their table in the Lord Mayor's Hall. The large globular bowl rests on four legs, in the form of dolphins, connected by a wire ring and is decorated with applied SPOON-HANDLE STRAPS and with chased STRAPWORK and shells. Standing upright from the rim of the bowl are four double-scroll BRACKETS, each with a terminal at the top in the form of a female head. The piece, now at the Mansion House, London, is said to be the most important surviving work of Augustine Courtauld and the last of the great ceremonial salts made in England. A similar salt, at Windsor Castle, made by PAUL STORR was formerly attributed to Courtauld. *See* E. Alfred Jones, 'The Silver State Salt of the Lord Mayor of London' in *The Connoisseur*, March 1942, p. 19.

sword-hilt. The handle of a SWORD, including the various parts, i.e., the pommel (top ornament), grip, quillons (forming the cross guard), knuckle bows (loops to protect the knuckles), and *pas d'âne* (guard just above the blade). The parts of the hilt of a small sword, especially those used on ceremonial occasions and those of naval officers, have been made of silver or silver gilt, and are usually ornately decorated with embossed and engraved designs and also sometimes embellished with gemstones. The grip is sometimes wound with braided wire. The hilt of a dagger or of a rapier is sometimes of silver and similarly decorated and jewelled. *See* John A. Atkinson, 'Swords for Dueling and Display' in *Country Life*, 19 October 1964, p. 876; John K. Lattimer, 'Sword Hilts of Early American Silversmiths' in *Antiques*, February 1965, p. 196.

Syng, Philip, Jr (1703–89). A silversmith, born in Cork, Ireland, who emigrated with his parents to Annapolis, Maryland, in 1714. By 1720 the family had moved to Philadelphia, where the father (1676–1739) established himself as a silversmith, but he returned to Annapolis *c.* 1725–30, and the son took over the Philadelphia business. He devoted only a small part of his time to the trade, as he was a friend of Benjamin Franklin and a business associate in many ventures. Only a few pieces of silverware are known to have been made by him, the most famous being the SYNG INKSTAND.

Syng Inkstand. The INKSTAND believed to have been used for the signing, on 4 July 1776, of the Declaration of Independence, and in 1787 for the signing of the United States Constitution, both at Philadelphia, Pennsylvania. The piece consists of a tray upon which rest three baluster-shaped writing accessories, a central QUILL-POT and at its sides a smaller INKPOT and 'sander' (POUNCE-POT). The set was made by PHILIP SYNG, JR, in 1752 for the Speaker's Table of the Pennsylvania Assembly. It was owned by the State of Pennsylvania and used at its capital, Harrisburg, until given in 1875 to the City of Philadelphia, where it is now kept in Independence Hall.

T

table. An article of FURNITURE consisting of a smooth, flat, and horizontal surface resting on legs or other type of support and variously used, as for writing, eating or to support ornaments. Some examples are made with a wood and iron frame, entirely covered (sheathed) with silver. An outstanding example is a table presented to William III by the Corporation of London, and now at Windsor Castle; made *c.*1690 by ANDREW MOORE, it has cast legs in the form of CARYATIDS, the cross-point of the stretchers is masked by a pineapple, and the top is engraved with the Royal arms, monogram, and badges of William and Mary (an ELECTROFORM copy is in the Victoria and Albert Museum, London). Another table, *c.*1715, made for Edward Harley, 2nd Earl of Oxford, now belongs to the Duke of Portland, and other examples are at Knole House, Sevenoaks, Kent, at Welbeck Abbey, Nottinghamshire, and at Ham House, Richmond, Surrey. A silver pier table, *c.*1700, with a pier glass mirror, is at Windsor Castle (an electroform copy being in the Victoria and Albert Museum). *See* TEA TABLE; WRITING TABLE; 'SLEEP' TABLE.

table bell. A type of BELL having an inverted cup-like (krater) shape and a vertical handle. The handle is usually baluster-shaped (of circular or hexagonal section), but sometimes ring-shaped or made in some fanciful form, such as a human figure (*see* FIGURAL BELL). Usually the finial of the handle is merely a ball, often of ivory or ebony. The waist and shoulder are usually undecorated but some have EMBOSSING or ENGRAVING. Such bells are usually from 7·5 to 12·5 cm high. Some Victorian examples (sometimes called a 'tea bell') were gilded. Similar smaller bells were often a central unit of an INKSTAND (hence sometimes called an 'inkstand bell') but, being separate pieces, they have often survived apart from the inkstand; such bells were generally for use in calling a servant to do an errand. Some examples have at the top of the handle a socket for a taper. *See* G. Bernard Hughes, 'Silver Table Bells' in *Country Life*, 20 December 1956, p. 1449. *See* HAND BELL.

table bell. Louise Courtauld, London, 1766-7. H. 13 cm. Ashmolean Museum, Oxford.

table candlestick. A type of CANDLESTICK usually having a flat-bottomed base (rarely, having tripod feet) for resting on a table. The stem (shaft) has been made in a great variety of forms and styles, ranging from a simple knopped stem to a stem with flared or baluster sections, knops, and ROCOCO STYLE ornamentation, and including examples of special types, e.g., a COLUMN CANDLESTICK, a FIGURAL CANDLESTICK, a PALM-TREE CANDLESTICK, and a TELESCOPIC CANDLESTICK. The base may be circular, lobed, square, polygonal,

table. Sheathed with silver, Andrew Moore, London, *c.* 1690. H. 85 cm. Windsor Castle; reproduced by gracious permission of Her Majesty the Queen.

or in other shapes, and sometimes has a flat top, a concave ('dished') top, or a convex (domed) top. *See* SUNKEN-BASE CANDLESTICK.

table fountain. A type of highly ornamental receptacle, made since the Middle Ages as a dinner-table or sideboard CENTREPIECE, originally intended to be used for table ablutions instead of a EWER and BASIN. The form has varied but usually such pieces had a container for water that poured into a bowl in which the fountain stood. Such pieces were often of silver gilt, and sometimes were enriched with enamelling and gemstones. Seven English examples were described in a 1574 inventory of Elizabeth I. An example given by Anne Boleyn to Henry VIII in 1534, and made from a design by Hans Holbein the Younger, provides for water to flow into the basin from the breasts of female figures. A later one, 1670, with maker's mark 'IC', is at Penshurst Place, Tonbridge, Kent; it was made for Philip Stanhope, Earl of Chesterfield (1633–1713). A modern one, in ART NOUVEAU STYLE, has a central column rising from a shallow bowl (lined with mother-of-pearl), from which water (propelled upward by an electric motor in the base) is ejected from the mouths of dolphins on the column, below the figures of standing nude boys; it was designed and made by Frederick Courthope, London, 1903. *See* WINE FOUNTAIN; ALHAMBRA TABLE FOUNTAIN.

table pomander. A type of POMANDER, having a large receptacle supported by an attached or separate stemmed foot, to be placed on a table.

table snuffer. A type of large SNUFFER, up to 30 cm long, accompanied by a conforming SNUFFER TRAY and usually placed on a table between two TABLE CANDLESTICKS.

tablespoon. A type of large SPOON having an oval bowl, normally with a capacity three times that of a DESSERT SPOON.

tableware. Articles, collectively, that are generally used for serving meals at table, including various types of drinking and pouring vessels, PLATES, BOWLS, FLATWARE, and accessories, such as SALTS, CASTERS, PLACE MATS, TRIVETS, and COASTERS, but not necessarily constituting a SERVICE.

Talisman Centrepiece. A silver-gilt CENTREPIECE, in sculptural form, with four figures in-the-round depicting a scene from *The Talisman* by Sir Walter Scott. It was designed by EDMUND COTTERILL and made in 1834 by ROBERT GARRARD II for GARRARD & CO.

tang. The shank forming the extension from the blade of a knife or the head of a fork and connecting it to the handle; usually it is tapered and inserted into the handle.

tankard. A type of drinking vessel, usually not as high as a FLAGON, that is generally of cylindrical shape, sometimes narrower at the top with inward-sloping sides, and having one handle and a hinged lid with a THUMBPIECE. The form developed from medieval wooden drinking vessels, and the staves and the binding hoops of a barrel were often adapted as the decoration of tankards. The early form with straight sides was briefly superseded by a slightly pyriform shape (sometimes called a 'hanse pot'), but by the end of the 18th century the style of straight sides was resumed. Many examples have a flat bottom, but some are supported by three small feet or by a SKIRT FOOT to raise the bottom of the vessel from the table. The lid may be flat, low-domed, stepped (single- or double-stepped), or of CUSHION SHAPE with a narrow horizontal encircling flange, and some pieces have a decorative ornament, such as a lion couchant, atop the hinge, sometimes to conform with the style of the three feet. Some have a peak at the front of the lid. The handle is usually massive, either a SCROLL HANDLE or DOUBLE-SCROLL HANDLE, extending from the rim down to the base, and is often made with a curved section upon which is applied a shorter strengthening section. The thumbpiece occurs in various shapes, e.g., a CORKSCREW THUMBPIECE or of volute, scroll, or double-pomegranate shape. Tankards have been made of silver or silver gilt, about 15 to 20 cm high; some are made of glass with silver mounts (*see* SUDELEY TANKARD). The prescribed capacity for the old tankard was one quart, but the overall range is from about one pint to, rarely, eight pints. Similar smaller vessels, of half-pint capacity, are about 12·5 cm high and have a hinged lid but no thumbpiece; although sometimes called a 'half-pint tankard', an example in this size is preferably called a MUG. Tankards have been decorated with REPOUSSÉ work, ENGRAVING, and CUT CARD work, but more often they have a plain body encircled by raised bands of ribs, or occasionally a band of alternating ANTHEMION leaves and PALMETTES encircling the lower half. Some have a coin set in the lid or affixed to the handle as a termi-

table candlestick. George Wickes, London, 1742-3. H. 25·5 cm. Ashmolean Museum, Oxford.

Talisman Centrepiece. Silver gilt, Robert Garrard II, London, 1834. H. 76 cm. Courtesy, Garrard & Co. Ltd, London.

nal. Late examples made by PAUL STORR and the Regency silversmiths were ornately decorated, to be used more as presentation pieces than as drinking vessels. Some, mainly from the 18th century, have a lid that can be removed to allow the piece to be used as a mug; *see* TANKARD CUP. *See* G. Bernard Hughes, 'Old English Silver Tankards' in *Country Life*, 14 September 1951, p. 815; A. G. Grimwade, 'English Silver Tankards' in *Apollo*, December 1963, p. 117; Judith Banister, 'Old England's Good Cheer' in *Country Life*, 2 December 1965, p. 1517; Allen Wardwell, 'One Hundred Years of American Tankards' in *Antiques*, July 1966, p. 80. *See* PEG TANKARD; SCANDINAVIAN-TYPE TANKARD; SPOUT TANKARD; ASTON TANKARD; CUMBERLAND TANKARD; WENMAN TANKARD; SERPENTINE OBJECTS.

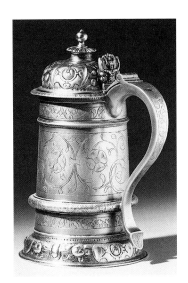

tankard. Silver gilt, London, 1591. H. 18 cm. Courtesy, Brand Inglis Ltd, London.

tankard cup. A type of TANKARD, made between *c.* 1675 and *c.* 1800, that has a loose hinge-pin attached by a chain to the handle, so that its withdrawal would permit the lid to be removed and the tankard to be used as a MUG.

Tanqueray, David (fl. 1713–24). A Huguenot silversmith, born in St Lô, Normandy, apprenticed in London in 1708 under DAVID WILLAUME I, naturalized, and freed in 1722. His first mark was entered in 1713, with address at Green St, and a second one in 1720, with address Pall Mall. In 1717 he married his master's eldest and only surviving daughter, Anne (1691–1733). He is recorded as Subordinate Goldsmith to the King in 1729 and 1732 (although probably deceased before the latter date). His best-known surviving work is the silver-gilt WINE COOLER, 1718, now at Chatsworth; other pieces by him are mainly standard cups, salvers, and salt-cellars. Upon his death, the business was carried on by his widow Anne, with the assistance of her brother, DAVID WILLAUME II; she was probably not a goldsmith, and the pieces that bear her mark (some highly regarded sauce-boats and inkstands) were made by journeymen employed by her.

tantalus frame. A receptacle for holding a square decanter (or up to four such decanters placed in a line), having an overhead hinged frame that can be locked when vertical and swung sideways when unlocked to permit removal of the decanter(s). Sometimes called 'the Butler's Enemy'.

tap. A type of tubular device inserted into the side of a barrel or other receptacle that permits the outflow of the liquid contents, with usually a SPIGOT to control the rate of the flow. It generally has a down-curved SPOUT. Sometimes the tap and the spigot are collectively termed a 'faucet'. *See* BARREL TAP.

taper-box. The same as a BOUGIE-BOX.

taperstick. A type of utensil similar to and usually in the style of various types of CANDLESTICK, but smaller, being about 10 cm high, for holding a taper (a thin candle). Such pieces usually have a flat circular or shaped base and a SOCKET of narrow diameter. They are usually now found singly, not as one of a pair, as one usually suffices for the intended use. Some have the stem in the form of a human figure (sometimes a harlequin or mandarin). They do not usually have a DRIP-PAN, but some (especially those having a figural stem) do have one. The socket is sometimes lined with paper in order to hold securely the tall thin taper. The taperstick is sometimes accompanied by a chained CANDLE EXTINGUISHER. The taper (made of wax and non-odorous) was used mainly for melting sealing wax and for lighting candles, tobacco pipes, etc., and not as a source of illumination, hence the piece was sometimes called a 'tobacco candlestick'. A taperstick was sometimes a unit of an INKSTAND (2). *See* Charles R. Beard, 'Taper-Sticks' in *The Connoisseur*, November 1931, p. 302 (including wax-jacks).

taperstick. With chained candle extinguisher, J. Shepherd, 1699. W. 8·8 cm. Ashmolean Museum, Oxford.

targe. A type of Scottish shield, sometimes decorated with silver ornaments. An example, made of wood covered with pigskin, is decorated with numerous small silver ornaments, some in the form of military trophies, and bears a silver mask of Medusa in whose open mouth is a socket into which to screw a spike, now missing. It is traditionally said to have been lost at the battle of Culloden Moor (1746) by Prince Charles Edward Stuart (1720–88), the 'Young Pretender'. Although it is sometimes thought to be French, it has been attributed probably to English make, *c.* 1740. It was sold at Sotheby's, London, on 23 May 1928, and is now in the National Museum of Antiquities of Scotland, Edinburgh. A similar article is at Warwick Castle.

tarnish. The altered LUSTRE or blackish surface colour of silver, due either to a slight alteration, as by chemical reaction caused by contact with sulphurous fumes (or egg-yolks) forming silver sulphide, or to a thin surface deposit, e.g., of dust. Tarnish on silver is not due, as often stated, to oxidation (hence the term 'OXIDIZED SILVER' is an incorrect name for tarnished silver). It can be removed by a liquid, cream, foam or dip that releases the sulphur, and can be avoided by frequent use and polishing or permanently prevented by plating the silver with rhodium. *See* PATINA.

Tassie silver medallion. A silver stamped medallion based on the moulded medallions made of paste by James Tassie (1735–99) and his nephew William (1777–1860) in cameo or intaglio form; such silver medallions were manufactured wholesale by W. Brown and others and mounted on JUGS, TUREENS, and other forms of ADAM SILVERWARE. Such decorated ware was a speciality of ANDREW FOGELBERG.

Tassie silver medallion. Cream-jug, Andrew Fogelberg and Stephen Gilbert, London, 1780–1, with medallion by W. Brown. H. 13·5 cm. Victoria and Albert Museum, London.

tastevin (sometimes spelled *tâtevin*). The French term for a WINE TASTER.

Tatton Cup. A silver-gilt TWO-HANDLED CUP standing on a base in the form of rocks encrusted with animal life and plants, with the stem and the baluster-shaped bowl encircled with relief decoration of fruiting vine stalks. The FLYING SCROLL HANDLES, in the form of twisting TERMS facing in opposite directions, represent Pan and a Bacchante, the latter holding in her upraised left hand a tabor engraved with the crest and (on the reverse) a variant of the arms of the Tattons, of Wythenshawe, near Manchester. The figure of Pan holds pipes in his right hand and a bunch of grapes in his upraised left hand. The unmarked cup was very probably made by THOMAS HEMING, *c.*1760–1. The family of William Tatton (1703–76) owned during his lifetime an unpretentious property at Wythenshawe, and so, it has been suggested, probably no member of his family could have afforded to acquire the cup at the time of its production, indicating that the arms were not engraved contemporaneously with the making of the cup. It seems unlikely that the cup was made in 1745, as has been sometimes said, as Heming registered his first mark only in that year, and several other comparable cups, similar in form and decoration, made by or attributed to him, are dated *c.*1750–71 (*see* HEMING TWO-HANDLED CUPS). The cup was acquired in 1978 from Brand Inglis Ltd by the City Art Gallery, Manchester. *See* Hilary Young, 'Thomas Heming and the Tatton Cup' in *Burlington Magazine*, May 1983, p. 285.

tau handle. A type of vertical HANDLE found on some COFFEE-POTS, JUGS, etc., the handle being in the shape of the Greek letter *tau* (T) and having at the bottom of the vertical section an outward curve that is affixed to the body. It differs from a SQUARE HANDLE by having only two straight sides. Sometimes called a 'T-shaped handle'.

Tatton Cup. Silver gilt, probably Thomas Heming, *c.* 1760–1. H. 42 cm. City Art Gallery, Manchester.

Taylor, Samuel (fl. 1744–73). A London silversmith, apprenticed to John Newton in 1737 and freed in 1744, and a Liveryman in 1751. His first mark was entered in 1744 and his second mark in 1757, both at the address of Maiden Lane, Wood St, which was the address of Newton, to whose business he succeeded. Both men specialized in making TEA-CADDIES and SUGAR-BOWLS, usually decorated with floral chasing, and Taylor's marks are rarely found on other ware.

tazza. (1) A type of drinking cup having a wide shallow bowl that is supported by a short stem with a central knop (so shaped to afford a secure grip) rising from a spreading foot or domed base. The side of the bowl is either straight (the piece being called a 'flat-cupped tazza') or curves upward from the bottom (a 'shallow-bowl tazza'). The bowl is often decorated – the exterior being usually plain – with engraved or hammered work; often there are, in the centre, a BOSS or an embossed motif depicting the head of a Roman warrior in profile within an embossed circular frame and, in the bottom of the bowl and on the rim, concentric bands of STRAPWORK and arabesques. The tazza has no handles, and only rarely has a cover (*see* COVERED TAZZA). The form is based on an ancient prototype and was reintroduced as a type of WINE-CUP on the Continent and in England in the 16th century by Renaissance goldsmiths. The name is the Italian word for 'cup', and the silver examples are in the form of the Italian maiolica prototypes. Sometimes called in England a STANDING DISH. *See* ARLINGTON TAZZA; CRIPPLEGATE TAZZA; ROCHESTER CATHEDRAL TAZZE; SOUTHAMPTON TAZZA. (2) A misnomer for a flat SALVER supported by a stemmed foot (sometimes erroneously called a 'tazza salver') and sometimes for a PATEN with a stemmed foot.

tea-and-coffee service. A combined SERVICE for serving tea and coffee, including, when complete, the articles in a TEA SERVICE and also a COFFEE-POT. Some four-piece services omit the SLOP-BASIN and CREAM-JUG. *See* LINCOLN TEA-AND-COFFEE SERVICE.

tea ball. A type of TEA INFUSER.

tea-bowl. A small semi-spheroidal CUP without a handle, used for drinking tea, such as those made of porcelain in the Far East and also commonly made by many European porcelain factories in the 18th century, some accompanied (unlike the Chinese prototypes) by a SAUCER. An early example, 1683, is decorated with CHINOISERIES executed by FLAT CHASING. Another, with sides completely formed by FLUTING and with a conforming saucer, was made in 1700 by Mark Paillet, London. A hexagonal cup without handle, together with its accompanying saucer, early 18th century, may (by analogy with the Chinese tea-bowl) have been intended for tea; it is in the Victoria and Albert Museum, London. Due to the heat-conducting quality of silver, such bowls were impracticable and the few known examples were probably used to serve tepid tea. *See* TEACUP.

tea-caddy. A closed container for dry tea (*see* CADDY), used at a tea table as part of a TEA SERVICE. It was until the late 18th century called a 'tea-canister'. Such pieces have been made in many styles, shapes, and sizes. The early examples were in the form of the Chinese porcelain tea-jars, having a flat rectangular or octagonal base with vertical sides and shoulders sloping to a narrow neck with a high-domed cover; the cover was used as a measure. Later some examples were shaped like urns and vases, having a stemmed foot, and from *c.*1800 they were made in the form of a box with vertical (sometimes corrugated) sides and a square, rectangular, circular, oval or polygonal section; some were made in BOMBÉ shape or as cubes in the form of the wooden chests in which tea was exported from China. Decoration was in many styles, including EMBOSSING, ENGRAVING, FLAT CHASING, and BRIGHT CUTTING, in ROCOCO STYLE and later in NEO-CLASSICAL STYLE, and often featured CHINOISERIE motifs. The small SLIP-ON COVER or hinged lid is usually flat-topped but is sometimes dome-shaped, decorated with a finial. Some examples have a sliding top or a slide-in base to facilitate filling the narrow-mouthed caddy; this type (sometimes having a lead liner) was often accompanied by a CADDY SPOON which could be kept inside the caddy. Caddies were made in sets for different kinds of tea, some marked 'B' and 'G' for 'black' and 'green', or sometimes 'Bohea', 'Hyson', etc.; these were provided with a TEA-CHEST, for two or three caddies, with its lock and key. Later the caddy was made with two compartments and each had its own lock (tea then being a costly luxury). In England the tea-caddy was sometimes erroneously called a TEAPOY. *See* Charles C. Oman, 'English 18th-century Tea Caddies' in *Apollo*, September 1931, p. 132; Judith Banister, 'Sixty Glorious Years of Silver Tea Caddies' in *Antique Dealer & Collectors Guide*, April 1967, p. 44. *See* DOUBLE TEA-CADDY; TEA-VASE.

tea-canister. A receptacle for dry tea leaves, originally in the form of the Chinese porcelain bottle-shaped tea container, and later generally vase- or urn-shaped, resting on a SPLAYED base and having a domed cover. The shape and style have evolved into many different forms. Since the late 18th century the term TEA-CADDY has generally been used for such pieces. *See* TEA-VASE.

tea-chest. A wooden container to hold two or more TEA-CADDIES (for different types of tea, to be chosen or blended according to taste), together with various related accessories, such as a SUGAR-BOWL, SUGAR-BOX, CREAM-JUG, SUGAR TONGS, and MOTE STRAINER, as well as a set of TEASPOONS, and generally provided with a lock to prevent pilferage of the tea. Such chests were usually covered with shagreen and had silver mounts on the rim. *See* G. Bernard Hughes, 'Tea Chests for the Georgian Hostess' in *Country Life*, 5 September 1957, p. 439.

tea equipage. The various articles that constitute a TEA SERVICE and also ancillary articles, such as sometimes a TEA-URN or a COFFEE-AND-TEA MACHINE, and TEASPOONS. Occasionally a fitted case is provided.

tea infuser. A type of implement, with a hinged container having pierced decoration, used for infusing a small quantity of tea. There are two basic forms: (1) A globular 'tea ball' consisting of hinged hemispheres, and having a suspensory chain for dipping the container into hot water in a cup or teapot (comparable to a modern teabag). A modern novelty version is in the form of a tiny teapot with pierced holes and a suspensory chain. (2) A hinged double-bowl spoon having an extended handle.

tea-jar. A vase-shaped type of TEA-CADDY.

tea kettle. A type of KETTLE for hot water, to be used to replenish the TEAPOT when brewing tea. The form is usually pear-shaped (circular or octagonal in section), spherical, BULLET-SHAPED, or MELON-SHAPED. It has a

tau handle. Covered jug, David Mosely, Boston, Mass., *c.* 1805–15. Yale University Art Gallery (Mabel Brady Garvan Collection), New Haven, Conn.

tea-bowl. Fluted sides and scalloped edge, with conforming saucer (detail), Mark Paillet, London, 1750. H. 5·4 cm. Holburne of Menstrie Museum (University of Bath).

tea-caddy. Sliding-top type, John Jacob, 1745. H. 11 cm. Ashmolean Museum, Oxford.

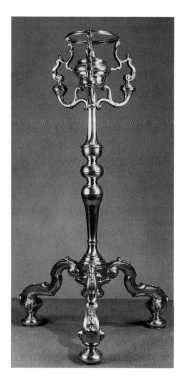

tea-kettle tripod table. Table with supporting ring for kettle, unmarked, *c.* 1725. H. 70 cm. Victoria and Albert Museum, London.

curved SPOUT (often with a moulded MOUNT as reinforcement at its base), a fixed or swivelling BAIL HANDLE (sometimes with a wooden, ivory or wicker GRIP), and a COVER with a FINIAL. Some early examples were accompanied by a small footed SALVER, to be used to protect the surface of the table from the heat of the kettle, but later kettles were supported by a stand provided with a spirit lamp for keeping the contents warm. *See* TEA KETTLE WITH STAND; TEA-URN.

tea-kettle salver. A type of small SALVER that was placed under a TEA KETTLE or a TEA KETTLE WITH STAND to protect the surface of the table from heat. Some are circular but others are triangular (to conform to the tripod form of the stand).

tea-kettle tripod table. A type of three-footed table, about 65 to 75 cm high, upon which to rest a TEA KETTLE WITH STAND, having at the top sometimes a small flat table top with a surface area sufficient only for the kettle and stand, but sometimes a frame of four curved brackets, with a ring at the top to support the kettle and a smaller ring below to support the heating lamp. A complete set, with table, kettle, and stand, of the former type, made by SIMON PANTIN, London, 1724, is in the Untermyer Collection at the Metropolitan Museum of Art, New York. Another, by John Corporon, is in the Collection of the Duke of Northumberland. One such table *c.* 1725, of the latter type and without the kettle and stand, is in the Victoria and Albert Museum, London, and another is in the Collection of the Duke of Buccleuch and Queensberry.

tea kettle with stand. A TEA KETTLE that rests on a STAND equipped with a warming device. Such stands were originally basin-shaped to contain smokeless charcoal, but later were three- or four-legged to support a spirit lamp. The kettle has a flat bottom and fits within a low ridge encircling the stand. The later stands usually have legs that are joined by arms which are connected to a central ring upon which the heating lamp rests. Some stands have an encircling descending pierced gallery that serves as a shield to protect the flame and to conceal the lamp. Some lamps have a hinged dome-shaped LID to extinguish and cover the wick. Sometimes the stand is provided with two hinged side handles so that it and the kettle can be carried together; and some stands have silver pegs (attached by chains) to be passed through holes in the foot-ring of the kettle and in the ridge of the stand so that the whole apparatus can be carried by the BAIL HANDLE of the kettle. Some examples have the kettle hinged to the stand at the front so that it may be tipped for pouring (antedating the TEA-URN), with two side chains to prevent over-tipping; in some other cases the kettle tilts between two upright posts to facilitate pouring. A few examples are provided with a footed SALVER as further protection for the table. *See* TEAPOT WITH STAND; TEA-URN WITH STAND; KANDLER TEA KETTLE; KETTLE WITH STAND.

tea ladle. The same as a CADDY-SPOON.

tea service (or **tea set**). A type of SERVICE, intended for serving tea, the components of which vary according to the individual needs, taste, and means of the owner. Among the articles from which a tea service might be composed are a TEAPOT (occasionally two, for different teas), TEA KETTLE (or TEA-URN), TEA-CADDY (or set of two caddies), SUGAR-BOWL, MUFFIN-DISH, CAKE-BASKET, HOT-WATER JUG, MILK-JUG, CREAMER (CREAM-JUG, CREAM-BOAT, or COW CREAMER), SLOP-BASIN, SUGAR TONGS, SPOON TRAY, and a TEA TRAY (or TEA TABLE), but not the articles of CUTLERY or FLATWARE. For afternoon tea, a fairly complete service is not unusual; but for morning tea, or for use by one person, a service is usually of three pieces – the teapot, sugar-bowl, and creamer – with sometimes a hot-water jug. *See* CABARET SERVICE; SOLITAIRE SERVICE; TÊTE-À-TÊTE SET. Often a service is made EN SUITE, but in many such cases it is composed of pieces made by different silversmiths and at different dates. Some tea services are combined with a COFFEE SERVICE. *See* COMPOSITE SERVICE; MATCHED SERVICE.

tea set. *See* TEA SERVICE.

tea strainer. A type of small flat utensil having in a central circular well patterned holes, and used for straining the leaves and motes from brewed tea when pouring it from a TEAPOT into a TEACUP. It has a wide rim and one flat horizontal handle, and it can be rested on the rim of a teacup while the tea is being poured. Some are accompanied by a small bowl, upon which to rest the used strainer and catch drips. A variant form is a small globular strainer that can be suspended from the spout of the teapot by a spring pin. *See* MOTE SKIMMER.

tea table. (1) A small table on which to rest a TEA SERVICE; a few examples have a wood core sheathed with silver and the top so made that it could be lifted off for separate use as a TRAY or WAITER. *See* TEA-KETTLE TRIPOD TABLE. (2) A type of handleless waiter, called in the 18th century a 'table', 'tea table' or 'tea board', that was made to fit on a wooden stand and upon which a tea service is placed. Some examples are oblong (later versions have two horizontal end-handles), but most are circular, oval or polygonal; they are large enough to accommodate a tea service. Some were made to fit on the circular top of a wooden tripod stand having a PIECRUST RIM of the same shape as that of the waiter, with the waiter sometimes having four short legs that fit into carved recesses in the rim of the stand; two examples were owned by the Earl of Warrington, and are at Dunham Massey Hall, Altrincham, Cheshire. *See* TEA TRAY.

tea tongs. The same as SUGAR TONGS; a term applied when the tongs form part of a TEA SERVICE.

tea tray. A type of TRAY upon which to rest a TEA SERVICE. The tray (called in the 18th century a 'table', 'tea table' or 'tea board') was made in various shapes, circular, oval, square or polygonal, and sometimes hexafoil or octofoil with lobed sides. Large examples usually have a GALLERY and two (rarely four) handles. Early trays generally have no decoration except an elaborate engraved COAT OF ARMS or CARTOUCHE in the centre; later examples have designs in BRIGHT CUTTING. *See* TEA TABLE.

tea urn. A type of vessel for dispensing, originally, hot water for making tea or, later, hot tea; it has (instead of the SPOUT of a TEAPOT or a TEA KETTLE) a TAP and a SPIGOT that enable the contents to be dispensed without lifting or tilting the heavy piece. In order to permit use of the tap, the urn is elevated on a stemmed foot or on legs rising from a footed base, or sometimes on a STAND equipped with a heating device. The early examples were placed on a low table and used for heating water (the water to be poured over the tea leaves); the heat was provided by burning smokeless charcoal in a BRAZIER upon which the urn rested. Hot air rising from the brazier passed through a fixed vertical copper tube inside the urn, heating the surrounding water before escaping through a pierced finial on the cover. A later method of heating the water made use of an iron rod (BILLET), previously heated in the kitchen, that was placed in a cylindrical socket (FIRE-BOX) affixed vertically inside the urn.

In the 1790s the vessel was used to keep hot the tea made in it; the heat was then provided continuously by a spirit lamp set on a flat base or in a frame or separate stand placed under the urn. The receptacles were of various shapes, globular, vase-chaped, pear-shaped, etc., and were decorated in NEO-CLASSICAL STYLE or ROCOCO STYLE, with FLUTING, REEDING, EMBOSSING, and applied ornaments. The tap was placed as low as possible on the urn, and was made sometimes of pewter or of hollow silver filled with pewter. The spigot was usually made of silver, wood or ivory in the form of a T, but some were in ornate form, such as an animal head, and some were a patented U-shaped lever that operated by being pulled down. The urn

tea-kettle with stand. Two forms: With brazier for charcoal, Gabriel Sleath, London, 1715; courtesy, Spink & Son Ltd, London. Decagonal, with conforming lampstand, Jacob Margas, London, 1715; British Museum, London.

tea service. Five-piece service, John Vernon, New York, *c.* 1695. Wadsworth Atheneum, Hartford, Conn.

sometimes has fixed side handles or DROP-RING HANDLES; such handles were made of silver, wood or ivory. As the spigot would sometimes drip, a small drip-bowl was often placed under the tap, resting on a slide-out shelf. The capacity of such an urn ranged from about two to four quarts. The early examples were called a 'tea kitchen'. *See* G. Bernard Hughes, 'The Georgian Vogue of the Tea Urn' in *Country Life*, 25 October 1962, p.1026. *See* COFFEE-URN; COFFEE-AND-TEA MACHINE; GODMAN TEA-URN.

tea-vase. A type of covered TEA-CADDY or TEA-JAR, ovoid in shape and having a small MOUTH intended for pouring out dry tea leaves rather than spooning them.

tea warmer. A type of VEILLEUSE, the upper part of which is a teapot, known in France as a *veilleuse-théière*. The only *veilleuses* known to have been made in silver are two English examples that are in the same form as the creamware tea warmers made from 1802 by Wedgwood, consisting of a cylindrical pedestal supporting a large teapot modelled to carry upward the lines of the pedestal and having a three-sectioned fixed BAIL HANDLE; the pedestals have vertical loop handles and pierced designs similar to the pierced leafage sprays on Wedgwood *veilleuses*. Both known examples bear a Royal cipher and crown; one was made by JOHN EMES in 1807 (its *godet* in 1812), the other by REBECCA(H) EMES and Edward Barnard I in 1813.

tea warmer. Pedestal with teapot, Rebecca(h) Emes and Edward Barnard I, London, 1813. H. 33 cm. National Library of Australia (Rex Nan Kivell Collection), Canberra.

teacup. A type of CUP for drinking tea, usually of semi-spheroidal form, having one vertical loop handle and usually accompanied by a saucer. Few, if any, English silver teacups have been made, due to the impracticability (arising from the heat-conducting quality of silver) of drinking from a hot cup and holding a hot handle. A few silver cups without a handle, resembling the Chinese porcelain TEA-BOWL, are recorded from the period 1660–85, but they were more likely intended to be used as a bowl. Some early recorded examples may have been made for tea-drinking, but they were probably melted down when porcelain teacups were introduced. *See* COFFEE-CUP; TREMBLEUSE.

teapot. A type of covered vessel, made in a great variety of shapes, styles, and sizes, used for brewing and serving tea (but early examples were used to pour hot water on to tea leaves in the teacups). The body of the early examples is globular, pear-shaped or square, or sometimes has vertical sides and is oval, hexagonal or octagonal in section; later ones are bullet-shaped and, in the neo-classical period, vase-shaped. The SPOUT is usually straight, ATTENUATED or curved, and on the opposite side of the teapot is the handle (loop, scroll, tau-shaped, foliated, etc.). The spout is usually attached near the bottom of the body so as to drain the infused tea without disturbing any floating tea leaves. The pot has an interior strainer of small holes at the junction of the spout and the body to prevent tea leaves from being poured into the cup with the liquid. Such pots are decorated in many styles, including having EMBOSSING, GADROONING, RIBBING or CHASING. Early examples have a flat or skirted bottom and a few later ones have small feet, but many have a FOOT-RING; those with a flat bottom are sometimes accompanied by a small stand that supports a heating device such as a spirit lamp (*see* TEAPOT WITH STAND). The COVER often fits flush with the rim of the body and has a decorative finial. A few teapots have, instead of a spout, a large BEAK, as on a JUG. The capacity is usually one to one-and-a-half pints. Teapots have been made of silver, silver gilt, or SHEFFIELD PLATE; and some of ceramic ware are fitted with silver MOUNTS, including the foot-ring, cover, handle, and the tip of the spout. *See* BULLET TEAPOT; CAPE TEAPOT; BACHELOR TEAPOT; BARREL TEAPOT; MELON TEAPOT; DRUM-SHAPED TEAPOT; PARAPET TEAPOT; CORRUGATED TEAPOT; BERKELEY TEAPOT; CERAMIC-STYLE SILVERWARE.

teapot with stand. Teapot with rounded bottom, stand with no heating device, Andrew Fogelberg and Stephen Gilbert, London, 1784-5. Victoria and Albert Museum, London.

teapot stand. A type of low flat utensil having short legs, upon which to rest a teapot in order to protect the surface of a table from the heat. *See* TRIVET. It is to be distinguished from a shaped stand in which to rest a teapot or an elevated stand equipped with a heating device; *see* TEAPOT WITH STAND.

teapot with stand. A type of TEAPOT that rests on a STAND usually having a heating device such as a small spirit lamp. Such a teapot has a flat bottom and the stand usually has either three or four legs (sometimes with decorative feet) joined at the bottom by arms that connect with a central ring in which the burner rests; the top of the stand is encircled by a grooved ring to support the teapot. It is similar to the large TEA KETTLE WITH STAND. Sometimes the stand is merely to support the teapot without any heating device; such a teapot may have a rounded bottom, as it rests on the stand rather than on a flat surface.

teapoy. A type of small lightweight table for individual use in the late 18th century when being served afternoon tea. It has three legs, is about 75 cm high, and its top is usually octagonal. Silver examples were made in the Queen Anne period, *c.* 1702–14. The type must be distinguished from the low and wider tables, intended to support a TEA SERVICE, for use by a seated hostess. The original form of a teapoy was modified from *c.* 1810 into a stand having a central pillar which supported, not a table top, but a fixed wooden chest which had compartments for TEA-CADDIES, SUGAR-BOWL, TONGS, CADDY SPOONS, and a BOWL in which to blend different teas. The term 'teapoy' has sometimes been erroneously applied to a tea-caddy, a TEA-CANISTER or a TEA-JAR; it is derived from Hindi words for 'table' and 'three', and hence has no connection with tea other than its use. *See* G. Bernard Hughes, 'Old English Teapoys' in *Country Life,* 8 September 1955, p. 504.

teaspoon. A type of SPOON having an oval bowl, normally with a capacity one-quarter or (modern) one-third that of a TABLESPOON, and used mainly for stirring in a teacup or a coffee-cup.

teething stick. A stalk of coral for an infant to teeth on, with a silver handle from which the coral extends. Most examples are a part of a RATTLE, and some are an extension of the handle of a WHISTLE. Sometimes called a 'gum-stick'. *See* WHISTLE WITH CORAL AND BELLS.

telescopic candelabrum. A type of CANDELABRUM having a telescopic stem with two or three slides, the lowest of which descended into the tall foot and the topmost had an urn-shaped SOCKET that supported a two-light arm and had a central socket for a third candlestick. Such pieces were made in the first quarter of the 19th century, with a square or circular base and variously decorated. *See* TELESCOPIC CANDLESTICK.

telescopic candlestick. Stem extended, John Roberts & Co., Sheffield, 1806. H. 9·5 cm. City Museum, Sheffield.

telescopic candlestick. A type of TABLE CANDLESTICK, the height of which is adjustable from about 5 to 50 cm to suit the needs of the user when writing, sewing, etc. and to maintain the same height for the light as the candle burns down. The stem is a cylinder having two to five interior telescopic slides rising from a base, the shape of which may be circular, square or lobed; but the earliest example used the Archimedean spiralling screw principle to raise the nozzle by turning the stem. Such candlesticks were patented in 1795; several patented techniques have been employed to adjust the height. The interior of the stem is usually lined with fabric to avoid binding and to ensure a close fit. The telescopic principle has also been used in a TELESCOPIC CANDELABRUM and a TRAVELLER'S CANDLESTICK. Sometimes called a 'sliding candlestick'. *See* G. Bernard Hughes, 'Candlesticks with a telescopic stem' in *Country Life,* 18 April 1968, p. 996.

Temple Bar Inkstand. An INKSTAND having, on a rectangular platform, a silver model of Temple Bar, a gateway built *c.* 1672 by Sir Christopher Wren (1632–1723) on the site of one of the City of London's entrances that was destroyed in the Great Fire of 1666. The platform is chased with the City arms, and the cover of the inkpot bears a reproduction of the City seal. The piece, which was made by ELKINGTON & CO., 1908, is at the Mansion House, London.

temple centrepiece. *See* COLONNADE CENTREPIECE.

Ten Eyck (family). Two generations of New York silversmiths. Koenraet Ten Eyck (1678–1753), born in Albany, New York, was a silversmith and a merchant. His two sons, Jacob (1705–93) and Barent (1714–95), each made pieces now in museums in the United States.

Teniers silverware. Articles of silverware that are decorated with peasant scenes reproduced from French prints of paintings by the Flemish painter David Teniers the Younger (1610–90). The decoration is on a plaque, made by CASTING and also EMBOSSING, which is then affixed to the piece (e.g., a COFFEE-POT).

Teniers silverware. Silver-gilt coffee-pot with lamp-stand, maker's mark 'IRS', London, 1850. H. 35·5 cm. Courtesy, Spink & Son Ltd, London.

term. Strictly, in architectural usage, a tall quadrangular pillar tapering downward (the gaine) and surmounted by a bust or figure of classical derivation. The word is a shortened form of the expression 'terminal figure', and originally applied to an ancient Roman boundary post. The pillar is about twice the height of the figure surmounting it. The figure is usually head and shoulders only, but sometimes includes considerably more of the body, gradually merging with the formal pillar. Some silver handles were made in this form, usually FLYING SCROLL HANDLES, e.g., addorsed figures on some examples of HEMING TWO-HANDLED CUPS.

terminal. An applied ornament at the end of a part of a vessel, such as the lower end of a vertical handle at the point where it joins the body and sometimes begins to curve away from it. It usually takes the form of an ornamental relief detail, often floral, but sometimes a human mask or a bird's head. Sometimes called an 'antefix'.

testimonial silverware. Any article of silverware, usually a VASE, SALVER or other imposing piece, presented formally to a person as a token of admiration for services rendered, civic or military, and usually with an apposite decoration and inscription; examples include the WELLINGTON PLATE, LLOYD'S PATRIOTIC FUND VASES, EGLINTON TESTIMONIAL, GLADSTONE TESTIMONIAL, KEAN TESTIMONIAL, MACREADY TESTIMONIAL, MONTEFIORE CANDELABRUM, MONTEFIORE CENTREPIECE, TYNG CUP, and WEBSTER VASE. Comparable articles are those made to honour the memory of a deceased person, e.g., the COWPER CUP and the SHAKESPEARE VASE.

tête-à-tête set. A type of CABARET SERVICE for two persons, for use at breakfast or for tea, usually consisting of a small COFFEE-POT or TEAPOT, a CREAM-JUG, and a SUGAR-BOWL. *See* LINCOLN TÊTE-À-TÊTE SET; SOLITAIRE SERVICE.

texturing. Giving a textured appearance to the surface of silverware. *See* ELECTRO-TEXTURING.

Thanet Service. An important silver DINNER SERVICE consisting of 110 known surviving pieces made by PAUL DE LAMERIE, 1742-6, for Sackville Tufton, 7th Earl of Thanet. It includes 72 dinner plates, 6 meat plates, 4 second-course plates, 2 soup-tureens with ladles, 4 sauce-boats with ladles, 6 salt-cellars with 5 salt spoons, 2 mazarines, 2 serving platters, and a covered supper dish, generally decorated with GADROONING. It is one of the few known silver dinner services made by a single silversmith; *see* LEINSTER SERVICE. The service descended from the Earl of Thanet, of Hothfield, in Kent, through Sir Richard Tufton, 1st Bt (said to have been the illegitimate son of the 11th and last Earl of Thanet), finally passing to his great-grandson, Henry, 3rd Baron Hothfield. It thus remained in the same family until sold in one lot by the Trustee of the 3rd Baron Hothfield's Will Trust on 22 November 1984 at Sotheby's, London; it was bought for £825,000 ($1,039,000) – a record price for a single lot of silverware – by the London silverware dealer E. & C. T. Koopman & Son Ltd. A few pieces by de Lamerie similar to some articles in the service have been recorded.

Theed, William (I) (d. 1772). A shopman of Henry Hurt who in 1758 became joint owner with WILLIAM PICKETT of the firm in which PHILIP RUNDELL became a partner in 1772, and which later became RUNDELL, BRIDGE & RUNDELL.

Theed, William (II) (1764-1817). An English artist and sculptor who, after studying in 1786 at the Royal Academy Schools, London, and from 1790 to 1794 in Rome, designed and modelled ceramic ware for Josiah Wedgwood II from 1799 until 1803 and, from 1803 to 1817, silverware for RUNDELL, BRIDGE & RUNDELL, becoming the head of their design department and chief modeller (some of his designs being executed by PAUL STORR and also by BENJAMIN SMITH I and DIGBY SCOTT). In 1808 he became a partner in the firm, but died impoverished. He was probably the modeller of the MERCURY CANDELABRUM and the GARDEN OF THE HESPERIDES CANDELABRUM.

Theocritus Cups. Several CUPS in the form of a Greek pottery calyx-type krater, having two vertical twisted vine-stem handles extending from the bottom of the bowl halfway up the sides. Each is decorated with two scenes in low relief; on one side, a maiden between two suitors (after the 'Orpheus' relief in the Villa Albani, Rome), and on the other side, an old fisherman gathering a net, a seated boy, and two foxes – all within a border of vines. The cups were made by PAUL STORR, for RUNDELL, BRIDGE & RUNDELL, from a design by JOHN FLAXMAN II, based on the description of a pottery cup in the First Idyll of Theocritus (*c.*300-260 BC), the Alexandrian pastoral poet:
    (1) One, marked London 1811-12 (accompanied by a PLINTH marked 1812-13; *see* below), presented in 1811 by officials of the City of Liverpool to Thomas Earle (1754-1822) in recognition of his services as an Alderman; it was sold at Sotheby's, London, on 24 October 1973, and is now owned by the Merseyside County Museums, Liverpool. (2) One, marked 1811-12, now in the Henry E. Huntington Museum and Art Gallery, San Marino, California. (3) One, marked 1811-12, that belonged to William Stanley Goddard (Headmaster of Winchester College, 1793-1810) and was acquired in 1911 by Francis G. Morgan. (4) One, marked 1812-13, bearing the engraved cipher of Queen Charlotte (consort of George III), for whom it was made,

Theocritus Cups. Cup, 1811-12, viewed from both sides, and plinth, 1812-13 (*top*), Paul Storr for Rundell, Bridge & Rundell, H. (overall) 36·3 cm. Merseyside County Museums, Liverpool.

and the badge of the Prince of Wales (later George IV), to whom she gave it; it is now in the Royal Collection. A silver-gilt pair of reproductions, made in 1868 by ROBERT GARRARD II for R. & S. Garrard & Co., were sold at Christie's, London, on 24 April 1974. The plinth associated with the cup now in Liverpool is four-sided and two-tiered, and has four curved legs (each surmounted by a ram's-head mask and terminating in a hoof) and a central foliated support; although it bears a later date than the cup, it was possibly made by Storr earlier and was probably not designed by Flaxman. The other cups listed do not have a plinth but each may have had one originally.

A variant of the Theocritus Cups, in the same shape and style, and made by Paul Storr, 1817–18, for Rundell, Bridge & Rundell, is inscribed 'Bequeathed to Elizth. Saltren by Charles Earl Manvers, her brother-in-law … 1816'; it differs in its decoration, having – on a granulated ground – classical figures of, on one side, two toga-clad women pouring libations on an altar, and, on the other, a semi-nude figure, reclining on a rock and leaning on an inverted torch, between two cypress trees, with a butterfly above some tall reeds. Dr N. M. Penzer (*Paul Storr*, 1964, 1971, p. 196, pl. LIX) has suggested that the figures represent, respectively, 'An Offering to the Departed' and 'The Departed in the Lower World', such motifs being appropriate for a memorial gift. The 1816 bequest is said to have been £100, with which the cup was purchased (or ordered to be made) by Elizabeth Saltren, sister of the widow of Charles Pierrepont, 1st Earl Manvers; the cup passed to the Earl's grand-daughter Augusta Sophia Anne (only child of his third son, Henry Pierrepont), who in 1844 married Lord Charles Wellesley (1808–58), the second son of the 1st Duke of Wellington. The cup passed to the Wellesley family, descending to the present Duke; it is kept at Stratfield Saye, his country seat near Reading, where it has always been known as the 'Flaxman Cup', and was so called in 19th-century wills (there being, however, no known record of its having been designed by Flaxman).

An earlier silver-gilt cup, dated 1814, similar in form and decoration to the Wellington example, and also made by Paul Storr for Rundell, Bridge & Rundell (with a liner, 1812), was unrecorded until sold at Sotheby's, London, on 23 May 1985, at which time it was suggested that this cup may have been a companion piece to one of the Theocritus Cups. It differs from the Wellington example in that the bowl has a plain ground, the posture of the reclining figure is not the same, the vines encircling the rim are less detailed, and there are no reeds behind the butterfly. It was bought by E. & C. T. Koopman & Son Ltd and Armitage, London silverware dealers.

Theocritus Cups. Variant, silver gilt, viewed from both sides, Paul Storr for Rundell, Bridge & Rundell, 1814. Courtesy, Sotheby's, London.

thimble. A protective cover worn, while hand-sewing, on the finger used to push the needle through the material. Thimbles are usually of metal, with the top pitted to prevent the head of the needle from slipping. Luxury examples are of silver (or gold), and sometimes the side is decorated with enamelling, a gold band, or several small gemstones. Sometimes a thimble is kept in a needle-case, and some thimbles hold a spool of thread. During the 16th century thimbles were made by vertically seaming a flat plate, and later by hammering a disk into a series of concave moulds of increasingly large size; in the 19th century they were made mechanically. Decoration was done by hand until the second quarter of the 19th century, when designs were impressed by a roller. *See* Elizabeth Galbraith Sickels, 'Thimblemakers in America' in *Antiques,* September 1967, p. 372.

thimble cover. A type of circular COVER, for a teapot or other receptacle, having a flat top much narrower than the receptacle to which the cover belongs, and fitting over a central vertical cylindrical opening.

thin plate. Any area of an article of silverware that is thinner than the surrounding part, resulting from the removal of an ARMORIAL, monogram, inscription, etc., the metal sometimes having become so thin that it is no longer rigid. Also, any article having such a thin area.

thistle cup. (1) A type of CUP, indigenous to Scotland, which is small, about 7 cm high, and of inverted-bell shape; the lower part of its bowl is decorated with a calyx-type band of applied upright lobes giving it the appearance of a thistle. It has an EVERTED rim and a vertical SCROLL HANDLE. Such cups were made in the late-17th and early-18th centuries. (2) A type of STANDING CUP of which the bowl is in the form of a thistle, made in the 16th century; its height ranges from about 30 to 50 cm *See* MANCROFT THISTLE CUP.

thistle cup (1). Alexander Forbes, Edinburgh, 1696-7, H. 7 cm. Royal Scottish Museum, Edinburgh.

Thistle Hallmark. The STANDARD HALLMARK used at the EDINBURGH ASSAY OFFICE for silver from 1759 (replacing the 'Deacon's Mark') but discontinued from 1 January 1975, when the LION RAMPANT HALLMARK was substituted as the mark for STERLING SILVER (differing from the LION PASSANT HALLMARK used from 1975 at the English Assay Offices).

Thistle Hallmark

Thomas Mazer. Miniature, silver band and foot-ring, Richard Sibley, London, 1847. D: 9 cm. Goldsmiths' Company, London.

Thomas Mazer. A miniature MAZER, 9 cm wide, of the type used for drinking the health of an infant. It has a wide encircling silver band engraved with the arms of John William Thomas and of the Goldsmiths' Company, Thomas having been a goldsmith elected to the Livery of the Company in 1839 and to its Court in 1851, as recorded in an engraved inscription on the base of the mazer. On the band is an engraved inscription recording that the cup was used by Thomas when the health of Albert, Prince of Wales (later Edward VII), was first drunk on 9 November 1841 (the day of his birth) on board the barge of the Company pursuant to the ancient, but since abandoned, custom of accompanying the Lord Mayor from the City of London to Westminster. The silver band and foot-ring were made by Richard Sibley, 1847. The cup is owned by the Goldsmiths' Company.

Thomas Wager Cup. A silver-gilt WAGER CUP in the form of a female figure in Elizabethan dress holding aloft a swivel cup between two upraised oak branches. It was made in London by William Eaton, 1829, and bears the engraved arms of Francis Boone Thomas, who donated it to the Goldsmiths' Company, London, of which he was Prime Warden in 1881. The cup bears in relief the arms of the Company, and also the engraved details of the donor's career in the Company.

Thomason Cup. A silver-gilt STANDING CUP, 1830, having a bowl of inverted-bell shape resting in an embossed CALYX decorated with ACANTHUS leaves. It is inscribed as the gift in 1831 from the Tsar of Russia to Sir Edward Thomason (1769–1849), a Birmingham silversmith. He had made sets of sixty silver medals depicting reproductions of paintings of biblical scenes, and donated a set to each of the reigning Sovereigns of Europe, and received in return knighthoods and gifts; the cup was commissioned by the Tsar in reciprocity, but from the rival firm of RUNDELL, BRIDGE & RUNDELL, rather than from Thomason's own workshop. The cup was bought at Sotheby's, London, in December 1970 for the City Museums and Art Gallery, Birmingham.

threading. A decorative border motif in the form of one or two thin closely spaced lines found along the entire length of both edges of the stem (handle) of some KNIVES, FORKS, and SPOONS. Sometimes called a 'threaded edge'. *See* FIDDLE PATTERN.

Three Kings Mazer. (1) A MAZER, *c*. 1490 (unmarked), the wooden bowl having an encircling silver-gilt collar engraved with the names of the Three Kings, Jasper *(sic)*, Melchior, and Balthasar, and having a PRINT in the bottom enclosing a plate enamelled in green depicting a squirrel sitting on a fish. The piece has a silver-gilt footed stem (detachable by a BAYONET JOINT), enabling it to be used as a STANDING CUP (hence it is sometimes called the 'Cup of the Three Kings'); the stem is decorated with six spiralling rounded flutes increasing in size as they descend toward the base, which is decorated with a band of CRESTING. It is owned by Corpus Christi College, Cambridge. (2) A mazer made by OMAR RAMSDEN, 1937, to commemorate the year in which Great Britain had three kings (1936). The maple bowl, resting on a low foot, is encircled by a silver band decorated with engraved leaves and having on it at equal intervals relief busts of George V, Queen Mary, Edward VIII, George VI, Queen Elizabeth, and the Princesses Elizabeth and Margaret. The mazer was a gift in 1940 from Harold Sidney Harmsworth (1868–1940), 1st Viscount Rothermere, to the Honourable Society of the Middle Temple, London.

three-handled cup. A variation of the TWO-HANDLED cup, an example of which was introduced in recent years at the Mansion House, London, for use as a LOVING CUP or a GRACE CUP for the benefit of its female guests. *See* HOARE LOVING CUPS; CAMBON CUP.

throne. A royal seat, of which none made of silver is known or recorded as being in England, but one, having a wood frame completely overlaid with silver plates, was made in 1713–14, with a foot-stool EN SUITE, upon the order of Peter the Great of Russia, by the London silversmith NICHOLAS CLAUSEN. Its CABRIOLE legs have CLAW-AND-BALL FEET, with eagle's claws; the decoration consists of foliated scrolls on a DIAPER ground and the Imperial arms of Russia surmounted by a crown, and each of the arms terminates with an eagle's head. The pieces originally stood, as a symbol of the Russian Empire, in the large Throne Room of St George's Hall in the Winter Palace, St Petersburg (now Leningrad), were moved to the small Throne Room of the Winter Palace, and are now preserved in the Hermitage Museum, Leningrad. *See* A. G. Grimwade, 'Peter the Great's Throne' in *The Connoisseur Year Book*, 1962, p. 192.

Thomason Cup. Silver gilt, Rundell, Bridge & Rundell, London, 1830. H. 34 cm. City Museums and Art Gallery, Birmingham.

thumbpiece. (1) A flat area, on the top of some HANDLES or the rim of some PLATES, on which to rest the user's thumb for better support, as on a CHAMBER-CANDLESTICK or a BOURDALOU. (2) A projection on the hinged LID of some drinking vessels (e.g., a TANKARD), by which the lid is raised when pressure is applied by the drinker's thumb. Formerly sometimes called a 'purchase', 'billet' or 'lever'. Such thumbpieces are made in a great variety of forms, including a lion sejant, a lion couchant, a vertical scroll, a pomegranate, etc. *See* CORKSCREW THUMBPIECE; GRIP. (3) A small projecting knob, to be pressed by the thumb to release a catch, as on some BOXES.

Tichborne Spoons. A set of twelve silver-gilt spoons, each with the London hallmark for 1592–3 and having as the finial on the stem a cast full-length figure in-the-round depicting a biblical or historical character, including nine known as 'The Nine Worthies' (as referred to by Shakespeare and Dryden), viz. 'The Three Pagans'–Hector of Troy, Alexander the Great, and Julius Caesar; 'The Three Jews'–Joshua, King David, and Judas Maccabaeus; and 'The Three Christian Knights'–King Arthur, Charlemagne, and Godfrey de Bouillon (sometimes considered to be Guy of Warwick), together with the 'Mystical Figures'–Christ and St Peter–and (presumably to provide twelve figures for a dozen spoons) Elizabeth I. The original set, known as 'The Tichborne Celebrities', was made by William Cowdell (although formerly thought to be by Christopher Wace), and is said to have been presented in 1657 by the Corporation of London to Sir Robert Tichborne, then Lord Mayor of London. The original set, which passed to his sister Sarah Sharp, was later sold at Christie's, London, on 19 April 1858 for £430, on 15 June 1914 for £2,000, and on 26 June 1974 for £70,000; after a resale to an overseas buyer and the refusal to grant an export licence, a public subscription of £85,000 ensured that the set would remain in England, and it is now in the County Museum of Hampshire, in Winchester. Reproductions in silver, silver gilt, and gold have been produced in a limited edition of 5,050 sets.

Tiffany & Co. A leading American silversmith and jewelry firm, founded in New York City in 1837 by Charles Lewis Tiffany (1812–1902) with John B. Young, the firm, known as Tiffany & Young, selling miscellaneous inexpensive wares, but soon thereafter expanding to offer jewelry, diamonds, and watches. In 1841 J. L. Ellis became a partner, the firm being called Tiffany, Young & Ellis. From 1848 to 1851 the firm employed the German, Gustav Herter, to design silverware. In 1851 Tiffany made an arrangement with John C. Moore for the latter's company to manufacture silverware for the firm, and from that year Moore's son, Edward Chandler Moore (1827–91), designed exclusively for Tiffany. He influenced the introduction of Japanese styles and became responsible for the growth of the firm's silverware business. In 1853 Tiffany gained sole control, the firm being known thereafter as Tiffany & Co., and it moved to 550 Broadway. By 1852 it had introduced the English STERLING SILVER standard, which was later legalized by the American Government. In 1868 Edward C. Moore & Co. was merged with Tiffany & Co., Moore became head of the art department, and the firm became the most important silverware firm in the United States. Moore was succeeded in 1891 by John T. Curran. Tiffany's son, Louis Comfort Tiffany (1844–1933), an early exponent of the ART NOUVEAU STYLE, introduced

thumbpiece. Tankard with thumbpiece in the form of a lion couchant, Robert Smythier, London, 1685. Courtesy, Garrard & Co. Ltd, London.

Three Kings Mazer (1). Mazer with detachable stem, silver gilt, unmarked, *c.* 1490. H. 13·3 cm. Corpus Christi College, Cambridge.

Three Kings Mazer (2). Omar Ramsden, London, 1937. D. 32·5 cm. Middle Temple, London (photo courtesy, Goldsmiths' Company, London).

tigerware jug. Rhenish stoneware jug with English silver mounts, *c.* 1580. H. 23 cm. Courtesy, Asprey & Co. Ltd, London.

Titan Vase. Matt silver with black-oxidized figures in high relief, Antoine Vechte, London, 1847. H. 75·5 cm. Goldsmiths' Company, London.

c. 1892 the Favrile iridescent glassware, and *c.* 1900 joined the firm, succeeding his father as Director in 1902. Thereafter the firm became the leader in designing and producing Art Nouveau silverware. In 1940, the firm, having acquired an international reputation for its silverware, jewelry, and gemstones, moved to its present luxurious premises at 5th Avenue and 57th St. The firm is noted for its many flatware patterns (*see* TIFFANY FLATWARE) and also for its PRESENTATION CUPS and presentation SWORDS. It sold some ware produced by ELECTROPLATING made by others (mainly by Thomas Shaw & Co., of Providence, Rhode Island, from 1870, acquiring that firm *c.* 1885) and made by itself from 1885, but ceased making electroplated ware in 1931. In the period 1910–25 it made silverware in the Colonial Revival style, some being shown at the 1939 New York World's Fair. In the 1930s–40s a small amount of ware was made in ART DECO STYLE, designed by A. L. Barney. In the 1950s William T. Lusk, great-grandson of Charles L. Tiffany, became President. In 1955 Walter Hoving took control from the Tiffany and Moore families; on his retirement he was succeeded by Henry B. Platt (great-great-grandson of Charles L. Tiffany), who is no longer with the company. The firm has branches in several United States cities, as well as in Paris (since 1850) and London (since 1868). *See* Charles H. Carpenter, Jr, *Tiffany Silver* (1978); —,'Tiffany Silver in the Japanese Style' in *The Connoisseur,* January 1979, p. 42. *See* BRYANT VASE; GLADSTONE TESTIMONIAL; MAGNOLIA VASE; VIKING PUNCH BOWL; MACKAY SERVICE.

Tiffany flatware. Various types of FLATWARE sold by TIFFANY & CO. The early examples, 1848–68, were produced by other manufacturers. The first standard Tiffany pattern was made in 1869, called 'Tiffany' (it was modified and its name was changed in 1936 to 'Beekman'); this and nine other patterns were designed and patented for Tiffany in the period 1869–89 by Edward C. Moore, and thirteen in the period 1880–6 by Charles T. Grosjean (1841–88), who succeeded Moore as designer, and by others thereafter, including Burnett Y. Tiffany, youngest son of Charles L. Tiffany. The firm has produced flatware in more than forty patterns, in addition to some 'custom-designed private patterns' and some 'hand-worked patterns' for wealthy clients. The popular CHRYSANTHEMUM PATTERN, introduced in 1880, is still being made.

tigerware jug. A type of JUG made of Rhenish stoneware (sometimes called 'tygerware') with a mottled brown, purple or blackish glaze over a greyish body, occasionally having English silver mounts. The mounts comprise usually a neck-band (wide to narrow), a hinged lid with a finial and a THUMB-PIECE, and a base rim. The mounts were decorated with ENGRAVING, EMBOSSING or STAMPING. The top of the handle is often only 2·5 cm below the rim of the jug, so that the hinge of the domed lid had to be raised on a box-like mount. On some examples there are vertical straps connecting a central band with the base rim; as such straps could not be soldered to affix them to the ceramic piece, they are attached by hinged pins. The stoneware body was made in the style of jugs made in Germany, at Nuremberg and Augsburg. Many examples were mounted in the second half of the 16th century, such as: (1) the FRANCES JUG; (2) a similar piece with mounts by William Cocknidge, 1576–7, now in the Wadsworth Atheneum, Hartford, Connecticut; (3) a jug, also having mounts by Cocknidge, now in the Metropolitan Museum of Art, New York; and (4) two jugs with silver-gilt mounts by John Eydes, Exeter, *c.* 1580, the other, *c.* 1560, smaller and without a box hinge. *See* G. Bernard Hughes, 'The Brilliance of Tigerware' in *Country Life,* 23 October 1969, p. 1048. *See* STONEWARE JUG; HAUNCE POT; MOUNTED OBJECTS.

tilting water set. A receptacle for holding and pouring water, being in the form of a JUG suspended in a frame so that it can be tilted for pouring. An example, in the Yale University Art Gallery, was made in 1891 by Simpson, Hall and Miller, of Wallingford, Connecticut; it rests on a square base upon which are depressions to position a silver SLOP-BOWL and two silver BEAKERS. Related to it is a silver jug on wheels (locally called a 'tipping water pitcher') that was shown in an 1876 catalogue of REED & BARTON.

tincture. In heraldry, the colour of, or painted on, an object, especially a COAT OF ARMS. In uncoloured printed or engraved renderings, white or silver (ARGENT) is represented by a plain surface (tinctureless), gold by small dots, and colours by horizontal, vertical or diagonal lines (called HATCHING); such representations are found on silverware decorated with an engraved coat of arms.

tinder-box. A metal box in which tinder (e.g., an inflammable piece of linen) is kept, together with steel and flint for striking a spark to kindle a fire. An example made of silver has compartments for the materials; made by Joseph Richardson, Jr (*see* RICHARDSON), it is in the Museum of Fine Arts, Boston, Massachusetts.

tine. One of the thin pointed prongs, usually from two to four in number, on a FORK.

tinning. The process of lining the interior of certain articles of HOLLOW WARE made of PLATED METAL, and occasionally the bottom of some such flat articles, with tin so as to afford protection against any health risks arising from food or drink being in contact with copper. The tin lining was cheaper and more easily kept clean than additional plating with silver. The technique involved thoroughly cleaning the area to be tinned, then protecting the remaining area with a covering against any spilled molten tin, sprinkling the area to be tinned with sal ammoniac, heating the article, and pouring molten pure tin over the entire copper area. Tinned bottoms were polished to resemble the silver top. Re-tinning was required as the tin wore off with use.

tipstaff. A type of STAFF that is tipped with a metal ornament (in England, often a crown) and is carried as a symbol of authority. It is less massive and ornate than a MACE, and is carried by officials of lower rank. Such tipstaffs were carried by the beadles of certain Livery Companies or corporations. Some have a concealed miniature OAR to evidence the authority of a water-bailiff. *See* BEADLE'S STAFF; PORTER'S STAFF; VERGE.

Titan Vase. A VASE in Etruscan form, made by ANTOINE VECHTE and considered to be his most important work, commissioned by John Samuel Hunt, of HUNT & ROSKELL, on his visit to Paris in 1844. The vase is of matt silver with *repoussé* black-oxidized figures in high relief. The decoration, in the style of Michelangelo, shows the defeat of the Titans by Zeus, who is depicted on the cover hurling thunderbolts on them from Mount Olympus. On each side of the bowl are groups of Titans, some climbing upward, others crushed by rocks hurled by Zeus. On the two vertical handles are Titans menacing Zeus, and on the base are the fallen figures of Vice and Presumption. On the neck in non-oxidized low relief are figures of Time and Fate, and elsewhere are such figures of Neptune and Pan, as well as of fabulous monsters. The vase was completed in 1847 and was exhibited by Hunt & Roskell in Paris in 1847, also at the Great Exhibition in London in 1851, and again in Paris in 1855 and in London in 1862. It was purchased by the Goldsmiths' Company, London, along with the VECHTE SHIELD, in 1890.

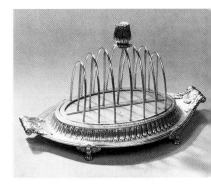

toast-rack. One of a pair, silver gilt, with loop partitions and acanthus finial, on separate base, Paul Storr, London, 1810. W. 27·5 cm. Courtesy, Partridge (Fine Arts) Ltd, London.

toast-rack. A type of utensil having vertical openwork partitions for holding and serving several (usually four to eight) slices of toast, one slice standing upright in each space, and usually having a central vertical ring for carrying. Early examples were in the form of a single row of vertical posts on a wire-ring base that supported the slices, but later ones have circular wire loops (occasionally flat openwork partitions) to separate the slices. The stand (sometimes a separate piece) rests usually on four feet, and often has a flat-bottomed tray to support the slices instead of the simple wire ring. Some toast-racks are combined with an EGG-CUP STAND, and some were made in expanding form (so as to occupy less storage space) by means of an accordion wire frame. *See* BANNOCK-RACK; LETTER-RACK.

toasting fork. A type of implement for holding a slice of bread to be toasted before an open fire. It usually has a wooden haft, about 75 to 100 cm long, fitted with a FERRULE into which is fixed a fork having two or three long tines; sometimes there is a hook attached to the ferrule, by which to hang the fork when not in use, or there may be a suspensory ring at the end of the haft. Examples are known from the 16th century, but such pieces became popular in the 18th century. A variant form, called a 'toaster', has no tines to hold the slice but instead has attached to the handle a U-shaped rack into which the slice is suspended; an example, made by ANTHONY NELME, 1700–1, is at Queens' College, Cambridge. Later examples, *c*.1800, were made with a telescopic handle having three or four slides so as to reduce its length when not in use to about 30 cm. *See* Charles C. Oman, 'Antique Silver Toasting Forks' in *Antique Collector,* February 1963, p. 24.

tobacco-box (1). Oval box, London, 1652. Courtesy, Brand Inglis Ltd, London.

tobacco-box. (1) A type of small BOX used for carrying smoking tobacco, usually differing from a SNUFF-BOX in having an unattached fitted COVER instead of a hinged LID (the reason being that a snuff-taker needed to keep one hand free while holding and opening the box to take snuff, but a pipe-smoker, using both hands to fill his pipe, could rest the box and cover on a table). Tobacco-boxes were usually oval, about 7·5 to 10 cm long and 2·5 cm deep, until *c*. 1750, and thereafter were made in various shapes and sizes.

toilet mirror. Silver frame with scroll feet and with armorial cresting, attributed to Paul de Lamerie, London, *c.* 1730. H. 66 cm. Courtesy, Partridge (Fine Arts) Ltd, London.

Tompion (Mostyn) Clock. Parcel-gilt decoration and silver mounts, *c.* 1695. H. 71 cm. British Museum, London.

They were made of silver, and also of many other materials, and were variously decorated. *See* GRANT TOBACCO-BOX. (2) A large type of box, for use on a table, to contain smoking tobacco. Such boxes are circular or of other form, with a flat bottom and a close-fitting LID or COVER, but not distinguishable from boxes for toilet or other use unless accompanied by a pipe-tamper or other smoking implement or being significantly decorated or being provided with a weighted plate to press down the tobacco. *See* TOBACCO STAND.

tobacco rasper. A type of implement for rasping (grating) tobacco, similar to a NUTMEG GRATER but larger and for finer grating.

tobacco stand. A type of table receptacle for holding smoking tobacco and also sometimes having provision for smoking accessories, such as an ash-tray or a pipe-rest. An example, at Clare College, Cambridge, donated by Sir William Peere Williams, is in the form of a vertical barrel with a demi-lion finial, standing on a tray and accompanied by two silver ash-trays; it was made by Phillips Garden, bears a London mark, 1757–8, and is decorated on the barrel and tray with the arms of the donor.

toddy ladle. A type of LADLE used for serving hot toddy from a PUNCH-BOWL into drinking glasses. It is similar to but shorter than a PUNCH LADLE. A plated rod was sometimes inserted in the FERRULE so as to raise the join of the wooden handle to a point above the level where it would dip into the hot toddy; in this way the join was protected from the effects of repeated expansion and contraction of the metal in contact with the hot liquid, which would otherwise cause the handle to become loose. In the 1760s the use of wood for the handle was sometimes superseded by whalebone, the handle being circular or square near the ferrule, but having the upper part twisted to afford a firm grip. In the 1800s some such ladles were made with a silver handle, slightly curved, joining the bowl at right-angles to its width and at a 135° upward angle. The bowl sometimes has a pouring lip, occasionally two. Such toddy ladles were made mainly in Scotland or for sale in the Scottish market. They were largely superseded in the 1820s by the introduction of the TODDY LIFTER.

toddy lifter. A hollow utensil used for transferring hot toddy from a bowl into drinking glasses. It is usually shaped like a small decanter with a long thin neck, bulbous at one end and with a hole in each end. The bulbous end was dipped into the bowl until the object filled (capacity, about a wine glass), when a thumb was used to close the opposite hole until removed to release the toddy into the glass. Some examples have, at the middle of the neck, a collar as a finger grip. The toddy lifter is said to have been invented in Scotland, and they were made in England in the 18th and early-19th centuries. Sometimes called a 'punch filler'. *See* DECANTING SIPHON.

toddy warmer. A type of utensil for warming toddy over a flame. Such pieces are similar to a CHAFING DISH, being in the form of a receptacle placed over a BRAZIER or other type of heating device. Sometimes the receptacle has a rounded bottom and rests in a ring over the flame, but some have a flat bottom and are supported by three brackets. *See* BRANDY WARMER.

toilet accessories. Various small toilet articles made of or mounted with silver, such as hair-brushes, combs, manicuring sets. Such articles are beyond the scope of this book, except when part of a TOILET SERVICE.

toilet mirror. A type of MIRROR to be stood on a toilet table, and often a part of a TOILET SERVICE. The frame for some such mirrors has been made of silver; it is usually square or rectangular, sometimes shaped, and has an easel support at the back. Some frames are not of solid silver, but are of wood, covered with velvet, and have applied a die-stamped openwork silver decoration. Some examples have attached at each side, to afford good illumination, a MIRROR SCONCE of the pilaster type with a single branch.

toilet service. A set of articles for a lady's toilet, including usually a TOILET MIRROR, HAND MIRROR, SCENT-BOTTLE, EYE BATH, CASKET (for jewels), COMB-BOX, patch-box, pin-cushion, SALVERS, pomade-jar, toilet jar, brush, comb, and small covered bowls. Such articles were made of silver or silver gilt in complete matching sets of up to thirty pieces. The early sets were decorated with only an engraved cipher or COAT OF ARMS, but later decoration was more elaborate, with FLAT CHASING of patterns in CHINOISERIE style or with overall EMBOSSING. Although a number of such services are known to have been made in England, only one (made by Colin McKenzie, Edinburgh, 1702, and consisting of 16 pieces, 7 being undecorated) is known from Scotland. Many silver articles were later replaced by those of glass with silver

MOUNTS. *See* J. Starkie Gardner, 'Silver Toilet Services' in *The Connoisseur,* May-August 1905, p. 95; Edward Wenham, 'Silver Toilet Services' in *Antique Collector,* May-June 1948, p. 102; Arthur G. Grimwade, 'Royal Toilet Services in Scandinavia' in *The Connoisseur,* April 1956, p. 175. *See* CALVERLEY TOILET SERVICE; NORFOLK TOILET SERVICE; TREBY TOILET SERVICE; CAROLINE MATHILDA TOILET SERVICE; SOPHIA MAGDALENA TOILET SERVICE; WILLIAMS-WYNN TOILET SERVICE.

toilet-water label. A type of BOTTLE TICKET made for a bottle of toilet water, a known example being for Hungary Water.

Tollemache Dessert Dish. One of a SET of four DESSERT DISHES made by PAUL STORR in 1838 after he had left RUNDELL, BRIDGE & RUNDELL. It is in the form of a SCALLOP shell being drawn over a rocky base by a sculptured figure of a Triton blowing a conch-shell. It was formerly in the Tollemache Collection.

Tompion (Mostyn) Clock. A historically important bracket clock made by Thomas Tompion (1639-1713), one of the world's greatest clock-makers. It has a rectangular ebony-veneered case decorated with PARCEL GILDING and silver MOUNTS, made by an unidentified silversmith, and based probably on a design by Daniel Marot (1663-1752), a leading French designer who, as a Huguenot, came to London and worked for the Court of William III, 1694-8. The case has four scroll feet and on the upper corners are figures of a lion and a unicorn (the supporters of the Royal coat of arms), as well as a rose and thistle; it is surmounted by a standing figure of Britannia holding a spear. The clock was made in England *c.* 1695 for the bedchamber of William III, who bequeathed it to Henry Seymour, Earl of Romney, from whom it descended to Lord Mostyn. It was purchased in 1982 by the British Museum, London. (A different Tompion Clock, similarly decorated, is at Colonial Williamsburg, Virginia.)

Tong Cup. A silver-gilt STANDING CUP having a rock-crystal cylindrical bowl enclosed by three straps decorated with lion's-head masks and resting on a vase-shaped stem on a domed foot. The bowl has a wide everted silver-gilt rim of the same diameter as the low-domed cover, which has a bracketed spool-shaped finial surmounted by a ball. The stem, base, and cover are decorated with applied scrolling and berried foliage. The piece, *c.* 1610, is unmarked and is owned by the church at Tong, Shropshire. Cups, *c.* 1611, with similar decoration are at Christ's College, Cambridge, and in the Victoria and Albert Museum, London, and a salt so decorated is owned by the Duke of Bedford; all are apparently by the same maker.

tongs. (1) A type of utensil for lifting and holding some article of food (such as a lump of sugar, a piece of ice, or an asparagus stalk), usually consisting of two arms joined at one end by a pivot, hinged together midway like a pair of scissors, or made in U-shape with arms that spring back into parallel position when hand pressure is released. Sometimes referred to as a 'pair of tongs'. *See* SERVING TONGS; SUGAR TONGS; ICE TONGS; ASPARAGUS HOLDER. (2) A similar type of utensil for use at a fireplace, for lifting coals or firewood. Some small such pieces, about 12·5 cm long and made of silver, were used to hold a burning ember while lighting a tobacco pipe. One example has a thin rod between the blades, to be used to clean the stem of the pipe.

tontine ware. Articles of silver (or gold) of various types, that bear an inscription with the names of the members of a tontine (an arrangement by which each member of a group of subscribers participates in the income of a fund during his lifetime, the balance of the assets going to the last one, or few, to survive; it was invented by Lorenzo Tonti, a Neapolitan banker who initiated the scheme in France in 1653). The earliest-known example of such an article is a gold TUMBLER CUP, 1702, made by PIERRE HARACHE II and now in the Museum of Fine Arts, Boston, Massachussetts. Such articles made of silver in the 18th century include a WAITER, an INKSTAND, and a TWO-HANDLED CUP.

toothbrush set. A traveller's set that includes a toothbrush (sometimes double-headed) and a container for tooth powders (sometimes double-hinged for two varieties of powder), and occasionally a tongue scraper (flat, narrow, and flexible) The set is fitted into a pocket container. Examples are known from *c.* 1780 to *c.* 1830.

toothpick. A thin pointed instrument for removing particles of food lodged between the teeth. Examples made of silver (or gold) were popular in Eng-

Tong Cup. Silver gilt with rock-crystal bowl, *c.* 1610. Parish church, Tong, Shropshire (photo courtesy, Historic Churches Preservation Trust, London).

land during the Renaissance period. They were sometimes included in the equipment of a CANTEEN or a TRAVELLER'S DINING SET. Occasionally, a toothpick had, at the opposite end, an EAR-PICK. Some examples made from *c.* 1800 to the present consist of a decorative case containing a retractable point.

toothpick-case. A type of BOX, usually oblong and with a LID having a BLIND HINGE, for carrying TOOTHPICKS. Examples have been made in France and England since the 18th century, some of gold or silver and variously decorated – with enamelling, with a Wedgwood jasper plaque, set with gemstones, or with engraved decoration in BRIGHT CUTTING. *See* WHISTLE.

topographical ware. Articles of silver which are decorated by EMBOSSING or CHASING with depictions of palaces, castles, manor houses, cathedrals, and scenic views, such as the lids of some SNUFF-BOXES (including large examples for table use, as well as those of pocket size), and VINAIGRETTES. A specialist in such work was Nathaniel Mills, of Birmingham, in the 1830s. Some large SALVERS were so decorated. *See* CASTLE-TOP WARE.

Torah bells. Rimmonim in campanile form, with crown and flaming-urn finial, Abraham de Oliveyra, London, 1724. H. 45·5 cm. Jewish Museum, London (photo courtesy, Warburg Institute, University of London).

Torah bells. A pair of vertical ornaments (in Hebrew, *rimmonim*) called the 'Crowns of the Law' which, in western Jewish communities, are placed as a finial atop the two rollers upon which is wound the scroll of the Torah ('The Scroll of the Law'), the Jewish Pentateuch or Law of Moses, which, when not being read as a part of the religious service, is kept covered with an embroidered mantle and ornamented on the front by a suspended TORAH BREASTPLATE and TORAH POINTER. The *rimmonim* are in architectural form, made usually of silver but sometimes of silver gilt, and have a silver FERRULE (sometimes having chased decoration) to fit over the top of each roller (also often of silver). They are usually made in ROCOCO STYLE, the early examples – in the form of arcades in several tiers of openwork – being suggestive of a campanile or in bulbous form, and always having attached several small bells. Later the campanile form was abandoned for an open bowl covered by an openwork or filigree canopy having a tall finial and resting on several scroll brackets. The finial is usually in the form of a crown, occasionally with a Lion of Judah or a flaming urn. The earliest-known English silver example was made (after a Dutch prototype) by Samuel Wastell, 1712, and other early examples were made in 1719 by GABRIEL SLEATH and by William Sparkman, one in 1724 by ABRAHAM DE OLIVEYRA, and three – in 1758, 1767, and 1768 – by William Grundy; a later American example was made in 1772 by MYER MYERS for the Synagogue of Newport, Rhode Island. Examples made in the 19th century vary considerably in form and decoration. Sometimes there was used, instead of the *rimmonim*, a type of crown. The term '*rimmonim*', Hebrew for 'pomegranates', is related not to the shape of the piece, but to the fact that the seeds in a dried pomegranate rattle, and hence pomegranates and bells were attached to a rabbi's garment *(ephod)* to announce his arrival. *See* JEWISH RITUAL SILVERWARE.

Torah breastplate. An ornamental shield that in a synagogue is suspended by chains over the front of the Torah. It is usually ornately decorated with embossing to depict symbolic motifs, such as two columns reminiscent of the columns of the Temple of Jerusalem, the Tablet of the Ten Commandments, or the Lion of Judah. Attached is a removable small plate upon which is indicated the part of the Torah for current reading. Some such shields have suspended bells. An example has been made by GERALD BENNEY. *See* JEWISH RITUAL SILVERWARE.

Torah pointer. A decorated rod used in a synagogue to indicate the text of the Torah that is to be read in the day's service and so avoid the Torah being touched by hand. It usually has at the head a representation of a hand with a pointing index finger, and at the other end a suspension ring by which to hang it, when not in use, on the Torah. Examples in many forms and materials are known from Continental countries; an English silver example was made by Duncan Urquhart and Napthali Hart, London, 1798, and one made in London, 1797-8, is in the Victoria and Albert Museum. *See* JEWISH RITUAL SILVERWARE

Torah pointer. Duncan Urquhart and Napthali Hart, London, 1798. L. 27·3 cm. Jewish Museum, London (photo courtesy, Warburg Institute, University of London).

torchère (French). A type of tripod table having a small circular surface, about 20 cm in diameter, and being about 1·15 m high, usually with the stem decorated with baluster-shaped and knopped ornaments and with three scroll-shaped feet; used to support a lamp, candlestick or candelabrum, such pieces were popular in the 17th/18th centuries, being made usually as a pair, to stand one on each side of a wall mirror. Examples made of silver are rare: an English pair, 1676, 1·14 m high, is at Knole House, Sevenoaks, Kent, and another pair, presented by Charles II, 1660–85, to the Corporation of the City of London, and now in the Royal Collection, is at Windsor Castle. Sometimes called a 'candlestand'.

In England in recent years the term GUÉRIDON has sometimes been applied to such tables, but the word is preferably used to refer to a type of table that is usually lower, has a larger top surface, and has a columnar stem (often in the form of a kneeling blackamoor supporting the table top on his upraised arms), and that is used to support an ornament. The term is derived from the name of the character Guéridon (a Moor) in a French play of the late 17th century, confirming that it should be applied to tables of that form rather than to a *torchère* as defined above. In France the term *guéridon* was sometimes used for a tall candlestand before 1696, when the term *torchère* became accepted there in the *Dictionnaire de l'Académie;* this earlier practice possibly accounts for the occasional use of *guéridon* in England in recent years (and for its support by Norman M. Penzer in *The Connoisseur,* March 1961, p. 88, note 4).

tot-cup. A type of small drinking CUP of no specified form. The term has been applied to a small one-handled cup possibly used as a STIRRUP CUP, but there seems no basis for calling such a cup a stirrup cup.

touch. (1) The mark stamped on silver to attest its quality, such as the British STANDARD HALLMARK. (2) The standard or degree of FINENESS of a piece of silver stamped with a Standard Hallmark. (3) The act of ASSAYING. The term is derived from the ancient practice of rubbing a piece of silver (or gold) on a TOUCHSTONE to test its composition.

touchstone. Generally, a black siliceous stone (usually basanite) related to flint, used in the oldest-known method of testing the purity of a silver (or gold) ALLOY by examining the narrow streak left on the stone after it has been rubbed with the metal. The method involved the use of a set of 'touch-needles', each made of an alloy containing a known proportion of the base metal; these would be scratched on the touchstone, and the colour of the marks compared with that made by the metal being tested. Sometimes there is little difference in the colours, but an expert can judge by the sensation of greasiness or dryness imparted by the scratching, or by the resulting smoothness or roughness.

torchère. One of a pair, London, *c.* 1676. H. 1·14 m. Knole House, Sevenoaks, Kent.

toy. A term used in England in the 18th century in respect of: (1) miniature versions of articles of many types; and (2) types of household articles and personal trinkets which, although small, were full-size, such as were made by a 'toyman', examples being CADDY-SPOONS, NUTMEG GRATERS, VINAIGRETTES, WINE LABELS, SNUFF-BOXES, WATCH-CASES, BUCKLES, SEALS, RATTLES, CARD-CASES, TOOTHPICK-CASES, etc. Many of the latter group were made in Birmingham (known as the 'toy-making capital of the world') from *c.*1750 to *c.*1850; the leading makers were Samuel Pendleton, Joseph Taylor, and Nathaniel Mills. Today the first category is known as MINIATURE SILVERWARE and the second as SMALLWARE. Small silver articles were required to be hallmarked until, under the Act of 1738, some types were listed as being exempt; the Act of 1790 repealed that provision, however, and thereafter silver articles weighing less than 5 dwt were exempt with the exception of certain specified types, including caddy-spoons, BOTTLE TICKETS, and TEA STRAINERS.

Trafalgar Vase. *See* LLOYD'S PATRIOTIC FUND VASES.

traveller's candlestick. A type of CANDLESTICK for use by a traveller to afford better lighting than locally provided in an inn or tavern. There are at least three types: (1) A TELESCOPIC CANDLESTICK made in pairs so that after the two candlesticks have been dismantled by removing the telescopic stems, with the sockets, the two stems can be enclosed in the two joined deep bases. Sometimes such a pair is accompanied by a shagreen or leather case which also accommodates a CANDLE EXTINGUISHER. (2) A candlestick on a small circular base, having as a cover for the candle a cylindrical SNUFFER with a rounded top; the snuffer can also be screwed into the side of the base to serve as a horizontal handle. (3) A CHAMBER CANDLESTICK made so that the small candle socket is hinged and can be folded down into the bowl-shaped base.

Treby Armorial Dish. Paul de Lamerie, London, 1723–4. D. 61 cm. British Museum, London.

Treby Helmet Jug. Paul de Lamerie, London, 1724–5. H. 21·5 cm. Ashmolean Museum, Oxford.

traveller's dining set. A SET of dining articles for personal use to be taken on a journey. It often includes a BEAKER or TUMBLER CUP, KNIFE, FORK, and SPOON (sometimes with folding or detachable handles), SPICE-BOX (for salt and pepper), CORER, CORKSCREW, TOOTHPICK, NUTMEG GRATER, etc., all sometimes fitted into the beaker or the tumbler cup, and also a TRAVELLER'S CANDLESTICK. The set is sometimes provided with a shagreen case, occasionally having silver mounts. Also called a 'travelling set'; a less complete set is sometimes called a CAMPAIGN ÉTUI or a 'camp canteen'. See BEAKER SET.

traveller's tea set. A type of small portable TEA SERVICE for use while travelling. One such set consisting of a TEAPOT, MILK-JUG, and SLOP-BOWL made with the handles slotted for removal and compact packing, was used by the Duke of Wellington; made in London, 1811–15, and bearing the mark 'MS' (possibly for May Sumner), it is in the Wellington Museum, Apsley House, London. A rare example consists of a teapot into which can be fitted three bowls (without handles) which nest into each other – two for use as drinking cups, and one divided midway to permit filling with two types of tea or with tea and sugar; it was made in Edinburgh, 1817. Another rare example, made of SHEFFIELD PLATE, *c.*1810, consists of an oval teapot into which nest a slop-bowl, a CREAMER (with a tiny lip), and a SUGAR-BOWL.

tray. A type of flat utensil for carrying articles used for food or drink, made in many sizes and styles, but usually rectangular with rounded or slightly indented corners and having on each narrow end a horizontal loop handle or an extended hand-grip; but some examples are circular or oval with two such handles. The length ranges from about 50 to 75 cm, but some trays are up to 1·22 m long, those over 75 cm usually having four handles. Some trays have at the sides an encircling vertical pierced GALLERY edged with a rim of GADROONING or BEADING, and some have a rim with ROCOCO mounts. Decoration of the surface is by ENGRAVING, CHASING or BRIGHT CUTTING, often with an engraved ARMORIAL. A tray was often made EN SUITE with, and large enough to hold all the pieces of, a SERVICE. Some small so-called trays are not for serving; *see* PEN TRAY, SNUFFER TRAY, SPOON TRAY. *See* also BREAD TRAY; WAITER; SALVER.

tray candlestick. A type of CANDLESTICK that is similar to a CHAMBER CANDLESTICK, but has a larger tray, sometimes of lobed shape, to which the socket is affixed.

tray snuffer. A type of SNUFFER that rests horizontally on a SNUFFER TRAY. Such snuffers usually have three short feet, one under each handle and one under the pointed end, provided to facilitate picking up the snuffer from the tray.

treasure. An article, or group of articles, found after being lost or having been buried for a purpose other than mere concealment (such as funerary articles), as distinguished from a HOARD. *See* MILDENHALL TREASURE.

Treasury inkstand. A type of INKSTAND in the form of a low oblong casket resting on four feet and, in most examples, having the interior divided into compartments for ink, pounce, sealing-wax, seals, and pens. Some examples have a single hinged LID, others have a double lid centrally hinged back-to-back, and occasionally an upright handle. It is so called because such inkstands were first made, pursuant to an order of 13 May 1686 by the Lord Chamberlain, for the Treasury or the Privy Council, those for the Treasury having one compartment, those for the Privy Council two.

Treby Armorial Dish. A large DISH of ARMORIAL PLATE decorated only with an applied plaque bearing the coat of arms of the Rt Hon. George Treby, M.P. It was made by PAUL DE LAMERIE, London, 1723, with engraving in the style of WILLIAM HOGARTH (but attribution questioned). It is owned by the British Museum. London.

Treby Basin. A large BASIN, having a shallow bowl (and hence not unlike a large DISH), made in 1725 by PAUL DE LAMERIE for the Rt Hon. George Treby, M.P.; in the centre there is a cast and chiselled ESCUTCHEON with the Treby coat of arms, executed in high relief and enclosed within an elaborate CARTOUCHE in BAROQUE STYLE. It was last recorded as being in a private collection.

Treby Helmet Jug. A HELMET JUG that is part of the TREBY TOILET SERVICE. It has a FLYING SCROLL HANDLE and the lower portion of the bowl is decorated with SPOON-HANDLE STRAPS. It was made by PAUL DE LAMERIE, London, 1724–5.

Treby Toilet Service. One of the most complete surviving TOILET SERVICES, made in 1724–5 by PAUL DE LAMERIE on order from the Rt Hon. George Treby, M.P., as a wedding gift for his wife, Charity Hele. It consists of 28 pieces, all hallmarked in the same year, including a silver-mounted MIRROR, four square TRAYS, a pair of CANDLESTICKS, the TREBY HELMET JUG, a pair of pomade-jars, four circular BOXES, two whisks, two clothes brushes, two CANISTERS, a pair of SNUFFERS with trays, two glass jars, and three CASKETS. The pieces are decorated with applied STRAPWORK, medallions, and scrolls, but not similar on the various objects, suggesting that the service was assembled from individual pieces available. It is now in the Ashmolean Museum, Oxford, together with the original bill (specifying the charge by weight plus an extra for 'FASHION').

tree platter. A type of WELL PLATTER having several grooves for draining gravy from a roast into a deeper WELL at one end. Examples have a straight central groove and two or three branches on each side (giving the appearance of a tree), and sometimes there is a vertical pierced straining divider to separate the deep well from the shallower grooves. Such pieces are decorated in various styles with GADROONING, BEADING and elaborate MOUNTS. *See* WELL DISH; VENISON DISH.

trefid spoon. *See* TRIFID SPOON.

trellis work. A type of decoration in the form of a band formed by horizontal, vertical, and diagonal lines crossing each other, or sometimes consisting only of diagonal lines forming a DIAPER PATTERN of a series of lozenge shapes with an ornament in the interstices; some examples are supplemented by larger diagonal lines superimposed on the band, and sometimes with interspersed masks and leaves. The style was popular in Ireland, but used mainly in the period 1735–7; it is found on some JUGS, covers of KETTLES, and rims of SALVERS.

trembleuse (French). In ceramic ware, a *trembleuse* is a COFFEE-CUP with a SAUCER *(soucoupe)*, the saucer having either a vertically projecting ring into which the cup fits or a deep well to position the cup, to prevent spilling of the contents caused by a shaky hand. As coffee-cups are not known to have been made of English silver, the same result was sometimes achieved by making an openwork silver stand that was attached to a silver (or porcelain) saucer and that served to hold a porcelain cup (of BEAKER or TEA-BOWL form) without a handle. Such a stand was in the form of a circular base from which arose three or four vertical supports for an attached ring that served to hold the cup in place, the supports being so shaped that they project outwards to provide the user with a grip when drinking from the cup. An English pair of such stands in silver gilt (used with contemporary Fukien *blanc de Chine* porcelain tea-bowls) was made by DAVID TANQUERAY, 1718, and probably used for hot chocolate; they were sold at Sotheby's, London, on 31 January 1946, and were acquired by the British Museum, London, as part of the 1969 Wilding Bequest. Sometimes called a 'teacup stand'. *See* CHOCOLATE-CUP; MANCERINA.

Trenchard Bowl. A Chinese blue-and-white porcelain bowl dating from the Ming dynasty (though bearing no reign mark) with silver-gilt MOUNTS, London, 1577 or 1599. The bowl (said to have been one of a pair, the other without mounts) is hemispherical, being decorated in underglaze blue with lotus (or peony) flowers on the outside and with fish and seaweed motifs on the interior. The mounts consist of a band around the rim connected to a base

trembleuse. Pair, silver gilt (with Chinese porcelain tea-bowls), David Tanqueray, London, 1718. H. (of saucer) 5·8 cm. British Museum, London.

trencher salt. Paul de Lamerie, London, 1712. Ashmolean Museum, Oxford.

Trewhiddle Chalice. Origin uncertain, 9th century. H. 12·5 cm. British Museum, London.

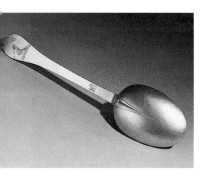

trifid spoon. Rat-tail on back of bowl, maker's mark 'IL', *c.* 1680. Courtesy, Asprey & Co. Ltd, London.

by four vertical straps (each decorated with a nude female figure in relief) hinged at top and bottom, with two CARYATID HANDLES (each in the form of a mermaid with a twisting bifurcated tail). The piece is 16·6 cm high and the mounts bear the unidentified maker's mark 'IH' (the same as that on the mounts of the ROBINSON BOWL).

Traditionally, the bowls (with other items) were said to have been given in 1506 by Philip, Archduke of Austria and by marriage King of Castile, and his wife Joanna, Queen of Castile, to Sir Thomas Trenchard, High Sheriff of Dorset, in appreciation of his hospitality at Wolfeton House, near Dorchester, when they had been forced by a storm at sea to land at Weymouth. The known bowl has been attributed to the Xuande (Hsüan Tê) period, 1426–35 (*see* Yvonne Hackenbroch, 'Chinese Porcelain in European Silver Mounts' in *The Connoisseur,* June 1955, p. 22) – in which case the gift could have been made in 1506 – but, in the light of more recent research, to the later years of the Jia Jing (Chia Ching) period, 1522–66 (*see* Philippa Glanville, 'Chinese Porcelain and English Goldsmiths *c.*1560 to *c.*1660' in *V & A Album.* 3, 1984, p. 247 and fig. 1) – thus ruling out, as noted by Miss Glanville, the possibility of the gift having been made in 1506. The bowl has been said to have been in the possession of a Dorset family since the 16th century; it was acquired by private treaty in 1983 by the Victoria and Albert Museum, London. *See* WARHAM BOWL; PORCELAIN OBJECTS.

trencher. Originally, from *c.* 1450, a flat circular piece of wood or tough coarse bread, placed beneath meat when being carved, to protect the table or tablecloth from knife marks. Later, from *c.*1550, such flat articles were made of silver, either circular (called 'roundels') or rectangular, and were used for serving cheese and fruit after the sweet (then called 'trencher plates'). One example is listed in a Scottish inventory of 1553, and examples were assayed in the 17th century. Some examples had the upper side gilded and engraved with the owner's coat of arms. *See* G. Bernard Hughes, 'The Use of Trenchers' in *Country Life,* 27 August 1953, p. 630.

trencher salt. An early type of SALT-CELLAR which has a SELF BASE, being without legs or feet and resting flat on the table. Such salts occur in many shapes, i.e., square, triangular, circular, oval, lobed or polygonal (with up to 8 or 12 sides). The sides are vertical or slope inward from the base, and sometimes the corners are chamfered or recessed. Such pieces have been made with one, two or three circular or oval wells, and were often made in sets. They are usually from 7·5 to 10 cm wide and about 2·5 cm high. Some are gilded to afford protection from corrosion by damp salt. Early examples have little decoration, but later ones have shaped or waisted sides, the base being wider than the rim. Such salts have long been popular (Edward III having had over 500 in 1329), but especially in the period 1640–1750. *See* DOUBLE SALT.

Trewhiddle Chalice. A CHALICE dating from Anglo-Saxon times, possibly of foreign make but found with a HOARD that was discovered at Trewhiddle, near St Austell, Cornwall, in 1774, and possibly deposited *c.* 875. It has a hemispherical bowl resting on a short knopped stem and domed base, and is entirely undecorated. It has been suggested that it was possibly a chalice intended for use by a travelling ecclesiastic. It is owned by the British Museum, London.

trifid (or trefid) spoon. A type of SPOON having a flat stem that widens at the top and has two notches that form it into a three-lobed shape suggestive of a cleft hind's hoof (hence the French term *'pied-de-biche'*). Such spoons often have on the back of the oval bowl a RAT-TAIL pattern, extending about halfway down the bowl, and are sometimes decorated with ENGRAVING, foliage in relief, or a lace pattern (*see* LACE-BACK SPOON). They are found in three lengths: large, 19 to 21·5 cm; medium, 16·5 cm; and, occasionally, short, 7·5 to 10 cm.

Trinity Hall Cup. A HEMING TWO-HANDLED CUP, 1771, differing from other such cups in that the cup itself is in NEO-CLASSICAL STYLE, being urn-shaped with a circular spreading foot that rests on a square PLINTH. The two vertical handles are in ROCOCO STYLE, each with an encircling snake. The front of the bowl is decorated with a low-relief roundel depicting three bewigged men seated around a table and drinking. The domed cover has a finial in the form of a figure of a youthful Bacchus, seated and holding aloft a bunch of grapes. The cup is owned by Trinity Hall, Cambridge.

triple salt. A type of SALT-CELLAR that has three wells for salt. An unmarked example, *c.*1745, with ROCOCO STYLE bowls and dolphin feet, is in the Metropolitan Museum of Art, New York. *See* DOUBLE SALT.

triptych. A picture or a carving made on three panels hinged together, sometimes of equal size and folding over each other completely, but more often consisting of a central panel and two narrower flanking panels that fold over it. Such pieces were probably derived from the two-panel consular diptychs which were used in churches in the Middle Ages to record the names of those commemorated in the Mass, and later were used as covers on gospel books. Some triptychs were made of silver with various types of decoration. One, from the late 14th century, having on the central panel a relief depiction of St George slaying the Dragon, was probably used as a PAX; it is in the Victoria and Albert Museum, London.

trivet. A type of ornamental flat dinner-table or sideboard accessory, resting on short legs, and used to support a hot PLATTER, BOWL, TUREEN or other receptacle and so protect the surface from being damaged by heat. Some examples are divided into two sections and are fitted with telescoping horizontal rods on the bottom so that they can be adjusted for use with receptacles of different lengths. *See* COASTER; TEAPOT STAND; DISH CROSS; DISH STAND; DISH RING.

trophy. A type of VASE, CUP, TAZZA, BOWL, SALVER, ARROW or other article, made in many shapes, styles, and sizes, awarded as a prize for a wide variety of sporting competitions, such as horse-racing (*see* HORSE-RACING TROPHY), sailing (*see* AMERICA'S CUP; WEYMOUTH REGATTA CUP), golf (*see* GOLF TROPHY), tennis (*see* WIMBLEDON CUP; DAVIS CUP), archery (*see* SCORTON ARROW), motor racing (*see* BORG-WARNER TROPHY), American football (Tiffany Superbowl Cup), cricket (*see* MENZIES MEMORIAL TROPHY), backgammon (University Club Trophy), and coursing (*see* DOG COLLAR), as well as for industrial accomplishment (e.g., the Carnegie Steel Safety Award), etc. Some such pieces are permanent trophies, held by or for successive winners, while others – especially those for horse racing – are awarded annually, to be retained by the winner, and so – being the work of various designers and makers – differ in form.

trowel. A type of hand tool used by bricklayers and stonemasons, having a flat, triangular, pointed metal blade attached to a wooden handle. Examples used since the early 19th century on ceremonial occasions to lay a foundation stone or cornerstone have often been made of silver or silver gilt, and engraved with an inscription commemorating the occasion. Sometimes a FISH SLICE was so used and inscribed. *See* BUTTER TROWEL; ICE SPADE.

trumpet. A musical wind instrument consisting of a long metal tube, once or twice curved, and ending in a bell, and having a cup-shaped mouthpiece. Modern examples have pistons. Trumpets have been made entirely of silver. Extant examples include one by William Bull, *c.*1655, four by William Shaw, *c.*1787, and one by THOMAS HEMING, 1780. A set of sixteen (the earliest dated 1780, and the others from 1804 to 1813, including a set of four made in 1813, presumably made at the command of the Prince Regent) is in the Royal Collection, but no longer used. *See* LUCK OF WOODSOME HALL; FIREMAN'S TRUMPET; TRUMPET MOUNTS; MUSICAL WARE.

trumpet foot. A type of FOOT that flares outward from the point where it joins the body of the piece or its stem, curving downward to the base.

trumpet mounts. Decorative silver garnishments on a brass TRUMPET, placed midway along the upper tube, on the mouthpiece, and on the bell (mouth). Such English mounts made of engraved silver are known from the time of Charles II, 1660–85; *see* LUCK OF WOODSOME HALL.

tucked in. Shaped, as a MUG, with sides that curve sharply inward just above the FOOT-RING, the upper part being straight and vertical.

Trinity Hall Cup. Thomas Heming, London, 1771. H. 33 cm. Trinity Hall, Cambridge.

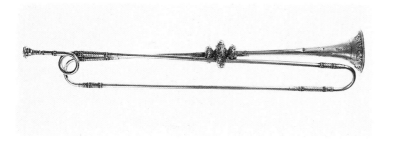

trumpet. William Bull, *c.* 1655. L. 85 cm. Ashmolean Museum, Oxford.

Tudor Clock Salt. Silver gilt, French, *c.* 1530, before and after restoration *c.* 1970. H. 34 cm and 39 cm, respectively. Photos courtesy, Christie's, London (*top*), and Goldsmiths' Company, London.

Tudor Clock Salt. A silver-gilt CLOCK SALT of French make, *c.* 1530, but included here because of two English restorations and its English historical associations. The piece in its original form is recorded in an inventory of 1550 as having been owned by Henry VIII and in inventories of 1559 and 1574 of the Royal Plate of England. When under the Commonwealth pieces in the Jewel House were sold, it was bought by a Mr Smith in 1649. In 1862 it was shown at the South Kensington Loan Exhibition by W. B. Stopford, of Drayton House, Northamptonshire, whose wife, Caroline Harriet Sackville, had inherited it. The latter's grandson, Col. Nigel Stopford Sackville, sold the piece at Christie's, London. on 12 July 1967, for 7,000 guineas (\$20,580), to Ronald Lee, from whom it was purchased (after an export licence had been refused) by its present owner, the Goldsmiths' Company, London. Research in 1972 by J. F. Hayward led him to suggest that the piece was made, on the order of Francis I, by a goldsmith employed by the French Court, and that it was given by the French king to Henry VIII.

The piece has a hexagonal base, resting on six CLAW-AND-BALL FEET (the balls being of agate) and decorated with six high-relief agate cameo busts, above which six BRACKETS enclose the clock movement that rests on a crystal column. The salt was extensively altered in the early 18th century from its original form; this alteration involved changing the movement and also removing the octagonal receptacle for the salt and the cover upon which was a figure of a man sitting on an eagle, and substituting a white enamelled rotating globe within the metal arms at the top, with the hour numerals on a band encircling the globe and the hour being indicated by the figure of a Roman soldier pointing with a lance. The globe had been removed when the piece was acquired by the Goldsmiths' Company, leaving at the top an empty crystal cylinder and the metal calyx for the globe. Later the original appearance was restored as far as possible, except for the man on the cover (perhaps a group representing the Rape of Ganymede), substituting for him temporarily the figure of a standing woman. The base and cover are set with garnets (in lieu of false emeralds on the original form), and are without the original pendent pearls.

See Norman M. Penzer, 'A Clock Salt' in *Apollo,* June 1956, p. 183; J. F. Hayward, 'The Restoration of the Tudor Clock-Salt' in the *Goldsmiths' Company Review,* 1972–3, p. 27.

Tudor silverware. Articles of silverware made in England in the Tudor period, during the reigns, 1485–1558, of Henry VII, Henry VIII, Edward VI, and Mary I, and thereafter until *c.* 1600. Surviving examples, some bearing unidentified marks, are very rare and in some cases unique. The articles include MAZERS, TIGERWARE JUGS, and some GREAT SALTS, COMMUNION CUPS, CASTING BOTTLES, BELL SALTS, PEDESTAL SALTS, 'FONT-SHAPED' CUPS, STANDING CUPS, COCONUT CUPS, and EWERS. Much silverware was imported from the Continent (mainly from Germany) and many Continental silversmiths came to England, so that the earlier Gothic style was influenced by the RENAISSANCE STYLE. Many large pieces, often of SILVER GILT, were made primarily for display (and later melting down and conversion into ingots when funds were needed). *See* Victoria and Albert Museum booklet, *Tudor Domestic Silver* (1970). *See* CAMPION CUP; HOWARD GRACE CUP; MOSTYN SALT; SMELT CUP; VYVYAN SALT.

tumbler. A type of drinking vessel without a stem, foot or handle, and having a flat base. It is usually of circular section and may be cylindrical, waisted or barrel-shaped or have sides that taper slightly inward toward the base. The base is usually thicker and heavier than the sides, to provide stability and prevent spilling. Although made in many styles and sizes, such vessels do not have a flared mouth as does a BEAKER. Some were made to form a box when two were fitted together mouth to mouth; some were part of a TRAVELLER'S DINING SET; and occasionally several fit as a NEST one above the other with a cover for the one uppermost. *See* G. Bernard Hughes, 'Silver Tumblers' in *Country Life,* 10 November 1955, p. 1084. *See* TUMBLER CUP; TUMBLER STAND.

tumbler cup. A type of drinking vessel that has no stem, foot or handle; its sides are convex or are straight with an inward curve toward the base. Such cups are not as tall as a TUMBLER, and range in height from 5 to 10 cm. They were made with a weighted bottom so that they would readily 'tumble' and not overturn if tilted, and so were used at sea to withstand the rolling of a ship. They were intended to be drained (quaffed) at a single draught and handed back empty to the server. Most examples are undecorated, with only an engraved coat of arms, a crest, or the owner's name for identification; some have a design on the base, indicating that they were expected to be placed rim down when not in use. Some were made in sets of up to eight, sometimes fitting together as a NEST.

tumbler stand. A type of BOTTLE STAND, from *c.* 1780, in which to rest a TUMBLER, having a low gallery and a base resting on three low scroll feet.

tun. An archaic term for a drinking cup, beaker or bowl. It is still used for a silver drinking cup holding about one-third of a quart at Magdalen College, Oxford, some such cups being dated in the late 17th century, and at Christ's College, Cambridge, and Trinity Hall, Cambridge. *See* COLLEGE CUP; BEAUFORT BEAKER.

tumbler cup. Marmaduke Best, 1682. D. 8·8 cm. Ashmolean Museum, Oxford.

tureen. A circular or oval deep serving BOWL, for soup, stew or sauce. Although tureens were often made of porcelain or pottery, many have been made of silver or silver gilt. They usually have four short feet or a spreading foot, a domed cover with a lifting handle, and two opposed handles. Some silver examples have an accompanying flat-bottomed STAND decorated EN SUITE, some a LADLE, and occasionally there is a silver TUREEN LINER. Large and small examples are now called, respectively, a SOUP-TUREEN and a SAUCE-TUREEN. The French distinguish between the circular and oval soup-tureens, calling the former a *pot-à-oille* (used for a spiced stew) and the latter a *terrine* (used for soup). The name 'tureen' is derived from the Latin *terrenus* (earthen); but the bowl has sometimes been said to have been named after the Vicomte de Turenne (1611–75), Marshal of France, who – legend has it – used his helmet for his soup. *See* Judith Banister, 'A Century of Tureens' in *Antique Dealer & Collectors Guide,* December 1966, p. 68.

tureen liner. A LINER for a SOUP-TUREEN, made of silver or, often, silver-plated, and conforming in shape to that of the tureen; it usually has two end-handles for lifting it from the tureen. A silver liner was often the work of a different maker and made at a later date than the tureen.

Turkish coffee-pot. (1) A type of COFFEE-POT that has, instead of a long curving spout extending from the bottom of the pot, a pouring LIP or a BEAK SPOUT. Such a pot was more suitable for Turkish coffee, with its heavy sediment. The form is similar to a HOT-WATER JUG. Sometimes called a 'Turky coffee-pot'. (2) A type of coffee-pot in Islamic or Persian form, having a bowl tapering upward to form a very tall neck connected to the bowl by a loop-handle, and having a tall curved spout. Such pots were a speciality of the GORHAM COMPANY in the period 1880–90, being made in various styles and finishes, some of copper with silver mounts, and some with decoration in Japanese style.

two-handled cup. With cover and double-scroll handles, Paul de Lamerie, London, 1740. H. 18·3 cm. Ashmolean Museum, Oxford.

turned-out rim. A type of RIM which extends outwards at right-angles at the top of the vertical wall of some receptacles, e.g., a DECANTER STAND. *See* EVERTED.

turtle tureen. A type of SOUP-TUREEN made in the form of a large turtle in-the-round. Examples have been made in England, and in the United States a comparable tureen in the form of a terrapin was made in 1890 by the GORHAM COMPANY.

tutorial silverware. Any article of silverware that has been presented to a tutor by a group of his students, usually bearing an appropriate inscription with the name of the recipient and the date of the gift, or sometimes the Latin phrase *'Donum Pupillorum'.*

two-handled cup. A type of CUP usually of inverted-bell shape or BOMBÉ shape, having two opposed loop handles and generally resting on a footed base (later examples having a short stem), and sometimes having a cover with a decorative finial. The two handles are in the form of scrolls of various shapes, some being of the SCROLL HANDLE, DOUBLE-SCROLL HANDLE or S-SCROLL HANDLE type, others being HARP-SHAPED HANDLES or FLYING SCROLL HANDLES. The covers of such cups are flat or nearly so when of CAROLINE SILVERWARE, but in HUGUENOT SILVERWARE they expand in height to a pronounced dome. Later examples, after *c.* 1700, have a band or girdle, plain or with GADROONING, encircling the body midway. Such cups were made in England in great numbers from the mid-17th century until the mid-18th century. They are usually elaborately decorated, with applied vertical SPOON-HANDLE STRAPS, CUT CARD work, LANCEOLATE motifs, gadrooning or reversed LAMBREQUIN motifs on the cup and with cut-card work or applied leaves on the cover; the cut-card work and the strapwork were often further embellished with applied relief motifs, PIERCED WORK or GUILLOCHE decoration. In addition, some examples have ENGRAVING, EMBOSSING or CHASING. Such cups were used as a LOVING CUP on ceremonial occasions, as a prize for competitions, as awards on special occasions, or merely as ornaments. Cups of such form but of much smaller size (*see* SMALL TWO-HANDLED CUP) are

Tyndale Flagon. Parcel-gilt haunce pot, London, 1567. H. 18 cm. Armourers and Brasiers' Company, London (photo courtesy, Goldsmiths' Company, London).

Tyng Cup. Jacob Hurd, Boston, Mass., 1744. H. 38·3 cm. Yale University Art Gallery (Mabel Brady Garvan Collection), New Haven, Conn.

sometimes called a POSSET-POT or a CAUDLE-CUP, and too often in England have confusedly been called a PORRINGER. *See* CORONATION CUP; COLLEGE CUP; HEMING TWO-HANDLED CUPS; FISHER CUP; TYNG CUP; BRIDGE CUP; KIDNEY CUP; THREE-HANDLED CUP.

Tyndale Flagon. A parcel-gilt, pear-shaped HAUNCE POT decorated with chased foliage and a wide vertical stripe of STRAPWORK on each side, and having a hinged lid. It bears the mark 'RD' for Robert Danbe(?), 1567, and is inscribed 'The Gifte of Thomas Tyndale Bachelar, 1574'. It is now owned by the Armourers and Brasiers' Company, London.

Tyng Cup. A TWO-HANDLED CUP, in the style of QUEEN ANNE SILVERWARE, having a cylindrical bowl resting on a high-domed STEPPED foot and with two scroll handles and having a high-domed stepped cover and a knob finial. Between the rim of the cup and encircling moulded band applied midway there is an engraved CARTOUCHE enclosing an inscription recording the original gift of the cup to Edward Tyng (1683-1755), a naval commander, by several merchants of Boston, Massachusetts, in acknowledgment of his services 'done the trade' in capturing the first French privateer on 24 June 1744. The cup, made by JACOB HURD, 1744, was in the Tyng family until acquired by Francis P. Garvan, who donated it to the Yale University Art Gallery, New Haven, Connecticut. It has sometimes been called the 'Bishop Cup' as it was used to drink bishop (a beverage of port wine, orange or lemon juice, and sugar). Hurd also made three similar but smaller cups.

U

United States silverware. Tankard with coin mount on handle, Nicholas Roosevelt, New York, *c.* 1745-60, height 19 cm; and jug, Paul Revere II, Boston, *c.* 1805, height 16 cm. Yale University Art Gallery (Mabel Brady Garvan Collection), New Haven, Conn.

United States silver marks. In the United States there is no official ASSAYING of silver or other precious metals, hence there are no legally authorized HALLMARKS. The only hallmarks used there were those in Baltimore from 1814 to 1830, consisting of a town mark with a date letter. However, many silversmiths stamp on the articles of silver or PLATED METAL made by them their name, initials, trade-mark, symbol or other identifying mark, and sometimes the place of manufacture. Although purchasers do not have the protection of official assaying and related hallmarks, they do have a legal remedy (a) in cases where the maker stamps an article 'Sterling' (as many do), but the standard for STERLING SILVER is not complied with, and (b) if the maker has forged the name or mark of another maker. On some pieces there appears 'Coin' or 'Pure coin' or merely 'D' (for dollar) or 'C' (for coin) to indicate the source and standard of the metal (from 1792 to 1837 of ·892 FINENESS, thereafter ·900).

United States silverware. Articles of silverware made in various centres in the United States (and often too broadly referred to as 'American silverware'), including mainly cities on the Eastern seaboard. The early silverware in the American Colonies was almost entirely imported from England and continental Europe, and – as there was no silver available locally – the earliest ware made in the Colonies was produced from melted-down foreign coinage, some being executed *c.* 1652 in Massachusetts by JOHN HULL and ROBERT SANDERSON. Hull and Sanderson had numerous apprentices who became native silversmiths and greatly extended the scope and decorative style of the articles locally produced. The local silversmiths were originally influenced by ware imported from England and Holland from Colonial days until the early 19th century and the development of the local FEDERAL STYLE. The articles made in the Colonial and post-Revolutionary periods included a wide range of household and personal ware, but mainly SPOONS, PORRINGERS, BEAKERS, MUGS, and TEA SERVICES, often in forms inspired by English and Dutch prototypes. Many silversmiths after the Revolution worked as designer-makers and as hand craftsmen, but later they became employed by companies, and mass-production was introduced and greatly extended after the mid-19th century. Among the leading firms for many years and still designing and making silverware are the GORHAM COMPANY and TIFFANY & CO. *See* C. L. Avery, *Early American Silver* (1930); Edward Wenham, 'American XVIIIth Century Silver in England' in *The Connoisseur*, July-December 1934, pp. 17, 87; —, 'American XVIIIth Century Silver Teapots' in *Apollo*, December 1938, p. 292; John Marshall Phillips, *American Silver* (1949); Gregor Norman-Wilcox, 'The American Silversmith in the 18th Century' in *The Connoisseur*, February 1955, p. 72; Katherine Morrison McClintock, 'American Presentation Silver' in *The Connoisseur*, December 1967, p. 256, January 1968, p. 58, and August 1971, p. 287; Kathryn C. Buhler and Graham Hood, '*American Silver, Yale University Art Gallery Collection* (1970); Graham Hood, *American Silver* (1971); Dorothy T. Rainwater, *Encyclopedia of American Silver Manufacturers* (1966, 1975), with extensive list of makers and comprehensive bibliography. *See* CONNECTICUT SILVERWARE; GEORGIA SILVERWARE; MARYLAND SILVERWARE; MASSACHUSETTS SILVERWARE; NEW ORLEANS SILVERWARE; NEW YORK SILVERWARE; PHILADELPHIA SILVERWARE; RHODE ISLAND SILVERWARE; ST LOUIS SILVERWARE; VIRGINIA SILVERWARE; UNITED STATES SILVER MARKS.

urn. As to silverware: (1) a receptacle for dispensing a liquid by means of a TAP and SPIGOT, usually elevated from the table by resting on a stand and often having a heating device. *See* COFFEE-URN; TEA-URN; HOT-WATER URN; COFFEE-AND-TEA MACHINE. (2) A receptacle of classical form in various shapes and styles; usually the body is globular or ovoid and curved inward toward a stemmed foot, the mouth is smaller in diameter than the body, and it has two side handles. The term is sometimes applied to a receptacle in the form of a Greek vase (*see* GREEK-VASE SILVERWARE).

V

van Vianen, Christian (1598–*c.* 1666). A silversmith from Utrecht, Netherlands, the son of Adam van Vianen (1565-1627) and nephew of Paulus van Vianen (*c.* 1568/70-1613), both recognized goldsmiths (as was their father, Willem Eersterz). Christian worked for his uncle, was apprenticed in 1616, and was freed and became a Master Goldsmith in 1628. The early pieces that he made in Utrecht bear his father's mark. Before March 1630 he emigrated to London, where he was employed by (and received in 1630 a pension from) Charles I, and received commissions from titled patrons, including the 10th Earl of Northumberland. He returned to Utrecht by 1631, but by 1633/4 was back in London. In 1634 he was a resident of Westminster and was awarded an order to make a 17-piece silver altar service for St George's Chapel, Windsor, for the Order of the Garter; completed in 1637, the service was looted by Cromwell's troops and melted down in 1641. He left London again before 1643, settled in Utrecht from 1647 to 1652, but his whereabouts thereafter is unknown until *c.* 1660, when he returned to London once more and did work for Charles II. He was appointed 'Silversmith in Ordinary' to the King until replaced in 1661 and was last heard of in 1666. His most important extant English work is a large silver basin signed and dated 1635, but he also made a number of SALVERS, covered BOWLS, and EWERS. He developed the AURICULAR STYLE, the use of which in silverware is said to have been initiated, *c.* 1613, by his uncle Paulus, and was used also by his father. He is not mentioned in the records of the Goldsmiths' Company, London; he signed his pieces, but did not use or enter a MAKER'S MARK, perhaps as his work for the Crown did not need to be assayed. Some of his work may bear the mark of a London goldsmith who, in order to help a foreigner, had the pieces assayed for him (*see* SPONSOR'S MARK). Much of his work is now in the Rijksmuseum, Amsterdam. *See* R. W. Lightbown, 'Christian van Vianen at the Court of Charles I' in *Apollo*, June 1968, p. 426.

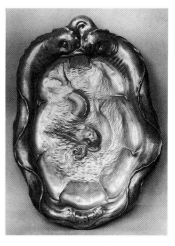

Van Vianen, Christian. Dish in auricular style, with *repoussé* decoration of dolphins in and encircling a pool, London, 1633. L. 49 cm. Victoria and Albert Museum, London.

vandyke band. A type of band, applied as a rim or encircling decoration, that is in the form of a series of adjacent pointed motifs, sometimes engraved. The term is derived from the scalloped lace collars depicted in portraits by Sir Anthony Van Dyck (Vandyke) (1549-1641).

vase. A type of vessel made in many forms, styles, sizes, and sections, but usually cylindrical and taller than it is wide. It is used mainly for ornamental or flower-display purposes. Some examples have an ornamental cover. Vases made of silver gilt and decorated with relief ACANTHUS leaves rising from the base, and with floral festoons near the top, were popular in England *c.* 1660-85. Such vases, together with GINGER-JARS decorated EN SUITE, were often used as a GARNITURE DE CHEMINÉE or a GARNITURE DE TABLE. Some so-called vases were made to be presented as awards (*see* LLOYD'S PATRIOTIC FUND VASES) and some for use as ornaments (*see* WARWICK VASE; PORTLAND VASE; MAGNOLIA VASE). *See* TROPHY; LEKANE VASE.

vase-shaped caster. A type of CASTER of which the upper half of the body and the pierced cover rise in cylindrical or polygonal form from a wider hemispherical section that rests on a footed base. The cover has a small finial and pierced openings arranged in various patterns, sometimes with stripes of spiral FLUTING bordering foliage motifs and small holes between the fluted stripes. The size of the holes differs on casters intended for sprinkling salt and pepper. Some examples are of silver gilt and some have, encircling the lower part of the base, relief decoration of garlands with masks at intervals. Some pieces of similar shape decorated in ROCOCO STYLE or in NEO-CLASSICAL STYLE, and sometimes referred to as a 'vase' or a 'condiment vase', have, instead of a pierced cover for sprinkling, a cover with a notch to accommodate the handle of a small ladle; such pieces are used for sugar, wet mustard or coarse ground pepper. *See* Michael Snodin, 'Silver Vases and their Purposes' in *The Connoisseur,* January 1977, p. 37.

vase-shaped mustard pot. A type of MUSTARD-POT that is vase-shaped, having a footed base, a low-domed hinged LID with a THUMBPIECE, and a curved handle. Such pieces are sometimes decorated on the foot, rim, and handle, and have an ornamental finial. In some cases the interior is of silver gilt. In later examples the indentation in the lid, for the handle of a MUSTARD SPOON, was omitted so as to make the receptacle air-tight. Sometimes called a 'mustard tankard'.

vase-shaped standing cup. A type of STANDING CUP of which the bowl is shaped in the form of a traditional semi-elliptical vase and rests on a spreading foot; it usually has a high-domed cover with a pointed finial. *See* PRESENTATION CUP.

vase-shaped caster. Paul de Lamerie, London, 1735, H. 20·3 cm. Ashmolean Museum, Oxford.

Vechte, Antoine (1799–1868). A French designer and maker of silverware who came to London after 1848 to work for HUNT & ROSKELL at its Harrison St workshop. He had worked alone in Paris, acquiring a reputation as a designer and maker of armour, but in the 1820s and 1830s had passed off some of his work as that of Benvenuto Cellini. He was visited in Paris in 1844 by John Samuel Hunt, of Hunt & Roskell, who commissioned him to make the TITAN VASE. Hunt again visited him in Paris in 1849–50, and arranged to bring him to London and to provide him with his own workshop. In London he designed and made, in 1855, the VECHTE SHIELD. He developed a process for easier production of an embossed design, instead of hammering from the back, by making a model and from it a base-metal mould, and then beating the silver plate into the mould to create a positive pattern. He retired in 1862. *See* BREADALBANE CANDELABRUM.

Vechte Shield. A circular SHIELD dedicated to Shakespeare, Milton, and Newton, who are depicted in scenes in three oval plaques embossed with characters and episodes from their respective works and also in adjacent friezes around the rim, together with other figures in the interstices. In the centre are several decorative concentric circles. The shield is made of silver with iron bands DAMASCENED with gold, and is inscribed 'Antoine Vechte Fecit 1855'. It was designed and executed by ANTOINE VECHTE, but the three plaques bear the mark of John Samuel Hunt, of HUNT & ROSKELL, 1854. It was shown (unfinished) at Goldsmiths' Hall, London, in 1851, and (completed) in Paris in 1855 and in London in 1862, and was purchased, with the TITAN VASE, by the Goldsmiths' Company in 1890.

vegetable-dish. A type of DISH for serving vegetables, the usual form of which is circular (sometimes lobed) and shallow, sometimes with three interior dividers, and with a high-domed COVER. Some deep varieties have a detachable three-compartment divider, and have a central lifting handle and sometimes a glass LINER. Such dishes sometimes have detachable horizontal side handles (screwed into sockets), loop handles or sometimes DROP-RING HANDLES. The cover has a detachable (by a BAYONET JOINT) finial or handle, the removal of which permits the cover to be inverted and to serve as an extra vegetable-dish. A rectangular variant has only two compartments, being divided midway by a fixed partition. Some vegetable-dishes are accompanied by a supporting STAND to protect the table from the heat (but such a stand may be a later addition). *See* ENTRÉE-DISH.

vase-shaped standing cup. Cup with cover and plinth, Robert Hennell I, London, 1780–1. H. 27 cm. Wadsworth Atheneum (Elizabeth B. Miles Collection), Hartford, Conn.

veilleuse (French). A utensil, consisting of several parts, for keeping warm the contents of the bowl, teapot or cup which rests on a hollow pedestal containing a *godet* (lamp). Originally made to be used at the bedside to keep

Vechte Shield. Silver with iron bands damascened with gold, Antoine Vechte, cempleted 1855, with plaques bearing mark of John Samuel Hunt. D. 82·5 cm. Goldsmiths' Company, London.

food warm for an invalid or an infant, the *veilleuse* was (after *c.*1800) similarly used in the bedroom for keeping warm a beverage for one person. The name is derived form the verb *veiller,* to keep a night vigil. The characteristic feature is that the bowl or teapot is made with a projecting bottom which fits into the pedestal, bringing the contents nearer to the warming flame of the *godet.* There are three basic forms, almost always made of ceramic ware – (1) the food warmer, (2) the TEA WARMER (*veilleuse-théière*), and (3) the cup warmer; only the tea warmer is known to have been reproduced in silver. *See* Harold Newman, *Veilleuses* (2nd ed., 1987).

vegetable-dish. One of a set of four, Paul Storr, London, 1808 (on Sheffield plate warming stand). H. 25 cm. Courtesy, Garrard & Co. Ltd, London.

venison-dish. A type of DISH. usually from 45 to 60 cm in length, large enough to serve a haunch of venison and to hold it while it is being carved. Superseding the WELL PLATTER in the 1780s, it consists of two parts: (1) a shallow oval hot-water receptacle, of which the top is in the form of the earlier well dish and which has either on one side or at one end a filling orifice with a screw cap; and (2) a domed cover, sufficiently high to enclose the haunch of venison, surmounted by a vertical loop handle. The dish usually has two sturdy horizontal handles and rests on four feet so that it is elevated above the surface of the table; it sometimes has a vertical pierced divider in front of the well to strain the drippings, but occasionally there is an added piece, a MAZARINE, upon which to rest the venison. The piece is often decorated with GADROONING and FLUTING, and the cover almost always bears the

venison-dish. Dish (without cover) with well separated by vertical lattice divider, Paul Storr, for Rundell, Bridge & Rundell, London, 1814. L. 61 cm. Courtesy, Sotheby's, London.

coat of arms or the crest of the original or a later owner. Early examples were made of BRITANNIA METAL or of SHEFFIELD PLATE (the cover in the latter case being lined with tin); examples were also made of silver (a number by PAUL STORR, including four made in 1805 for the Earl of Bridgwater), and from the late 1840s they were made of SILVER-PLATED WARE. *See* G. Bernard Hughes, 'The dish to serve the venison on' in *Country Life,* 16 September 1971, p. 680. *See* BREAKFAST DISH; CARVING SKEWER.

verge (or **virge**). The tall STAFF carried by a verger (usually a church attendant) as the emblem of his office. Such articles were made of silver as early as 1465. There is a decorative ornament at each end. Six silver examples are still in use at St Paul's Cathedral, London (where the word is still spelled 'virge', from Latin *virga,* rod), ranging in length from 81·5 to 117 cm; one is dated 1781 and marked 'HB', probably for Hester Bateman (*see* BATEMAN), one 1782 (by Burrage Davenport), two 1821, and two modern, 1957 and 1964. *See* BEADLE'S STAFF; PORTER'S STAFF; TIPSTAFF.

vermeil. Gilded silver, i.e., silver covered with a layer of gold. The early processes of GILDING, developed in France in the 18th century, are seldom used today, being largely supplanted by ELECTRO-GILDING, the process used by TIFFANY & CO. (since its revival of the production of such gilded ware) and by others. The colour has a richer look than the brassy appearance of some of the earlier processes. The finish of the ware retards indefinitely the formation of TARNISH.

Verplanck Cup. A silver-gilt TWO-HANDLED CUP, undecorated except for the usual encircling ribbing midway, and having DOUBLE-SCROLL HANDLES and a STEPPED dome cover. It was made by Bartholomew Le Roux II (1717–63), of New York, *c.* 1737–51, for Giulian Verplanck (1698–1751), and descended through two centuries in the family, until acquired by the Henry Francis du Pont Winterthur Museum, near Wilmington, Delaware. *See* Louise C. Belden, 'The Verplanck Cup' in *Antiques,* December 1967, p. 840.

verrière (French). (1) A MONTEITH. (2) A wine-glass cooler in the form of a bowl having, on one or both sides, a lip or notch on the rim; when the piece is filled with iced water, the bowl of a wine-glass – the glass being inverted and suspended by its foot in the notch – can be immersed to be chilled. Examples with two notches (on opposite sides of the bowl) were used to place an emptied glass in the bowl for rinsing and chilling, while a second glass was removed, preparatory to serving a different wine to be drunk from it.

vervel. A type of small ring that is used to secure a falcon or hawk to its perch, being tied to the end of the jesses (short straps of leather or silk tied to the bird's legs) and attached to the swivel on the leash. Such rings, sometimes made of silver, are very small, about 1 to 1·5 cm in diameter, are usually made in pairs, and serve as a means of identification of the birds (identifying words being inscribed half on each ring of the pair). Some were flat rings, others were bands.

vesta-box. A type of small BOX made to hold short wax matches (called 'vestas', after the Roman goddess of the hearth). The earliest examples, made from the 1840s, were usually originally a SNUFF-BOX with an attached serrated steel striker. Later examples (sometimes called a 'matchbox') are of many shapes and styles, but usually are rectangular, with rounded corners, and have a narrow horizontal section; some are of fantasy shape, such as a horseshoe, heart, turtle, horn, or even a human head. The lid is hinged on one of the narrow sides, and is often surmounted by a small ring for suspension from a watch-chain. Some examples incorporate a rasp for striking and some have a gilded interior (to prevent a chemical reaction that would result from contact between the silver and the match heads). Such boxes date from *c.* 1850 to *c.* 1910, when safety matches came into general use, and with the advent of cigarette lighters they ceased to be made after World War I. *See* Roger Ashford, 'Striking an Elegant Lighter' in *Country Life,* 19 February 1976, p. 427.

Vickers Metal. An ALLOY resembling silver, made under a formula bought in 1769 by James Vickers, of Sheffield. Its main constituent was tin and it was introduced at Sheffield in 1787 under the name of 'Vickers Metal' or 'Vickers White Metal'. It was superseded in 1790 when Vickers developed BRITANNIA METAL.

Victoria, Queen. For silver articles associated with Queen Victoria, *see* QUEEN'S CUP; 'QUEEN VICTORIA'S DOGS' CENTREPIECE; JUBILEE CENTREPIECE; VICTORIA STATUETTE.

Viking Punch Bowl. Tiffany & Co., New York, 1892. Metropolitan Museum of Art (Purchase, the Edgar J. Kaufmann Foundation Gift, 1969), New York.

Victoria and Albert Museum Centrepiece. A CENTREPIECE made as a replica of the central octagonal turret of the Victoria and Albert Museum, London. It rests on a square stepped plinth of black marble with silver plaques on each side. It was designed by Jocelyn Burton and made in 1984. *See* ARCHITECTURAL SILVERWARE.

Victoria Statuette. A STATUETTE in the form of an equestrian figure of Queen Victoria in riding habit. It was made by ROBERT GARRARD II in 1840, and rests on an oval ebonized PLINTH inscribed 'Victoria Regina'. It is in the personal collection of Her Majesty the Queen.

Victorian silverware. Articles of silverware made in England during the reign of Queen Victoria, 1837–1901. The six decades produced few original styles, but the mingling of revived versions of the GOTHIC STYLE, RENAISSANCE STYLE, and ROCOCO STYLE led to the 'Revived Rococo Style' (and in the United States to the HIGH VICTORIAN STYLE), and the unrestrained taste for ornamentation that resulted in lavishly decorated ware that is fairly readily identifiable as Victorian, with its plethora of naturalistic, and later classical and Renaissance motifs, its use of elaborate EMBOSSING and ornate MOUNTS, and the frequency of examples of SCULPTURAL SILVERWARE. The increase in wealth of the middle classes, the popular urge to display affluence, and the impetus given by the Great Exhibition of 1851 and the International Exhibition of 1862 were met by the increased production of SILVER- PLATED pieces in mass-produced machine-made forms, not only in the newly created ware in a wide range of styles and prices (some made from melted-down outmoded pieces), but in converting old ware by adding new mounts to embellish more conservative and less ornate pieces from prior periods. Toward the end of the period, the influence of the ART NOUVEAU STYLE and the development of craft work under the Arts and Crafts Movement were manifested. *See* Patricia Wardle, *Victorian Silver and Silver-Plate* (1963).

Viking Punch Bowl. A PUNCH-BOWL of which the decoration is based on Viking motifs; the eight vertical loop handles extend upward through the flanged rim of the bowl, each symbolizing the prow of a Viking ship. The piece is made of 'decarbonized iron' etched and DAMASCENED with gold and silver, and has a plain silver lining. It was made in 1892 by TIFFANY & CO., to be shown in the World's Columbian Exposition held in Chicago in 1893. It is now owned by the Metropolitan Museum of Art, New York.

vinaigrette. A small receptacle to contain scented vinegar, formerly used by ladies (sometimes by men) to ward off faintness. Such pieces succeeded the POMANDER (which often included a vinaigrette). The earliest-known example in separate form dates from 1492. Such pieces were popular from the mid-18th century to the late-19th century. They were made in innumerable forms and styles (such as circular, oval, polygonal, heart-shaped or shell-shaped, and in fantasy forms, such as a shoe, book, watch-case, padlock, purse, cowrie shell, beehive, acorn, and flexible fish) in silver, gold or porce-

vinaigrette. Powder-horn ('bugle') form with built-in whistle, English, *c.* 1890. Courtesy, Cameo Corner, London.

Vintage Claret-Jug. Glass body with silver cagework, Joseph Angell III, London, 1851. H. 34·8 cm. Goldsmiths' Company, London.

Virgin spoon. Detail of finial, silver gilt, Salisbury(?), *c.* 1625, L. 17·5 cm. Holburne of Menstrie Museum (University of Bath).

lain, with a pierced metal grille (of silver, gold or pinchbeck) under the stopper or the securely hinged lid to cover a finely textured sponge saturated with a scented substance. Some were rectangular, having on the lid a topographical scene (*see* CASTLE-TOP WARE). Some were decorated with embossing, engraving or ENGINE-TURNING. The pierced work in the grille is found in many and diverse intricate patterns. The vinaigrette was usually carried loose in a pocket or handbag, but later sometimes worn on a fob or suspended by a chain from a bracelet. Some were made as a LOCKET so as to be exempt from hallmarking; the FINENESS of these was usually below the standard for STERLING SILVER. Some examples were made in the form of a POWDER-HORN (sometimes called a 'bugle') with a built-in whistle. *See* L. I. Middleton, 'The Vinaigrette' in *The Connoisseur*, November 1932, p. 308; E. Ellenbogen, *English Vinaigrettes* (1956); L. G. G. Ramsey, 'Vinaigrettes' in *The Connoisseur*, October 1956, p. 95; G. Bernard Hughes, 'Silver Vinaigrettes' in *Country Life*, 12 October 1961, p. 830. *See* VINEGAR STICK.

vine pattern. A pattern on FLATWARE, found usually on pieces in a DESSERT SERVICE, the handles being decorated with a continuous row of vine leaves and bunches of grapes. Services so decorated often include GRAPE SHEARS and a large SERVING SPOON, the bowl of which is made in the form of a vine leaf.

vinegar stick. A type of stick or cane of silver, having at one end a small pierced box to contain some aromatic substance to freshen the air. *See* POMANDER; VINAIGRETTE..

Vintage Claret-Jug. A CLARET-JUG having a tall glass body of hexagonal section widening toward the bottom and then narrowing to rest on a hexagonal base, and having silver MOUNTS. The glass jug is enclosed in a removable silver cage, partly frosted and decorated with numerous figures of boys, some with ladders, gathering grapes. It has a BEAK SPOUT and a long curved bifurcated handle extending upward from the widened part of the bowl to above the hinged lid. The finial is surmounted by a figure of a boy astride a barrel with a SPIGOT and TAP. The mounts bear the mark of Joseph Angell III (*see* ANGELL), London, 1851-2, and an inscription recording that the piece was purchased by William Quilter at the Great Exhibition of 1851. The jug is now owned by the Goldsmiths' Company, London.

Virgin spoon. A type of SPOON having a straight stem terminating in a finial, in the form of a female figure in-the-round with flowing hair, depicting the Virgin Mary; some related examples depict the Virgin holding the Child, or with an exposed Sacred Heart. A few examples from the 16th century are known, and there are later reproductions. The term 'Virgin spoon', when applied to a spoon having a finial depicting a female figure with plaited hair, is a misnomer, as sacred iconography allows such a hairstyle only to married women (*see* MAIDENHEAD SPOON).

Virginia silverware. Articles of silverware made in the state of Virginia. A number of pieces made by Charles A. Burnett (1785-1849), of Alexandria, have long been at the White House, Washington, D.C.; they include three SALT SPOONS, 1817-18, inscribed 'President's House'. *See* G. B. Cutten, *The Silversmiths of Virginia, 1694-1850* (1952); William de Matteo, *The Silversmith in Eighteenth-Century Williamsburg* (1956).

vision aids. Various articles with one or two glass lenses, used to assist an individual's short-range vision, have been made with silver frames, or silver mounts, including such articles as spectacles, lorgnettes, quizzers, opera-glasses, and spyglasses, as well as microscopes. They are beyond the scope of this book, as also are some long-range vision aids, such as a silver telescope recorded as made in 1840 as a wedding gift for Queen Victoria. Some spectacles were provided with a silver spectacle-case.

vitruvian scroll. A decorative motif in the form of a classical ornament of a continuous series of convoluted scrolls resembling stylized undulating waves. It is a feature of silverware in the ADAM STYLE. It was named after Marcus Vitruvius Pollio, a Roman architect of the age of Augustus, 27 BC – AD 14, whose writings had great influence on Renaissance and later decorative art. Also called 'wave pattern'. *See* ROYAL DISH WARMERS.

voider (or **voyder**). (1) A type of TRAY or BOWL, shallow and having a vertical rim, used by a servant to carry from the dinner table, after each course, the remains of food left on the plates and also to remove used knives and forks and soiled dishes. (2) A term sometimes applied to a SLOP-BOWL used at a tea table, also called a 'voiding bowl'.

voiding knife. A type of KNIFE that has a long flat blade with two straight sides and a rounded end, extending from a short straight handle. It was presumably used to clear the crumbs from a dinner table, as is done today by a CRUMBER. One silver example, 65·5 cm long, made in 1678 and said to be a replacement for one made in 1634, was owned by the Drapers' Company, London.

volute. A spiral curve, sometimes called a 'helix', derived from the ornament on Greek Ionic capitals. In silverware, it is sometimes found as two such curves joined in a continuous motif, called a 'double volute', and occasionally foliated.

Vyvyan Salt. A silver-gilt GREAT SALT in the form of a square COVERED STANDING SALT. It rests on a square base having four feet in the form of lions couchant. Each side of the body encloses a panel of glass decorated on the reverse with painting and metal foil *(verre églomisé)*; the paintings show, for example, a bunch of grapes with an inscription 'RUDENTES VINO ABSTINENT' and MORESQUE motifs adapted from Geoffrey Whitney's *A Choice of Emblemes and other Devices*, published in Leyden in 1586. Rising from the rim of the square body there are four vertical, cast, scroll BRACKETS that support the removable domed cover which is above the bowl for the salt. On the cover there are four circular medallions of *verre églomisé*, each painted with a portrait of a hero of antiquity–Ninus, Cyrus, Alexander the Great, and Julius Caesar, the four great founders of empires. The finial on the cover is surmounted by a standing figure of Justice. The piece bears the London mark of 1592–3 and the maker's mark 'WH'. It was for 250 years in the family of the Vyvyans of Trelowarren, Cornwall, until purchased in 1925 by the Victoria and Albert Museum, London.

W

wager cup. A type of drinking CUP, frequently found in Holland but also made in England, in the form of a standing woman (or, rarely, a man) with upraised arms which hold the side handles of a small gimbal-type drinking cup that swivels in a bracket frame. The woman's wide skirt (or the domed base under the man) is a fixed cup upside down. An English example, *c.*1680, in the form of a 17th-century milkmaid and known as the 'Milkmaid Cup', is owned by the Vintners' Company, London, whose Liverymen are required to drain both cups (in drinking a toast to the prosperity of the Company and the health of the Master) without spilling any wine. (The trick is to drain first the fixed large cup held uppermost and then reverse the piece carefully so that the swivel cup is turned to the top and remains upright while being drained.) In 1827 the Company commissioned from Joseph Angell II (*see* ANGELL) some replicas and these are still extant, as well as many copies made in the 20th century. Pieces in such form (but in some cases with only the swivelling cup) used jointly at a wedding by the bride and groom were called a 'Bridal Cup'. *See* THOMAS WAGER CUP.

waiter. A flat serving utensil, without a handle, and similar to but usually smaller than a SALVER. It was intended to be carried by a servant to present a cup, a letter, etc., or when serving at a dinner table. Some examples made of SHEFFIELD PLATE were covered with silver on both sides (the layer of silver on the upper surface being thicker, to withstand wear), so that only silver would be seen when a servant held it out to a seated person. To protect a table upon which it was placed, a waiter was often made with three or four supporting feet, variously decorated, or sometimes a spreading foot. The shape is usually circular (sometimes square or polygonal with rounded corners or lobed), and the size varies, generally from 15 to 25 cm in diameter. Decoration includes GADROONING, ENGRAVING, CHASING or BRIGHT CUTTING, and often includes an engraved COAT OF ARMS or crest. *See* TRAY.

Wakelin, Edward (fl. 1748–84). A London silversmith, apprenticed to John Le Sage (*see* LE SAGE) in 1730 and freed in 1748. His first mark was entered in 1747, in which year he joined GEORGE WICKES and Samuel Netherton (the latter a jeweller), with address at Panton St, Haymarket. Wickes renounced

wager cup. One of a pair, silver gilt, *c.* 1680. H. 17·8 cm. Vintners' Company, London.

Walker Art Gallery Replica. Detail showing model of building and part of plinth, silver on wood core, Elkington & Co., Birmingham, 1877–8. L. overall 66 cm. Merseyside County Art Galleries, Liverpool.

his interest in the silver part of the business in 1747, and some time after 1758 Wakelin entered his second mark in partnership with JOHN PARKER, at the same address, the firm being called from 1761 Parker & Wakelin. Edward Wakelin and Parker retired in 1776, and in 1777 his son, JOHN WAKELIN, with William Taylor, succeeded to the business. Edward Wakelin was an aggressive businessman, and obtained orders from some members of the nobility, his firm becoming, after the death of PAUL DE LAMERIE in 1751, the leading London firm in competition with that of PAUL CRESPIN. *See* SHAVING SET.

Wakelin, John (fl. 1776–1805). A London silversmith, the son of EDWARD WAKELIN, apprenticed in 1766 to his father and freed in 1779. His first and second marks were entered in partnership with William Taylor in 1776 and 1777, both with address at Panton St, Haymarket; the firm, called Wakelin & Taylor, succeeded in 1777 that of Parker & Wakelin and continued until 1792. A third mark was entered by John Wakelin in 1792 in partnership with ROBERT GARRARD I, which firm continued until 1805 when Garrard obtained control. John Wakelin was in 1797 Goldsmith and Jeweller to George III. The firm of Wakelin & Taylor employed the silversmiths Sebastian and James Crespel to supply plates and dishes, their speciality, and from 1782 to 1805 all their ware was sold through the firm.

Wakely & Wheeler Ltd. A London silversmith firm whose origins go back to 1791, when John Lias began in business as a buckle-maker at 15 Great Sutton St. In 1818 he took as his partner his son Henry Lias I (freed in 1816), and they were joined, from 1823 to 1837, by another son, Charles. Henry Lias I and his son Henry Lias II were partners from 1850; in 1875 they moved from 7 Salisbury Court to St Brides St, Ludgate Circus. In 1879, upon the death of his father, Henry Lias II formed a firm with James Wakely; in 1884 that firm consisted of James Wakely and Frank Wheeler, its name becoming Wakely & Wheeler in 1909, at which time Arthur Wakely replaced his father James and the firm moved to 27 Red Lion Square. It remained at that address until 1937, when it moved to 14/22 Ganton St. The firm, which manufactures all types of silverware except flatware, made the ELIZABETH II CORONATION CUP in 1953. In 1957 the business was acquired by Padgett & Braham Ltd (founded in 1870), which subsequently also acquired several other silversmith firms, including EDWARD BARNARD & SONS LTD. The group's present offices and factory at 10 Shacklewell Road, London, were acquired in 1974, and a new showroom at 54 Hatton Garden was established in 1977. The constituent firms retain, however, their separate identities. In recent years Wakely & Wheeler have made silverware designed by, among others, ROBERT Y. GOODDEN and LESLIE G. DURBIN.

Walker Salt. Silver gilt and rock crystal, London, 1549. H. 22·8 cm. Trinity College, Oxford.

Walker Art Gallery Replica. A CASKET surmounted by a silver miniature replica of the Walker Art Gallery, Liverpool, which was presented in 1877 by local townsmen to Andrew Barclay Walker (who had contributed substantially toward the cost of building the gallery) and which was donated to the gallery in 1956 by Walker's descendant, Sir Ian Walker-Okeover. The replica, made in meticulous detail from the model by William Goodall from the architect's plans, rests on a large and elaborately decorated plinth. Both pieces, of silver on a wood core, were made in 1877 by ELKINGTON & CO. The plinth, measuring 66 × 53·5 cm, has decoration of motifs associated with Liverpool or Walker. *See* Mary Bennett, 'An Art Gallery in Silver' in *Country Life*, 5 December 1957, p. 1239. *See* ARCHITECTURAL SILVERWARE.

Walker Salt. A silver-gilt PILLAR SALT having its stem made of a hollow cylindrical pillar of rock crystal (perhaps surviving from a destroyed RELIQUARY) in which is enclosed a silver standing female figure, sometimes said to represent Lucretia (the legendary Roman virtuous wife – the eponymous subject of Shakespeare's *The Rape of Lucrece* – who stabbed herself after being raped). The pillar rests on a spreading foot and supports a circular silver receptacle for salt. The hemispherical cover encloses a dome-shaped piece of rock crystal, above which the finial is in the form of a similar silver female figure standing on crossed arches. On the base, and supporting the pillar, are three scroll BRACKETS, each surmounted by a female TERM. The piece, the design of which is based on a drawing by Hans Holbein the Younger, is marked London, 1549. It was bequeathed in 1949 by Sir Bernard Eckstein to Trinity College, Oxford, and is hence sometimes called the 'Trinity College Salt'; the College has no record of how the name Walker came to be associated with the piece.

wall mirror. A type of MIRROR that is in a frame, to be hung on a wall for a decorative as well as for a utilitarian purpose. Some such mirrors have a frame made entirely of silver, examples being in many sizes, shapes, and styles. Two examples are in the Royal Collection: one, *c.* 1665, 2·10 m high, made for Charles II; the other, *c.* 1690, 2·25 m high, bearing the arms and cipher of William and Mary, made (EN SUITE with a silver TABLE) by ANDREW MOORE.

wall sconce. A type of SCONCE to be hung on a wall, having a shaped reflector back-plate and one or more candle SOCKETS. There are three basic silver types: (1) a back-plate with a small horizontal tray at the bottom, upon which rests a candle socket (only a few English examples are recorded); (2) a rounded plate from which extend one or more curved branches with sockets; and (3) a pilaster plate, upright and rectangular, from which extends a single branch with a socket. Sometimes the plate of types (2) and (3) is ornately decorated (reducing its reflective quality) and has attached figures of cherubs; in some cases it has a mounted rear mirror (to improve reflection). *See* ARM SCONCE; JUDGMENT OF SOLOMON SCONCES.

Walpole Inkstand. A rectangular INKSTAND, probably the largest-known example, that belonged to Sir Robert Walpole (1676-1745), 1st Earl of Orford, possibly received from Queen Caroline (1683-1737), his strong supporter. It was given by Walpole to Peter Burrell I (1692-1756), of Langley Park, Beckenham, Kent (hence it is sometimes called the 'Burrell Inkstand'); who was the brother of Sir Merrik Burrell, a Director, 1742-64, and Governor, 1758-60, of the Bank of England (the present owner of the piece). It was made by PAUL DE LAMERIE, 1733-4. It rests on four scroll feet, has a double LID hinged lengthwise along the centre, and has on one side a pen tray and on the other side five compartments, the two at the ends each holding a POUNCE-POT and the central three empty, presumably for INKWELLS (now missing). The lid is decorated with simple FLAT CHASING of rococo shells and foliated scrolls; one side of the piece bears a CARTOUCHE enclosing Walpole's monogram and two engraved collars (within each of which is the monogram 'PB') of the Order of the Garter (conferred on Walpole in 1726), and the other side bears the arms of Peter Burrell I and his motto, both probably

wall sconce. (1) With drip-pan supporting socket, John Bernard, London, 1669-70. H. 30 cm. Bank of England, London. (2) Pair with ornately decorated backplates and branches, English, *c.* 1685-90. H. 20 cm. Courtesy, Brand Inglis Ltd, London.

Walpole Inkstand. Paul de Lamerie, London, 1733-4. L. 38·5 cm. Bank of England, London.

added later by his son, Peter Burrell II (1724–75). The subsequent history of the piece until 1937 is uncertain. It has been said to have been sold by the first daughter of Peter Burrell II at Christie's, London, on 7 April 1836, but there is no record of such a sale. It has been suggested by E. Alfred Jones that the piece was probably inherited by the second daughter, Isabelle Susanna, wife of Algernon Percy (1750–1830, created 1st Earl of Beverley in 1790), and that it descended to his fourth son, Vice-Admiral Josceline Percy (1784–1856), from whom it descended by inheritance to Sir Edward Durand, who sold it at Christie's, London, on 5 May 1937. *See* E. Alfred Jones, 'An Historic Silver Inkstand made by Paul de Lamerie' in *The Connoisseur*, September 1936, p. 140; Charles C. Oman, *Plate Belonging to the Bank of England* (1967), pl. 176.

Walpole Salver. (1) A SEAL SALVER that was made probably from the metal of the first Exchequer Seal of George I, made for Sir Robert Walpole (1676–1745), Chancellor of the Exchequer, 1715–17 and 1721–42. It was made by William Lukin and engraved and signed by JOSEPH SYMPSON. Its whereabouts today is unknown. (2) A square silver-gilt salver that was made from the metal of the second and last Exchequer Seal of George I, made for Sir Robert Walpole. It was made by PAUL DE LAMERIE, 1728–9, with engraving formerly doubtfully attributed to, but now confirmed by Charles Oman as being by, WILLIAM HOGARTH. It has within an upcurved rim a TRELLIS-WORK border of FLAT CHASING and ENGRAVING, with four CARTOUCHES enclosing male and female heads. On the large central medallion are depicted the obverse and reverse of the seal, above which is the mythological figure of Fortune and below which are three figures representing Hercules between Calumny and Envy, against a background panorama of London. It was probably made for sideboard display, not for use. It is now in the Victoria and Albert Museum, London.

Walrus and Carpenter Claret-Jugs. A pair of CLARET-JUGS in the form of the characters, as drawn by Sir John Tenniel to illustrate Lewis Carroll's *Through the Looking Glass*. Both jugs are of glass with silver mounts. The Walrus Jug, resting horizontally, was made in 1881 under a Patent Office Design Registry mark of 22 September 1878 and bears the maker's mark of William Leuchars; the Carpenter Jug, standing vertically, is dated 1886 and bears the maker's mark of H. W. Griffin.

Wantage Cup. A silver-gilt HORSE-RACING CUP having two large vertical handles and a high-domed cover. The decoration is in NEO-CLASSICAL STYLE. The

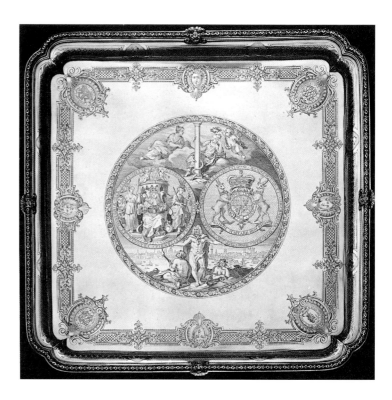

Walpole Salver (2). Seal ware, Paul de Lamerie, 1728–9, with engraving by William Hogarth. W. 49 cm. Victoria and Albert Museum, London.

Walrus and Carpenter Claret-Jugs. Glass with silver mounts, with maker's marks of, respectively, William Leuchars, 1881, and H. W. Griffin, 1886. H. (of Carpenter Jug) 23 cm. Courtesy, Lowe of Chester.

cup bears an engraved scene of a horse race and commemorates a race in 1795 at Wantage, a town near the training grounds on the Berkshire Downs. The cup, dated 1795-6, was made by Peter and Ann Bateman (*see* BATEMAN), and was awarded on 22 September 1795. It was donated by Mrs Henry Belinda du Pont to the Philadelphia Museum of Art. *See* note in *The Connoisseur*, December 1946, p. 126.

Warden Hill's Salt. A silver-gilt HOURGLASS SALT, *c.* 1490, of which the body is in the form of an hourglass, encircled by swirling and lobed REEDING, with midway a foliated knop. The circular base and the top rim of the hourglass are decorated, respectively, with CRESTING and inverted cresting. The cover is a hexagonal pyramid, with six reticulated triangular panels filled with purple glass decorated with a DIAPER PATTERN and separated by CROCKETS; its finial is foliated and topped by a seeded berry. The salt receptacle is a shallow bowl. Encircling the base is an inscription in Lombardic characters on a cross-hatched ground, 'Super WA montes TER stabunt HIL aque M' (The waters stood above the hills), a punning allusion - from Psalm 104, v. 6, in the Vulgate - to Walter Hill, Warden of New College, Oxford, 1475-94, by whom the salt was donated to the College.

Warden's Grace Cup. A silver-gilt GRACE CUP in the form of a STANDING CUP having an inverted bell-shaped bowl, detachable from a tall trumpet-shaped stem upon which are eight small balls supporting the bowl. The two-tiered cover has decoration of foliage topped by a melon-shaped finial. The base and the rim of the cover are decorated with an encircling band of CRESTING. The entire piece is decorated with a flatly embossed pattern of leaves with interspersed pineapple-shaped (or pine-cone-shaped) motifs. The piece, dating from *c.* 1480, is unmarked; it is owned by New College, Oxford, whose records indicate that, despite its current name, the cup was a gift to the College rather than to its Warden.

Warham Bowl. A BOWL of Chinese greyish-green celadon porcelain set in unmarked silver-gilt MOUNTS, *c.* 1506-30. The bowl, 12·5 cm wide, is of hemispherical shape with an everted rim; it is attributed to the early Ming period, *c.* 1368-1505. The mounts include a narrow plain lip rim, a wider neck band with a lower edge of cut work, a plain wide low stem with a spreading base, and three openwork vertical hinged straps connecting the neck band with the stem. The piece was named after William Warham (1450-1532), Archbishop of Canterbury, 1504-32, who is said by tradition (based on his name being scratched on the bottom of the base) to have bequeathed the bowl to New College, Oxford, of which he was a member between 1473 and 1488. It is also the tradition (but without factual basis) that the bowl was given to Warham by Archduke Philip of Austria, King of Castile, in 1506 (after being forced by a storm at sea to land at Weymouth on the Dorset coast) during his resulting stay in England with Sir Thomas Trenchard at Wolfeton House (*see* TRENCHARD BOWL). *See* CELADON OBJECTS.

Warden Hill's Salt. Silver gilt, *c.* 1490. H. 36·8 cm. New College, Oxford.

Warden's Grace Cup. Silver gilt, *c.* 1480.
H. 40 cm. New College, Oxford.

warming pan. Seth Lofthouse, 1715. D.
28 cm. Royal Collection; reproduced by
gracious permission of Her Majesty the
Queen.

warming pan. A household accessory, used to warm a bed, having a
covered circular pan (in which were placed hot coals), and a long, straight
detachable handle of turned wood. The pan, although usually made of brass
or copper, was sometimes made of silver in England from the late 16th century, often bearing the engraved badge of a nobleman or the coat of arms of
one of the Livery Companies. Rare existing examples with a silver pan have
a hinged lid with pierced holes forming elaborate decorative patterns, and
some have the pan protected by crossed strong wire bands attached to the
rim and extending above and across the pan; some have a small ring on the
far end to facilitate opening the pan. The handle could be taken off when
necessary to facilitate the removal of FIRE MARKS caused by oxidation from
the burning coals. Such warming pans were widely used, e.g., one was
owned by Samuel Pepys and one by Nell Gwynn. An example made in 1715
by Seth Lofthouse for the Princess of Wales (later Queen Caroline, consort
of George II) is at Buckingham Palace; an inscription on the pan states that
it formerly belonged to Queen Caroline. *See* Charles R. Beard, 'English
Warming Pans of the 17th Century' in *The Connoisseur*, January 1933, p. 4;
G. Bernard Hughes, 'Old English Warming Pans' in *Country Life*, 18 November 1949, p. 1502; —, 'Warming Pans' in *Country Life*, 6 August 1953, p. 426.

Warrington Wine Fountain. A WINE FOUNTAIN made (according to an in-
scription inside the foot) by PETER ARCHAMBO I, 1728, for George Booth, 2nd
Earl of Warrington. The body (having a SPIGOT and TAP) and cover are
chased with shells, palm leaves, and STRAPWORK, and the DROP-RING
HANDLES are suspended from demi-figures of rampant boars, the supporters
of the Warrington arms. The domed cover is surmounted by an earl's coronet.
A small disc, marked 1728, had been inserted in the base by Archambo, a
DUTY DODGER, to minimize duty; this was removed and the piece was assayed in 1729 and then given a new date mark. The piece has been on loan
from the Goldsmiths' Company, London, to Dunham Massey Hall (formerly
owned by the Booth family), at Altrincham, Cheshire.

Warwick Cruet Stand. A CRUET STAND made by ANTHONY NELME, 1715, for
the 1st Earl of Warwick and now in the possession of the 8th Earl. The
stand, with a cinquefoil tray, supports three silver CASTERS and two glass
CRUETS with silver mounts, and has a centre vertical post with a ring handle.
The name has been applied, as a generic term, to stands of the same type in
the belief that the Nelme example was the first of the type, but the form had
been made earlier. Two later examples, owned by the Goldsmiths' Company
and bearing a plaque with its arms, were made in 1740 by Richard Bailey;
the cinquefoil frame rests on four bracketed shell-shaped feet and has an
overhead scroll handle and two outside rings for stoppers, and is accompanied by three silver casters and two glass cruets with silver mounts. The type
is sometimes called a 'condiment stand' or 'condiment frame'.

'Warwick Vase'. In silverware, one of a number of copies or adaptations in
silver, silver gilt or SHEFFIELD PLATE, of a Greek marble vase, 2nd–4th century AD, of krater (campana type) form, discovered in fragments in a pool at
Hadrian's Villa (the Villa Adriana) at Tivoli, near Rome, and bought in
1770 by Gavin Hamilton. The marble vase was restored for Sir William Hamilton (1730–1803), British envoy to Naples, who, being unable to agree on a
price to sell it to the British Museum, sold it to his nephew, George Gre-
ville, 2nd Earl of Warwick. The latter brought it to England and by 1774 had
it set up at Warwick Castle. Permission was granted in 1813 by Warwick to
the 1st Earl of Lonsdale (1757–1844) to have a full-scale copy cast in silver,
but after the wax model was made for RUNDELL, BRIDGE & RUNDELL by WIL-
LIAM THEED II, together with PAUL STORR, Lord Lonsdale abandoned the project; however, the moulds were used later in France to make two bronze
copies. The marble vase was sold in 1978 to the Metropolitan Museum of
Art, New York, but an export licence was refused; it was then acquired by
the Burrell Collection, and is now in the Burrell Museum, Glasgow.
    Numerous copies and adaptations in silver or silver gilt, as well as some
in SHEFFIELD PLATE, bronze, or porcelain, have been made; these are
usually basically in the original form with an oval bowl, two side vine-stem
bifurcated handles, a trumpet foot, four relief masks on each side of the
bowl (masks of Hercules and Bacchus between masks of bearded satyrs), and
the pelt of the Nemean lion below the central pair of masks. The earliest silver adaptations are WINE COOLERS, ICE-PAILS, BOWLS, and TUREENS made from
c. 1812 by Paul Storr for Rundell, Bridge & Rundell and for GREEN, WARD
& GREEN, based on three engravings by G. B. PIRANESI. Among the known silver versions in the form of the marble vase are twelve of silver gilt made by
Storr, 1812–23, for the Prince Regent (later George IV), of which ten are in
the Royal Collection; others are owned by the Goldsmiths' Company, London, the Los Angeles County Art Museum, the Art Institute of Chicago, and

the 8th Earl of Warwick in Warwickshire. A silver-gilt pair made by Storr, 1823-6, as wine coolers with detachable rims and liners, is in an English private collection, and two were sold in 1965 by the Earl of Harewood. A modified version, made by PHILIP RUNDELL, 1820, resting on a stand having three figures of leopards sejant made by John Tapley, 1838, is now owned by the Goldsmiths' Company. More recent English copies include two made in 1901 and one in 1906 by Carrington & Co., London, and one in 1912 by EDWARD BARNARD & SONS LTD. Silver adaptations were also made in the United States, such as the CLINTON VASE and the WEBSTER VASE. Copies were also made in Sheffield plate, probably from *c*.1820, sometimes with applied ornamentation in silver. Many of the reproductions are not accurate copies of the marble vase but are merely in its basic form, sometimes substantially modified. *See* Norman M. Penzer, 'Copies of the Warwick Vase' in *Apollo*, March 1956, p. 71. *See* WATERLOO VASE.

Warrington Wine Fountain. Peter Archambo I, London, 1728. H. 70·5 cm. Goldsmiths' Company, London.

wash bowl. A type of BOWL with everted rim, suitable for washing. An example made by JOHN BRIDGE for Rundell, Bridge & Co., 1833, bears an inscription 'AR to WR / 21st August 1833 / Brighton', indicating that it was a gift from Queen Adelaide to William IV on his 68th birthday that day; it was sold at Sotheby's, London, on 22 November 1984. SEE FOOTBATH

wassail-bowl. A type of BOWL, similar to a PUNCH-BOWL, made of hardwood (lignum-vitae or maple), sometimes with silver MOUNTS, and having a cover. It was used for mixing and serving wassail (a festive drink served in olden times in England from Christmas to Twelfth Night, consisting of wine or ale, flavoured with spices, sugar, toast, roasted apples, etc.) drunk to toast good health *('Wass hail')*. One example, bearing the arms of James II, as Duke of York, and having on the interior a PRINT of a Tudor rose, has silver mounts (some now missing); it bears the mark 'IR' for John Ruslen, *c*.1680-85 (*see* C. R. Beard, 'A Royal Wassail-Bowl' in *The Connoisseur*, December 1937, p. 316). Other examples have mounts of silver (one formerly in the William Randolph Hearst Collection) or mounts of ivory (one owned in 1955 by Lord Cullen of Ashbourne, acquired by his ancestor in 1645, together with the complete wassail equipment – a wassail table, silver-rimmed wassail TUMBLERS or GOBLETS, and two CANDELABRA or CANDLESTICKS); *see* H. Clifford Smith, 'A Royal Wassail Table' in *The Connoisseur*, March 1927, p. 158, fig. III. The cover of a wassail-bowl often has, atop it, a box for spices and, affixed to it, a silver plate bearing the owner's arms, engraved or painted. *See* G. Bernard Hughes, 'Old English Wassail Bowls' in *Country Life*, 1 December 1955, p. 1320.

Warwick Cruet Stand. Three casters and two cruets, Richard Bailey, London, 1740. H. 25·5 cm. Goldsmiths' Company, London.

wassail-horn. *See* DRINKING HORN.

watch-case. The metal case enclosing the works of a watch, the case often being of a different date from the movement. Examples have been made of many materials, including some of silver or silver gilt; some have a silver dial, occasionally engraved. Although generally circular, cases have been made in many shapes, including fantasy shapes (known as a 'form watch'). Some are open-face, with the case exposing the glass-covered dial, but some have a front cover ('half hunter') or also an extra hinged back cover to pro-

'Warwick Vase'. One of a pair of silver-gilt wine coolers, Paul Storr, *c*. 1823-6. H. 24 cm. Private Collection; photo courtesy, Partridge (Fine Arts) Ltd, London.

Waterloo Vase. Silver-gilt vase made by Benjamin Smith II, for Green, Ward & Green, London, 1824–5; plinth by Robert Garrard II, 1825–6. H. (of vase) 64·7 cm. Wellington Museum, Apsley House, London (photo Victoria and Albert Museum).

tect the decorated inner cover ('hunter watch'). Some cases, especially that of a 'repeater', are pierced. Some watches have two cases (a 'pair-case watch'), the outer one decorated but the inner one (the 'box') plain, unless pierced for a repeater. Silver cases are not required to be assayed and only occasionally bear a hallmark. *See* CLOCK-CASE.

water leaf. A stylized form of leaf ornament, somewhat resembling an ivy leaf. It was a popular motif in the period of the NEO-CLASSICAL STYLE and the following decades.

Waterloo Vase. A silver-gilt VASE similar in form to the WARWICK VASE, having an oval bowl resting on a SPLAYED foot and two vertical handles, in the form of foliated scrolls, on top of each of which sits a figure of a goddess of Victory. The bowl is decorated with an encircling relief frieze depicting fighting warriors. The vase was designed by THOMAS STOTHARD, modelled by his son Alfred Joseph Stothard, and made by BENJAMIN SMITH II, 1824–5, to the order of GREEN, WARD & GREEN. It rests on a square PLINTH made by ROBERT GARRARD II, 1825–6. It was presented in 1825 to the Duke of Wellington, by a group of 'noblemen and gentlemen' who had served as officers with him in the Peninsular War or at Waterloo, to commemorate the Battle of Waterloo; their names are inscribed on the square base below the vase. On one side of the plinth there is a historical inscription, and on the opposite side a battle scene. The vase is in the Wellington Museum, Apsley House, London.

waterman's badge. A type of BADGE worn by Thames River Watermen of the various London Livery Companies, each example bearing the emblem of the particular Company and the identifying numeral of the waterman. A distinctive badge was worn by the barge-master of each Company. *See* BARGE-MASTER'S BADGE; DOGGETT'S BADGE; ADMIRALTY BARGE BADGE.

wavy-end spoon. A type of SPOON that is a modified version of the TRIFID SPOON, the terminal of the stem being undulating, with the lobes merging into each other. Also called 'shield-top spoon'.

wax-ball taper holder. A type of frame to hold a ball of wax taper, having at the top an opening for the taper to emerge. Some examples are designed to hold the ball within a wire globe that opens across the centre to allow the ball to be inserted. This type of taper holder superseded the WAX-JACK in the 1770s, when it was realized that the coiled taper tended to adhere, hence a loosely wound ball was substituted.

wax-jack. A device to hold a coiled turpentined-wax taper so as to permit it to be extended upward while burning. There are three basic types: (1) a circular base having a central vertical post with a reel around which the taper is wound in a horizontal coil, emerging upward through a small tube or a scissors-like split drip-pan that rotates on the threaded post; (2) a base with a support for a reel around which the taper is wound in a vertical coil, similarly emerging through a small tube, and having at one end of the axis of the reel a handle for turning it; and (3) a frame with a horizontal SNUFFER through the two blades of which the coiled taper emerges and can be cut. Some examples have a ring or clip from which to hang a small CANDLE EXTINGUISHER, and some have, attached to the circular base, a ring handle with a THUMBPIECE. Also called a 'wax-taper stand/holder/winder'. *See* Charles R. Beard, 'Taper Sticks' in *The Connoisseur*, November 1931, p. 302 (including wax-jacks); G. Bernard Hughes, 'Wax Taper Winders and Holders' in *Country Life*, 22 November 1956, p. 84. *See* WAX-BALL TAPER HOLDER; BOUGIE-BOX.

wax-jack. (1) With horizontal drip-pan, Dublin, 1786, height 9 cm. (2) With reel and candle extinguisher attached by chain, Dublin, 1813, height 10 cm. Both National Museum of Ireland, Dublin.

Webster Vase. A bowl in the form of the WARWICK VASE but having different relief decoration. It was made by OBADIAH RICH and Samuel L. Ward, 1835, for presentation on 12 October 1835 to Daniel Webster (1782–1852), American statesman, by the citizens of Boston, Massachusetts, in recognition of his defence of the Constitution, and bears on the base a commemorative inscription. In 1865 it was acquired by a group of subscribers and was presented to the City of Boston on 10 March 1865, with the request that it be placed in the Boston Public Library, where it now is.

wedding knife. A type of KNIFE that, in the 16th and early-17th centuries, was presented in a pair by a bridegroom to his bride. The pair was provided with either a sheath or an embroidered bag with chains or strings for suspending it from a girdle in the manner of a CHATELAINE. The haft (handle), made of silver (or ivory, amber, ebony, etc.) was inscribed with the name of the bride and the date of the wedding, and usually a symbolic motif, e.g., a dove or a heart. Often one of a pair of such knives was converted to a fork by cutting and filing its blade to form tines. Several pairs are owned by the Cutlers' Company, London, and were included in the Exhibition of Cutlery at the Victoria and Albert Museum, London, in 1979. *See* G. Bernard Hughes, 'English Wedding Knives' in *Country Life*, 25 March 1949, p. 666.

wedge-shaped spout. A type of SPOUT, found on some Renaissance-style EWERS, *c.* 1550, that is affixed to the body along its entire height, extending from the bottom of the bowl to the rim, and slanting outward to the pointed beak-shaped mouth. *See* HENSLOWE EWER AND BASIN; PARKER EWER.

weight. As to silverware, the weight of an article, usually expressed in troy ounces (oz.) and PENNYWEIGHTS (dwt) and now also often in metric grams (20 dwt = 1 oz. = 31·1035 grams). When silverware is offered for sale, it is customary to specify the present-day weight (which, as a result of wear and polishing, is often less than the original weight), as this is indicative of the quantity and thickness (GAUGE) of the silver in an article and thus of its minimum value as metal, although the PRICE is also affected by other factors. Occasionally, the weight of an article is engraved or scratched on the underside. *See* WOOD OBJECTS.

Welch, Robert (1929–). An English silversmith, born in Hereford, who trained at the Birmingham School of Art and, in 1952/5, at the Royal College of Art, London. After working in 1953 in Sweden and in 1954 in Norway, he established a workshop at Chipping Campden, Gloucestershire. He thereafter designed ware in stainless steel, cast iron, pottery, and glass, and established an association with a Swedish manufacturing firm, but always continued working as a silversmith. He made important pieces, commissioned by the Goldsmiths' Company, London, and other patrons (*see* WELCH CANDELABRA), emphasizing boldly rounded forms with an almost total absence of ornamentation. *See* Graham Hughes, 'Robert Welch' in *The Connoisseur*, July 1963, p. 190.

Welch Candelabra. A pair of CANDELABRA, commissioned by the Victoria and Albert Museum, London, for its own use, designed by ROBERT WELCH, and made in Welch's workshop by John Limbrey. They bear the SPONSOR'S MARK of Welch, who in December 1979 produced five sketches for the selection of a design, and later many detailed drawings and sketches of the chosen design. Each piece has a straight stem with three knops of oblate-globular shape and resting on a circular base, and each has a similar oblate-globular finial; each has, in circular arrangement, eight straight horizontal branches supporting the bowl-shaped candle SOCKETS within which are the candle NOZZLES. Encircling the base is an engraved Latin inscription translated as 'I put darkness to flight, rejoice the eyes, crowning the night. R. S. [Roy Strong] had me made, V & A, 1980'.

Welch Candelabra. One of the pair, designed by Robert Welch, made by John Limbrey, London, 1980. H. 38 cm. Victoria and Albert Museum, London.

Welford Cup. A miniature 'FONT-SHAPED' cup of silver gilt, having a wide stem and no decoration other than a wide band encircling the bowl, with a reserved inscription 'VERBVM/DOMINE/MANET/ETERNV' in plain lettering on a STIPPLED ground. The cup, made in London in 1518, was found at Welford, Northamptonshire, in 1968; it was purchased in 1968 by the British Museum, London.

well. (1) The depressed central portion of a PLATE, a DISH or a CHARGER, within the LEDGE or MARLI. (2) The shallow concave portion of certain receptacles, such as a TRENCHER SALT or a WELL PLATTER.

well dish. A type of large oval DISH upon which to serve and carve a haunch of venison; it supplanted the large TRENCHER previously so used. It is in the form of a TREE PLATTER, and was used from the 1720s by being placed over a DISH CROSS which, from the 1750s, was accompanied by a LAMP-STAND for keeping warm the drippings from the meat being carved. Later it was integrated into a VENISON DISH.

well platter. A type of PLATTER having a WELL at one end for holding gravy. *See* TREE PLATTER; WEDGE.

Wellington Ambassadorial Service. Articles of AMBASSADORIAL SILVERWARE provided by the nation to the 1st Duke of Wellington when he was appointed Ambassador to Paris in 1814 and to the Congress of Verona in 1822, as part of the service, technically loaned to him while Ambassador but, by custom, retained by him as a perquisite of office. All the pieces bear the engraved Royal arms. The pieces, taken together, bear the MAKER'S MARKS of fourteen different goldsmiths, and formed a COMPOSITE SERVICE. It included the following: (1) A pair of silver-gilt SALVERS with the mark of BENJAMIN

Welford Cup. Silver gilt, London, 1518. H. 9·8 cm. British Museum, London.

SMITH I, 1808, each decorated with the Royal arms in the centre, and with, around the rim, two circular bands, the inner one of VITRUVIAN SCROLLS, the outer one of clusters of grapes and leaves. (2) A silver-gilt FRUIT-BOWL resting on a high stand, the bowl having an everted rim (formed of openwork made of interlaced vertical stripes of RIBBING) and containing a glass LINER; the stand has a tripod base with a lion's-head mask at each corner, connected by floral swags, and above are three draped classical female figures upon whose heads rests a circular band, decorated with a Vitruvian scroll, that supports the bowl. The piece bears the crest of Sir Arthur Wellesley (Wellington) within the insigne of the Order of the Garter. It was made by RUNDELL, BRIDGE & RUNDELL for the Prince Regent (later George IV). (3) One of the REGENCY SUGAR-VASES made by BENJAMIN SMITH I and James Smith. Some of the pieces are now in the Wellington Museum, Apsley House, London, and some – personally owned by the descendants of Wellington – are at Stratfield Saye, the family country seat, near Reading. *See* WELLINGTON COASTER; WELLINGTON PLATE.

Wellington Centrepieces. Two large parcel-gilt CENTREPIECES that were presented to Lt-Gen. Sir Arthur Wellesley (later, 1st Duke of Wellington), from separate funds, by officers in the Peninsular Army that he commanded in 1808 (after landing at Mondego Bay, Portugal, in order to oust from that country the French Army sent by Napoleon under the command of General Andoche Junot, the British forces had defeated the French at Vimeiro on 21 August). The gifts were intended to evidence, against the public outcry, the support of the officers for Wellesley's having joined in signing the lenient Convention of Cintra, 1808, that ended the invasion by permitting the French Army to withdraw. Both centrepieces were inspired by JOHN BRIDGE, were designed by JOHN FLAXMAN II, and were made – in 1810-11 and 1811-12, respectively – by PAUL STORR for RUNDELL, BRIDGE & RUNDELL. They are now in the Wellington Museum, Apsley House, London. *See* WELLINGTON PLATE.

(1) The piece presented by the General Officers in 1810 has a circular base upon which there are three figures of lions couchant, alternating with the Royal arms, encircling a tripod pedestal which supports a column in the form of a palm tree around which are three full-length draped and winged figures, each depicting Victory holding a laurel wreath. At the top of the column is an oval tureen decorated with a band of chased bay leaves, having two vertical loop handles and a cover with a finial in the form of a vertical ring chased as a wreath.

(2) The piece presented by the Field Generals in 1811 has a square plinth with CHAMFERED CORNERS, at each of which stand three stacked rifles and a banner. Resting on the plinth is an oval tureen with vertical loop handles and a rim encircled with an identical band of chased bay leaves. On a globe on the cover stands a winged figure of Victory holding aloft a laurel wreath. The piece was to commemorate the victories at the battles at Roliça and Vimeiro against General Junot in August 1808.

Wellington Coaster. A silver-gilt BOTTLE COASTER, having the sides decorated with EMBOSSING and PIERCED WORK. It was made by PAUL STORR for RUNDELL, BRIDGE & RUNDELL, 1814-15, and after 1842 copies were made by G. R. Collis & Co., of Birmingham, from a model that the Collis company acquired at the sale of Storr models by the Rundell firm. The original, part of the WELLINGTON AMBASSADORIAL SERVICE, is in the Wellington Museum, Apsley House, London.

Wellington Decanter Wagons. A pair of silver-gilt DECANTER WAGONS devised and made in 1838 by Sir Edward Thomason, of Birmingham, upon the order of Lord Rolle, who wished to comply with a wish expressed by George IV. Each piece has two coaster-shaped silver-gilt stands for cut-glass decanters, and each of the stands is decorated with an encircling band of medals made by Thomason to commemorate the 1st Duke of Wellington's victories over Napoleon. The pair were later presented to Wellington by George IV; they are now kept at Stratfield Saye, the Wellington country seat, near Reading.

Wellington Deccan Service. A large and elaborate SERVICE of parcel-gilt silver that was presented to Sir Arthur Wellesley (created 1st Duke of Wellington in 1814), after his return to England from India in 1805, by fellow officers in the army which – under the command of his brother, Richard Colley Wellesley (1760-1842), with the aid of Sir Arthur (then Major-General) – had defeated Tippoo Sahib, Sultan of Mysore, and the Mahratta chiefs in the Deccan in southern India in the years 1796-1805. The service was made, 1804-14, by four London silversmiths, William Fountain, John Moore, John Edwards, and JOSEPH PREEDY, but it is not known who super-

Wellington Centrepieces. Paul Storr, for Rundell, Bridge & Rundell, London: (1) 1810-11, height 55 cm (*top*); and (2) 1812-13, height 83·8 cm. Both Wellington Museum, Apsley House, London (photos Victoria and Albert Museum).

vised its production. It includes two CANDELABRA and four TUREENS (see below), four SALT-CELLARS (each resting on a figure of an elephant and having a serpent handle), and other articles. Part of the service is now in the Wellington Museum, Apsley House, London, and part at Stratfield Saye, the Wellington country seat near Reading.

candelabra. A pair of candelabra, each having a tripod base with CHAMFERED CORNERS and having, on each concave side, a low-relief frieze; from the base rises a column in the form of the ancient Roman fasces, surmounted by a tall battle-axe, supporting six foliated branches, each with a candle SOCKET. On each corner of the base there is a seated figure of a soldier, and on the plinth of the column there are four standing figures of soldiers (a Highlander, a Light Dragoon, an Indian trooper, and a sepoy), each with his right arm upraised and holding aloft a wreath. The pieces bear the maker's mark of Joseph Preedy, London, 1806-7.

tureens. Two covered SOUP-TUREENS and two similar SAUCE-TUREENS, each in the form of a hemispherical bowl resting on four standing figures of elephants on a wide circular base, and each having two lateral loop handles in the form of intertwined serpents. Each cover has a finial in the form of a wide horizontal disc decorated as a lotus leaf, upon which is a seated female figure holding aloft a parasol. The pieces bear the maker's mark of John Edwards, London, 1806-7.

Wellington Plate. Various articles of silver, or silver gilt or parcel gilding, that were presented to Sir Arthur Wellesley, from 1814 1st Duke of Wellington (1769-1852), to commemorate victories while he was Major-General in India, 1796-1805, Lieutenant-General in the Peninsular War in Spain and Portugal, 1808-13, and Commander of the British Army at the Battle of Waterloo in 1815, as well as the WELLINGTON AMBASSADORIAL SERVICE. The various gifts include the WELLINGTON DECCAN SERVICE, the WELLINGTON PORTUGUESE SERVICE, the WELLINGTON SHIELD, the WATERLOO VASE, and the WELLINGTON WATERLOO CANDELABRA. Most of such pieces were donated to the nation in 1947 by the 7th Duke of Wellington and are now in the Wellington Museum, Apsley House, London; some pieces not selected by the Victoria and Albert Museum for the gift are kept by the present Duke at Stratfield Saye, the Wellington country seat, near Reading. *See* Charles C. Oman, *The Wellington Plate* (Victoria and Albert Museum), 1954; —, 'The Plate at the Wellington Museum' in *Apollo*, September 1973, p. 197. *See* WELLINGTON DECANTER WAGONS.

Wellington Portuguese Service. A monumental parcel-gilt SERVICE presented in 1816 to the 1st Duke of Wellington by the Prince Regent of Portugal, Dom João, later João (John) VI, to commemorate the landing of the British Peninsular. Army on 1 August 1808 under Lt-Gen. Sir Arthur Wellesley (later 1st Duke of Wellington) at Mondego Bay in Portugal, his victories at the battles of Roliça and Vimeiro, and his defeating the French Army sent by Napoleon under General Junot that led to the French evacuation of Portugal in 1808 after the Convention of Cintra. The service was designed in NEO-CLASSICAL STYLE by Domingos Antonio de Sequeira (1768-1837), a Portuguese painter and sculptor, who also supervised the production. It was authorized by the Council of Regency which in March 1811 directed the Military Arsenal at Lisbon to make the service. The sculpture was executed, 1811-16, principally by Vicente Pires de Gama and João Teixeira Pinto. It was started in 1813, completed in 1816, after certain pieces had been redesigned to meet criticisms by Wellington, and arrived at Portsmouth in 55 crates in 1816. The service is now in the Wellington Museum, Apsley House, London, where it was used by Wellington at an annual banquet held on the anniversary of the Battle of Waterloo; it proved inadequate for such occasions, however, and in 1819 Wellington ordered additional matching tureens, hot plates, and salt-cellars to be made by GARRARD & CO. (perhaps executed by PAUL STORR) which are identifiable only by the HALLMARKS they bear.

The service now stands on a shaped PLATEAU, 29·12 m long, consisting of thirteen panels. It includes:

(1) A CENTREPIECE resting on an octagonal base that is supported by eight sphinxes, upon which stands a central column composed of four fasces bearing the arms of Britain, Spain, and Portugal and surmounted by a terrestrial globe upon which stands a winged figure of Victory and around the base of which are four allegorical figures symbolic of Europe, Asia (with a horse), Africa (with a camel), and America (an Indian).

(2) Two CANDELABRA, each in the form of a palm tree, from the top of which extend twelve branches (symbolizing the twelve most sanguinary battles of the Peninsular War) for candle sockets, all resting on a large square base upon which there are four dancing nymphs (without floral garlands originally intended for them).

Wellington Deccan Service. One of the pair of candelabra, Joseph Preedy, London, 1806-7, height 79 cm; and a sauce-tureen, John Edwards, London, 1806-7. Both Wellington Museum, Apsley House, London (photos Victoria and Albert Museum).

Wellington Portuguese Service. Centrepiece with allegorical figures of Four Continents. H. 1·08 m. Portugal, 1814. Wellington Museum, Apsley House, London (photo Victoria and Albert Museum).

(3) Four crowned griffins supporting plaques bearing the names and dates of the main battles.

(4) Two SOUP-TUREENS, each supported by four reclining mermaids on a circular base and encircled by a laurel border and a band of adjacent coats of arms, and each having a domed cover with a pineapple finial.

(5) Two SAUCE-TUREENS, each supported by four reclining Tritons and having a cover similar to (4) above.

(6) Several large triangular and oblong DISHES, each with a domed cover having a pineapple finial.

(7) Several figures of 'Tagides' (nymphs of the River Tagus), each holding aloft a wreath, of nymphs dancing and blowing trumpets, and of *putti* ('geniuses') playing musical instruments.

(8) Candelabra with six branches, having a central pillar encircled by three tall spears.

(9) Additional candelabra and candlesticks, tureens, dishes, Victory columns, and knives, forks, and spoons.

See Charles C. Oman, *The Wellington Plate: Portuguese Service* (1914).

(Note: Although the service was not made in Britain, it is discussed here because of its historical associations and the supplementary pieces made by Garrard & Co. in London.)

Wellington Shield. A large silver-gilt SHIELD having a central medallion, against a background of radiating reeding, of figures in high relief and in-the-round depicting the 1st Duke of Wellington on horseback surrounded by his officers, also mounted, and at the bottom three recumbent nude figures symbolic of fallen adversaries. The wide border is composed of ten adjacent embossed panels, most depicting battle scenes of horsemen and foot soldiers. The piece is from a winning design (perhaps inspired by the ACHILLES SHIELD) by THOMAS STOTHARD in 1814 and was to have been modelled by Tollemache (an employee of Stothard), but upon his sudden death Stothard himself modelled it (the only piece he ever modelled). It was made, 1821–2, by BENJAMIN SMITH II for GREEN, WARD & GREEN, whose signature is on it, with some chasing and embossing by WILLIAM PITTS II. It was presented in 1822 to the 1st Duke of Wellington by the Merchants and Bankers of the City of London; it is in the Wellington Museum, Apsley House, London.

Wellington Statuette. An equestrian STATUETTE depicting the 1st Duke of Wellington astride his horse 'Copenhagen', made by ROBERT GARRARD II, 1838.

Wellington Waterloo Candelabra. A pair of silver-gilt CANDELABRA, marked 1816–17, with sculptural decoration by an unknown designer; they

Wellington Portuguese Service. Soup-tureen supported by figures of mermaids. H. 39·3 cm. Portugal, 1814. Wellington Museum, Apsley House, London (photo Victoria and Albert Museum).

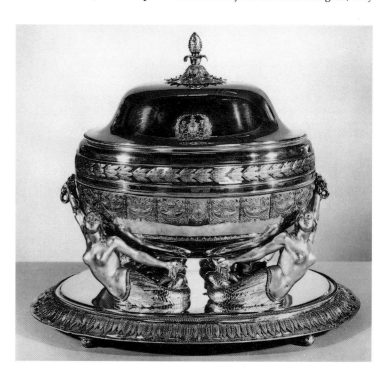

Wellington Shield. Silver gilt, designed by Thomas Stothard, made by Benjamin Smith II, 1821-2, for Green, Ward & Green, London. D. 1·03 m. Wellington Museum, Apsley House, London (photo Victoria and Albert Museum).

were made by BENJAMIN SMITH I for GREEN, WARD & GREEN, and were presented in 1816 as a gift from the Merchants and Bankers of the City of London to the 1st Duke of Wellington in recognition of his victory at the Battle of Waterloo in 1815. Each piece, 1·45 m high, has a tripod base having at each corner a cannon, trophies, and arms, and on the base, surrounding the central stem, three soldiers (on one, a Portuguese soldier, a sepoy, and a Spanish guerrilla; on the other, an English, an Irish, and a Scottish infantryman) holding ensigns and rifles. Each stem, which supports six branches for candle sockets (adapted in 1824-5 for oil-burning lamps), is surmounted by a winged figure of Victory holding a wreath. Encircling the base is a low-relief frieze. The pieces are in the Wellington Museum, Apsley House, London. *See* WELLINGTON PLATE.

Welsh silverware. Articles of silverware made by Welsh silversmiths, of whom several produced quality ware in the 16th and 17th centuries. The leading silversmiths were Morgan Phillips (fl. 1520-53), Sir Hugh Myddleton, Bt (1555-1631), John Williams (fl. 1604-36), and John Edwards (fl. 1697-1738). Later several Welsh apprentices worked in England at nearby Chester and Shrewsbury, and also in Dublin. *See* E. Alfred Jones 'Welsh Goldsmiths' in *The Connoisseur*, February 1942, p. 112. *See* MYDDLETON CUP.

Wenman Tankard. A large TANKARD of cylindrical shape, having a flat lid with a THUMBPIECE in the form of a lion couchant and around the base an encircling band of ACANTHUS leaves. It has an engraved inscription stating it to be the gift in 1679 by Sir Richard Wenman, Bt (d. 1691) to Oriel College, Oxford. It is hallmarked London, 1678, but bears an unidentified maker's mark; it was formerly attributed to English make (*see* G. E. P. How, in *Apollo*, January 1945, p. 171), but Charles C. Oman dissented and attributed it to French origin (*ibid.*, July 1945, p. 272). It has a capacity of about one gallon, hence has been called 'The Great Lion Tankard'. It is distinct from a STANDING CUP with a cover and lobed rim, also at Oriel College, but both have been referred to as 'The Founder's Cup, Oriel College'.

Westbury Cup. A silver-gilt ACORN CUP bearing London hallmarks for 1585-6. It has, encircling the upper part of the bowl, an engraved inscription 'Given to the Church of Westbury by Colonel Wancklen and Mary Contes of Marlbrou. 1671' and on the cover the initials 'TW' and 'MM' (the initials of his deceased wife). The cup was presented to the parish church of Westbury, Wiltshire, by Wancklen, whose wife Mary (the widow of the 2nd Earl

Wellington Waterloo Candelabra. One of the pair, silver gilt, Benjamin Smith I for Green, Ward & Green, London, 1816-17. H. 1·45 m. Wellington Museum, Apsley House, London (photo Victoria and Albert Museum).

of Marlborough) had died in 1670 before the gift was made; in order to conceal the fact of her death, Wancklen had secretly buried her body – an action intended to prolong her life interest in certain property – and had provided the elaborate inscription to create the impression that she was still alive at the time the gift was made in 1671. The cup, after being owned by the church for some two hundred years, came into private ownership, and was at one time in the collection of Sir Charles Robinson; it is now owned by the Museum of Fine Arts, Boston, Massachusetts.

Westminster Bridge Wine Cistern. The same as the JERNINGHAM-KANDLER WINE COOLER.

Westminster Monstrance. A MONSTRANCE having a cruciform base and stem, with canopied niches framing statuettes of Saints Peter, Francis, Clare, and Colette. It was made, from silver plate and gemstones contributed by a Franciscan nun, by OMAR RAMSDEN and ALWYN CARR, 1907, and is partially enamelled by Jeanne Etève. It was bequeathed by Carr in 1940 to Westminster Cathedral, London.

Westminster Tobacco Box. A BOX (and group of related silverware made from 1720 to the present century) owned by the Past Overseers' Society of St Margaret and St John, Westminster, London, and on loan to the Westminster City Council, being occasionally displayed at its City Hall. The box is of HORN and was a gift in 1713 from Henry Monck, an Overseer of St Margaret's (the parish church). In 1720 silver mounts were added. In 1749 an oval case was provided for the box and the case was later raised on to a plinth; thereafter a plate of inscribed silver was affixed annually to each side of the plinth. Subsequent periodical gifts added five silver cases. The box is surmounted by a figure of Queen Victoria, added in 1887. A canopy was provided in 1913, and in 1936 several silver dishes, designed by Sir Edwin Lutyens in the shape of the Tudor rose. *See* Peter Winckworth, 'The Westminster Tobacco Box' in *The Connoisseur*, May 1965, p. 19.

Westwell flagons. Two silver-gilt FLAGONS, originally secular flagons of the type known as a LIVERY POT. Each has a different maker's mark, and they are dated 1594 and 1595, respectively. Each has a pear-shaped body, supported by a spool-shaped stem resting on a TRUMPET FOOT, both the body and the cushion-shaped hinged lid being decorated with chased STRAPWORK and foliage on a matted ground. Each has a SCROLL HANDLE, and each lid has a thumbpiece decorated with a cherub mask. Both were owned by the parish church at Westwell, near Ashford, Kent, where the 1630 register records that they were given to the church by George Baker, Lord of the Manor of Ripple, in that parish, whose family had purchased the manor in 1553. The flagons were sold by the church at Sotheby's, London, on 4 July 1968 and were acquired by the Goldsmiths' Company, London.

Weymouth Regatta Cup. A silver-gilt circular, covered WINE-COOLER in the form of a Greek krater of the calyx type, having two uplifted horizontal side handles at the lower part of the bowl, each cast as a garland of flowers. Encircling the body are bands of at least ten different types of foliate motifs – including ACANTHUS leaves, roses, grapes, and lotus – cast and chased, together with a view of Weymouth with sailing boats in the harbour. The finial on the cover is a figure of a standing sailor beside an anchor. The cup, dated 1827–8, was made by REBECCA(H) EMES and Edward Barnard, and is inscribed 'Weymouth Regatta 1827'. It is in the Victoria and Albert Museum, London.

whistle. An instrument that produces a shrill sound when air (or steam) is blown through it. Air whistles were made in ornamental form from the 16th century, to be hung as a pendant or from a girdle or CHATELAINE (and sometimes used for calling domestics), and are shown in Renaissance paintings and in engravings by Dürer. Some were made of gold or silver with CHASING or enamelled decoration, and some carved from boxwood. One made for Henry VIII, set in a finger-ring, was decorated with diamonds and a ruby. Examples were hung with silver bells to ward off the 'evil eye', and some were in the form of a case to hold TOOTHPICKS and EAR-PICKS. *See* BOSUN'S CALL; WHISTLE WITH CORAL AND BELLS.

whistle tankard. A term sometimes used for a tankard having a BLOW HOLE at the base of the handle.

whistle with coral and bells. A small WHISTLE having, extending from the end of its handle, a coral stalk for teething (sometimes called a 'gumstick') and several free-swinging pellet-bells attached as a RATTLE. It has been a

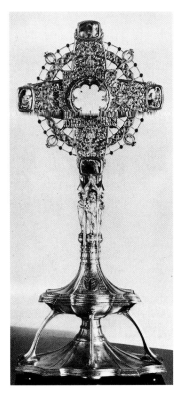

Westminster Monstrance. Silver with gemstones and enamelling, Omar Ramsden and Alwyn Carr, London, 1907. H. 76·2 cm. Westminster Cathedral, London.

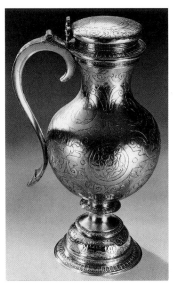

Westwell flagons. One of the pair, silver gilt, 1594. H. 30 cm. Goldsmiths' Company, London.

popular gift for use by infants. The length (exclusive of the coral) ranges from 5 to 20 cm. Often called merely 'coral and bells'. *See* Berenice Ball, 'Whistles with Coral and Bells' in *Antiques*, December 1961, p. 552. *See* TEETHING STICK.

white ware. (1) Unburnished silverware. (2) Any silverware other than SILVER GILT ware.

Whittington College Badge. A silver-gilt BADGE, one of thirteen given on 15 February 1625 to 'the poor men of Whittington College almshouse' by John Banckes, mercer. Of three large and nine small examples, all dated 1625, only three survive, now owned by the Mercers' Company, London. They are decorated with the busts of crowned maidens with flowing hair, as on the Common Seal of the Company and as on two MACES owned by it and made in 1679 by Edward Pinfold. The badges bear the inscription 'THINCKE AND THANCKE GOD', the motto of Banckes.

wick trimmer. A type of scissors-like implement used to cut off the end of a candle wick that is not charred, i.e., that of an unused hand-dipped candle (unlike the snuff, which would be trimmed with a SNUFFER). The wick trimmer has one blunt blade and one sharpened blade. *See* DOUTER.

wickerwork silverware. Articles of silverware decorated to resemble the type of basketwork made by encircling strands, interlacing or criss-crossing, of wicker (osier). Such decoration is found on some baskets by PAUL DE LAMERIE, 1731-2, and was a speciality of Robert Hennell IV (*see* HENNELL), *c.* 1850-60. *See* WICKERWORK TEAPOT; ORTOLAN BASKET.

wickerwork teapot. A type of TEAPOT with overall decoration in the form of basketwork. A small teapot so decorated made by Robert Hennell IV (*see* HENNELL), London, 1859, is in the Victoria and Albert Museum, London. *See* WICKERWORK SILVERWARE.

Wickes, George (1698-1761). A leading London silversmith, the son of James Wickes, apprenticed in 1712 to Samuel Wastell, a London silversmith; he received his freedom in 1720, and registered his first and second marks in 1722 when working in Threadneedle St. By 1730 he took into partnership John Craig (with no recorded joint mark) and moved to Norris St, near Haymarket. Upon Craig's death in 1735, Wickes registered his third mark and opened his own workshop in Panton St, corner of Haymarket, and he registered a fourth mark in 1739. He prospered and in 1747 took as his partner EDWARD WAKELIN, who assumed control of the business. They took as a partner Samuel Netherton, a jeweller, and Wickes renounced the silver part of the business to Wakelin in 1747, retiring in 1759. The firm of Wickes and Wakelin (which later became GARRARD & CO. LTD) and its successors prospered, receiving orders from members of the nobility and from bishops, as well as from Frederick Louis, Prince of Wales, from 1735 until his death in 1751, and then from his widow and their children. His largest surviving

Weymouth Regatta Cup. Silver-gilt covered wine cooler, Rebecca(h) Emes and Edward Barnard, London, 1827-8. H. 39·5 cm. Victoria and Albert Museum, London.

Wickes, George. Cake-basket with bail handle and pierced decoration, London, 1743. Courtesy, Garrard & Co. Ltd, London.

wickerwork silverware. Basket with openwork sides, Paul de Lamerie, London, 1731-2. L. 37·5 cm. Ashmolean Museum, Oxford.

Whittington College Badge. Silver gilt, 1625. Mercers' Company, London.

work is the LEINSTER SERVICE. From 1735 the production of the Wickes firm equalled in quantity and quality that of PAUL DE LAMERIE. Wickes often collaborated with other silversmiths, e.g., PETER ARCHAMBO I, by assigning some commissions to them, and by acquiring for his shop articles made by others. In some instances he was a DUTY DODGER. *See* Elaine Barr, *George Wickes, Royal Goldsmith, 1698-1761* (1980); Judith Banister, 'Master of Rococo Style' in *Country Life*, 6 November 1980, p. 1644.

Willaume, David (I) (1658-1740). A Huguenot silversmith from Metz, in Lorraine (or possibly from Mers), France, who emigrated between 1674 and 1686 to London and there took out his Letters of Denization in 1687. He worked near Charing Cross, 1688-92, and was freed by redemption in 1693, his name being recorded as David Williamme. He entered his first mark *c.* 1697, and later marks in 1718 and 1720, with address after 1720 in St James's St. He was the most prolific of the Huguenot silversmiths (having as apprentices his son, DAVID WILLAUME II, DAVID TANQUERAY, and Lewis Mettayer, all of whom later made very fine ware in his style), and was among the early ones to develop new forms and styles, featuring GADROONING. His work included imposing WINE COOLERS (a pair were made in 1698 for the Duke of Devonshire, and one in 1708 for the 5th Earl of Meath which was later acquired by the Prince of Wales, the future George II) and HELMET EWERS, as well as household ware, the pieces being of the highest quality of design and execution; much of his work, *c.* 1698-1726, was for wealthy clients. He sometimes collaborated with Augustin(e) Courtauld II (*see* COURTAULD), e.g., in making an important TOILET SERVICE, and apparently they used moulds lent by PAUL DE LAMERIE. He became prosperous as a banker and retired in 1728 to the Manor of Tingrith in Bedfordshire. Sometimes pieces made by him were signed by his son, and as a result their work has occasionally been the subject of wrong attributions. *See* Edward Wenham, 'David Willaume and his pupils' in *Antique Collector*, May–June 1945, p. 80; Christopher Lever, 'David Willaume' in *Apollo*, January 1975, p. 19; Judith Banister, 'The Founder of a Dynasty' in *Antique Dealer & Collectors Guide*, June 1985, p. 62.

Willaume, David (II) (1692-1761). A London silversmith, son of DAVID WILLAUME I, who was apprenticed to his father in 1706 and obtained his freedom by patrimony in 1723. He registered, from his father's address in St James's St, his first and second marks in 1728, upon the retirement of his father, and a third in 1739. In 1744 and 1746 he was a Subordinate Goldsmith to the King, being designated David Williams. His designs show much less of the Huguenot influence than do those of his father, and much of his work may have been executed by English journeymen.

William and Mary silverware. Articles of silverware made in England in the reign of William III and Mary I, 1689-1702. The style of the period, which continued until *c.* 1705, featured decoration of EMBOSSING composed of FLUTING and GADROONING, alternately convex and concave, and running vertically, obliquely or spirally.

Williams-Wynn Toilet Service. A silver-gilt 29-piece TOILET SERVICE made in 1768 by THOMAS HEMING for the marriage in 1769 of Sir Watkin Williams-Wynn, 4th Baronet, to Henrietta, fifth daughter of the 4th Duke of Beaufort. (The SNUFF-BOX bears the mark of EMICK ROMER.) The service descended to the present Baronet, of Llangedwyn, Oswestry, Shropshire, from whom it had been on loan to the old London Museum until it was sold in April 1963 to the National Museum of Wales, Cardiff. *See* Peter Hughes, 'Williams-Wynn Silver in the National Museum of Wales' in *The Connoisseur*, September 1973, p. 33. For an almost identical toilet service, also by Thomas Heming, *see* CAROLINE MATHILDA TOILET SERVICE.

Williamsburg Centrepiece. A COLONNADE CENTREPIECE which includes a water fountain. Within the encircling colonnade with a domed roof and resting on a rotating circular mirrored base there is a glass globular receptacle in which there is an upright tube upon which sits a figure of a *putto* astride a dolphin and holding aloft a conch-shell. The fountain is operated by filling, through an aperture in the roof under the finial, the water reservoir in the dome; the water descends to the reservoir in the base through a pipe in one of the columns and, by seeking its own level, then ascends through the pipe supporting the figure and out through the conch-shell, the flow being regulated by a valve at the base of the column. The upper surface of the base is depressed to receive the surplus water, and the underside of the base has a drainage valve. Two of the columns are detachable to permit removal of the glass bowl. The piece, of SILVER-PLATED WARE, was made at Sheffield or Birmingham, *c.* 1800-15, and is at Colonial Williamsburg, Virginia.

wickerwork teapot. Robert Hennell IV, London, 1859. H. 11·5 cm. Victoria and Albert Museum, London.

Williams-Wynn Toilet Service. Silver gilt, Thomas Heming, London, 1768. National Museum of Wales, Cardiff.

Willms, Auguste Adolphe (1823-99). A French sculptor and designer of silverware who studied in Paris and came to England in 1848 to work for Jean-Valentin Morel (1794-1860), a silversmith and jeweller of Paris who came to London, also in 1848, worked at 7 Burlington St, and exhibited at the Great Exhibition of 1851. When Morel dissolved his firm in London and returned to Paris, Willms also returned to Paris, to work for Christofle & Cie., François-Désiré Froment-Meurice, and Victor Paillard, designing pieces for the Paris Exposition of 1855. He was employed in 1859 by ELK-INGTON & CO., and returned to London, becoming head of the design department, which post he held until his death. The firm exhibited much of his work at the London International Exhibition of 1862 and the Paris Expositions of 1867 and 1878, including pieces designed in the then popular Japanese style, and also work decorated with enamelling and gemstones, some of which were executed in REPOUSSÉ work by LÉONARD MOREL-LADEUIL. His work was exhibited at the Philadelphia Exhibition of 1876 (a feature was an elaborate mirror of silver and DAMASCENED steel). In 1897 he designed a MACE for the City of Birmingham. He was a leader in developing the production of silverware decorated with CLOISONNÉ and CHAMPLEVÉ enamelling. *See* JASMINE VASE.

Wimbledon Cup. A TROPHY in the form of a silver-gilt TWO-HANDLED CUP presented annually by the All England Lawn Tennis Club to the winner of the Men's Singles Tennis Tournament held at Wimbledon, in London, but never retained by him. The cup, made by ELKINGTON & CO., *c.* 1883, was purchased by the Club in 1887. It is inscribed 'All England Lawn Tennis Club – Single Handed Championship of the World', with the names and dates of all winners since 1877. It replaced two previous cups permanently kept by the winner, W. Renshaw, in 1877–83.

Wine-and-Water Ewers. Pairs of EWERS of vase shape, each with an extended lip and a wavy loop handle and standing on a square plinth. The one for wine has on the sides grape-vine swags and on the shoulder, within the handle and embracing the neck, a seated figure of Bacchus (Dionysus); the one for water has on the sides swags of aquatic leaves and a seated figure of a Triton. The pairs were made by Messrs Carrington (the firm of JOHN BOD-MAN CARRINGTON), being adaptations of the ceramic Wine-and-Water Ewers

Williamsburg Centrepiece. Colonnade centrepiece, Sheffield or Birmingham, *c.* 1800-15. H. 85 cm. Colonial Williamsburg, Va.

Wine-and-Water Ewers. Pair with symbolic figures and swags, Carrington & Co., London, 1905–6. H. (without plinth) 44·5 cm. Courtesy, Christie's, London.

wine-bottle coaster. One of a set of four, silver gilt, with openwork frieze, Benjamin Smith I, London 1807. H. 7·8 cm. Courtesy, Partridge (Fine Arts) Ltd, London.

wine cooler. One of a pair, silver gilt, in form of Greek krater vase (calyx type), Paul Storr, London, 1810–11. H. 27·3 cm. Goldsmiths' Company, London.

originally made by Wedgwood & Bentley at Etruria from plaster casts made in 1775 by JOHN FLAXMAN I from designs by Claude Michel (1738–1814), called Clodion; the silver pairs differ by substituting for the ornament on the front of the shoulder a bunch of grapes instead of the original ram's-head mask and substituting leaves instead of a dolphin mask, by varying the positions of the head and hands of the figures, by altering the forms of the swags, and by changing the pattern of the bands encircling the bowl. (Wedgwood pairs were made at various times from *c.* 1778 for almost 200 years, some of jasper ware, some of black basaltes.) A silver pair, marked Carringtons, 1905 and 1906, was sold at Christie's, London, on 27 March 1905. Two identical silver examples of the wine type, with the Carrington mark, 1899–1900, bear the engraved arms of the Carpenters' Company, London, their present owner. *See* CERAMIC-STYLE SILVERWARE.

wine-bottle. An adaptation of the PILGRIM FLASK, made of silver in the late-17th century and early-18th century, having a large compressed, rounded body, a long neck, and two short chains extending from lugs at the side of the body and sometimes connected to the stopper. Rare examples exist, their original use being uncertain, but it is generally believed that they were made solely for display or perhaps to be filled with wine and immersed, suspended by the chains, in cold water in order to cool the contents. They are elaborately ornamented, especially those made by Huguenot silversmiths, and some weigh as much as 400 to 483 troy ounces. *See* PILGRIM BOTTLE; CASTING BOTTLE.

wine-bottle coaster. A type of COASTER having a GALLERY (its height being less than its diameter) in which to stand a wine-bottle on a dinner table. The gallery is often ornately decorated with PIERCED WORK, EMBOSSING or ENGRAVING. *See* HOCK-BOTTLE COASTER; WINE-BOTTLE STAND.

wine-bottle cork. A type of decorated cork having at its top a silver cap surmounted by an ornament such as (1) a figure or a vine leaf, (2) a decorated vertical ring for extracting the cork, or (3) a vertical disc or shell inscribed with the name of the wine. A functional variation is in the form of a hollow cork surmounted by a silver pouring tube, to which is attached a hinged ball which can be rotated to close the tube and so protect the wine for a brief period; sometimes called a 'wine pourer'.

wine-bottle holder. A type of receptacle for holding vertically and for pouring a bottle of white wine, being in the form of a flat-bottomed cylindrical stand to fit the bottle (narrow diameter for hock, wide for champagne) from which extends upward a tall curved HANDLE, at the top of which there is a hinged ring that fits around the neck of the bottle and secures it. *See* WINE CRADLE.

wine-bottle stand. A type of COASTER having a high GALLERY (its height being greater than its diameter) in which to stand a wine-bottle on a dinner table. The gallery of some examples is up to 18 cm high, and is often decorated ornately with PIERCED WORK, EMBOSSING or ENGRAVING. *See* WINE-BOTTLE COASTER.

wine cistern. *See* WINE COOLER.

wine cooler. A type of receptacle for holding iced water and lumps of ice to chill one or more bottles of wine. There are two forms:
(1) To stand on a table or sideboard. Early examples made in the 1790s, were straight-sided, tapering slightly inward to a flat base, similar to an ICE-PAIL but larger; In the period 1800–10 some were shaped like a barrel, decorated with encircling hoops. In the 1820s some were made with a footed base, decorated at the bottom with GADROONING and having two upward-slanting horizontal handles or two DROP-RING HANDLES; some were shaped like an urn or inverted bell, with two side handles, midway like a Greek krater of the calyx type, and after *c.* 1820 the form became more elaborate, adapted from the WARWICK VASE, with relief decoration of ACANTHUS leaves, grapes, floral patterns, as well as mythological friezes and applied MASKS. Inside a wine cooler of this type there is sometimes a separate cylindrical metal LINER, into which a wine-bottle can be placed to be kept cool and dry, holding back the ice so that the bottle can be readily replaced. The liner originally had an everted collar that covered the iced water, but later the collar was made separate and was removable, or was dispensed with. Such wine coolers were often sold in pairs in a fitted case, or sometimes in sets of four or more. They were, until the 1840s, called in 'ice-pail' of 'ice-bucket', but thereafter catalogued as a 'wine cooler'. *See* DOUBLE WINE COOLER; WEYMOUTH REGATTA CUP.

(2) To stand on the floor: a large oval receptacle, in the form of a deep basin, for holding iced water and ice to chill several bottles or FLAGONS of wine. The oval bowl has a bulging body that forms a convex surface and rests on four feet or a spreading base; it has a slightly everted rim and two large carrying handles at the narrow ends. The handles vary in form, from drop-ring handles and FLYING SCROLL HANDLES to horizontal scroll handles surmounted by animal or mythological figures, such as a unicorn and a griffin or a crowned lion. The bowl is decorated in various styles, sometimes with applied acanthus leaves, gadrooning or SPOON-HANDLE STRAPS, as well as with EMBOSSING and ENGRAVING. Such pieces, sometimes called a 'bath', were sometimes used for washing plates and glasses, as shown in many paintings. They were of great weight, some ranging from 1,000 to 3,700 oz. (exceptional ones even more), hence many were melted down and few have survived. English examples were made (often as a pair) by the leading silversmiths for wealthy owners in the period after the Restoration, *c.*1660–1720, and some later, in ROCOCO STYLE, in the 18th century (in 1957 a total of 26 extant English examples, 1700–34, were listed by Norman M. Penzer), after which time they were largely replaced by the above-mentioned small type (1). The large pieces were not usually a permanent item of furnishing but were brought in from the pantry when needed. A notable example, made by CHARLES KANDLER, 1734, is now in the Hermitage, Leningrad (*see* JERNINGHAM-KANDLER WINE COOLER). Such large oval wine coolers have sometimes been called a 'wine cistern', but as a cistern is a receptacle intended for an unbottled liquid, such as water used for washing, a large example for cooling bottles is preferably called a 'wine cooler'. Some such coolers are sometimes accompanied by a related WINE FOUNTAIN; *see* EXETER WINE COOLER AND FOUNTAIN. *See* Norman M. Penzer, 'The Great English Wine Coolers' in *Apollo*, August 1957, p. 3, and September 1957, p. 46; G. Bernard Hughes, 'Wine Cisterns and Cellarettes' in *Country Life*, 8 December 1955, p. 1381; —, 'Elegance of Georgian Wine-Coolers' in *Country Life*, 15 February 1968, p. 366. *See* ROYAL WINE COOLER; SPEAKER'S WINE COOLER; SUTHERLAND WINE COOLER; BANK OF ENGLAND WINE COOLER.

wine cradle. An oblong basket-like receptacle with one overhead HANDLE, for holding in a nearly horizontal position a bottle of red wine, so that, while the wine is being carried, any sediment in the bottle remains undisturbed. Some have plain sides, but some are made of WIREWORK. *See* WINE-BOTTLE HOLDER.

wine-cup. A type of drinking vessel in the form of a GOBLET, but having a small bowl (made in various shapes) which rests on a stem with a base that is usually circular but generally conforms to the bowl. Silver examples date from the mid-15th century and were popular in England from *c.*1600 until they were largely replaced by those of glass in the 18th century. The shape of the bowl is usually semi-ovoid, hemispherical, saucer-shaped (the form often associated with one type of champagne glass), funnel-shaped, inverted-bell-shaped, beaker-shaped or, rarely, polygonal or four-lobed; its interior is sometimes gilded. The stem is usually BALUSTER-shaped (thick or thin) and solid, usually with a knop, and sometimes with collars and mereses (as on some glass goblets), or trumpet-shaped (hollow), and has a circular foot that is flat, spreading or low-domed. Early examples (called 'quaffing cups') are low, about 10 cm high, but later examples are up to 20 cm high. The cups are decorated with EMBOSSING, ENGRAVING, BRIGHT CUTTING or CHASING, sometimes with MATTING or PUNCHING. Sometimes called a 'goblet'. *See* G. Bernard Hughes, 'When wine was drunk from silver' in *Country Life*, 11 November 1965, p. 1262. *See* MARSTON CUP; CHALICE; COMMUNION CUP; WAGER CUP.

wine fountain. A type of receptacle for holding and dispensing wine, having near the bottom a TAP and a SPIGOT (sometimes two). Such pieces were made to be (1) placed on a serving table or a sideboard, or (2) suspended on a wall (rare). The former are large and massive, of cylindrical or baluster form or urn-shaped, with a low stem, spreading foot, two side handles (rarely four), and a high-domed cover; some have an interior chamber for ice, in which case the cover is in two parts, one opening for pouring in wine, the other for inserting ice, and there is a plug for draining water from the melted ice. The wall-mounted type has a flat back. The height of both types is usually about 70 cm, but some range up to 1·30 m; and the capacity is often 2 gallons. They are ornately decorated with EMBOSSING and some with FIGURAL HANDLES; the owner's crest is sometimes on the finial and the spigot. They were sometimes made as a pair, and some are accompanied by a matching BASIN, WINE COOLER or EWER. Most were made *c.*1660–1750; later wine fountains were made of glass with silver mounts, but without an ice chamber (these are urn-shaped or in the form of a horizontal barrel). From

wine cup. Hexagonal bowl and foot, chased decoration on matt ground, maker's mark 'TH', 1617. H. 22·2 cm. Cripplegate Foundation, London.

the wine fountain was evolved the TEA-URN. *See* G. Bernard Hughes, 'Old English Wine Fountains' in *Country Life*, 10 February 1955, p. 390. *See* CORONATION 'WINE FOUNTAIN'; WARRINGTON WINE FOUNTAIN; TABLE FOUNTAIN; SHAFTESBURY.

wine funnel. A type of FUNNEL used for decanting red wine from its bottle. It has a tapering spout that is curved near its opening, the tip being cut vertically so that the opening is at right-angles to the mouth of the funnel. Such funnels are made in two forms, and, in order to remove any sediment in the wine, each is provided with a strainer: (1) having a bowl that is detachable from the spout, and having a pierced bottom; and (2) having a removable inner bowl that has a pierced bottom and fits within the outer bowl. In both forms a piece of muslin is fitted between the strainer and the spout; this muslin is analogous to the conical muslin strainer (Hippocrates's sleeve) that was fitted into earlier types of funnel. Some wine funnels have a ring (bezel) to secure the muslin in position. The spout is curved to minimize aeration of the wine by causing it to flow down the side of the DECANTER or CLARET-JUG instead of splashing straight down into the already decanted wine. Sometimes such a funnel is accompanied by a circular stand upon which to place the inverted funnel after use. Such funnels are about 15 cm high. Sometimes a funnel of the second form has, on the rim of the removable inner bowl, a hook by which it can be suspended on the rim of a PUNCH-BOWL and used to strain orange juice, etc., into the punch. Such funnels are sometimes called a 'port strainer' when used to strain crusted port. *See* PERFUME FUNNEL.

wine funnel. Funnel and strainer, Sheffield plate, *c.* 1815. L. 15 cm. City Museum, Sheffield.

wine-jug. A type of JUG for pouring wine, having a vertical loop handle or scroll handle, a pouring lip, and a hinged LID that extends over the lip and has a thumbpiece. *See* CLARET-JUG.

wine label. The modern name for a BOTTLE TICKET of the type used on a wine-bottle. *See* DECANTER LABEL.

wine taster. A small shallow circular CUP used by oenophiles, vintners, and wine stewards to judge the quality of a wine by examining its colour, clarity, and taste. Some pieces so called, made in England in the 17th century, usually have two opposed vertical scroll handles, often of twisted wire or shaped like a snake, and are decorated with EMBOSSING of ornate patterns on the bottom and sides; it has been questioned whether these were for wine-tasting, and those having a smooth flat bottom were more probably drinking vessels. The basic French form, sometimes made in England, has one flat horizontal handle, level with the rim and supported by a vertical ring (to be held by the forefinger and thumb), or occasionally a vertical ring handle; it is characteristically modelled with a slightly bossed bottom and with dimpled recesses or hollow GADROONING in order 'to break the wine' so that the colour and clarity of the wine, when twirled, can be best examined. The width ranges from 7·5 to 10 cm. The French forms are usually attached to a chain or ribbon, so as to be worn suspended around the neck. The French term is *tastevin* (sometimes spelled *tâtevin*). *See* G. Bernard Hughes, 'English Silver Wine-tasters' in *Country Life*, 28 June 1951, p. 2034.

wine taster. Cup with gadrooning and caryatid handle, Samuel Wastel, London, 1701. D. 7·6 cm. Courtesy, Brand Inglis Ltd, London.

Winslow, Edward (1669–1753). A leading silversmith of Boston, Massachusetts, perhaps once apprenticed to JEREMIAH DUMMER, and a local judge from 1743 until his death. Many pieces of silverware, both ecclesiastical and secular, made by him survive in several United States museums.

Winslow Sugar Box. An elaborately decorated, oval SUGAR-BOX, having FLUTING on the sides and resting on four scroll feet. The hinged LID is domed, with a hasp at the front and decorated overall with granulation within a border of GADROONING; its finial is a vertical scrolled ring. It was made by EDWARD WINSLOW, *c.* 1700–10, for his own use, and descended in his family until 1935. It is now in the Garvan Collection at the Yale University Art Gallery. New Haven, Connecticut.

Winslow Sugar Box. Edward Winslow, Boston, Mass., *c.* 1700–10. H. 13·5 cm. Yale University Art Gallery (Mabel Brady Garvan Collection), New Haven, Conn.

wire. Metal in the form of a thread or very slender rod or ribbon, usually flexible and of various sectional shapes; although usually circular in section, it is sometimes half-round, oval, square, triangular, flat, L-shaped, U-shaped or angular, sometimes with curved upper surfaces or with ribbing, and sometimes twisted. Silver wire was used by silversmiths in making pieces composed of or decorated with WIREWORK. Such wire was made originally by rolling a hammered thin strip of sheet metal between two very hard surfaces (e.g., stone or bronze) until circular in section, or by twisting a thin strip of metal into a spiral. Later, in the Roman period and from the Middle Ages, a draw-plate (whittle) was used, pulling the wire through successively smaller holes to reduce its thickness and to stretch it. Thick wire was made by CAST-ING and hollow wire (tubing) either by hammering strips into grooves in wood or metal moulds or by wrapping a strip around a mandrel and hammering it into shape. Beaded wire was formerly made by pressing wire into a beading tool on which depressions had been engraved. Today solid silver wire manufactured in many GAUGES is available to silversmiths from rolling mills and metal refiners. *See* PLATED WIRE.

wire handle. A type of vertical handle made of a shaped length of WIRE, usually twisted.

wirework. The framework, decoration or supports made of silver or plated silver wire and used for various articles, such as an openwork CAKE-BASKET, TOASTER, SUGAR-BASKET, FRUIT-DISH or EPERGNE. (1) When wire was used to form the body of such hollow pieces or the gallery of a DECANTER STAND, the process involved cutting the wire into short lengths, curving them, and SOL-DERING the ends into holes drilled in the base and rim of the article to form the side of the piece. Later, the wire strips were curved into hairpin shapes and affixed side-by-side, and next a single long strip was formed into a continuous series of curves, soldered at intervals to the base and rim without holes. Sometimes the wire was interlaced or formed into a hexagonal DIAPER PATTERN. (2) When used to strengthen the joints of pieces, wire was produced in a variety of curved and angled forms. (3) When used to decorate the exterior of silverware, it was soldered on, in patterns as desired, such as encircling bands. (4) When used to strengthen the edges of CUPS, BOWLS, etc., it was soldered along the rim. For the methods of drawing and using silver wire, *see* G. Bernard Hughes. 'The Ancient Art of the Wire-Drawers' in *Country Life*, 19 April 1956, p. 817; —, 'Wire-work in Sheffield Plate' in *Country Life*, 8 February 1968, p. 288.

wire handle. Detail of two-handled bowl, Jacob Boelen, New York, *c.* 1790-1800. Yale University Art Gallery (Mabel Brady Garvan Collection), New Haven, Conn.

Woburn Salt. A GREAT SALT of silver gilt, *c.* 1610, unmarked, having a circular spreading base, a pillar of rock crystal enclosed within an openwork sheath, and a wide top, upon which rests a stepped cover with a vase-shaped finial. It is at Woburn Abbey, the seat of the Dukes of Bedford. *See* CRYSTAL OBJECTS.

wodewose spoon. A type of SPOON having a finial in the form of a figure in-the-round depicting a wodewose (woodwose, a satyr or wild man) wearing a fur skin and holding a club. An example is known from *c.* 1460. *See* MONKEY SALT.

women silversmiths. Women who have become silversmiths, either (1) as an apprentice and later a freed silversmith registering her own mark, or (2) as a widow who carried on the business of her late husband, sometimes as an active craftsman but often in a managerial capacity for the surviving business. (Under an English Act of 1562 a widow could take over the privileges of her husband who had been a freeman for seven years, and so-although not a trained silversmith herself-could enter her mark and continue the business.) Among leading English women silversmiths were: Louisa Perina Courtauld (*see* COURTAULD), Hester Bateman (*see* BATEMAN), REBECCA(H) EMES, Anne Tanqueray (widow of DAVID TANQUERAY), Mary Pantin (*see* PAN-TIN), and Eliza Buteaux-Godfrey (widow of Abraham Buteaux and later of Benjamin Godfrey). The Goldsmiths' Company, London, has accepted many women apprentices, a large number of whom have become freemen by servitude. *See* Edward Wenham, 'Women recorded as silversmiths' in *Antique Collector*, March–April 1946, p. 60; Eric J. G. Smith, 'Women Silversmiths' in *Antique Dealer & Collectors Guide*, May 1969, p. 67, and September 1969, p. 81; A. Bennett, 'English Women Silversmiths' in *Country Life*, 20 January 1977, p. 140; Margaret Holland, 'Women Silversmiths' in *Canadian Collector*, July/August 1985, p. 72.

Wood, Samuel (*c.* 1704-94). A London silversmith, apprenticed in 1721 and freed in 1730/1. He entered his first and second marks in 1733 and 1737/8, address Gutter Lane, Cheapside, a third mark in 1739, and, after moving to Foster Lane, a fourth in 1754 and a fifth in 1756. He specialized in making CRUETS and CASTERS, producing them in large numbers and in attractive designs.

wood objects. Articles made of wood and having silver MOUNTS, such as a MAZER or CUP. Many objects of silverware have handles made of wood (boxwood or ebony), such as those on TEAPOTS, JUGS, etc., a wooden handle being easier to hold than one made of heat-conducting silver, as well as being more economical to make; likewise, some finials are made of wood. (Such handles and finials of wood, when permanently affixed by riveting, are al-

wood objects. Mahogany cup with silver mounts, English, 17th century. H. 9·5 cm. British Museum, London.

ways included in the stated WEIGHT of a piece of silver.) Some WINE-CUPS were made of wood, with silver mounts, for the coronation in 1820 of George IV. Articles made of wood are generally referred to as 'treen'. *See* MONYMUSK RELIQUARY; MOUNTED OBJECTS.

wrigglework. A decorative pattern in the form of a zigzag or sinuous line, or two such intertwined lines, and sometimes found between two parallel straight lines.

writhen. Twisting, as the form of the spiral stem of some STANDING CUPS or the finial of some spoons.

writing accessories. For some articles used in connection with writing, *see* INKSTAND and LIBRARY SET. In general, writing implements, even those made of or mounted with silver, such as pens, quills, and pencils, are beyond the scope of this book.

writing table. A type of small table, generally used by a lady for writing. An inlaid ebony example, with a conforming chair, was designed by WILLIAM CHRISTMAS CODMAN and made in 1903 by the GORHAM COMPANY, the two pieces having ornamental mounts and inlays of silver (760 oz.) in the form of various flowers; they were purchased by a Lady Esther (formerly Antoinette Heckscher), and sold at Christie's, London, in 1954 to Mr and Mrs Frederic B. Thurber, of Providence, R.I., who donated them to the Rhode Island School of Design.

Wrothe Salt. A SCROLL SALT of circular spool-shaped form, bearing the maker's mark 'CT' (or 'CF') and the London date mark 1633. It has been said to be probably the earliest extant English example of a scroll salt. It has three upright scroll-terminal brackets and is undecorated except for an encircling inscription referring to its being a gift to the town of Bridgwater, Somerset, in 1638 by 'Tho:Wrothe'.

wrought (past tense of 'work'). Worked into shape, as by HAMMERING, RAISING, SPINNING, SINKING or STAMPING. 'Wrought silver' has been shaped by such means; 'hand-wrought silver' has been shaped by the use of hand tools rather than by machine (e.g., by stamping).

Wykeham, William of, Crosier. A silver-gilt CROSIER, *c.* 1367, reputed to have been bequeathed to New College, Oxford, by William of Wykeham (1324–1404), Bishop of Winchester in 1367, Chancellor in 1389–91, and founder of New College in 1379 and of Winchester College in 1387. The crosier is divided into three sections: the lowest terminating in a ribbed knop and a spike, and decorated with panels with REPOUSSÉ lilies; the middle section rising to several rows of Gothic niches in each of which stands a figure of a saint or an angel; and the crook being decorated with CRESTING and a continuous vertical series of panels in which are figures of angels, the last panel being surmounted by a praying figure. Much of the piece was originally decorated with blue and green enamelling. The crosier fell into decay after the Reformation and was restored in 1753.

Wyndham Ewer. A silver-gilt EWER, made in London, 1554–5, accompanied by a BASIN, London, 1607–8. The ewer has an ovoid bowl decorated with two wide encircling bands of embossing between which is an engraved band and with a mask on the neck; it rests on a domed foot, and has a large vertical loop handle in the form of a female TERM, a grotesque animalistic spout, and a hinged lid. The basin, made by Symon Owen, has decoration of overall embossing in three concentric bands depicting four flying dragons, and has a central boss. The ewer is the second-oldest English ewer extant and the oldest known piece with decoration in MANNERIST STYLE. The ewer bears the arms of Thomas More, of Heytesbury, Wiltshire, whose grand-daughter married Thomas Wyndham. The ewer and basin were owned by the Wyndham family until this century; they were purchased in 1977 by the British Museum, London.

Wyndham Ewer. Silver gilt, London, 1554–5. H. 35 cm. British Museum, London.

Y

Yateley Cup. A silver-gilt STANDING CUP having a rock-crystal bowl of compressed globular shape enclosed by four straps and resting on a stem with a faceted crystal knop between brackets. The domed foot is chased with cherub masks and fruit. The cover (a modern replacement for one damaged in the 19th century) is surmounted by a crystal shaft enclosed in CAGEWORK supported by brackets on a row of miniature figures. The cup, unmarked, *c.*1600, was a gift of Mrs Sarah Cocks to the parish church of Yateley, Hampshire. *See* CRYSTAL ARTICLES.

York, Duke of, Soup Tureens. A pair of covered oval SOUP-TUREENS WITH STAND, made by EDWARD FARRELL, London, 1823 (one bearing the mark of KENSINGTON LEWIS), for Frederick, Duke of York (1763–1827), second son of George III. The tureens are of BOMBÉ shape, each resting on four knurled feet, having two horizontal loop handles, and having on the front a cartouche with an applied crown, coronet, and rose. Their covers are of low-domed shape, each with a finial formed as cast and applied vegetables (one has a foliate vertical ring handle). The stands are of cushion shape, each resting on four scroll feet and bearing on the top the Royal coat of arms. The tureens, covers, and stands are elaborately decorated with repoussé and chased assorted vegetables and foliage; each has a plain liner with two ring handles. The two pieces had become separated (having been sold at Christie's, London, on 19 March 1827), but by coincidence were offered for sale by their respective owners at Christie's, New York, on 15 October 1985, when they were acquired by a European private collector and so reunited.

York Chamber Pot. A circular CHAMBER POT, having two opposed horizontal uplifted handles, and having a cover decorated with GADROONING and an ornamental finial; it rests on a circular tray. The piece, made of BRITANNIA SILVER, was owned by Richard York, of Wighill Park, York, High Sheriff of York in 1832, and was carried in the mayoral coach when he was Lord Mayor of York. It is said to have been made by ROBERT GARRARD II, 1818. It was sold at Sotheby's, London, in 1966 by a descendant of Richard York.

York silverware. Articles of silverware made at York, in northern England, which had an ASSAY OFFICE from the mid-16th century. Its early mark, *c.*1560–1698, was a circle divided midway vertically, having in the left side half of a fleur de lis and in the right side half of a crowned leopard's head (the latter changed later to half a seeded rose crowned). Thereafter, 1700–17, the mark was the city arms, a Greek cross charged with five small lions passant; later, 1778–87 (after the office had been temporarily closed), the same mark was enclosed in a shield, and then, 1787–1856, enclosed in a circle. The office was finally closed in 1856. The ware resembled Scandinavian work, and consisted mainly of CHURCH PLATE and domestic ware, the latter made mainly by the firm of J. Hampston & J. Prince, *c.*1776–85.

Yateley Cup. Silver gilt and rock crystal, *c.* 1600 (the cover a modern replacement). H. 44·5 cm. Parish church, Yateley, Hampshire (photo courtesy, Historic Churches Preservation Trust, London).

York, Duke of, Soup Tureens. Edward Farrell, London, 1823. Courtesy, Christie's, New York.